# Contents

## Part 1: General Family Statutes

## Part 2: Other Statutes

## Part 3: Court Rules

## Part 4: European Union Legislation

## Part 5: Miscellaneous

# Irish Family Law Handbook

## Fourth Edition

*Edited by*

### DEIRDRE KENNEDY

*BA (Hons), LLM, DipArb, DipIntArb, ACI Arb,
Barrister at Law, Accredited Mediator (Friary Law)*

*and*

### ELIZABETH MAGUIRE

*LLB, MA, MLitt,
Barrister at Law, Accredited Mediator (CEDR)*

Bloomsbury Professional

**Published by**
**Bloomsbury Professional**
**Maxwelton House**
**41–43 Boltro Road**
**Haywards Heath**
**West Sussex**
**RH16 1BJ**

**Bloomsbury Professional**
**The Fitzwilliam Business Centre**
**26 Upper Pembroke Street**
**Dublin 2**

ISBN: 978 1 84766 932 2

© Bloomsbury Professional Limited 2011

Bloomsbury Professional, an imprint of Bloomsbury Publishing Plc

**British Library Cataloguing-in-Publication Data**
A catalogue record for this book is available from the British Library

Typeset by Marlex Editorial Services Ltd, Dublin, Ireland
Printed and bound by CPI Group (UK) Ltd, Croydon, CR0 4YY

# List of Abbreviations

**Statutes**

| | |
|---|---|
| BÉ 1937 | Bunreacht na hÉireann 1937 |
| CAECOA 1991 | Child Abduction and Enforcement of Custody Orders Act 1991 |
| CPCROCA 2010 | Civil Partnership and Certain Rights and Obligations of Cohabitants Act 2010 |
| CRA 2004 | Civil Registration Act 2004 |
| DRFDA 1986 | Domicile and Recognition of Foreign Divorces Act 1986 |
| DVA 1996 | Domestic Violence Act 1996 |
| ECHRA 2003 | European Convention on Human Rights Act 2003 |
| FLA 1981 | Family Law Act 1981 |
| FLA 1988 | Family Law Act 1988 |
| FLA 1995 | Family Law Act 1995 |
| FL(D)A 1996 | Family Law (Divorce) Act 1996 |
| FL(MP)A 1997 | Family Law (Miscellaneous Provisions) Act 1997 |
| FL(MSC)A 1976 | Family Law (Maintenance of Spouses and Children) Act 1976 |
| FHPA 1976 | Family Home Protection Act 1976 |
| GIA 1964 | Guardianship of Infants Act 1964 |
| JCEJA 1998 | Jurisdiction of Courts and Enforcement of Judgments Act 1998 |
| JSFLRA 1989 | Judicial Separation and Family Law Reform Act 1989 |
| LCLRA 2009 | Land and Conveyancing Law Reform Act 2009 |
| MA 1994 | Maintenance Act 1994 |
| MAO 1974 | Maintenance Orders Act 1974 |

| | |
|---|---|
| PA 1868 | Partition Act 1868 |
| PA 1876 | Partition Act 1876 |
| RBA 1996 | Registration of Births Act 1996 |
| SCA 1987 | Status of Children Act 1987 |
| TCA 1997 | Taxes Consolidation Act 1997 |

## Court Rules

| | |
|---|---|
| CCR 2001 | Circuit Court Rules 2001 |
| CCR (RP) 2008 | Circuit Court Rules (Recording of Proceedings) 2008 |
| RSC | Rules of the Superior Courts |

## European Union Legislation

| | |
|---|---|
| CR(EC) No 2201/2003 | Council Regulation (EC) No 2201/2003 |
| EC(M)R SI 274/2011 | European Communities (Maintenance) Regulations 2011 (SI 274/2011) |

## Miscellaneous

| | |
|---|---|
| CAECOA 1991(S4)(HC)O 2008 SI 220/2008 | Child Abduction and Enforcement of Custody Orders Act 1991 (Section 4) (Hague Convention) Order 2008 (SI 220/2008) |
| CAECOA 1991(S4)(HC)O 2011 SI 400/2011 | Child Abduction and Enforcement of Custody Orders Act 1991 (Section 4) (Hague Convention) Order 2011 (SI 400/2011) |

# Useful Websites

| | |
|---|---|
| British and Irish Legal Information Institute | **www.bailii.org** |
| Bar Council of Ireland | **www.lawlibrary.ie** |
| Citizens Information | **www.citizensinformation.ie** |
| Commonwealth Legal Information Institute | **www.commonlii.org** |
| Courts Service of Ireland | **www.courts.ie** |
| Data Protection Commissioner | **www.dataprotection.ie** |
| Department of Justice, Equality and Defence | **www.justice.ie** |
| EUR-lex – the access to European Law | **www.eur-lex.europa.eu** |
| Europa – The European Union Online | **www.europa.eu** |
| European Court of Human Rights | **www.echr.coe.int** |
| Ex Tempore | **www.extempore.ie** |
| Government of Ireland website | **www.irlgov.ie** |
| Hague Conference on Private International Law | **www.hcch.net** |
| Houses of the Oireachtas, Parliament of Ireland – Tithe an Oireachtais | **www.oireachtas.ie** |
| Iris Oifigiúil | **www.irisoifigiuil.ie** |
| Irish Human Rights Commission | **www.ihrc.ie** |
| Irish Law site | **www.irish-law.org** |
| Irish Statute Book | **www.irishstatutebook.ie** |

| IRLII.org – Irish Legal Information Initiative | **www.irlii.org** |
|---|---|
| Law Society of Ireland | **www.lawsociety.ie** |
| Legal Aid Board | **www.legalaidboard.ie** |
| Legal and technology articles and resources for librarians, lawyers and law firms | **www.LLRX.com** |
| Office of the Attorney General | **www.attorneygeneral.ie** |
| Property Registration Authority | **www.prai.ie** |
| The Court of Justice of the European Union | **www.curia.europa.eu** |
| The Hague Conference on Private International Law – the International Child Abduction Database | **www.incadat.com** |
| World Legal Information Institute | **www.worldlii.org** |

**Note**: The reader should note that sums in punts have been changed to euros throughout. This amendment was provided for by SI 585/2001. Euro conversions may not always be referenced within the footnotes.

# Part 1: General Family Statutes

# Guardianship of Infants Act 1964

*Number 7 of 1964*

ARRANGEMENT OF SECTIONS

## PART I
### PRELIMINARY AND GENERAL

## PART II
### GUARDIANSHIP

## PART III
### ENFORCEMENT OF RIGHT OF CUSTODY

*An Act to consolidate with amendments the enactments relating to the custody and guardianship of infants. [25th March, 1964]*

*Be it enacted by the Oireachtas as follows:-*

## PART I
## PRELIMINARY AND GENERAL

**1      Short Title**

This Act may be cited as the Guardianship of Infants Act, 1964.[1]

---

**NOTES**

1   Commencement: See the Judicial Separation and Family Law Reform Act 1989, s 45 and the Courts Act 1981, s 16.

---

**[2      Interpretation**

(1) In this Act, except where the context otherwise requires—

"**the Act of 1987**" means the Status of Children Act, 1987;

["adoption order" means—

    (a)  an adoption order within the meaning of the Adoption Act 2010; or

    (b)  an intercountry adoption effected outside the State and recognised under that Act;

and for the time being in force;][1]

"**child**" means a person who has not attained full age;

"**father**"[2] includes a male adopter under an adoption order, but, subject to section 11(4), does not include the father of a child who has not married that child's mother unless either—

    (a)  an order under section 6A (inserted by the Act of 1987) is in force in respect of that child,

    (b)  the circumstances set out in subsection (3) of this section apply, or

    (c)  the circumstances set out in subsection (4) of this section apply;

"**maintenance**" includes education;

"**mother**" includes a female adopter under an adoption order;

"**parent**" means a father or mother as defined by this subsection;

"**testamentary guardian**" includes a guardian appointed by deed or will;

"**welfare**", in relation to a child, comprises the religious, moral, intellectual, physical and social welfare of the child.

(2) A reference, however, expressed, in this Act to a child whose father and mother have not married each other shall, except in a case to which subsection (3) relates, be construed in accordance with section 4 of the Act of 1987.

(3)  (a)  The circumstances referred to in paragraph (b) of the definition of "father" in subsection (1) of this section are that the father and mother of the child concerned have at some time gone through a ceremony of marriage and the ceremony resulted in—

        (i)  a voidable marriage in respect of which a decree of nullity was granted after, or at some time during the period of 10 months before, the birth of the child, or

        (ii)  a void marriage which the father reasonably believed (whether or not such belief was due to a mistake of law or of fact) resulted in a valid marriage—

            (I)  where the ceremony occurred before the birth of the child, at some time during the period of 10 months before that birth, or

            (II)  where the ceremony occurred after the birth of the child, at the time of that ceremony.

  (b)  It shall be presumed for the purposes of subparagraph (ii) of paragraph (a), unless the contrary is shown, that the father reasonably believed that the

5

ceremony of marriage to which that paragraph relates resulted in a valid marriage.

(4) The circumstances referred to in paragraph (c) of the definition of "father" in subsection (1) are that the father and mother of the child concerned, not being a father or mother to whom the circumstances set out in subsection (3) apply—

    (a)  have not married each other,

    (b)  declare that they are the father and mother of the child concerned,

    (c)  agree to the appointment of the father as a guardian of the child,

    (d)  have entered into arrangements regarding the custody of and, as the case may be, access to the child, and

    (e)  have made a statutory declaration to that effect as may be prescribed by the Minister for Justice, Equality and Law Reform[3].

(5) In this Act—

    (a)  a reference to a Part or section is a reference to a Part or section of this Act, unless it is indicated that a reference to some other enactment is intended,

    (b)  a reference to a subsection or paragraph is a reference to the subsection or paragraph of the provision in which the reference occurs, unless it is indicated that a reference to some other provision is intended, and

    (c)  a reference to any enactment shall be construed as a reference to that enactment as amended by or under any subsequent enactment.][4]

---

**Notes**

1   The definition of "adoption order" was substituted by the Adoption Act 2010, s 162.

2   See also the Protection of Children (Hague Convention) Act 2000, s 3(2)(e), which provides as follows: The definition of "father" in section 2 (inserted by the Children Act, 1997) of the Guardianship of Infants Act 1964, shall include the father of a child who has, by virtue of Article 16, acquired parental responsibility corresponding to guardianship in relation to the child by operation of the law of a state other than the State, and section 8(4) (which provides that certain guardians may be removed from office only by the court), as so inserted, of that Act shall apply in relation to such a father.

3   See also SI 5/1998 which prescribes the form for the statutory declaration referred to in paragraph (e) of section 2(4).

4   Section 2 was substituted by the Children Act 1997, s 4.

---

**3      Welfare of [child][1] to be paramount**

Where in any proceedings before any court the custody, guardianship or upbringing of a [child][1], or the administration of any property belonging to or held on trust for a [child][1], or the application of the income thereof, is in question, the court, in deciding that question, shall regard the welfare of the [child][1] as the first and paramount consideration.[2]

---

**Notes**

1  The word "child" was substituted for "infant" (also in the plural), by the Children Act 1997, s 12.

2  See the Adoption Act 2010, s 51(3).

---

## [3A    Proof of paternity in certain proceedings

Where in any proceedings before any court on an application for an order under this Act (other than so much of any proceedings as section 15 of the Act of 1987 relates to) in respect of a [child][1] whose father and mother have not married each other, a person (being a party to the proceedings) is alleged to be, or alleges that he is, the father of the [child][1] but that allegation is not admitted by a party to the proceedings, the court shall not on that application make any final order which imposes any obligation or confers any right on that person unless it is proved on the balance of probabilities that he is the father of the [child][1]:

Provided that this section applies only where the fact that that person is or is not the father of the [child][1] is material to the proceedings.][2]

---

**Notes**

1  The word "child" was substituted for "infant" (also in the plural), by the Children Act 1997, s 12.

2  Section 3A was inserted by the Status of Children Act 1987, s 10.

---

## 4    Repeals

Each enactment specified in the Schedule is hereby repealed to the extent indicated in the third column of the Schedule.

# PART II
## GUARDIANSHIP

## [5    Jurisdiction in guardianship matters

(1) Subject to subsection (2) of this section, the jurisdiction conferred on a court by this Part may be exercised by the Circuit Court or the District Court.

(2) The District Court and the Circuit Court on appeal from the District Court, shall not have jurisdiction to make an order under this Act for the payment of a periodical sum at a rate greater than [€150.00][1] per week towards the maintenance of a [child][2].

(3) The jurisdiction conferred by this Part is in addition to any other jurisdiction to appoint or remove guardians or as to the wardship of [children][2] or the care of [children's][2] estates.][3]

---

**Notes**

1   Subsection (2) was amended by the Courts Act 1991, s 12 and by the Courts and Court Officers Act 2002, s 21 (substitution of €150 for £60).

2   The word "child" was substituted for "infant" (also in the plural), by the Children Act 1997, s 12.

3   Section 5 was substituted by the Courts Act 1981, s 15(1)(a).

---

## 6        Rights of parents to guardianship

(1) The father and mother of a [child][1] shall be guardians of the [child][1] jointly.

(2) On the death of the father of a [child][1] the mother, if surviving, shall be guardian of the [child][1], either alone or jointly with any guardian appointed by the father or by the court.

(3) On the death of the mother of a [child][1] the father, if surviving, shall be guardian of the [child][1], either alone or jointly with any guardian appointed by the mother or by the court.

[(4) Where the mother of a child has not married the child's father, she, while living, shall alone be the guardian of the child unless the circumstances set out in section 2(4) apply or there is in force an order under section 6A (inserted by the Act of 1987) or a guardian has otherwise been appointed with this Act.][2]

---

**Notes**

1   The word "child" was substituted for "infant" (also in the plural), by the Children Act 1997, s 12.

2   Section 6(4) was inserted by the Children Act 1997, s 5.

---

## [6A        Power of court to appoint certain fathers as guardians[1]

(1) Where the father and mother of a child have not married each other and have not made a declaration under section 2(4), or where the father was a guardian of the child by virtue of a declaration under section 2(4) but was removed from office under section 8(4), the court may, on the application of the father, by order, appoint the father to be a guardian of the child.

(2) Without prejudice to the provisions of section 5(3) (inserted by the Courts Act, 1981), 8(4) and 12 of this Act, the appointment by the court under this section of the father of a [child][2] as his guardian shall not affect the prior appointment of any person as

a guardian of the [child]² under section 8(1) of this Act unless the court otherwise orders.

(3) ...]³

---

**Notes**

1  Commencement: 14 December 1987.

2  The word "child" was substituted for "infant" (also in the plural), by the Children Act 1997, s 12.

3  Section 6A was inserted by the Status of Children Act 1987, s 12. Subsection (1) was substituted by the Children Act 1997, s 6(a). Subsection (3) was repealed by the Children Act 1997, s 6(b).

---

**7**  **Power of father and mother to appoint testamentary guardians**

(1) The father of a [child]¹ may by deed or will appoint a person or persons to be guardian or guardians of the [child]¹ after his death.

(2) The mother of a [child]¹ may by deed or will appoint a person or persons to be guardian or guardians of the [child]¹ after her death.

(3) A testamentary guardian shall act jointly with the surviving parent of the [child]¹ so long as the surviving parent remains alive unless the surviving parent objects to his so acting.

(4) If the surviving parent so objects or if a testamentary guardian considers that the surviving parent is unfit to have the custody of the [child]¹, the testamentary guardian may apply to the court for an order under this section.

(5) The court may—

    (a)  refuse to make an order (in which case the surviving parent shall remain sole guardian), or

    (b)  make an order that the testamentary guardian shall act jointly with the surviving parent, or

    (c)  make an order that he shall act as guardian of the [child]¹ to the exclusion, so far as the court thinks proper, of the surviving parent.

(6) In the case mentioned in paragraph (c) of subsection (5) the court may make such order regarding the custody of the [child]¹ and the right of access to the [child]¹ of the surviving parent as the court thinks proper, and the court may further order that the surviving parent shall pay to the guardian or guardians, or any of them, towards the maintenance of the [child]¹ such weekly or other periodical sum as, having regard to the means of the surviving parent, the court considers reasonable.

(7) [...]²

(8) An appointment of a guardian by deed may be revoked by a subsequent deed or by will.

**Notes**

1   The word "child" was substituted for "infant" (also in the plural), by the Children Act 1997, s 12.

2   Subsection (7) was repealed by the Succession Act 1965, s 8.

## 8      Appointment and removal of guardians by court

(1) Where a [child][1] has no guardian, the court, on the application of any person or persons, may appoint the applicant or applicants or any of them to be the guardian or guardians of the [child][1].

(2) When no guardian has been appointed by a deceased parent or if a guardian so appointed dies or refuses to act, the court may appoint a guardian or guardians to act jointly with the surviving parent.

(3) A guardian appointed by the court to act jointly with a surviving parent shall continue to act as guardian after the death of the surviving parent.

[(4) A guardian appointed by will or deed or order of court, or holding office by virtue of the circumstances set out in section 2(4) (inserted by the Children Act, 1997) applying to him, may be removed from office only by the court.][2]

(5) The court may appoint another guardian in place of a guardian so removed or in place of a guardian appointed by any such order who dies.

**Notes**

1   The word "child" was substituted for "infant" (also in the plural), by the Children Act 1997, s 12.

2   Subsection (4) was substituted by the Children Act 1997, s 7.

## 9      Provisions where two or more guardians appointed

(1) Where two or more persons are appointed to be guardians they shall act jointly and on the death of any of them the survivor or survivors shall continue to act.

(2) Where guardians are appointed by both parents the guardians so appointed shall after the death of the surviving parent act jointly.

## 10      Powers and duties of guardians

(1) Every guardian under this Act shall be a guardian of the person and of the estate of the [child][1] unless, in the case of a guardian appointed by deed, will or order of the court, the terms of his appointment otherwise provide.

(2) Subject to the terms of any such deed, will or order, a guardian under this Act—

   (a)  as guardian of the person, shall, as against every person not being, jointly with him, a guardian of the person, be entitled to the custody of the [child][1] and shall be entitled to take proceedings for the restoration of his custody of the [child][1] against any person who wrongfully takes away or detains the [child][1] and for the recovery, for the benefit of the [child][1], of damages for any injury to or trespass against the person of the [child][1];

   (b)  as guardian of the estate, shall be entitled to the possession and control of all property, real and personal, of the [child][1] and shall manage all such property and receive the rents and profits on behalf and for the benefit of the [child][1] until the [child][1] attains the age of twenty-one years or during any shorter period for which he has been appointed guardian and may take such proceedings in relation thereto as may by law be brought by any guardian of the estate of a [child][1].

(3) The provisions of this section are without prejudice to the provisions of any other enactment or to any other powers or duties conferred or imposed by law on parents, guardians or trustees of the property of [children][1].

---

**Notes**

1   The word "child" was substituted for "infant" (also in the plural), by the Children Act 1997, s 12.

---

## 11      Applications to court[1]

(1) Any person being a guardian of a [child][2] may apply to the court for its direction on any question affecting the welfare of the [child][2] and the court may make such order as it thinks proper.

(2) The court may by an order under this section—

   (a)  give such directions as it thinks proper regarding the custody of the [child][2] and the right of access to the [child][2] of his father or mother;

   (b)  order the father or mother to pay towards the maintenance of the [child][2] such weekly or other periodical sum as, having regard to the means of the father or mother, the court considers reasonable.

[(3) An order under this section may be made on the application of either parent notwithstanding that the parents are then residing together, but an order made under paragraph (a) of subsection (2) shall not be enforceable and no liability thereunder shall accrue while they reside together, and the order shall cease to have effect if for a period of three months after it is made they continue to reside together.][3]

[(4) In the case of a [child][2] whose father and mother have not married each other, the right to make an application under this section regarding the custody of the [child][2] and the right of access thereto of his father or mother shall extend to the father who is not a guardian of the [child]² and for this purpose references in this section to the father or parent of a [child]² shall be construed as including him.]⁴

[(5) A reference in subsection 2(b) to a child shall include a reference to a person who—

    (a)  has not attained the age of 18 years, or—

    (b)  has attained the age of 18 years and is or will be, or if any order were made under this Act providing for payment of maintenance for the benefit of the person, would be, receiving full-time education or instruction at a university, college, school or other educational establishment, and who has not attained the age of 23 years.

(6) Subsection (2)(b) shall apply to and in relation to a person who has attained the age of 18 years and has a mental or physical disability to such extent that it is not reasonably possible for the person to maintain himself or herself fully, as it applies to a child.]⁵

[(7) A copy of any report prepared under subsection (5) shall be made available to the barrister or solicitor, if any, representing each party in the proceedings or, if any party is not so represented, to that party and may be received in evidence in the proceedings.

(8) Where any person prepares a report pursuant to a request under subsection (5) of this section, the fees and expenses of that person shall be paid by such party or parties to the proceedings as the court shall order.

(9) The court may, if it thinks fit, or either party to the proceedings may, call the person making the report as a witness.]⁶,⁷

---

**Notes**

1    Commencement: See the Family Law (Amendment) Act 1995, s 35(1)(aa) as amended by the Family Law (Amendment) Act 1996, s 52(e)(ii).

2    The word "child" was substituted for "infant" by the Children Act 1997, s 12.

3    Subsection (3) was substituted by the Age of Majority Act 1985, s 6.

4    Subsection (4) was substituted by the Status of Children Act 1987, s 13.

5    Subsections (5)–(6) were inserted by the Children Act 1997, s 8.

6    Subsections (7)–(9) were inserted by the Judicial Separation and Family Law Reform Act 1989, s 40.

7    See the Family Law Act 1995, s 47, the Domestic Violence Act 1996, s 9 and the Family Law (Divorce) Act 1996, s 43.

---

**[11A    Custody may be granted to father and mother jointly**

For the avoidance of doubt, it is hereby declared that the court, in making an order under section 11, may, if it thinks it appropriate, grant custody of a child to the child's father and mother jointly.]¹

**Notes**

1    Section 11A was inserted by the Children Act 1997, s 9.

**[11B    Relatives may apply for access to child**

(1) Any person who—

    (a)  is a relative of a child, or,

    (b)  has acted *in loco parentis* to a child,

and to whom section 11 does not apply may, subject to subsection (3), apply to the court for an order giving that person access to the child on such terms and conditions as the court may order.

(2) A person may not make an application under subsection (1) unless the person has first applied for and has been granted by the court leave to make the application.

(3) In deciding whether to grant leave under subsection (1), the court shall have regard to all the circumstances, including in particular—

    (a)  the applicant's connection with the child,

    (b)  the risk, if any, of the application disrupting the child's life to the extent that the child would be harmed by it,

    (c)  the wishes of the child's guardians.

(4) In this section, a relative of a child who is the subject of an adoption order includes:

    (a)  a relative of the child's adoptive parents,

    (b)  the adoptive parents of the child's parents, or

    (c)  a relative of the adoptive parents of the child's parents.][1]

**Notes**

1    Section 11B was inserted by the Children Act 1997, s 9.

**[11C    Operation of order not to be stayed pending appeal unless so ordered**

The operation of an order under this Act shall not be stayed pending the outcome of an appeal against the order unless the court that made the order or the court to which the appeal is brought directs otherwise.][1]

**Notes**

1    Section 11C was inserted by the Children Act 1997, s 9.

13

**[11D Provision relating to orders under sections 6A, 11, 14 and 16**

In considering whether to make an order under section 6A, 11, 14 or 16 the court shall have regard to whether the child's best interests would be served by maintaining personal relations and direct contact with both his or her father and mother on a regular basis.][1]

**Notes**

1   Section 11D was inserted by the Children Act 1997, s 9.

**12 Variation and discharge of court orders**

The court may vary or discharge any order previously made by the court under this Part.

## PART III
## ENFORCEMENT OF RIGHT OF CUSTODY

**13 Definitions for Part III**

In this Part—

["**the court**" means the Circuit Court or the District Court;][1]

"**health authority**" has the meaning assigned to it by subsection (1) of section 2 of the Health Act, 1947, as amended by section 9 of the Health Authorities Act, 1960;

"**parent**" includes a guardian of the person and any person at law liable to maintain a [child][2] or entitled to his custody;

"**person**" includes any school or institution.

**Notes**

1   The definition of "the court" was amended by the Courts Act 1981, s 15(1)(b).

2   The word "child" was substituted for "infant" (also in the plural), by the Children Act 1997, s 12.

**14 Power of court as to production of [child][1]**

Where a parent of a [child][1] applies to the court for an order for the production of the [child][1] and the court is of opinion that that parent has abandoned or deserted the [child][1] or that he has otherwise so conducted himself that the court should refuse to enforce his right to the custody of the [child][1], the court may in its discretion decline to make the order.

**Notes**

1    The word "child" was substituted for "infant" (also in the plural), by the Children Act 1997, s 12.

**15        Power to court to order repayment of costs of bringing up [child]**[1]

[(1) Where, upon application by a parent for the production of a child, the court finds that the child is being brought up at the expense of another person, the court may, in its discretion if it orders that the child be given up to the parent, further order that the parent shall pay to that person the whole of the costs properly incurred by the person in bringing up the child, or such portion of those costs as the court considers reasonable.

(2) Where, upon application by a parent for the production of a child, the court finds that—

    (a)   assistance has been provided for the child at any time by a health authority under section 55 of the Health Act 1953,

    (b)   the child has been maintained in the care of a health board under section 4 of the Child Care Act 1991 at any time before the amendment of that provision by the Health Act 2004, or

    (c)   the child has been maintained in the care of the Health Service Executive under section 4 of the Child Care Act 1991 at any time after the amendment of that provision by the Health Act 2004,

the court may, in its discretion if it orders that the child be given up to the parent, further order that the parent shall pay to the Health Service Executive the whole of the costs properly incurred by the health authority in providing such assistance or by the health board or the Executive in maintaining the child in care or such portion of those costs as the court considers reasonable.

(3) In determining the amount to be repaid under this section, the court shall have regard to the circumstances of the case including, in particular, the means of the parent.][2]

**Notes**

1    The word "child" was substituted for "infant" (also in the plural), by the Children Act 1997, s 12.

2    Section 15 was substituted by the Health Act 2004, s 75 and Schedule 7 and is commenced under the Health Act 2004 (Commencement) (No 2) Order 2004 (SI 887/2004).

**16        Court in making order to have regard to conduct of parent**

Where a parent has—

    (a)   abandoned or deserted a [child][1], or

(b) allowed a [child]¹ to be brought up by another person at that person's expense, or to be provided with assistance by a health authority under section 55 of the Health Act, 1953, [to be maintained as described in section 15(2)(b) or (c) in the care of a health board or the Health Service Executive]² for such a length of time and under such circumstances as to satisfy the court that the parent was unmindful of his parental duties,

the court shall not make an order for the delivery of the [child]¹ to the parent unless the parent has satisfied the court that he is a fit person to have the custody of the [child]¹.

**Notes**

1    The word "child" was substituted for "infant" (also in the plural), by the Children Act 1997, s 12.

2    Section 16(b) was amended by the Health Act 2004, s 75 and Schedule 7 and is commenced under the Health Act 2004 (Commencement) (No 2) Order 2004 (SI 887/2004).

## 17    Power of court as to [child's]¹ religious education

(1) Upon any application by a parent for the production or custody of a [child]¹, if the court is of opinion that that parent ought not to have the custody of the [child]¹, the court shall have power to make such order as it thinks fit to secure that the [child]¹ be brought up in the religion in which the parents, or a parent, have or has a legal right to require that the [child]¹ should be brought up.

(2) [...]²

**Notes**

1    The word "child" was substituted for "infant" (also in the plural), by the Children Act 1997, s 12.

2    Subsection (2) was deleted by the Children Act 1997, s 10.

## 18    Custody where parents are separated

(1) In any case where a decree for divorce *a mensa et thoro* is pronounced, the [Circuit]¹ Court may thereby declare the parent by reason of whose misconduct the decree is made to be a person unfit to have the custody of the children (if any) of the marriage or of any children adopted under the Adoption Act, 1952, by the parents jointly; and in such case, the parent so declared to be unfit shall not, on the death of the other parent, be entitled as of right to the custody of the children.

(2) A provision contained in any separation agreement made between the father and mother of a [child]² shall not be invalid by reason only of its providing that one of them shall give up the custody or control of the [child]² to the other.

**Notes**

1  Subsection (1) was amended by the Courts Act 1981, s 15(1)(c), and was repealed by the Judicial Separation and Family Law Reform Act 1989, s 41(3), except in relation to an action instituted before the commencement of the 1989 Act.

2  The word "child" was substituted for "infant" (also in the plural), by the Children Act 1997, s 12.

# [PART IV]¹
## SAFEGUARDING INTERESTS OF CHILDREN

**Notes**

1  Part IV was inserted by the Children Act 1997, s 11.

## 19      Definitions

In this Part—

**"the Act of 1976"** means the Family Law (Maintenance of Spouses and Children) Act, 1976;

**"the Act of 1989"** means the Judicial Separation and Family Law Reform Act, 1989;

**"the Act of 1995"** means the Family Law Act, 1995;

**"the Act of 1996"** means the Family Law (Divorce) Act, 1996.

## 20      Safeguards to ensure applicant's awareness of alternatives to custody, access and guardianship proceedings and to assist attempts at agreement

(1) In this section **"the applicant"** means a person who has applied, is applying or proposes to apply to the court for directions under section 6A, 11 or 11B.

(2) If a solicitor is acting for the applicant, the solicitor shall, before the institution of proceedings under section 6A, 11 or 11B, discuss with the applicant the possibility of the applicant—

    (a)  engaging in counselling to assist in reaching an agreement with the respondent about the custody of the child, the right of access to the child or any other question affecting the welfare of the child and give to the applicant the name and address of persons qualified to give counselling on the matter,

    (b)  engaging in mediation to help to effect an agreement between the applicant and the respondent about the custody of the child, the right of access to the child or any question affecting the welfare of the child, and give to the applicant the name and addresses of persons qualified to provide an appropriate mediation service, and

(c) where appropriate, effecting a deed or agreement in writing executed or made by the applicant and the respondent and providing for the custody of the child, the right of access to the child or any question affecting the welfare of the child.

(3) If a solicitor is acting for the applicant—

(a) the original documents by which the proceedings under section 6A, 11 or 11B are instituted shall be accompanied by a certificate signed by the solicitor indicating, if it be the case, that the solicitor has complied with subsection (2) in relation to the matter and, if the document is not so accompanied, the court may adjourn the proceedings for such period as it considers reasonable to enable the solicitor to engage in the discussions referred to in subsection (2),

(b) if the solicitor has complied with paragraph (a), any copy of the original document served on any person or left in an office of the court shall be accompanied by a copy of that certificate.

(4) The solicitor shall be deemed to have complied with subsection (3) in relation to the requirement of a certificate where the application under section 6A, 11 or 11B is made in proceedings for the grant of—

(a) a decree of judicial separation under the Act of 1989 and section 5(2) of that Act has been complied with by the solicitor, or

(b) a decree of divorce under the Act of 1996 and section 6(4) of that Act has been complied with by the solicitor.

**21      Safeguards to ensure respondent's awareness of alternatives to custody, access and guardianship proceedings and to assist attempts at agreement**

(1) In this section "**the respondent**" means a respondent in proceedings in the court under section 6A, 11 or 11B.

(2) If a solicitor is acting for the respondent, the solicitor shall, as soon as practicable after receiving instructions from the respondent in relation to proceedings under section 6A, 11 or 11B discuss with the respondent the possibility of the respondent—

(a) engaging in counselling to assist in reaching an agreement with the applicant about the custody of the child, the right of access to the child or any other question affecting the welfare of the child and give to the respondent the name and addresses of persons qualified to give counselling on the matter,

(b) engaging in mediation to help to effect an agreement between the respondent and the applicant about the custody of the child, the right of access to the child or any question affecting the welfare of the child and where appropriate give to the respondent the name and addresses of persons qualified to provide an appropriate mediation service, and

(c) where appropriate, effecting a deed or agreement in writing executed or made by the respondent and the applicant and providing for the custody of the child, the right of access to the child or any question affecting the welfare of the child.

(3) If a solicitor is acting for the respondent—

    (a)  the memorandum or other documents delivered to the appropriate officer of the court for the purpose of the entry of an appearance by the respondent in proceedings under section 6A, 11 or 11B shall be accompanied by a certificate signed by the solicitor indicating, if it be the case, that the solicitor has complied with subsection (2) in relation to the matter and, if the document is not so accompanied, the court may adjourn the proceedings for such period as it considers reasonable to enable the solicitor to engage in the discussions referred to in subsection (2),

    (b)  if the solicitor has complied with paragraph (a), any copy of the original document given or sent to the applicant or his solicitor shall be accompanied by a copy of that certificate.

(4) The solicitor shall be deemed to have complied with subsection (3) in relation to the requirement of a certificate where the application under section 6A, 11 or 11B is made in proceedings for the grant of—

    (a)  a decree of judicial separation under the Act of 1989 and section 6(2) of that Act has been complied with by the solicitor, or

    (b)  a decree of divorce under the Act of 1996 and section 7(4) of that Act has been complied with by the solicitor.

**22      Adjournment of proceedings to assist agreement on custody or guardianship of or access to child**

(1) Where, in proceedings under section 6A, 11 or 11B it appears to the court that agreement between the parties on the subject matter of the proceedings may be effected, it may adjourn or further adjourn the proceedings for the purpose of enabling attempts to be made by the parties, if they wish, to reach agreement, with or without the assistance of a third party, on some or all of the issues which are in dispute.

(2) If proceedings are adjourned pursuant to subsection (1), any party may at any time request that the hearing of the proceedings be resumed as soon as practicable and, if such a request is made, the court shall, subject to any other power of the court to adjourn proceedings, resume the hearing.

(3) The powers conferred by this section are additional to any other power of the court to adjourn proceedings.

(4) Where the court adjourns proceedings under this section, it may, at its discretion, advise the parties concerned to seek the assistance of a third party in relation to the effecting of an agreement between them on all or any of its terms.

**23      Non-admissibility as evidence of certain communications relating to agreement**

An oral or written communication between any of the parties concerned and a third party for the purpose of seeking assistance to reach agreement between them regarding the custody of the child, the right of access to the child or any question affecting the welfare of the child (whether or not made in the presence or with the knowledge of the other party) and any record of such communication, made or caused to be made by any of the parties concerned or such third party, shall not be admissible as evidence in any court.

## 24     Orders in respect of custody or access agreements

Where—

    (a)  the parties to a dispute relating to the welfare of a child enter into an agreement in writing that includes—

        (i)  a provision whereby one party undertakes, or both parties undertake, to take custody of the child, or

       (ii)  a provision governing the rights of access of parties,

      and

    (b)  an application is made by any party to the court for an order making the agreement a rule of court,

the court may make such an order if is satisfied that the agreement is a fair and reasonable one which in all the circumstances adequately protects the interests of the parties and the child, and such order shall, in so far as it relates to a provision specified in subparagraph (i) or (ii) of paragraph (a), be deemed to be an order under section 11(2)(a) or 11B as appropriate.

## 25     Wishes of child

In any proceedings to which section 3 applies, the court shall, as it thinks appropriate and practicable having regard to the age and understanding of the child, take into account the child's wishes in the matter.

## 26     Social reports

For the purposes of the application of section 47 of the Act of 1995 to proceedings under this Act, "**court**" includes the District Court.[1]

---

**Note**

1   This section is not yet in force.

---

## 27     Power to proceed in absence of child

(1) It shall not be necessary in proceedings under section 6A, 11 or 11B for the child to whom the proceedings relate to be brought before the court or to be present for all or any part of the hearing unless the court, either of its own motion or at the request of any of the parties to the proceedings, is satisfied that it is necessary for the proper disposal of the proceedings.

(2) Where the child requests to be present during the hearing or a particular part of the hearing of the proceedings, the court shall grant the request unless it appears to it that,

having regard to the age of the child or the nature of the proceedings, it would not be in the child's best interests to accede to the request.

## 28 Appointment of guardian *ad litem* for a child and provision for separate representation

(1) If in proceedings under section 6A, 11 or 11B the child to whom the proceedings relate is not a party, the court may, if satisfied that having regard to the special circumstances of the case it is necessary in the best interests of the child to do so, appoint a guardian *ad litem* for the child.

(2) Without prejudice to the generality of subsection (1), in deciding whether to appoint a guardian *ad litem*, the court shall, in particular, have regard to—

    (a) the age and understanding of the child,

    (b) any report on any question affecting the welfare of the child that is furnished to the court under section 47 of the Act of 1995,

    (c) the welfare of the child,

    (d) whether and to what extent the child should be given the opportunity to express the child's wishes in the proceedings, taking into account any statement in relation to those matters in any report under section 47 of the Act of 1995, and

    (e) any submission made in relation to the matter of the appointment as a guardian ad litem that is made to the court by or on behalf of a party to the proceedings or any other person to whom they relate.

(3) For the purposes of this section, the court may appoint as a guardian *ad litem* the person from whom, under section 47(1) of the Act of 1995, a report on any question affecting the welfare of the child was procured, or such other person as it thinks fit.

(4) If having regard to the gravity of the matters that may be in issue or any other special circumstances relating to the particular case, it appears to the court that it is necessary in the best interests of the child that the guardian *ad litem* ought to be legally represented, the court may order that the guardian *ad litem* be so represented in the proceedings.

(5) The fees and expenses of a guardian *ad litem* appointed pursuant to subsection (1) and the costs of obtaining legal representation pursuant to an order under subsection (4) shall be paid by such parties to the proceedings concerned, and in such proportions, or by such party to the proceedings, as the court may determine.[1]

---

**Note**

1   This section is not yet in force.

---

## 29 Cost of mediation and counselling services

The cost of any mediation or counselling services provided for an applicant or respondent who is or becomes a party to proceedings under this Act, or for the child to whom the proceedings relate, shall be in the discretion of the court concerned.

**30      Jurisdiction**

(1) Subject to subsection (2), the jurisdiction conferred on a court by this Part may be exercised by the Circuit Court or the District Court.

(2) Where the agreement referred to in section 24 is a separation agreement, the application for an order in respect of that agreement shall be made to the Circuit Court.

(3) Where an application is made to the court for an order under section 24, the court may, in the same proceedings, if it appears to it to be proper to do so, make an order under section 8 or 8A of the Act of 1976 without the institution of proceedings under that Act.

(4) Where an application is made to the court for an order under section 8 or 8A of the Act of 1976, the court may, in the same proceedings, if it appears to it to be proper to do so, make an order under section 24 without the institution of proceedings under this Act.[1]

**Note**

1    This section is not yet in force.

**SCHEDULE**
**REPEALS**

Section 4

| Session and Chapter | Short Title | Extent of Repeal |
|---|---|---|
| 14 & 15 Chas. 2, sess. 4, c. 19. | Tenures Abolition Act, 1662. | Sections 6, 7, 15 and 16. |
| 36 Vict. c. 12. | Custody of Infants Act, 1873. | The whole Act. |
| 49 & 50 Vict. c. 27. | Guardianship of Infants Act, 1886. | The whole Act. |
| 54 Vict. c. 3. | Custody of Children Act, 1891. | The whole Act. |

# Maintenance Orders Act 1974

[…][1]

---

## Notes

1 Maintenance Orders Act 1974 was repealed by European Communities (Maintenance) Regulations 2011 (SI 274/2011), reg 25.

---

# Family Law (Maintenance of Spouses And Children) Act 1976

*Number 11 of 1976*

*An Act to make provision for periodical payments by a spouse for the support of the other spouse and any dependent children of the family of the spouses in certain cases of failure by the spouse to provide reasonable maintenance, to enable payments to be made by an employer, by deductions from an employee's earnings, to a person entitled under certain court orders to periodic payments for maintenance from the employee, to provide for other matters connected with the matters aforesaid and to amend in other respects the law relating to parents and children. [6th April, 1976]*

*Be it enacted by the Oireachtas as follows:*

# PART I
## PRELIMINARY AND GENERAL

**1        Short title**

This Act may be cited as the Family Law (Maintenance of Spouses and Children) Act, 1976.[1]

---

**Notes**

1   See the Status of Children Act 1987, s 15, the Judicial Separation and Family Law Reform Act 1989, ss 39 and 45, the Family Law Act 1995, ss 41, 42 and 47, the Family Law (Divorce) Act 1996, s 26(1) and the Domestic Violence Act 1996, s 9.

---

## 2     Commencement

This Act shall come into operation on the day that is one month after the date of its passing.[1]

---

### Notes

1    Commencement: 6 May 1976.

---

## 3     Interpretation

(1) In this Act, save where the context otherwise requires—

**"antecedent order"**[1] means—

(a)   a maintenance order,

(b)   a variation order,

(c)   an interim order,

(d)   an order under section 8 of this Act (in so far as it is deemed under that section to be a maintenance order),

(e)   an order deemed under section 30 of this Act to be a maintenance order,

(f)   an order providing for a periodical payment under the Illegitimate Children (Affiliation Orders) Act, 1930,

(g)   an order for maintenance under section 11(2)(b) of the Guardianship of Infants Act, 1964,

(h)   an enforceable maintenance order under the Maintenance Orders Act, 1974,

[(i)   an order for alimony pending suit;][2]

[(j)   an order for maintenance pending suit under the Judicial Separation and Family Law Reform Act, 1989, or a periodical payments order under that Act,][3]

[(k)   a maintenance pending suit order under the Family Law Act, 1995, or a periodical payments order under that Act;

(l)   a maintenance pending suit order under the Family Law (Divorce) Act, 1996, or a periodical payments order under that Act;][4]

**"attachment of earnings order"** means an order under section 10 of this Act;

**"Court"** shall be construed in accordance with section 23 of this Act;

["**dependent child**" means any child (including a child whose parents are not married to each other) who is under the age of [18][5] years, or, if he has attained that age—

(a)   is or will be or, if an order were made under this Act providing for periodical payments for his support, would be receiving full-time education or instruction at any university, college, school or other educational establishment and is under the age of [23][5] years, or

27

(b) is suffering from mental or physical disability to such extent that it is not reasonably possible for him to maintain himself fully;]⁵

["**dependent child of the family**", in relation to a spouse or spouses, means any dependent child—

(a) of both spouses, or adopted by both spouses under the Adoption Acts, 1952 to 1976, or in relation to whom both spouses are *in loco parentis*, or

(b) of either spouse, or adopted by either spouse under the Adoption Acts, 1952 to 1976, or in relation to whom either spouse is *in loco parentis*, where the other spouse, being aware that he is not the parent of the child, has treated the child as a member of the family,]⁵

who is under the age of [18]⁵ years, or, if he has attained that age—

(i) is or will be or, if an order were made under this Act providing for periodical payments for his support, would be receiving full-time education or instruction at any university, college, school or other educational establishment and is under the age of [23]⁵ years, or

(ii) is suffering from mental or physical disability to such extent that it is not reasonably possible for him to maintain himself fully;

"**desertion**" includes conduct on the part of one spouse that results in the other spouse, with just cause, leaving and living separately and apart from him, and cognate words shall be construed accordingly;

"**earnings**" means any sums payable to a person—

(a) by way of wages or salary (including any fees, bonus, commission, overtime pay or other emoluments payable in addition to wages or salary or payable under a contract of service);

(b) by way of pension or other like benefit in respect of employment (including an annuity in respect of past services, whether or not rendered to the person paying the annuity, and including periodical payments by way of compensation for the loss, abolition or relinquishment, or diminution in the emoluments, of any office or employment);

"**interim order**" means an order under section 7 of this Act;

["**lump sum order**" means an order under section 21A of this Act;]⁵

"**maintenance creditor**", in relation to an order under this Act (other than an order under section 22 of this Act), or to proceedings arising out of such an order, means a person on whose application there has been made such an order;

"**maintenance debtor**", in relation to an attachment of earnings order, or to proceedings in which a Court has power to make such an order, or to proceedings arising out of such an order, means the spouse by whom payments are required by the relevant antecedent order to be made and, in relation to any other order under this Act (other than an order under section 22 of this Act) or to proceedings in which a Court has power to make such an order, or to proceedings arising out of such an order, means a spouse who is or, if it were made, would be required by such an order to make periodical payments for the support of persons named in the order;

["**maintenance order**" means, where the context requires, an order under either section 5 or 5A of this Act;][5]

"**normal deduction rate**" and "**protected earnings rate**" have the meanings respectively assigned to them by section 10 of this Act;

["**parent**", in relation to a dependent child, includes a person who has adopted the child under the Adoption Acts, 1952 to 1976, but does not include a person who is a parent of the child adopted under those Acts where the person is not an adopter of the child;][5]

"**variation order**" means an order under section 6 of this Act varying a maintenance order.

(2) Subject to section 16 of this Act, the relationship of employer and employee shall be regarded as subsisting between two persons if one of them as a principal and not as a servant or agent pays earnings to the other.

(3) References in this Act to a District Court clerk include references to his successor in the office of District Court clerk and to any person acting on his behalf.

(4) References in this Act to any enactment shall be construed as references to that enactment as amended by any subsequent enactment, including this Act.[6]

**Notes**

1 See the European Communities (Maintenance) Regulations 2011 (SI 274/2011), reg 8(4), 23(2) and European Communities (Mediation) Regulations 2011 (SI 209/2011), reg 5(3)(b).

2 Section 3(1)(i) was inserted by the Judicial Separation and Family Law Reform Act 1989, s 25(1).

3 Section 3(1)(j) and (k) were inserted by the Family Law Act 1995, s 43(a).

4 Section 3(1)(l) was inserted by the Family Law (Divorce) Act 1996, s 27.

5 Definitions of "dependent child", "dependent child of the family", "lump sum order", "maintenance order" and "parent" were inserted by the Status of Children Act 1987, s 16. The definition of "dependent child" was amended by the Family Law Act 1995, s 43(a) and the Family Law (Divorce) Act 1996, s 52(o)(i) by the substitution of "23" for "twenty-one" and "18" for "sixteen".

6 See the Judicial Separation and Family Law Reform Act 1989, s 25(2).

**4      Commencement of periodical payments**

[A periodical payment under an order under this Act shall commence on the date that is specified in the order being a date which may be before or after the date on which the order is made but which shall not be earlier than the date of the application for the order.][1]

**Notes**

1   Section 4 was substituted by the Social Welfare (Miscellaneous Provisions) Act 2002, s 16 and Sch.

# PART II
## MAINTENANCE OF SPOUSES AND DEPENDENT CHILDREN[1]

### 5   Maintenance order

(1) (a) Subject to subsection (4) of this section, where it appears to the Court, on application to it by a spouse, that the other spouse has failed to provide such maintenance for the applicant spouse and any dependent children of the family as is proper in the circumstances, the Court may make an order (in this Act referred to as a maintenance order) that the other spouse make to the applicant spouse periodical payments, for the support of the applicant spouse and of each of the dependent children of the family, for such period during the lifetime of the applicant spouse, of such amount and at such times, as the Court may consider proper.

   (b) Subject to subsection (4) of this section, where a spouse—

      (i)   is dead,

      (ii)  has deserted, or has been deserted by, the other spouse, or

      (iii) is living separately and apart from the other spouse,

   and there are dependent children of the family (not being children who are being fully maintained by either spouse), then, if it appears to the Court, on application to it by any person, that the surviving spouse or, as the case may be, either spouse has failed to provide such maintenance for any dependent children of the family as is proper in the circumstances, the Court may make an order (in this Act referred to as a maintenance order) that that spouse make to that person periodical payments, for the support of each of those dependent children, for such period during the lifetime of that person, of such amount and at such times, as the Court may consider proper.

   (c) A maintenance order [under this section][2] or a variation order shall specify each part of a payment under the order that is for the support of a dependent child [of the family][2] and may specify the period during the lifetime of the person applying for the order for which so much of a payment under the order as is for the support of a dependent child [of the family][2] shall be made.

(2) The Court shall not make a maintenance order for the support of a spouse where the spouse has deserted and continues to desert the other spouse [unless, having regard to all the circumstances (including the conduct of the other spouse), the Court is of the opinion that it would be repugnant to justice not to make a maintenance order.][3]

(3) [...][4]

[(4) The Court, in deciding whether to make a maintenance order under this section and, if it decides to do so, in determining the amount of any payment, shall have regard to all the circumstances of the case and, in particular, to the following matters—

(a)  the income, earning capacity (if any), property and other financial resources of—

   (i)   the spouses and any dependent children of the family, and

   (ii)  any other dependent children of which either spouse is a parent,

   including income or benefits to which either spouse or any such children are entitled by or under statute, and

(b)  the financial and other responsibilities of—

   (i)   the spouses towards each other and towards any dependent children of the family, and,

   (ii)  each spouse as a parent towards any other dependent children,

   and the needs of any such children, including the need for care and attention.]⁵

[(c)  the conduct of each of the spouses, if that conduct is such that in the opinion of the Court it would in all the circumstances be repugnant to justice to disregard it.]⁶

## Notes

1   See the European Communities (Civil and Commercial Judgments) Regulations 2002 (SI 52/2002), reg 6(7). The application of s 5 is extended by European Communities (Maintenance) Regulations 2011 (SI 274/2011), reg 10.

2   The words "of the family" and "under this section" were inserted by the Status of Children Act 1987, s 15.

3   Subsection (2) was amended by the Judicial Separation and Family Law Reform Act 1989, s 38.

4   Subsection (3) was repealed by the Judicial Separation and Family Law Reform Act 1989, s 38.

5   Subsection (4)(a), (b) was substituted by the Status of Children Act 1987, s 17.

6   Subsection (4)(c) was inserted by the Judicial Separation and Family Law Reform Act 1989, s 38.

## [5A     Maintenance Order (provision for certain dependent children)¹

(1) Subject to subsection (3) of this section, where, in respect of a dependent child whose parents are not married to each other, it appears to the Court on application to it by either parent of the child that the other parent has failed to provide such maintenance for the child as is proper in the circumstances, the Court may make an order (in this Act referred to as a maintenance order) that the other parent make to the applicant parent periodical payments, for the support of the child as aforesaid, for such period during the

lifetime of the applicant parent, of such amount and at such times, as the Court may consider proper.

(2) Subject to subsections (3) and (4) of this section, where in respect of a dependent child whose parents are not married to each other it appears to the Court, on application to it by any person other than a parent, that a parent of a child (not being a child who is being fully maintained by the other parent) has failed to provide such maintenance for the child as is proper in the circumstances, the Court may make an order (in this Act referred to as a maintenance order) that the parent make to that person periodical payments for the support of the child for such period during the lifetime of that person, of such amount and at such times as the Court may consider proper.

(3) The Court, in deciding whether to make a maintenance order under this section and, if it decides to do so, in determining the amount of any payment, shall have regard to all the circumstances of the case and, in particular, to the following matters—

    (a)  the income, earning capacity (if any), property and other financial resources of—

        (i)  each parent,

        (ii)  the dependent child in respect of whom the order is sought, and

        (iii)  any other dependent children of either parent,

        including income or benefits to which either parent, the dependent child as aforesaid or such other dependent children are entitled by or under statute, and

    (b)  the financial and other responsibilities of each parent towards—

        (i)  a spouse,

        (ii)  the dependent child in respect of whom the order is sought, and

        (iii)  any other dependent children of either parent,

        and the needs of any dependent child as aforesaid or of any such other dependent children, including the need for care and attention.

(4) The Court shall not make a maintenance order under subsection (2) of this section in relation to a parent of a dependent child if a maintenance order under subsection (1) of this section requiring that parent to make periodical payments for the support of the child is in force or that parent has made provision for the child by an agreement under which, at or after the time of the hearing of the application for the order under the said subsection (2), payments fall to be made and in relation to which an order under section 8A of this Act has been made unless—

    (a)  the parent is not complying with the order under the said subsection (1) or the agreement, as the case may be, and

    (b)  the Court, having regard to all the circumstances, thinks it proper to do so,

but, if the Court makes the order under the said subsection (2), any amounts falling due for payment under the order under the said subsection (1) or the agreement, as the case may be, on or after the date of the making of the order under the said subsection (2) shall not be payable.][2]

**Notes**

1    Commencement: 14 December 1987.

2    Section 5A was inserted by the Status of Children Act 1987, s 18. See the Family Law Act 1995, s 53(1)(aa) (as amended by the Family Law (Divorce) Act 1996, s 52(l)(ii)), the Domestic Violence Act 1996, s 9 and the Family Law (Divorce) Act 1996, s 26. See the European Communities (Civil and Commercial Judgments) Regulations 2002 (SI 52/2002), reg 6(7), (18). The application of s 5A is extended by European Communities (Maintenance) Regulations 2011 (SI 274/2011), reg 10.

**6      Discharge, variation and termination of maintenance order[1]**

(1) The Court may—

   (a)   discharge a maintenance order at any time after one year from the making thereof, on the application of the maintenance debtor, where it appears to the Court that, having regard to the maintenance debtor's record of payments pursuant to the order and to the other circumstances of the case, the persons for whose support it provides will not be prejudiced by the discharge thereof or

   (b)   discharge or vary a maintenance order at any time, on the application of either party, if it thinks it proper to do so having regard to any circumstances not existing when the order was made [(including the conduct of each of the spouses, if that conduct is such that in the opinion of the Court it would in all the circumstances be repugnant to justice to disregard it)][2] or, if it has been varied, when it was last varied, or to any evidence not available to that party when the maintenance order was made or, if it has been varied, when it was last varied.

(2) Notwithstanding anything contained in subsection (1) of this section, the Court shall, on application to it under that subsection, discharge that part of a maintenance order which provides for the support of a maintenance creditor where it appears to it that the maintenance creditor, being the spouse of the maintenance debtor, has deserted and continues to desert the maintenance debtor [unless, having regard to all the circumstances (including the conduct of the other spouse) the Court is of opinion that it would be repugnant to justice to do so.][2]

(3) That part of a maintenance order which provides for the support of a dependent child shall stand discharged when the child ceases to be a dependent child by reason of his attainment of the age of [18][2] years or [23][2] years, as the case may be, and shall be discharged by the Court, on application to it under subsection (1) of this section, if it is satisfied that the child has for any reason ceased to be a dependent child [for the purposes of the order.][3]

(4) [...][4]

(5) Desertion [by, or conduct of,]⁵ a spouse shall not be a ground for discharging or varying any part of a maintenance order that provides for the support of dependent children of the family.

**Notes**

1   See the Domestic Violence Act 1996, s 9 and the Family Law (Divorce) Act 1996, s 26(1).

2   Subsection (1)(b) and subsection (2) were amended by the Judicial Separation and Family Law Reform Act 1989, s 38. Subsection (3) was amended by the Family Law Act 1995, s 43(b) by the substitution of "18" for "sixteen" and "23" for "twenty-one".

3   Subsection (3) was amended by the Status of Children Act 1987, s 19 and by the Family Law Act 1995, s 43(b).

4   Subsection (4) was repealed by the Judicial Separation and Family Law Reform Act 1989, s 38.

5   Subsection (5) was amended by the Judicial Separation and Family Law Reform Act 1989, s 38.

**7      Interim order**

On an application to the Court for a maintenance order, the Court, before deciding whether to make or refuse to make the order, may, if it appears to the Court proper to do so having regard to the needs of the persons for whose support the maintenance order is sought and the other circumstances of the case, make an order (in this Act referred to as an interim order) for the payment to the applicant by the maintenance debtor, for a definite period specified in the order or until the application is adjudicated upon by the Court, of such periodical sum as, in the opinion of the Court, is proper.[1]

**Notes**

1   See the Family Law Act 1995, s 35(1)(aa) as amended by the Family Law (Divorce) Act 1996, s 52(l)(ii), the Domestic Violence Act 1996, s 9, and the Family Law (Divorce) Act 1996, s 26.

**8      Orders in respect of certain marital agreements**

Where—

   (a)  the parties to a marriage enter into an agreement in writing (including a separation agreement) after the commencement of this Act that includes either or both of the following provisions, that is to say—

         (i)  a provision whereby one spouse undertakes to make periodical payments towards the maintenance of the other spouse or of any dependent children of the family or of both that other spouse and any dependent children of the family,

> (ii) a provision governing the rights and liabilities of the spouses towards one another in respect of the making or securing of payments (other than payments specified in paragraph (a)(i) of this section), or the disposition or use of any property, and

(b) an application is made by one or both of the spouses to the High Court or the [Circuit Court or, in relation to an agreement other than a separation agreement, the District Court][1] for an order making the agreement a rule of court,

the Court may make such an order if it is satisfied that the agreement is a fair and reasonable one which in all the circumstances adequately protects the interests of both spouses and the dependent children (if any) of the family, and such order shall, in so far as it relates to a provision specified in paragraph (a)(i) of this section, be deemed, for the purpose of section 9 and Part III of this Act, to be a maintenance order.

---

**Notes**

1    Section 8(b) was amended by the Children Act 1997, s 15.

---

## [8A    Orders in respect of certain other agreements

Where—

(a) the parents of a dependent child who are not married to each other enter into an agreement in writing after the commencement of Part IV of the Status of Children Act, 1987, that includes either or both of the following provisions, that is to say—

> (i) a provision whereby a parent undertakes to make periodical payments towards the maintenance of a child,

> (ii) a provision affecting the interests of the child which governs the rights and liabilities of the parents towards one another in respect of the making or securing of payments (other than payments specified in paragraph (a)(i) of this section), or the disposition or use of any property,

and,

(b) an application is made by one or both of the parents to the High Court or the [Circuit Court or, in relation to an agreement other than a separation agreement, the District Court][1] for an order making the agreement a rule of court,

that Court may make such an order if it is satisfied that the agreement is a fair and reasonable one which in all the circumstances adequately protects the interests of the child and such order shall, in so far as it relates to a provision specified in paragraph (a)(i) of this section, be deemed, for the purposes of section 9 and Part III of this Act, to be a maintenance order.][2]

**Notes**

1   Section 8A(b) was amended by the Children Act 1997, s 15.

2   Commencement: 14 December 1987. Section 8A was inserted by the Status of Children Act 1987, s 20.

**[8B    Preservation of pension entitlements in separation agreements**

(1) Subject to the provisions of this section, on an application to the High Court or the Circuit Court under section 8 of this Act, the Court may, on application to it in that behalf by either of the spouses concerned, make an order directing the trustees of a pension scheme of which either or both of the spouses are members, not to regard the separation of the spouses by agreement as a ground for disqualifying either of them for the receipt of a benefit under the scheme a condition for the receipt of which is that the spouses should be residing together at the time when the benefit becomes payable.

(2) Notice of an application under subsection (1) shall be given by the spouse concerned to the trustees of the pension scheme concerned and, in deciding whether to make an order under subsection (1), the Court shall have regard to any order made, or proposed to be made, by it in relation to the application by the spouse or spouses concerned under section 8 of this Act and any representations made by those trustees in relation to the matter.

(3) Any costs incurred by the trustees of a pension scheme under subsection (2) or in complying with an order under subsection (1) shall be borne, as the court may determine, by either of the spouses concerned or by both of the spouses and in such proportions and such manner as the Court may determine.

(4) In this section **"pension scheme"** has the meaning assigned to it by the Family Law Act, 1995.][1]

**Notes**

1   Commencement: 1 August 1996. Commencement order: SI 46/1996. Section 8B was inserted by the Family Law Act 1995, s 43(c).

**9    Transmission of payments through District Court clerk**

(1) Where the Court makes a maintenance order, a variation order or an interim order under this Act, the Court shall—

(a) thereupon direct that payments under the order shall be made to the District Court clerk, unless the maintenance creditor requests it not to do so and the Court considers that it would be proper not to do so, and

(b) in a case in which the Court has not given a direction under paragraph (a) of this subsection, direct, at any time thereafter on the application of the maintenance creditor, that the payments aforesaid shall be made to the District Court clerk.

(2) Where payments to the District Court clerk under this section are in arrear, the District Court clerk shall, if the maintenance creditor so requests in writing, take such steps as he considers reasonable in the circumstances to recover the sums in arrear whether by proceeding in his own name for an attachment of earnings order or otherwise.

(3) Where a direction has been given under subsection (1) of this section, the Court, on the application of the maintenance debtor and having afforded the maintenance creditor an opportunity to oppose the application, may, if it is satisfied that, having regard to the record of the payments made to the District Court clerk and all the other circumstances, it would be proper to do so, discharge the direction.

(4) The District Court clerk shall transmit any payments made to him by virtue of this section to the maintenance creditor.

(5) Nothing in this section shall affect any right of a person to take proceedings in his own name for the recovery of any sum payable, but not paid, to the District Court clerk by virtue of this section.

(6) References in this section, in relation to any proceedings, to the District Court clerk are references to such District Court clerk in such District Court district as may be determined from time to time by the Court concerned.

(7) Nothing in subsection (1) or (2) of this section shall affect paragraph (a) or (b) of section 14 (8) of the Maintenance Orders Act, 1974, No. 16, 1974.

(8) Section 14(8) of the Maintenance Orders Act, 1974, is hereby amended by the insertion in paragraph (b) after "application under" of "section 10 of the Family Law (Maintenance of Spouses and Children) Act, 1976, or" and by the substitution of "the said section 8" for "that section" and the said paragraph (b), as so amended, is set out in the Table to this section.

## TABLE

(b) The district court clerk shall, if any sum payable by virtue of an enforceable maintenance order is not duly paid and if the maintenance creditor so requests in writing, make an application under section 10 of the Family Law (Maintenance of Spouses and Children) Act, 1976, or section 8 (which relates to the enforcement of certain maintenance orders) of the Enforcement of Court Orders Act, 1940, and for that purpose the references in the said section 8 (other than subsections (4) and (5)) to the applicant shall be construed as references to the district court clerk.[1]

**Notes**

1   See the Family Law (Divorce) Act 1996, s 28.

**[9A   Failure to make payments to be contempt of court**

(1) Subject to this section it shall be contempt of court for a maintenance debtor to fail to make a payment due under an antecedent order.

(2) As respects a contempt of court arising pursuant to this section, a judge of the District Court shall, subject to this section, have such powers, including the power to impose a sanction, as are exercisable by a judge of the High Court in relation to contempt of court in proceedings before the High Court.

(3) Where a payment under an antecedent order made by the District Court has not been made, the maintenance creditor may apply to the District Court clerk concerned for the issue of a summons directing the maintenance debtor to appear before the District Court.

(4) A summons referred to in subsection (3) shall—

    (a)   be issued by the District Court clerk concerned,

    (b)   contain a statement that failure to make a payment in accordance with the order concerned constitutes a contempt of court and giving details of the consequences of the court finding that a contempt of court has taken place including in particular the possibility of imprisonment,

    (c)   state that the maintenance debtor may be arrested if he or she fails to appear before the District Court as directed in the summons, and

    (d)   be served on the maintenance debtor personally, or in such other manner authorised by a judge of the District Court.

(5) If the maintenance debtor fails, without reasonable excuse, to appear before the court in answer to the summons, the judge of the District Court, on the application of the maintenance creditor, shall, if satisfied that the debtor was served with the summons, issue a warrant for the arrest of the maintenance debtor.

(6) A maintenance debtor arrested pursuant to a warrant issued under subsection (5) shall be brought as soon as practicable before the District Court.

(7) Where a maintenance debtor is arrested and brought before the District Court under subsection (6), the judge shall fix a new date for the hearing of the summons and direct that the creditor be informed by the District Court by notice in writing of the date so fixed, and shall explain to the debtor in ordinary language—

    (a)   that he or she is required to attend before the court at the date next fixed for the hearing of the summons,

    (b)   that failure to attend may in itself constitute a contempt of court and the consequences of such contempt, including in particular the possibility of imprisonment, and that such contempt and the consequences which may follow are in addition to the consequences arising by reason of failure to make a payment under the antecedent order, and

(c) that he or she is entitled to apply for legal advice and legal aid under the Civil Legal Aid Act 1995.

(8) At the hearing of the summons, before hearing evidence from any party the judge shall explain to the debtor in ordinary language—

(a) the consequences, and in particular the possibility of imprisonment, which may follow a failure to make a payment in accordance with an antecedent order, and

(b) unless the maintenance debtor has already been so informed under subsection (7), that he or she is entitled to apply for legal advice and legal aid under the Civil Legal Aid Act 1995.

(9) On the hearing of the summons, having given to the maintenance debtor the explanations referred to in subsection (8), having given the maintenance debtor an opportunity to apply for legal advice and legal aid, and having heard such evidence as may be adduced by the maintenance creditor and the maintenance debtor, if the judge is satisfied that the payment concerned has not been made, and—

(a) that the failure to make the payment concerned is due to—

(i) the inability of the maintenance debtor to make the payment concerned by reason of a change in his or her financial circumstances which occurred since the antecedent order or an order varying that order was last made (whichever is the later), or

(ii) some other reason not attributable to any act or omission of the maintenance debtor,

the judge may, where he or she believes that to do so would improve the likelihood of the payment concerned being made within a reasonable period, adjourn the hearing—

(I) to enable the outstanding payment to be made, or

(II) to enable an application to be made for an attachment of earnings order under section 10,

(b) that the failure to make the payment concerned is due to the inability of the maintenance debtor to make the payment concerned by reason of a change in his or her financial circumstances which occurred since the antecedent order or an order varying that order was last made (whichever is the later) the judge may, where the antecedent order was made by the District Court, treat the hearing as an application to vary the antecedent order, and having heard evidence as to the financial circumstances of both the maintenance debtor and the maintenance creditor, make an order varying the antecedent order.

(10) Where on the hearing of the summons, having given to the maintenance debtor the explanations referred to in subsection (8), having given the maintenance debtor an opportunity to apply for legal advice and legal aid, and having heard such evidence as may be adduced by the maintenance creditor and the maintenance debtor, the judge is

satisfied that the payment concerned has not been made and that the failure to make the payment concerned is not due to—

(a) the inability of the maintenance debtor to make the payment concerned by reason of a change in his or her financial circumstances which occurred since the antecedent order or an order varying that order was last made (whichever is the later), or

(b) some other reason not attributable to any act or omission of the maintenance debtor,

the judge may treat the failure by the maintenance debtor to make the payment concerned as constituting contempt of court and the judge may deal with the matter accordingly.

(11) Where a maintenance debtor to whom subsection (7) applies does not attend court on the date fixed for the hearing of the summons the judge may treat such failure to attend court as constituting contempt of court and the judge may deal with the matter accordingly.

(12) In this section '**financial circumstances**' means, in relation to a person—

(a) the amount of the person's annual income,

(b) the aggregate value of all property (real and personal) belonging to the person,

(c) the aggregate of all liabilities of the person including any duty (moral or legal) to provide financially for members of his or her family or other persons,

(d) the aggregate of all monies owing to the person, the dates upon which they fall due to be paid and the likelihood of their being paid, and

(e) such other circumstances as the court considers appropriate.

(13) This section does not apply unless the antecedent order concerned was actually made by the District Court.

## 9B     Certificate of outstanding payments

Where, pursuant to section 9, a court has made a maintenance order, a variation order or an interim order and directed that payments under the order be made to the District Court clerk, in any proceedings under this Act or under the Enforcement of Court Orders Acts 1926 to 2009, a certificate purporting to be signed by the relevant District Court clerk as to the amount of monies outstanding on foot of such order shall, until the contrary is shown, be evidence of the matters stated in the certificate.][1]

---

**Notes**

1   Sections 9A and 9B were inserted by the Civil Law (Miscellaneous Provisions) Act 2011, s 31.

---

PART III

ATTACHMENT OF EARNINGS

**10     Attachment of earnings order**

(1)  (a)  On application—

    (i)   to the High Court by a person on whose application the High Court has made an antecedent order,

    (ii)  to the Circuit Court by a person on whose application the Circuit Court has made an antecedent order,

    (iii) to the District Court—

        (I)   by a person on whose application the District Court has made an antecedent order, or

        (II)  by a District Court clerk to whom payments under an antecedent order are required to be made,

the Court to which the application is made (subsequently referred to in this section as "the Court") may, to secure payments under the antecedent order, if it is satisfied that the maintenance debtor is a person to whom earnings fall to be paid, make an attachment of earnings order.

  (b)  References in this subsection to an antecedent order made by any Court include references to such an order made, varied or affirmed on appeal from that Court.

[(1A)(a) Where a court has made an antecedent order, it shall in the same proceedings, subject to subsection (3), make an attachment of earnings order in order to secure payments under the antecedent order if it is satisfied that the maintenance debtor is a person to whom earnings fall to be paid.

  (b)  References in this subsection to an antecedent order made by a court include references to such an order made, varied or affirmed on appeal from that court.]¹

(2) An attachment of earnings order shall be an order directed to a person who (at the time of the making of the order or at any time thereafter) has the maintenance debtor in his employment [or is a trustee (within the meaning of the Family Law Act, 1995) of a pension scheme (within the meaning aforesaid) under which the maintenance debtor is receiving periodical pension benefits]², and shall operate as a direction to that person to make, at such times as may be specified in the order, periodical deductions of such amounts (specified in the order) as may be appropriate, having regard to the normal deduction rate and the protected earnings rate, from the maintenance debtor's earnings and to pay the amounts deducted, at such times as the Court may order—

  (a)  in case the relevant antecedent order is an enforceable maintenance order, to the District Court clerk specified by the attachment of earnings order for transmission to the person entitled to receive payments made under the relevant antecedent order,

41

(b) in any other case, to the person referred to in paragraph (a) of this subsection or, if the Court considers proper, to the District Court clerk specified by the attachment of earnings order for transmission to that person.

[(3) (a) Before deciding whether to make or refuse to make an attachment of earnings order, the court shall give the maintenance debtor concerned an opportunity to make the representations specified in paragraph (b) in relation to the matter and shall have regard to any such representations made by the maintenance debtor.

(b) The representations referred to in paragraph (a) are representations relating to the questions—

(i) whether the spouse concerned is a person to whom such earnings as aforesaid fall to be paid, and

(ii) whether he or she would make the payments to which the relevant order relates.][2]

(4) An attachment of earnings order shall—

(a) specify the normal deduction rate, that is to say, the rate at which the Court considers it reasonable that the earnings to which the order relates should be applied in satisfying the relevant antecedent order, not exceeding the rate appearing to the Court to be necessary for the purpose of—

(i) securing payment of the sums falling due from time to time under the relevant antecedent order, and

(ii) securing payment within a reasonable period of any sums already due and unpaid under the relevant antecedent order and any costs incurred in proceedings relating to the relevant antecedent order which are payable by the maintenance debtor,

(b) specify the protected earnings rate, that is to say, the rate below which, having regard to the resources and the needs of the maintenance debtor, the Court considers it proper that the relevant earnings should not be reduced by a payment made in pursuance of the attachment of earnings order,

(c) contain so far as they are known to the Court such particulars as it considers appropriate for the purpose of enabling the maintenance debtor to be identified by the person to whom the order is directed.

(5) Payments under an attachment of earnings order shall be in lieu of payments of the like total amount under the relevant antecedent order that have not been made and that, but for the attachment of earnings order, would fall to be made under the relevant antecedent order.[3]

---

**Notes**

1    Subsection (1A) was inserted by the Family Law Act 1995, s 43(d).

2    Subsection (2) was amended and subsection (3) was substituted by the Family Law Act 1995, s 43(d).

3   See the European Communities (Civil and Commercial Judgments) Regulations 2002 (SI 52/
    2002), reg 6(10)(b) and the European Communities (Maintenance) Regulations 2011 (SI 274/
    2011), reg 10(9)(b).

## 11      Compliance with attachment of earnings order

(1) Where an attachment of earnings order or an order varying it is made, the employer for the time being affected by it shall, if it has been served upon him, comply with it; but he shall be under no liability for non-compliance therewith before ten days have elapsed since the service.

(2) Where an attachment of earnings order is served on any person and the maintenance debtor is not in his employment or the maintenance debtor subsequently ceases to be in his employment, that person shall (in either case), within ten days from the date of service or, as the case may be, the cesser, give notice of that fact to the Court.

(3) On any occasion when a person makes, in compliance with an attachment of earnings order, a deduction from a maintenance debtor's earnings, he shall give to the maintenance debtor a statement in writing of the total amount of the deduction.

(4) Such court registrar or court clerk as may be specified by an attachment of earnings order shall cause the order to be served on the employer to whom it is directed and on any subsequent employer of the maintenance debtor concerned of whom the registrar or clerk so specified becomes aware and such service may be effected by leaving the order or a copy of the order at, or sending the order or a copy of the order by registered prepaid post to, the residence or place of business in the State of the person to be served.

## 12      Application of sums received by District Court clerk

Any payments made to a District Court clerk under an attachment of earnings order shall, when transmitted by him to the person entitled to receive those payments, be deemed to be payments made by the maintenance debtor so as to discharge—

(a) firstly, any sums payable under the relevant antecedent order, and

(b) secondly, any costs in proceedings relating to the relevant antecedent order payable by the maintenance debtor when the attachment of earnings order was made or last varied.

## 13      Statement as to earnings

(1) In relation to an attachment of earnings order or an application for such an order, the Court that made the order or to which the application is made may, before or at the hearing or while the order is in force—

(a) order the maintenance debtor to give to the Court, within a specified period, a statement in writing signed by him of—

(i) the name and address of any person by whom earnings are paid to him,

(ii) specified particulars as to his earnings and expected earnings and as to his resources and needs, and

      (iii)   specified particulars for enabling the maintenance debtor to be identified by any employer of his,

  (b)   order any person appearing to the Court to have the maintenance debtor in his employment to give to the Court, within a specified period, a statement signed by that person, or on his behalf, of specified particulars of the maintenance debtor's earnings and expected earnings.

(2) Notice of an application for an attachment of earnings order served on a maintenance debtor may include a requirement that he shall give to the Court, within the period and in the manner specified in the notice, a statement in writing of the matters referred to in subsection (1)(a) of this section and of any other matters which are or may be relevant to the determination of the normal deduction rate and the protected earnings rate to be specified in the order.

(3) In any proceedings in relation to an attachment of earnings order, a statement given to the Court in compliance with an order under paragraph (a) or (b) of subsection (1) of this section or with a requirement under subsection (2) of this section shall be admissible as evidence of the facts stated therein, and a document purporting to be such a statement shall be deemed, unless the contrary is shown, to be a statement so given.

**14**     **Notification of changes of employment and earnings**

Where an attachment of earnings order is in force:

  (a)   the maintenance debtor shall notify in writing the Court that made the order of every occasion on which he leaves any employment, or becomes employed or re-employed, not later (in each case) than ten days from the date on which he does so,

  (b)   the maintenance debtor shall, on any occasion on which he becomes employed or re-employed, include in his notification under paragraph (a) of this section particulars of his earnings and expected earnings from the relevant employment,

  (c)   any person who becomes an employer of the maintenance debtor and knows that the order is in force and by what Court it was made shall, within ten days of his becoming the maintenance debtor's employer or of acquiring that knowledge (whichever is the later), notify that Court in writing that he is the debtor's employer, and include in his notification a statement of the debtor's earnings and expected earnings.

**15**     **Power to determine whether particular payments are earnings**

(1) Where an attachment of earnings order is in force, the Court that made the order shall, on the application of the employer concerned or the maintenance debtor or the person to whom payments are being made under the order, determine whether payments (or any portions thereof) to the maintenance debtor of a particular class or description specified by the application are earnings for the purpose of the order, and the employer shall give effect to any determination for the time being in force under this section.

(2) Where an application under this section is made by the employer, he shall not incur any liability for non-compliance with the order as respects any payments (or any portions thereof) of the class or description specified by the application which are made by him to the maintenance debtor while the application or any appeal in consequence thereof or any decision in relation to the application or appeal is pending, but this shall not, unless the Court otherwise orders, apply as respects such payments (or any portions thereof) if the employer subsequently withdraws the application or, as the case may be, abandons the appeal.

**16     Persons in service of State, local authority, etc**

(1) Where a maintenance debtor is in the service of the State, a local authority for the purposes of the Local Government Act, 1941, a harbour authority within the meaning of the Harbours Act, 1946, [the Health Service Executive][1], a vocational education committee established by the Vocational Education Act, 1930, or a committee of agriculture established by the Agriculture Act, 1931, or is a member of either House of the Oireachtas—

(a)  in a case where a maintenance debtor in the service of the State is employed in a department, office, organisation, service, undertaking or other body, its chief officer (or such other officer as the Minister of State by whom the department, office, organisation, service, undertaking or other body is administered may from time to time designate) shall, for the purposes of this Act, be regarded as having the maintenance debtor in his employment,

(b)  in a case where a maintenance debtor is in the service of such an authority, board or committee, its chief officer shall, for the purposes of this Act, be regarded as having the maintenance debtor in his employment,

(c)  in any other case, where a maintenance debtor is paid out of the Central Fund or out of moneys provided by the Oireachtas, the Secretary of the Department of Finance (or such other officer of the Minister for Finance as that Minister may from time to time designate) shall, for the purposes of this Act, be regarded as having the maintenance debtor in his employment, and

(d)  any earnings of a maintenance debtor paid out of the Central Fund or out of moneys provided by the Oireachtas shall be regarded as paid by the chief officer referred to in paragraph (a) or (b), as the case may be, of this subsection, the Secretary of the Department of Finance or such other officer as may be designated under paragraph (a) or (c), as the case may be, of this subsection, as may be appropriate.

(2) If any question arises in proceedings for or arising out of an attachment of earnings order as to what department, office, organisation, service, undertaking or other body a maintenance debtor in the service of the State is employed in for the purposes of this section, the question may be referred to and determined by the Minister for the Public Service, but that Minister shall not be under any obligation to consider a reference under this subsection unless it is made by the Court.

(3) A document purporting to contain a determination of the Minister for the Public Service under subsection (2) of this section and to be signed by an officer of the Minister for the Public Service shall, in any such proceedings as are mentioned in that subsection, be admissible in evidence and be deemed, unless the contrary is shown, to contain an accurate statement of that determination.

(4) In this section references to a maintenance debtor in the service of the State include references to a maintenance debtor to whom earnings are paid directly out of moneys provided by the Oireachtas.

**Note**

1   Section 16(1) was amended by s 75 and Schedule 6 of the Health Act 2004 by the substitution of "the Health Service Executive" for "health board".

### 17      Discharge, variation and lapse of attachment of earnings order

(1) The Court that made an attachment of earnings order may, if it thinks fit, on the application of the maintenance creditor, the maintenance debtor or the District Court clerk on whose application the order was made, make an order discharging or varying that order.

(2) Where an order varying an attachment of earnings order is made under this section, the employer shall, if it has been served upon him, comply with it, but he shall be under no liability for non-compliance before ten days have elapsed since the service.

(3) Where an employer affected by an attachment of earnings order ceases to have the maintenance debtor in his employment, the order shall, in so far as that employer is concerned, lapse (except as respects deductions from earnings paid after the cesser by that employer and payment to the person in whose favour the order was made of deductions from earnings made at any time by that employer).

(4) The lapse of an order under subsection (3) of this section shall not prevent its remaining in force for other purposes.

### 18      Cesser of attachment of earnings order

(1) An attachment of earnings order shall cease to have effect upon the discharge of the relevant antecedent order, except as regards payments under the attachment of earnings order in respect of any time before the date of the discharge.

(2) Where an attachment of earnings order ceases to have effect, the clerk or registrar of the Court that made the order shall give notice of the cesser to the employer.

### 19      Provisions in relation to alternative remedies

(1) Where an attachment of earnings order has been made, any proceedings commenced under section 8(1) of the Enforcement of Court Orders Act, 1940, for the enforcement of the relevant antecedent order shall lapse and any warrant or order issued or made under that section in any such proceedings shall cease to have effect.

(2) An attachment of earnings order shall cease to have effect upon the making of an order under section 8(1) of the Enforcement of Court Orders Act, 1940, for the enforcement of the relevant antecedent order.

## 20     Enforcement

(1) Where, without reasonable excuse, a person—

    (a)   fails to comply with subsection (1) or (2) of section 11 or section 14 or an order under section 13 or section 17(2) of this Act, or

    (b)   gives to a Court a statement pursuant to section 13(1) of this Act, or a notification under section 14 of this Act, that is false or misleading,

and a maintenance creditor as a result fails to obtain a sum of money due under an attachment of earnings order, that sum may be sued for as a simple contract debt in any court of competent jurisdiction by the maintenance creditor or the District Court clerk to whom such sum falls to be paid, and that court may order the person to pay to the person suing such amount (not exceeding the sum aforesaid) as in all the circumstances the court considers proper for distribution in such manner and in such amounts as the court may specify amongst the persons for whose benefit the attachment of earnings order was made.

(2) Where a person gives to a Court—

    (a)   a statement pursuant to section 13 of this Act, or

    (b)   a notification under section 14 of this Act,

that is to his knowledge false or misleading, he shall be guilty of an offence and shall be liable on summary conviction to a fine not exceeding [€253.93] or, at the discretion of the court, to imprisonment for a term not exceeding six months or to both.

(3) A person who contravenes section 11(3) of this Act shall be guilty of an offence and shall be liable on summary conviction to a fine not exceeding [€63.49].

# PART IV
## MISCELLANEOUS

## 21     Property in household allowance

Any allowance made by one spouse to the other spouse after the commencement of this Act for the purpose of meeting household expenses, and any property or interest in property acquired out of such allowance, shall, in the absence of any agreement, whether express or implied, between them to the contrary, belong to the spouses as joint owners.

## [21A     Birth and funeral expenses of dependent child[1]

(1) The Court may make an order (in this Act referred to as a lump sum order) where it appears to the Court on application by—

    (a)   in relation to a dependent child of the family, a spouse, or

    (b)   in relation to a dependent child whose parents are not married to each other, a parent, that the other spouse or parent, as the case may be, has failed to make such contribution as is proper in the circumstances towards the expenses incidental to either or both—

(i) the birth of a child who is a dependent child or who would have been a dependent child were he alive at the time of the application for a lump sum order,

(ii) the funeral of a child who was a dependent child or who would have been a dependent child had he been born alive,

and any lump sum order shall direct the respondent spouse or parent, as the case may be, to pay to the applicant a lump sum not exceeding [€4,000][2], but no such order shall direct the payment of an amount exceeding [€2,000][2] in respect of the birth of a child to whom this section relates or [€2,000][2] in respect of the funeral of such a child.

(2) Section 5(4)(as amended by the Status of Children Act, 1987) or 5A(3)(inserted by the said Act) of this Act, as may be appropriate, shall apply for the purpose of determining the amount of any lump sum under this section as it applies for the purpose of determining the amount of any payment under section 5 or 5A of this Act, as appropriate.

(3) (a) Nothing in this section, apart from this subsection, shall prejudice any right of a person otherwise to recover moneys expended in relation to the birth or funeral of a child.

(b) Where an application for a lump sum order has been determined, the applicant shall not be entitled otherwise to recover from the respondent moneys in relation to matters so determined.][3]

---

**Notes**

1   Commencement: 14 December 1987.

2   Section 21A(1) was amended by the Courts and Court Officers Act 2002, s 19.

3   Section 21A was inserted by the Status of Children Act 1987, s 21. See the Domestic Violence Act 1996, s 9. See the European Communities (Civil and Commercial Judgments) Regulations 2002 (SI 52/2002), reg 6(7) and European Communities (Maintenance) Regulations 2011 (SI 274/2011) reg 10.

---

**22      Barring of spouse from family home**

(1) On application to it by either spouse, the Court may, if it is of opinion that there are reasonable grounds for believing that the safety or welfare of that spouse or of any dependent child of the family requires it, order the other spouse, if he is residing at a place where the applicant spouse or that child resides, to leave that place, and, whether the other spouse is or is not residing at that place, prohibit him from entering that place until further order by the Court or until such other time as the Court shall specify.

(2) Either spouse may apply at any time to the Court that made it for the discharge of an order under this section, and the Court shall discharge the order if it is satisfied that it is

proper to do so and that the safety and welfare of the spouse on whose application the order was made or any dependent child will not be prejudiced by the discharge.

(3) Without prejudice to the law as to contempt of court, where a person—

    (a)   contravenes an order under this section, or

    (b)   while an order under this section directed against him is in force, molests or puts in fear his spouse or a dependent child,

he shall be guilty of an offence and shall be liable on summary conviction to a fine not exceeding [€253.93] or, at the discretion of the court, to imprisonment for a term not exceeding six months or to both

(4) In subsections (1) and (2) of this section "**the Court**" means the High Court, the Circuit Court or the District Court, and—

    (a)   the District Court shall have jurisdiction in relation to proceedings under this section irrespective of the rateable value of the place to which the proceedings relate, but any order made by the District Court shall, subject to subsection (5) of this section, expire three months after the date of its making but may be renewed from time to time by order of the District Court, on application to it by a person in whose favour the order was made, for further periods of three months but not exceeding three months in respect of any one renewal,

    (b)   the Circuit Court (except on appeal from an order of the District Court) shall not have jurisdiction in relation to proceedings under this section where the rateable value of the place to which the proceedings relate exceeds [€126.97],

    (c)   an order made by the Circuit Court on appeal from an order of the District Court under subsection (1) of this section in relation to a place the rateable value of which exceeds [€126.97] shall, subject to subsection (5) of this section, expire three months after the date of its making but may be renewed from time to time by order of the District Court, on application to it by a person in whose favour the order was made, for further periods of three months but not exceeding three months in respect of any one renewal.

(5) An order under this section shall expire upon the determination of any matrimonial cause or matter in the High Court between the spouses or of any proceedings between the spouses under the Guardianship of Infants Act, 1964, in the High Court or Circuit Court, and the Court determining any such cause, matter or proceedings may, in the cause, matter or proceedings, make an order under this section irrespective of the rateable value of the place to which the order relates.

(6) An appeal from an order under this section shall, if the court that made the order or the court to which the appeal is brought so determines, but not otherwise, stay the proceeding upon the order upon such terms (if any) as may be imposed by the court making the determination.

(7) Where, by reason only of an order under subsection (1) of this section, a person is not residing at a place during any period, he shall be deemed, for the purposes of any rights under the Landlord and Tenant Acts, 1931 to 1971, the Statute of Limitations,

1957, or the Rent Restrictions Acts, 1960 and 1967, to be residing at the place during that period.

## 23     Jurisdiction of courts

[(1) Subject to subsection (2) of this section, the Circuit Court and the District Court shall have jurisdiction to hear and determine proceedings under [sections 5, 5A, 6, 7, 9 and 21A]¹ of this Act.

(2) (a)  The District Court and the Circuit Court (on appeal from the District Court) shall not have jurisdiction to make an order under this Act for the payment of a periodical sum at a rate greater than [€500]¹ per week for the support of a spouse or [€150]¹ per week for the support of a child.

(b)  Subject to paragraph (d) of this subsection, nothing in subsection (1) of this section shall be construed as conferring on the District Court or on the Circuit Court jurisdiction to make an order or direction under section 5, 5A, 6, 7 or 21A of this Act in any matter in relation to which the High Court has made an order or direction under any of those sections.

(c)  Subject to paragraph (d) of this subsection, nothing in subsection (1) of this section shall be construed as conferring on the District Court jurisdiction to make an order or direction under section 5, 5A, 6, 7, or 21A of this Act in any matter in relation to which the Circuit Court (except on appeal from the District Court) has made an order or direction under any of those sections.

(d)  The District Court and the Circuit Court may vary or revoke an order or direction made by the High Court under section 5, 5A, 6, 7, 9 or 21A of this Act before the commencement of section 12 of the Courts Act, 1981, if—

(i)  the circumstances to which the order or direction of the High Court related have changed other than by reason of such commencement, and

(ii)  in the case of a variation or revocation of such an order or direction by the District Court, the provisions of the order or direction would have been within the jurisdiction of that Court if the said section 12 had been in operation at the time of the making of the order or direction.]¹

[(3) In proceedings under this Act—

(a)  each of the spouses concerned shall give to the other spouse and to, or to a person acting on behalf of, any dependent member of the family concerned, and

(b)  any dependent member of the family concerned shall give to, or to a person acting on behalf of, any other such member and to each of the spouses concerned,

such particulars of his or her property and income as may reasonably be required for the purpose of the proceedings.

(4) Where a person fails or refuses to comply with subsection (3), the Court, on application to it in that behalf by a person having an interest in the matter, may direct the person to comply with that subsection.

(5) Where a person fails or refuses to comply with subsection (4), the Court, on application to it in that behalf by a person having an interest in the matter, may direct the person to comply with that subsection.]²

## Notes

1   Subsections (1) and (2) substituted by the Courts Act 1981, s 12. Subsection (1) was amended by the Status of Children Act 1987, s 22. Subsection 2(a) was amended by the Courts Act 1991, s 11 and by the Courts and Court Officers Act 2002, s 20.

2   Subsections (3), (4) and (5) were inserted by the Family Law Act 1995, s 43(e) (as amended by the Family Law (Divorce) Act 1996, s 52(o)(ii)).

## 24   Payments to be without deduction of income tax

A periodical payment of money pursuant to a maintenance order, a variation order, an interim order, an order under section 8 [or 8A]¹ of this Act (in so far as it is deemed under [either of those sections]¹ to be a maintenance order), or an attachment of earnings order shall be made without deduction of income tax.

## Notes

1   Amended by the Status of Children Act 1987, s 23.

## 25   Conduct of Court proceedings¹

(1) Proceedings under this Act shall be conducted in a summary manner and shall be heard otherwise than in public.

(2) Proceedings in the High Court and the Circuit Court under this Act shall be heard in chambers.

## Notes

1   See Civil Liability and Courts Act 2004, s 40.

## 26   Costs

The costs of any proceedings under this Act shall be in the discretion of the Court.

## 27   Voidance of certain provisions of agreements

An agreement shall be void in so far as it would have the effect of excluding or limiting the operation of any provision of this Act (other than section 21).

## 28    Amendment of Illegitimate Children (Affiliation Orders) Act, 1930, and Courts Act, 1971

(1) [...

(2) ...]¹

(3) [...]²

---

**Notes**

1    Subsections (1) and (2) amend the Illegitimate Children (Affiliation Orders) 1930, which Act was repealed by the Status of Children Act 1987, s 25.

2    Subsection (3) amends the Courts Act 1971, s 19(3)(a) which related to orders made under the 1930 Act; see the Status of Children Act 1987, s 25.

---

## 29    Amendment of Enforcement Orders Act, 1940

The references in subsections (1) and (7) of section 8 of the Enforcement of Court Orders Act, 1940, to an order shall be construed as including references to a maintenance order, a variation order, an interim order, an order under section 8 of this Act (in so far as it is deemed under that section to be a maintenance order) or a direction under section 9 of this Act.

## 30    Repeals

(1) The Married Women (Maintenance in case of Desertion) Act, 1886, section 13 of the Illegitimate Children (Affiliation Orders) Act, 1930, section 7 of the Enforcement of Court Orders Act, 1940, and section 18 of the Courts Act, 1971, are hereby repealed, and the reference in section 98(1)(a) of the Defence Act, 1954, to an order made by a civil court under section I of the said Married Women (Maintenance in case of Desertion) Act, 1886, shall be construed as a reference to an order under section 5, 6, or 7 of this Act or an order under section 8 of this Act (in so far as it is deemed under that section to be a maintenance order).

(2) (a)    Any order made by a Court under the provisions repealed by this section and in force immediately before the commencement of this Act shall continue in force as if it was, and shall be deemed for all purposes to be, a maintenance order or an attachment of earnings order, as the case may be.

  (b)    Any proceedings initiated under the provisions repealed by this section and not completed before the repeal shall be deemed for all purposes to be proceedings under the corresponding provisions of this Act and may be continued accordingly.

# Family Home Protection Act 1976

*Number 27 of 1976*

*An Act to provide for the protection of the family home and for related matters. [12th July, 1976]*

*Be it enacted by the Oireachtas as follows:*

**1    Interpretation**

(1) In this Act, except where the context otherwise requires—

"**conduct**" includes an act and a default or other omission;

"**conveyance**" includes a mortgage, lease, assent, transfer, disclaimer, release and any other disposition of property otherwise than by a will or a *donatio mortis causa* and also includes an enforceable agreement (whether conditional or unconditional) to make any such conveyance, and "**convey**" shall be construed accordingly;

"**the court**" means the court having jurisdiction under section 10;

"**dependent child of the family**", in relation to a spouse or spouses, means any child—

(a) of both spouses, or adopted by both spouses under the Adoption Acts, 1952 to 1974, or in relation to whom both spouses are *in loco parentis*, or

(b) of either spouse, or adopted by either spouse under the Adoption Acts, 1952 to 1974, or in relation to whom either spouse is *in loco parentis,* where the other spouse, being aware that he is not the parent of the child, has treated the child as a member of the family,

who is under the age of sixteen years, or, if he has attained that age—

(i) is receiving full-time education or instruction at any university, college, school or other educational establishment and is under the age of twenty-one years, or

(ii) is suffering from mental or physical disability to such extent that it is not reasonably possible for him to maintain himself fully;

"**family home**" has the meaning assigned by section 2;

"**household chattels**" has the meaning assigned by section 9(7);

"**interest**" means any estate, right, title or other interest, legal or equitable;

"**mortgage**" includes an equitable mortgage, a charge on registered land and a chattel mortgage, and cognate words shall be construed accordingly;

"**rent**" includes a conventional rent, a rentcharge within the meaning of section 2(1) of the Statute of Limitations, 1957, and a terminable annuity payable in respect of a loan for the purchase of a family home.

(2) References in this Act to any enactment shall be construed as references to that enactment as amended or extended by any subsequent enactment, including this Act.

(3) (a) A reference in this Act to a section is a reference to a section of this Act, unless it is indicated that reference to some other enactment is intended.

(b) A reference in this Act to a subsection is a reference to the subsection of the section in which the reference occurs unless it is indicated that reference to some other section is intended.[1]

---

**Notes**

1 Commencement: 12 July 1976. See the Judicial Separation and Family Law Reform Act 1989, s 45 and the Family Law Act 1995, s 47.

---

**2     Family Home**

(1) In this Act "**family home**" means, primarily, a dwelling in which a married couple ordinarily reside. The expression comprises, in addition, a dwelling in which a spouse whose protection is in issue ordinarily resides or, if that spouse has left the other spouse, ordinarily resided before so leaving.

[(2) In subsection (1), "**dwelling**" means any building or part of a building occupied as a separate dwelling and includes any garden or other land usually occupied with the dwelling, being land that is subsidiary and ancillary to it, is required for amenity or convenience and is not being used or developed primarily for commercial purposes, and includes a structure that is not permanently attached to the ground and a vehicle, or vessel, whether mobile or not occupied as a separate dwelling.]¹

**Notes**

1  Subsection (2) was substituted by the Family Law Act 1995, s 54.

**3      Alienation of interest in family home**

(1) Where a spouse, without the prior consent in writing of the other spouse, purports to convey any interest in the family home to any person except the other spouse, then, subject to [subsections (2), (3) and (8)]¹ and section 4, the purported conveyance shall be void.

(2) Subsection (1) does not apply to a conveyance if it is made by a spouse in pursuance of an enforceable agreement made before the marriage of the spouses.

(3) No conveyance shall be void by reason only of subsection (1)—

    (a)   if it is made to a purchaser for full value,

    (b)   if it is made, by a person other than the spouse making the purported conveyance referred to in subsection (1), to a purchaser for value, or

    (c)   if its validity depends on the validity of a conveyance in respect of which any of the conditions mentioned in subsection (2) or paragraph (a) or (b) is satisfied.

(4) If any question arises in any proceedings as to whether a conveyance is valid by reason of subsection (2) or (3), the burden of proving that validity shall be on the person alleging it.

(5) In subsection (3), **"full value"** means such value as amounts or approximates to the value of that for which it is given.

(6) In this section **"purchaser"** means a grantee, lessee, assignee, mortgagee, chargeant or other person who in good faith acquires an estate or interest in property.

(7) For the purposes of this section, section 3 of the Conveyancing Act, 1882, shall be read as if the words "as such" wherever they appear in Paragraph (ii) of subsection (1) of that section were omitted.

[(8)  (a)   (i)   Proceedings shall not be instituted to have a conveyance declared void by reason only of subsection (1) after the expiration of 6 years from the date of the conveyance.

        (ii)   Subparagraph (i) does not apply to any such proceedings instituted by a spouse who has been in actual occupation of the land concerned from immediately before the expiration of 6 years from the date of the conveyance until the institution of the proceedings.

        (iii)   Subparagraph (i) is without prejudice to any right of the other spouse referred to in subsection (1) to seek redress for a contravention of that subsection otherwise than by proceedings referred to in that subparagraph.

(b) A conveyance shall be deemed not to be and never to have been void by reason of subsection (1) unless—

    (i) it has been declared void by a court by reason of subsection (1) in proceedings instituted—

        (I) before the passing of the Family Law Act, 1995, or

        (II) on or after such passing and complying with paragraph (a), or

    (ii) subject to the rights of any other person concerned, it is void by reason of subsection (1) and the parties to the conveyance or their successors in title so state in writing before the expiration of 6 years from the date of the conveyance.

(c) A copy of a statement made for the purpose of subparagraph (ii) of paragraph (b) and certified by, or by the successor or successors in title of, the party or parties concerned ("**the person or persons**") to be a true copy shall, before the expiration of the period referred to in that subparagraph, as appropriate, be lodged by the person or persons in the Land Registry for registration pursuant to section 69(1) of the Registration of Title Act, 1964, as if statements so made had been prescribed under paragraph (s) of the said section 69(1) or be registered by them in the Registry of Deeds.[2]

(d) Rules of court shall provide that a person who institutes proceedings to have a conveyance declared void by reason of subsection (1) shall, as soon as may be, cause relevant particulars of the proceedings to be entered as a *lis pendens* under and in accordance with the Judgments (Ireland) Act, 1844.

(9) If, whether before or after the passing of the Family Law Act, 1995, a spouse gives a general consent in writing to any future conveyance of any interest in a dwelling that is or was the family home of that spouse and the deed for any such conveyance is executed after the date of that consent, the consent shall be deemed, for the purposes of subsection (1) to be a prior consent in writing of the spouse to that conveyance.][1]

---

**Notes**

1  Subsection (1) was amended and sub-ss (8) and (9) were inserted by the Family Law Act 1995, s 54.

2  Form prescribed under the Registration of Deeds Rules 2008 (SI 52/2008), rule 17. See the Family Law Act 1981, s 10 and the Family Law Act 1995, s 54, sub-ss (2) and (3), the Housing Miscellaneous Provisions Act 2009, ss 46(13), 88(7), 98(15) and 99(10), and the Nursing Homes Support Scheme Act 2009, s 17(9).

---

**4 Consent of Spouse**

(1) Where the spouse whose consent is required under section 3(1) omits or refuses to consent, the court may, subject to the provisions of this section, dispense with the consent.

(2) The court shall not dispense with the consent of a spouse unless the court considers that it is unreasonable for the spouse to withhold consent, taking into account all the circumstances, including—

    (a) the respective needs and resources of the spouses and of the dependent children (if any) of the family, and

    (b) in a case where the spouse whose consent is required is offered alternative accommodation, the suitability of that accommodation having regard to the respective degrees of security of tenure in the family home and in the alternative accommodation.

(3) Where the spouse whose consent is required under section 3(1) has deserted and continues to desert the other spouse, the court shall dispense with the consent. For this purpose, desertion includes conduct on the part of the former spouse that results in the other spouse, with just cause, leaving and living separately and apart from him.

(4) Where the spouse whose consent is required under section 3(1) is incapable of consenting by reason of unsoundness of mind or other mental disability or has not after reasonable inquiries been found, the court may give the consent on behalf of that spouse, if it appears to the court to be reasonable to do so.

**5 Conduct leading to loss of family home**

(1) Where it appears to the court, on the application of a spouse, that the other spouse is engaging in such conduct as may lead to the loss of any interest in the family home or may render it unsuitable for habitation as a family home with the intention of depriving the applicant spouse or a dependent child of the family of his residence in the family home, the court may make such order as it considers proper, directed to the other spouse or to any other person, for the protection of the family home in the interest of the applicant spouse or such child.

(2) Where it appears to the court, on the application of a spouse, that the other spouse has deprived the applicant spouse or a dependent child of the family of his residence in the family home by conduct that resulted in the loss of any interest therein or rendered it unsuitable for habitation as a family home, the court may order the other spouse or any other person to pay to the applicant spouse such amount as the court considers proper to compensate the applicant spouse and any such child for their loss or make such other order directed to the other spouse or to any other person as may appear to the court to be just and equitable.[1]

**Notes**

1   See the Family Law (Divorce) Act 1996, s 15.

## 6     Payment of outgoings on family home

(1) Any payment or tender made or any other thing done by one spouse in or towards satisfaction of any liability of the other spouse in respect of rent, rates, mortgage payments or other outgoings affecting the family home shall be as good as if made or done by the other spouse, and shall be treated by the person to whom such payment is made or such thing is done as though it were made or done by the other spouse.

(2) Nothing in subsection (1) shall affect any claim by the first-mentioned spouse against the other to an interest in the family home by virtue of such payment or thing made or done by the first-mentioned spouse.

## 7     Adjournment of proceedings by mortgagee or lessor for possession or sale of family home

(1) Where a mortgagee or lessor of the family home brings an action against a spouse in which he claims possession or sale of the home by virtue of the mortgage or lease in relation to the non-payment by that spouse of sums due thereunder, and it appears to the court—

    (a)  that the other spouse is capable of paying to the mortgagee or lessor the arrears (other than arrears of principal or interest or rent that do not constitute part of the periodical payments due under the mortgage or lease) of money due under the mortgage or lease within a reasonable time, and future periodical payments falling due under the mortgage or lease, and that the other spouse desires to pay such arrears and periodical payments: and

    (b)  that it would in all the circumstances, having regard to the terms of the mortgage or lease, the interests of the mortgagee or lessor and the respective interests of the spouses, be just and equitable to do so,

the court may adjourn the proceedings for such period and on such terms as appear to the court to be just and equitable.

(2) In considering whether to adjourn the proceedings under this section and, if so, for what period and on what terms they should be adjourned, the court shall have regard in particular to whether the spouse of the mortgagor or lessee has been informed (by or on behalf of the mortgagee or lessor or otherwise) of the non-payment of the sums in question or of any of them.[1]

**Notes**

1    See the Family Law (Divorce) Act 1996, s 15 and the Land and Conveyancing Law Reform Act 2009, s 101(7).

## 8    Modification of terms of mortgage or lease as to payment of capital sum

(1) Where, on an application by a spouse, after proceedings have been adjourned under section 7, it appears to the court that—

   (a)    all arrears (other than arrears of principal or interest or rent that do not constitute part of the periodical payments due under the mortgage or lease) of money due under the mortgage or lease, and

   (b)    all the periodical payments due to date under the mortgage or lease, have been paid off

and that the periodical payments subsequently falling due will continue to be paid, the court may by order declare accordingly.

(2) If the court makes an order under subsection (1), any term in a mortgage or lease whereby the default in payment that gave rise to the proceedings under section 7 has, at any time before or after the initial hearing of such proceedings, resulted or would have resulted in the capital sum advanced thereunder (or part of such sum or interest thereon) or any sum other than the periodical payments, as the case may be, becoming due, shall be of no effect for the purpose of such proceedings or any subsequent proceedings in respect of the sum so becoming due.[1]

**Notes**

1    See the Land and Conveyancing Law Reform Act 2009, s 101(7).

## 9    Restriction on disposal of household chattels

(1) Where it appears to the court, on the application of a spouse, that there are reasonable grounds for believing that the other spouse intends to sell, lease, pledge, charge or otherwise dispose of or to remove such a number or proportion of the household chattels in a family home as would be likely to make it difficult for the applicant spouse or a dependent child of the family to reside in the family home without undue hardship, the court may by order prohibit, on such terms as it may see fit, the other spouse from making such intended disposition or removal.

(2) Where matrimonial proceedings have been instituted by either spouse, neither spouse shall sell, lease, pledge, charge or otherwise dispose of or remove any of the household chattels in the family home until the proceedings have been finally determined, unless—

(a) the other spouse has consented to such sale, lease, pledge, charge or other disposition or removal, or

(b) the court before which the proceedings have been instituted, on application to it by the spouse who desires to make such disposition or removal, permits that spouse to do so, which permission may be granted on such terms as the court may see fit.

(3) In subsection (2) "**matrimonial proceedings**" includes proceedings under section 12 of the Married Women's Status Act, 1957, under the Guardianship of Infants Act, 1964, or under section 21 or 22 of the Family Law (Maintenance of Spouses and Children) Act, 1976.

(4) A spouse who contravenes the provisions of subsection (2) shall, without prejudice to any other liability, civil or criminal, be guilty of an offence and shall be liable on summary conviction to a fine not exceeding [€126.97] or to imprisonment for a term not exceeding six months or to both.

(5) Where it appears to the court, on application to it by either spouse, that the other spouse—

(a) has contravened an order under subsection (1) or the provisions of subsection (2), or

(b) has sold, leased, pledged, charged or otherwise disposed of or removed such a number or proportion of the household chattels in the family home as has made or is likely to make it difficult for the applicant spouse or a dependent child of the family to reside in the family home without undue hardship,

the court may order that other spouse to provide household chattels for the applicant spouse, or a sum of money in lieu thereof, so as to place the applicant spouse or the dependent child of the family as nearly as possible in the position that prevailed before such contravention, disposition or removal.

(6) Where a third person, before a sale, lease, pledge, charge or other disposition of any household chattel to him by a spouse, is informed in writing by the other spouse that he intends to take proceedings in respect of such disposition or intended disposition, the court in proceedings under this section may make such order, directed to the former spouse or the third person, in respect of such chattel as appears to it to be proper in the circumstances.

(7) For the purposes of this section "**household chattels**" means furniture, bedding, linen, china, earthenware, glass, books and other chattels of ordinary household use or ornament and also consumable stores, garden effects and domestic animals, but does not include any chattels used by either spouse for business or professional purposes or money or security for money.[1]

---

**Notes**

1  See the Domestic Violence Act 1996, ss 8 and 9, and the Family Law (Divorce) Act 1996, s 15.

---

## 10  Jurisdiction

(1) The jurisdiction conferred on a court by this Act may be exercised by the High Court.

(2) Subject to subsections (3) and (4), the Circuit Court shall concurrently with the High Court have all the jurisdiction of the High Court to hear and determine proceedings under this Act.

(3) Where either spouse is a person of unsound mind and there is a committee of the spouse's estate, the jurisdiction conferred by this Act may, subject to subsection (4), be exercised by the court that has appointed the committee.

[(4) Where the rateable value of the land to which the proceedings relate exceeds [€253.93] and the proceedings are brought in the Circuit Court, that Court shall, if a defendant so requires, before the hearing thereof, transfer the proceedings to the High Court but any order made or act done in the course of such proceedings before such transfer shall be valid unless discharged or varied by order of the High Court.]¹

[(5) (a)  The District Court shall, subject to subsection (3), have all the jurisdiction of the High Court to hear and determine proceedings under this Act where the rateable valuation of the land to which proceedings relate does not exceed [€25.39].

(b)  The District Court shall, subject to subsection (3), have jurisdiction to deal with the question arising under section 9 where the value of the household chattels intended to be disposed of or removed or actually disposed of or removed, as the case may be, does not exceed [€20,000]² or where such chattels are or immediately before such disposal or removal, were in a family home the rateable valuation of which does not exceed [€25.39].

(c)  The District Court may, for the purpose of determining whether it has jurisdiction in proceedings under this Act in relation to a family home that has not been given a rateable valuation or is the subject with other land of a rateable valuation, determine that its rateable valuation would exceed, or would not exceed, [€25.39].]³

(6) Proceedings under or referred to in this Act in which each spouse is a party (whether by joinder or otherwise) shall be conducted in a summary manner and shall be heard otherwise than in public.

(7) Proceedings in the High Court and in the Circuit Court under or referred to in this Act in which each spouse is a party (whether by joinder or otherwise) shall be heard in chambers.

---

**Notes**

1  Subsection (4) was substituted by the Courts Act 1981, s 13.
2  Subsection (5)(b) was amended by the Courts and Court Officers Act 2002, s 14.
3  Subsection (5) was inserted by the Family Law Act 1995, s 54.

---

## 11    Joinder of parties

In any proceedings under or referred to in this Act each of the spouses as well as any third person who has or may have an interest in the proceedings may be joined—

   (a)   by service upon him of a third-party notice by an existing party to the proceedings, or

   (b)   by direction of the court.

## 12    Registration of notice of existence of marriage

(1) A spouse may register in the Registry of Deeds pursuant to the Registration of Deeds Act, 1707 (in the case of unregistered property) or under the Registration of Title Act 1964 (in the case of registered land) a notice stating that he is married to any person, being a person having an interest in such property or land.

(2) The fact that notice of a marriage has not been registered under subsection (1) shall not give rise to any inference as to the non-existence of a marriage.

(3) No stamp duty, Registry of Deeds fee or land registration fee shall be payable in respect of any such notice.[1]

**Notes**

1   Form prescribed under Registration of Deeds Rules 2008, (SI 52/2008), rule 16.

## 13    Restriction of section 59(2) of Registration of Title Act, 1964

Section 59(2) of the Registration of Title Act, 1964 (which refers to noting upon the register provisions of any enactment restricting dealings in land) shall not apply to the provisions of this Act.

## 14    Creation of joint tenancy in family home, exemption from stamp duty and fees

No land registration fee, Registry of Deeds fee or court fee shall be payable on any transaction creating a joint tenancy between spouses in respect of a family home where the home was immediately prior to such transaction owned by either spouse or by both spouses otherwise than as joint tenants.[1]

**Notes**

1   The words "stamp duty" were removed by the Finance Act 1998, s 125, Sch 8.

## 15    Offences

Where any person having an interest in any premises, on being required in writing by or on behalf of any other person proposing to acquire that interest to give any information necessary to establish if the conveyance of that interest requires a consent under section 3(1), knowingly gives information which is false or misleading in any material particular, he shall be guilty of an offence and shall be liable—

(a) on summary conviction, to a fine not exceeding [€253.93] or to imprisonment for a term not exceeding twelve months or to both, or

(b) on conviction on indictment, to imprisonment for a term not exceeding five years,

without prejudice to any other liability, civil or criminal.

**16      Short title**

This Act may be cited as the Family Home Protection Act, 1976.

# Family Law Act 1981

*Number 22 of 1981*

**Acts referred to**

| | |
|---|---|
| Married Women's Status Act, 1957 | 1957, No. 5 |
| Courts (Supplemental Provisions) Act, 1961 | 1961 No 39 |
| Family Home Protection Act, 1976 | 1976, No. 27 |

*An Act to abolish actions for criminal conversation, enticement and harbouring of a spouse and breach of promise of marriage, to make provision in relation to the property of, and gifts to and between, persons who have been engaged to be married and in relation to the validity of the consent of a minor spouse for the purposes of the Family Home Protection Act, 1976; and to provide for related matters. [23rd June, 1981]*

*Be it enacted by the Oireachtas as follows:*

**1    Abolition of actions for criminal conversation, enticement and harbouring of spouse[1]**

(1) After the passing of this Act, no action shall lie for criminal conversation, for inducing a spouse to leave or remain apart from the other spouse or for harbouring a spouse.

(2) Subsection (1) shall not have effect in relation to any action that has been commenced before the passing of this Act.[2]

---

**Notes**

1    Commencement: 23 June 1981.

2    See the Judicial Separation and Family Law Reform Act 1989, s 45.

---

**2        Engagements to marry not enforceable at law**

(1) An agreement between two persons to marry one another, whether entered into before or after the passing of this Act, shall not under the law of the State have effect as a contract and no action shall be brought in the State for breach of such an agreement, whatever the law applicable to the agreement.

(2) Subsection (1) shall not have effect in relation to any action that has been commenced before the passing of this Act.

**3        Gifts to engaged couples by other persons**

Where two persons have agreed to marry one another and any property is given as a wedding gift to either or both of them by any other person, it shall be presumed, in the absence of evidence to the contrary, that the property so given was given—

    (a)   to both of them as joint owners, and

    (b)   subject to the condition that it should be returned at the request of the donor or his personal representative if the marriage for whatever reason does not take place.

**4        Gifts between engaged couples**

Where a party to an agreement to marry makes a gift of property (including an engagement ring) to the other party, it shall be presumed, in the absence of evidence to the contrary, that the gift—

    (a)   was given subject to the condition that it should be returned at the request of the donor or his personal representative if the marriage does not take place for any reason other than the death of the donor, or

    (b)   was given unconditionally, if the marriage does not take place on account of the death of the donor.

**5        Property of engaged couples**

(1) Where an agreement to marry is terminated, the rules of law relating to the rights of spouses in relation to property in which either or both of them has or have a beneficial interest shall apply in relation to any property in which either or both of the parties to the agreement had a beneficial interest while the agreement was in force as they apply in relation to property in which either or both spouses has or have a beneficial interest.[1]

(2) Where an agreement to marry is terminated, section 12 of the Married Women's Status Act, 1957 (which relates to the determination of questions between husband and wife as to property) shall apply, as if the parties to the agreement were married, to any dispute between them, or claim by one of them, in relation to property in which either or both had a beneficial interest while the agreement was in force as they apply in relation to property in which either or both spouses has or have a beneficial interest.

**Notes**

1   See the Family Law Act 1995, s 48.

**6       Application to the court in case of substantial benefit to a party to a broken engagement**

Where an agreement to marry is terminated and it appears to the court, on application made to it in a summary manner by a person other than a party to the agreement, that a party to the agreement has received a benefit of a substantial nature (not being a gift to which section 3 applies) from the applicant in consequence of the agreement, the court may make such order (including an order for compensation) as appears to it just and equitable in the circumstances.

**7       Application to the court in case of substantial expenditure incurred by or on behalf of a party to a broken engagement**

Where an agreement to marry is terminated and it appears to the court, on application made to it in a summary manner by a party to the agreement or another person, that, by reason of the agreement—

(a)   in the case of the party to the agreement, expenditure of a substantial nature has been incurred by him, or

(b)   in the case of the other person, expenditure of a substantial nature has been incurred by him on behalf of a party to the agreement,

and that the party by whom or on whose behalf the expenditure was incurred has not benefited in respect of the expenditure, the court may make such order (including an order for the recovery of the expenditure) as appears to it just and equitable in the circumstances.

**8       Jurisdiction (sections 6 and 7)**

(1) The Circuit Court shall, concurrently with the High Court, have jurisdiction to hear and determine proceedings under section 6 or 7 subject, in the case of a claim exceeding [€100,000][1], to the like consents as are required for the purposes of section 22 of the Courts (Supplemental Provisions) Act, 1961.

(2) The District Court shall have jurisdiction to hear and determine proceedings under section 6 or 7 where the amount claimed does not exceed [€20,000][1].

**Notes**

1 Amended by the Courts Act 1991, s 13 and the Courts and Court Officers Act 2002, ss 13 and 14.

**9 Limitation period for proceedings under this Act**

Proceedings to enforce a right conferred by this Act arising out of the termination for whatever reason of an agreement to marry shall not be brought after the expiration of three years from the date of the termination of the agreement.

**10 Consent by minor spouse to disposal of family home, etc**

(1) No consent given by a spouse, whether before or after the passing of this Act, for the purposes of section 3(1) of the Family Home Protection Act, 1976 (which provides that a conveyance by one spouse of an interest in the family home without the written consent of the other spouse shall be void) or of section 9(2) of that Act (which restricts the right of a spouse to dispose of household chattels without the consent of the other spouse) shall be, or shall be taken to have been, invalid by reason only that it is or was given by a spouse who has not or had not attained the age of majority.

(2) Subsection (1) shall apply to a consent given for the aforesaid purposes before the passing of this Act by a guardian or a court on behalf of a spouse who had not attained the age of majority as if the consent had been given by the spouse.

**11 Short title**

This Act may be cited as the Family Law Act, 1981.

# Domicile and Recognition of Foreign Divorces Act 1986

*Number 24 of 1986*

## ARRANGEMENT OF SECTIONS

Section

*An Act to amend the law relating to domicile and the recognition of foreign divorces.*
*[2nd July, 1986]*

*Be it enacted by the Oireachtas as follows:*

## 1    Abolition of wife's dependent domicile

(1) From the commencement of this Act the domicile of a married woman shall be an independent domicile and shall be determined by reference to the same factors as in the case of any other person capable of having an independent domicile and, accordingly, the rule of law whereby upon marriage a woman acquires the domicile of her husband and is during the subsistence of the marriage incapable of having any other domicile is hereby abolished.

(2) This section applies to the parties to every marriage, irrespective of where and under what law the marriage takes place and irrespective of the domicile of the parties at the time of the marriage.

## 2    Domicile before commencement of Act

The domicile that a person had at any time before the commencement of this Act shall be determined as if this Act had not been passed.

## 3    Domicile after commencement of Act

The domicile that a person has at any time after the commencement of this Act shall be determined as if this Act had always been in force.

## 4    Dependent domicile of minor

(1) The domicile of a minor at any time when his father and mother are living apart shall be that of his mother if—

(a)   the minor then has his home with her and has no home with his father, or

(b)   the minor has at any time had her domicile by virtue of paragraph (a) of this subsection and has not since had a home with his father.

(2) The domicile of a minor whose mother is dead shall be that which she last had before she died if at her death the minor had her domicile by virtue of subsection (1) of this section and has not since had a home with his father.

(3) This section shall not affect any existing rule of law as to the cases in which a minor's domicile is regarded as being, by dependence, that of his mother.

(4) In the application of this section to a minor who has been adopted, references to the father or mother of such minor shall be construed as references to the adoptive father or adoptive mother of such minor.

## 5     Recognition of foreign divorces[1]

(1) For the rule of law that a divorce is recognised if granted in a country where both spouses are domiciled, there is hereby substituted a rule that a divorce shall be recognised if granted in the country where either spouse is domiciled.

(2) In relation to a country which has in matters of divorce two or more systems applying in different territorial units, this section shall, without prejudice to subsection (3) of this section, have effect as if each territorial unit were a separate country.

(3) A divorce granted in any of the following jurisdictions—

    (a)  England and Wales,

    (b)  Scotland,

    (c)  Northern Ireland,

    (d)  the Isle of Man,

    (e)  the Channel Islands,

shall be recognised if either spouse is domiciled in any of those jurisdictions.

(4) In a case where neither spouse is domiciled in the State, a divorce shall be recognised if, although not granted in the country where either spouse is domiciled, it is recognised in the country or countries where the spouses are domiciled.

(5) This section shall apply to a divorce granted after the commencement of this Act.

(6) Nothing in this section shall affect a ground on which a court may refuse to recognise a divorce, other than such a ground related to the question whether a spouse is domiciled in a particular country, or whether the divorce is recognised in a country where a spouse is domiciled.

(7) In this section—

**"divorce"** means divorce *a vinculo matrimonii*;

**"domiciled"** means domiciled at the date of the institution of the proceedings for divorce.[2]

---

**Notes**

1   See the European Communities (Judgments in Matrimonial Matters and Matters of Parental Responsibility) Regulations 2002 (SI 472/2001), reg 3.

2. See also the European Communities (Judgments in Matrimonial Matters and Matters of Parental Responsibility) Regulations 2005 (SI 112/2005), reg 7.

## 6     Short title and commencement

(1) This Act may be cited as the Domicile and Recognition of Foreign Divorces Act, 1986.

(2) This Act shall come into operation on the day that is three months after the date of the passing of this Act.[1]

### Notes

1    Commencement: 2 October 1986.

# Status of Children Act 1987

*Number 26 of 1987*

## PART IX
### REGISTRATION AND RE-REGISTRATION OF BIRTHS

48. Re-registration of birth after declaration of parentage.

49. Amendment of Births and Deaths Registration Act (Ireland), 1880.

50. Construction and collective citation (Part IX).

### Acts Referred to

| | |
|---|---|
| Adoption Act, 1952 | 1952, No. 25 |
| Adoption Acts, 1952 to 1976 | |
| Age of Majority Act, 1985 | 1985, No. 2 |
| Births and Deaths Registration Act (Ireland), 1880 | 43 and 44 Vict., c. 13 |
| Births and Deaths Registration Acts, 1863 to 1972 | |
| Courts Act, 1981 | 1981, No. 11 |
| Defence Act, 1954 | 1954, No. 18 |
| Defence (Amendment) (No. 2) Act, 1979 | 1979, No. 28 |
| Evidence Further Amendment Act, 1869 | 32 and 33 Vict., c. 68 |
| Family Law (Maintenance of Spouses and Children) Act, 1976 | 1976, No. 11 |
| Friendly Societies Act, 1896 | 59 and 60 Vict., c. 25 |
| Guardianship of Infants Act, 1964 | 1964, No. 7 |
| Health Act, 1970 | 1970, No. 1 |
| Illegitimate Children (Affiliation Orders) Act, 1930 | 1930, No. 17 |
| Industrial and Provident Societies Act, 1893 | 56 and 57 Vict., c. 39 |
| Irish Nationality and Citizenship Acts, 1956 and 1986 | |
| Legitimacy Act, 1931 | 1931, No. 13 |
| Local Government (Superannuation) Act, 1956 | 1956, No. 10 |
| Provident Nominations and Small Intestacies Act, 1883 | 46 and 47 Vict., c. 47 |
| Savings Banks Act, 1887 | 50 and 51 Vict., c. 40 |
| Social Welfare (Consolidation) Act, 1981 | 1981, No. 1 |
| Succession Act, 1965 | 1965, No. 27 |
| Superannuation Act, 1887 | 50 and 51 Vict., c. 67 |

*An Act to equalise the rights of children and amend the law relating to their status and for those purposes to amend the law relating to legitimacy and to guardianship of infants, to amend and extend the Family Law (Maintenance Of Spouses And Children) Act, 1976, in relation to certain children and to amend further the law relating to maintenance, to amend the law relating to succession and other property rights, to provide for declarations of parentage and for the use of blood tests to assist in the determination of parentage, to amend the law relating to certain presumptions and evidence, to make further provision for the registration and re-registration of births and to provide for connected matters. [14th December, 1987]*

*Be it enacted by the Oireachtas as follows:*

# PART I
## PRELIMINARY AND GENERAL[1]

**1      Short title and commencement**

(1) This Act may be cited as the Status of Children Act, 1987.

(2) (a)   This Part (other than sections 3 and 4) shall come into operation on the passing of this Act and the said sections 3 and 4 shall come into operation one month after such passing.

    (b)   Parts II to IX shall come into operation six months after the passing of this Act or on such earlier day or days (not being earlier than one month after such passing) as may be fixed therefor by order or orders of the Minister for Justice, either generally or with reference to any particular Part or Parts.

---

**Notes**

1     Commencement: 14 December 1987 (Part I, except ss 3 and 4).

---

**2      Interpretation**

In this Act, a reference to a Part is to a Part of this Act unless the context requires that a reference to some other enactment is intended.

**3      Marital status of parents to be of no effect on relationships[1]**

(1) In deducing any relationship for the purposes of this Act or of any Act of the Oireachtas passed after the commencement of this section, the relationship between every person and his father and mother (or either of them) shall, unless the contrary intention appears, be determined irrespective of whether his father and mother are or have been married to each other, and all other relationships shall be determined accordingly.

(2) (a)   An adopted person shall, for the purposes of subsection (1) of this section, be deemed from the date of the adoption to be the child of the adopter or adopters and not the child of any other person or persons.

    [(b)   In this subsection 'adopted person' means a person who has been adopted under an adoption order within the meaning of section 3 (1) of the Adoption Act 2010 or, where the person has been adopted outside the State, whose adoption is recognised by virtue of the law for the time being in force in the State.][2]

**Notes**

1  Commencement of s 3: 14 January 1988.

2  Amended and substituted by Adoption Act 2010, s 172(a). See the Finance Act 1988, s 74 re the construction of certain Acts in accordance with this section.

**4**      **Construction of references to persons whose parents have or have not married each other, etc**

In this Act and in every Act of the Oireachtas passed after the commencement of this section—

(a)  a reference, however expressed, to a person whose parents have not married each other shall, unless the contrary intention appears, be construed as including a reference to a person whose parents are or have been married to each other but between whom there has been no subsisting marriage at any time during the period of ten months before the person's birth, or during the person's lifetime, and

(b)  a reference, however expressed, to a person whose parents have married each other shall, unless the contrary intention appears, be construed as excluding a reference to a person in respect of whom paragraph (a) of this section applies.[1]

**Notes**

1  Commencement of s 4: 14 January 1988.

**5**      **Meaning of father, mother, parent in Irish Nationality and Citizenship Acts, 1956 and 1986**

It is hereby declared that, in relation to a child, any reference to "father", "mother" or "parent" in the Irish Nationality and Citizenship Acts, 1956 and 1986, includes and shall be deemed always to have included the father, mother or parent, as the case may require, who was not married to the child's other parent at the time of the child's birth or at any time during the period of ten months preceding the birth.

## PART II
### AMENDMENT OF THE ACT OF 1931

**6**      **Definition (Part II)**

In this Part **"the Act of 1931"** means the Legitimacy Act, 1931.

## 7 Amendment of section 1 of the Act of 1931

(1) Section 1(2) of the Act of 1931 (which precludes the operation of that Act in the case of a person whose father and mother could not have been lawfully married to one another at the time of his birth or at some time during the period of ten months preceding such birth) is hereby repealed.

(2) In the case of a person to whom this section relates, the Act of 1931 shall have effect as if for the references in sections 1(1) and 5 of that Act to the commencement of that Act there were substituted a reference to the commencement of this Part.

## PART III
## GUARDIANSHIP[1]

**Notes**

1 Part III (ss 8–13) amends the Guardianship of Infants Act 1964; see the amended Act.

## PART IV
## MAINTENANCE[1]

**Notes**

1 Sections 14–23 amend the Family Law (Maintenance of Spouses and Children) Act 1976; see the amended Act.

## 24 Amendment of Defence Act, 1954

(1) The reference in section 98(1)(d) of the Defence Act, 1954, to an order made by a civil court under section 3, 6 or 7 of the Illegitimate Children (Affiliation Orders) Act, 1930, shall be construed as a reference to an order under section 5A, 6, 7 or 21A of the Act of 1976 (as amended by this Part) or an order under section 8A (inserted by this Part) of the Act of 1976 (in so far as it is deemed under that section to be a maintenance order).

(2) Section 99 (as extended to women by virtue of sections 2 and 5 of the Defence (Amendment) (No. 2) Act, 1979) of the Defence Act, 1954 (which relates to deductions from the pay of certain members of the Permanent Defence Force in respect of maintenance of a spouse or legitimate children) is hereby amended by the substitution in subsection (1) of "his spouse or any of his children (including any of his children in respect of whom his spouse is not a parent and any children he has adopted under the Adoption Acts, 1952 to 1976)" for "his wife or any of his legitimate children" and of "the spouse or any such children" for "the wife or such legitimate children".

**25        Repeal of the Act of 1930 and consequential provisions**

(1) The Illegitimate Children (Affiliation Orders) Act, 1930 (hereafter in this section referred to as "the Act of 1930") is hereby repealed.

(2) Any order made by a court under the provisions of the Act of 1930 and in force immediately before the commencement of this Part shall, in so far as such order could have been made under section 5A (inserted by this Part) of the Act of 1976 had it been in operation when that order was made, be deemed for all purposes to be an order made under the said section 5A.

(3) Any proceedings initiated under the provisions of the Act of 1930 and not completed before the commencement of this Part shall, in so far as such proceedings could have been initiated under section 5A of the Act of 1976 had it been in operation at such initiation, be deemed for all purposes to be proceedings under the said section 5A and may be continued accordingly.

(4) Subsections (2) and (3) of this section are without prejudice to any proceedings initiated, or any order or part of such order made, under the Act of 1930 to which those subsections do not relate.

# PART V
## PROPERTY RIGHTS

**26        Definition (Part V)**

In this Part "**the Act of 1965**" means the Succession Act, 1965.

**27        Construction of dispositions, etc**

(1) In any disposition (including a disposition creating an entailed estate) made after the commencement of this Part, references, however expressed, to relationships between persons shall be construed in accordance with section 3 of this Act.

(2) The following provisions of section 3 of the Legitimacy Act, 1931, namely—

  (a)   subsection (1)(b) (which relates to the effect of dispositions where a person has been legitimated),

  (b)   subsection (1)(c) (which relates to the effect of legitimation on entailed estates), and

  (c)   subsection (2) (which provides that, where the right to any property depends on the relative seniority of the children of any person, legitimated persons shall rank as if born on the date of legitimation),

shall not apply—

  (i)   in the case of the said subsection (1)(b), to a disposition made after the commencement of this Part,

  (ii)   in the case of the said subsection (1)(c), in relation to any entitlement under an entailed estate created by a disposition made after the commencement of this Part, and

(iii) in the case of the said subsection (2), in relation to any right conferred by a disposition made after the commencement of this Part,

except as respects any interest in relation to which the disposition refers only to persons who are, or whose relationship is deduced through, legitimate persons.

(3) For the purpose of any property right to which this section or section 4A (inserted by this Act) of the Act of 1965 relates, [section 60 of the Adoption Act 2010 (which relates to the property rights of persons adopted under the Adoption Act 2010)][1] shall be construed as applying also to any person adopted outside the State whose adoption is recognised by virtue of the law for the time being in force in the State.

(4) (a) Subject to paragraph (b) of this subsection, this section is without prejudice to [section 60 (as construed in accordance with subsection (3) of this section) of the Adoption Act 2010][2].

(b) An adopted person shall, unless the contrary intention appears, be entitled to take under a disposition made after the commencement of this Part in the same manner as he would have been entitled to so take if, at the date of the adoption order, he had been born in lawful wedlock to the person or persons who so adopted him.

(5) Any rule of law that a disposition in favour of illegitimate children not in being when the disposition takes effect is void as contrary to public policy is hereby abrogated as respects such dispositions made after the commencement of this Part.

(6) In relation to any disposition made before the commencement of this Part—

(a) nothing in this section shall affect the operation or construction of, or any entitlement under, any disposition so made, and

(b) where such a disposition creates a special power of appointment, nothing in this section shall be interpreted as extending the class of persons in whose favour the appointment may be made so as to include any person who is not a member of that class.

(7) (a) In this section **"disposition"** means a disposition, including an oral disposition, of real or personal property whether *inter vivos* or by will or codicil.

(b) Notwithstanding any rule of law, a disposition made by will or codicil executed before the commencement of this Part shall not be treated for the purposes of this section as made on or after that date by reason only that the will or codicil is confirmed by a codicil executed on or after that date.

---

**Notes**

1  Subsection 3 amended by Adoption Act 2010, s 172(b).

2  Subsection 4(a) amended by Adoption Act 2010, s 172(c).

## 28      Amendment of section 3 of the Act of 1965

Section 3 of the Act of 1965 is hereby amended—

(a)  by the insertion in subsection (1) after the definition of "an intestate" of the following:

> "'**issue**' shall be construed in accordance with section 4A (inserted by the Status of Children Act, 1987);",

and

(b)  by the insertion of the following subsection after subsection (1):

> "(1A) In this Act a reference, however expressed, to a person whose parents have married or have not married each other shall be construed in accordance with section 4 of the Status of Children Act, 1987.".

## 29      Succession rights

The Act of 1965 is hereby amended by the insertion after section 4 of the following section:

"4A.  (1)  In deducing any relationship for the purposes of this Act, the relationship between every person and his father and mother shall, subject to section 27A of this Act (inserted by the Act of 1987), be determined in accordance with section 3 of the Act of 1987, and all other relationships shall be determined accordingly.

(2)  Where a person whose father and mother have not married each other dies intestate, he shall be presumed not to have been survived by his father, or by any person related to him through his father, unless the contrary is shown.

(3)  The reference in section 75(1) to Part VI and the reference in the said section 75(1) to the foregoing provisions of the said Part VI shall, in relation to an instrument *inter vivos* made, or a will coming into operation, after the commencement of Part V of the Act of 1987, be construed as including references to this section.

(4)  This section is without prejudice to section 26 (which, as construed in accordance with section 27(3) of the Act of 1987, relates to the property rights of adopted persons) of the Adoption Act, 1952.

(5)  This section shall not affect any rights under the intestacy of a person dying before the commencement of Part V of the Act of 1987.

(6)  In this section '**the Act of 1987**' means the Status of Children Act, 1987."

## 30      Entitlement to grant of probate or administration

The Act of 1965 is hereby amended by the insertion after section 27 of the following section:

"27A. For the purpose of the application of section 26 or 27 in respect of the estate of a deceased person, the deceased shall be presumed, unless the contrary is shown, not to have been survived by any person related to him whose parents have not married each other or by any person whose relationship with the deceased is deduced through a person whose parents have not married each other.".

**31 Amendment of section 117 of the Act of 1965**

Section 117 of the Act of 1965 is hereby amended by the insertion of the following subsection after subsection (1):

"(1A)(a) An application made under this section by virtue of Part V of the Status of Children Act, 1987, shall be considered in accordance with subsection (2) irrespective of whether the testator executed his will before or after the commencement of the said Part V.

(b) Nothing in paragraph (a) shall be construed as conferring a right to apply under this section in respect of a testator who dies before the commencement of the said Part V.".

**32 Repeals relating to property rights**

The provisions of the following enactments are hereby repealed to the extent specified:

(a) in the Provident Nominations and Small Intestacies Act, 1883, section 8;

(b) in the Savings Banks Act, 1887, the words ", or in case of any illegitimacy of the deceased person or his children, to or among such person or persons as may be directed by the said regulations," in section 3(2);

(c) in the Superannuation Act, 1887, the words ", or in case of the illegitimacy of the deceased person or his children, to or among such persons as the department may think fit," in section 8;

(d) in the Industrial and Provident Societies Act, 1893, section 27(2);

(e) in the Friendly Societies Act, 1896, section 58(2);

(f) in the Legitimacy Act, 1931, sections 1(3) and 9;

(g) in the Local Government (Superannuation) Act, 1956, the words "or, in the case of the illegitimacy of the deceased, to or among such persons as the local authority think fit," in section 61(1)(e);

(h) in the Act of 1965, section 110.

## PART VI
### DECLARATIONS OF PARENTAGE

**33 Definitions (Part VI)**

In this Part—

**"the Court"** means the Circuit Court;

**"prescribed"** means prescribed by rules of court.

**34      Jurisdiction and venue (Part VI)**

(1) The Court shall have jurisdiction to grant a declaration under this Part.

(2) The jurisdiction conferred on the Court by this section shall be exercised by the judge of the circuit where any party to the proceedings ordinarily resides or carries on any profession, business or occupation or, where no party to the proceedings ordinarily resides or carries on any profession, business or occupation in the State, by a judge assigned to the Dublin Circuit.

(3) The jurisdiction conferred by this section is in addition to any other jurisdiction to grant a declaration of parentage or to make an order which has the effect of such a declaration.

**35      Declaration of parentage**

(1)  (a)   A person (other than an adopted person) born in the State, or

(b)   any other person (other than an adopted person),

may apply to the Court in such manner as may be prescribed for a declaration under this section that a person named in the application is his father or mother, as the case may be, or that both the persons so named are his parents.

(2) An application may be made under subsection (1) of this section notwithstanding the fact that any person named in the application as the father or the mother or a parent, as the case may be, is not, or may not be, alive.

(3) Where a person not born in the State makes an application for a declaration by virtue of subsection (1)(b) of this section, he shall specify in the application the reasons for seeking the declaration from the Court, and the Court shall refuse to hear or refuse to continue hearing, as the case may be, the application if at any stage it considers that there are no good and proper reasons for seeking the declaration.

(4) Where a person makes an application for a declaration under this section by his next friend the Court shall refuse to hear or refuse to continue hearing, as the case may be, the application if at any stage the Court considers that it would be against the interests of the applicant to determine the application.

(5) On an application under this section the Court may at any stage of the proceedings, of its own motion or on the application of any party to the proceedings, direct that all necessary papers in the matter be sent to the Attorney General.

(6) Where on an application under this section the Attorney General requests to be made a party to the proceedings, the Court shall order that he shall be added as a party, and, whether or not he so requests, the Attorney General may argue before the Court any question in relation to the application which the Court considers necessary to have fully argued and take such other steps in relation thereto as he thinks necessary or expedient.

(7) The Court may direct that notice of any application under this section shall be given in the prescribed manner to such other persons as the Court thinks fit and where notice is so given to any person the Court may, either of its own motion or on the application of that person or any party to the proceedings, order that that person shall be added as a party to those proceedings.

(8) Where on an application under this section it is proved on the balance of probabilities that—

    (a)  a person named in the application is the father, or

    (b)  a person so named is the mother, or

    (c)  persons so named are the parents,

of the applicant, the Court shall make the declaration accordingly.

(9) Any declaration made under this section shall be in a form to be prescribed and shall be binding on the parties to the proceedings and any person claiming through a party to the proceedings, and where the Attorney General is made a party to the proceedings the declaration shall also be binding on the State.

### 36    Supplementary provisions to section 35

(1) Rules of court may provide that any application for a declaration under section 35 of this Act shall contain such information as may be prescribed.

(2) Where any costs are incurred by the Attorney General in connection with any application for a declaration under section 35 of this Act, the Court may make such order as it considers just as to the payment of those costs by other parties to the proceedings.

(3) No proceedings on an application under section 35 of this Act shall affect any final judgment or decree already pronounced or made by any court of competent jurisdiction.

(4) On the hearing of an application under section 35 of this Act the Court may direct that the whole or any part of the proceedings shall be heard otherwise than in public, and an application for a direction under this subsection shall be so heard unless the Court otherwise directs.

(5) Where a declaration is made by the Court under section 35 of this Act, notification of that decision shall be given to an tArd-Chláraitheoir and shall be given in such manner as may be prescribed.

## PART VII
### BLOOD TESTS IN DETERMINING PARENTAGE IN CIVIL PROCEEDINGS

### 37    Definitions (Part VII)

In this Part—

"**blood samples**" means blood taken for the purpose of blood tests;

"**blood test**" means any test carried out under this Part and made with the object of ascertaining inheritable characteristics;

"**excluded**" means excluded subject to the occurrence of mutation;

"**the Minister**" means the Minister for Justice.

### 38    Direction by court on blood tests

(1) In any civil proceedings before a court in which the parentage of any person is in question, the court may, either of its own motion or on an application by any party to the

proceedings, give a direction for the use of blood tests for the purpose of assisting the court to determine whether a person named in the application or a party to the proceedings, as the case may be, is or is not a parent of the person whose parentage is in question, and for the taking, within a period to be specified in the direction, of blood samples from the person whose parentage is so questioned, from any person alleged to be a parent of that person and from any other person who is a party to the proceedings, or from any of those persons.

(2) Where, on the application of any party to proceedings—

    (a) a direction is given under subsection (1) of this section, such party shall pay the costs of taking and testing blood samples for the purpose of giving effect to the direction (including any expenses reasonably incurred by any person in taking any steps required of him for that purpose) and of making a report to the court under section 40(2) of this Act,

    (b) such party obtains, under section 40(4) of this Act, a written statement explaining or supplementing any statement made in a report under the said section 40(2), that party shall, subject to any direction by the court, pay the costs (if any) of obtaining the written statement (including any expenses reasonably incurred by any person in taking any steps required by him for that purpose),

but any amount paid or to be paid by virtue of this subsection shall be treated as costs incurred by such party in the proceedings.

(3) The court may at any time revoke or vary a direction previously given by it under this section.

## 39    Consent to, and taking, of blood samples

(1) Subject to subsection (3) of this section, a blood sample which is required to be taken from any person for the purpose of giving effect to a direction under section 38 of this Act shall not be taken from that person except with his consent.

(2) Where for the purpose of giving effect to a direction under section 38 of this Act a blood sample is required to be taken from a person who is not of full age and the court considers that he is in the circumstances capable of giving or refusing the necessary consent, any consent given or refused by him shall be as effective as it would be if he were of full age.

(3) For the purpose of giving effect to a direction under section 38 of this Act—

    (a) a blood sample may be taken from a minor, other than one to whom subsection (2) of this section relates, if the person having charge of or control over the minor consents:

        Provided that where more than one person has charge of or control over the minor and they disagree as to whether consent should be given, the minor shall be treated as not having consented;

    (b) a blood sample may be taken from a person of full age who is, in the opinion of the court, incapable of understanding the nature and purpose of blood tests if the person having charge of or control over him consents and any medical practitioner in whose care he may be has certified that the taking of a blood sample from him will not be prejudicial to his proper care and treatment:

Provided that where more than one person has charge of or control over the person concerned and they disagree as to whether consent should be given, the person concerned shall be treated as not having consented.

## 40    Blood tests and reports

(1) Where blood samples are taken for the purpose of giving effect to a direction of a court under section 38(1) of this Act, they shall be tested—

(a)  under the control of such person (including a person to whom subsection (6) of this section relates) as all the parties to the proceedings before the court agree to, or

(b)  where the parties are not in agreement,

   (i)   under the control of such person to whom subsection (6) of this section relates, or

   (ii)  under the control of such other person,

as the court shall direct.

(2) The person under whose control blood samples are to be tested by virtue of subsection (1) of this section shall make to the court by which the direction was given a report in which he shall state—

(a)  in relation to each person from whom blood samples were so taken, the results of the tests, and

(b)  in relation to each person (other than the person whose parentage is in question) from whom blood samples were so taken—

   (i)   whether the person to whom the report relates is or is not excluded by the results from being a parent of the person whose parentage is in question, and

   (ii)  if the person to whom the report relates is not so excluded, the value, if any, of the results in determining whether that person is a parent of the person whose parentage is in question,

and the report shall be received by the court as evidence in the proceedings of the matters stated therein.

(3) A report under subsection (2) of this section shall be in the form prescribed by regulations made under section 41 of this Act.

(4) Where a report has been made to a court under subsection (2) of this section, any party may, with the leave of the court, or shall, if the court so directs, obtain from the person who made the report a written statement explaining or supplementing any statement made in the report, and that statement shall be deemed for the purposes of this section (other than subsections (3) and (6)) to form part of the report made to the court.

(5) Where a direction is given under section 38(1) of this Act in any proceedings and the blood samples to which the direction relates have been tested by virtue of this section, a party to the proceedings, unless the court otherwise directs, shall not be entitled to call

as a witness the person under whose control the blood samples were tested for the purpose of giving effect to that direction, or any person by whom any thing necessary for the purpose of enabling those tests to be carried out was done, unless within 14 days after receiving a copy of the report he serves notice on the other parties to the proceedings, or on such of them as the court may direct, of his intention to call that person as a witness and, where that person is so called, the party who called him shall be entitled to cross-examine him.

(6) (a) The Minister may, for the purpose of subsection (1) of this section, appoint a person or category of persons under whose control blood tests may be carried out.

(b) The Minister may at any time amend or revoke an appointment under this subsection but such amendment or revocation shall not affect any blood test carried out, or the testing of any blood sample for the purpose of this Part which was submitted for testing, before such amendment or revocation.

(c) Notice of an appointment, or the amendment or revocation of any appointment, shall be published by the Minister in the *Iris Oifigiúil*.

## 41 Regulations for purpose of giving effect to this Part

(1) The Minister may make regulations for the purpose of giving effect to this Part.

(2) Without prejudice to the generality of subsection (1) of this section, regulations made under this section may in particular—

(a) regulate the taking, identification and transport of blood samples;

(b) require the production at the time when a blood sample is to be taken of such evidence of the identity of the person from whom it is to be taken as may be prescribed by the regulations;

(c) require any person from whom a blood sample is to be taken, or, in such cases as may be prescribed by the regulations, such other person as may be so prescribed, to state in writing whether he or the person from whom the sample is to be taken, as the case may be, had during such period as may be specified in the regulations suffered from any such illness as may be so specified or received a transfusion of blood;

(d) prescribe the form of any report to be made to a court under this Part.

(3) Every regulation made under this section shall be laid before each House of the Oireachtas as soon as may be after it is made and, if a resolution annulling the regulation is passed by either such House within the next 21 days on which that House has sat after the regulation is laid before it, the regulation shall be annulled accordingly, but without prejudice to the validity of anything previously done thereunder.

## 42 Failure to comply with direction on blood tests

(1) Where a court gives a direction under section 38 of this Act and any person fails to take any step required of him for the purpose of giving effect to the direction, the court may draw such inferences, if any, from that fact as appear proper in the circumstances.

(2) Where in proceedings on an application under section 35 of this Act a court gives a direction under section 38 of this Act for the taking of blood samples then, if any person named in the direction fails, within such period as may be specified by the court, to take any step required of him for the purpose of giving effect to the direction, the court may dismiss the application.

(3) Where in any civil proceedings in which the parentage of any person falls to be determined by the court hearing those proceedings there is, by virtue of section 46 of this Act, a presumption of paternity relating to such person, then if—

(a) a direction is given under section 38 of this Act in those proceedings, and

(b) any party who is claiming any relief in the proceedings and who for the purpose of obtaining that relief is entitled to rely on the presumption fails to take any step required of him for the purpose of giving effect to the direction,

the court may adjourn the hearing for such period as it thinks fit to enable that party to take that step, and if at the end of that period he has failed without reasonable cause to take it the court may, without prejudice to subsection (1) of this section, dismiss his claim for relief notwithstanding the absence of evidence to rebut the presumption.

(4) Where any person named in a direction under section 38 of this Act fails to consent to the taking of a blood sample from himself or from any person named in the direction whom he has charge of or control over, he shall be deemed for the purposes of this section to have failed to take a step required of him for the purpose of giving effect to the direction.

**43      Penalty for personation for blood test purposes**

If, for the purpose of providing a blood sample for a test under section 40 of this Act, any person personates another or proffers another knowing him not to be the person named in the direction, he shall be liable—

(a) on summary conviction, to a fine not exceeding [€1,269.74] or to imprisonment for a term not exceeding 12 months, or to both;

(b) on conviction on indictment, to a fine not exceeding [€3,174.35] or to imprisonment for a term not exceeding two years or to both.

## PART VIII
### PRESUMPTIONS AND EVIDENTIAL PROVISIONS

**44      Abrogation of presumption of legitimacy or illegitimacy**

Any presumption of law as to the legitimacy or illegitimacy of any person is hereby abrogated.

**45      Finding of parentage as evidence in other proceedings**

(1) Where, either before or after the commencement of this Part, a person has been found or adjudged to be a parent of a child in any civil proceedings before a court relating to guardianship of infants or maintenance (including affiliation) or under section 215 of the Social Welfare (Consolidation) Act, 1981, such a finding or

adjudication shall, notwithstanding the fact that that person did or did not offer any defence to the allegation of parentage or was or was not a party to those proceedings, be admissible in evidence in any subsequent civil proceedings for the purpose of proving that that person is or, where not alive, was a parent of that child:

Provided that no finding or adjudication as aforesaid other than a subsisting one shall be admissible in evidence by virtue of this section.

(2) Where evidence that a person has been found or adjudged to be a parent of a child has been submitted in subsequent proceedings by virtue of subsection (1) of this section, then—

(a)  that person shall be taken to be or, where he is not alive, to have been a parent of that child, unless the contrary is proved on the balance of probabilities, and

(b)  in relation to the prior court proceedings the contents of any document which was before that court, or which contains any pronouncement of that court, shall, without prejudice to the submission of any other admissible evidence for the purpose of identifying the facts on which the finding or adjudication was based, be admissible for that purpose.

(3) Where in subsequent civil proceedings the contents of any document are admissible in evidence by virtue of subsection (2) of this section, a copy of that document, or of the material part thereof, purporting to be certified or otherwise authenticated by or on behalf of the court or authority having custody of that document shall be admissible in evidence and shall be taken to be a true copy of that document or part unless the contrary is shown.

## 46 Presumptions of paternity and non-paternity

(1) Where a woman gives birth to a child—

(a)  during a subsisting marriage to which she is a party, or

(b)  within the period of ten months after the termination, by death or otherwise, of a marriage to which she is a party,

then the husband of the marriage shall be presumed to be the father of the child unless the contrary is proved on the balance of probabilities.

(2) Notwithstanding subsection (1) of this section, where a married woman, being a woman who is living apart from her husband under—

(a)  a decree of divorce *a mensa et thoro*, or

(b)  a deed of separation,

gives birth to a child more than ten months after the decree was granted or the deed was executed, as the case may be, then her husband shall be presumed not to be the father of the child unless the contrary is proved on the balance of probabilities.

(3) Notwithstanding subsection (1) of this section, where—

(a)  the birth of a child is registered in a register maintained under the Births and Deaths Registration Acts, 1863 to 1987, and

(b)  the name of a person is entered as the father of the child on the register so maintained,

then the person whose name is so entered shall be presumed to be the father of the child unless the contrary is proved on the balance of probabilities.

(4) For the purposes of subsection (1) of this section **"subsisting marriage"** shall be construed as including a voidable marriage and the expression **"the termination, by death or otherwise, of a marriage"** shall be construed as including the annulment of a voidable marriage.

## 47  Admissibility of certain evidence

(1) The evidence of a husband or wife shall be admissible in any proceedings to prove that marital intercourse did or did not take place between them during any period.

(2) The proviso to section 3 of the Evidence Further Amendment Act, 1869, is hereby repealed.

# PART IX
## REGISTRATION AND RE-REGISTRATION OF BIRTHS

## 48  Re-registration of birth after declaration of parentage

[...]¹

**Notes**

1  Repealed by Schedule 2 of the Civil Registration Act 2004.

## 49  Amendment of Births and Deaths Registration Act (Ireland), 1880

The Births and Deaths Registration Act (Ireland), 1880, is hereby amended by the substitution for section 7 of the following sections:

> **"7. Registration of father where parents not married**
>
> (1) In the case of a child whose parents were not married to each other at the date of his birth or at any time during the period of ten months before his birth, no person shall as father of the child be required to give information concerning the birth.
>
> (2) The registrar shall not enter in the register the name of a person as father of a child to whom subsection (1) of this section relates except—
>
> (a)  at the joint request of the mother and the person acknowledging himself to be the father of the child, or
>
> (b)  at the request of the mother on production of—
>
> (i)  a declaration in the prescribed form made by the mother stating that that person is the father of the child, and

    (ii)    a statutory declaration made by that person acknowledging himself to be the father of the child, or

  (c)  at the request of that person on production of—

    (i)    a declaration in the prescribed form by that person acknowledging himself to be the father of the child, and

    (ii)    a statutory declaration made by the mother stating that that person is the father of the child, or

  (d)  at the request of the mother or that person, which shall in either case be made in writing, on production of a certified copy of any court order in respect of proceedings to which section 45 of the Status of Children Act, 1987, relates, naming that person as the father of the child.

(3) Where the mother of a child to whom subsection (1) of this section relates was married at the date of the birth of the child or at some time during the period of ten months before that birth, the registrar shall not, in respect of a request made by virtue of paragraph (a), (b) or (c) of subsection (2) of this section, register the name of a person as father except, in addition to the said paragraph (a), (b) or (c) being complied with, on production of—

  (a)  a statutory declaration by the husband of the mother stating that he is not the father of the child, or

  (b)  a statutory declaration by the mother stating that she has been living apart from her husband under a decree of divorce *a mensa et thoro* or a deed of separation, as the case may be, for more than ten months before the birth of the child.

(4) On registration of the birth of a child under this section, the register shall be signed by—

  (a)  the registrar,

  (b)  the mother of the child, where she has made a request for registration in accordance with subsection (2) of this section, and

  (c)  the person acknowledging himself to be the father of the child, where he has made a request for registration in accordance with subsection (2) of this section.

(5) Where a person acknowledging himself to be the father of a child (being a child to whom subsection (1) of this section relates) makes a request to the registrar in accordance with subsection (2)(c) or (2)(d) of this section, he shall be treated as a qualified informant concerning the birth of the child for the purposes of this Act.

### 7A. Re-registration of birth so as to show who is father

(1) Where the birth of a child (being a child whose parents were not married to each other at the date of his birth or at any time during the period of ten months before his birth) has been registered under this Act, but no person has been registered as the child's father, the registrar shall re-register the birth so as to show the name of a person as father—

(a) at the joint request of the mother and that person (being a person who acknowledges himself to be the father of the child), or

(b) at the request of the mother on production of—

    (i) a declaration in the prescribed form made by the mother stating that that person is the father of the child, and

    (ii) a statutory declaration made by that person acknowledging himself to be the father of the child, or

(c) at the request of that person on production of—

    (i) a declaration in the prescribed form by that person acknowledging himself to be the father of the child, and

    (ii) a statutory declaration made by the mother stating that that person is the father of the child, or

(d) at the request of the mother or that person, which shall in either case be made in writing, on production of a certified copy of any court order in respect of proceedings to which section 45 of the Status of Children Act, 1987, relates, naming that person as the father of the child,

but no birth shall be re-registered under this section except in the prescribed manner and with the authority of an tArd-Chláraitheoir.

(2) Where the mother of a child to whom subsection (1) of this section relates was married at the date of the birth of the child or at some time during the period of ten months before that birth, the registrar shall not, in respect of a request made by virtue of paragraph (a), (b) or (c) of the said subsection (1), re-register the birth so as to show the name of a person as father except, in addition to the said paragraph (a), (b) or (c) being complied with, on production of—

(a) a statutory declaration by the husband of the mother stating that he is not the father of the child, or

(b) a statutory declaration by the mother stating that she has been living apart from her husband under a decree of divorce *a mensa et thoro* or a deed of separation, as the case may be, for more than ten months before the birth of the child.

(3) On re-registration of the birth of a child under this section, the register shall be signed by—

(a) the registrar,

(b) the mother of the child, where she has made a request for re-registration in accordance with subsection (1) of this section, and

(c) the person acknowledging himself to be the father of the child, where he has made a request for re-registration in accordance with subsection (1) of this section."

## 50    Construction and collective citation

The Births and Deaths Registration Acts, 1863 to 1972, and this Part shall be construed together as one and may be cited together as the Births and Deaths Registration Acts, 1863 to 1987.

# Family Law Act 1988

*Number 31 of 1988*

*An Act to abolish proceedings for restitution of conjugal rights. [23rd November, 1988]*

*Be it enacted by the Oireachtas as follows:*

## 1    Abolition of proceedings for restitution of conjugal rights

After the passing of this Act, no person shall be entitled to institute proceedings for restitution of conjugal rights.[1]

---

**Notes**

1   Commencement: 23 November 1988.

---

## 2    Short title

This Act may be cited as the Family Law Act, 1988.

# Judicial Separation and Family Law Reform Act 1989

*Number 6 of 1989*

---

**Notes**

1 Part II (with the exception of s 25) was repealed by the Family Law Act 1995, s 3.

---

34. Privacy.

35. Costs.

36. Rules of court.

## PART IV
### MISCELLANEOUS

37. Saver for existing law.

38. Amendment of sections 5 and 6 of Family Law (Maintenance of Spouses and Children) Act, 1976.

39. Discharge of orders under Family Law (Maintenance of Spouses and Children) Acts 1976.

40. Reports on children in guardianship cases.

41. Custody of dependent children.

42. Amendment of section 120(2) of Succession Act, 1965.

43. Divorce *a mensa et thoro* decrees and alimony orders.

44. Collusion, condonation, recrimination, connivance.

45. Conduct of District Court family proceedings.

46. Short title and commencement.[1]

## Acts referred to

| | |
|---|---|
| Adoption Acts, 1952 to 1988 | |
| Defence Act, 1954 | 1954, No. 18 |
| Enforcement of Court Orders Act, 1940 | 1940, No. 23 |
| Family Home Protection Act, 1976 | 1976, No. 27 |
| Family Law Act, 1981 | 1981, No. 22 |
| Family Law (Maintenance of Spouses and Children) Act, 1976 | 1976, No. 11 |
| Family Law (Protection of Spouses and Children) Act, 1981 | 1981, No. 21 |
| Guardianship of Infants Act, 1964 | 1964, No. 7 |
| Legitimacy Declaration Act (Ireland), 1868 | 1868, c. 20 |
| Married Women's Status Act, 1957 | 1957, No. 5 |
| Matrimonial Causes and Marriage Law (Ireland) Amendment Act, 1870 | 1870, c. 110 |
| Partition Act, 1868 | 1868, c. 40 |
| Partition Act, 1876 | 1876, c. 17 |
| Status of Children Act, 1987 | 1987, No. 26 |
| Succession Act, 1965 | 1965, No. 27 |

*An Act to amend the grounds for judicial separation: to facilitate reconciliation between estranged spouses: to provide for the making of ancillary orders in separation proceedings: to amend the law relating to the courts' family law jurisdiction and to provide for connected matters. [19th April, 1989]*

*Be it enacted by the Oireachtas as follows:*

---

**Notes**

1   Commencement: 19 October 1989.

---

## PART I
### THE OBTAINING OF A DECREE OF SEPARATION

**1      Definition**

In this Act, except where the context otherwise requires—

**"the court"** means the court having jurisdiction under Part III of this Act.

**2      Application for a decree of judicial separation**

(1) An application by a spouse for a decree of judicial separation from the other spouse may be made to the court having jurisdiction to hear and determine proceedings under Part III of this Act on one or more of the following grounds:

(a)   that the respondent has committed adultery;

(b)   that the respondent has behaved in such a way that the applicant cannot reasonably be expected to live with the respondent;

(c)   subject to subsection (2) of this section, that there has been desertion by the respondent of the applicant for a continuous period of at least one year immediately preceding the date of the application;

(d)   subject to subsection (2) of this section, that the spouses have lived apart from one another for a continuous period of at least one year immediately preceding the date of the application and the respondent consents to a decree being granted;

(e)   subject to subsection (2) of this section, that the spouses have lived apart from one another for a continuous period of at least three years immediately preceding the date of the application;

(f)   that the marriage has broken down to the extent that the court is satisfied in all the circumstances that a normal marital relationship has not existed between the spouses for a period of at least one year immediately preceding the date of the application.

(2) In considering for the purposes of subsection (1) of this section, whether—

(a) in the case of paragraph (c) of that subsection, the period for which the respondent has deserted the applicant, or

(b) in the case of paragraph (d) or (e) of that subsection, the period for which the spouses have lived apart,

has been continuous, no account shall be taken of any one period (not exceeding 6 months) or of any two or more periods (not exceeding 6 months in all) during which the spouses resumed living with each other, but no such period or periods during which the spouses lived with each other shall count as part of the period of desertion or the period for which the spouses have lived apart, as the case may be:

Provided that this subsection shall only apply where the spouses are not living with each other at the time the application is made.

(3) (a) In this section spouses shall be treated as living apart from each other unless they are living with each other in the same household, and references to spouses living with each other shall be construed as references to their living with each other in the same household.

(b) In this section "**desertion**" includes conduct on the part of one spouse that results in the other spouse, with just cause, leaving and living apart from that other spouse.

**3        Grant of decree of judicial separation, custody, etc of children**

(1) Where, on an application under section 2 of this Act, the court is satisfied that any of the grounds referred to in subsection (1) of that section which have been relied on by the applicant have been proved on the balance of probabilities, the court shall, subject to subsection (2) of this section and sections 5 and 6 of this Act, grant a decree of judicial separation in respect of the spouses concerned.

(2) (a) Where there are, in respect of the spouses concerned, any dependent children of the family, the court shall not grant a decree of judicial separation unless the court—

[(i)   is satisfied that such provision exists or has been made, or][1]

(ii)   intends by order upon the granting of the decree to make such provision,

for the welfare of those children as is proper in the circumstances.

(b) In this subsection—

"**dependent children of the family**" has the same meaning as it has for the purposes of Part II of this Act;

"**welfare**" comprises the religious and moral, intellectual, physical and social welfare of the children concerned.

(3) Upon the granting of a decree of judicial separation by the court, the court may, where appropriate, by order give such directions under section 11 of the Guardianship of Infants Act, 1964, as it thinks proper regarding the welfare or custody of, or right of

access to, an infant (being an infant within the meaning of that Act) as if an application had been made under that section.[2]

**Notes**

1  Subsection 2(a)(i) was substituted by the Family Law (Divorce) Act 1996, s 45.

2  See the Child Care Act 1991, s 20.

**4      Supplemental provisions as to proof of adultery and unreasonable behaviour**

(1) Where the spouses have lived with each other for more than 1 year after it became known to the applicant that the respondent had committed adultery the applicant shall not be entitled to rely on that adultery for the purposes of section 2(1)(a) although that adultery may be one of the factors that the applicant may rely on for the purposes of section 2(1)(b) together with other matters.

(2) Where the applicant alleges that the respondent has behaved in such a way that the applicant cannot reasonably be expected to cohabit with him but the spouses have cohabited for a period or periods after the date of the occurrence of the final incident relied on by the applicant and held by the court to support his allegation, such cohabitation shall be disregarded in determining for the purpose of section 2(1)(b) of this Act whether the applicant cannot be reasonably expected to live with the respondent if the length of the period or of those periods of cohabitation together was or were 6 months or less.

**5      Safeguards to ensure applicant's awareness of alternatives to separation proceedings and to assist attempts at reconciliation**

(1) A solicitor, if any, acting for an applicant for a decree of judicial separation shall, prior to the making of an application for a decree of judicial separation—

(a)   discuss with the applicant the possibility of reconciliation and give to him the names and addresses of persons qualified to help effect a reconciliation between spouses who have become estranged, and

(b)   discuss with the applicant the possibility of engaging in mediation to help effect a separation on an agreed basis with an estranged spouse and give to him the names and addresses of persons and organisations qualified to provide a mediation service, and

(c)   discuss with the applicant the possibility of effecting a separation by the negotiation and conclusion of a separation deed or written separation agreement.

(2) An application for judicial separation shall be accompanied by a certificate by the solicitor, if any, acting on behalf of the applicant that he has complied with the provisions of subsection (1) of this section and, where a solicitor does not so certify, the court may adjourn the proceedings for such period as it deems reasonable for the

applicant's solicitor to discuss with the applicant the matters referred to in that subsection.

(3) Provision shall be made by rules of court for the certification required for the purposes of subsection (2) of this section.

**6    Safeguards to ensure respondent's awareness of alternatives to separation proceedings and to assist attempts at reconciliation**

(1) A solicitor, if any, acting for a respondent in an application for a decree of judicial separation shall, as soon as possible after receiving instructions from the respondent—

(a)  discuss with the respondent the possibility of reconciliation and give to him the names and addresses of persons qualified to help effect a reconciliation between parties to a marriage who have become estranged, and

(b)  discuss with the respondent the possibility of engaging in mediation to help effect a separation on an agreed basis with an estranged spouse and give to him the names and addresses of persons and organisations qualified to provide a mediation service, and

(c)  discuss with the respondent the possibility of effecting a separation by the negotiation and conclusion of a separation deed or written separation agreement.

(2) An Entry of Appearance or a Notice of Intention to Defend an application for judicial separation shall be accompanied by a certificate by the solicitor, if any, acting on behalf of the respondent, that he has complied with the provisions of subsection (1) of this section and where a solicitor does not so certify, the court may adjourn the proceedings for such period as it deems reasonable for the respondent's solicitor to discuss with the respondent the matters referred to in that subsection.

(3) Provision shall be made by rules of court for the certification required for the purposes of this section.

**7    Adjournment of proceedings to assist reconciliation or agreements on separation**

(1) Where an application is made under this Act to the court for a decree of judicial separation, the court shall give consideration to the possibility of a reconciliation of the spouses concerned and, accordingly, may adjourn the proceedings at any time for the purpose of affording the spouses an opportunity, if they both so wish, to consider a reconciliation between themselves with or without the assistance of a third party.

(2) If during any adjournment of proceedings to which subsection (1) of this section relates the spouses resume living with each other, no account shall be taken of that fact for the purposes of those proceedings.

(3) Where on an application made under this Act for a decree of judicial separation it appears to the court that no reconciliation of the spouses concerned is possible, it may adjourn or further adjourn the proceedings for the purpose of affording the spouses an opportunity, if they both so wish, to establish agreement (with or without the assistance of a third party) on the terms, so far as is possible, of the separation.

(4) If an adjournment has taken place by virtue of subsection (1) or (3) of this section, either or both of the spouses may request that the hearing of the application be proceeded with and, without prejudice to subsection (5) of this section, the court shall resume hearing the application as soon as is practicable.

(5) The power of adjournment exercisable under subsections (1) and (3) of this section is in addition to and not in substitution for any other power of adjournment exercisable by the court.

(6) Where the court adjourns proceedings under subsection (1) or (3) of this section, it may at its discretion advise the spouses concerned to seek the assistance of a third party for the purpose set out in the appropriate subsection.

(7) [...]¹

**Notes**

1   Subsection (7) was repealed by the Family Law (Divorce) Act 1996, s 45.

**[7A    Non-admissibility as evidence of certain communications relating to reconciliation or separation**

An oral or written communication between either of the spouses concerned and a third party for the purpose of seeking assistance to effect a reconciliation or to reach agreement between them on some or all the terms of a separation (whether or not made in the presence or with the knowledge of the other spouse), and any record of such a communication, made or caused to be made by either of the spouses concerned or such a third party, shall not be admissible as evidence in any court.]¹

**Notes**

1   Commencement: 27 February 1997. Section 7A was inserted by the Family Law (Divorce) Act 1996, s 45.

**8    Effect of judicial separation and rescission of decree of separation and ancillary orders upon reconciliation**

(1) Where the court grants a decree of judicial separation it shall no longer be obligatory for the spouses who were the parties to such proceedings to cohabit.

(2) Following the granting of a decree of judicial separation the applicant and the respondent in the separation proceedings may at any future date by consent apply to the court to rescind the decree of separation granted and such order of rescission shall be made by the court upon it being satisfied that a reconciliation has taken place between the applicant and the respondent and that they have already resumed or again wish to resume cohabiting as husband and wife.

(3) Upon making an order of rescission under subsection (2) of this section the court may also make such necessary ancillary order or orders as it deems proper in the circumstances with regard to any orders previously made under Part II of this Act.

**9      Abolition of decree of divorce *a mensa et thoro*, etc**

(1) After the commencement of this Act, no action shall lie for divorce *a mensa et thoro*.

(2) Subsection (1) of this section shall not have effect in relation to any action instituted before the commencement of this Act.

# PART II
## ANCILLARY FINANCIAL, PROPERTY, CUSTODY AND OTHER ORDERS.[1]

**Notes**

1   Part II has been repealed by the Family Law Act 1995, s 3, other than s 25.

**25      Amendment of section 3 of Family Law (Maintenance of Spouses and Children) Act, 1976[1]**

**Notes**

1   Section 25 amends the Family Law (Maintenance of Spouses and Children) Act 1976; see the amended Act.

# PART III
## COURT JURISDICTION

**30      Definition**

In this Part **"family law proceedings"**, in relation to a court, means proceedings before a court of competent jurisdiction under—

    (a)   this Act,

    (b)   the Adoption Acts, 1952 to 1988,

    (c)   the Family Home Protection Act, 1976,

    (d)   the Family Law (Maintenance of Spouses and Children) Act, 1976,

    (e)   the Family Law (Protection of Spouses and Children) Act, 1981,

    (f)   the Family Law Act, 1981,

    (g)   the Guardianship of Infants Act, 1964,

    (h)   the Legitimacy Declaration Act (Ireland), 1868,

(i)   the Married Women's Status Act, 1957, or

(j)   the Status of Children Act, 1987,

or between spouses under the Partition Act, 1868, and the Partition Act, 1876, where the fact that they are married to each other is of relevance to the proceedings.

## 31      Courts, jurisdiction and venue

(1) The Circuit Court shall be known as "the Circuit Family Court" when exercising its jurisdiction to hear and determine family law proceedings or, where provided for, when transferring family law proceedings to the High Court.

(2) Subject to the other provisions of this section, the Circuit Family Court shall, concurrently with the High Court, have jurisdiction to hear and determine proceedings under this Act for a decree of judicial separation.

(3) Where in proceedings under this Act for a decree of judicial separation an order could be made in respect of land whose rateable valuation exceeds [€253.93] and an application commencing those proceedings is made to the Circuit Family Court, that Court shall, if the respondent so requires before the hearing thereof, transfer those proceedings to the High Court, but any order made (including an interim order) or act done in the course of those proceedings before such transfer shall be valid unless discharged or varied by order of the High Court.

(4) The jurisdiction referred to in subsection (2) of this section shall only be exercisable where either of the spouses is domiciled in the State on the date of the application commencing proceedings or is ordinarily resident in the State throughout the period of one year ending on that date.[1]

(5) The jurisdiction referred to in subsection (2) of this section shall, in the Circuit Family Court, be exercised by the judge of the circuit where either spouse to the proceedings ordinarily resides or carries on any profession, business or occupation.

---

### Notes

1   See the Family Law (Divorce) Act 1996, s 39(4).

---

## 32      Hearing of proceedings

The Circuit Family Court shall sit to hear and determine proceedings instituted under this Act and under the Acts referred to in section 30 of this Act in a different place or at different times or on different days from those on which the ordinary sittings of the Circuit Court are held.

## 33      Conduct of family proceedings in Circuit and High Courts

(1) Circuit Family Court proceedings shall be as informal as is practicable and consistent with the administration of justice.

(2) Neither judges sitting in the Circuit Family Court nor barristers nor solicitors appearing in such courts shall wear wigs or gowns.

(3) Family law proceedings before the High Court shall be as informal as is practicable and consistent with the administration of justice.

(4) In hearing and determining such proceedings as are referred to in subsection (3) of this section neither judges sitting in the High Court nor barristers nor solicitors appearing in such proceedings shall wear wigs or gowns.

## 34 Privacy

Proceedings under this Act shall be heard otherwise than in public.

## 35 Costs

The costs of any proceedings under this Act shall be at the discretion of the court.

## 36 Rules of court

(1) Rules of court shall provide for the documentation required for the commencement of proceedings under this Act in a summary manner.

(2) The rules of court, and any established form or course of pleading, practice or procedure, for the purposes of any enactment or jurisdiction affected by this Act shall, pending the due making of rules of court, apply for such purposes with such adaptations as may be necessary.

# PART IV
## MISCELLANEOUS

## 37 Saver for existing law

Save in so far as otherwise provided in this Act, the law relating to proceedings for divorce *a mensa et thoro* shall, so far as applicable, apply in relation to proceedings for judicial separation.

## 38 Amendment of sections 5 and 6 of Family Law (Maintenance of Spouses and Children) Act, 1976[1]

---

**Notes**

1 Section 38 amends the Family Law (Maintenance of Spouses and Children) Act 1976; see the amended Act.

---

## 39 Discharge of orders under Family Law (Maintenance of Spouses and Children) Act, 1976

[...][1]

## 40 Reports on children in guardianship cases

[...][1]

**Notes**

1   Sections 39 and 40 of this Part were repealed by the Family Law Act 1995, s 3.

## 41   Custody of dependent children

[(1) In this section "**dependent member of the family**" has the meaning assigned to it by section 2 of the Family Law Act, 1995.

(2) Where the court grants a decree of judicial separation, it may declare either of the spouses concerned to be unfit to have custody of any dependent member of the family who is minor and, if it does so and the spouse to whom the declaration related is a parent of a dependent member of the family who is a minor, that spouse shall not, on the death of the other spouse, be entitled as of right to the custody of that minor.]¹

(3) Section 18(1) of the Guardianship of Infants Act, 1964, is hereby repealed except in relation to an action instituted before the commencement of this Act.

**Notes**

1   Subsections (1) and (2) were substituted by the Children Act 1997, s 16.

## 42   Amendment of section 120(2) of Succession Act, 1965

(1) Section 120(2) of the Succession Act, 1965 is hereby amended by the deletion of the words from "against whom the deceased obtained a decree of divorce *a mensa et thoro*," to "and a spouse".

(2) Subsection (1) of this section shall not have effect in relation to a decree of divorce *a mensa et thoro* granted in proceedings instituted before the commencement of this Act.

## 43   Divorce *a mensa et thoro* decrees and alimony orders

Any order made by either the Circuit Court or the High Court granting a decree of divorce *a mensa et thoro* in proceedings issued before the commencement of this Act shall not be affected by this Act save that any alimony order made subsequent to the granting of such decree shall be deemed for all purposes to be an order made under section 14(1)(a) of this Act.

## 44   Collusion, condonation, recrimination, connivance

(1) Collusion between the spouses in connection with an application for a judicial separation or, subject to subsection (2) of this section, any conduct (including condonation or recrimination) on the part of the applicant shall not be a bar to the grant of a decree of judicial separation.

(2) Where an application for a decree of judicial separation is made on the ground of adultery and the respondent proves that the adultery was committed with the connivance of the applicant the court may refuse the application.

## 45      Conduct of District Court family proceedings

(1) Proceedings before the District Court under the Guardianship of Infants Act, 1964, the Family Law (Maintenance of Spouses and Children) Act, 1976, the Family Home Protection Act, 1976, section 9 of the Family Law Act, 1981, the Family Law (Protection of Spouses and Children) Act, 1981[, the Status of Children Act, 1987, and the Child Abduction and Enforcement of Custody Orders, 1991][1] shall be as informal as is practicable and consistent with the administration of justice.

(2) Neither district justices hearing and determining such proceedings as are referred to in subsection (1) of this section nor barristers nor solicitors appearing in such proceedings shall wear wigs or gowns.

**Notes**

1    Section 45(1) was amended by the Child Abduction and Enforcement of Custody Orders 1991, s 39.

## 46      Short title and commencement

(1) This Act may be cited as the Judicial Separation and Family Law Reform Act, 1989.

(2) This Act shall come into operation on the day that is 6 months after the date of the passing of this Act.[1]

**Notes**

1    Commencement: 19 October 1989.

# Child Abduction and Enforcement of Custody Orders Act 1991

*Number 6 of 1991*

## PART IV
### SUPPLEMENTARY

## PART V
### MISCELLANEOUS

## FIRST SCHEDULE
### TEXT OF THE CONVENTION ON THE CIVIL ASPECTS OF INTERNATIONAL CHILD ABDUCTION

## SECOND SCHEDULE
### TEXT OF THE EUROPEAN CONVENTION ON RECOGNITION AND ENFORCEMENT OF DECISIONS CONCERNING CUSTODY OF CHILDREN AND ON RESTORATION OF CUSTODY OF CHILDREN

## Acts Referred to

| | |
|---|---|
| Children Act 1908 | 1908 c. 67 |
| Courts (Supplemental Provisions) Acts | 1961 to 1988 |
| Guardianship of Infants Act, 1964 | 1964 No. 7 |
| Health Act, 1970 | 1970 No. 1 |
| Judicial Separation and Family Law Reform Act, 1989 | 1989 No. 6 |

*An Act to give the force of law to the Convention on the Civil Aspects of International child Abduction signed at The Hague on the 25th day of October, 1980, and the European Convention on Recognition and Enforcement of Decisions concerning Custody of Children and on Restoration of Custody of Children signed at Luxembourg on the 20th day of May, 1980, and to provide for matters consequent upon and otherwise related to the matters aforesaid. [27th March, 1991]*

*Be It enacted by the Oireachtas As follows:*

## PART I
### PRELIMINARY AND GENERAL

**1**     **Short title, construction and commencement**

(1) This Act may be cited as the Child Abduction and Enforcement of Custody Orders Act, 1991.

(2) The Courts (Supplemental Provisions) Acts, 1961 to 1988, and this Act, insofar as it affects the jurisdiction or procedure of any court in the State, shall be construed together as one.

(3) This Act shall come into operation on such day or days as the Minister shall fix by order or orders either generally or with reference to any particular purpose or provision and different days may be so fixed for different purposes and different provisions.

**2**     **Interpretation**

(1) In this Act—

**"Central Authority in the State"** shall be construed in accordance with section 8 or 22 (as may be appropriate) of this Act;

**"child"** where used in the context of the Children Act, 1908, includes a young person within the meaning of that Act;

[**"Council Regulation"** means Council Regulation (EC) No. 2201/2003 of 27 November 2003;][1]

**"the Court"** means the High Court;

**"the Hague Convention"** means the Convention on the Civil Aspects of International Child Abduction, signed at The Hague on the 25th day of October, 1980;

"**the Luxembourg Convention**" means the European Convention on Recognition and Enforcement of Decisions concerning Custody of Children and on Restoration of Custody of Children, signed at Luxembourg on the 20th day of May, 1980;

"**the Minister**" means the Minister for [Justice, Equality and Law Reform][2];

"**prescribed**" means prescribed by regulations made by the Minister under this Act;

"**probation and welfare officer**" means a person appointed by the Minister [for Justice, Equality and Law Reform][2] to be a probation and welfare officer or to be a welfare officer or probation officer.

[(2) References in this Act to the Hague Convention shall, where the context requires in relation to applications under the Hague Convention to which the Council Regulation relates, be deemed to include references to the Council Regulation.][3]

**Notes**

1    Definition of "Council Regulation" and subsection (2) inserted by the European Communities (Judgments in Matrimonial Matters and Matters of Parental Responsibility) Regulations 2005 (SI 112/2005), reg 8.

2    Definitions of "the Minister" and "probation and welfare officer" amended by the Family Law Act 1995, s 55 and the Children Act 1997, s 18.

3    The definition of "health board" was deleted by Schedule 6 of the Health Act 2004.

## PART II[1]
## THE HAGUE CONVENTION

**Notes**

1    See the Child Abduction and Enforcement of Custody Orders Act 1991 (Section 4) (Hague Convention) Order 2011 (SI 400/2011) which specifies the Contracting States for the purpose of Part II of this Act.

**3      "Contracting State"**

In this Part "Contracting State" means a state in respect of which the Hague Convention is in force in accordance with the provisions of that Convention and shall be construed so that this Act shall have effect in relation to—

(a)   the states which have acceded to that Convention, or any states which may accede to that Convention, and in respect of which the State has made a declaration pursuant to Article 38 of that Convention, and

(b)   the places as respects which that Convention has effect by virtue of Articles 39 and 40 of that Convention.

**4      Contracting States and declarations, reservations, withdrawals and denunciations under Hague Convention**

(1) The Minister for Foreign Affairs may by order declare—

    (a)   that any state specified in the order is a Contracting Stale, or

    (b)   that—

        (i)   a declaration (the text of which shall be set out in the order) has been made pursuant to Article 38, 39 or 40 of the Hague Convention, or

        (ii)   a reservation, or a withdrawal thereof (the text of which shall be set out in the order) has been made pursuant to Article 24, 26 or (in the case of a withdrawal) 42 of that Convention, or

        (iii)   a denunciation (the text of which shall be set out in the order) has been made pursuant to Article 44 of that Convention,

    to the Ministry of Foreign Affairs of the Kingdom of the Netherlands.

(2) An order that is in force under subsection (1) of this section shall, as the case may be, be evidence—

    (a)   that any state specified in the order is a Contracting State;

    (b)   that a declaration, a reservation, a withdrawal of a reservation or a denunciation set out in the order was made and of its contents.

(3) The Minister for Foreign Affairs may by order amend or revoke an order under this section (including an order under this subsection).

**5      Evidence of decisions and determinations of authorities of Contracting States and other matters relating to Hague Convention**

(1) For the purposes of Article 14 of the Hague Convention a document, duly authenticated, which purports to be a copy of a decision or determination of a judicial or administrative authority of a Contracting State other than the State shall without further proof be deemed to be a true copy of the decision or determination, unless the contrary is shown.

(2) For the purposes of Articles 14 and 30 of the Hague Convention the original or a copy of any such document as is mentioned in Article 8 of that Convention shall be admissible—

    (a)   insofar as it consists of a statement of fact, as evidence of that fact, and

    (b)   insofar as it consists of a statement of opinion, as evidence of that opinion.

(3) A document which—

    (a)   purports to be a translation of a decision or determination of a judicial or administrative authority of a Contracting State other than the State or of a document mentioned in Article 8 of the Hague Convention, and

    (b)   is certified as correct by a person competent to do so,

shall be admissible as evidence of the translation.

(4) A document purporting to be a copy of a decision, determination or declaration of a judicial or administrative authority of a Contracting State shall, for the purposes of this Part, be regarded as being duly authenticated if it purports—

    (a)   to bear the seal of that authority, or

    (b)   to be certified by a person in his capacity as a judge or officer of that authority to be a true copy of a decision, determination or declaration of that authority.

## 6     Hague Convention to have the force of law

(1) Subject to the provisions of [the Council Regulation and this Part]¹, the Hague Convention shall have the force of law in the State and judicial notice shall be taken of it.

(2) The text of the Hague Convention in the English language is set out for convenience of reference in the First Schedule to this Act.

---

**Notes**

1     The words "the Council Regulation and this Part" substituted for "this Part" by the European Communities (Judgments in Matrimonial Matters and Matters of Parental Responsibility) Regulations 2005 (SI 112/2005), reg 8.

---

## 7     Jurisdiction of the Court for purposes of Part II

(1) For the purposes of this Part and the Hague Convention the Court shall have jurisdiction to hear and determine applications under that Convention.

[(2) For the purposes of such applications—

    (a)   references to 'judicial or administrative authority' in the Hague Convention, and

    (b)   references to 'competent authorities in a Member State' and to 'court' in Article 11 of the Council Regulation,

shall be construed as references to the Court unless the context otherwise requires.]¹

---

**Notes**

1     Subsection (2) substituted by the European Communities (Judgments in Matrimonial Matters and Matters of Parental Responsibility) Regulations 2005 (SI 112 of 2005), reg 8.

---

## 8     Central Authority for purposes of Hague Convention

(1) The Minister may by order appoint a Central Authority (referred to in this Part as the Central Authority in the State) to discharge the functions under the Hague Convention of a Central Authority.

(2) Notwithstanding subsection (1) of this section, unless and until the Minister appoints a Central Authority under this section, the said functions shall be discharged by the Minister and references in this Part to the Central Authority in the State shall be construed, accordingly, as references to the Minister.

(3) The Minister may by order amend or revoke an order under this section (including an order under this subsection).

**9        Application for return of child removed to the State**

(1) Any application, in such form as may be prescribed, made under the Hague Convention in respect of a child removed to the State may be addressed to the Central Authority in the State.

(2) Where the Central Authority in the State receives any such application and is satisfied that the application is an application to which the Hague Convention applies, it shall take action or cause action to be taken under that Convention to secure the return of the child.

**10       Application for return of child removed from the State**

(1) Any application, in such form as may be prescribed, made under the Hague Convention in respect of a child removed from the State to another Contracting State may be addressed to the Central Authority in the State.

(2) Where the Central Authority in the State receives any such application and is satisfied that the application is an application to which the Hague Convention applies, it shall, on behalf of the applicant, take any action required to be taken by a Central Authority under that Convention.

(3) Nothing in subsection (1) of this section shall prevent the Central Authority in the State from dealing with any application made under the Hague Convention by or on behalf of a person in respect of a child removed from a Contracting State (not being the State) to another Contracting State (not being the State).

**11       Operation of this Part not to affect jurisdiction of the Court**

Nothing in this Part shall prevent a person from applying in the first instance to the Court, whether or not under the Hague Convention, in respect of the breach of rights of custody of, or breach of rights of access to, a child removed to the State.

**12       Interim powers of the Court for the purposes of Part II**

(1) Where an application has been made or is about to be made to the Court under the Hague Convention, the Court may of its own motion or on an application under this section, at any time before the application is determined, give such interim directions as it thinks fit for the purpose of securing the welfare of the child concerned, or preventing prejudice to interested persons or changes in the circumstances relevant to the determination of the application.

(2) An application for interim directions under this section may, where the case is one of urgency, be made ex parte.

**13 Notice and stay of certain proceedings for purposes of Part II**

(1) Any person who has an interest in proceedings in the Court or in proceedings about to be commenced in the Court under this Part in respect of a child removed to the State shall, where he knows that an application relating to the custody of the child is pending in or before any court in the State, give notice to that court of the proceedings, or pending proceedings (as the case may be), under the Hague Convention and that court, having notified the parties to the proceedings before it of that notice, shall stay in accordance with Article 16 of that Convention all further proceedings in the matter and shall notify the Court of the stay.

(2) For the purpose of this section an application relating to custody of a child shall be construed as including a reference to an application for—

(a) an order making, varying or discharging an order regarding the custody of, or the right of access to, a child under the Guardianship of Infants Act, 1964;

(b) an order made pursuant to Part II or IV of the Children Act, 1908, in relation to the care of a child;

(c) the recognition or enforcement of a decision relating to custody under Part III of this Act.

**14 Reports for purposes of Part II**

Where the Central Authority in the State is requested to provide information relating to a child under Article 7d of the Hague Convention it may—

(a) request a probation and welfare officer to make a report to it in writing with respect to any matter relating to the child which appears to it to be relevant;

(b) request [the Health Service Executive][1] to arrange for a suitably qualified person to make such a report to it; or

(c) request any court to which a written report relating to the child has been made to send it a copy of the report,

and any such request shall be duly complied with.

**Notes**

1   Amended by s 75 and Schedule 6 of the Health Act 2004, substituting "[the Health Service Executive]" for "health board".

**15 Declaration by the Court of wrongful removal of child**

[(1) The Court may, on an application made for the purposes of Article 15 of the Hague Convention y any person appearing to the Court to have an interest in the matter, make a declaration that the removal of any child from, or his retention outside, the State was—

(a) in the case of a removal to or a retention in a Member State, a wrongful removal or retention within the meaning of Article 2 of the Council Regulation, or

(b) in any other case, wrongful within the meaning of Article 3 of the Hague Convention.][1]

(2) The Central Authority in the State shall take action or cause action to be taken to assist the person referred to in subsection (1) of this section in making an application under this section if a request for such assistance, in such form as may be prescribed, is made by him or on his behalf by the Central Authority of another Contracting State.

**Notes**

1   Subsection (1) substituted by the European Communities (Judgments in Matrimonial Matters and Matters of Parental Responsibility) Regulations 2005 (SI 112/2005), reg 8.

## 16      Provision of certain documents by courts in the State for purposes of Hague Convention

As respects a decision relating to custody made by a court in the State (including a declaration made by the Court under section 15 of this Act) the registrar or clerk of the court shall, at the request of a person who wishes to make an application under the Hague Convention in a Contracting State other than the State or at the request on his behalf of the Central Authority in the State and subject to any conditions that may be specified by rules of court, give to the person or the Central Authority, as the case may be, the following documents—

(a)   a copy of the decision duly authenticated;

(b)   where the decision was given in default of appearance, the original or a copy, certified by the registrar or clerk of the court to be a true copy, of a document establishing that notice of the institution of proceedings was served on the person in default.

# PART III
## THE LUXEMBOURG CONVENTION[1]

**Notes**

1   See the Child Abduction and Enforcement of Custody Orders Act 1991(Section 18) (Luxembourg Convention) Order 2001 (SI 508/2001) for the Contracting States under Part III.

## 17      Interpretation of Part III

In this Part—

**"Contracting State"** means a state in respect of which the Luxembourg Convention is in force in accordance with the provisions of that Convention and shall be construed so that this Part shall have effect in relation to the places as respects which that Convention has effect by virtue of Articles 24 and 25 of that Convention;

"**decision relating to custody**" has the meaning given to it in Article 1 of the Luxembourg Convention;

"**enforcement order**" means an order of the Court for the recognition or enforcement of a decision relating to custody to which either Article 7 or 12 of the Luxembourg Convention applies.

## 18      Contracting States and declarations, reservations, withdrawals, notifications and denunciations under Luxembourg Convention

(1) The Minister for Foreign Affairs may by order declare—

    (a)  that any state specified in the order is a Contracting State, or

    (b)  that—

        (i)  a reservation, or a withdrawal thereof (the text of which shall be set out in the order) has been made pursuant to Article 6.3, 17, 18 or (in the case of a withdrawal) 27 of the Luxembourg Convention, or

        (ii)  a declaration (the text of which shall be set out in the order) has been made pursuant to Article 24 or 25 of that Convention, or

        (iii)  a notification (the text of which shall be set out in the order) has been received pursuant to Article 2 of that Convention, or

        (iv)  a notification of a decision or of an alteration or revocation of a decision (the text of which shall be set out in the order) has been made pursuant to Article 20 of that Convention, or

        (v)  a denunciation (the text of which shall be set out in the order) has been made pursuant to Article 29 of that Convention,

    to or by, as the case may be, the Secretary General of the Council of Europe.

(2) An order that is in force under subsection (1) of this section shall, as the case may be, be evidence—

    (a)  that any state specified in the order is a Contracting State;

    (b)  that a reservation, a withdrawal of a reservation, a declaration, a notification or a denunciation set out in the order was made or received and of its contents.

(3) The Minister for Foreign Affairs may by order amend or revoke an order under this section (including an order under this subsection).

## 19      Evidence of decisions and declarations of authorities of Contracting States and other matters relating to Luxembourg Convention

(1) For the purposes of the Luxembourg Convention—

    (a)  a document, duly authenticated, which purports to be a copy of a decision or declaration relating to custody of a judicial or administrative authority of a Contracting State other than the State shall without further proof be deemed to be a true copy of the decision or declaration, unless the contrary is shown; and

    (b)  the original or a copy of any other document as is mentioned in Article 13 of the Luxembourg Convention shall be admissible—

        (i)  insofar as it consists of a statement of fact, as evidence of that fact, and

    (ii)   insofar as it consists of a statement of opinion, as evidence of that opinion.

(2) A document which—

    (a)   purports to be a translation of a decision or declaration of a judicial or administrative authority of a Contracting State other than the State or any other document mentioned in Article 13 of the Luxembourg Convention, and

    (b)   is certified as correct by a person competent to do so,

shall be admissible as evidence of the translation.

(3) A document purporting to be a copy of a decision or declaration relating to custody made by a judicial or administrative authority of a Contracting State shall, for the purposes of this Part, be regarded as being duly authenticated if it purports—

    (a)   to bear the seal of that authority, or

    (b)   to be certified by a person in his capacity as a judge or officer of that authority to be a true copy of a decision or declaration of that authority.

## 20    Application of this Part

This Part applies to any decision relating to custody (by whatever name called) that is a decision relating to custody for the purposes of the Luxembourg Convention.

## 21    Luxembourg Convention to have the force of law.

(1) Subject to the provisions of this Part (including the restrictions on recognition and enforcement of a decision relating to custody contained in section 28 of this Act), the Luxembourg Convention shall have the force of law in the State and judicial notice shall be taken of it.

(2) The text of the Luxembourg Convention in the English language is set out for convenience of reference in the Second Schedule to this Act.

## 22    Central Authority for purposes of Luxembourg Convention

(1) The Minister may by order appoint a Central Authority (referred to in this Part as the Central Authority in the State) to discharge the functions under the Luxembourg Convention of a Central Authority.

(2) Notwithstanding subsection (1) of this section, unless and until the Minister appoints a Central Authority under this section, the said functions shall be discharged by the Minister and references in this Part to the Central Authority in the State shall be construed, accordingly, as references to the Minister.

(3) The Minister may by order amend or revoke an order under this section (including an order under this subsection).

## 23    Jurisdiction of the Court for purposes of Part III

For the purposes of this Part and the Luxembourg Convention the Court shall have jurisdiction to hear and determine applications under that Convention for the recognition or enforcement of a decision relating to custody.

**24 Applications for recognition and enforcement of custody decisions in the State**

(1) Any application, in such form as may be prescribed, made by or on behalf of a person on whom any rights are conferred by a decision relating to custody made by an authority in a Contracting State other than the State for the recognition or enforcement of the decision in the State may be addressed to the Central Authority in the State.

(2) Where the Central Authority in the State receives any such application and is satisfied that the application is an application to which the Luxembourg Convention applies, it shall take action or cause action to be taken under that Convention to secure the recognition or enforcement of the decision.

**25 Applications in the first instance to the Court**

Nothing in this Part shall prevent a person from applying in the first instance to the Court under the Luxembourg Convention for the recognition or enforcement of a decision relating to custody made by an authority in a Contracting State, other than the State.

**26 Interim powers of the Court for the purposes of Part III**

(1) Where an application has been made or is about to be made to the Court under the Luxembourg Convention for the recognition or enforcement of a decision relating to custody, the Court may of its own motion or on an application under this section, at any time before the application is determined, give such interim directions as it thinks fit for the purpose of securing the welfare of the child concerned, or preventing prejudice to interested persons or changes in the circumstances relevant to the determination of the application.

(2) An application for interim directions under this section may, where the case is one of urgency, be made ex parte.

**27 Notice and stay of certain proceedings for purposes of Part III**

(1) Any person who has an interest in proceedings in the Court under this Part for the recognition or enforcement of a decision relating to custody made by an authority in a Contracting State other than the State shall, where he knows that an application relating to custody of the child is pending in or before any court in the State and such proceedings were commenced before the proceedings in the Contracting State which resulted in the decision in respect of which recognition or enforcement is sought were instituted, give notice to the Court of those proceedings and the Court may stay all further proceedings in the application for recognition or enforcement until the other proceedings have been determined.

(2) Any person who has an interest in proceedings in the Court under this Part for the recognition or enforcement of a decision relating to custody made by an authority in a Contracting State other than the State shall, where he knows that an application relating to custody of the child is pending in or before any court in the State and such proceedings were commenced after the proceedings in the Contracting State which resulted in the decision in respect of which recognition or enforcement is sought were

instituted, give notice to that court of the proceedings under the Luxembourg Convention and that court having notified the parties to the proceedings before it of that notice shall stay all further proceedings in the matter until the Court determines the application for recognition or enforcement. The court concerned shall notify the Court of the stay.

(3) For the purpose of this section an application relating to custody of a child shall be construed as including a reference to an application for—

(a)  an order making, varying or discharging an order regarding the custody of, or the right of access to, a child under the Guardianship of Infants Act, 1964;

(b)  an order made pursuant to Part II or IV of the Children Act, 1908, in relation to the care of a child.

**28     Refusal of application for recognition or enforcement of custody decision in the State**

(1) The Court shall refuse an application made under this Part for recognition or enforcement in the State of a decision relating to custody where—

(a)  in relation to a decision to which Article 8 of the Luxembourg Convention applies, the Court is of opinion on any of the grounds specified in Article 10.1. a, b, c or d of that Convention that the decision should not be recognised or enforced in the State;

(b)  in relation to a decision to which Article 9 or 10 of that Convention applies, the Court is of opinion on any of the grounds specified in the said Articles that the decision should not be recognised or enforced in the State;

(c)  the Court is of opinion that the decision is not enforceable in the Contracting State where it was made and is not a decision to which Article 12 of the Convention applies.

(2) Where an application is made to the Court under this Part for recognition or enforcement in the State of a decision relating to custody and an application to the Court in respect of the child is pending under Part II of this Act the Court shall stay all further proceedings under this Part until the other proceedings have been determined.

(3) The references in Article 9.1.c of the Luxembourg Convention to the removal of the child are to his improper removal within the meaning of that Convention.

(4) For the purposes of this section a decision relating to custody includes a decision varying that decision.

**29     Enforcement of custody decisions**

A decision relating to custody in respect of which an enforcement order has been made shall be of the same force and effect and, as respects the enforcement of the decision, the Court shall have the same powers, and proceedings may be taken, as if the decision was a decision of the Court.

**30     Reports for purposes of Part III**

Where the Central Authority in the State is requested to make enquiries about a child under Article 15.1.b of the Luxembourg Convention the Central Authority may—

    (a)   request a probation and welfare officer to make a report to it in writing with respect to any matter relating to the child which appears to it to be relevant;

    (b)   request [the Health Service Executive][1] to arrange for a suitably qualified person to make such a report to it;

    (c)   request any court to which a written report relating to the child has been made to send it a copy of the report,

and any such request shall be duly complied with.

---

**Notes**

1    Amended by s 75 and Schedule 6 of the Health Act 2004, substituting "[the Health Service Executive]" for "health board".

---

**31     Variation and revocation of custody decisions**

(1) Where a decision relating to custody is varied or revoked by an authority in the Contracting State in which it was made, any person appearing to the Court to have an interest in the matter may make an application to the Court for an order for variation or revocation of the order of recognition or enforcement of that decision.

(2) Where an application is made under subsection (1) of this section for revocation of an order the Court shall, if it is satisfied that the decision (in respect of which the order of recognition or enforcement was made) has been revoked by an authority in the Contracting State in which it was made, discharge the order and the decision shall cease to be enforceable in the State.

(3) Where an application is made under subsection (1) of this section for variation of an order, the Court may, if it is satisfied that the decision has been varied by an authority in the Contracting State in which it was made and, subject to the grounds of refusal specified in section 28 (1) of this Act, make an order varying the order and a decision so varied shall be of the same force and effect, and as respects the enforcement of the decision so varied, the Court shall have the same powers and proceedings may be taken, as if the decision so varied was a decision of the Court.

(4) The Central Authority in the State shall assist the person referred to in subsection (1) of this section if a request for such assistance, in such form as may be prescribed, is made by him or on his behalf by the Central Authority of the Contracting State in question.

**32    Applications for recognition and enforcement of custody decisions in another Contracting State**

(1) A person on whom any rights are conferred by a decision relating to custody made by a court in the State or by an authority within the meaning of the Luxembourg Convention in another Contracting State may make an application, in such form as may be prescribed, to the Central Authority in the State under Article 4 of the Luxembourg Convention with a view to securing its recognition or enforcement in another Contracting State.

(2) Where the Central Authority in the State receives any such application and is satisfied that the application is an application to which Article 4 of the Luxembourg Convention applies it shall, on behalf of the applicant, take any action required to be taken by a Central Authority under that Convention.

**33    Provision of certain documents by courts in the State for purposes of Luxembourg Convention**

As respects a decision relating to custody made by a court in the State (including a declaration made by a court under section 34 of this Act), the registrar or clerk of the court shall, at the request of a person who wishes to make an application under the Luxembourg Convention in a Contracting State other than the State or at the request on his behalf of the Central Authority in the State and subject to any conditions that may be specified by rules of court, give to the person or the Central Authority, as the case may be, all or any of the documents referred to in Article 13. 1. b, c and d of that Convention, that is to say—

(a)   a copy of the decision duly authenticated;

(b)   a certificate signed by the registrar or clerk of the court stating—

    (i)    the nature of the proceedings,

    (ii)   the date on which the time for the lodging of an appeal against the decision will expire or, if it has expired, the date on which it expired,

    (iii)  whether notice of appeal against, or, in any case where the defendant does not appear, a notice to set aside, the decision has been entered, and

    (iv)   such particulars (if any) as may be specified by rules of court,

and

(c)   in case the decision was given in default of appearance, the original or a copy, certified by the registrar or clerk of the court to be a true copy, of a document establishing that notice of the institution of proceedings was served on the person in default.

**34    Declaration by a court of unlawful removal of child**

(1) Where a court in the State makes a decision relating to the custody of a child who has been removed from the State that court may also, on an application made by any person for the purposes of Article 12 of the Luxembourg Convention, make a declaration that the removal of the child from the State was unlawful if it is satisfied that the applicant has an interest in the matter and that the child has been taken from or sent

or kept out of the State without the consent of any of the persons having the right to determine the child's place of residence under the law of the State.

(2) The Central Authority in the State shall take action or cause action to be taken to assist the person referred to in subsection (1) of this section in making an application under this section if a request for such assistance, in such form as may be prescribed, is made by him or on his behalf by the Central Authority of another Contracting State.

## PART IV
### SUPPLEMENTARY

**35        Termination of existing custody orders**

Where the Court makes—

(a)  an order for the return of a child under Part II of this Act; or

(b)  an order recognising or enforcing a decision relating to the custody of a child (other than a decision relating only to rights of access) under Part III of this Act,

the Court may, on notice to any interested parties, discharge any order regarding the custody of, or the right of access to, the child.

**36        Power of the Court to order disclosure of child's whereabouts**

(1) Where—

(a)  in proceedings for the return of a child under Part II of this Act, or

(b)  on an application for the recognition or enforcement of a decision in respect of a child under Part III of this Act,

there is not available to the Court adequate information as to the whereabouts of the child, the Court may order any person who, it has reason to believe, may have relevant information to disclose it to the Court.

(2) Any person who is the subject of an order under subsection (1) of this section may, notwithstanding production of the child, be ordered to disclose any information that is relevant to proceedings under Part II or III of this Act.

(3) Where—

(a)  in proceedings in a Contracting State other than the State for the return of a child under the Hague Convention, or

(b)  in proceedings for the recognition or enforcement of a decision in a Contracting State other than the State in respect of a child under the Luxembourg Convention,

or where such proceedings are about to be commenced, there is not available to the authorities in the Contracting State adequate information as to the whereabouts of the child, the Court may, on application made to it by any person, if it is satisfied that the applicant has an interest in the matter and that the child has been taken from or sent or kept out of the State without the consent of any of the persons having the right to determine the child's place of residence under the law of the State, order any person who, it has reason to believe, may have relevant information to disclose it to the Court.

(4) Any person who is the subject of an order under subsection (3) of this section may, notwithstanding production of the child in the Contracting State, be ordered to disclose any information that is relevant to proceedings in that state.

(5) A person shall not be excused from complying with any order under this section by reason that to do so may incriminate him or his spouse of an offence; but a statement or admission made in compliance with any such order shall not be admissible in evidence against either of them in proceedings for an offence other than perjury.

**37    Power of Garda Síochána to detain a child and matters consequential upon such detention**

(1) A member of the Garda Síochána shall have power to detain a child who he reasonably suspects is about to be or is being removed from the State in breach of any of the following orders of a court in the State—

(a) an order regarding the custody of, or right of access to, the child (whether or not such an order contains an order prohibiting the removal of the child from the jurisdiction without leave of the court) or any order relating to the child made by the court in the exercise of its jurisdiction relating to wardship of a child;

(b) an order made pursuant to Part II or IV of the Children Act, 1908, in relation to the care of the child;

(c) an order made under section 12 of this Act or an order made for return of the child under Part II of this Act;

(d) an order made under section 26 of this Act or an order made for recognition or enforcement of a decision relating to custody under Part III of this Act,

or while proceedings for one of those orders are pending or an application for one of those orders is about to be made.

[(2) Where a child is detained under this section a member of the Garda Síochána shall as soon as possible—

(a) return the child to the custody of a person (not being the Health Service Executive) in favour of whom a court has made an order referred to in subsection (1) of this section unless the member has reasonable grounds for believing that such person will act in breach of such order, or

(b) where the child has been in the care of the Health Service Executive, return the child to it, or

(c) in a case other than one to which paragraph (a) or (b) of this subsection applies, or where the member is of the belief referred to in the said paragraph (a), deliver the child into the care of the Health Service Executive.][1]

(3) Where a member of the Garda Síochána delivers into the care of [the Health Service Executive][1] a child in accordance with subsection (2)(c) of this section, he shall as soon as possible inform or cause to be informed—

(a) a parent of the child, or

(b) a person acting in loco parentis, or

(c) the Central Authority referred to in section 8 (in a case to which subsection (1)(c) of this section applies) or section 22 (in a case to which subsection (1)(d) of this section applies) of this Act, of such delivery.

(4) Where any child is delivered into the care of [the Health Service Executive][1] in accordance with subsection (2)(c) of this section [the Health Service Executive][1] shall arrange suitable care and accommodation for the child, which may include placing the child in foster care or residential care, pending the determination of an application under subsection (5) of this section by [the Health Service Executive][1].

(5) Where a child is delivered into the care of [the Health Service Executive][1] under subsection (2)(c) of this section [the Health Service Executive][1] shall apply at the next sitting of the District Court or, in the event that the next sitting is not due to be held within three days of the date on which the child is delivered into the care of [the Health Service Executive][1], at a specially arranged sitting of the District Court held within the said three days, for directions as to the child's release from such care or otherwise in relation to the child's care and the District Court may make such order as it thinks proper in the circumstances regarding custody of and, where appropriate, access to, the child, taking into account any order referred to in subsection (1) of this section relating to the child and without prejudice to proceedings that may be pending or any application that is about to be made for one of those orders in relation to the child.

(6) Any order containing a direction under subsection (5) of this section shall be of the same force and effect as if it were an order made by the District Court under section 11 of the Guardianship of Infants Act, 1964.

(7) The jurisdiction of the District Court in respect of proceedings under subsection (5) of this section may be exercised by the justice of the District Court for the time being assigned to the district court district where the child resides or was at a material time residing and where a justice for the district in which the proceedings are brought is not immediately available, an order may be made by any justice of the District Court.

---

**Notes**

1   Subsection (2) inserted and the words "the Health Service Executive" substituted, wherever occurring, by s 75 and Schedule 6 of the Health Act 2004.

---

PART V

MISCELLANEOUS

**38      Rules of court**

(1) Proceedings under Part II or III of this Act shall be commenced in a summary manner.

(2) Rules of court may make provision for the expeditious hearing of an application under Part II or III of this Act.

### 39 Amendment of Judicial Separation and Family Law Reform Act, 1989

(1) In this section "the Act of 1989" means the Judicial Separation and Family Law Reform Act, 1989.

(2) The proceedings to which subsections (3) and (4) of section 33 (conduct of family proceedings in the High Court) of the Act of 1989 apply shall be deemed to include proceedings under this Act.

(3) Section 45 of the Act of 1989 is hereby amended by the substitution of the following for "and the Status of Children Act, 1987" in subsection (1):

> "the Status of Children Act, 1987, and the Child Abduction and Enforcement of Custody Orders Act, 1991,".

### 40 Costs

(1) The costs of any proceedings under any provision of this Act shall be in the discretion of the court concerned.

(2) Without prejudice to the generality of subsection (1) of this section, a court in making an order for costs in any proceedings under this Act—

  (a) may direct the person who removed or retained a child, or who prevented the exercise of rights of access in relation to a child, to pay any necessary expenses incurred by or on behalf of the applicant in the proceedings, including travel expenses, any costs incurred or payments made for locating the child, the costs of legal representation of the applicant and those of returning the child;

  (b) shall otherwise have regard to the provisions of Article 26 of the Hague Convention (where proceedings under Part II of this Act are concerned) or Article 5.3 of the Luxembourg Convention (where proceedings under Part III of this Act are concerned).

### 41 Regulations

(1) The Minister may make regulations for the purpose of giving effect to this Act.

(2) Without prejudice to the generality of subsection (1) of this section, regulations under this section may prescribe forms to be used in connection with any of the provisions of this Act.

### 42 Laying of orders and regulations before Houses of Oireachtas

Every order or regulation made by the Minister under this Act (other than an order made under section 1 (3) of this Act) shall be laid before each House of the Oireachtas as soon as may be after it is made and, if a resolution annulling the order or regulation is passed by either such House within the next subsequent twenty-one days on which that House has sat after the order or regulation is laid before it, the order or regulation shall be annulled accordingly, but without prejudice to the validity of anything previously done thereunder.

## 43      Expenses

The expenses incurred in the administration of this Act by the Minister or a Central Authority appointed under section 8 or 22 of this Act shall, to such extent as may be sanctioned by the Minister for Finance, be paid out of moneys provided by the Oireachtas.

### FIRST SCHEDULE
TEXT OF THE CONVENTION ON THE CIVIL ASPECTS OF INTERNATIONAL CHILD ABDUCTION

The States signatory to the present Convention

Firmly convinced that the interests of children are of paramount importance in matters relating to their custody,

Desiring to protect children internationally from the harmful effects of their wrongful removal or retention and to establish procedures to ensure their prompt return to the State of their habitual residence, as well as to secure protection for rights of access,

Have resolved to conclude a Convention to this effect, and have agreed upon the following provisions—

*Chapter I*
*Scope of the Convention*

*Article 1*

The objects of the present Convention are:

(a)  to secure the prompt return of children wrongfully removed to or retained in any Contracting State; and

(b)  to ensure that rights of custody and of access under the law of one Contracting State are effectively respected in the other Contracting States.

*Article 2*

Contracting States shall take all appropriate measures to secure within their territories the implementation of the objects of the Convention. For this purpose they shall use the most expeditious procedures available.

*Article 3*

The removal or the retention of a child is to be considered wrongful where:

(a)  it is in breach of rights of custody attributed to a person, an institution or any other body, either jointly or alone, under the law of the State in which the child was habitually resident immediately before the removal or retention; and

(b)  at the time of removal or retention those rights were actually exercised, either jointly or alone, or would have been so exercised but for the removal or retention.

The rights of custody mentioned in sub-paragraph (a) above, may arise in particular by operation of law or by reason of a judicial or administrative decision, or by reason of an agreement having legal effect under the law of that State.

### Article 4

The Convention shall apply to any child who was habitually resident in a Contracting State immediately before any breach of custody or access rights. The Convention shall cease to apply when the child attains the age of 16 years.

### Article 5

For the purposes of this Convention:

(a) 'rights of custody' shall include rights relating to the care of the person of the child and, in particular, the right to determine the child's place of residence;

(b) 'rights of access' shall include the right to take a child for a limited period of time to a place other than the child's habitual residence.

### CHAPTER II
### Central Authorities

### Article 6

A Contracting State shall designate a Central Authority to discharge the duties which are imposed by the Convention upon such authorities.

Federal States, States with more than one system of law or States having autonomous territorial organizations shall be free to appoint more than one Central Authority and to specify the territorial extent of their powers. Where a State has appointed more than one Central Authority, it shall designate the Central Authority to which applications may be addressed for transmission to the appropriate Central Authority within that State.

### Article 7

Central Authorities shall co-operate with each other and promote co-operation amongst the competent authorities in their respective State to secure the prompt return of children and to achieve the other objects of this Convention.

In particular, either directly or through any intermediary, they shall take all appropriate measures—

(a) to discover the whereabouts of a child who has been wrongfully removed or retained;

(b) to prevent further harm to the child or prejudice to interested parties by taking or causing to be taken provisional measures;

(c) to secure the voluntary return of the child or to bring about an amicable resolution of the issues;

(d) to exchange, where desirable, information relating to the social background of the child;

(e)  to provide information of a general character as to the law of their State in connection with the application of the Convention;

(f)  to initiate or facilitate the institution of judicial or administrative proceedings with a view to obtaining the return of the child and, in a proper case, to make arrangements for organizing or securing the effective exercise of rights of access;

(g)  where the circumstances so require, to provide or facilitate the provision of legal aid and advice, including the participation of legal counsel and advisers;

(h)  to provide such administrative arrangements as may be necessary and appropriate to secure the safe return of the child;

(i)  to keep each other informed with respect to the operation of this Convention and, as far as possible, to eliminate any obstacles to its application.

*Chapter III*
*Return of Children*

*Article 8*

Any person, institution or other body claiming that a child has been removed or retained in breach of custody rights may apply either to the Central Authority of the child's habitual residence or to the Central Authority of any other Contracting State for assistance in securing the return of the child.

The application shall contain—

(a)  information concerning the identity of the applicant, of the child and of the person alleged to have removed or retained the child;

(b)  where available, the date of birth of the child;

(c)  the grounds on which the applicant's claim for return of the child is based;

(d)  all available information relating to the whereabouts of the child and the identity of the person with whom the child is presumed to be.

The application may be accompanied or supplemented by—

(e)  an authenticated copy of any relevant decision or agreement;

(f)  a certificate or an affidavit emanating from a Central Authority, or other competent authority of the State of the child's habitual residence, or from a qualified person, concerning the relevant law of that State;

(g)  any other relevant document.

*Article 9*

If the Central Authority which receives an application referred to in Article 8 has reason to believe that the child is in another Contracting State, it shall directly and without delay transmit the application to the Central Authority of that Contracting State and inform the requesting Central Authority, or the applicant, as the case may be.

*Article 10*

The Central Authority of the State where the child is shall take or cause to be taken all appropriate measures in order to obtain the voluntary return of the child.

*Article 11*

The judicial or administrative authorities of Contracting States shall act expeditiously in proceedings for the return of children.

If the judicial or administrative authority concerned has not reached a decision within six weeks from the date of commencement of the proceedings, the applicant or the Central Authority of the requested State, on its own initiative or if asked by the Central Authority of the requesting State, shall have the right to request a statement of the reasons for the delay. If a reply is received by the Central Authority of the requested State, that Authority shall transmit the reply to the Central Authority of the requesting State, or to the applicant, as the case may be.

*Article 12*

Where a child has been wrongfully removed or retained in terms of Article 3 and, at the date of the commencement of the proceedings before the judicial or administrative authority of the Contracting State where the child is, a period of less than one year has elapsed from the date of the wrongful removal or retention, the authority concerned shall order the return of the child forthwith.

The judicial or administrative authority, even where the proceedings have been commenced after the expiration of the period of one year referred to in the preceding paragraph, shall also order the return of the child, unless it is demonstrated that the child is now settled in its new environment.

Where the judicial or administrative authority in the requested State has reason to believe that the child has been taken to another State, it may stay the proceedings or dismiss the application for the return of the child.

*Article 13*

Notwithstanding the provisions of the preceding Article, the judicial or administrative authority of the requested State is not bound to order the return of the child if the person, institution or other body which opposes its return establishes that—

    (a)  the person, institution or other body having the care of the person of the child was not actually exercising the custody rights at the time of removal or retention, or had consented to or subsequently acquiesced in the removal or retention; or

    (b)  there is a grave risk that his or her return would expose the child to physical or psychological harm or otherwise place the child in an intolerable situation.

The judicial or administrative authority may also refuse to order the return of the child if it finds that the child objects to being returned and has attained an age and degree of maturity at which it is appropriate to take account of its views.

In considering the circumstances referred to in this Article, the judicial and administrative authorities shall take into account the information relating to the social background of the child provided by the Central Authority or other competent authority of the child's habitual residence.

### Article 14

In ascertaining whether there has been a wrongful removal or retention within the meaning of Article 3, the judicial or administrative authorities of the requested State may take notice directly of the law of, and of judicial or administrative decisions, formally recognized or not in the State of the habitual residence of the child, without recourse to the specific procedures for the proof of that law or for the recognition of foreign decisions which would otherwise be applicable.

### Article 15

The judicial or administrative authorities of a Contracting State may, prior to the making of an order for the return of the child, request that the applicant obtain from the authorities of the State of the habitual residence of the child a decision or other determination that the removal or retention was wrongful within the meaning of Article 3 of the Convention, where such a decision or determination may be obtained in that State. The Central Authorities of the Contracting States shall so far as practicable assist applicants to obtain such a decision or determination.

### Article 16

After receiving notice of a wrongful removal or retention of a child in the sense of Article 3, the judicial or administrative authorities of a Contracting State to which the child has been removed or in which it has been retained shall not decide on the merits of rights of custody until it has been determined that the child is not to be returned under this Convention or unless an application under this Convention is not lodged within a reasonable time following receipt of the notice.

### Article 17

The sole fact that a decision relating to custody has been given in or is entitled to recognition in the requested State shall not be a ground for refusing to return a child under this Convention, but the judicial or administrative authorities of the requested State may take account of the reasons for that decision in applying this Convention.

### Article 18

The provisions of this Chapter do not limit the power of a judicial or administrative authority to order the return of the child at any time.

### Article 19

A decision under this Convention concerning the return of the child shall not be taken to be a determination on the merits of any custody issue.

*Article 20*

The return of the child under the provisions of Article 12 may be refused if this would not be permitted by the fundamental principles of the requested State relating to the protection of human rights and fundamental freedoms.

CHAPTER IV
*Right of Access*

*Article 21*

An application to make arrangements for organizing or securing the effective exercise of rights of access may be presented to the Central Authorities of the Contracting States in the same way as an application for the return of a child.

The Central Authorities are bound by the obligations of co-operation which are set forth in Article 7 to promote the peaceful enjoyment of access rights and the fulfilment of any conditions to which the exercise of those rights may be subject. The Central Authorities shall take steps to remove, as far as possible, all obstacles to the exercise of such rights.

The Central Authorities, either directly or through intermediaries, may initiate or assist in the institution of proceedings with a view to organising or protecting these rights and securing respect for the conditions to which the exercise of these rights may be subject.

CHAPTER V
*General Provisions*

*Article 22*

No security, bond or deposit, however described, shall be required to guarantee the payment of costs and expenses in the judicial or administrative proceedings falling within the scope of this Convention.

*Article 23*

No legalization or similar formality may be required in the context of this Convention.

*Article 24*

Any application, communication or other document sent to the Central Authority of the requested State shall be in the original language, and shall be accompanied by a translation into the official language or one of the official languages of the requested State or, where that is not feasible, a translation into French or English.

However, a Contracting State may, by making a reservation in accordance with Article 42, object to the use of either French or English, but not both, in any application, communication or other document sent to its Central Authority.

*Article 25*

Nationals of the Contracting States and persons who are habitually resident within those States shall be entitled in matters concerned with the application of this Convention to legal aid and advice in any other Contracting State on the same conditions as if they themselves were nationals of and habitually resident in that State.

### Article 26

Each Central Authority shall bear its own costs in applying this Convention.

Central Authorities and other public services of Contracting States shall not impose any charges in relation to applications submitted under this Convention. In particular, they may not require any payment from the applicant towards the costs and expenses of the proceedings or, where applicable, those arising from the participation of legal counsel or advisers. However, they may require the payment of the expenses incurred or to be incurred in implementing the return of the child.

However, a Contracting State may, by making a reservation in accordance with Article 42, declare that it shall not be bound to assume any costs referred to in the preceding paragraph resulting from the participation of legal counsel or advisers or from court proceedings, except in so far as those costs may be covered by its system of legal aid and advice.

Upon ordering the return of a child or issuing an order concerning rights of access under this Convention, the judicial or administrative authorities may, where appropriate, direct the person who removed or retained the child, or who prevented the exercise of rights of access, to pay necessary expenses incurred by or on behalf of the applicant, including travel expenses, any costs incurred or payments made for locating the child, the costs of legal representation of the applicant, and those of returning the child.

### Article 27

When it is manifest that the requirements of this Convention are not fulfilled or that the application is otherwise not well founded, a Central Authority is not bound to accept the application. In that case, the Central Authority shall forthwith inform the applicant or the Central Authority through which the application was submitted, as the case may be, of its reasons.

### Article 28

A Central Authority may require that the application be accompanied by a written authorisation empowering it to act on behalf of the applicant, or to designate a representative so to act.

### Article 29

This Convention shall not preclude any person, institution or body who claims that there has been a breach of custody or access rights within the meaning of Article 3 or 21 from applying directly to the judicial or administrative authorities of a Contracting State, whether or not under the provisions of this Convention.

*Article 30*

Any application submitted to the Central Authorities or directly to the judicial or administrative authorities of a Contracting State in accordance with the terms of this Convention, together with documents and any other information appended thereto or provided by a Central Authority, shall be admissible in the courts or administrative authorities of the Contracting States.

*Article 31*

In relation to a State which in matters of custody of children has two or more systems of law applicable in different territorial units—

(a) any reference to habitual residence in that State shall be construed as referring to habitual residence in a territorial unit of that State;

(b) any reference to the law of the State of habitual residence shall be construed as referring to the law of the territorial unit in that State where the child habitually resides.

*Article 32*

In relation to a State which in matters of custody of children has two or more systems of law applicable to different categories of persons, any reference to the law of that State shall be construed as referring to the legal system specified by the law of that State.

*Article 33*

A State within which different territorial units have their own rules of law in respect of custody of children shall not be bound to apply this Convention where a State with a unified system of law would not be bound to do so.

*Article 34*

This Convention shall take priority in matters within its scope over the Convention of 5 October 1961 concerning the powers of authorities and the law applicable in respect of the protection of minors, as between Parties to both Conventions. Otherwise the present Convention shall not restrict the application of an international instrument in force between the State of origin and the State addressed or other law of the State addressed for the purposes of obtaining the return of a child who has been wrongfully removed or retained or of organising access rights.

*Article 35*

This Convention shall apply as between Contracting States only to wrongful removals or retentions occurring after its entry into force in those States.

Where a declaration has been made under Article 39 or 40 the reference in the preceding paragraph to a Contracting State shall be taken to refer to the territorial unit or units in relation to which this Convention applies.

*Article 36*

Nothing in this Convention shall prevent two or more Contracting States, in order to limit the restrictions to which the return of the child may be subject, from agreeing among themselves to derogate from any provisions of this Convention which may imply such a restriction.

*Chapter VI*
*Final Clauses*

*Article 37*

The Convention shall be open for signature by the States which were Members of the Hague Conference on Private International Law at the time of its Fourteenth Session.

It shall be ratified, accepted or approved and the instruments of ratification, acceptance or approval shall be deposited with the Ministry of Foreign Affairs of the Kingdom of the Netherlands.

*Article 38*

Any other State may accede to the Convention.

The instruments of accession shall be deposited with the Ministry of Foreign Affairs of the Kingdom of the Netherlands.

The Convention shall enter into force for a State acceding to it on the first day of the third calendar month after the deposit of its instrument of accession.

The accession will have effect only as regards the relations between the acceding State and such Contracting States as will have declared their acceptance of the accession. Such a declaration will also have to be made by any Member State ratifying, accepting or approving the Convention after an accession. Such declaration shall be deposited at the Ministry of Foreign Affairs of the Kingdom of the Netherlands; this Ministry shall forward, through diplomatic channels, a certified copy to each of the Contracting States.

The Convention will enter into force as between the acceding State and the State that has declared its acceptance of the accession on the first day of the third calendar month after the deposit of the declaration of acceptance.

*Article 39*

Any State may, at the time of signature, ratification, acceptance, approval or accession, declare that the Convention shall extend to all the territories for the international relations of which it is responsible, or to one or more of them. Such a declaration shall take effect at the time the Convention enters into force for that State.

Such declaration, as well as any subsequent extension, shall be notified to the Ministry of Foreign Affairs of the Kingdom of the Netherlands.

*Article 40*

If a Contracting State has two or more territorial units in which different systems of law are applicable in relation to matters dealt with in this Convention, it may at the time of signature, ratification, acceptance, approval or accession declare that this Convention shall extend to all its territorial units or only to one or more of them and may modify this declaration by submitting another declaration at any time. Any such declaration shall be notified to the Ministry of Foreign Affairs of the Kingdom of the Netherlands and shall state expressly the territorial units to which the Convention applies.

### *Article 41*

Where a Contracting State has a system of government under which executive, judicial and legislative powers are distributed between central and other authorities within that State, its signature or ratification, acceptance or approval of, or accession to this Convention, or its making of any declaration in terms of Article 40 shall carry no implication as to the internal distribution of powers within that State.

### *Article 42*

Any State may, not later than the time of ratification, acceptance, approval or accession, or at the time of making a declaration in terms of Article 39 or 40, make one or both of the reservations provided for in Article 24 and Article 26, third paragraph. No other reservation shall be permitted.

Any State may at any time withdraw a reservation it has made. The withdrawal shall be notified to the Ministry of Foreign Affairs of the Kingdom of the Netherlands.

The reservation shall cease to have effect on the first day of the third calendar month after the notification referred to in the preceding paragraph.

### *Article 43*

The Convention shall enter into force on the first day of the third calendar month after the deposit of the third instrument of ratification, acceptance, approval or accession referred to in Articles 37 and 38.

Thereafter the Convention shall enter into force—

(1)  for each State ratifying, accepting, approving or acceding to it subsequently, on the first day of the third calendar month after the deposit of its instrument of ratification, acceptance, approval or accession;

(2)  for any territory or territorial unit to which the Convention has been extended in conformity with Article 39 or 40, on the first day of the third calendar month after the notification referred to in that Article.

### *Article 44*

The Convention shall remain in force for five years from the date of its entry into force in accordance with the first paragraph of Article 43 even for States which subsequently have ratified, accepted, approved it or acceded to it.

If there has been no denunciation, it shall be renewed tacitly every five years.

Any denunciation shall be notified to the Ministry of Foreign Affairs of the Kingdom of the Netherlands at least six months before the expiry of the five year period. It may be limited to certain of the territories or territorial units to which the Convention applies.

The denunciation shall have effect only as regards the State which has notified it. The Convention shall remain in force for the other Contracting States.

*Article 45*

The Ministry of Foreign Affairs of the Kingdom of the Netherlands shall notify the States Members of the Conference, and the States which have acceded in accordance with Article 38, of the following:—

(1) the signatures and ratifications, acceptances and approvals referred to in Article 37;

(2) the accessions referred to in Article 38;

(3) the date on which the Convention enters into force in accordance with Article 43;

(4) the extensions referred to in Article 39;

(5) the declarations referred to in Articles 38 and 40;

(6) the reservations referred to in Article 24 and Article 26, third paragraph, and the withdrawals referred to in Article 42;

(7) the denunciations referred to in Article 44.

In Witness Whereof the undersigned, being duly authorised thereto, have signed this Convention.

Done at The Hague, on the 25th day of October, 1980, in the English and French languages, both texts being equally authentic, in a single copy which shall be deposited in the archives of the Government of the Kingdom of the Netherlands, and of which a certified copy shall be sent, through diplomatic channels, to each of the States Members of the Hague Conference on Private International Law at the date of its Fourteenth Session and to each other State having participated in the preparation of this Convention at this Session.

(Here follow signatures on behalf of certain States.)

## SECOND SCHEDULE
EUROPEAN CONVENTION ON RECOGNITION AND ENFORCEMENT OF DECISIONS
CONCERNING CUSTODY OF CHILDREN AND ON RESTORATION OR CUSTODY OF
CHILDREN

Section 21

The member States of the Council of Europe, signatory hereto,

Recognising that in the member States of the Council of Europe the welfare of the child is of overriding importance in reaching decisions concerning his custody;

Considering that the making of arrangements to ensure that decisions concerning the custody of a child can be more widely recognised and enforced will provide greater protection of the welfare of children;

Considering it desirable, with this end in view, to emphasise that the right of access of parents is a normal corollary to the right of custody;

Noting the increasing number of cases where children have been improperly removed across an international frontier and the difficulties of securing adequate solutions to the problems caused by such cases;

Desirous of making suitable provision to enable the custody of children which has been arbitrarily interrupted to be restored;

Convinced of the desirability of making arrangements for this purpose answering to different needs and different circumstances;

Desiring to establish legal co-operation between their authorities,

Have agreed as follows:

*Article 1*

For the purposes of this Convention:

   a.  child means a person of any nationality, so long as he is under 16 years of age and has not the right to decide on his own place of residence under the law of his habitual residence, the law of his nationality or the internal law of the State addressed;

   b.  authority means a judicial or administrative authority;

   c.  decision relating to custody means a decision of an authority in so far as it relates to the care of the person of the child, including the right to decide on the place of his residence, or to the right of access to him;

   d.  improper removal means the removal of a child across an international frontier in breach of a decision relating to his custody which has been given in a Contracting State and which is enforceable in such a State; improper removal also includes:

      i.  the failure to return a child across an international frontier at the end of a period of the exercise of the right of access to this child or at the end of any other temporary stay in a territory other than that where the custody is exercised;

     ii.  a removal which is subsequently declared unlawful within the meaning of Article 12.

## PART I
### CENTRAL AUTHORITIES

*Article 2*

1. Each Contracting State shall appoint a central authority to carry out the functions provided for by this Convention.

2. Federal States and States with more than one legal system shall be free to appoint more than one central authority and shall determine the extent of their competence.

3. The Secretary General of the Council of Europe shall be notified of any appointment under this Article.

*Article 3*

1. The central authorities of the Contracting States shall co-operate with each other and promote co-operation between the competent authorities in their respective countries. They shall act with all necessary despatch.

2. With a view to facilitating the operation of this Convention, the central authorities of the Contracting States:

    a.  shall secure the transmission of requests for information coming from competent authorities and relating to legal or factual matters concerning pending proceedings;

    b.  shall provide each other on request with information about their law relating to the custody of children and any changes in that law;

    c.  shall keep each other informed of any difficulties likely to arise in applying the Convention and, as far as possible, eliminate obstacles to its application.

*Article 4*

1. Any person who has obtained in a Contracting State a decision relating to the custody of a child and who wishes to have that decision recognised or enforced in another Contracting State may submit an application for this purpose to the central authority in any Contracting State.

2. The application shall be accompanied by the documents mentioned in Article 13.

3. The central authority receiving the application, if it is not the central authority in the State addressed, shall send the documents directly and without delay to that central authority.

4. The central authority receiving the application may refuse to intervene where it is manifestly clear that the conditions laid down by this Convention are not satisfied.

5. The central authority receiving the application shall keep the applicant informed without delay of the progress of his application.

*Article 5*

1. The central authority in the State addressed shall take or cause to be taken without delay all steps which it considers to be appropriate, if necessary by instituting proceedings before its competent authorities, in order:

 a. to discover the whereabouts of the child;

 b. to avoid, in particular by any necessary provisional measures, prejudice to the interests of the child or of the applicant;

 c. to secure the recognition or enforcement of the decision;

 d. to secure the delivery of the child to the applicant where enforcement is granted;

 e. to inform the requesting authority of the measures taken and their results.

2. Where the central authority in the State addressed has reason to believe that the child is in the territory of another Contracting State it shall send the documents directly and without delay to the central authority of that State.

3. With the exception of the cost of repatriation, each Contracting State undertakes not to claim any payment from an applicant in respect of any measures taken under paragraph 1 of this Article by the central authority of that State on the applicant's behalf, including the costs of proceedings and, where applicable the costs incurred by the assistance of a lawyer.

4. If recognition or enforcement is refused, and if the central authority of the State addressed considers that it should comply with a request by the applicant to bring in that State proceedings concerning the substance of the case, that authority shall use its best endeavours to secure the representation of the applicant in the proceedings under conditions no less favourable than those available to a person who is resident in and a national of that State and for this purpose it may, in particular, institute proceedings before its competent authorities.

*Article 6*

1. Subject to any special agreements made between the central authorities concerned and to the provisions of paragraph 3 of this Article:

 a. communications to the central authority of the State addressed shall be made in the official language or in one of the official languages of that State or be accompanied by a translation into that language;

 b. the central authority of the State addressed shall nevertheless accept communications made in English or in French or accompanied by a translation into one of these languages.

2. Communications coming from the central authority of the State addressed, including the results of enquiries carried out, may be made in the official language or one of the official languages of that State or in English or French.

3. A Contracting State may exclude wholly or partly the provisions of paragraph 1 (b) of this Article. When a Contracting State has made this reservation any other Contracting State may also apply the reservation in respect of that State.

## PART II
### RECOGNITION AND ENFORCEMENT OF DECISIONS AND RESTORATION OF CUSTODY OF CHILDREN

*Article 7*

A decision relating to custody given in a Contracting State shall be recognised and, where it is enforceable in the State of origin, made enforceable in every other Contracting State.

*Article 8*

1. In the case of an improper removal, the central authority of the State addressed shall cause steps to be taken forthwith to restore the custody of the child where:

   a. at the time of the institution of the proceedings in the State where the decision was given or at the time of the improper removal, if earlier, the child and his parents had as their sole nationality the nationality of that State and the child had his habitual residence in the territory of that State, and

   b. a request for the restoration was made to a central authority within a period of six months from the date of the improper removal.

2. If, in accordance with the law of the State addressed, the requirements of paragraph 1 of this Article cannot be complied with without recourse to a judicial authority, none of the grounds of refusal specified in this Convention shall apply to the judicial proceedings.

3. Where there is an agreement officially confirmed by a competent authority between the person having the custody of the child and another person to allow the other person a right of access, and the child, having been taken abroad, has not been restored at the end of the agreed period to the person having the custody, custody of the child shall be restored in accordance with paragraphs 1 b and 2 of this Article. The same shall apply in the case of a decision of the competent authority granting such a right to a person who has not the custody of the child.

*Article 9*

1. In cases of improper removal, other than those dealt with in Article 8, in which an application has been made to a central authority within a period of six months from the date of the removal, recognition and enforcement may be refused only if:

   a. in the case of a decision given in the absence of the defendant or his legal representative, the defendant was not duly served with the document which instituted the proceedings or an equivalent document in sufficient time to enable him to arrange his defence; but such a failure to effect service cannot constitute a ground for refusing recognition or enforcement where service was not effected because the defendant had concealed his whereabouts from the person who instituted the proceedings in the State of origin:

b.  in the case of a decision given in the absence of the defendant or his legal representative, the competence of the authority giving the decision was not founded:

 i.  on the habitual residence of the defendant, or

 ii.  on the last common habitual residence of the child's parents, at least one parent being still habitually resident there, or

 iii.  on the habitual residence of the child;

c.  the decision is incompatible with a decision relating to custody which became enforceable in the State addressed before the removal of the child, unless the child has had his habitual residence in the territory of the requesting State for one year before his removal.

2. Where no application has been made to a central authority, the provisions of paragraph 1 of this Article shall apply equally, if recognition and enforcement are requested within six months from the date of the improper removal.

3. In no circumstances may the foreign decision be reviewed as to its substance.

## Article 10

1. In cases other than those covered by Articles 8 and 9, recognition and enforcement may be refused not only on the grounds provided for in Article 9 but also on any of the following grounds:

a.  if it is found that. the effects of the decision are manifestly incompatible with the fundamental principles of the law relating to the family and children in the State addressed;

b.  if it is found that by reason of a change in the circumstances including the passage of time not including a mere change in the residence of the child after an improper removal, the effects of the original decision are manifestly no longer in accordance with the welfare of the child;

c.  if at the time when the proceedings were instituted in the State of origin:

 i.  the child was a national of the State addressed or was habitually resident there and no such connection existed with the State of origin:

 ii.  the child was a national both of the State of origin and of the State addressed and was habitually resident in the State addressed:

d.  if the decision is incompatible with a decision given in the State addressed or enforceable in that State, after being given in a third State, pursuant to proceedings begun before the submission of the request for recognition or enforcement, and if the refusal is in accordance with the welfare of the child.

2. In the same cases, proceedings for recognition or enforcement may be adjourned on any of the following grounds:

a.  if an ordinary form of review of the original decision has been commenced;

b.  if proceedings relating to the custody of the child, commenced before the proceedings in the State of origin were instituted, are pending in the State addressed;

c.  if another decision concerning the custody of the child is the subject of proceedings for enforcement or of any other proceedings concerning the recognition of the decision.

### *Article 11*

1. Decisions on rights of access and provisions of decisions relating to custody which deal with the right of access shall be recognised and enforced subject to the same conditions as other decisions relating to custody.

2. However, the competent authority of the State addressed may fix the conditions for the implementation and exercise of the right of access taking into account, in particular, undertakings given by the parties on this matter.

3. Where no decision on the right of access has been taken or where recognition or enforcement of the decision relating to custody is refused, the central authority of the State addressed may apply to its competent authorities for a decision on the right of access, if the person claiming a right of access so requests.

### *Article 12*

Where, at the time of the removal of a child across an international frontier, there is no enforceable decision given in a Contracting State relating to his custody, the provisions of this Convention shall apply to any subsequent decision, relating to the custody of that child and declaring the removal to be unlawful, given in a Contracting State at the request of any interested person.

## PART III
## PROCEDURE

### *Article 13*

1. A request for recognition or enforcement in another Contracting State of a decision relating to custody shall be accompanied by:

a.  a document authorising the central authority of the State addressed to act on behalf of the applicant or to designate another representative for that purpose;

b.  a copy of the decision which satisfies the necessary conditions of authenticity;

c.  in the case of a decision given in the absence of the defendant or his legal representative, a document which establishes that the defendant was duly served with the document which instituted the proceedings or an equivalent document;

d.  if applicable, any document which establishes that, in accordance with the law of the State of origin, the decision is enforceable;

e.  if possible, a statement indicating the whereabouts or likely whereabouts of the child in the State addressed; proposals as to how the custody of the child should be restored.

2. The documents mentioned above shall, where necessary, be accompanied by a translation according to the provisions laid down in Article 6.

### *Article 14*

Each Contracting State shall apply a simple and expeditious procedure for recognition and enforcement of decisions relating to the custody of a child. To that end it shall ensure that a request for enforcement may be lodged by simple application.

### *Article 15*

1. Before reaching a decision under paragraph 1 b of Article 10, the authority concerned in the State addressed:

a.  shall ascertain the child's views unless this is impracticable having regard in particular to his age and understanding; and

b.  may request that any appropriate enquiries be carried out.

2. The cost of enquiries in any Contracting State shall be met by the authorities of the State where they are carried out.

Requests for enquiries and the results of enquiries may be sent to the authority concerned through the central authorities.

### *Article 16*

For the purposes of this Convention, no legalisation or any like formality may be required.

## PART IV
## RESERVATIONS

### *Article 17*

1. A Contracting State may make a reservation that, in cases covered by Articles 8 and 9 or either of these Articles, recognition and enforcement of decisions relating to custody may be refused on such of the grounds provided under Article 10 as may be specified in the reservation.

2. Recognition and enforcement of decisions given in a Contracting State which has made the reservation provided for in paragraph 1 of this Article may be refused in any other Contracting State on any of the additional grounds referred to in that reservation.

*Article 18*

A Contracting State may make a reservation that it shall not be bound by the provisions of Article 12. The provisions of this Convention shall not apply to decisions referred to in Article 12 which have been given in a Contracting State which has made such a reservation.

## PART V
### OTHER INSTRUMENTS

*Article 19*

This Convention shall not exclude the possibility of relying on any other international instrument in force between the State of origin and the State addressed or on any other law of the State addressed not derived from an international agreement for the purpose of obtaining recognition or enforcement of a decision.

*Article 20*

1. This Convention shall not affect any obligations which a Contracting State may have towards a non-contracting State under an international instrument dealing with matters governed by this Convention.

2. When two or more Contracting States have enacted uniform laws in relation to custody of children or created a special system of recognition or enforcement of decisions in this field, or if they should do so in the future, they shall be free to apply, between themselves, those laws or that system in place of this Convention or any part of it. In order to avail themselves of this provision the States shall notify their decision to the Secretary General of the Council of Europe. Any alteration or revocation of this decision must also be notified.

## PART VI
### FINAL CLAUSES

*Article 21*

This Convention shall be open for signature by the member States of the Council of Europe. It is subject to ratification, acceptance or approval. Instruments of ratification, acceptance or approval shall be deposited with the Secretary General of the Council of Europe.

*Article 22*

1. This Convention shall enter into force on the first day of the month following the expiration of a period of three months after the date on which three member States of the Council of Europe have expressed their consent to be bound by the Convention in accordance with the provisions of Article 21.

2. In respect of any member State which subsequently expresses its consent to be bound by it, the Convention shall enter into force on the first day of the month following the expiration of a period of three months after the date of the deposit of the instrument of ratification, acceptance or approval.

### Article 23

1. After the entry into force of this Convention, the Committee of Ministers of the Council of Europe may invite any State not a member of the Council to accede to this Convention, by a decision taken by the majority provided for by Article 20.d of the Statute and by the unanimous vote of the representatives of the Contracting States entitled to sit on the Committee.

2. In respect of any acceding State, the Convention shall enter into force on the first day of the month following the expiration of a period of three months after the date of deposit of the instrument of accession with the Secretary General of the Council of Europe.

### Article 24

1. Any State may at the time of signature or when depositing its instrument of ratification, acceptance, approval or accession, specify the territory or territories to which this Convention shall apply.

2. Any State may at any later date, by a declaration addressed to the Secretary General of the Council of Europe, extend the application of this Convention to any other territory specified in the declaration. In respect of such territory, the Convention shall enter into force on the first day of the month following the expiration of a period of three months after the date of receipt by the Secretary General of such declaration.

3. Any declaration made under the two preceding paragraphs may, in respect of any territory specified in such declaration, be withdrawn by a notification addressed to the Secretary General. The withdrawal shall become effective on the first day of the month following the expiration of a period of six months after the date of receipt of such notification by the Secretary General.

### Article 25

1. A State which has two or more territorial units in which different systems of law apply in matters of custody of children and of recognition and enforcement of decisions relating to custody may, at the time of signature or when depositing its instrument of ratification, acceptance, approval or accession, declare that this Convention shall apply to all its territorial units or to one or more of them.

2. Such a State may at any later date, by a declaration addressed to the Secretary General of the Council of Europe, extend the application of this Convention to any other territorial unit specified in the declaration. In respect of such territorial unit the Convention shall enter into force on the first day of the month following the expiration of a period of three months after the date of receipt by the Secretary General of such declaration.

3. Any declaration made under the two preceding paragraphs may, in respect of any territorial unit specified in such declaration, be withdrawn by notification addressed to the Secretary General. The withdrawal shall become effective on the first day of the month following the expiration of a period of six months after the date of receipt of such notification by the Secretary General.

## Article 26

1. In relation to a State which has in matters of custody two or more systems of law of territorial application:

   a. reference to the law of a person's habitual residence or to the law of a person's nationality shall be construed as referring to the system of law determined by the rules in force in that State or, if there are no such rules, the system of law with which the person concerned is most closely connected;

   b. reference to the State of origin or to the State addressed shall be construed as referring, as the case may be, to the territorial unit where the decision was given or to the territorial unit where recognition or enforcement of the decision or restoration of custody is requested.

2. Paragraph 1.a of this Article also applies mutatis mutandis to States which have in matters of custody two or more systems of law of personal application.

## Article 27

1. Any State may, at the time of signature or when depositing its instrument of ratification, acceptance, approval or accession, declare that it avails itself of one or more of the reservations provided for in paragraph 3 of Article 6, Article 17 and Article 18 of this Convention. No other reservation may be made.

2. Any Contracting State which has made a reservation under the preceding paragraph may wholly or partly withdraw it by means of a notification addressed to the Secretary General of the Council of Europe. The withdrawal shall take effect on the date of receipt of such notification by the Secretary General.

## Article 28

At the end of the third year following the date of the entry into force of this Convention and, on his own initiative, at any time after this date the Secretary General of the Council of Europe shall invite the representatives of the central authorities appointed by the Contracting States to meet in order to study and to facilitate the functioning of the Convention. Any member State of the Council of Europe not being a party to the Convention may be represented by an observer. A report shall be prepared on the work of each of these meetings and forwarded to the Committee of Ministers of the Council of Europe for information.

*Article 29*

1. Any Party may at any time denounce this Convention by means of a notification addressed to the Secretary General of the Council of Europe.

2. Such denunciation shall become effective on the first day of the month following the expiration of a period of six months after the date of receipt of the notification by the Secretary General.

*Article 30*

The Secretary General of the Council of Europe shall notify the member States of the Council and any State which has acceded to this Convention, of:

   a.  any signature;

   b.  the deposit of any instrument of ratification, acceptance, approval or accession;

   c.  any date of entry into force of this Convention in accordance with Articles 22, 23, 24 and 25;

   d.  any other act, notification or communication relating to this Convention.

In witness whereof the undersigned, being duly authorised thereto, have signed this Convention.

Done at Luxembourg, the 20th day of May 1980, in English and French, both texts being equally authentic, in a single copy which shall be deposited in the archives of the Council of Europe. The Secretary General of the Council of Europe shall transmit certified copies to each member State of the Council of Europe and to any State invited to accede to this Convention.

(Here follow signatures on behalf of certain States.)

# Maintenance Act 1994

*Number 28 of 1994*

## PART I
### PRELIMINARY

## PART II
### RECOVERY OF MAINTENANCE (RECIPROCATING JURISDICTIONS)

## PART III
### RECOVERY OF MAINTENANCE
### (DESIGNATED JURISDICTION)

## PART IV
### PROVISIONS COMMON TO RECIPROCATING AND DESIGNATED JURISDICTIONS

## PART V
### MISCELLANEOUS

22.   Enforceability of foreign maintenance orders.

23.   Currency of payments under foreign maintenance orders.

24.   Saving.

25.   Expenses.

## FIRST SCHEDULE
### TEXT OF ROME CONVENTION

## SECOND SCHEDULE
### TEXT OF NEW YORK CONVENTION

### Acts Referred to

| | |
|---|---|
| Central Bank Act, 1989 | 1989, No. 16 |
| Courts Act, 1971 | 1971, No. 36 |
| Enforcement of Court Orders Act, 1940 | 1940, No. 23 |
| Family Law (Maintenance of Spouses and Children) Act, 1976 | 1976, No. 11 |
| Jurisdiction of Courts and Enforcement of Judgments Act, 1993 | 1993, No 9 |
| Jurisdiction of Courts and Enforcement of Judgments (European Communities) Act, 1988 | 1988, No. 3 |
| Maintenance Orders Act, 1974 | 1974, No. 16 |
| Social Welfare (Consolidation) Act, 1993 | 1993, No. 27 |
| Status of Children Act, 1987 | 1987, No. 26 |

*An Act to enable effect to be given to the Convention between the Member States of the European Communities on the simplification of procedures for the recovery of maintenance payments done at Rome on the 6th day of November, 1990, and the Convention On The Recovery Abroad Of Maintenance done at New York on the 20th day of June, 1956, and to provide for other matters related to the recovery of maintenance. [23rd November, 1994]*

*Be it enacted by the Oireachtas as follows:*

## PART I
### PRELIMINARY[1]

**1      Short title**

This Act may be cited as the Maintenance Act, 1994.

**Notes**

1 Commencement: 25 November 1995 (SI 288/1995). See the European Communities (Maintenance) Regulations 2011 (SI 274/2011) at Part 4 of this handbook. This SI provides at section 22 as follows:

(1) The Maintenance Act 1994 shall cease to apply in relation to the State and Member States for the purposes of Chapter VII of the Maintenance Regulation with effect from 18 June 2011.

(2) The Act of 1994 applies to Denmark, except where a request for the recovery of maintenance is received under section 14 of that Act from the Central Authority of Denmark, the Central Authority shall transmit that request to the Master of the High Court for determination under Regulation 9.

## 2 Commencement

This Act shall come into operation on such day or days as the Minister shall fix by order or orders either generally or with reference to any particular purpose or provision and different days may be so fixed for different purposes and different provisions.

## 3 Interpretation

(1) In this Act, unless the context otherwise requires—

**"the Act of 1976"** means the Family Law (Maintenance of Spouses and Children) Act, 1976;

["**the Act of 1998**" means the Jurisdiction of Courts and Enforcement of Judgments Act, 1998;][2]

["**the Act of 1995**" means the Family Law Act, 1995;][1]

["**the Act of 1996**" means the Family Law (Divorce) Act, 1996;][1]

["**the Brussels I Regulation**" means Council Regulation (EC) No 44/2001 of 22 December 2000 on jurisdiction and the recognition and enforcement of judgments in civil and commercial matters;][3]

**"the Central Authority"** has the meaning assigned to it by section 4;

**"court"**, in relation to a jurisdiction other than the State, means any authority competent under the law of that jurisdiction to make an order for the recovery of maintenance;

**"designated jurisdiction"** has the meaning assigned to it by section 13;

**"the Minister"** means the Minister for Equality and Law Reform;

**"the New York Convention"** has the meaning assigned to it by section 13;

**"reciprocating jurisdiction"** has the meaning assigned to it by section 6;

**"the Rome Convention"** has the meaning assigned to it by section 6.

(2) In this Act a reference to a Part or section is to a Part or section of this Act, unless it is indicated that reference to some other enactment is intended.

(3) In this Act a reference to a subsection or paragraph is to the subsection or paragraph of the provision in which the reference occurs, unless it is indicated that reference to some other provision is intended.

(4) In this Act a reference to any enactment includes a reference to that enactment as amended or adapted by any other enactment including this Act.

(5) This Act is without prejudice to the provisions of the Maintenance Orders Act, 1974.

---

**Notes**

1   Subsection (1) was amended by the Family Law Act 1995, s 45(a), and by the Family Law (Divorce) Act 1996, s 53(a).

2   Definition of "Act of 1998" was substituted by the Jurisdiction of Courts and Enforcement of Judgments Act 1998, s 22.

3   The definition of "Brussels I Regulation" was inserted by the European Communities (Civil and Commercial Judgments) Regulations 2002 (SI 52/2002), reg 13(1)(a).

---

**4      Central Authority**

(1) (a)   The Minister may by order appoint a Central Authority ("the Central Authority") to discharge the functions required of it under this Act or required of a central authority under the Rome Convention or of a transmitting agency or receiving agency under the New York Convention.

   (b)   Pending the appointment of a Central Authority the Minister shall discharge its functions, and references in this Act to the Central Authority shall be construed accordingly as references to the Minister.

   (c)   The Minister may by order amend or revoke an order made under this section.

(2) [(a)   (i)   For the purposes of section 8 of the Enforcement of Court Orders Act 1940, the Acts of 1976, 1995, 1996 and 1998, the Brussels I Regulation and this Act the Central Authority shall have authority to act on behalf of a maintenance creditor or of a claimant (as defined in section 13(1)), and references therein to a maintenance creditor or to such a claimant shall be construed as including references to that Authority

           (ii)   In subparagraph (i) "maintenance creditor" means, in the context of the Brussels I Regulation, a maintenance creditor referred to in Article 5(2) of that Regulation.]¹

   (b)   Where the Central Authority so acts, payments of maintenance shall be made directly to the maintenance creditor or claimant unless the Central Authority requests that they be made to a public authority in the jurisdiction where the maintenance creditor or claimant resides.

**Notes**

1 Subsection (2)(a) was substituted by the European Communities (Civil and Commercial) Regulation 2002 (SI 52/2002), reg 13(1)(b).

## PART II
## RECOVERY OF MAINTENANCE (RECIPROCATING JURISDICTIONS)

**5 Construction of Part II**

This Part shall be construed as one with the Jurisdiction of Courts and Enforcement of Judgments Act, 1998 [and the Brussels I Regulation]¹.

**Notes**

1 Section 5 was amended by the Jurisdiction of Courts and Enforcement of Judgments Act 1998, s 22 and by the European Communities (Civil and Commercial Judgments) Regulation 2002 (SI 52/2002), reg 13(1)(c).

**6 Interpretation of Part II**

(1) In this Part—

["**the Brussels Convention**" means—

    (a) the 1968 Convention, and

    (b) the Accession Conventions,

as defined in the Act of 1998, and a reference to an Article of the Brussels Convention shall be construed as including a reference to the corresponding Article of the Lugano Convention;]¹

"**central authority of a reciprocating jurisdiction**" means—

    (a) the central authority of such a jurisdiction which has been designated pursuant to paragraph 1 or, where appropriate, paragraph 2 of Article 2 of the Rome Convention, or

    (b) an authority of such a jurisdiction with functions corresponding to those exercisable by the Central Authority within the State;

["**the Lugano Convention**" has the meaning assigned to it by the Act of 1998;]¹

"**maintenance creditor**" includes any body which, under the law of a reciprocating jurisdiction, is entitled to exercise the rights of redress of, or to represent, the creditor;

["**reciprocating jurisdiction**" means a Contracting State within the meaning of the Act of 1998 or, as appropriate, a member state within the meaning of the Brussels I Regulation;]²

"**the Rome Convention**" means the Convention between the member states of the European Communities on the simplification of procedures for the recovery of maintenance payments done at Rome on the 6th day of November, 1990, the text of which in the English language is set out, for convenience of reference, in the First Schedule to this Act.

(2) (a) The Minister for Foreign Affairs may by order declare that any Contracting State (within the meaning of the [Act of 1998]¹) specified in the order is a reciprocating jurisdiction.

   (b) An order that is in force under this subsection shall be evidence that any state specified in the order is a reciprocating jurisdiction.

   (c) The Minister for Foreign Affairs may by order amend or revoke an order under this subsection.

(3) If a judgment or an instrument or settlement referred to in Article 50 or 51 of the Brussels Convention does not relate solely to maintenance, this Part shall apply only to those parts that relate to maintenance.

(4) A word or expression in this Part which is used in the Rome Convention has the same meaning as it has in that Convention and for this purpose the report by Mr. J. Martin and Mr. C. Ó hUiginn on the Convention, a copy of which has been placed in the Oireachtas Library, may be considered by any court when interpreting such word or expression and shall be given such weight as is appropriate in the circumstances.

---

**Notes**

1   Definitions of "Brussels Convention" and "Lugano Convention" were inserted by the Jurisdiction of Courts and Enforcement of Judgments Act 1998, s 22(4).

2   Definition of "reciprocating jurisdiction" substituted by the European Communities (Civil and Commercial Judgments) Regulation 2002 (SI 52/2002), reg 13(1)(d).

---

**7    Application from reciprocating jurisdiction**

(1) The Central Authority may, on receipt of an application for the recognition or enforcement in the State of a maintenance order which has been transmitted by a central authority of a reciprocating jurisdiction, send the application to the Master of the High Court for determination in accordance with section [7 of the Act of 1998 or with the Brussels I Regulation.]¹

(2) [In the case of an application under the Brussels Convention or the Lugano Convention the Master shall consider it]² privately and shall make an enforcement order unless it appears to the Master from the application and accompanying documents or from the Master's own knowledge that its recognition and enforcement are prohibited by the Brussels Convention or the Lugano Convention.

[(2A) In the case of an application under the Brussels I Regulation the Master shall determine it in accordance with Regulation 4 of the European Communities (Civil and Commercial Judgments) Regulations, 2002.][3]

(3) The Master shall cause the decision on the request to be brought to the notice of the Central Authority and, if an enforcement order has been made, shall cause notice thereof to be served on the maintenance debtor.

(4) (a) The notice to be served on a maintenance debtor under subsection (3) shall include a statement of the provisions of Article 36 (right of appeal against enforcement order) of the Brussels Convention [or Article 43 (right of appeal against declaration of enforceability) of the Brussels I Regulation, as appropriate.][2]

    (b) Service of the notice may be effected personally or in any manner in which service of a superior court document within the meaning of section 23 of the Courts Act, 1971, may be effected.

(5) The Master may—

    (a) accept an application under subsection (1) [or (2)][2] as having been transmitted by the central authority of the reciprocating jurisdiction concerned, and

    (b) accept the documents accompanying the application, namely—

        (i) a request that the application be processed in accordance with the provisions of the Rome Convention,

        (ii) a letter delegating to the Central Authority authority to act, or cause action to be taken, on behalf of the maintenance creditor, including specific authority to enable enforcement proceedings to be taken,

        (iii) a document containing the name, date of birth, nationality and description of the maintenance debtor and all other relevant information regarding the identity, whereabouts or location of the assets, of the maintenance debtor,

        (iv) a document required under Article 46 or 47 of the Brussels Convention [or Article 53, 54 or 57 of the Brussels I Regulation, as appropriate,][2] to be produced by a party seeking recognition or applying for enforcement of a judgment, and

        (v) any translation of such a document,

    as being such request, letter, document or translation, as the case may be.

(6) If any of the documents mentioned in subsection (5)(b) are not produced, the Master may allow time for their production, accept equivalent documents or, if the Master considers that there is sufficient information available, dispense with their production.

(7) [...][4]

**Notes**

1   Section 7(1) was amended by the Jurisdiction of Courts and Enforcement of Judgments Act 1998, s 22(5) and the European Communities (Civil and Commercial Judgments) Regulation 2002 (SI 52/2002), reg 13(1)(e).

2   Sections 7(2), 7(4), 7(5) were amended by the European Communities (Civil and Commercial Judgments) Regulation 2002 (SI 52/2002), reg 13(1)(e).

3   Section 7(2A) was inserted by the European Communities (Civil and Commercial Judgments) Regulations 2002, (SI 52/2002), reg 13(1)(e).

4   Section 7(7) was repealed by Jurisdiction of Courts and Enforcement of Judgments Act 1998, s 23.

**8       Evidence proceedings**

Subject to section 21(4), in any proceedings under this Part, unless the court sees good reason to the contrary—

(a)   a document purporting to be an application for the recognition or enforcement in the State of a maintenance order and to have been transmitted by a central authority of a reciprocating jurisdiction may be admitted as evidence that it is such an application and has been so transmitted, and

(b)   a document purporting to be a document accompanying such an application and to be—

(i)    a request that the application be processed in accordance with the provisions of the Rome Convention,

(ii)   a letter delegating to the Central Authority authority to act, or cause action to be taken, on behalf of the maintenance creditor, including specific authority to enable enforcement proceedings to be taken, and

(iii)  a document containing the name, date of birth, nationality and description of the maintenance debtor and all other relevant information regarding the identity, whereabouts, or location of the assets, of the maintenance debtor,

may be admitted as evidence of any matter to which it relates.

**9       Amendment of section 1 of Act of 1988**

[...]¹

**Notes**

1   Repealed by the Jurisdiction of Courts and Enforcement of Judgments Act 1998, s 23.

## 10 Amendment of section 6 of Act of 1988

[...]¹

---

**Notes**

1  Repealed by the Jurisdiction of Courts and Enforcement of Judgments Act 1998, s 23.

---

## 11 Amendment of section 7 of the Act of 1988

[...]¹

---

**Notes**

1  Repealed by the Jurisdiction of Courts and Enforcement of Judgments Act 1998, s 23.

---

## 12 Amendment of section 11 of Act of 1993

[...]¹

---

**Notes**

1  Repealed by the Jurisdiction of Courts and Enforcement of Judgments Act 1998, s 23.

---

PART III

RECOVERY OF MAINTENANCE (DESIGNATED JURISDICTIONS)

## 13 Interpretation of Part III

(1) In this Part, unless the context otherwise requires—

**"central authority of a designated jurisdiction"** means—

(a) a transmitting agency or receiving agency in a state which is a contracting party to the New York Convention, or

(b) an authority of a designated jurisdiction with functions corresponding to those exercisable by the Central Authority within the State;

**"claimant"** means, according to the context, either—

(a) a person residing in a designated jurisdiction (including any body which under the law of that jurisdiction is entitled to exercise the rights of redress of, or to represent, that person) and claiming pursuant to this Part to be entitled to receive maintenance from a person residing in the State, or

(b) a person residing in the State (including a competent authority within the meaning of Part IX (Liability to Maintain Family) of the Social Welfare (Consolidation) Act, 1993) and claiming pursuant to this Part to be entitled to recover maintenance from a person residing in a designated jurisdiction;

**"designated jurisdiction"** means—

(a) any state which is a contracting party to the New York Convention, or

(b) any other state or jurisdiction which is declared by order of the Minister for Foreign Affairs to be a designated jurisdiction for the purposes of this Part;

**"the New York Convention"** means the Convention on the recovery abroad of maintenance done at New York on the 20th day of June, 1956, the text of which in the English language is set out, for convenience of reference, in the Second Schedule to this Act;

**"respondent"** means, according to the context, either—

(a) a person residing in the State from whom maintenance is sought to be recovered pursuant to this Part by a person residing in a designated jurisdiction, or

(b) a person residing in a designated jurisdiction from whom maintenance is sought to be recovered pursuant to this Part by a person residing in the State.

(2) (a) The Minister for Foreign Affairs may by order declare that any state or jurisdiction specified in the order is a designated jurisdiction.

(b) An order that is in force under this subsection shall be evidence that any state or jurisdiction specified in the order is a designated jurisdiction.

(c) The Minister for Foreign Affairs may by order amend or revoke an order under this subsection.

(3) Subject to subsection (1), a word or expression in this Part which is used in the New York Convention has the same meaning as it has in that Convention.

**14    Application for maintenance from designated jurisdiction**

(1) On receipt of a request by the Central Authority from a central authority of a designated jurisdiction on behalf of a claimant for the recovery of maintenance from a person for the time being residing in the State ("the respondent") the Central Authority may—

[(a) if the request is accompanied by an order of a court in a Contracting State (as defined in the Act of 1998*),* transmit the request to the Master of the High Court for determination in accordance with section 7 of the Act of 1998 and Part II of this Act, and the other provisions of the Act of 1998 shall apply accordingly, with any necessary modifications,][1]

[(aa) if the request is accompanied by an order of a court of a member state (as defined in the Brussels I Regulation), transmit the request to the Master of the High Court for determination in accordance with that Regulation.][2]

(b) if the request is accompanied by an order made by any other court and the Central Authority is of opinion that the order may be enforceable in the State, apply to the District Court for the enforcement of the order, or

(c) if either the request is not accompanied by such an order or enforcement of the order is refused—

[(i) if the amount of the maintenance sought to be recovered exceeds the maximum amount which the District Court has jurisdiction to award under the Act of 1976 or the request is for a relief order (within the meaning of the Act of 1995) or a maintenance pending suit order, a periodical payments order, a secured periodical payments order or a lump sum order (within the meaning, in each case, of the Act of 1996), make an application to the Circuit Court,]³

(ii) in any other case, make an application to the District Court, for the recovery of maintenance in accordance with the request.

(2) The District Court, on an application to it under subsection (1)(b), may, if it considers that the order of the court in the designated jurisdiction for the recovery of maintenance is enforceable in the State, make an order for its enforcement and thereupon—

[(a) the order of the District Court shall be deemed to be an enforceable maintenance order as defined in the Act of 1998, and

(b) sections 8, 9 and 10 of that Act shall apply in relation to the order, with any necessary modifications]¹.

[(3) An application referred to in subsection (1)(c) shall be deemed to be an application for a maintenance order under section 5 or section 5A or 21A (inserted by the Status of Children Act, 1987) of the Act of 1976, or the appropriate order referred to subsection (1)(c), as may be appropriate, and to have been made on the date on which the request of the claimant for the recovery of maintenance was received by the Central Authority of the designated jurisdiction concerned.]³

(4) The court, on an application to it under subsection (1)(c) may, subject to subsection (5)—

(a) take evidence from the respondent by way of affidavit or on sworn deposition,

(b) cause a copy of the affidavit or deposition to be sent to the Central Authority for transmission to the Central Authority of the designated jurisdiction with a request that the claimant provide an answering affidavit,

(c) send letters of request pursuant to section 17 for the taking of further evidence in a designated jurisdiction,

(d) take the evidence of the claimant or of any witness residing in a designated jurisdiction through a live television link,

[(e) pending the final determination of the application, make an interim order under section 7 of the Act of 1976 or an order under section 24 of the Act of 1995.]⁴

(5) Where it appears to the court that the claimant or respondent *bona fide* desires to cross-examine a witness and the witness is available for the cross-examination, whether through a live television link or otherwise, the court shall decline to permit the evidence of the witness to be given by affidavit.

(6) Notice of an application under paragraph (b) or (c) of subsection (1) shall be given to the respondent by the Central Authority and shall be accompanied by a copy of the documents proposed to be given in evidence by the Central Authority at the hearing of the application.

(7) Where—

    (a) on an application pursuant to subsection (1)(c) it is necessary to take the evidence of the claimant or of any witness through a live television link, and

    (b) facilities for doing so are not available in the circuit or district court district concerned,

the court may by order transfer the proceedings to a circuit or district court district where those facilities are available.

(8) The provisions of this section shall also apply as appropriate to a request made to the Central Authority to vary or discharge an order made on an application under subsection (1)(c).

(9) Where an order of a court which accompanies a request referred to in subsection (1) includes provision for matters other than those relating to maintenance, this section shall apply to the order only in so far as it relates to maintenance.

[(9A) In subsections (1)(a) and (9) a reference to an order of, or made by, a court shall be construed as including a reference to—

    (a) an instrument or settlement within the meaning of the Brussels Convention, as defined in Part II, or the Brussels I Regulation,

    (b) an arrangement relating to maintenance obligations concluded with or authenticated by an administrative authority, as referred to in Article 10 of the 1996 Accession Convention as defined in section 2 of the Act of 1998.][5]

(10) Section 8 and section 8A (inserted by the Status of Children Act, 1987) of the Act of 1976 shall apply and have effect in relation to any agreement in writing which contains a provision mentioned in paragraph (a) of either section and is made—

    (a) between a claimant and respondent, notwithstanding that one of them may at the time of the making of the agreement be resident outside the State, and

    (b) between a respondent and a person or body in the State where such a person or body has been authorised to enter into such an agreement on behalf of the claimant,

and an application may be made by the Central Authority to the Circuit Court under paragraph (b) of either section for an order making such an agreement a rule of court.

(11) The jurisdiction conferred by this section may be exercised—

    (a) in the case of the Circuit Court, by the judge of the circuit, and

(b) in the case of the District Court, by the judge of the District Court assigned to the district court district,

in which the respondent resides or carries on any profession, business or occupation or, as the case may be, to which proceedings have been transferred under subsection (7).

**Notes**

1 Section 14(1)(a) and (2)(a) and (b) were substituted by the Jurisdiction of Courts and Enforcement of Judgments Act 1998, s 22(6).

2 Section 14(1)(aa) was inserted by the European Communities (Civil and Commercial Judgments) Regulations 2002, (SI 52/2002) reg 13(1)(f).

3 Section 14(1)(c)(i) and (3) were inserted by the Family Law (Divorce) Act 1996, s 53(c).

4 Section 14(4) was amended by the Family Law Act 1995, s 45(c).

5 Subsection 14(9A) was inserted by the Jurisdiction of Courts and Enforcement of Judgments Act 1998, s 22(6)(c) and amended by the European Communities (Civil and Commercial Judgments) Regulations 2002, (SI 52/2002), reg 13(1)(f).

**15      Application for maintenance in designated jurisdiction**

(1) A claimant who wishes to recover maintenance from a respondent residing in a designated jurisdiction may apply to the Central Authority to have the claim transmitted to the central authority in that jurisdiction notwithstanding the existence of a maintenance order made against the respondent by a court in the State.

(2) (a) Such a claimant may give evidence on sworn deposition before the District Court as to the facts relating to the claim, and the Court, if satisfied that the deposition sets forth facts from which it may be determined that the respondent concerned owes a duty to maintain the claimant, may certify accordingly.

(b) The district court clerk concerned shall give to the claimant a certified copy of the deposition and certificate.

(c) The jurisdiction conferred on the District Court by this subsection may be exercised by the judge of the District Court assigned to the district court district in which the claimant resides or carries on any profession, business or occupation.

(3) As respects an order for the recovery of maintenance or an order varying such an order made by a court in the State on the application of the claimant, the registrar or clerk of the court shall, at the request of the claimant and subject to any conditions that may be specified by rules of court, give to the claimant—

(a) a copy of the order duly authenticated,

(b) a certificate signed by the registrar or clerk stating—

(i) the date on which the time for lodging an appeal against the order will expire or, if it has expired, the date on which it expired,

(ii) whether notice of appeal against the order has been entered,

     (iii)   the amount of any arrears under the order, and

     (iv)   such other particulars (if any) as may be specified by rules of court, and

  (c)   in case the order was made in default of appearance, the original or a copy, certified by the registrar or clerk to be a true copy, of a document establishing that notice of the institution of proceedings was served on the respondent.

## 16     Evidence in proceedings

Subject to section 21(4), in any proceedings under this Part, unless the court sees good reason to the contrary—

  (a)   a document purporting to be an application by a claimant who is residing in a designated jurisdiction to the central authority of that jurisdiction for the recovery of maintenance from a respondent residing in the State, or for the variation or revocation of an order made on such an application, and to have been transmitted by that authority to the Central Authority may be admitted as evidence that it is such an application and has been so transmitted;

  (b)   a document purporting to be signed by or on behalf of the claimant and to authorise the Central Authority to act, or to appoint some other person to act, on behalf of the claimant may be admitted as evidence of such authorisation;

  (c)   a document purporting to be an order for the payment of maintenance by the respondent, or an order varying or discharging such an order, made by a court in a designated jurisdiction and to be signed by a judge, magistrate or officer of that court may be admitted as evidence that the order was so made and—

     (i)   that the respondent is liable to maintain the claimant and, where appropriate, a child of the claimant, and

     (ii)   that the claimant was resident or present in that jurisdiction at the date of the commencement of the relevant proceedings;

  (d)   a document purporting to be—

     (i)   a petition which has been filed in a court in a designated jurisdiction seeking an order for the recovery of maintenance against a person alleged in the petition to have a duty of support,

     (ii)   a certificate by a judge, magistrate or officer of that court to the effect that the petition sets forth facts from which it may be determined that the person owes such a duty of support,

may be admitted as evidence of the matters to which the document relates;

  (e)   a document purporting to be signed by a judge, magistrate or officer of a court in a designated jurisdiction and to be—

     (i)   a document setting out or summarising evidence given in proceedings in that court or evidence taken in that jurisdiction for the purpose of maintenance proceedings in that jurisdiction or elsewhere,

     (ii)   a document which has been received in evidence in proceedings in that court, or

(iii) if an order for the recovery of maintenance from the respondent has been made in default of the respondent's appearance by a court in that jurisdiction, a document which establishes that notice of the institution of proceedings was served on the respondent,

may be admitted as evidence of the matters to which the document relates;

(f) a document purporting to be signed on behalf of a central authority of a designated jurisdiction and to certify that the request of a specified claimant for the recovery of maintenance from a specified respondent residing in the State was received by that central authority on a specified date may be admitted as evidence that the request was so received on that date.

## 17 Obtaining of evidence from designated jurisdiction

(1) A court may, for the purpose of any proceedings under this Part, address letters of request for further evidence, documentary or otherwise, either to the appropriate court of a designated jurisdiction or to any other authority or institution designated in that behalf by that jurisdiction.

(2) Letters of request under subsection (1) may also be sent to the Central Authority for transmission to the court, authority or institution concerned.

## 18 Provisional, including protective, measures

Where the Central Authority has received a request under this Part from a central authority of a designated jurisdiction for the recovery of maintenance, the High Court may, on application to it by the Central Authority, grant provisional, including protective, measures of any kind that the Court has power to grant in proceedings that are within its jurisdiction.

## 19 Taking of evidence for proceedings in designated jurisdiction

(1) Where a request is made to the Central Authority by or on behalf of a court in a designated jurisdiction ("the requesting authority") to obtain the evidence of a person residing in the State for the purposes of any proceedings in that jurisdiction for the recovery of maintenance the provisions of this section shall have effect.

(2) If the request is in order the Central Authority shall refer the request to the Master of the High Court, who shall request a judge of the District Court to take the evidence.

(3) The judge shall cause notice of the time and place at which evidence is to be taken to be given to the person concerned, to the Central Authority for communication to the requesting authority, to the Master of the High Court and to such other persons as the judge thinks fit.

(4) The judge shall take the evidence and cause a record thereof to be sent to the Central Authority for transmission to the requesting authority.

(5) If it is not possible to take the evidence within four months of the receipt of the request by the Central Authority, the judge shall cause the reasons for the non-execution of the request or for the delay in executing it to be sent to the Central Authority for transmission to the requesting authority.

(6) The judge shall have the same powers in relation to compelling the attendance of persons and the production of documents and in relation to the taking of evidence as the District Court has on the hearing of an action.

(7) Where any person, not being a party to proceedings referred to in subsection (1), attends pursuant to a request under that subsection, the judge may order that there shall be paid to that person out of public funds such sum by way of expenses as the District Court may order to be paid in respect of a witness on the hearing of an action.

(8) If the Central Authority or the judge is of the view that the authenticity of the request is not established or that the execution of the request would compromise the sovereignty or safety of the State the execution of the request shall not be proceeded with.

(9) Where the requesting authority makes a request for the taking of evidence directly to a court in the State—

(a) if that court is the District Court, the evidence shall be taken by a judge of that Court, and

(b) in any other case, the court addressed may refer the request to the Master of the High Court,

and this section shall apply in relation to such a request with the necessary modifications.

## PART IV
### PROVISIONS COMMON TO RECIPROCATING AND DESIGNATED JURISDICTIONS

**20     Obtaining information on debtor**

[(1) The Central Authority may, for the purposes of obtaining any information that is necessary or expedient for the performance of its functions, require any holder of a public office or body financed wholly or partly by means of moneys provided by the Oireachtas to provide it with any information in the possession or procurement of the holder or body as to the whereabouts, place of work, or location and extent of the assets, of a person who is liable to make payments under a maintenance order (the maintenance debtor) or respondent, and the holder or body shall, as soon as practicable, comply with the requirement.]¹

(2) If the District Court, on application to it by the Central Authority, is of opinion that any person or body (not being a person or body mentioned in subsection (1)) is likely to have information as to the matters referred to in that subsection and that the Central Authority requires the information for the purposes so referred to, the Court may order that person or body to provide it to the Central Authority within such period as may be specified in the order.

(3) The jurisdiction conferred on the District Court by subsection 20(2) may be exercised by the judge of the District Court for the time being assigned to the district court district in which the person or body to whom the order sought is to be directed resides or carries on any profession, business or occupation.

**Notes**

1   Section 20(1) was substituted by the European Communities (Civil and Commercial Judgments) Regulations 2002, (SI 52/2002), reg 13(1)(g).

## 21     Evidence in proceedings

(1) Subject to subsection (4), in any proceedings under Part II or III, unless the court sees good reason to the contrary, a document—

    (a) purporting to be signed by a judge, magistrate or officer of a court in a reciprocating jurisdiction or designated jurisdiction and to be a statement of arrears under an order of that court for the recovery of maintenance, or

    (b) purporting to be—

        (i) a tax assessment or other statement or certificate relating to tax,

        (ii) a statement or certificate of earnings,

        (iii) a medical certificate,

        (iv) a statement or certificate that a person was employed or was unemployed for a specified period,

        (v) a letter written by a party to maintenance proceedings who is residing in a reciprocating jurisdiction or designated jurisdiction,

        (vi) an affidavit or other document made or signed by such a party, or a witness, residing in such a jurisdiction,

        (vii) a document establishing a marital relationship between parties to such proceedings or a relationship between the parties, or one of the parties, and a child for whom maintenance is sought in the proceedings, or

        (viii) a document establishing that a person or body is entitled to exercise, under the law of the state in which that party resides, the rights of the party seeking maintenance,

may, unless the contrary is proved, be admitted as evidence that it is such a document and as evidence of any matter to which it relates subject to such authentication, if any, as the court may require.

(2) A document purporting to be—

    (a) a translation of a document mentioned in subsection (1) or in section 8 or 16, and

    (b) certified as correct by a person competent to do so, may be admitted as evidence of any matter to which it relates.

(3) (a) Where a document is admissible in evidence by virtue of subsection (1) or of section 8 or 16, it may be given in evidence, whether or not the document is still in existence, by producing a copy of the document, or of the material part of it, authenticated in such manner as the court may approve.

(b) It is immaterial for the purposes of paragraph (a) how many removes there are between the copy and the original or by what means (which may include facsimile transmission) the copy produced or any intermediate copy was made.

(4) In estimating in the weight (if any) to be attached to a statement in a document admitted in evidence by virtue of subsection (1) or of section 8 or 16, regard shall be had to any other evidence available to the court and to any circumstances from which any inference can reasonably be drawn as to the accuracy or otherwise of the statement, including (except in the case of a court order or a certificate or other document prepared by or on behalf of a court or public authority) the question whether the maker of the statement had any incentive to conceal or misrepresent facts and whether or not it was made on oath.

# PART V
## MISCELLANEOUS

**22      Enforceability of foreign maintenance orders**

Recognition or enforcement of an order (other than a provisional order) for recovery of maintenance made by a court in a jurisdiction other than the State may not be refused—

(a) by reason only of the fact that the court which made the order had power to vary or revoke it, or

(b) on the ground that, under the rules of private international law of the State, the court concerned had not jurisdiction by reason of the fact that the respondent was not resident or present in that jurisdiction at the date of the commencement of the relevant proceedings, provided that at that date the claimant was resident there.

**23      Currency of payments under foreign maintenance orders**

(1) An amount payable in the State under an order for recovery maintenance which is made by a court in a jurisdiction other than the State and is enforceable in the State shall be paid in the currency of the State and, if the amount is stated in the order in a currency other than the currency of the State, the payment shall be made on the basis of the exchange rate prevailing, on the date of the making of an order by a court in the State for the enforcement of the order, between that currency and the currency of the State.

(2) For the purposes of this section, a certificate purporting to be signed by an officer of a bank in the State and to state the exchange rate prevailing on a specified date between a specified currency and the currency of the State shall be evidence of the facts stated in the certificate.

(3) In this section "**bank**" means the holder of a banker's licence within the meaning of the Central Bank Act, 1989.

**24      Saving**

Nothing in this Act shall prevent the recognition or enforcement of an order for recovery of maintenance which is made in a reciprocating jurisdiction or designated jurisdiction and which, apart from this Act, would be recognised or enforceable in the State.

## 25 Expenses

The expenses incurred in the administration of this Act shall, to such extent as may be sanctioned by the Minister for Finance, be paid out of moneys provided by the Oireachtas.

### FIRST SCHEDULE

Section 6

## TEXT OF ROME CONVENTION

## CONVENTION BETWEEN THE MEMBER STATES OF THE EUROPEAN COMMUNITIES ON THE SIMPLIFICATION OF PROCEDURES FOR THE RECOVERY OF MAINTENANCE PAYMENTS

### PREAMBLE

*The Member States of the European Communities,* hereinafter referred to as "The Member States",

*Mindful* of the close links existing between their peoples,

*Having regard to* the developments tending to the elimination of obstacles to the free movement of persons between Member States,

*Convinced* of the need to simplify among the Member States the procedures for securing the reciprocal recognition and enforcement of judgments relating to maintenance,

*Desiring* for this purpose to complement with administrative arrangements the provisions of the Brussels Convention of 27 September 1968 on jurisdiction and the enforcement of judgments in civil and commercial matters, as amended by the Accession Conventions under the successive enlargements of the European Communities,

Have agreed as follows:

### *Article 1*
### *Scope and Application*

1. This Convention may be applied to any judgment relating to maintenance which comes within the scope of the Convention on jurisdiction and the enforcement of judgments in civil and commercial matters signed at Brussels on 27 September 1968 and as subsequently amended (hereinafter referred to as "the Brussels Convention").

2. The judgment may be a judgment given before or after this Convention enters into force provided it is a judgment that is enforceable in the State addressed under the Brussels Convention or a convention concluded between the State of origin and the State addressed.

3. If the judgment does not relate solely to maintenance the Convention shall only apply to those parts of the judgment which relate to maintenance.

4. For the purpose of this Convention **"judgment"** shall include an authentic instrument or court settlement within the meaning of Articles 50 and 51 of the Brussels Convention.

5. Any body which, under the law of a Contracting State, is entitled to exercise the rights of redress of the creditor or to represent him shall benefit from the provisions of this Convention.

## *Article 2*
### *Central Authorities*

1. Each Contracting State shall designate a Central Authority to carry out or arrange to have carried out the functions provided for by this Convention.

2. Federal States and States with more than one legal system shall be free to appoint more than one Central Authority. Where a State has appointed more than one Central Authority it shall designate the Central Authority to which applications under this Convention may be addressed for transmission to the appropriate Central Authority within that State.

3. Central Authorities shall not charge any fees in respect of services rendered by them under this Convention.

## *Article 3*

1. The Central Authorities shall co-operate with each other and promote co-operation between the competent authorities in their respective states in order to facilitate the recovery of maintenance payments due.

2. On receipt of the application mentioned in Article 5 the Central Authority in the State addressed shall take or cause to be taken without delay all appropriate and useful measures to:

    (i)   seek out and locate the debtor or his assets;

    (ii)  obtain, where appropriate, relevant information from Government Departments or agencies in relation to the debtor;

    (iii)  have the judgment registered or declared enforceable, where appropriate;

    (iv)  facilitate the transfer of maintenance payments to the creditor or body referred to in Article 1(5); and

    (v)  ensure, where the payments due to the maintenance creditor are not made, the use of all appropriate means of enforcement provided for in the State addressed which are applicable and which might permit recovery of these sums.

3. The Central Authority in the State addressed shall keep the Central Authority in the State of origin informed of the measures taken under paragraph 2 and their results.

## *Article 4*

Each Contracting State shall take the necessary administrative and legal measures, including the provision of effective enforcement measures, to enable the Central Authority to fulfil its obligations under this Convention.

*Article 5*

*Applications*

1. Where a maintenance creditor or body referred to in Article 1(5) obtains in a Contracting State a judgment relating to maintenance and wishes to have that judgment recognised or enforced in another Contracting State, the maintenance creditor or body may submit a request for this purpose to the Central Authority in the State of origin.

2. Before transmitting an application to the State addressed, the Central Authority in the State of origin shall ensure that the application and the accompanying documents are in accordance with paragraph 3 of this Article and with Article 6.

3. The application shall contain:

   (i)  a request that it be processed in accordance with the provisions of this Convention;

  (ii)  a letter delegating to the Central Authority addressed authority to act, or cause action to be taken, on behalf of the maintenance creditor including specific authority to enable enforcement proceedings to be taken;

 (iii)  the name, date of birth, nationality and description of the debtor and all other relevant information regarding his identity or whereabouts or the location of his assets;

 (iv)  the documentation required under Section 3 of Title III of the Brussels Convention.

*Article 6*

*Language*

The documentation referred to in Article 5 and any correspondence between the Central Authorities relating to the application shall, unless otherwise agreed between the Central Authorities concerned, be in, or shall be accompanied by a translation into, the official language or one of the official languages of the State addressed or any other language that the State addressed has declared it will accept.

*Article 7*

*Relationship with other Conventions*

The provisions of this Convention are in addition to the provisions of the Brussels Convention and are without prejudice to other existing international instruments.

*Article 8*

*Standing Committee*

1. A Standing Committee shall be set up for the purposes of exchanging views on the functioning of the Convention and resolving any difficulties which arise in practice. The Committee may issue recommendations on the implementation of the Convention or recommend changes in the Convention.

2. The Committee shall be composed of representatives appointed by each Member State. The Commission of the European Communities may attend meetings as observers.

3. The Presidency of European Political Co-operation shall convene meetings of the Committee at least once every two years and otherwise at its discretion. In this regard it shall pay due regard to any requests made by other Member States.

### Article 9
### Final Provisions

1. This Convention shall be open for signature by the Member States. It shall be subject to ratification, acceptance or approval. The instruments of ratification, acceptance or approval shall be deposited with the Ministry of Foreign Affairs of the Italian Republic.

2. This Convention shall enter into force 90 days after the date of deposit of the instruments of ratification, acceptance or approval by all the States which are members of the European Communities on the date on which it is opened for signature.

3. Each Member State may, when depositing its instrument of ratification, acceptance or approval, or at any later date, declare that the Convention shall apply to it in its relations with other states which have made the same declaration 90 days after the date of deposit.

4. A Member State which has not made such a declaration may apply the Convention with other contracting Member States on the basis of bilateral agreements.

5. (i) Each Member State shall at the time of the deposit of its instrument of ratification, acceptance or approval inform the Ministry of Foreign Affairs of the Italian Republic of the following—

   (a) the designation of a Central Authority pursuant to Article 2 and

   (b) any declarations pursuant to Article 6.

   (ii) Any such designation or declaration may at a later date be changed, and any new declaration may be made, by notification addressed to the Ministry of Foreign Affairs of the Italian Republic.

6. The Ministry of Foreign Affairs of the Italian Republic shall notify all the Member States of any signature, deposit of instruments, declaration or designation.

### Article 10

1. This Convention shall be open to accession by any State which becomes a member of the European Communities. The instruments of accession shall be deposited with the Ministry of Foreign Affairs of the Italian Republic.

2. This Convention shall enter into force in respect of any State which accedes to it 90 days after the date of deposit of that State's instrument of accession.

Done at Rome on the sixth day of November in the year one thousand nine hundred and ninety, in the Danish, Dutch, English, French, German, Greek, Irish, Italian, Portuguese and Spanish languages, each text being equally authentic, in a single original which shall be deposited in the archives of the Ministry of Foreign Affairs of the Italian Republic.

The Ministry of Foreign Affairs of the Italian Republic shall transmit certified copies of the Convention to the Government of each Member State.

## SECOND SCHEDULE

Section 13

### TEXT OF NEW YORK CONVENTION

### CONVENTION ON THE RECOVERY ABROAD OF MAINTENANCE DONE AT NEW YORK ON 20 JUNE 1956

#### PREAMBLE

*Considering* the urgency of solving the humanitarian problem resulting from the situation of persons in need dependent for their maintenance on persons abroad,

*Considering* that the prosecution or enforcement abroad of claims for maintenance gives rise to serious legal and practical difficulties, and

*Determined* to provide a means to solve such problems and to overcome such difficulties,

The Contracting Parties have agreed as follows:

#### *Article 1*
#### *Scope of the Convention*

1. The purpose of this Convention is to facilitate the recovery of maintenance to which a person, hereinafter referred to as claimant, who is in the territory of one of the Contracting Parties, claims to be entitled from another person, hereinafter referred to as respondent, who is subject to the jurisdiction of another Contracting Party. This purpose shall be effected through the offices of agencies which will hereinafter be referred to as Transmitting and Receiving Agencies.

2. The remedies provided for in this Convention are in addition to, and not in substitution for, any remedies available under municipal or international law.

#### *Article 2*
#### *Designation of Agencies*

1. Each Contracting Party shall, at the time when the instrument of ratification or accession is deposited, designate one or more judicial or administrative authorities which shall act in its territory as Transmitting Agencies.

2. Each Contracting Party shall, at the time when the instrument of ratification or accession is deposited, designate a public or private body which shall act in its territory as Receiving Agency.

3. Each Contracting Party shall promptly communicate to the Secretary-General of the United Nations the designations made under paragraphs 1 and 2 and any changes made in respect thereof.

4. Transmitting and Receiving Agencies may communicate directly with Transmitting and Receiving Agencies of other Contracting Parties.

### Article 3
#### Application to Transmitting Agency

1. Where a claimant is in the territory of one Contracting Party, hereinafter referred to as the State of the claimant, and the respondent is subject to the jurisdiction of another Contracting Party, hereinafter referred to as the State of the respondent, the claimant may make application to a Transmitting Agency in the State of the claimant for the recovery of maintenance from the respondent.

2. Each Contracting Party shall inform the Secretary-General as to the evidence normally required under the law of the State of the Receiving Agency for the proof of maintenance claims, of the manner in which such evidence should be submitted, and of other requirements to be complied with under such law.

3. The application shall be accompanied by all relevant documents, including, where necessary, a power of attorney authorising the Receiving Agency to act, or to appoint some other person to act, on behalf of the claimant. It shall also be accompanied by a photograph of the claimant and, where available, a photograph of the respondent.

4. The Transmitting Agency shall take all reasonable steps to ensure that the requirements of the law of the State of the Receiving Agency are complied with; and, subject to the requirements of such law, the application shall include:

    (a) the full name, address, date of birth, nationality, and occupation of the claimant, and the name and address of any legal representative of the claimant;

    (b) the full name of the respondent, and, so far as known to the claimant, his addresses during the preceding five years, date of birth, nationality, and occupation;

    (c) particulars of the grounds upon which the claim is based and of the relief sought, and any other relevant information such as the financial and family circumstances of the claimant and the respondent.

### Article 4
#### Transmission of Documents

1. The Transmitting Agency shall transmit the documents to the Receiving Agency of the State of the respondent, unless satisfied that the application is not made in good faith.

2. Before transmitting such documents, the Transmitting Agency shall satisfy itself that they are regular as to form, in accordance with the law of the State of the claimant.

3. The Transmitting Agency may express to the Receiving Agency an opinion as to the merits of the case and may recommend that free legal aid and exemption from costs be given to the claimant.

### Article 5
#### Transmission of Judgments and other Judicial Acts

1. The Transmitting Agency shall, at the request of the claimant, transmit under the provisions of article 4, any order, final or provisional, and any other judicial act, obtained by the claimant for the payment of maintenance in a competent tribunal of any

of the Contracting Parties, and, where necessary and possible, the record of the proceedings in which such order was made.

2. The orders and judicial acts referred to in the preceding paragraph may be transmitted in substitution for or in addition to the documents mentioned in article 3.

3. Proceedings under article 6 may include, in accordance with the law of the State of the respondent, exequatur or registration proceedings or an action based upon the act transmitted under paragraph 1.

### Article 6
### Functions of the Receiving Agency

1. The Receiving Agency shall, subject always to the authority given by the claimant, take, on behalf of the claimant, all appropriate steps for the recovery of maintenance, including the settlement of the claim and, where necessary, the institution and prosecution of an action for maintenance and the execution of any order or other judicial act for the payment of maintenance.

2. The Receiving Agency shall keep the Transmitting Agency currently informed. If it is unable to act, it shall inform the Transmitting Agency of its reasons and return the documents.

3. Notwithstanding anything in this Convention, the law applicable in the determination of all questions arising in any such action or proceedings shall be the law of the State of the respondent, including its private international law.

### Article 7
### Letters of Request

If provision is made for letters of request in the laws of the two Contracting Parties concerned, the following rules shall apply:

(a) A tribunal hearing an action for maintenance may address letters of request for further evidence, documentary or otherwise, either to the competent tribunal of the other Contracting Party or to any other authority or institution designated by the other Contracting Party in whose territory the request is to be executed.

(b) In order that the parties may attend or be represented, the requested authority shall give notice of the date on which and the place at which the proceedings requested are to take place to the Receiving Agency and the Transmitting Agency concerned, and to the respondent.

(c) Letters of request shall be executed with all convenient speed; in the event of such letters of request not being executed within four months from the receipt of the letters by the requested authority, the reasons for such non-execution or for such delay shall be communicated to the requesting authority.

(d) The execution of letters of request shall not give rise to reimbursement of fees or costs of any kind whatsoever.

(e) Execution of letters of request may only be refused:

    (1) If the authenticity of the letters is not established;

    (2) If the Contracting Party in whose territory the letters are to be executed deems that its sovereignty or safety would be compromised thereby.

## Article 8
### Variation of Orders

The provisions of this Convention apply also to applications for the variation of maintenance orders.

## Article 9
### Exemptions and Facilities

1. In proceedings under this Convention, claimants shall be accorded equal treatment and the same exemptions in the payment of costs and charges as are given to residents or nationals of the State where the proceedings are pending.

2. Claimants shall not be required, because of their status as aliens or non-residents, to furnish any bond or make any payment or deposit as security for costs or otherwise.

3. Transmitting and Receiving Agencies shall not charge any fees in respect of services rendered under this Convention.

## Article 10
### Transfer of Funds

A Contracting Party, under whose law the transfer of funds abroad is restricted, shall accord the highest priority to the transfer of funds payable as maintenance or to cover expenses in respect of proceedings under this Convention.

## Article 11
### Federal State Clause

In the case of a Federal or non-unitary State, the following provisions shall apply:

    (a) With respect to those articles of this Convention that come within the legislative jurisdiction of the federal legislative authority, the obligations of the Federal Government shall to this extent be the same as those of Parties which are not Federal States;

    (b) With respect to those articles of this Convention that come within the legislative jurisdiction of constituent States, provinces or cantons which are not, under the constitutional system of the Federation, bound to take legislative action, the Federal Government shall bring such articles with a favourable recommendation to the notice of the appropriate authorities of States, provinces or cantons at the earliest possible moment;

    (c) A Federal State Party to this Convention shall, at the request of any other Contracting Party transmitted through the Secretary-General, supply a statement of the law and practice of the Federation and its constituent units in regard to any particular provision of the Convention, showing the extent to which effect has been given to that provision by legislative or other action.

## Article 12
### Territorial Application

The provisions of this Convention shall extend or be applicable equally to all non-self-governing, trust or other territories for the international relations of which a Contracting Party is responsible, unless the latter, on ratifying or acceding to this Convention, has given notice that the Convention shall not apply to any one or more of such territories. Any Contracting Party making such a declaration may, at any time thereafter, by notification to the Secretary-General, extend the application of the Convention to any or all of such territories.

## Article 13
### Signature, Ratification and Accession

1. This Convention shall be open for signature until 31 December 1956 on behalf of any Member of the United Nations, any non-member State which is a Party to the Statute of the International Court of Justice, or member of a specialized agency, and any other non-member State which has been invited by the Economic and Social Council to become a Party to the Convention.

2. This Convention shall be ratified. The instruments of ratification shall be deposited with the Secretary-General.

3. This Convention may be acceded to at any time on behalf of any of the States referred to in paragraph 1 of this article. The instruments of accession shall be deposited with the Secretary-General.

## Article 14
### Entry Into Force

1. This Convention shall come into force on the thirtieth day following the date of deposit of the third instrument of ratification or accession in accordance with article 13.

2. For each State ratifying or acceding to the Convention after the deposit of the third instrument of ratification or accession, the Convention shall enter into force on the thirtieth day following the date of the deposit by such State of its instrument of ratification or accession.

## Article 15
### Denunciation

1. Any Contracting Party may denounce this Convention by notification to the Secretary-General. Such denunciation may also apply to some or all of the territories mentioned in article 12.

2. Denunciation shall take effect one year after the date of receipt of the notification by the Secretary-General, except that it shall not prejudice cases pending at the time it becomes effective.

*Article 16*
*Settlement of Disputes*

If a dispute should arise between Contracting Parties relating to the interpretation or application of this Convention, and if such dispute has not been settled by other means, it shall be referred to the International Court of Justice. The dispute shall be brought before the Court either by the notification of a special agreement or by a unilateral application of one of the parties to the dispute.

*Article 17*
*Reservations*

1. In the event that any State submits a reservation to any of the articles of this Convention at the time of ratification or accession, the Secretary-General shall communicate the text of the reservation to all States which are Parties to this Convention, and to the other States referred to in article 13. Any Contracting Party which objects to the reservation may, within a period of ninety days from the date of the communication, notify the Secretary-General that it does not accept it, and the Convention shall not then enter into force as between the objecting State and the State making the reservation. Any State thereafter acceding may make such notification at the time of its accession.

2. A Contracting Party may at any time withdraw a reservation previously made and shall notify the Secretary-General of such withdrawal.

*Article 18*
*Reciprocity*

A Contracting Party shall not be entitled to avail itself of this Convention against other Contracting Parties except to the extent that it is itself bound by the Convention.

*Article 19*
*Notification by the Secretary-general*

1. The Secretary-General shall inform all Members of the United Nations and the non-member States referred to in article 13:

(a) of communications under paragraph 3 of article 2;

(b) of information received under paragraph 2 of article 3;

(c) of declarations and notifications made under article 12;

(d) of signatures, ratifications and accessions under article 13;

(e) of the date on which the Convention has entered into force under paragraph 1 of article 14;

(f) of denunciations made under paragraph 1 of article 15;

(g) of reservations and notifications made under article 17.

2. The Secretary-General shall also inform all Contracting Parties of requests for revision and replies thereto received under article 20.

*Article 20*
*Revision*

1. Any Contracting Party may request revision of this Convention at any time by a notification addressed to the Secretary-General.

2. The Secretary-General shall transmit the notification to each Contracting Party with a request that such Contracting Party reply within four months whether it desires the convening of a Conference to consider the proposed revision. If a majority of the Contracting Parties favour the convening of a Conference it shall be convened by the Secretary-General.

*Article 21*
*Languages and Deposit of Convention*

The original of this Convention, of which the Chinese, English, French, Russian and Spanish texts are equally authentic, shall be deposited with the Secretary-General, who shall transmit certified true copies thereof to all States referred to in article 13.

# Family Law Act 1995

*Number 26 of 1995*

ARRANGEMENT OF SECTIONS

## PART I
### PRELIMINARY AND GENERAL

## PART II
### PRELIMINARY AND ANCILLARY ORDERS IN OR AFTER PROCEEDINGS FOR JUDICIAL SEPARATION

## PART III
### RELIEF AFTER DIVORCE OR SEPARATION OUTSIDE STATE

## PART IV
### DECLARATIONS AS TO MARITAL STATUS

## PART V
### MARRIAGE

## PART VI
### MISCELLANEOUS

## SCHEDULE
### ENACTMENTS REPEALED

### Acts Referred To

| | |
|---|---|
| Adoption Acts, 1952 to 1991 | |
| Capital Acquisitions Tax Act, 1976 | 1976, No. 8 |
| Child Abduction and Enforcement of Custody Orders Act, 1991 | 1991, No. 6 |
| Defence Act, 1954 | 1954, No. 18 |
| Enforcement of Court Orders Act, 1940 | 1940, No. 23 |
| Family Home Protection Act, 1976 | 1976, No. 27 |
| Family Law Act, 1981 | 1981, No. 22 |
| Family Law (Maintenance of Spouses and Children) Act, 1976 | 1976, No. 11 |
| Family Law (Protection of Spouses and Children) Act, 1981 | 1981, No. 21 |
| Finance (1909-10) Act, 1910 | 10 Edw. 7, c. 8 |
| Finance Act, 1972 | 1972, No. 19 |
| Finance Act, 1983 | 1983, No. 15 |
| Finance Act, 1993 | 1993, No. 13 |
| Finance Act, 1994 | 1994, No. 13 |
| Guardianship of Infants Act, 1964 | 1964, No. 7 |
| Income Tax Act, 1967 | 1967, No. 6 |
| Insurance Act, 1989 | 1989, No. 3 |
| Judgments (Ireland) Act, 1844 | 1844, c. 90 |
| Judicial Separation and Family Law Reform Act, 1989 | 1989, No. 6 |
| Jurisdiction of Courts and Enforcement of Judgments Acts, 1988 and 1993 | |
| Legitimacy Declaration Act, (Ireland), 1868 | 1868, c. 20 |
| Maintenance Act, 1994 | 1994, No. 28 |
| Marriages Act, 1972 | 1972, No. 30 |
| Marriages (Ireland) Act, 1844 | 1844, c. 81 |
| Marriage Law (Ireland) Amendment Act, 1863 | 1863, c. 27 |
| Married Women's Status Act, 1957 | 1957, No. 5 |

**Acts Referred To**

| | |
|---|---|
| Matrimonial Causes and Marriage Law (Ireland) Amendment Act, 1870 | 1870, c. 110 |
| Partition Act, 1868 | 1868, c. 40 |
| Partition Act, 1876 | 1876, c. 17 |
| Pensions Act, 1990 | 1990, No. 25 |
| Registration of Marriages (Ireland) Act, 1863 | 1863, c. 90 |
| Registration of Title Act, 1964 | 1964, No. 16 |
| Status of Children Act, 1987 | 1987, No. 26 |
| Succession Act, 1965 | 1965, No. 27 |

*An Act to make further provision in relation to the jurisdiction of the courts to make preliminary and ancillary orders in or after proceedings for judicial separation, to enable such orders to be made in certain cases where marriages are dissolved, or as respects which the spouses become judicially separated, under the law of another state, to make further provision in relation to maintenance under the Family Law (Maintenance of Spouses and Children) Act, 1976, and in relation to marriage and to provide for connected matters. [2nd October, 1995]*

*Be it enacted by the Oireachtas as follows:*

## PART I
### PRELIMINARY AND GENERAL

**1        Short title and commencement[1]**

(1) This Act may be cited as the Family Law Act, 1995—

(2) (a)   This Act shall come into operation on such day or days as, by order or orders made by the Minister for Equality and Law Reform under this section, may be fixed therefor either generally or with reference to any particular purpose or provision and different days may be so fixed for different purposes and different provisions.

   (b)   An order under paragraph (a) relating to, or in so far as it relates to, section 32 shall not be made without the consent of the Minister for Health.

---

**Notes**

1   Commencement: 1 August 1996 (SI 46/1996).

---

## 2      Interpretation

(1) In this Act, save where the context otherwise requires:

**"the Act of 1964"** means the Guardianship of Infants Act, 1964;

**"the Act of 1965"** means the Succession Act, 1965;

**"the Act of 1976"** means the Family Law (Maintenance of Spouses and Children) Act, 1976;

[...][1]

**"the Act of 1989"** means the Judicial Separation and Family Law Reform Act, 1989;

[**"the Act of 1996"** means the Domestic Violence Act, 1996;][2]

**"conveyance"** includes a mortgage, lease, assent, transfer, disclaimer, release and any other disposition of property otherwise than by a will or a *donatio mortis causa* and also includes an enforceable agreement (whether conditional or unconditional) to make any such disposition;

**"the court"** shall be construed in accordance with section 38;

[**"civil partnership"** has the meaning assigned to it by the Civil Partnership and Certain Rights and Obligations of Cohabitants Act 2010;][3]

**"decree of judicial separation"** means a decree under section 3 of the Act of 1989;

**"decree of nullity"** means a decree granted by a court declaring a marriage to be null and void;

**"dependent member of the family"**, in relation to a spouse, or the spouses, concerned, means any child—

(a) of both spouses or adopted by both spouses under the Adoption Acts, 1952 to 1991, or in relation to whom both spouses are *in loco parentis*, or

(b) of either spouse or adopted by either spouse under those Acts or in relation to whom either spouse is *in loco parentis*, where the other spouse, being aware that he or she is not the parent of the child, has treated the child as a member of the family,

who is under the age of 18 years or if the child has attained that age—

(i) is or will be or, if an order were made under this Act providing for periodical payments for the benefit of the child or for the provision of a lump sum for the child, would be receiving full-time education or instruction at any university, college, school or other educational establishment and is under the age of 23 years, or

(ii) has a mental or physical disability to such extent that it is not reasonably possible for the child to maintain himself or herself fully;

**"family home"** has the meaning assigned to it by section 2 of the Family Home Protection Act, 1976, with the modification that the references to a spouse in that section shall be construed as references to a spouse within the meaning of this Act;

**"financial compensation order"** has the meaning assigned to it by section 11;

**"Land Registry"** and **"Registry of Deeds"** have the meanings assigned to them by the Registration of Title Act, 1964;

"**lump sum order**" means an order under section 8(1)(c);

"**maintenance pending suit order**" means an order under section 7;

"**maintenance pending relief order**" means an order under section 24;

"**member**", in relation to a pension scheme, means any person who, having been admitted to membership of the scheme under its rules, remains entitled to any benefit under the scheme;

"**pension adjustment order**" means an order under section 12:

"pension scheme" means—

    (a)  an occupational pension scheme (within the meaning of the Pensions Act, 1990), or

    (b)  (i)  an annuity contract approved by the Revenue Commissioners under section 235 of the Income Tax Act, 1967, or a contract so approved under section 235A of that Act,

          (ii)  a trust scheme, or part of a trust scheme, so approved under subsection (4) of the said section 235 or subsection (5) of the said section 235A, or

          (iii)  a policy or contract of assurance approved by the Revenue Commissioners under Chapter II of Part I of the Finance Act, 1972, or

  [(bb)  a PRSA contract within the meaning of Part X of the Pensions Act, 1990, or][4]

    (c)  any other scheme or arrangement (including a personal pension plan and a scheme or arrangement established by or pursuant to statute or instrument made under statute other than under the Social Welfare Acts) that provides or is intended to provide either or both of the following, that is to say:

          (i)  benefits for a person who is a member of the scheme or arrangement ("the member") upon retirement at normal pensionable age or upon earlier or later retirement or upon leaving, or upon the ceasing of, the relevant employment,

          (ii)  benefits for the widow, widower or dependants of the member, or for any other persons, on the death of the member;

"**periodical payments order**" and "**secured periodical payments order**" have the meanings assigned to them by section 8(1);

"**property adjustment order**" has the meaning assigned to it by section 9;

[**"registration"**, with respect to a civil partnership, includes entering into a relationship of a class of legal relationships that is the subject of an order made under section 5 of the Civil Partnership and Certain Rights and Obligations of Cohabitants Act 2010;][5]

"**relief order**" means an order under Part 11 made by virtue of section 23;

"**trustees**", in relation to a scheme that is established under a trust, means the trustees of the pension scheme and, in relation to a pension scheme not so established, means the persons who administer the scheme.

(2) In this Act, where the context so requires—

    (a)  a reference to a marriage includes a reference to a marriage that has been dissolved under the law of a country or jurisdiction other than the State,

(b) a reference to a remarriage includes a reference to a marriage that takes place after a marriage that has been dissolved under the law of a country or jurisdiction other than the State,

(c) a reference to a spouse includes a reference to a person who is a party to a marriage that has been dissolved under the law of a country or jurisdiction other than the State,

(d) a reference to a family includes a reference to a family as respects which the marriage of the spouses concerned has been dissolved under the law of a country or jurisdiction other than the State,

(e) a reference to an application to a court by a person on behalf of a dependent member of the family includes a reference to such an application by such a member and a reference to a payment, the securing of a payment, or the assignment of an interest, to a person for the benefit of a dependent member of the family includes a reference to a payment, the securing of a payment, or the assignment of an interest, to such a member,

and cognate words shall be construed accordingly.

(3) In this Act—

(a) a reference to any enactment shall, unless the context otherwise requires, be construed as a reference to that enactment as amended or extended by or under any subsequent enactment including this Act,

(b) a reference to a Part or section is a reference to a Part or section of this Act unless it is indicated that reference to some other enactment is intended,

(c) a reference to a subsection, paragraph, subparagraph or clause is a reference to the subsection, paragraph, subparagraph or cause of the provision in which the reference occurs unless it is indicated that reference to some other provision is intended.

---

**Notes**

1   Reference to the Family Law (Protection of Spouses and Children) Act 1981 was deleted by the Domestic Violence Act 1996, s 21.

2   Reference to the Domestic Violence Act 1996 was inserted by the Domestic Violence Act 1996, s 21.

3   Definition of "civil partnership" was inserted by the Civil Partnership and Certain Rights and Obligations of Cohabitants Act 2010, s 159.

4   Section 2(1)(bb) was inserted by the Pensions (Amendment) Act 2002, s 57.

5   Definition of "registration" was inserted by the Civil Partnership and Certain Rights and Obligations of Cohabitants Act 2010, s 159.

---

## 3      Repeals

(1) The enactments specified in the Schedule to this Act are hereby repealed to the extent specified in the third column of that Schedule.

(2) Notwithstanding subsection (1)—

    (a)    orders made before the commencement of Part II under a provision of the Act of 1989 repealed by subsection (1) shall continue in force and be treated after such commencement as if made under the corresponding provision of this Act,

    (b)    (i)    orders or decrees made or exceptions granted under section 1 of the Legitimacy Declaration Act (Ireland), 1868, section 1 of the Marriages Act, 1972, or section 12 of the Married Women's Status Act, 1957, before such commencement shall continue in force after such commencement,

            (ii)    proceedings instituted under any of those sections before such commencement may be continued and determined after such commencement, and

            (iii)    orders or decrees made or exceptions granted after such commencement in those proceedings shall be in force,

    (c)    proceedings instituted before such commencement under a provision of the Act of 1989 repealed by subsection (1) may be continued and determined as if instituted under the corresponding provision of this Act and orders made in those proceedings after such commencement shall be in force and be treated as if made under the corresponding provision of this Act.

## 4      Expenses

The expenses incurred by the Minister for Equality and Law Reform, the Minister for Health or the Minister for Justice in the administration of this Act shall, to such extent as may be sanctioned by the Minister for Finance, be paid out of moneys provided by the Oireachtas.

# PART II
## PRELIMINARY AND ANCILLARY ORDERS IN OR AFTER PROCEEDINGS FOR JUDICIAL SEPARATION

## 5      Application (sections 6 to 14)

Each of the following sections, that is to say, sections 6 to 14, applies to a case in which proceedings for the grant of a decree of judicial separation are instituted after the commencement of that section.

## 6      Preliminary orders in proceedings for judicial separation

Where an application is made to the court for the grant of a decree of judicial separation, the court, before deciding whether to grant or refuse to grant the decree, may, in the same proceedings and without the institution of proceedings under the Act concerned, if it appears to the court to be proper to do so, make one or more of the following orders—

(a) [an order under section 2, 3, 4 or 5 of the Act of 1996,][1]

(b) an order under section 11 of the Act of 1964,[2]

(c) an order under section 5 or 9 of the Family Home Protection Act, 1976.

**Notes**

1   Section 6(a) was substituted by the Domestic Violence Act 1996, s 21(b).

2   Section 6(b) – see the Child Care Act 1991, s 20.

## 7   Maintenance pending suit orders

(1) Where an application is made to the court for the grant of a decree of judicial separation, the court may make an order for maintenance pending suit, that is to say, an order requiring either of the spouses concerned to make to the other spouse such periodical payments or lump sum payments for his or her support and, where appropriate, to make to such person as may be specified in the order such periodical payments for the benefit of such (if any) dependent member of the family and, as respects periodical payments, for such period beginning not earlier than the date of the application and ending not later than the date of its determination, as the court considers proper and specifies in the order.

(2) The court may provide that payments under an order under this section shall be subject to such terms and conditions as it considers appropriate and specifies in the order.

## 8   Periodical payments and lump sum orders

(1) On granting a decree of judicial separation [or at any time thereafter][1], the court, on application to it in that behalf by either of the spouses concerned or by a person on behalf of a dependent member of the family, may, during the lifetime of the other spouse or, as the case may be, the spouse concerned, make one or more of the following orders, that is to say:

   (a) a periodical payments order, that is to say—

      (i) an order that either of the spouses shall make to the other spouse such periodical payments of such amount, during such periods and at such times as may be specified in the order, or

      (ii) an order that either of the spouses shall make to such person as may be so specified for the benefit of such (if any) dependent member of the family such periodical payments of such amount, during such period and at such times as may be so specified,

   (b) a secured periodical payments order, that is to say—

      (i) an order that either of the spouses shall secure, to the satisfaction of the court, to the other spouse such periodical payments of such amounts during such period and at such times as may be so specified, or

(ii) an order that either of the spouses shall secure, to the satisfaction of the court, to such person as may be so specified for the benefit of such (if any) dependent member of the family such periodical payments of such amounts, during such period and at such times as may be so specified,

(c) (i) an order that either of the spouses shall make to the other spouse a lump sum payment or lump sum payments of such amount or amounts and at such time or times as may be so specified [or][1],

(ii) an order that either of the spouses shall make to such person as may be so specified for the benefit of such (if any) dependent member of the family a lump sum payment or lump sum payments of such amount or amounts and at such time or times as may be so specified.

(2) The court may—

(a) order a spouse to pay a lump sum to the other spouse to meet any liabilities or expenses reasonably incurred by that other spouse before the making of an application by that other spouse for an order under subsection (1) in maintaining himself or herself or any dependent member of the family, or

(b) order a spouse to pay a lump sum to such person as may be specified to meet any liabilities or expenses reasonably incurred by or for the benefit of a dependent member of the family before the making of an application on behalf of the member for an order under subsection (1).

(3) An order under this section for the payment of a lump sum may provide for the payment of the lump sum by instalments of such amounts as may be specified in the order and may require the payment of the instalments to be secured to the satisfaction of the court.

(4) The period specified in an order under paragraph (a) or (b) of subsection (1) shall begin not earlier than the date of the application for the order and shall end not later than the death of [the spouse, or any dependent member of the family, in whose favour the order is made or the other spouse concerned.][1]

(5) (a) Upon the remarriage [or registration in a civil partnership][2] of the spouse in whose favour an order is made under paragraph (a) or (b) of subsection (1), the order shall, to the extent that it applies to that spouse, cease to have effect, except as respects payments due under it on the date of the remarriage [or civil partnership registration][2].

(b) If, after the grant of a decree of judicial separation, either of the spouses concerned remarries [or registers in a civil partnership][3], the court shall not, by reference to that decree, make an order under subsection (1) in favour of that spouse.

(6) (a) Where a court makes an order under subsection (1)(a), it shall in the same proceedings, subject to paragraph (b), make an attachment of earnings order (within the meaning of the Act of 1976) to secure payments under the first-mentioned order if it is satisfied that the person against whom the order is made is a person to whom earnings (within the meaning aforesaid) fall to be paid.

(b) Before deciding whether to make or refuse to make an attachment of earnings order by virtue of paragraph (a), the court shall give the spouse concerned an opportunity to make the representations specified in paragraph (c) in relation to the matter and shall have regard to any such representations made by that spouse.

(c) The representations referred to in paragraph (b) are representations relating to the questions—

    (i) whether the spouse concerned is a person to whom such earnings as aforesaid fall to be paid, and

    (ii) whether he or she would make the payments to which the relevant order under subsection (1)(a) relates.

(d) References in this subsection to an order under subsection (1)(a) include references to such an order as varied or affirmed on appeal from the court concerned or varied under section 18.

## Notes

1   Subsections (1) and (4) were amended by the Family Law (Divorce) Act 1996, s 52(a).

2   Subsection (5)(a) was amended by the Civil Partnership and Certain Rights and Obligations of Cohabitants Act 2010, s 160(a).

3   Subsection (5)(b) was amended by the Civil Partnership and Certain Rights and Obligations of Cohabitants Act 2010, s 160(b).

## 9    Property adjustment orders

(1) On granting a decree of judicial separation [or any time thereafter][1], the court, on application to it in that behalf by either of the spouses concerned or by a person on behalf of a dependent member of the family, may, during the lifetime of the other spouse or, as the case may be, the spouse concerned, make a property adjustment order, that is to say, an order providing for one or more of the following matters:

(a) the transfer by either of the spouses to the other spouse, to any dependent member of the family or to any other specified person for the benefit of such a member of specified property, being property to which the first-mentioned spouse is entitled either in possession or reversion;

(b) the settlement to the satisfaction of the court of specified property, being property to which either of the spouses is so entitled as aforesaid, for the benefit of the other spouse and of any dependent member of the family or of any or all of those persons;

(c) the variation for the benefit of either of the spouses and of any dependent member of the family or of any or all of those persons of any ante-nuptial or post-nuptial settlement (including such a settlement made by will or codicil) made on the spouses;

(d) the extinguishment or reduction of the interest of either of the spouses under any such settlement.

(2) An order under paragraph (b), (c) or (d) may restrict to a specified extent or exclude the application of section 18 in relation to the order.

(3) If, after the grant of a decree of judicial separation, either of the spouses concerned remarries [or registers in a civil partnership][2], the court shall not, by reference to that decree, make a property adjustment order in favour of that spouse.

(4) Where a property adjustment order is made in relation to land, a copy of the order certified to be a true copy by the registrar or clerk of the court concerned shall, as appropriate, be lodged by him or her in the Land Registry for registration pursuant to section 69(1)(h) of the Registration of Title Act, 1964, in a register maintained under that Act or be registered in the Registry of Deeds.

[(4A) Where a property adjustment order lodged under subsection (4) and registered pursuant to section 69(1)(h) of the Registration of Title Act 1964 or in the Registry of Deeds has been complied with, the Property Registration Authority shall, on being satisfied that the order has been complied with—

(a) cancel the entry made in the register under the Registration of Title Act 1964, or

(b) note compliance with the order in the Registry of Deeds.][3]

(5) Where—

(a) a person is directed by an order under this section to execute a deed or other instrument in relation to land, and

(b) the person refuses or neglects to comply with the direction or, for any other reason, the court considers it necessary to do so,

the court may order another person to execute the deed or instrument in the name of the first-mentioned person; and a deed or other instrument executed by a person in the name of another person pursuant to an order under this subsection shall be as valid as if it had been executed by that other person.

(6) Any costs incurred in complying with a property adjustment order shall be borne, as the court may determine, by either of the spouses concerned, or by both of them in such proportions as the court may determine, and shall be so borne in such manner as the court may determine.

(7) This section shall not apply in relation to a family home in which, following the grant of a decree of judicial separation either of the spouses concerned, having remarried, ordinarily resides with his or her spouse.[4]

---

**Notes**

1  Subsection (1) was amended by the Family Law (Divorce) Act 1996, s 52(b).

2  Subsection (3) was amended by the Civil Partnership and Certain Rights and Obligations of Cohabitants Act 2010, s 161.

3  Subsection (4A) inserted by Civil Law (Miscellaneous Provisions) Act 2008, s 74(a).

4    See Registration of Deeds Rules 2008, rule 14(2), Land Registration Rules 2009, rule 5 and Registration of Deeds Rules 2009, rule 3.

## 10    Miscellaneous

(1) On granting a decree of judicial separation [or at any time thereafter][1], the court, on application to it in that behalf by either of the spouses concerned or by a person on behalf of a dependent member of the family, may, during the lifetime of the other spouse or, as the case may be, the spouse concerned, make one or more of the following orders:

(a) an order—

    (i) providing for the conferral on one spouse either for life or for such other period (whether definite or contingent) as the court may specify the right to occupy the family home to the exclusion of the other spouse, or

    (ii) directing the sale of the family home subject to such conditions (if any) as the court considers proper and providing for the disposal of the proceeds of the sale between the spouses and any other person having an interest therein,

(b) an order under section 36,

(c) an order under section 4, 5, 7 or 9 of the Family Home Protection Act, 1976,

(d) [an order under section 2, 3, 4 or 5 of the Act of 1996,][2]

(e) an order [under section 31 of the Land and Conveyancing Law Reform Act 2009][3],

(f) an order under section 11 of the Act of 1964.

(2) The court, in exercising its jurisdiction under subsection (1)(a), shall have regard to the welfare of the spouses and any dependent member of the family and, in particular, shall take into consideration—

(a) that, where a decree of judicial separation is granted, it is not possible for the spouses concerned to continue to reside together, and

(b) that proper and secure accommodation should, where practicable, be provided for a spouse who is wholly or mainly dependent on the other spouse and for any dependent member of the family.

[(3) Subsection (1)(a) shall not apply in relation to a family home in which, following the grant of a decree of judicial separation, either of the spouses concerned, having remarried, ordinarily resides with his or her spouse.][1]

### Notes

1    Subsection (1) was amended and subsection (3) was inserted by the Family Law (Divorce) Act 1996, s 52(c).

2    Subsection (1)(d) was amended and substituted by the Domestic Violence Act 1996, s 21(c).

3   Subsection (1)(e) was amended by the Land and Conveyancing Law Reform Act 2009, schedule 1.

---

## 11     Financial compensation orders

(1) Subject to the provisions of this section, on granting a decree of judicial separation or at any time thereafter, the court, on application to it in that behalf by either of the spouses concerned or by a person on behalf of a dependent member of the family, may, during the lifetime of the other spouse or, as the case may be, the spouse concerned, if it considers—

> (a) that the financial security of the spouse making the application ("the applicant") or the dependent member of the family ("the member") can be provided for either wholly or in part by so doing, or

> (b) that the forfeiture, by reason of the decree of judicial separation, by the applicant or the dependent, as the case may be, of the opportunity or possibility of acquiring a benefit (for example, a benefit under a pension scheme) can be compensated for wholly or in part by so doing,

make a financial compensation order, that is to say, an order requiring either or both of the spouses to do one or more of the following:

> (i)   to effect such a policy of life insurance for the benefit of the applicant or the member as may be specified in the order,

> (ii)  to assign the whole or a specified part of the interest of either or both of the spouses in a policy of life insurance effected by either or both of the spouses to the applicant or to such person as may be specified in the order for the benefit of the member,

> (iii) to make or to continue to make to the person by whom a policy of life insurance is or was issued the payments which either or both of the spouses is or are required to make under the terms of the policy.

(2) (a) The court may make a financial compensation order in addition to or in substitution in whole or in part for orders under sections 8 to 10 and 12 and in deciding whether or not to make such an order it shall have regard to whether [proper provision, having regard to the circumstances][1] exists or can be made for the spouse concerned or the dependent member of the family concerned by orders under those sections.

> (b) An order under this section shall cease to have effect on the remarriage, [registration in a civil partnership][2] or death of the applicant in so far as it relates to the applicant.

> (c) The court shall not make an order under this section if the spouse who is applying for the order has remarried [or registered in a civil partnership][3].

> (d) An order under section 18 in relation to an order under paragraph (i) or (ii) of subsection (1) may make such provision (if any) as the court considers appropriate in relation to the disposal of—

(i)  an amount representing any accumulated value of the insurance policy effected pursuant to the order under the said paragraph (i), or

(ii)  the interest or the part of the interest to which the order under the said paragraph (ii) relates.

**Notes**

1  Subsection (2)(a) was amended by the Family Law (Divorce) Act 1996, s 52(d).

2  Subsection (2)(b) was amended by the Civil Partnership and Certain Rights and Obligations of Cohabitants Act 2010, s 162(a).

3  Subsection (2)(c) was amended by the Civil Partnership and Certain Rights and Obligations of Cohabitants Act 2010, s 162(b).

**12  Pension adjustment orders**

(1) In this section, save where the context otherwise requires—

**"the Act of 1990"** means the Pensions Act, 1990;

**"active member"**, in relation to a scheme, means a member of the scheme who is in reckonable service;

**"actuarial value"** means the equivalent cash value of a benefit (including, where appropriate, provision for any revaluation of such benefit) under a scheme calculated by reference to appropriate financial assumptions and making due allowance for the probability of survival to normal pensionable age and thereafter in accordance with normal life expectancy on the assumption that the member concerned of the scheme, at the effective date of calculation, is in a normal state of health having regard to his or her age;

**"approved arrangement"**, in relation to the trustees of a scheme, means an arrangement whereby the trustees, on behalf of the person for whom the arrangement is made, effect policies or contracts of insurance that are approved of by the Revenue Commissioners with, and make the appropriate payments under the policies or contracts to, one or more undertakings;

**"contingent benefit"** means a benefit payable under a scheme, other than a payment under subsection (7) to or for one or more of the following, that is to say, the widow or the widower and any dependants of the member spouse concerned and the personal representative of the member spouse, if the member spouse dies while in relevant employment and before attaining any normal pensionable age provided for under the rules of the scheme;

["**defined contribution scheme**" has the same meaning as in the Pensions Act 1990;][1]

**"designated benefit"**, in relation to a pension adjustment order, means an amount determined by the trustees of the scheme concerned, in accordance with relevant guidelines, and by reference to the period and the percentage of the retirement benefit specified in the order concerned under subsection (2);

"**member spouse**", in relation to a scheme, means a spouse who is a member of the scheme;

"**normal pensionable age**" means the earliest age at which a member of a scheme is entitled to receive benefits under the rules of the scheme on retirement from relevant employment, disregarding any such rules providing for early retirement on grounds of ill health or otherwise;

"**occupational pension scheme**" has the meaning assigned to it by section 2(1) of the Act of 1990;

"**reckonable service**" means service in relevant employment during membership of any scheme;

"**relevant guidelines**" means any relevant guidelines for the time being in force under [paragraph (c) or (cc) of section 10(1)]² of the Act of 1990;

"**relevant employment**", in relation to a scheme, means any employment (or any period treated as employment) or any period of self employment to which a scheme applies;

"**retirement benefit**", in relation to a scheme, means all benefits (other than contingent benefits) payable under the scheme;

"**rules**", in relation to a scheme, means the provisions of the scheme, by whatever name called;

"**scheme**" means a pension scheme;

"**transfer amount**" shall be construed in accordance with subsection (4);

"**undertaking**" has the meaning assigned to it by the Insurance Act, 1989.

(2) Subject to the provisions of this section, where a decree of judicial separation ("the decree") has been granted, the court, if it so thinks fit, may, in relation to retirement benefit under a scheme of which one of the spouses concerned is a member, on application to it in that behalf at the time of the making of the order for the decree or at any time thereafter during the lifetime of the member spouse by either of the spouses or by a person on behalf of a dependent member of the family, make an order providing for the payment, in accordance with the provisions of this section, to either of the following, as the court may determine, that is to say:

(a) the other spouse and, in the case of the death of that spouse, his or her personal representative, and

(b) such person as may be specified in the order for the benefit of a person who is, and for so long only as he or she remains, a dependent member of the family,

of a benefit consisting, either, as the court may determine, of the whole, or such part as the court considers appropriate, of that part of the retirement benefit that is payable (or which, but for the making of the order for the decree, would have been payable) under the scheme and has accrued at the time of the making of the order for the decree and, for the purpose of determining the benefit, the order shall specify—

(i) the period of reckonable service of the member spouse prior to the granting of the decree to be taken into account, and

(ii)  the percentage of the retirement benefit accrued during that period to be paid to the person referred to in paragraph (a) or (b), as the case may be.

(3) Subject to the provisions of this section, where a decree of judicial separation ("the decree") has been granted, the court, if it so thinks fit, may, in relation to a contingent benefit under a scheme of which one of the spouses concerned is a member, on application to it in that behalf not more than one year after the making of the order for the decree by either of the spouses or by a person on behalf of a dependent member of the family concerned, make an order providing for the payment, upon the death of the member spouse, to either of the following, or to both of them in such proportions as the court may determine, that is to say:

(a)  the other spouse, and

(b)  such person as may be specified in the order for the benefit of a dependent member of the family,

of, either, as the court may determine, the whole, or such part (expressed as a percentage) as the court considers appropriate, of that part of any contingent benefit that is payable (or which, but for the making of the order for the decree, would have been payable) under the scheme.

(4) Where the court makes an order under subsection (2) in favour of a spouse and payment of the designated benefit concerned has not commenced, the spouse in whose favour the order is made shall be entitled to the application in accordance with subsection (5) of an amount of money from the scheme concerned (in this section referred to as a "transfer amount") equal to the value of the designated benefit, such amount being determined by the trustees of the scheme in accordance with relevant guidelines.

(5) Subject to subsection (17), where the court makes an order under subsection (2) in favour of a spouse and payment of the designated benefit concerned has not commenced, the trustees of the scheme concerned shall, for the purpose of giving effect to the order—

(a)  on application to them in that behalf at the time of the making of the order or at any time thereafter by the spouse in whose favour the order was made ("the spouse"), and

(b)  on the furnishing to them by the spouse of such information as they may reasonably require,

apply in accordance with relevant guidelines the transfer amount calculated in accordance with those guidelines either—

(i)  if the trustees and the spouse so agree, in providing a benefit for or in respect of the spouse under the scheme aforesaid that is of the same actuarial value as the transfer amount concerned, or

(ii)  in making a payment either to—

(I)  such other occupational pension scheme, being a scheme the trustees of which agree to accept the payment, or

(II)   in the discharge of any payment falling to be made by the trustees under any such other approved arrangement,

as may be determined by the spouse.

(6) Subject to subsection (17), where the court makes an order under subsection (2) in relation to a defined contribution scheme and an application has not been brought under subsection (5), the trustees of the scheme may, for the purpose of giving effect to the order, if they so think fit, apply in accordance with relevant guidelines the transfer amount calculated in accordance with those guidelines in making a payment to—

(a)   such other occupational pension scheme, being a scheme the trustees of which agree to accept the payment, or

(b)   in the discharge of any payment falling to be made by the trustees under such other approved arrangement,

as may be determined by the trustees.

(7) Subject to subsection (17), where—

(a)   the court makes an order under subsection (2), and

(b)   the member spouse concerned dies before payment of the designated benefit concerned has commenced,

the trustees shall, for the purpose of giving effect to the order, within 3 months of the death of the member spouse, provide for the payment to the person in whose favour the order is made of an amount that is equal to the transfer amount calculated in accordance with relevant guidelines.

(8) Subject to subsection (17), where—

(a)   the court makes an order under subsection (2), and

(b)   the member spouse concerned ceases to be a member of the scheme otherwise than on death,

the trustees may, for the purpose of giving effect to the order, if they so think fit, apply, in accordance with relevant guidelines, the transfer amount calculated in accordance with those guidelines either, as the trustees may determine—

(i)   if the trustees and the person in whose favour the order is made ("the person") so agree, in providing a benefit for or in respect of the person under the scheme aforesaid that is of the same actuarial value as the transfer amount concerned, or

(ii)   in making a payment, either to—

(I)   such other occupational pension scheme, being a scheme the trustees of which agree to accept the payment, or

(II)   in the discharge of any payment falling to be made under such other approved arrangement,

as may be determined by the trustees.

(9) Subject to subsection (17), where—

(a) the court makes an order under subsection (2) in favour of a spouse ("the spouse"), and

(b) the spouse dies before payment of the designated benefit has commenced,

the trustees shall, within 3 months of the death of the spouse, provide for the payment to the personal representative of the spouse of an amount equal to the transfer amount calculated in accordance with relevant guidelines.

(10) Subject to subsection (17), where—

(a) the court makes an order under subsection (2) in favour of a spouse ("the spouse"), and

(b) the spouse dies after payment of the designated benefit has commenced,

the trustees shall, within 3 months of the death of the spouse, provide for the payment to the personal representative of the spouse of an amount equal to the actuarial value, calculated in accordance with relevant guidelines, of the part of the designated benefit which, but for the death of the spouse, would have been payable to the spouse during the lifetime of the member spouse.

(11) Where—

(a) the court makes an order under subsection (2) for the benefit of a dependent member of the family ("the person"), and

(b) the person dies before payment of the designated benefit has commenced,

the order shall cease to have effect in so far as it relates to that person.

(12) Where—

(a) the court makes an order under subsection (2) or (3) in relation to an occupational pension scheme, and

(b) the trustees of the scheme concerned have not applied the transfer amount concerned in accordance with subsection (5), (6), (7), (8) or (9), and

(c) after the making of the order, the member spouse ceases to be an active member of the scheme,

the trustees shall, within 12 months of the cessation, notify the registrar or clerk of the court concerned and the other spouse of the cessation.

(13) Where the trustees of a scheme apply a transfer amount under subsection (6) or (8), they shall notify the spouse (not being the spouse who is the member spouse) or other person concerned and the registrar or clerk of the court concerned of the application and shall give to that spouse or other person concerned particulars of the scheme or undertaking concerned and of the transfer amount.

(14) Where the court makes an order under subsection (2) or (3) for the payment of a designated benefit or a contingent benefit, as the case may be, the benefit shall be payable or the transfer amount concerned applied out of the resources of the scheme concerned and, unless otherwise provided for in the order or relevant guidelines, shall be

payable in accordance with the rules of the scheme or, as the case may be, applied in accordance with relevant guidelines.

(15) Where the court makes an order under subsection (2), the amount of the retirement benefit payable, in accordance with the rules of the scheme concerned to, or to or in respect of, the member spouse shall be reduced by the amount of the designated benefit payable pursuant to the order.

(16)(a)   Where the court makes an order under subsection (3), the amount of the contingent benefit payable, in accordance with the rules of the scheme concerned in respect of the member spouse shall be reduced by an amount equal to the contingent benefit payable pursuant to the order.

   (b)   Where the court makes an order under subsection (2) and the member spouse concerned dies before payment of the designated benefit concerned has commenced, the amount of the contingent benefit payable in respect of the member spouse in accordance with the rules of the scheme concerned shall be reduced by the amount of the payment made under subsection (7).

(17) Where, pursuant to an order under subsection (2), the trustees of a scheme make a payment or apply a transfer amount under subsections (5), (6), (7), (8), (9) or (10), they shall be discharged from any obligation to make any further payment or apply any transfer amount under any other of those subsections in respect of the benefit payable pursuant to the order.

(18) A person who makes an application under subsection (2) or (3) or an application for an order under section 18(2) in relation to an order under subsection (2) shall give notice thereof to the trustees of the scheme concerned and, in deciding whether to make the order concerned and in determining the provisions of the order, the court shall have regard to any representations made by any person to whom notice of the application has been given under this section or section [40][3].

(19) An order under subsection (3), shall cease to have effect on the death or remarriage [or registration in a civil partnership][4] of the person in whose favour it was made in so far as it relates to that person.

(20) The court may, in a pension adjustment order or by order made under this subsection after the making of a pension adjustment order, give to the trustees of the scheme concerned such directions as it considers appropriate for the purposes of the pension adjustment order including directions compliance with which occasions non-compliance with the rules of the scheme concerned or the Act of 1990; and a trustee of a scheme shall not be liable in any court or other tribunal for any loss or damage caused by his or her non-compliance with the rules of the scheme or with the Act of 1990 if the non-compliance was occasioned by his or her compliance with a direction of the court under this section.

(21) The registrar or clerk of the court concerned shall cause a copy of a pension adjustment order to be served on the trustees of the scheme concerned.

(22)(a)   Any costs incurred by the trustees of a scheme under subsection (18) or in complying with a pension adjustment order or a direction under subsection (20) or (25) shall be borne, as the court may determine, by the member spouse or by the other person concerned or by both of them in such proportion as the court may determine and, in the absence of such determination, those costs shall be borne by them equally.

(b) Where a person fails to pay an amount in accordance with paragraph (a) to the trustees of the scheme concerned, the court may, on application to it in that behalf by the trustees, order that the amount be deducted from the amount of any benefit payable to the person under the scheme or pursuant to an order under subsection (2) or (3) and be paid to the trustees.

(23)(a) The court shall not make a pension adjustment order if the spouse who applies for the order has remarried [or registered in a civil partnership][5].

(b) The court may make a pension adjustment order in addition to or in substitution in whole or in part for an order or orders under section 8, 9, 10 or 11 and, in deciding whether or not to make a pension adjustment order, the court shall have regard to the question whether [proper provision, having regard to the circumstances][6] exists or can be made for the spouse concerned or the dependent member of the family concerned by an order or orders under any of those sections.

(24) Section 54 of the Act of 1990 and any regulations under that section shall apply with any necessary modifications to a scheme if proceedings for the grant of a decree of judicial separation to which a member spouse is a party have been instituted and shall continue to apply notwithstanding the grant of a decree of judicial separation in the proceedings.

(25) For the purposes of this Act, the court may, of its own motion, and shall, if so requested by either of the spouses concerned or any other person concerned, direct the trustees of the scheme concerned to provide the spouses or that other person and the court, within a specified period of time—

(a) with a calculation of the value and the amount, determined in accordance with relevant guidelines, of the retirement benefit, or contingent benefit, concerned that is payable (or which, but for the making of the order for the decree of judicial separation concerned, would have been payable) under the scheme and has accrued at the time of the making of that order, and

(b) with a calculation of the amount of the contingent benefit concerned that is payable (or which, but for the making of the order for the decree of judicial separation concerned, would have been payable) under the scheme.

(26) An order under this section may restrict to a specified extent or exclude the application of section 18 in relation to the order.

---

**Notes**

1    Definition of "defined contribution scheme" was inserted by Social Welfare and Pensions Act 2008, s 30.

2    Subsection (1) was amended by the Family Law (Divorce) Act 1996, s 52(e)(i).

3　Subsection (18) was amended by the Family Law (Divorce) Act 1996, s 52(e)(ii).

4　Subsection 19 was amended by the Civil Partnership and Certain Rights and Obligations of Cohabitants Act 2010, s 163(a).

5　Subsection 23(a) was amended by the Civil Partnership and Certain Rights and Obligations of Cohabitants Act 2010, s 163(b).

6　Subsection 23(b) was amended by the Family Law (Divorce) Act 1996, s 52(d).

---

## 13　Preservation of pension entitlement after judicial separation

(1) Subject to the provisions of this section, on granting a decree of judicial separation or at any time thereafter, the court may, in relation to a pension scheme, on application to it in that behalf by either of the spouses concerned, make during the lifetime of the spouse who is a member of the scheme ("the member spouse") an order directing the trustees of the scheme not to regard the separation of the spouses resulting from the decree as a ground for disqualifying the other spouse for the receipt of a benefit under the scheme a condition for the receipt of which is that the spouses should be residing together at the time the benefit becomes payable.

(2) Notice of an application under subsection (1) shall be given by the spouse concerned to the trustees of the pension scheme concerned and, in deciding whether to make an order under subsection (1), the court shall have regard to any representations made by any person to whom notice of the application has been given under this section or section 40.

(3) Any costs incurred by the trustees of a pension scheme under subsection (2) or in complying with an order under subsection (1) shall be borne, as the court may determine, by either of the spouses concerned or by both of the spouses and in such proportion and manner as the court may determine.

(4) The court may make an order under this section in addition to or in substitution in whole or in part for orders under sections 8 to 11 and, in deciding whether or not to make such an order, it shall have regard to the question whether adequate and reasonable financial provision exists or can be made for the spouse concerned by orders under those sections.

## 14　Orders extinguishing succession rights on judicial separation

On granting a decree of judicial separation or at any time thereafter, the court may, on application to it in that behalf by either of the spouses concerned, make an order extinguishing the share that either of the spouses would otherwise be entitled to in the estate of the other spouse as a legal right or on intestacy under the Act of 1965 if—

(a) it is satisfied that adequate and reasonable financial provision exists or can be made under section 8, 9, 10(1)(a), 11, 12 or 13 for the spouse whose succession rights are in question ("the spouse concerned"),

(b) the spouse concerned is a spouse for the support of whom the court refused to make an order under section 8, 9, 10(1)(a), 11, 12 or 13, or

(c) it is satisfied that the spouse concerned is not a spouse for whose benefit the court would, if an application were made to it in that behalf, make an order under section 8, 9, 10(1)(a), 11, 12 or 13.

## 15 Orders for sale of property

(1) Where the court makes a secured periodical payments order, a lump sum order or a property adjustment order, thereupon, or at any time thereafter, it may make an order directing the sale of such property as may be specified in the order, being property in which, or in the proceeds of sale of which, either or both of the spouses concerned has or have a beneficial interest, either in possession or reversion.

(2) The jurisdiction conferred on the court by subsection (1) shall not be so exercised as to affect a right to occupy the family home of the spouse concerned that is enjoyed by virtue of an order under this Part.

(3) (a) An order under subsection 11 may contain such consequential or supplementary provisions as the court considers appropriate.

 (b) Without prejudice to the generality of paragraph (a), an order under subsection (1) may contain—

   (i) a provision specifying the manner of sale and some or all of the conditions applying to the sale of the property to which the order relates,

   (ii) a provision requiring any such property to be offered for sale to a person, or a class of persons, specified in the order,

   (iii) a provision directing that the order, or a specified part of it, shall not take effect until the occurrence of a specified event or the expiration of a specified period,

   (iv) a provision requiring the making of a payment or payments (whether periodical payments or lump sum payments) to a specified person or persons out of the proceeds of the sale of the property to which the order relates, and

   (v) a provision specifying the manner in which the proceeds of the sale of the property concerned shall be disposed of between the following persons or such of them as the court considers appropriate, that is to say, the spouses concerned and any other person having an interest therein.

(4) A provision in an order under subsection (1) providing for the making of periodical payments to one of the spouses concerned out of the proceeds of the sale of property shall, on the death or remarriage [or registration in a civil partnership][1] of that spouse, cease to have effect except as respects payments due on the date of the death or remarriage [or civil partnership registration][1].

(5) Where a spouse has a beneficial interest in any property, or in the proceeds of the sale of any property, and a person (not being the other spouse) also has a beneficial interest in that property or those proceeds, then, in considering whether to make an order under this section or section 9 or [10(1)(a)][2] in relation to that property or those proceeds, the court shall give to that person an opportunity to make representations with respect to the making of the order and the contents thereof, and any representations

made by such a person shall be deemed to be included among the matters to which the court is required to have regard under section 16 in any relevant proceedings under a provision referred to in that section after the making of those representations.

[(6) This section shall not apply in relation to a family home in which, following the grant of a decree of judicial separation either of the spouses concerned, having remarried, ordinarily resides with his or her spouse.]²

---

**Notes**

1 Subsection (4) was amended by the Civil Partnership and Certain Rights and Obligations of Cohabitants Act 2010, s 164.

2 Subsection (5) was amended and subsection (6) was inserted by the Family Law Divorce Act 1996, s 52(f).

---

**[15A  Orders for provision for spouse out of estate of other spouse**

(1) Subject to the provisions of this section, where, following the grant of a decree of judicial separation, a court makes an order under section 14 in relation to the spouses concerned and one of the spouses dies, the court, on application to it in that behalf by the other spouse ("the applicant") not more that six months after representation is first granted under the Act of 1965 in respect of the estate of the deceased spouse, may by order make such provision for the applicant out of the estate of the deceased spouse as it considers appropriate having regard to the rights of any other person having an interest in the matter and specifies in the order if it is satisfied that proper provision in the circumstances was not made for the applicant during the lifetime of the deceased spouse under section 8, 9, 10(1)(a), 11 or 12 for any reason (other than conduct referred to in subsection (2)(i) of section 16 of the applicant).

(2) The court shall not make an order under this section if the applicant concerned has remarried [or registered in a civil partnership]¹ since the granting of the decree of judicial separation concerned.

(3) In considering whether to make an order under this section the court shall have regard to all the circumstances of the case including—

(a)  any order under paragraph (c) of section 8(1) or a property adjustment order in favour of the applicant, and

(b)  any devise or bequest made by the deceased spouse to the applicant.

(4) The provision made for the applicant concerned by an order under this section together with any provision made for the applicant by an order referred to in subsection (3)(a) (the value of which for the purposes of this subsection shall be its value on the date of the order) shall not exceed in total the share (if any) of the applicant in the estate of the deceased spouse to which the applicant was entitled or (if the deceased spouse died intestate as to the whole or part of his or her estate) would have been entitled under the Act of 1965 if the court had not made an order under section 14.

(5) Notice of an application under this section shall be given by the applicant to the spouse (if any) of the deceased spouse concerned and to such (if any) other persons as the court may direct and, in deciding whether to make the order concerned and in determining the provisions of the order, the court shall have regard to any representations made by the spouse of the deceased spouse and any other such persons as aforesaid.

(6) The personal representative of a deceased spouse in respect of whom a decree of judicial separation has been granted shall make a reasonable attempt to ensure that notice of his or her death is brought to the attention of the other spouse concerned and, where an application is made under this section, the personal representative of the deceased spouse shall not, without the leave of the court, distribute any of the estate of that spouse until the court makes or refuses to make an order under this section.

(7) Where the personal representative of a deceased spouse in respect of whom a decree of judicial separation has been granted gives notice of his or her death to the other spouse concerned ("the spouse") and—

    (a)   the spouse intends to apply to the court for an order under this section,

    (b)   the spouse has applied for such an order and the application is pending, or

    (c)   an order has been made under this section in favour of the spouse,

the spouse shall, not later than one month after receipt of the notice, notify the personal representative of such intention, application or order, as the case may be and, if he or she does not do so, the personal representative shall be at liberty to distribute the assets of the deceased spouse, or any part thereof, amongst the parties entitled thereto.

(8) The personal representative shall not be liable to the spouse for the assets or any part thereof so distributed unless, at the time of such distribution he or she had notice of the intention, application or order aforesaid.

(9) Nothing in subsection (7) or (8) shall prejudice the right of the spouse to follow such assets into the hands of any person who may have received them.

(10) On granting a decree of judicial separation or at any time thereafter, the court, on application to it in that behalf by either of the spouses concerned, may, during the lifetime of the other spouse or, as the case may be, the spouse concerned, if it considers it just to do so, make an order that either or both spouses shall not, on the death of either of them, be entitled to apply for an order under this section.]²

---

**Notes**

1    Section 15A(2) was amended by the Civil Partnership and Certain Rights and Obligations of Cohabitants Act 2010, s 165.

2    Section 15A was inserted by the Family Law (Divorce) Act 1996, s 52(g).

---

**16     Provisions relating to certain orders under sections 7 to 13 and 18**

(1) In deciding whether to make an order under sections 7, 8, 9, 10(1)(a), 11, 12, 13, 14, [15A][1], 18 or 25 and in determining the provisions of such an order, the court shall endeavour to ensure that such provision [exists or will be made][1] for each spouse concerned and for any dependent member of the family concerned as is [proper][1] having regard to all the circumstances of the case.

(2) Without prejudice to the generality of subsection (1), in deciding whether to make such an order as aforesaid and in determining the provisions of such an order, the court shall, in particular, have regard to the following matters—

  (a) the income, earning capacity, property and other financial resources which each of the spouses concerned has or is likely to have in the foreseeable future,

  (b) the financial needs, obligations and responsibilities which each of the spouses has or is likely to have in the foreseeable future (whether in the case of the remarriage of the spouse or otherwise),

  (c) the standard of living enjoyed by the family concerned before the proceedings were instituted or before the spouses separated, as the case may be,

  (d) the age of each of the spouses and the length of time during which the spouses lived together,

  (e) any physical or mental disability of either of the spouses,

  (f) the contributions which each of the spouses has made or is likely in the foreseeable future to make to the welfare of the family, including any contribution made by each of them to the income, earning capacity, property and financial resources of the other spouse and any contribution made by either of them by looking after the home or caring for the family,

  (g) the effect on the earning capacity of each of the spouses of the marital responsibilities assumed by each during the period when they lived together and, in particular, the degree to which the future earning capacity of a spouse is impaired by reason of that spouse having relinquished or foregone the opportunity of remunerative activity in order to look after the home or care for the family,

  (h) any income or benefits to which either of the spouses is entitled by or under statute,

  (i) the conduct of each of the spouses, if that conduct is such that in the opinion of the court it would in all the circumstances of the case be unjust to disregard it,

  (j) the accommodation needs of either of the spouses,

  (k) the value to each of the spouses of any benefit (for example, a benefit under a pension scheme) which by reason of the decree of judicial separation concerned that spouse will forfeit the opportunity or possibility of acquiring,

  (l) the rights of any person other than the spouses but including a person to whom either spouse is remarried.

(3) (a) The court shall not make an order under a provision referred to in subsection (1) for the support of a spouse if the spouse had deserted the other spouse before the institution of proceedings for the decree or, as the case may be, a decree, specified in that provision and had continued such desertion up to the time of the institution of such proceedings unless, having regard to all the circumstances of the case (including the conduct of the other spouse), the court is of opinion that it would be unjust not to make the order.

(b) A spouse who, with just cause, leaves and lives apart from the other spouse because of conduct on the part of that other spouse shall not be regarded for the purposes of paragraph (a) as having deserted that spouse.

(4) Without prejudice to the generality of subsection (1), in deciding whether to make an order referred to in that subsection in favour of a dependent member of the family concerned and in determining the provisions of such an order, the court shall, in particular, have regard to the following matters:

(a) the financial needs of the member,

(b) the income, earning capacity (if any), property and other financial resources of the member,

(c) any physical or mental disability of the member,

(d) any income or benefits to which the member is entitled by or under statute,

(e) the manner in which the member was being and in which the spouses concerned anticipated that the member would be educated or trained,

(f) the matters specified in paragraphs (a), (b) and (c) of subsection (2),

(g) the accommodation needs of the member.

(5) The court shall not make an order under a provision referred to in subsection (1) unless it would be in the interests of justice to do so.

(6) In this section **"desertion"** includes conduct on the part of one of the spouses concerned that results in the other spouse, with just cause, leaving and living apart from the first-mentioned spouse.

---

**Notes**

1    Subsection (1) was amended by the Family Law (Divorce) Act 1996, s 52(h).

---

**17      Retrospective periodical payments orders**

(1) Where, having regard to all the circumstances of the case, the court considers it appropriate to do so, it may, in a periodical payments order, direct that—

(a) the period in respect of which payments under the order shall be made shall begin on such date before the date of the order, not being earlier than the time of the institution of the proceedings concerned for the grant of a decree of judicial separation, as may be specified in the order,

(b) any payments under the order in respect of a period before the date of the order be paid in one sum and before a specified date, and

(c) there be deducted from any payments referred to in paragraph (b) made to the spouse concerned an amount equal to the amount of such (if any) payments made to that spouse by the other spouse as the court may determine, being payments made during the period between the making of the order for the grant of the decree aforesaid and the institution of the proceedings aforesaid.

(2) The jurisdiction conferred on the court by subsection (1)(b) is without prejudice to the generality of section 8(1)(c).

**18      Variation, etc of certain orders under this Part**

(1) This section applies to the following orders—

(a) a maintenance pending suit order,

(b) a periodical payments order,

(c) a secured periodical payments order,

(d) a lump sum order if and in so far as it provides for the payment of the lump sum concerned by instalments or requires the payment of any such instalments to be secured,

(e) an order under paragraph (b), (c) or (d) of section 9(1) in so far as such application is not restricted or excluded pursuant to section 9(2),

(f) an order under subparagraph (i) or (ii) of section 10(1)(a),

(g) a financial compensation order,

(h) an order under subsection (2) of section 12, [in so far as such application is not restricted or excluded by section 12(26)][1],

(i) an order under section 13,

(j) an order under this section.

(2) Subject to the provisions of this section and section 16 and any restriction pursuant to section 9(2) and without prejudice to section 11(2)(d), the court may, on application to it in that behalf by either of the spouses concerned or, in the case of the death of either of the spouses, by any other person who, in the opinion of the court, has a sufficient interest in the matter or by a person on behalf of a dependent member of the family concerned, if it considers it proper to do so having regard to any change in the circumstances of the case and to any new evidence, by order vary or discharge an order to which this section applies, suspend any provision of such an order or any provision of such an order temporarily, revive the operation of such an order or provision so suspended, further vary an order previously varied under this section or further suspend or revive the operation of an order or provision previously suspended or revived under this section; and, without prejudice to the generality of the foregoing, an order under this section may require the divesting of any property vested in a person under or by virtue of an order to which this section applies.

(3) Without prejudice to the generality of section 7 or 8, that part of an order to which this section applies which provides for the making of payments for the support of a dependent member of the family shall stand discharged if the member ceases to be a dependent member of the family by reason of his or her attainment of the age of 18 years or 23 years, as may be appropriate, and shall be discharged by the court, on application to it under subsection (2), if it is satisfied that the member has for any reason ceased to be a dependent member of the family.

(4) The power of the court under subsection (2) to make an order varying, discharging or suspending an order referred to in subsection (1)(e) shall be subject to any restriction or exclusion specified in that order and shall (subject to the limitation aforesaid) be a power—

(a) to vary the settlement to which the order relates in any person's favour or to extinguish or reduce any person's interest under that settlement, and

(b) to make such supplemental provision (including a further property adjustment order or a lump sum order) as the court thinks appropriate in consequence of any variation, extinguishment or reduction made pursuant to paragraph (a),

and section 15 shall apply to a case where the court makes such an order as aforesaid under subsection (2) as it applies to a case where the court makes a property adjustment order with any necessary modifications.

(5) The court shall not make an order under subsection (2) in relation to an order referred to in subsection (1)(e) unless it appears to it that the order will not prejudice the interests of any person who—

(a) has acquired any right or interest in consequence of the order referred to in subsection (1)(e), and

(b) is not a party to the marriage concerned or a dependent member of the family concerned.

(6) This section shall apply, with any necessary modifications, to instruments executed pursuant to orders to which this section applies as it applies to those orders.

(7) Where the court makes an order under subsection (2) in relation to a property adjustment order relating to land a copy of the order under subsection (2) certified to be a true copy by the registrar or clerk of the court concerned shall, as appropriate, be lodged by him or her in the Land Registry for registration pursuant to section 69(1)(h) of the Registration of Title Act, 1964, in a register maintained under that Act or be registered in the Registry of Deeds.

[(8) Where a property adjustment order lodged under section 9(4) and duly registered pursuant to section 69(1)(h) of the Registration of Title Act 1964 is varied, discharged, suspended or revived by an order under subsection (2) and the second-mentioned order has been duly lodged for such registration pursuant to subsection (7), the Property Registration Authority shall—

(a) amend or cancel the entry made in the register, pursuant to section 9(4), under the Registration of Title Act 1964 accordingly, or

(b) note the position in the Registry of Deeds.][2]

**Notes**

1   Subsection (1)(h) was amended by the Family Law (Divorce) Act 1996, s 52(i).

2   Subsection (8) inserted by Civil Law (Miscellaneous Provisions) Act 2008, s 74(b).

**19      Restriction in relation to orders for benefit of dependent members of the family**

In deciding whether—

(a)  to include in an order under section 7 a provision requiring the making of periodical payments for the benefit of a dependent member of the family,

(b)  to make an order under paragraph (a)(ii), (b)(ii) or (c)(ii) of section 8(1),

(c)  to make an order under section 18 varying, discharging or suspending a provision referred to in paragraph (a) or an order referred to in paragraph (b),

the court shall not have regard to conduct by the spouse or spouses concerned of the kind specified in subsection (2)(i) of section 16 or desertion referred to in subsection (3) of that section.

**20      Transmission of periodical payments through District Court clerk**

Notwithstanding anything in this Act, section 9 of the Act of 1976 shall apply in relation to an order ("the relevant order"), being a maintenance pending suit order, a periodical payments order or a secured periodical payments order or any such order as aforesaid as affected by an order under section 18, with the modifications that—

(a)  the reference in subsection (4) of the said section 9 to the maintenance creditor shall be construed as a reference to the person to whom payments under the relevant order concerned are required to be made,

(b)  the other references in the said section 9 to the maintenance creditor shall be construed as references to the person on whose application the relevant order was made, and

(c)  the reference in subsection (3) of the said section 9 to the maintenance debtor shall be construed as a reference to the person to whom payments under the relevant order are required by that order to be made,

and with any other necessary modifications.

**21      Application of maintenance pending suit and periodical payment orders to certain members of Defence Forces**

The reference in section 98(1)(h) of the Defence Act, 1954, to an order for payment of alimony shall be construed as including a reference to a maintenance pending suit order, a periodical payments order and a secured periodical payments order.

## 22 Amendment of Enforcement of Court Orders Act, 1940

The references in subsections (1) and (7) of section 8 of the Enforcement of Court Orders Act, 1940 (as amended by section 29 of the Act of 1976), to an order shall be construed as including references to a maintenance pending suit order and a periodical payments order.

# PART III
## RELIEF AFTER DIVORCE OR SEPARATION OUTSIDE STATE

### 23 Relief orders where marriage dissolved or spouses legally separated outside State

(1) This section applies to a marriage that has been dissolved, or as respects which the spouses have been legally separated, after the commencement of this section under the law of a country or jurisdiction other than the State, being a divorce or legal separation that is entitled to be recognised as valid in the State.

(2) (a) Subject to the provisions of this Part, the court may, in relation to a marriage to which this section applies, on application to it in that behalf by either of the spouses concerned or by a person on behalf of a dependent member of the family concerned, make any order under Part II (other than an order under section 6 or a maintenance pending suit order) (in this Act referred to as a relief order) that it could have made if the court had granted a decree of judicial separation in relation to the marriage.

(b) Part II shall apply and have effect in relation to relief orders and applications therefor as it applies and has effect in relation to orders under Part II and applications therefor with the modifications that—

    (i) subsections (4) and (5) of section 8, section 10(1)(c) and section 13 shall not apply in relation to a marriage that has been dissolved under the law of a country or jurisdiction other than the State,

    (ii) section 15 shall not apply in relation to a family home in which, following the dissolution of the marriage under such a law, either spouse, having remarried, ordinarily resides with his or her spouse, and

    (iii) the modifications specified in paragraph (c) and any other necessary modifications.

(c) Section 16 shall apply in relation to a relief order subject to the modifications that—

    (i) it shall be construed as including a requirement that the court should have regard to the duration of the marriage,

    (ii) the reference in subsection (2)(k) to the forfeiture of the opportunity or possibility of acquiring any benefit shall be construed as a reference to such forfeiture by reason of the divorce or legal separation concerned, and

      (iii)   the reference in subsection (3) to proceedings shall be construed as a reference to the proceedings for the divorce concerned or, as the case may be, for the legal separation concerned.

  (d)  Where a [person][1] whose marriage has been dissolved in a country or jurisdiction other than the State has remarried [or registered in a civil partnership][1], the court may not make a relief order in favour of that [person][1] in relation to a previous marriage of that [person][1].

(3)  (a)  An application shall not be made to the court by a person for a relief order unless, prior to the application, the court, on application to it *ex parte* in that behalf by that person, has by order granted leave for the making of the first-mentioned application and the court shall not grant such leave unless it considers that there is a substantial ground for so doing and a requirement specified in section 27 is satisfied.

  (b)  The court may make the grant of leave under this subsection subject to such (if any) terms and conditions as it considers appropriate and specifies in its order.

  (c)  The court may grant leave under this subsection to a person notwithstanding that an order has been made by a court of a country or jurisdiction other than the State requiring the spouse concerned to make a payment or transfer property to the person.

  (d)  This subsection does not apply to an application for a relief order made pursuant to a request under section 14 of the Maintenance Act, 1994.

(4) In determining, for the purposes of this section, the financial resources of a spouse or a dependent member of the family in a case in which payments are required to be made or property is required to be transferred to the spouse or to the member by the other spouse under an order of a court of a country or jurisdiction other than the State or an agreement in writing, the court shall have regard to the extent to which the order or agreement has been complied with or, if payments are required to be made, or property is required to be transferred, after the date of the order made by virtue of this section under Part II, is likely to be complied with.

(5) The period specified in a periodical payments order made by virtue of this section under paragraph (a) or (b) of section 8(1) shall begin not earlier than the date of the application for the order and shall end not later than the death of either of the spouses concerned or, if the order is made on or after the dissolution of the marriage, the remarriage [or registration in a civil partnership][2] of the spouse in whose favour the order was made.

(6)  (a)  Where, by virtue of this section, the court makes a periodical payments order or a secured periodical payments order on or after the dissolution of the marriage concerned, it may direct that the person in whose favour the order is made shall not apply for an order under section 18 extending the period specified in the order and, if the court so directs, such an order under section 18 shall not be made.

(b) Where, by virtue of this section, the court makes a periodical payments order or a secured periodical payments order in favour of a spouse other than on or after the dissolution of the marriage of the spouse and the marriage is dissolved subsequently, the order, if then in force, shall cease to have effect on the remarriage [or registration in a civil partnership]³ of that spouse, except as respects payments due under it on the date of the remarriage [or registration in a civil partnership]³.

(c) If, after the dissolution of a marriage to which this section applies, either of the spouses concerned remarries [or registers in a civil partnership]³, the court shall not, by reference to that dissolution, make by virtue of this section such an order as aforesaid, or a property adjustment order, in favour of that spouse.

---

**Notes**

1   Subsection 2(d) was amended by the Civil Partnership and Certain Rights and Obligations of Cohabitants Act 2010, s 166(a).

2   Subsection 5 was amended by the Civil Partnership and Certain Rights and Obligations of Cohabitants Act 2010, s 166 (b).

3   Subsection 6 was amended by the Civil Partnership and Certain Rights and Obligations of Cohabitants Act 2010, s 166 (c).

---

**24      Maintenance pending relief orders**

(1) Where leave is granted to a person under section 23(3) for the making of an application for a relief order, the court may, subject to subsection (3), on application to it in that behalf by the person, if it appears to it that a spouse, or a dependent member of the family, concerned is in immediate need of financial assistance make an order for maintenance pending relief, that is to say, an order requiring the other spouse or either of the spouses, as may be appropriate, to make to the person such periodical payments or lump sum payments for his or her support or, as may be appropriate, for the benefit of the dependent member of the family as it considers proper and, as respects any periodical payments, for such period beginning not earlier than the date of such grant and ending not later than the date of the determination of the application as it considers proper.

(2) The court may, on application to it in that behalf, provide that payments under an order under this section shall be subject to such terms and conditions as it considers appropriate and specifies in the order.

(3) The court shall not make an order under this section in a case where neither of the requirements specified in paragraphs (a) and (b) of section 27(1) is satisfied.

**25      Orders for provision for spouse out of estate of other spouse**

(1) Subject to the provisions of this section, where a spouse whose marriage has been dissolved in a country or jurisdiction other than the State dies, the court, on application

to it in that behalf by the other spouse ("the applicant") not more than [6 months][1] after representation is first granted under the Act of 1965 in respect of the estate of the deceased spouse, may by order make such provision for the applicant out of the estate of the deceased spouse as it considers appropriate having regard to the rights of any other person having an interest in the matter and specifies in the order if it is satisfied that it was not possible to provide [proper provision, having regard to the circumstances][1] for the applicant during the lifetime of the deceased spouse under sections 8 to 12 for any reason (other than conduct referred to in subsection (2)(i) of section 16 or desertion referred to in subsection (3) of that section by the applicant).

(2) The court shall not make an order under this section if the applicant concerned has remarried [or registered in a civil partnership][2] since the granting of the decree of divorce concerned.

(3) In considering whether to make an order under this section, the court shall have regard to all the circumstances of the case including—

    (a)  any order under paragraph (c) of section 8(1) or a property adjustment order in favour of the applicant, and

    (b)  any devise or bequest made by the deceased spouse to the applicant.

(4) The provision made for the applicant concerned by an order under this section together with any provision made for the applicant by an order referred to in subsection (3)(a) (the value of which for the purposes of this subsection shall be its value on the date of the order) shall not exceed in total the share (if any) of the applicant in the estate of the deceased spouse to which the applicant was entitled or (if the deceased spouse died intestate as to the whole or part of his or her estate) would have been entitled under the Act of 1965 if the marriage had not been dissolved.

(5) Section 121 of the Act of 1965 shall apply with any necessary modifications to a disposition referred to in subsection (1) of that section in respect of which the court is satisfied that it was made for the purpose of defeating or substantially diminishing the provision which the court would make for the applicant concerned under this section if the disposition had not been made.

(6) Notice of an application under this section shall be given by the applicant to the spouse (if any) or civil partner (if any) of the deceased spouse concerned and to such (if any) other persons as the court may direct and, in deciding whether to make the order concerned and in determining the provisions of the order, the court shall have regard to any representation made by the spouse [or civil partner][3] of the deceased spouse and any other such persons as aforesaid.

[(7) The personal representative of a deceased spouse in respect of whom a decree of divorce has been granted in a country or jurisdiction other than the State shall make a reasonable attempt to ensure that his or her death is brought to the attention of the other spouse concerned and, where an application is made under this section, the personal representative of the deceased spouse shall not, without the leave of the court, distribute any of the estate of that spouse until the court makes or refuses to make an order under this section.

(8) Where the personal representative of a deceased spouse in respect of whom a decree of divorce has been granted in a country or jurisdiction other than the State gives notice of his or her death to the other spouse concerned ("the spouse") and—

(a)　the spouse intends to apply to the court for an order under this section,

(b)　the spouse has applied for such an order and the application is pending, or

(c)　an order has been made under this section in favour of the spouse,

the spouse shall, not later than one month after receipt of the notice, notify the personal representative of such intention, application or order, as the case may be, and, if he or she does not do so, the personal representative shall be at liberty to distribute the assets of the deceased spouse, or any part thereof, amongst the parties entitled thereto.

(9) The personal representative shall not be liable to the spouse for the assets or any part thereof so distributed unless, at the time of such distribution, he or she had notice of the intention, application or order aforesaid.

(10) Nothing in subsection (8) or (9) shall prejudice the right of the spouse to follow any such assets into the hands of any person who may have received them.][4]

---

**Notes**

1　Subsection (1) was amended by the Family Law (Divorce) Act 1996, s 52(d), (j)(i).

2　Subsection (2) was amended by the Civil Partnership and Certain Rights and Obligations of Cohabitants 2010, s 167(1).

3　Subsection (6) was amended by the Civil Partnership and Certain Rights and Obligations of Cohabitants 2010, s 167(2).

4　Subsection (7) was substituted and sub-ss (8), (9) and (10) were inserted by the Family Law (Divorce) Act 1996, s 52(j)(ii). See the Finance Act 1997, s 142.

---

**26　　Appropriateness of making relief order in State**

The court shall not make a relief order unless it is satisfied that in all the circumstances of the particular case it is appropriate that such an order should be made by a court in the State and, without prejudice to the generality of the foregoing, in deciding whether to make a relief order, the court shall, in particular, have regard to the following matters:

(a)　the connection which the spouses concerned have with the State,

(b)　the connection which the spouses have with the country or jurisdiction other than the State in which the marriage concerned was dissolved or in which they were legally separated,

(c)　the connection which the spouses have with any country or jurisdiction other than the State,

(d)　any financial benefit which the spouse applying for the making of the order ("the applicant") or a dependent member of the family has received, or is likely to receive, in consequence of the divorce or legal separation concerned or by virtue of any agreement or the operation of the law of a country or jurisdiction other than the State,

(e) in a case where an order has been made by a court in a country or jurisdiction other than the State requiring a spouse, or the spouses, concerned to make any payment or transfer any property for the benefit of the applicant or a dependent member of the family, the financial relief given by the order and the extent to which the order has been complied with or is likely to be complied with,

(f) any right which the applicant or a dependent member of the family has, or has had, to apply for financial relief from a spouse or the spouses under the law of any country or jurisdiction other than the State and, if the applicant or dependent member of the family has omitted to exercise any such right, the reason for that omission,

(g) the availability in the State of any property in respect of which a relief order in favour of the applicant or dependent member of the family could be made,

(h) the extent to which the relief order is likely to be enforceable,

(i) the length of time which has elapsed since the date of the divorce or legal separation concerned.

## 27 Jurisdiction of court to make relief orders

(1) Subject to subsection (2), the court may make a relief order if, but only if, at least one of the following requirements is satisfied:

(a) either of the spouses concerned was domiciled in the State on the date of the application for an order under section 23(3) in relation to the relief order or was so domiciled on the date on which the divorce or judicial separation concerned took effect in the country or jurisdiction in which it was obtained,

(b) either of the spouses was ordinarily resident in the State throughout the period of one year ending on either of the dates aforesaid,

(c) on the date of the institution of the proceedings aforesaid either or both of the spouses had a beneficial interest in land situated in the State.

(2) Subsection (1) does not apply in relation to a case to which the Jurisdiction of Courts and Enforcement of Judgments Acts, 1988 and 1993, apply or to a relief order that is the subject of a request under section 14 of the Maintenance Act, 1994.

## 28 Restriction of jurisdiction of court to make relief orders

(1) Where the jurisdiction of the court to make a relief order is conferred by virtue only of section 27(1)(c), the court may make any of the following relief orders, but no others:

(a) a lump sum order,

(b) a property adjustment order providing for one or more of the matters specified in paragraphs (b), (c) and (d) of section 9(1),

(c) an order under section 14,

(d) an order under section 25,

(e)  an order directing the sale of the interest of either of the spouses concerned in the family home concerned.

(2) Where, in the circumstances referred to in subsection (1), the court makes one or more lump sum orders, the amount or aggregate amount of the sum or sums to which the order or orders relate shall not exceed—

(a)  in case the interest of the spouse liable to make the payment or payments under the order or orders in the family home concerned is sold whether in pursuance of an order of the court or otherwise, the amount of the proceeds of the sale after deduction therefrom of the costs thereof, or

(b)  in any other case, such amount as, in the opinion of the court, represents the value of that interest.

(3) The reference in subsection (1)(e) to the interest of either of the spouses concerned shall, in relation to a case where the interest of a spouse in the family home concerned is held under a joint tenancy or a tenancy in common with another person or other persons, be construed as including a reference to the interest of the other person or persons in the home.

## PART IV
## DECLARATIONS AS TO MARITAL STATUS

**29      Declarations as to marital status**

(1) The court may, on application to it in that behalf by either of the spouses concerned or by any other person who, in the opinion of the court, has a sufficient interest in the matter, by order make one or more of the following declarations in relation to a marriage, that is to say:

(a)  a declaration that the marriage was at its inception a valid marriage,

(b)  a declaration that the marriage subsisted on a date specified in the application,

(c)  a declaration that the marriage did not subsist on a date so specified, not being the date of the inception of the marriage,

(d)  a declaration that the validity of a divorce, annulment or legal separation obtained under the civil law of any other country or jurisdiction in respect of the marriage is entitled to recognition in the State,

(e)  a declaration that the validity of a divorce, annulment or legal separation so obtained in respect of the marriage is not entitled to recognition in the State.

(2) The court may grant an order under subsection (1) if, but only if, either of the spouses concerned—

(a)  is domiciled in the State on the date of the application,

(b)  has been ordinarily resident in the State throughout the period of one year ending on that date, or

(c)  died before that date and either—

(i)  was at the time of death domiciled in the State, or

(ii) had been ordinarily resident in the State throughout the period of one year ending on that date.

(3) The other spouse or the spouses concerned or the personal representative of the spouse or each spouse, within the meaning of the Act of 1965, shall be joined in proceedings under this section.

(4) The court may, at any stage of proceedings under this section of its own motion or on application to it in that behalf by a party thereto, order that notice of the proceedings be given to the Attorney General or any other person and that such documents relating to the proceedings as may be necessary for the purposes of his or her functions shall be given to the Attorney General.

(5) The court shall, on application to it in that behalf by the Attorney General, order that he or she be added as a party to any proceedings under this section and, in any such proceedings, he or she shall, if so requested by the court, whether or not he or she is so added to the proceedings, argue any question arising in the proceedings specified by the court.

(6) Where notice of proceedings under this section is given to a person (other than the Attorney General), the court may, of its own motion or on application to it in that behalf by the person or a party to the proceedings, order that the person be added as a party to the proceedings.

(7) Where a party to proceedings under this section alleges that the marriage concerned is or was void, or that it is voidable, and should be annulled, the court may treat the application under subsection (1) as an application for a decree of nullity of marriage and may forthwith proceed to determine the matter accordingly and may postpone the determination of the application under subsection (1).

(8) A declaration under this section shall be binding on the parties to the proceedings concerned and on any person claiming through such a party and, if the Attorney General is a party to the proceedings, the declaration shall also be binding on the State.

(9) A declaration under this section shall not prejudice any person if it is subsequently proved to have been obtained by fraud or collusion.

(10) Where proceedings under this section, and proceedings in another jurisdiction, in relation to the same marriage have been instituted but have not been finally determined, the court may stay the first-mentioned proceedings until the other proceedings have been finally determined.

[(11) In this section a reference to a spouse includes a reference to a person who is a party to a marriage that has been dissolved under the Family Law (Divorce) Act, 1996.]¹

---

**Notes**

1 Subsection (11) was inserted by the Family Law (Divorce) Act 1996, s 52(k). See the European Communities (Judgments in Matrimonial Matters and Matters of Parental Responsibility) Regulations 2001 (SI 472/2001), reg 3.

**30     Provisions supplementary to section 29**

(1) Rules of court may make provision as to the information to be given in an application under section 29(1) including particulars of any previous or pending proceedings in relation to any marriage concerned or to the matrimonial status of a party to any such marriage.

(2) The court may make such order (if any) as it considers just for the payment of all or part of any costs incurred by the Attorney General in proceedings under this section by other parties to the proceedings.

(3) Without prejudice to the law governing the recognition of decrees of divorce granted by courts outside the State, a declaration under section 29 conflicting with a previous final judgment or decree of a court of competent jurisdiction of a country or jurisdiction other than the State shall not be made unless the judgment or decree was obtained by fraud or collusion.

(4) Notification of a declaration under section 29 (other than a declaration relating to a legal separation) shall be given by the registrar of the court to an tArd-Chláraitheoir.

# PART V
## MARRIAGE

**31     Age of marriage**

(1)   (a)   (i)   A marriage solemnised, after the commencement of this section, between persons either of whom is under the age of 18 years shall not be valid in law.

      (ii)   Subparagraph (i) applies to any marriage solemnised—

            (I)     in the State, irrespective of where the spouses or either of them are or is ordinarily resident, or

            (II)    outside the State, if at the time of the solemnisation of the marriage, the spouses or either of them are or is ordinarily resident in the State.

   (b)   Paragraph (a) does not apply if exemption from it was granted under section 33 before the marriage concerned.

   (c)   The requirement in relation to marriage arising by virtue of paragraph (a) is hereby declared to be a substantive requirement for marriage.

(2) Any person to whom application is made in relation to the solemnisation of an intended marriage may, if he or she so thinks fit, request the production of evidence of age with respect to either or both of the parties concerned.

(3) Where a request is made under subsection (2)—

   (a)   refusal or failure to comply with the request shall be a proper reason for refusal of the application concerned, and

   (b)   if the request is complied with and the evidence shows that either or both of the parties is or are under the age of 18 years, the application shall be refused.

(4) Where a person knowingly—

    (a)  solemnises or permits the solemnisation of a marriage which, consequent on the provisions of this section, is not valid in law, or

    (b)  is a party to such a marriage,

the person shall be guilty of an offence and shall be liable on summary conviction to a fine not exceeding [€634.87].

## 32     Notification of intention to marry

[...][1]

**Notes**

1   Subsection 5(1) was amended and sub-s 6(1) was inserted by the Family Law (Miscellaneous Provisions) Act 1997, s 2(1)(a), and subsequently repealed by s 4 and Second Schedule of the Civil Registration Act 2004.

## 33     Exemption of certain marriages from sections 31(1) and 32(1)

(1) The court may, on application to it in that behalf by both of the parties to an intended marriage, by order exempt the marriage from the application of section 31(1)(a) [...].[1]

(2) The following provisions shall apply in relation to an application under subsection (1):

    (a)  it may be made informally,

    (b)  it may be heard and determined otherwise than in public,

    (c)  a court fee shall not be charged in respect of it, and

    (d)  it shall not be granted unless the applicant shows that its grant is justified by serious reasons and is in the interests of the parties to the intended marriage.

**Notes**

1   Section 33(1) amended by s 4 and the Second Schedule of the Civil Registration Act 2004.

## 34     Abolition of right to petition for jactitation of marriage

No person shall after the commencement of this Act be entitled to petition a court for jactitation of marriage.

PART VI

MISCELLANEOUS

**35     Powers of court in relation to transactions intended to prevent or reduce relief**

(1) In this section—

"**disposition**" means any disposition of property howsoever made other than a disposition made by a will or codicil;

"**relief**" means the financial or other material benefits conferred by—

(a) an order under section 7, 8 or 9, paragraph (a) or (b) of section 10(1) or section 11, 12, 13, [15A]¹, 17, 18 (other than an order affecting an order referred to in subsection (1) (e) thereof), 24 or 25, or

[(aa) an order under section 11(2)(b) of the Act of 1964 or sections 5, 5A or 7 of the Act of 1976, or]¹

(b) a relief order (other than an order under section 18 affecting an order referred to in subsection (1)(e) thereof),

and references to defeating a claim for relief are references to—

(i) preventing relief being granted to the person concerned, whether for the benefit of the person or a dependent member of the family concerned,

(ii) limiting the relief granted, or

(iii) frustrating or impeding the enforcement of an order granting relief;

"**reviewable disposition**", in relation to proceedings for the grant of relief brought by a spouse, means a disposition made by the other spouse concerned or any other person but does not include such a disposition made for valuable consideration (other than marriage) to a person who, at the time of the disposition acted in good faith and without notice of an intention on the part of the respondent to defeat the claim for relief.

(2) (a) The court, on the application of a person ("the applicant") who—

(i) has instituted proceedings that have not been determined for the grant of relief,

(ii) has been granted leave under section 23(3) to institute such proceedings, or

(iii) intends to apply for such leave upon the completion of one year's ordinary residence in the State—

may—

(I) if it is satisfied that the other spouse concerned or any other person, with the intention of defeating the claim for relief, proposes to make any disposition of or to transfer out of the jurisdiction or otherwise deal with any property, make such order as it thinks fit for the purpose of restraining that other spouse or other person from so doing or otherwise for protecting the claim,

(II)  if it is satisfied that that other spouse or other person has, with that intention, made a reviewable disposition and that, if the disposition were set aside, relief or different relief would be granted to the applicant, make an order setting aside the disposition.

(b)  Where relief has been granted by the court and the court is satisfied that the other spouse concerned or another person has, with the intention aforesaid, made a reviewable disposition, it may make an order setting aside the disposition.

(c)  An application under paragraph (a) shall, in a case in which proceedings for relief have been instituted, be made in those proceedings.

(3) Where the court makes an order under paragraph (a) or (b) of subsection (2), it shall include in the order such provisions (if any) as it considers necessary for its implementation (including provisions requiring the making of any payments or the disposal of any property).

(4) In a case where neither of the conditions specified in paragraphs (a) and (b) of section 27(1) is satisfied, the court shall not make an order under subsection (2) in respect of any property other than the family home concerned.

(5) Where an application is made under subsection (2) with respect to a disposition that took place less than 3 years before the date of the application or with respect to a disposition or other dealing with property that the other spouse concerned or any other person proposes to make and the court is satisfied—

(a)  in case the application is for an order under subsection (2)(a)(I), that the disposition or other dealing concerned would (apart from this section) have the consequence, or

(b)  in case the application is for an order under paragraph (a)(II) or (b) of subsection (2), that the disposition has had the consequence,

of defeating the applicant's claim for relief, it shall be presumed, unless the contrary is shown, that that other spouse or other person disposed of or otherwise dealt with the property concerned, or, as the case may be, proposes to do so, with the intention of defeating the applicant's claim for relief.

[(6) An application shall not be made for an order setting aside a disposition by reason only of subsection (2)(a)(II) or (b) after the expiration of 6 years from the date of the disposition.][2]

---

**Notes**

1  Subsection (1) was amended by the Family Law (Divorce) Act 1996, s 52(1).

2  Subsection (6) inserted by Civil Law (Miscellaneous Provisions) Act 2008, s 74(c).

---

**36    Determination of questions between spouses in relation to property**

(1) Either spouse may apply to the court in a summary manner to determine any question arising between them as to the title to or possession of any property.

(2) On application to it under subsection (1), the court may—

(a)  make such order with respect to the property in dispute (including an order that it be sold or partitioned) and as to the costs consequent upon the application, and

(b)  direct such inquiries, and give such other directions, in relation to the application,

as the court considers proper.

(3) Either spouse or a child of a deceased spouse (in this section referred to subsequently as "the plaintiff spouse") may make an application specified in subsection (1) where it is claimed that the other spouse (in this section referred to subsequently as "the defendant spouse") has had in his or her possession or under his or her control—

(a)  money to which, or to a share of which, the plaintiff spouse was beneficially entitled whether by reason of the fact that it represented the proceeds of property to which, or to an interest in which, the plaintiff spouse was beneficially entitled or for any other reason, or

(b)  property (other than money) to which, or to an interest in which, the plaintiff spouse was beneficially entitled,

and that either that money or other property has ceased to be in the possession or under the control of the defendant spouse or that the plaintiff spouse does not know whether it is still in the possession or under the control of the defendant spouse.

(4) Where an application under subsection (1) is made by virtue of subsection (3) and the court is satisfied that—

(a)    (i)   the defendant spouse concerned has had in his or her possession or under his or her control money or other property to which paragraph (a) or (b) of subsection (3) relates, or

(ii)  the defendant spouse has in his or her possession or under his or her control property that represents the whole or part of the money or other property aforesaid,

and

(b)  the defendant spouse has not made to the plaintiff spouse concerned such payment or disposition (not being a testamentary disposition) as would have been appropriate in all the circumstances,

the court may make an order under subsection (2) in relation to the application and may, in addition to or in lieu of such an order, make an order requiring the defendant spouse to pay to the plaintiff spouse either, as the case may be—

(i)   such sum in respect of the money to which the application relates, or the plaintiff spouse's share thereof, or

(ii) such sum in respect of the value of the property (other than money) referred to in paragraph (a), or the plaintiff spouse's interest therein,

as the court considers proper.

(5) In any proceedings under this section, a person (other than the plaintiff spouse concerned or the defendant spouse concerned) who is a party thereto shall, for the purposes of costs or any other matter, be treated as a stakeholder only.

(6) This section is without prejudice to section 2 (which prescribes the legal capacity of married women) of the Married Women's Status Act, 1957.

(7) (a) Where a marriage—

    (i) has been annulled [or dissolved][1] under the law of the State, or

    (ii) has been annulled or dissolved under the law of a country or jurisdiction other than the State and is, by reason of that annulment or divorce, not or no longer a subsisting valid marriage under the law of the State,

an application under this section shall not be made by either of the spouses more than 3 years after the date of the annulment or divorce.

(b) Where a marriage is void but has not been so declared under the law of the State or another state, an application shall not be made under this section by either of the spouses more than 3 years after the parties have ceased to be ordinarily resident together.

(8) In this section references to a spouse include references to—

(a) a personal representative of a deceased spouse,

(b) either of the parties to a void marriage, whether or not it has been declared to be void under the law of the State or a country or jurisdiction other than the State,

(c) either of the parties to a voidable marriage that has been annulled under the law of the State,

[(cc) either of the parties to a marriage that has been dissolved under the law of the State,][1]

(d) either of the parties to a marriage that has been annulled under the law of another state and that is, by reason of the annulment, not a subsisting valid marriage under the law of the State, and

(e) either of the parties to a marriage that has been dissolved under the law of another state and that is, by reason of the divorce, no longer a subsisting valid marriage under the law of the State.

---

**Notes**

1   Subsections (7) and (8) were amended by the Family Law (Divorce) Act 1996, s 52(m).

---

## 37    Payments to be made without deduction of income tax

[...]¹

---

**Notes**

1    Section 37 was repealed by the Taxes Consolidation Act 1997, s 1098, Sch 4 with effect from 6 April 1997.

---

## 38    Jurisdiction of courts and venue

(1) Subject to the provisions of this section, the Circuit Court shall, concurrently with the High Court, have jurisdiction to hear and determine proceedings under this Act and shall, in relation to that jurisdiction, be known as the Circuit Family Court.

(2) Subject to the other provisions of this section, the Circuit Family Court shall, concurrently with the High Court, have jurisdiction to hear and determine proceedings for a decree of nullity.

(3) Where the rateable valuation of any land to which proceedings in the Circuit Family Court under this Act relate exceeds [€253.95], that Court shall, if an application is made to it in that behalf by any person having an interest in the proceedings, transfer the proceedings to the High Court, but any order made or act done in the course of such proceedings before the transfer shall be valid unless discharged or varied by the High Court by order.

[(4) The jurisdiction conferred on the Circuit Family Court by this Act may be exercised—

(a)   in the case of an application under section 33, by the judge of any circuit, and

(b)   in any other case, by the judge of the circuit in which any of the parties to the proceedings ordinarily resides or carries on any business, profession or occupation.]¹

(5) The Circuit Family Court may, for the purposes of subsection (3) and section 31 (3) of the Act of 1989 in relation to land that has not been given a rateable valuation or is the subject with other land of a rateable valuation, determine that its rateable valuation would exceed, or would not exceed, [€253.95].

(6) Section 32 of the Act of 1989 shall apply to proceedings under this Act in the Circuit Family Court and sections 33 to 36 of that Act shall apply to proceedings under this Act in that Court and in the High Court.

(7) In proceedings under section 8, 9, 10(1)(a), 11, 12, 13, 14, [15A]², 18, 23 or 25—

(a)   each of the spouses concerned shall give to the other spouse and to, or to a person acting on behalf of, any dependent member of the family concerned, and

(b) any dependent member of the family concerned shall give to, or to a person acting on behalf of, any other such member and to each of the spouses concerned,

such particulars of his or her property and income as may reasonably be required for the purposes of the proceedings.

(8) Where a person fails or refuses to comply with subsection (7), the court, on application to it in that behalf by a person having an interest in the matter, may direct the person to comply with that subsection.

**Notes**

1 Subsection (4) was substituted by the Family Law (Miscellaneous Provisions) Act 1997, s 2(2).

2 Subsection (7) was amended by the Family Law (Divorce) Act 1996, s 52(n).

### 39 Exercise of jurisdiction by court in relation to nullity[1]

(1) The court may grant a decree of nullity if, but only if, one of the following requirements is satisfied:

(a) either of the spouses concerned was domiciled in the State on the date of the institution of the proceedings concerned,

(b) either of the spouses was ordinarily resident in the State throughout the period of one year ending on that date,

(c) either of the spouses died before that date and—

(i) was at the time of death domiciled in the State, or

(ii) had been ordinarily resident in the State throughout the period of one year ending on that date.

(2) Where proceedings are pending in a court in respect of an application for the grant of a decree of nullity or in respect of an appeal from the determination of such an application and the court has or had, by virtue of subsection (1), jurisdiction to determine the application, the court, notwithstanding section 31(4) of the Act of 1989, shall have jurisdiction to determine an application for the grant of a decree of judicial separation in respect of the marriage concerned.

**Notes**

1 See European Communities (Judgments in Matrimonial Matters and Matters of Parental Responsibility) Regulations 2001 (SI 472/2001), reg 3.

**40 Notice of proceedings under Act**

Notice of any proceedings under this Act shall be given by the person bringing the proceedings to—

(a) the other spouse concerned or, as the case may be, the spouses concerned, and

(b) any other person specified by the court.

**41 Secured maintenance orders**

Where, in proceedings under any other Act, the court or the District Court makes or has made an order providing for the payment—

(a) by a spouse to the other spouse of periodical payments for the support or maintenance of that other spouse, or[1]

(b) by a parent to the other parent or to another person specified in the order of periodical payments for the support or maintenance of a child—

    (i) of both parents or adopted by both parents under the Adoption Acts, 1952 to 1991, or in relation to whom both parents are *in loco parentis*, or

    (ii) Of either parent or adopted by either parent under those Acts or in relation to whom either parent is *in loco parentis* where the other parent being aware that he or she is not the parent of the child has treated the child as a member of the family,

the court by which the order was made may in those proceedings or subsequently, on application to it by any person having an interest in the proceedings, order the spouse or parent liable to make the payments under the order to secure them to the other spouse or parent or the other person specified in the order to the satisfaction of the court.

**Notes**

1 See Finance Act 1997, s 142(1)(c) regarding orders made under s 41(a).

**42 Lump sum maintenance orders**

(1) Where, in proceedings under any other Act, an order providing for the periodical payments referred to in paragraph (a) or (b) of section 41 would, apart from this section, fall to be made, the court may in addition to, or instead of such an order, make an order providing for the making by the person concerned to the person concerned of a lump sum payment or lump sum payments of such amount or amounts and at such time or times as may be specified in the order.

(2) The amount or aggregate amount of a lump sum payment or of lump sum payments to a person under an order under this section shall be—

(a) if the order is instead of an order for the making of periodical payments to the person, such amount as the court considers appropriate having regard to the amount of the periodical payments that would have been made, and the periods during which and the times at which they would have been made, but for this section, and

(b) if the first-mentioned order is in addition to an order for the making of periodical payments to the person, such amount as the court considers appropriate having regard to the amount of the periodical payments and the periods during which and the times at which they will be made.

(3) In this section "**the court**" includes the District Court.

(4) The amount or aggregate amount of a lump sum payment or of lump sum payments provided for in an order of the District Court under this section shall not exceed [€20,000][1].

**Notes**

1 Section 42(4) was amended by the Courts and Court Officers Act 2002, s 14 and Sch 2, Pt 2, col (3).

**43 Amendment of Act of 1976[1]**

**Notes**

1 This section amends the Family Law (Maintenance of Spouses and Children) Act 1976; see the amended Act. Section 43 was amended by the Family Law (Divorce) Act 1996, s 52(o)(ii).

**44 Discharge of orders under Act of 1976**

Where, while a maintenance order, an order varying a maintenance order, or an interim order, under the Act of 1976 is in force, an application is made to the court by a spouse to whom the order aforesaid relates for an order granting a decree of judicial separation or an order under Part II or III, the court may by order discharge the order aforesaid under the Act of 1976 as on and from such date as may be specified in the order.

**45 Amendment of Maintenance Act 1994[1]**

**Notes**

1 This section amends the Maintenance Act 1994; see the amended Act.

**46 Custody of dependent members of the family after decree of nullity**

Where the court makes an order for the grant of a decree of nullity, it may declare either of the spouses concerned to be unfit to have custody of any dependent member of the family who is a minor and, if it does so and the spouse to whom the declaration relates is a parent of any dependent member of the family who is a minor, that spouse shall not, on the death of the other spouse, be entitled as of right to the custody of that minor.

## 47 Social reports in family law proceedings

(1) In proceedings to which this section applies, the court may, of its own motion or on application to it in that behalf by a party to the proceedings, by order give such directions as it thinks proper for the purpose of procuring a report in writing on any question affecting the welfare of a party to the proceedings or any other person to whom they relate from—

    (a) such probation and welfare officer (within the meaning of the Child Abduction and Enforcement of Custody Orders Act, 1991) as the Minister for Justice may nominate,

    [(b) such person nominated by the Health Service Executive specified in the order as the Health Service Executive may nominate, being a person who, in it's opinion is suitably qualified for the purpose, or]¹

    (c) any other person specified in the order.

(2) In deciding whether or not to make an order under subsection (1), the court shall have regard to any submission made to it in relation to the matter by or on behalf of a party to the proceedings concerned or any other person to whom they relate.

(3) A copy of a report under subsection (1) shall be given to the parties to the proceedings concerned and (if he or she is not a party to the proceedings) to the person to whom it relates and may be received in evidence in the proceedings.

(4) The fees and expenses incurred in the preparation of a report under subsection (1) shall be paid by such parties to the proceedings concerned and in such proportions, or by such party to the proceedings, as the court may determine.

(5) The court or a party to proceedings to which this section applies may call as a witness in the proceedings a person who prepared a report under subsection (1) pursuant to an order under that subsection in those proceedings.

(6) [This section]² applies to proceedings—

    (a) under the Act of 1964,

    (b) under the Act of 1976,

    (c) under the Family Home Protection Act, 1976,

    (d) [under the Act of 1996,]³

    (e) under the Status of Children Act, 1987,

    (f) under the Act of 1989,

    (g) under the Child Abduction and Enforcement of Custody Orders Act, 1991,

    (h) in relation to an application for a decree of nullity, and

    (i) under this Act.

(7) [...]⁴

**Notes**

1    Subsection (1)(b) was substituted by s 75 and Schedule 6 of the Health Act 2004.

2    Subsection (6) was amended by the Family Law (Divorce) Act 1996, s 52(p)(a).

3    Subsection (6)(d) was amended and substituted by the Domestic Violence Act 1996, s 21(d).

4    Subsection (7) was amended by the Family Law (Divorce) Act 1996, s 52(p)(b) and subsequently repealed by s 75 and Schedule 6 of the Health Act 2004.

## 48    Property of engaged couples

For the avoidance of doubt, it is hereby declared that the reference in section 5(1) of the Family Law Act, 1981, to the rules of law relating to the rights of spouses in relation to property in which either or both of them has or have a beneficial interest shall relate and be deemed always to have related only to the rules of law for the determination of disputes between spouses, or a claim by one of them, in relation to the beneficial ownership of property in which either or both of them has or have a beneficial interest and, in particular, does not relate, and shall be deemed never to have related, to the rules of law relating to the rights of spouses under the Act of 1965, the Family Home Protection Act, 1976, the Act of 1989 or this Act.

## 49    Income tax treatment of persons divorced outside State

[…][1]

**Notes**

1    Section 49 was repealed by the Finance Act 1997, s 5.

## 50    Exemption of certain transfers from stamp duty

[…][1]

**Notes**

1    Section 50 was repealed by the Finance Act 1997, s 127(4).

## 51    Exemption of certain transfers from capital acquisitions tax

[…][1]

**Notes**

1   Section 51 was repealed by the Finance Act 1997, s 142(3).

**52        Capital gains tax treatment of certain disposals by spouses**

[...]¹

**Notes**

1   Section 52 was repealed by the Finance Act 1997, s 72(4) and (5) with effect from 1 August 1996.

**53        Abatement and postponement of probate tax on property the subject of an order under section 25**

[...]¹

**Notes**

1   Section 53 was repealed by the Finance Act 1997, s 143(2).

**54        Amendment of Family Home Protection Act, 1976, and Act of 1989**

(1) ...¹

(2) The amendment effected by subsection (1)(a) does not apply in relation to—

(a)  any conveyances referred to in section 3 of the Family Home Protection Act, 1976, the dates of which are,

(b)  any proceedings under or referred to in that Act which are instituted,

(c)  any thing referred to in section 6 of that Act which is done, and

(d)  any transactions referred to in section 14 of that Act which occur,

before the commencement of this section.

(3) Where a court, when granting a decree of judicial separation under the Act of 1989, orders that the ownership of the family home shall be vested in one of the spouses, it shall, unless it sees reason to the contrary, order that section 3(1) (prior consent of spouse to conveyance of interest in family home) of the Family Home Protection Act, 1976, shall not apply to any conveyance by that spouse of an interest in the home and, if the court so orders, the said section 3(1) shall have effect accordingly.

**Notes**

1    Subsection (1) amends the Family Home Protection Act 1976; see amended Act.

## 55    Amendment of Child Abduction and Enforcement of Custody Orders Act 1991

Section 2 of the Child Abduction and Enforcement of Custody Orders Act, 1991, shall be amended as follows:

(a)    "'the Minister' means the Minister for Equality and Law Reform" shall be substituted for the definition of "the Minister", and

(b)    "the Minister for Justice" shall be substituted for "the Minister" in the definition of "probation and welfare officer".

SCHEDULE

Section 3

## ENACTMENTS REPEALED

| Year & Chapter or Number & Year | Short Title | Extent of Repeal |
|---|---|---|
| 1844, c.81 | Marriages (Ireland) Act, 1844 | In section 9, "and that they are both of the full age of twenty-one years, or, when either of the parties shall be under the age of twenty-one years, that the consent of the person or persons whose consent to such marriage is required by law has been obtained thereto, or that there is no person having authority to give such consent, or that such party is a widower or widow as the case may be" |
| | | Sections 19 and 25. In section 22, "and that they are both of the full age of twenty-one years, or, where either of the parties shall be under the age of twenty-one years, that the consent of the person or persons whose consent to such marriage is required by law has been obtained thereto, or that there is no person having authority to give such consent, or that such party is a widower or widow, as the case may be" |
| 1868, c.20 | Legitimacy Declaration Act, (Ireland), 1868 | Section 1 |

| Year & Chapter or Number & Year | Short Title | Extent of Repeal |
| --- | --- | --- |
| 1863, c 27 | Marriage Law (Ireland) Amendment Act, 1863 | In section 4, the words from "and when either of the Parties intending marriage" to "whose consent to such Marriage is by Law required;"<br><br>In Schedule (B), the fourth paragraph |
| 1870 c.110 | Matrimonial Causes and Marriage Law (Ireland) Amendment Act, 1870 | In section 35, the words "Whenever a marriage shall not be had within three calendar months after the notice shall have been so given to the person so appointed as aforesaid, the notice, and any licence which may have been granted thereupon, shall be utterly void" and the words and "that they are both of the full age of twenty-one years, or, where either of the parties shall be under the age of twenty-one years, that the consent of the person or persons whose consent to such marriage is required by law has been obtained thereto, or that there is no person having authority to give such consent, or that such person is a widower or widow, as the case may be" |
| No. 5 of 1957 | Married Women's Status Act, 1957 | Section 12 |
| No. 30 of 1972 | Marriages Act, 1972 | Sections 1 and 18 |
| No 6 of 1989 | Judicial Separation and Family Law Reform Act, 1989 | Part II (other than section 25) and sections 39 and 40 |

# Domestic Violence Act 1996

*Number 1 of 1996*

ARRANGEMENT OF SECTIONS

## Acts referred to

*An Act to make provision for the protection of a spouse and any children or other dependent persons, and of persons in other domestic relationships, whose safety or welfare requires it because of the conduct of another person in the domestic relationship concerned and for that purpose to repeal and re-enact with amendments the provisions of the Family Law (Protection of Spouses and Children) Act, 1981, to provide for arrest without warrant in certain circumstances, to provide for the hearing at the same time of certain applications to a court under more than one enactment for orders relating to domestic relationships and to provide for other connected matters. [27th February, 1996]*

*Be it enacted by the Oireachtas as follows:*

## 1    Interpretation[1]

(1) In this Act, except where the context otherwise requires—

["**Act of 2010**" means the Civil Partnership and Certain Rights and Obligations of Cohabitants Act 2010;][2]

"**applicant**", where appropriate, has the meaning assigned by either section 2 or 3 or by both of those sections and where an interim barring order has been made the applicant for the barring order to which the interim barring order relates shall be deemed to be the applicant for the interim barring order and where a protection order has been made the applicant for the safety order or the barring order to which the protection order relates shall be deemed to be the applicant for that protection order;

"**barring order**" has the meaning assigned by section 3;

["**civil partner**" has the meaning assigned to it by the Act of 2010 and includes a person who was a civil partner in a partnership that has been dissolved under that Act;][3]

"**civil proceedings** under this Act" means—

(a) proceedings for the making, variation or discharge of a safety order or a barring order,

(b) proceedings, consequent on the making of an application for a barring order, for the making, variation or discharge of an interim barring order which relates to the application,

(c) proceedings, consequent on the making of an application for a safety order or barring order, for the making, variation or discharge of a protection order which relates to the application,

(d) any proceedings by way of appeal or case stated which are related to proceedings to which paragraph (a), (b) or (c) applies;

"**the court**" means the Circuit Court or the District Court;

"**dependent person**", in relation to the applicant or the respondent or both of them, as the case may be, means any child—

(a) of the applicant and the respondent or adopted by both the applicant and the respondent under the Adoption Acts, 1952 to 1991, or under an adoption deemed to have been effected by a valid adoption order by virtue of section 2, 3, 4 or 5 of the Adoption Act, 1991, or in relation to whom both the applicant and the respondent are *in loco parentis*, or

(b) of the applicant or adopted by the applicant under the Adoption Acts, 1952 to 1991, or under an adoption deemed to have been effected by a valid adoption order by virtue of section 2, 3, 4 or 5 of the Adoption Act, 1991, or in relation to whom the applicant is *in loco parentis*, or

(c) of the respondent or adopted by the respondent under the Adoption Acts, 1952 to 1991, or under an adoption deemed to have been effected by a valid adoption order by virtue of section 2, 3, 4 or 5 of the Adoption Act, 1991, or in relation to whom the respondent is *in loco parentis*, and the applicant, while not in the same relationship to that child for the purposes of this paragraph as the respondent is in, is in respect of that child a person to whom paragraph (b) of this definition relates,

who is not of full age or if the child has attained full age has a physical or mental disability to such extent that it is not reasonably possible for the child to live independently of the applicant;

**"full age"** has the same meaning as it has in the Age of Majority Act, 1985:

**"functions"** includes powers and duties;

**"health board"** means a health board established under the Health Act, 1970:

**"interim barring order"** has the meaning assigned by section 4;

**"protection order"** has the meaning assigned by section 5;

**"respondent"**, where appropriate, has the meaning assigned by either section 2 or 3 or by both of those sections and where an interim barring order has been made the respondent to the application for the barring order to which the interim barring order relates shall be deemed to be the respondent to the interim barring order and where a protection order has been made the respondent to the application for the safety order or the barring order to which the protection order relates shall be deemed to be the respondent to that protection order;

**"safety order"** has the meaning assigned by section 2;

**"welfare"** includes the physical and psychological welfare of the person in question.

(2) (a) A reference in this Act to a section is a reference to a section of this Act unless it is indicated that a reference to some other Act is intended.

    (b) A reference in this Act to a subsection or to a paragraph is to the subsection or paragraph of the provision in which the reference occurs unless it is indicated that reference to some other provision is intended.

(3) Any reference in this Act to any other enactment shall, except where the context otherwise requires, be construed as a reference to that enactment as amended by or under any other enactment including this Act.

---

**Notes**

1 Commencement: 27 March 1996.

2 Definition of "Act of 2010" inserted by the Civil Partnership and Certain Rights and Obligations of Cohabitants Act 2010, s 91.

3 Definition of "civil partner" inserted by the Civil Partnership and Certain Rights and Obligations of Cohabitants Act 2010, s 91.

---

**2     Safety Order[1]**

(1) (a) In this section—

    **"the applicant"** means a person, other than a health board, who has applied or on whose behalf a health board has applied by virtue of section 6 for a safety order against another person (in this section referred to as "the respondent") and the person so applying or on whose behalf the health board has so applied—

    is the spouse of the respondent, or

[(ia) is the civil partner of the respondent, or a person who was a party to a civil partnership with the respondent that has been dissolved under the Act of 2010, or]²

[(ii) is not the spouse or civil partner within the meaning of the Act of 2010 of the respondent and is not related to the respondent within the prohibited degrees of relationship, but lived with the respondent in an intimate and committed relationship prior to the application for the safety order, or]³

(iii) is a parent of the respondent and the respondent is a person of full age who is not, in relation to the parent a dependent person, or

(iv) being of full age resides with the respondent in a relationship the basis of which is not [primarily contractual, or];³

[(v) is a parent of a child whose other parent is the respondent;]⁴

"**kindred**", in respect of two or more persons, means the relationship of each of those persons to the other person or to the rest of those persons by blood, adoption or marriage.

(b) In deciding whether or not a person is residing with another person in a relationship the basis of which is not primarily contractual, the court shall have regard to—

(i) the length of time those persons have been residing together,

(ii) the nature of any duties performed by either person for the other person or for any kindred person of that other person,

(iii) the absence of any profit or of any significant profit made by either person from any monetary or other consideration given by the other person in respect of residing at the place concerned,

(iv) such other matters as the court considers appropriate in the circumstances.

(2) Where the court, on application to it, is of the opinion that there are reasonable grounds for believing that the safety or welfare of the applicant or any dependent person so requires, it may, subject to section 7, by order (in this Act referred to as a "safety order") direct that the respondent to the application—

(a) shall not use or threaten to use violence against, molest or put in fear the applicant or that dependent person, and

(b) if he or she is residing at a place other than the place where the applicant or that dependent person resides, shall not watch or beset the place where the applicant or that dependent person resides,

and the court may make such order subject to such exceptions and conditions as it may specify.

(3) Where a safety order has been made, any of the following may apply to have it varied, that is to say:

(a) if the application for the order was made by a health board in respect of any dependent person by virtue of section 6—

(i) the health board,

      (ii)  the person referred to in subsection (1)(c) that section, or

      (iii)  the respondent to that application;

  (b)  if the application for the order was made by a health board in any other case by virtue of section 6:

      (i)  the health board,

      (ii)  the person who was the applicant for the order, or

      (iii)  the respondent to that application;

  (c)  in any other case—

      (i)  the person who was the applicant for the order, or

      (ii)  the person who was the respondent to the application for the order,

and the court upon hearing any such application shall make such order as it considers appropriate in the circumstances.

(4) For the purposes of subsection (3), a safety order made by a court on appeal from another court shall be treated as if it had been made by that other court.

(5) A safety order, if made by the District Court or by the Circuit Court on appeal from the District Court, shall, subject to subsection (6)(a) and section 13, expire five years after the date of its making or on the expiration of such shorter period as the court may provide for in the order.

(6) (a)  On or before the expiration of a safety order to which subsection (5) relates, a further safety order may be made by the District Court or by the Circuit Court on appeal from the District Court for a period of five years, or such shorter period as the court may provide for in the order, with effect from the expiration of the first-mentioned order.

  (b)  On or before the expiration of a safety order to which paragraph (a) does not relate, a further safety order may be made with effect from the- expiration of the first mentioned safety order.

(7) Notwithstanding subsection (5), so much of a safety order as was made for the benefit of a dependent person shall expire in accordance with such order or upon such person ceasing to be a dependent person, whichever first occurs.

(8) The court shall not make a safety order on an application for a barring order unless there is also an application for a safety order before the court concerning the same matter.

---

**Notes**

1   See the Family Law (Divorce) Act 1996, s 51.

2   Subsection 1(a)(i) was substituted by the Civil Partnership and Certain Rights and Obligations of Cohabitants Act 2010, s 92.

3   Subsection (1)(a)(ii) substituted by the Civil Law (Miscellaneous Provisions) Act 2011, s 60. Subsection 1(a)(iv) amended by the Civil Law (Miscellaneous Provisions) Act 2011, s 60.

4   Subsection (1)(a)(v) inserted by the Civil Law (Miscellaneous Provisions) Act 2011, s 60.

## 3   Barring order[1]

(1) In this section **"the applicant"** means a person, other than a health board, who has applied or on whose behalf a health board has applied by virtue of section 6 for a barring order against another person (in this section referred to as "the respondent") and the person so applying or on whose behalf the health board has so applied—

(a)  is the spouse of the respondent, or

[(aa)  is the civil partner of the respondent, or a person who was a party to a civil partnership with the respondent that has been dissolved under the Act of 2010, or][2]

[(b)  is not the spouse or civil partner within the meaning of the Act of 2010 of the respondent and is not related to the respondent within the prohibited degrees of relationship, but lived with the respondent in an intimate and committed relationship for a period of at least six months in aggregate during the period of nine months immediately prior to the application for the barring order, or][3]

(c)  is a parent of the respondent and the respondent is a person of full age who is not, in relation to the parent, a dependent person.

(2) (a)  Where the court, on application to it, is of the opinion that there are reasonable grounds for believing that the safety or welfare of the applicant or any dependent person so requires, it may, subject to section 7 and having taken into account any order made or to be made to which paragraph (a) or (d) of subsection (2) of section 9 relates, by order (in this Act referred to as a "barring order")—

(i)  direct the respondent, if residing at a place where the applicant or that dependent person resides, to leave such place, and

(ii)  whether the respondent is or is not residing at a place where the applicant or that dependent person resides, prohibit that respondent from entering such place until further order of the court or until such other time as the court shall specify.

(b)  In deciding whether or not to grant a barring order the court shall have regard to the safety and welfare of any dependent person in respect of whom the respondent is a parent or *in loco parentis*, where such dependent person is residing at the place to which the order, if made, would relate.

(3) A barring order may, if the court thinks fit, prohibit the respondent from doing one or more of the following, that is to say:

(a)  using or threatening to use violence against the applicant or any dependent person:

(b) molesting or putting in fear the applicant or any dependent person;

(c) attending at or in the vicinity of, or watching or besetting a place where, the applicant or any dependent person resides;

and shall be subject to such exceptions and conditions as the court may specify.

(4) (a) In respect of a person who is an applicant by virtue of paragraph (b) or (c) of subsection (1), the court shall not make a barring order in respect of the place where the applicant or dependent person resides where the respondent has a legal or beneficial interest in that place but—

    (i) the applicant has no such interest, or

    (ii) the applicant's interest is, in the opinion of the court, less than that of the respondent.

(b) Where in proceedings to which this section applies the applicant states the belief, in respect of the place to which paragraph (a) relates, that he or she has a legal or beneficial interest in that place which is not less than that of the respondent, then such belief shall be admissible in evidence.

(5) Without prejudice to section 22, nothing in this Act shall be construed as affecting the rights of any person, other than the applicant or the respondent, who has a legal or beneficial interest in a place in respect of which the court has made an order under this section.

(6) Where a barring order has been made, any of the following may apply to have it varied, that is to say:

(a) if the application for the order was made by a health board in respect of any dependent person by virtue of section 6—

    (i) the health board,

    (ii) the person referred to in subsection (1)(c) of that section, or

    (iii) the respondent to that application;

(b) if the application for the order was made by a health board in any other case by virtue of section 6—

    (i) the health board,

    (ii) the person who was the applicant for the order, or

    (iii) the respondent to that application;

(c) in any other case—

    (i) the person who was the applicant for the order, or

    (ii) the person who was the respondent to the application for the order.

and the court upon hearing any such application shall make such order as it considers appropriate in the circumstances.

(7) For the purposes of subsection (6), a barring order made by a court on appeal from another court shall be treated as if it had been made by that other court.

(8) A barring order, if made by the District Court or by the Circuit Court on appeal from the District Court, shall, subject to subsection (9)(a) and section 13, expire three years

after the date of its making or on the expiration of such shorter period as the court may provide for in the order.

(9) (a) On or before the expiration of a barring order to which subsection (8) relates, a further barring order may be made by the District Court or by the Circuit Court on appeal from the District Court for a period of three years, or such shorter period as the court may provide for in the order, with effect from the expiration of the first-mentioned order.

(b) On or before the expiration of a barring order to which paragraph (a) does not relate, a further barring order may be made with effect from the expiration of the first-mentioned barring order.

(10) Notwithstanding subsection (8), so much of a barring order as was made for the benefit of a dependent person shall expire in accordance with such order or upon such person ceasing to be a dependent person, whichever first occurs.

(11) The court shall not make a barring order on an application for a safety order unless there is also an application for a barring order before the court concerning the same matter.

(12) For the purposes of subsections (2) and (3), an applicant or a dependent person who would, but for the conduct of the respondent, be residing at a place shall be treated as residing at such place.

[(13) Where, by reason only of either or both of the following, that is to say, a barring order and an interim barring order, an applicant who is not the spouse of the respondent has not lived with the respondent as husband or wife for a period of at least six months in aggregate during the period of nine months immediately prior to the application for a further barring order under subsection (9), the applicant shall be deemed, for the purposes of this section, to have lived with the respondent as husband or wife for a period of at least six months in aggregate during the period of nine months immediately prior to the application.][4]

## Notes

1   See the Family Law (Divorce) act 1996, s 51.

2   Subsection (1)(aa) inserted by the Civil Partnership and Certain Rights and Obligations of Cohabitants Act 2010, s 93.

3   Subsection (3)(1)(b) substituted by the Civil Law (Miscellaneous Provisions) Act 2011, s 60.

4   Subsection (13) was inserted by Family Law (Miscellaneous Provisions) Act 1997, s 4.

## 4      Interim barring order

(1) If, on the making of an application for a barring order or between the making of such application and its determination, the court is of the opinion that there are reasonable grounds for believing that—

(a) there is an immediate risk of significant harm to the applicant or any dependent person if the order is not made immediately, and

(b) the granting of a protection order would not be sufficient to protect the applicant or any dependent person,

the court may, subject to section 7 and having taken into account any order made or to be made to which paragraph (a) or (d) of subsection (2) of section 9 relates, by order (in this Act referred to as an "interim barring order")—

(i) direct the respondent, if residing at a place where the applicant or that dependent person resides, to leave such place, and

(ii) whether the respondent is or is not residing at a place where the applicant or that dependent person resides, prohibit that respondent from entering such place until further order of the court or until such other time as the court shall specify.

(2) Subsections (3), (4), (5), (6), (7) and (12) of section 3 shall apply to an interim barring order as they apply to a barring order.

[(3) (a) An interim barring order may be made ex parte where, having regard to the circumstances of the particular case, the court considers it necessary or expedient to do so in the interests of justice.

(b) The application for such an order shall be grounded on an affidavit or information sworn by the applicant.

(c) If an interim barring order is made *ex parte*—

(i) a note of evidence given by the applicant shall be prepared forthwith—

(I) by the judge,

(II) by the applicant or the applicant's solicitor and approved by the judge, or

(III) as otherwise directed by the judge,

and

(ii) a copy of the order, affidavit or information and note shall be served on the respondent as soon as practicable.

(d) The order shall have effect for a period, not exceeding 8 working days, to be specified in the order, unless, on application by the applicant for the barring order and on notice to the respondent, the interim barring order is confirmed within that period by order of the court.

(e) The order shall contain a statement of the effect of paragraph (d).

(f) In paragraph (d) 'working days' means days other than Saturdays, Sundays or public holidays (within the meaning of the Organisation of Working Time Act 1997).][1]

(4) An interim barring order shall cease to have effect on the determination by the court of the application for a barring order.

(5) Notwithstanding subsection (4), so much of an interim barring order as was made for the benefit of a dependent person shall cease to have effect in accordance with that subsection or upon such person ceasing to be a dependent person, whichever first occurs.

**Notes**

1    Section 4(3) was substituted by the Domestic Violence (Amendment) Act 2002, s 1.

## 5       Protection order

(1) If, on the making of an application for a safety order or a barring order or between the making of such an application and its determination, the court is of the opinion that there are reasonable grounds for believing that the safety or welfare of the applicant for the order concerned or of any dependent person so requires, the court may by order (in this Act referred to as a "protection order") direct that the respondent to the application—

(a)   shall not use or threaten to use violence against, molest or put in fear the applicant or that dependent person, and

(b)   if he or she is residing at a place other than the place where the applicant or that dependent person resides, shall not watch or beset the place where the applicant or that dependent person resides,

and the court may make the protection order subject to such exceptions and conditions as it may specify.

(2) Where a protection order has been made, any of the following may apply to have it varied, that is to say:

(a)   if the application for the order was made by a health board in respect of any dependent person by virtue of section 6

(i)   the health board,

(ii)   the person referred to in subsection (1)(c) of that section, or

(iii)   the respondent to that application;

(b)   if the application for the order was made by a health board in any other case by virtue of section 6—

(i)   the health board,

(ii)   the person who was the applicant for the order, or

(iii)   the respondent to that application;

(c)   in any other case—

(i)   the person who was the applicant for the order, or

(ii)   the person who was the respondent to the application for the order,

and the court upon hearing any such application shall make such order as it considers appropriate in the circumstances.

(3) For the purposes of subsection (2), a protection order made by a court on appeal from another court shall be treated as if it had been made by that other court.

(4) A protection order may be made [*ex parte.*][1]

(5) A protection order shall cease to have effect on the determination by the court of the application for a safety order or a barring order.

(6) Notwithstanding subsection (5), so much of a protection order as was made for the benefit of a dependent person shall cease to have effect in accordance with that subsection or upon such person ceasing to be a dependent person, whichever first occurs.

(7) For the purposes of this section, an applicant or a dependent person who would, but for the conduct of the respondent, be residing at a place shall be treated as residing at such place.

**Notes**

1    Section 5(4) was amended by the Domestic Violence (Amendment) Act 2002, s 1.

**6        Power of health board to apply for certain orders[1]**

(1) Subject to subsections (2), (3) and (4), this section shall apply where a health board—

(a)  becomes aware of an alleged incident or series of incidents which in its opinion puts into doubt the safety or welfare of a person (in this section referred to as the "aggrieved person"),

(b)  has reasonable cause to believe that the aggrieved person has been subjected to molestation, violence or threatened violence or otherwise put in fear of his or her safety or welfare,

(c)  is of the opinion that there are reasonable grounds for believing that, where appropriate in the circumstances, a person would be deterred or prevented as a consequence of molestation, violence or threatened violence by the respondent or fear of the respondent from pursuing an application for a safety order or a barring order on his or her own behalf or on behalf of a dependent person, and

(d)  considers, having ascertained as far as is reasonably practicable the wishes of the aggrieved person or, where the aggrieved person is a dependent person, of the person to whom paragraph (c) relates in respect of such dependent person, that it is appropriate in all the circumstances to apply for a safety order or a barring order or both in accordance with this Act on behalf of the aggrieved person.

(2) A health board may apply to the court on behalf of the aggrieved person for a safety order or a barring order for which the aggrieved person or, where the aggrieved person is a dependent person, the person to whom subsection (1)(c) relates in respect of such dependent person could have applied.

(3) Where an application is made by a health board by virtue of this section, the court shall, in determining whether, and if so to what extent, to exercise any of its functions under section 2, 3, 4, 5 or 13, have regard to any wishes expressed by—

    (a)  the aggrieved person, or

    (b)  where the aggrieved person is a dependent person, the person to whom subsection (1)(c) relates in respect of such dependent person and, where the court considers it appropriate, such dependent person.

(4) The provisions of paragraphs (a) and (b) of subsection (1) need not be complied with—

    (a)  where the application relates to an aggrieved person who is a dependent person, or

    (b)  in respect of so much of an application as relates to an aggrieved person where such person is a dependent person,

if the court is of the opinion that there is reasonable cause to believe that

        (i)  such dependent person has been or is being assaulted, ill-treated, sexually abused or seriously neglected, or

        (ii)  such dependent person's health, development or welfare has been, is being or is likely to be avoidably impaired or seriously neglected,

and that if the order is made the likelihood of harm to such dependent person will not arise or will be materially diminished.

(5) The court shall not make a barring order or an interim barring order where the aggrieved person is a dependent person unless the health board satisfies the court that the person to whom subsection (1)(c) relates in respect of such dependent person is willing and able to provide reasonable care for such dependent person.

(6)  (a)  The functions of a health board by virtue of this section shall be functions of the chief executive officer of the board.

      (b)  In this subsection **"chief executive officer"** includes a person acting as deputy chief executive officer in accordance with section 13 of the Health Act, 1970.

---

**Notes**

1   Commencement: 1 January 1997.

---

**7     Power to make orders, etc, under Child Care Act, 1991**

(1) Where in proceedings for any order under this Act, other than proceedings to which section 6 relates, it appears to the court that it may be appropriate for a care order or a supervision order to be made under the Child Care Act, 1991, with respect to a dependent person concerned in the proceedings, the court may, of its own motion or on the application of any person concerned, adjourn the proceedings and direct the health board for the area in which such dependent person resides or is for the time being to

undertake an investigation or, as the case may be, further investigations of such dependent person's circumstances.

(2) Where proceedings are adjourned and the court gives a direction under subsection (1), the court may give such directions under the Child Care Act, 1991, as it sees fit as to the care and custody of, and may make a supervision order under that Act in respect of, the dependent person concerned pending the outcome of the investigation by the health board concerned.

(3) Where the court gives a direction under subsection (1) in respect of a dependent person, the health board concerned shall undertake an investigation of such dependent person's circumstances and shall consider if it should—

(a) apply for a care order or a supervision order under the Child Care Act, 1991,

(b) provide services or assistance for such dependent person's family, or

(c) take any other action in respect of such dependent person.

(4) Where a health board undertakes an investigation under this section and decides not to apply for a care order or supervision order under the Child Care Act, 1991, with respect to the dependent person concerned, it shall inform the court of—

(a) its reasons for so deciding,

(b) any service or assistance it has provided, or intends to provide, for such dependent person and his or her family, and

(c) any other action which it has taken, or proposes to take, with respect to such dependent person.

**8 Application of section 9(2) of Family Home Protection Act, 1976, to certain orders**

(1) Subsection (2) of section 9 (which restricts the right of a spouse to dispose of or remove household chattels pending the determination of matrimonial proceedings) of the Family Home Protection Act, 1976, shall apply between the making of an application, against the spouse of the applicant, for a barring order or a safety order and its determination, and if an order is made, while such order is in force, as it applies between the institution and final determination of matrimonial proceedings to which that section relates.

(2) For the avoidance of doubt, it is hereby declared that the court which is empowered under subsection (2)(b) of section 9 of the Family Home Protection Act, 1976, to grant permission for any disposition or removal of household chattels (being household chattels within the meaning of that section) is, notwithstanding anything in section 10 of that Act, the court before which the proceedings (including any proceedings for a barring order or a safety order) have been instituted.

**[8A Application of orders restricting disposal or removal of household chattels**

(1) Section 34(2) (which restricts the right of a civil partner to dispose of or remove household chattels) of the Act of 2010 shall apply between the making of an application against the civil partner of the applicant for a barring order or a safety order and its determination, and if an order is made, while the order is in force, as it applies between

the institution and final determination of dissolution proceedings to which that section relates.

(2) A court which is empowered under section 34(2)(b) of the Act of 2010 to grant permission for any disposition or removal of household chattels within the meaning of that section is, notwithstanding anything in section 140 of that Act, the court before which the proceedings (including any proceedings for a barring order or a safety order) have been instituted.][1]

**Notes**

1   Section 8A was inserted by Civil Partnership and Certain Rights and Obligations of Cohabitants Act 2010, s 94.

**9       Hearing of applications under various Acts together**

(1) Where an application is made to the court for an order under this Act, the court may, on application to it in the same proceedings and without the institution of proceedings under the Act concerned, if it appears to the court to be proper to do so, make one or more of the orders referred to in subsection (2).

(2) The provisions to which subsection (1) relates are as follows, that is to say:

   (a)   an order under section 11 (as amended by the Status of Children Act, 1987) of the Guardianship of Infants Act, 1964;

   (b)   an order under section 5, 5A, 6, 7 or 21A of the Family Law (Maintenance of Spouses and Children) Act, 1976 (as amended by the Status of Children Act, 1987);

   (c)   an order under section 5 or 9 of the Family Home Protection Act, 1976;

   [(cc)  an order under section 30, 34 or 45 of the Act of 2010;][1]

   (d)   an order under the Child Care Act, 1991.

**Notes**

1   Subsection (2)(cc) was inserted by Civil Partnership and Certain Rights and Obligations of Cohabitants Act 2010, s 95.

**10      Taking effect of orders**

(1) A safety order, barring order, interim barring order or protection order shall take effect on notification of its making being given to the respondent.

(2) Oral communication to the respondent by or on behalf of the applicant of the fact that a safety order, barring order, interim barring order or protection order has been made, together with production of a copy of the order, shall, without prejudice to the

sufficiency of any other form of notification, be taken to be sufficient notification to the respondent of the making of the order.

(3) If the respondent is present at a sitting of the court at which the safety order, barring order, interim barring order or protection order is made, that respondent shall be taken for the purposes of subsection (1) to have been notified of its making.

(4) An order varying a safety order, barring order, interim barring order or protection order shall take effect on notification of its making being given to the person who was the other party in the proceedings for the making of the safety order or barring order and for this purpose subsections (2) and (3) shall apply with the necessary modifications.

**11    Copies of orders to be given to certain persons**

(1) The court, on making, varying or discharging a safety order or a protection order, shall cause a copy of the order in question to be given or sent as soon as practicable—

   (a)  to the applicant for the safety order or, in respect of a protection order, the applicant for the safety order or barring order concerned,

   (b)  to the respondent to the application for the safety order or, in respect of a protection order, the respondent to the application for the safety order or barring order concerned,

   (c)  where a health board by virtue of section 6 made the application for the safety order or, in respect of a protection order, for the safety order or barring order, to the health board,

   (d)  to the member of the Garda Síochána in charge of the Garda Síochána station for the area in which the person for whose benefit the safety order or protection order was made resides, and

   (e)  where the order in question is a variation or discharge of a safety order or a protection order and the person for whose benefit the order was made had previously resided elsewhere, to the member of the Garda Síochána in charge of the Garda Síochána station for the area in which that person had so resided but only if that member had previously been sent under this subsection a copy of such safety order or protection order or any order relating thereto.

(2) The court on making, varying or discharging a barring order or an interim barring order shall cause a copy of the order in question to be given or sent as soon as practicable to—

   (a)  the applicant for the barring order,

   (b)  the respondent to the application for the barring order,

   (c)  where a health board by virtue of section 6 made the application for the barring order concerned, the health board,

   (d)  the member of the Garda Síochána in charge of the Garda Síochána station for the area in which is situate the place in relation to which the application for the barring order was made, and

   (e)  where the order in question is a variation or discharge of a barring order or an interim barring order and the place in respect of which the previous order was made is elsewhere, to the member of the Garda Síochána in charge of the Garda Síochána station for the area in which is situated that place but only if that member had previously been sent under this subsection a copy of such barring order or interim barring order or any order relating thereto.

(3) The court—

(a) on making a barring order, a safety order, an interim barring order or a protection order on the application of, or on behalf of, a person who is not of full age, or

(b) on varying or discharging an order to which paragraph (a) relates,

shall cause a copy of the order in question to be given or sent as soon as practicable to the health board for the area in which the person resides.

(4) The validity of any order to which this section relates shall not be affected by non-compliance with the other provisions of this section.

## 12    Effect of appeal from order

(1) An appeal from a safety order or a barring order shall, if the court that made the order or the court to which the appeal is brought so determines (but not otherwise), stay the operation of the order on such terms (if any) as may be imposed by the court making the determination.

(2) An appeal from a protection order or an interim barring order shall not stay the operation of the order.

## 13    Discharge of orders

(1) Where a safety order, barring order, interim barring order or protection order has been made, any of the following may apply to the court that made the order to have the order discharged, that is to say:

(a) if the application for the order was made by a health board in respect of any dependent person by virtue of section 6—

(i)   the health board,

(ii)  the person referred to in subsection (1)(c) of that section, or

(iii) the respondent to that application;

(b) if the application for the order was made by a health board in any other case by virtue of section 6—

(i)   the health board,

(ii)  the person who was the applicant for the order, or

(iii) the respondent to that application;

(c) in any other case—

(i)   the person who was the applicant for the order, or

(ii)  the person who was the respondent to the application for the order, and thereupon the court shall discharge the order if it is of the opinion that the safety and welfare of the applicant or such dependent person for whose protection the order was made does not require that the order should continue in force.

(2) On determination of any matrimonial cause or matter [or any annulment or dissolution proceedings under the Act of 2010,][1] between the applicant and the respondent or of any proceedings between them under the Guardianship of Infants Act, 1964, the court determining any such cause, matter or proceedings may, if it thinks fit, discharge any safety order, barring order, interim barring order or protection order.

(3) For the purposes of this section, an order made by a court on appeal from another court shall be treated as if it had been made by that other court.

**Notes**

1   Subsection (2) was amended by Civil Partnership and Certain Rights and Obligations of Cohabitants Act 2010, s 96.

## 14      Exercise of jurisdiction by court

(1) The jurisdiction of the court in respect of civil proceedings under this Act may be exercised—

   (a)   as regards the Circuit Court, by the judge of the circuit, and

   (b)   as regards the District Court, by the judge of the District Court for the time being assigned to the district court district,

where the applicant resides or, if the application is for a barring order, where there is situate the place in relation to which that application was made.

(2) For the purposes of subsection (1), the court may treat any person concerned as residing at a place where that person would, but for the conduct of the respondent, be residing at.

(3) Where a judge of the District Court to whom subsection (1) relates is not immediately available, the jurisdiction of the District Court under that subsection may be exercised by any judge of the District Court.

## 15      Rules of Court

(1) For the purpose of ensuring the expeditious hearing of applications under this Act, rules of court may make provision for the service of documents otherwise than under section 7 (as amended by section 22 of the Courts Act, 1971) of the Courts Act, 1964, in circumstances to which that section relates.

(2) This section is without prejudice to section 17 of the Interpretation Act, 1937, which provides for rules of court.

## 16      Hearing of civil proceedings, etc

(1) Civil proceedings under this Act shall be heard otherwise than in public.

(2) Where under section 9 the court hears together applications under several enactments, then the court shall as far as is practicable comply with the requirements relating to the hearing of applications under each of those enactments and the other relevant provisions of those Acts shall apply accordingly.

(3) (a) Civil proceedings under this Act before the District Court shall be as informal as is practicable and consistent with the administration of justice.

   (b) District Court judges hearing and determining civil proceedings under this Act and barristers and solicitors appearing in such proceedings shall not wear wigs or gowns.

(4) Civil proceedings under this Act before the Circuit Court shall be heard by the Circuit Family Court and, accordingly, the provisions of section 32 and subsection (1) and (2) of section 33 of the Judicial Separation and Family Law Reform Act, 1989, shall apply to such proceedings.

(5) The proceedings to which subsections (3) and (4) of section 33 of the Judicial Separation and Family Law Reform Act, 1989, apply shall be deemed to include civil proceedings under this Act.

## 17 Offences

(1) A respondent who—

   (a) contravenes a safety order, a barring order, an interim barring order or a protection order, or

   (b) while a barring order or interim barring order is in force refuses to permit the applicant or any dependent person to enter in and remain in the place to which the order relates or does any act for the purpose of preventing the applicant or such dependent person from so doing,

shall be guilty of an offence and shall be liable on summary conviction to a fine not exceeding [€1,904.61] or, at the discretion of the court, to imprisonment for a term not exceeding 12 months, or to both.

(2) Subsection (1) is without prejudice to the law as to contempt of court or any other liability, whether civil or criminal, that may be incurred by the respondent concerned.

## 18 Arrest without warrant

(1) (a) Where a member of the Garda Síochána has reasonable cause for believing that, in respect of an order under this Act, an offence is being or has been committed under section 17 the member may, on complaint being made to him or her by or on behalf of the person who was the applicant to which the order relates, arrest the respondent concerned without warrant.

   (b) For the purpose of arresting a respondent under paragraph (a), a member of the Garda Síochána may enter, if need be by force, and search any place where the member, with reasonable cause, suspects the respondent to be.

(2) Where a member of the Garda Síochána has reasonable cause for believing that a person (in this section referred to as "the first-mentioned person") is committing or has committed—

(a)  an assault occasioning actual bodily harm, or

(b)  an offence under section 20 (which relates to unlawfully and maliciously wounding or inflicting any grievous bodily harm) of the Offences against the Person Act, 1861,

against a person (in this section referred to as "the second-mentioned person") in circumstances which in the opinion of the member could give rise to the second-mentioned person applying for, or on whose behalf another person could in accordance with this Act apply for, a safety order or a barring order, then the member may—

(i)  arrest the first-mentioned person without warrant,

and

(ii)  for the purpose of making such an arrest, enter, if need be by force, and search any place where the member, with reasonable cause, suspects the first-mentioned person to be.

**19      Costs**

The costs of any civil proceedings under this Act shall be in the discretion of the court.

**20      Amendment of Judicial Separation and Family Law Reform Act, 1989**

The Judicial Separation and Family Law Reform Act, 1989, is hereby amended—

(a)  in section 11, by the substitution of the following paragraph for paragraph (a):

"(a)  a safety order, barring order, interim barring order or protection order pursuant to section 2, 3, 4 or 5, respectively, of the Domestic Violence Act, 1996;",

(b)  in section 16, by the substitution of the following paragraph for paragraph (e):

"(e)  an order under section 2, 3, 4 or 5 of the Domestic Violence Act, 1996;".

and

(c)  in section 19, by the substitution of "the Domestic Violence Act, 1996" for "the Family Law (Protection of Spouses and Children) Act, 1981".

**21      Amendment of Family Law Act, 1995[1]**

---

**Notes**

1   Section 21 amends the Family Law Act 1995, ss 2, 6, 10 and 47; see the amended Act.

---

**22      Saving provisions**

(1) Where, by reason only of an interim barring order or a barring order, a person is not residing at a place during any period, that person shall be deemed, for the purposes of any rights under the Statutes of Limitation, 1957 and 1991, the Landlord and Tenant Acts, 1967 to 1994, and the Housing (Private Rented Dwellings) Acts, 1982 and 1983, to be residing at that place during that period.

(2) Except in so far as the exercise by a respondent of a right to occupy the place to which a barring order or an interim barring order relates is suspended by virtue of the order, the order shall not affect any estate or interest in that place of that respondent or any other person.

## 23 Repeal and transitional provisions

(1) The Family Law (Protection of Spouses and Children) Act, 1981 (in this section referred to as "the Act of 1981"), is hereby repealed.

(2) (a) Subject to paragraph (b), this Act shall apply to a barring order made under the Act of 1981 and which is in force, or stayed by virtue of section 10 of that Act, at the commencement of this Act as if it were an order made under section 3.

    (b) For the purposes of a barring order to which paragraph (a) relates, the reference in section 3 (8) to the expiration of three years after the date of its making shall be construed as a reference to twelve months after the date of its making.

(3) An application made to the court under the Act of 1981 for a barring order and not determined before the commencement of this Act shall be treated as if it had been made under section 3.

(4) This Act shall apply to a protection order made under the Act of 1981 and which is in force at the commencement of this Act as if it were an order made under section 5.

## 24 Expenses

The expenses incurred by the Minister for Equality and Law Reform, the Minister for Health and the Minister for Justice in the administration of this Act shall, to such extent as may be sanctioned by the Minister for Finance, be paid out of moneys provided by the Oireachtas.

## 25 Commencement[1]

(1) Subject to sub-section (2), this Act shall come into operation one month after the date of its passing.

(2) Section 6 and so much of the other provisions of this Act as relate to that section shall come into operation on the 1st day of January, 1997.

**Notes**

1 Commencement: 27 March 1996: s 25.

## 26 Short Title

This Act may be cited as the Domestic Violence Act, 1996.

# Family Law (Divorce) Act 1996

*Number 33 of 1996*

## ARRANGEMENT OF SECTIONS

### PART I
### PRELIMINARY AND GENERAL

### PART II
### THE OBTAINING OF A DECREE OF DIVORCE

### PART III
### PRELIMINARY AND ANCILLARY ORDERS IN OR AFTER PROCEEDINGS FOR DIVORCE

## PART IV
### INCOME TAX, CAPITAL ACQUISITIONS TAX, CAPITAL GAINS TAX, PROBATE TAX AND STAMP DUTY

## PART V
### MISCELLANEOUS

## Acts referred to

| | |
|---|---|
| Adoption Acts, 1952 to 1991 | |
| Capital Acquisitions Tax Act, 1976 | 1976, No. 8 |
| Capital Gains Tax Acts | |
| Censorship of Publications Act, 1929 | 1929, No. 21 |
| Criminal Damage Act, 1991 | 1991, No. 31 |
| Criminal Evidence Act, 1992 | 1992, No. 12 |
| Defence Act, 1954 | 1954, No. 18 |
| Domestic Violence Act, 1996 | 1996, No. 1 |
| Enforcement of Court Orders Act, 1940 | 1940, No. 23 |
| Family Home Protection Act, 1976 | 1976, No. 27 |
| Family Law Act, 1995 | 1995, No. 26 |
| Family Law (Maintenance of Spouses and Children) Act, 1976 | 1976, No. 11 |
| Finance (1909-10) Act, 1910 | 1910, c. 8 |
| Finance Act, 1972 | 1972, No. 19 |
| Finance Act, 1983 | 1983, No. 15 |
| Finance Act, 1993 | 1993, No. 13 |
| Finance Act, 1994 | 1994, No. 13 |
| Guardianship of Infants Act, 1964 | 1964, No. 7 |
| Income Tax Act, 1967 | 1967, No. 6 |
| Income Tax Acts | |
| Insurance Act, 1989 | 1989, No. 3 |
| Judicial Separation and Family Law Reform Act, 1989 | 1989, No. 6 |
| Maintenance Act, 1994 | 1994, No. 28 |
| Partition Act, 1868 | 1868, c. 40 |
| Partition Act, 1876 | 1876, c. 17 |
| Pensions Act, 1990 | 1990, No. 25 |
| Pensions (Amendment) Act, 1996 | 1996, No. 18 |
| Powers of Attorney Act, 1996 | 1996, No. 12 |
| Registration of Title Act, 1964 | 1964, No. 16 |

**Acts referred to**

Social Welfare Acts

Status of Children Act, 1987                    1987, No. 26

Succession Act, 1965                             1965, No. 27

*An Act to make provision for the exercise by the courts of the jurisdiction conferred by the constitution to grant decrees of divorce, to enable the courts to make certain preliminary and ancillary orders in or after proceedings for divorce, to provide, as respects transfers of property of divorced spouses, for their exemption from, or for the abatement of, certain taxes (including stamp duty) and to provide for related matters. [27th November, 1996]*

*Be it enacted by the Oireachtas as follows:*

## PART I
### PRELIMINARY AND GENERAL

**1      Short title and commencement[1]**

(1) This Act may be cited as the Family Law (Divorce) Act, 1996.

(2) This Act shall come into operation on the day that is 3 months after the date of its passing.

---

**Notes**

1   Commencement: 27 February 1997.

---

**2      Interpretation**

(1) In this Act, save where the context otherwise requires—

**"the Act of 1964"** means the Guardianship of Infants Act, 1964;

**"the Act of 1965"** means the Succession Act, 1965;

**"the Act of 1976"** means the Family Law (Maintenance of Spouses and Children) Act, 1976;

**"the Act of 1989"** means the Judicial Separation and Family Law Reform Act, 1989;

**"the Act of 1995"** means the Family Law Act, 1995;

**"the Act of 1996"** means the Domestic Violence Act, 1996;

**["civil partnership"** has the meaning assigned to it by the Civil Partnership and Certain Rights and Obligations of Cohabitants Act 2010;][1]

**"conveyance"** includes a mortgage, lease, assent, transfer, disclaimer, release and any other disposition of property otherwise than by a will or a *donatio mortis causa* and also includes an enforceable agreement (whether conditional or unconditional) to make any such disposition; **"the court"** shall be construed in accordance with section 38;

**"decree of divorce"** means a decree under section 5;

**"decree of judicial separation"** means a decree under section 3 of the Act of 1989;

**"decree of nullity"** means a decree granted by a court declaring a marriage to be null and void;

**"dependent member of the family"**, in relation to a spouse, or the spouses, concerned, means any child—

(a) of both spouses or adopted by both spouses under the Adoption Acts, 1952 to 1991, or in relation to whom both spouses are *in loco parentis*, or

(b) of either spouse or adopted by either spouse under those Acts, or in relation to whom either spouse is *in loco parentis*, where the other spouse, being aware that he or she is not the parent of the child, has treated the child as a member of the family,

who is under the age of 18 years or if the child has attained that age—

(i) is or will be or, if an order were made under this Act providing for periodical payments for the benefit of the child or for the provision of a lump sum for the child, would be receiving full-time education or instruction at any university, college, school or other educational establishment and is under the age of 23 years, or

(ii) has a mental or physical disability to such extent that it is not reasonably possible for the child to maintain himself or herself fully;

**"family home"** has the meaning assigned to it by section 2 of the Family Home Protection Act, 1976, with the modification that the references to a spouse in that section shall be construed as references to a spouse within the meaning of this Act;

**"financial compensation order"** has the meaning assigned to it by section 16;

**"Land Registry"** and **"Registry of Deeds"** have the meanings assigned to them by the Registration of Title Act, 1964;

**"lump sum order"** means an order under section 13(1)(c);

**"maintenance pending suit order"** means an order under section 12;

**"member"**, in relation to a pension scheme, means any person who, having been admitted to membership of the scheme under its rules, remains entitled to any benefit under the scheme;

**"pension adjustment order"** means an order under section 17;

**"pension scheme"** means—

(a) an occupational pension scheme (within the meaning of the Pensions Act, 1990), or

(b) (i) an annuity contract approved by the Revenue Commissioners under section 235 of the Income Tax Act, 1967, or a contract so approved under section 235A of that Act,

      (ii)   a trust scheme, or part of a trust scheme, so approved under subsection (4) of the said section 235 or subsection (5) of the said section 235A, or

      (iii)  a policy or contract of assurance approved by the Revenue Commissioners under Chapter II of Part I of the Finance Act, 1972,

or

[(bb)  a PRSA contract within the meaning of Part X of the Pensions Act 1990, or]²

  (c)  any other scheme or arrangement (including a personal pension plan and a scheme or arrangement established by or pursuant to statute or instrument made under statute other than under the Social Welfare Acts) that provides or is intended to provide either or both of the following, that is to say:

      (i)  benefits for a person who is a member of the scheme or arrangement ("the member") upon retirement at normal pensionable age or upon earlier or later retirement or upon leaving, or upon the ceasing of, the relevant employment,

      (ii)  benefits for the widow, widower or dependants of the member, or for any other persons, on the death of the member;

**"periodical payments order"** and **"secured periodical payments order"** have the meanings assigned to them by section 13;

**"property adjustment order"** has the meaning assigned to it by section 14;

[**"registration"**, with respect to a civil partnership, includes entering into a relationship of a class of legal relationships that is the subject of an order made under section 5 of the Civil Partnership and Certain Rights and Obligations of Cohabitants Act 2010;]³

**"trustees"**, in relation to a scheme that is established under a trust, means the trustees of the scheme and, in relation to a pension scheme not so established, means the persons who administer the scheme.

(2) In this Act, where the context so requires—

  (a)  a reference to a marriage includes a reference to a marriage that has been dissolved under this Act,

  (b)  a reference to a remarriage includes a reference to a marriage that takes place after a marriage that has been dissolved under this Act,

  (c)  a reference to a spouse includes a reference to a person who is a party to a marriage that has been dissolved under this Act,

  (d)  a reference to a family includes a reference to a family as respects which the marriage of the spouses concerned has been dissolved under this Act,

  (e)  a reference to an application to a court by a person on behalf of a dependent member of the family includes a reference to such an application by such a member and a reference to a payment, the securing of a payment, or the assignment of an interest, to a person for the benefit of a dependent member of the family includes a reference to a payment, the securing of a payment, or the assignment of an interest, to such a member,

and cognate words shall be construed accordingly.

(3) In this Act—

    (a)  a reference to any enactment shall, unless the context otherwise requires, be construed as a reference to that enactment as amended or extended by or under any subsequent enactment including this Act,

    (b)  a reference to a Part or section is a reference to a Part or section of this Act unless it is indicated that reference to some other enactment is intended,

    (c)  a reference to a subsection, paragraph, subparagraph or clause is a reference to the subsection, paragraph, subparagraph or clause of the provision in which the reference occurs unless it is indicated that reference to some other provision is intended.

**Notes**

1   Definition of "civil partnership" was inserted by the Civil Partnership and Certain Rights and Obligations of Cohabitants Act 2010, s 150.

2   Section 2(1)(bb) was inserted by the Pensions (Amendment) Act 2002, s 57.

3   Definition of "registration" was inserted by the Civil Partnership and Certain Rights and Obligations of Cohabitants Act 2010, s 150.

**3      Repeal**

Section 14(2) of the Censorship of Publications Act, 1929, is hereby repealed.

**4      Expenses**

The expenses incurred by the Minister for Equality and Law Reform, the Minister for Health or the Minister for Justice in the administration of this Act shall, to such extent as may be sanctioned by the Minister for Finance, be paid out of moneys provided by the Oireachtas.

## PART II
### THE OBTAINING OF A DECREE OF DIVORCE

**5      Grant of decree of divorce and custody etc., of children**

(1) Subject to the provisions of this Act, where, on application to it in that behalf by either of the spouses concerned, the court is satisfied that—

    (a)  at the date of the institution of the proceedings, the spouses have lived apart from one another for a period of, or periods amounting to, at least four years during the previous five years,

    (b)  there is no reasonable prospect of a reconciliation between the spouses, and

    (c)  such provision as the court considers proper having regard to the circumstances exists or will be made for the spouses and any dependent members of the family, the court may, in exercise of the jurisdiction conferred by Article 41.3.2° of the Constitution, grant a decree of divorce in respect of the marriage concerned.

(2) Upon the grant of a decree of divorce, the court may, where appropriate, give such directions under section 11 of the Act of 1964 as it considers proper regarding the welfare (within the meaning of that Act), custody of, or right of access to, any dependent member of the family concerned who is an infant (within the meaning of that Act) as if an application had been made to it in that behalf under that section.

**6      Safeguards to ensure applicant's awareness of alternatives to divorce proceedings and to assist attempts at reconciliation**

(1) In this section **"the applicant"** means a person who has applied, is applying or proposes to apply to the court for the grant of a decree of divorce.

(2) If a solicitor is acting for the applicant, the solicitor shall, prior to the institution of the proceedings concerned under section 5—

(a) discuss with the applicant the possibility of a reconciliation and give to him or her the names and addresses of persons qualified to help to effect a reconciliation between spouses who have become estranged,

(b) discuss with the applicant the possibility of engaging in mediation to help to effect a separation (if the spouses are not separated) or a divorce on a basis agreed between the applicant and the other spouse and give to the applicant the names and addresses of persons qualified to provide a mediation service for spouses who have become estranged, and

(c) discuss with the applicant the possibility (where appropriate) of effecting a separation by means of a deed or agreement in writing executed or made by the applicant and the other spouse and providing for their separation.

(3) Such a solicitor shall also ensure that the applicant is aware of judicial separation as an alternative to divorce where a decree of judicial separation in relation to the applicant and the other spouse is not in force.

(4) If a solicitor is acting for the applicant—

(a) the originating document by which the proceedings under section 5 are instituted shall be accompanied by a certificate signed by the solicitor indicating, if it be the case, that he or she has complied with subsection (2) and, if appropriate, subsection (3) in relation to the matter and, if the document is not so accompanied, the court may adjourn the proceedings for such period as it considers reasonable to enable the solicitor to engage in the discussions specified in subsection (2), and, if appropriate, to make the applicant aware of judicial separation,

(b) if the solicitor has complied with paragraph (a), any copy of the originating document aforesaid served on any person or left in an office of the court shall be accompanied by a copy of the certificate aforesaid.

(5) A certificate under subsection (4)(a) shall be in a form prescribed by rules of court or a form to the like effect.

(6) The Minister may make regulations to allow for the establishment of a Register of Professional Organisations whose members are qualified to assist the parties involved in effecting a reconciliation, such register to show the names of members of those organisations and procedures to be put in place for the organisations involved to regularly update the membership lists.

**7       Safeguards to ensure respondent's awareness of alternatives to divorce proceedings and to assist attempts at reconciliation**

(1) In this section "**the respondent**" means a person who is the respondent in proceedings in the court under section 5.

(2) If a solicitor is acting for the respondent, the solicitor shall, as soon as may be after receiving instructions from the respondent in relation to the proceedings concerned under section 5—

   (a) discuss with the respondent the possibility of a reconciliation and give to him or her the names and addresses of persons qualified to effect a reconciliation between spouses who have become estranged,

   (b) discuss with the respondent the possibility of engaging in mediation to help to effect a separation (if the spouses are not separated) or a divorce on a basis agreed between the respondent and the other spouse and give to the respondent the names and addresses of persons qualified to provide a mediation service for spouses who have become estranged, and

   (c) discuss with the respondent the possibility (where appropriate) of effecting a separation by means of a deed or agreement in writing executed or made by the applicant and the other spouse and providing for their separation.

(3) Such a solicitor shall also ensure that the respondent is aware of judicial separation as an alternative to divorce where a decree of judicial separation is not in force in relation to the respondent and the other spouse.

(4) If a solicitor is acting for the respondent—

   (a) the memorandum or other document delivered to the appropriate officer of the court for the purpose of the entry of an appearance by the respondent in proceedings under section 5 shall be accompanied by a certificate signed by the solicitor indicating, if it be the case, that the solicitor has complied with subsection (2) and, if appropriate, subsection (3) in relation to the matter and, if the document is not so accompanied, the court may adjourn the proceedings for such period as it considers reasonable to enable the solicitor to engage in the discussions specified in subsection (2) and, if appropriate, to make the applicant aware of judicial separation,

   (b) if paragraph (a) is complied with, any copy of the document aforesaid given or sent to the other party to the proceedings or his or her solicitor shall be accompanied by a copy of the relevant certificate aforesaid.

(5) A certificate under subsection (4)(a) shall be in a form prescribed by rules of court or a form to the like effect.

**8      Adjournment of proceedings to assist reconciliation or agreements on the terms of the divorce**

(1) Where an application is made to the court for the grant of a decree of divorce, the court shall give consideration to the possibility of a reconciliation between the spouses concerned and, accordingly, may adjourn the proceedings at any time for the purpose of enabling attempts to be made by the spouses, if they both so wish, to effect such a reconciliation with or without the assistance of a third party.

(2) Where, in proceedings under section 5, it appears to the court that a reconciliation between the spouses cannot be effected, it may adjourn or further adjourn the proceedings for the purpose of enabling attempts to be made by the spouses, if they both so wish, to reach agreement, with or without the assistance of a third party, on some or all of the terms of the proposed divorce.

(3) If proceedings are adjourned pursuant to subsection (1) or (2), either or both of the spouses may at any time request that the hearing of the proceedings be resumed as soon as may be and, if such a request is made, the court shall, subject to any other power of the court to adjourn proceedings, resume the hearing.

(4) The powers conferred by this section are additional to any other power of the court to adjourn proceedings.

(5) Where the court adjourns proceedings under this section, it may, at its discretion, advise the spouses concerned to seek the assistance of a third party in relation to the effecting of a reconciliation between the spouses or the reaching of agreement between them on some or all of the terms of the proposed divorce.

**9      Non-admissibility as evidence of certain communications relating to reconciliation, separation or divorce**

An oral or written communication between either of the spouses concerned and a third party for the purpose of seeking assistance to effect a reconciliation or to reach agreement between them on some or all of the terms of a separation or a divorce (whether or not made in the presence or with the knowledge of the other spouse), and any record of such a communication, made or caused to be made by either of the spouses concerned or such a third party, shall not be admissible as evidence in any court.

**10      Effect of decree of divorce**

(1) Where the court grants a decree of divorce, the marriage, the subject of the decree, is thereby dissolved and a party to that marriage may marry again.

(2) For the avoidance of doubt, it is hereby declared that the grant of a decree of divorce shall not affect the right of the father and mother of an infant, under section 6 of the Act of 1964, to be guardians of the infant jointly.

## PART III
### PRELIMINARY AND ANCILLARY ORDERS IN OR AFTER PROCEEDINGS FOR DIVORCE

**Notes**

See Finance Act 1997, s 142(1)(d).

### 11 Preliminary orders in proceedings for divorce

Where an application is made to the court for the grant of a decree of divorce, the court, before deciding whether to grant or refuse to grant the decree, may, in the same proceedings and without the institution of proceedings under the Act concerned, if it appears to the court to be proper to do so, make one or more of the following orders—

(a) a safety order, a barring order, an interim barring order or a protection order under the Act of 1996,

(b) an order under section 11 of the Act of 1964,

(c) an order under section 5 or 9 of the Family Home Protection Act, 1976.

### 12 Maintenance pending suit orders

(1) Where an application is made to the court for the grant of a decree of divorce, the court may make an order for maintenance pending suit, that is to say, an order requiring either of the spouses concerned to make to the other spouse such periodical payments or lump sum payments for his or her support and, where appropriate, to make to such person as may be specified in the order such periodical payments for the benefit of such (if any) dependent member of the family and, as respects periodical payments, for such period beginning not earlier than the date of the application and ending not later than the date of its determination, as the court considers proper and specifies in the order.

(2) The court may provide that payments under an order under this section shall be subject to such terms and conditions as it considers appropriate and specifies in the order.

### 13 Periodical payments and lump sum orders

(1) On granting a decree of divorce or at any time thereafter, the court, on application to it in that behalf by either of the spouses concerned or by a person on behalf of a dependent member of the family, may, during the lifetime of the other spouse, or, as the case may be, the spouse concerned, make one or more of the following orders, that is to say—

(a) a periodical payments order, that is to say—

(i) an order that either of the spouses shall make to the other spouse such periodical payments of such amount, during such period and at such times as may be specified in the order, or

    (ii)  an order that either of the spouses shall make to such person as may be so specified for the benefit of such (if any) dependent member of the family such periodical payments of such amount, during such period and at such times as may be so specified,

  (b)  a secured periodical payments order, that is to say—

    (i)  an order that either of the spouses shall secure, to the satisfaction of the court, to the other spouse such periodical payments of such amounts, during such period and at such times as may be so specified, or

    (ii)  an order that either of the spouses shall secure, to the satisfaction of the court, to such person as may be so specified for the benefit of such (if any) dependent member of the family such periodical payments of such amounts, during such period and at such times as may be so specified,

  (c)  (i)  an order that either of the spouses shall make to the other spouse a lump sum payment or lump sum payments of such amount or amounts and at such time or times as may be so specified, or

    (ii)  an order that either of the spouses shall make to such person as may be so specified for the benefit of such (if any) dependent member of the family a lump sum payment or lump sum payments of such amount or amounts and at such time or times as may be so specified.

(2) The court may—

  (a)  order a spouse to pay a lump sum to the other spouse to meet any liabilities or expenses reasonably incurred by that other spouse before the making of an application by that other spouse for an order under subsection (1) in maintaining himself or herself or any dependent member of the family, or

  (b)  order a spouse to pay a lump sum to such person as may be specified to meet any liabilities or expenses reasonably incurred by or for the benefit of a dependent member of the family before the making of an application on behalf of the member for an order under subsection (1).

(3) An order under this section for the payment of a lump sum may provide for the payment of the lump sum by instalments of such amounts as may be specified in the order and may require the payment of the instalments to be secured to the satisfaction of the court.

(4) The period specified in an order under paragraph (a) or (b) of subsection (1) shall begin not earlier than the date of the application for the order and shall end not later than the death of the spouse, or any dependent member of the family, in whose favour the order is made or the other spouse concerned.

(5) (a)  Upon the remarriage [or registration in a civil partnership][1] of the spouse in whose favour an order is made under paragraph (a) or (b) of subsection (1), the order shall, to the extent that it applies to that spouse, cease to have effect, except as respects payments due under it on the date of the remarriage [or civil partnership registration][1].

(b) If, after the grant of a decree of divorce, either of the spouses concerned remarries [or registers in a civil partnership]², the court shall not, by reference to that decree, make an order under subsection (1) in favour of that spouse.

(6) (a) Where a court makes an order under subsection (1)(a), it shall in the same proceedings, subject to paragraph (b), make an attachment of earnings order (within the meaning of the Act of 1976) to secure payments under the first-mentioned order if it is satisfied that the person against whom the order is made is a person to whom earnings (within the meaning aforesaid) fall to be paid.

(b) Before deciding whether to make or refuse to make an attachment of earnings order by virtue of paragraph (a), the court shall give the spouse concerned an opportunity to make the representations specified in paragraph (c) in relation to the matter and shall have regard to any such representations made by that spouse.

(c) The representations referred to in paragraph (b) are representations relating to the questions—

(i) whether the spouse concerned is a person to whom such earnings as aforesaid fall to be paid, and

(ii) whether he or she would make the payments to which the relevant order under subsection (1)(a) relates.

(d) References in this subsection to an order under subsection (1)(a) include references to such an order as varied or affirmed on appeal from the court concerned or varied under section 22.

**Notes**

1   Subsection (5)(a) was amended by the Civil Partnership and Certain Rights and Obligations of Cohabitants Act 2010, s 151(a).

2   Subsection (5)(b) was amended by the Civil Partnership and Certain Rights and Obligations of Cohabitants Act 2010, s 151(b).

## 14      Property adjustment orders

(1) On granting a decree of divorce or at any time thereafter, the court, on application to it in that behalf by either of the spouses concerned or by a person on behalf of a dependent member of the family, may, during the lifetime of the other spouse or, as the case may be, the spouse concerned, make a property adjustment order, that is to say, an order providing for one or more of the following matters:

(a) the transfer by either of the spouses to the other spouse, to any dependent member of the family or to any other specified person for the benefit of such a member of specified property, being property to which the first-mentioned spouse is entitled either in possession or reversion,

(b) the settlement to the satisfaction of the court of specified property, being property to which either of the spouses is so entitled as aforesaid, for the benefit of the other spouse and of any dependent member of the family or of any or all of those persons,

(c) the variation for the benefit of either of the spouses and of any dependent member of the family or of any or all of those persons of any ante-nuptial or post-nuptial settlement (including such a settlement made by will or codicil) made on the spouses,

(d) the extinguishment or reduction of the interest of either of the spouses under any such settlement.

(2) An order under paragraph (b), (c) or (d) may restrict to a specified extent or exclude the application of section 22 in relation to the order.

(3) If, after the grant of a decree of divorce, either of the spouses concerned remarries [or registers in a civil partnership][1], the court shall not, by reference to that decree, make a property adjustment order in favour of that spouse.

(4) Where a property adjustment order is made in relation to land, a copy of the order certified to be a true copy by the registrar or clerk of the court concerned shall, as appropriate, be lodged by him or her in the Land Registry for registration pursuant to section 69(1)(h) of the Registration of Title Act, 1964, in a register maintained under that Act or be registered in the Registry of Deeds.

[(4A) Where a property adjustment order lodged under subsection (4) and registered pursuant to section 69(1)(h) of the Registration of Title Act 1964 or in the Registry of Deeds has been complied with, the Property Registration Authority shall, on being satisfied that the order has been complied with—

(a) cancel the entry made in the register under the Registration of Title Act 1964, or

(b) note compliance with the order in the Registry of Deeds.][2]

(5) Where—

(a) a person is directed by an order under this section to execute a deed or other instrument in relation to land, and

(b) the person refuses or neglects to comply with the direction or, for any other reason, the court considers it necessary to do so,

the court may order another person to execute the deed or instrument in the name of the first-mentioned person; and a deed or other instrument executed by a person in the name of another person pursuant to an order under this subsection shall be as valid as if it had been executed by that other person.

(6) Any costs incurred in complying with a property adjustment order shall be borne, as the court may determine, by either of the spouses concerned, or by both of them in such proportions as the court may determine, and shall be so borne in such manner as the court may determine.

(7) This section shall not apply in relation to a family home in which, following the grant of a decree of divorce, either of the spouses concerned, having remarried, ordinarily resides with his or her spouse.

---

**Notes**

1   Subsection (3) was amended by the Civil Partnership and Certain Rights and Obligations of Cohabitants Act 2010, s 152.

2   Subsection (4A) inserted by Civil Law (Miscellaneous Provisions) Act 2008, s 75(a).

---

**15     Miscellaneous ancillary orders**

(1) On granting a decree of divorce or at any time thereafter, the court, on application to it in that behalf by either of the spouses concerned or by a person on behalf of a dependent member of the family, may, during the lifetime of the other spouse or, as the case may be, the spouse concerned, make one or more of the following orders:

   (a)   an order—

       (i)   providing for the conferral on one spouse either for life or for such other period (whether definite or contingent) as the court may specify of the right to occupy the family home to the exclusion of the other spouse, or

       (ii)   directing the sale of the family home subject to such conditions (if any) as the court considers proper and providing for the disposal of the proceeds of the sale between the spouses and any other person having an interest therein,

   (b)   an order under section 36 of the Act of 1995,

   (e)   an order under section 5, 7 or 9 of the Family Home Protection Act, 1976,

   (d)   an order under section 2, 3, 4 or 5 of the Act of 1996,

   (e)   an order [under section 31 of the Land and Conveyancing Law Reform Act 2009][1],

   (f)   an order under section 11 of the Act of 1964,

and, for the purposes of this section, in paragraphs (b), (c) and (d), a reference to a spouse in a statute referred to in paragraph (b), (c) or (d) shall be construed as including a reference to a person who is a party to a marriage that has been dissolved under this Act.

(2) The court, in exercising its jurisdiction under subsection (1)(a), shall have regard to the welfare of the spouses and any dependent member of the family and, in particular, shall take into consideration—

   (a)   that, where a decree of divorce is granted, it is not possible for the spouses concerned to reside together, and

(b) that proper and secure accommodation should, where practicable, be provided for a spouse who is wholly or mainly dependent on the other spouse and for any dependent member of the family.

(3) Subsection (1)(a) shall not apply in relation to a family home in which, following the grant of a decree of divorce, either of the spouses concerned, having remarried, ordinarily resides with his or her spouse.

---

**Notes**

1   Subsection (1)(e) was amended by the Land and Conveyancing Law Reform Act 2009, schedule 1.

---

**16      Financial compensation orders**

(1) Subject to the provisions of this section, on granting a decree of divorce or at any time thereafter, the court, on application to it in that behalf by either of the spouses concerned or by a person on behalf of a dependent member of the family, may, during the lifetime of the other spouse or, as the case may be, the spouse concerned, if it considers—

(a) that the financial security of the spouse making the application ("the applicant") or the dependent member of the family ("the member") can be provided for either wholly or in part by so doing, or

(b) that the forfeiture, by reason of the decree of divorce, by the applicant or the member, as the case may be, of the opportunity or possibility of acquiring a benefit (for example, a benefit under a pension scheme) can be compensated for wholly or in part by so doing,

make a financial compensation order, that is to say, an order requiring the other spouse to do one or more of the following:

(i)   to effect such a policy of life insurance for the benefit of the applicant or the member as may be specified in the order,

(ii)  to assign the whole or a specified part of the interest of the other spouse in a policy of life insurance effected by that other spouse or both of the spouses to the applicant or to such person as may be specified in the order for the benefit of the member,

(iii) to make or to continue to make to the person by whom a policy of life insurance is or was issued the payments which that other spouse or both of the spouses is or are required to make under the terms of the policy.

(2) (a) The court may make a financial compensation order in addition to or in substitution in whole or in part for orders under section 13, 14, 15 or 17 and in deciding whether or not to make such an order it shall have regard to whether proper provision having regard to the circumstances exists or can be made for

the spouse concerned or the dependent member of the family concerned by orders under those sections.

(b)   An order under this section shall cease to have effect on the re-marriage or death, [registration in a civil partnership][1] of the applicant in so far as it relates to the applicant.

(c)   The court shall not make an order under this section in favour of a spouse who has remarried [or registered in a civil partnership][2].

(d)   An order under section 22 in relation to an order under paragraph (i) or (ii) of subsection (1) may make such provision (if any) as the court considers appropriate in relation to the disposal of—

  (i)   an amount representing any accumulated value of the insurance policy effected pursuant to the order under the said paragraph (i), or

  (ii)   the interest or the part of the interest to which the order under the said paragraph (ii) relates.

---

**Notes**

1   Subsection (2)(b) amended by the Civil Partnership and Certain Rights and Obligations of Cohabitants Act 2010, s 153(a).

2   Subsection (2)(c) amended by the Civil Partnership and Certain Rights and Obligations of Cohabitants Act 2010, s 153(b).

---

**17      Pension adjustment orders**

(1) In this section, save where the context otherwise requires-

**"the Act of 1990"** means the Pensions Act, 1990;

**"active member"** in relation to a scheme, means a member of the scheme who is in reckonable service;

**"actuarial value"** means the equivalent cash value of a benefit (including, where appropriate, provision for any revaluation of such benefit) under a scheme calculated by reference to appropriate financial assumptions and making due allowance for the probability of survival to normal pensionable age and thereafter in accordance with normal life expectancy on the assumption that the member concerned of the scheme, at the effective date of calculation, is in a normal state of health having regard to his or her age;

**"approved arrangement"**, in relation to the trustees of a scheme, means an arrangement whereby the trustees, on behalf of the person for whom the arrangement is made, effect policies or contracts of insurance that are approved of by the Revenue Commissioners with, and make the appropriate payments under the policies or contracts to, one or more undertakings;

**"contingent benefit"** means a benefit payable under a scheme, other than a payment under subsection (7) to or for one or more of the following, that is to say, the widow or the widower and any dependants of the member spouse concerned and the personal representative of the member spouse, if the member spouse dies while in relevant employment and before attaining any normal pensionable age provided for under the rules of the scheme;

["**defined contribution scheme**" has the same meaning as in the Pensions Act 1990;][1]

"**designated benefit**", in relation to a pension adjustment order, means an amount determined by the trustees of the scheme concerned, in accordance with relevant guidelines, and by reference to the period and the percentage of the retirement benefit specified in the order concerned under subsection (2);

"**member spouse**", in relation to a scheme, means a spouse who is a member of the scheme;

"**normal pensionable age**" means the earliest age at which a member of a scheme is entitled to receive benefits under the rules of the scheme on retirement from relevant employment, disregarding any such rules providing for early retirement on grounds of ill health or otherwise;

"**occupational pension scheme**" has the meaning assigned to it by section 2(1) of the Act of 1990;

"**reckonable service**" means service in relevant employment during membership of any scheme;

"**relevant guidelines**" means any relevant guidelines for the time being in force under paragraph (c) or (cc) of section 10(1) of the Act of 1990;

"**relevant employment**", in relation to a scheme, means any employment (or any period treated as employment) or any period of self-employment to which a scheme applies;

"**retirement benefit**", in relation to a scheme, means all benefits (other than contingent benefits) payable under the scheme;

"**rules**", in relation to a scheme, means the provisions of the scheme, by whatever name called;

"**scheme**" means a pension scheme;

"**transfer amount**" shall be construed in accordance with subsection (4);

"**undertaking**" has the meaning assigned to it by the Insurance Act, 1989.

(2) Subject to the provisions of this section, where a decree of divorce ("the decree") has been granted, the court, if it so thinks fit, may, in relation to retirement benefit under a scheme of which one of the spouses concerned is a member, on application to it in that behalf at the time of the making of the order for the decree or at any time thereafter during the lifetime of the member spouse by either of the spouses or by a person on behalf of a dependent member of the family, make an order providing for the payment, in accordance with the provisions of this section, to either of the following, as the court may determine, that is to say—

    (a)  the other spouse and, in the case of the death of that spouse, his or her personal representative, and

    (b)  such person as may be specified in the order for the benefit of a person who is, and for so long only as he or she remains, a dependent member of the family, of a benefit consisting, either, as the court may determine, of the whole, or such part as the court considers appropriate, of that part of the retirement benefit that is payable (or which, but for the making of the order for the decree, would have been payable) under the scheme and has accrued at the time of the making of the order for the decree and, for the purpose of determining the benefit, the order shall specify—

    (i)   the period of reckonable service of the member spouse prior to the granting of the decree to be taken into account, and

    (ii)  the percentage of the retirement benefit accrued during that period to be paid to the person referred to in paragraph (a) or (b), as the case may be.

(3) Subject to the provisions of this section, where a decree of divorce ("the decree") has been granted, the court, if it so thinks fit, may, in relation to a contingent benefit under a scheme of which one of the spouses concerned is a member, on application to it in that behalf not more than one year after the making of the order for the decree by either of the spouses or by a person on behalf of a dependent member of the family concerned, make an order providing for the payment, upon the death of the member spouse, to either of the following, or to both of them in such proportions as the court may determine, that is to say—

    (a)  the other spouse, and

    (b)  such person as may be specified in the order for the benefit of a dependent member of the family,

of, either, as the court may determine, the whole, or such part (expressed as a percentage) as the court considers appropriate, of that part of any contingent benefit that is payable (or which, but for the making of the order for the decree, would have been payable) under the scheme.

(4) Where the court makes an order under subsection (2) in favour of a spouse and payment of the designated benefit concerned has not commenced, the spouse in whose favour the order is made shall be entitled to the application in accordance with subsection (5) of an amount of money from the scheme concerned (in this section referred to as a "transfer amount") equal to the value of the designated benefit, such amount being determined by the trustees of the scheme in accordance with relevant guidelines.

(5) Subject to subsection (17), where the court makes an order under subsection (2) in favour of a spouse and payment of the designated benefit concerned has not commenced, the trustees of the scheme concerned shall, for the purpose of giving effect to the order—

    (a)  on application to them in that behalf at the time of the making of the order or at any time thereafter by the spouse in whose favour the order was made ("the spouse"), and

    (b)  on the furnishing to them by the spouse of such information as they may reasonably require,

apply in accordance with relevant guidelines the transfer amount calculated in accordance with those guidelines either—

    (i)  if the trustees and the spouse so agree, in providing a benefit for or in respect of the spouse under the scheme aforesaid that is of the same actuarial value as the transfer amount concerned, or

    (ii)  in making a payment either to

        (I)  such other occupational pension scheme, being a scheme the trustees of which agree to accept the payment, or

        (II)  in the discharge of any payment falling to be made by the trustees under any such other approved arrangement,

as may be determined by the spouse.

(6) Subject to subsection (17), where the court makes an order under subsection (2) in relation to a defined contribution scheme and an application has not been brought under subsection (5), the trustees of the scheme may, for the purpose of giving effect to the order, if they so think fit, apply in accordance with relevant guidelines the transfer amount calculated in accordance with those guidelines, in making a payment—

    (a)  such other occupational pension scheme, being a scheme the trustees of which agree to accept the payment, or

    (b)  in the discharge of any payment falling to be made by the trustees under such other approved arrangement,

as may be determined by the trustees.

(7) Subject to subsection (17), where—

    (a)  the court makes an order under subsection (2), and

    (b)  the member spouse concerned dies before payment of the designated benefit concerned has commenced,

the trustees shall, for the purpose of giving effect to the order, within 3 months of the death of the member spouse, provide for the payment to the person in whose favour the order was made of an amount that is equal to the transfer amount calculated in accordance with relevant guidelines.

(8) Subject to subsection (17), where—

    (a)  the court makes an order under subsection (2), and

    (b)  the member spouse concerned ceases to be a member of the scheme otherwise than on death,

the trustees may, for the purpose of giving effect to the order, if they so think fit, apply, in accordance with relevant guidelines, the transfer amount calculated in accordance with those guidelines either, as the trustees may determine—

    (i)  if the trustees and the person in whose favour the order is made ("the person") so agree, in providing a benefit for or in respect of the person under the scheme aforesaid that is of the same actuarial value as the transfer amount concerned, or

    (ii)  in making a payment, either to

        (I)  such other occupational pension scheme, being a scheme the trustees of which agree to accept the payment, or

> > (II)    in the discharge of any payment falling to be made under such other approved arrangement,

as may be determined by the trustees.

(9) Subject to subsection (17), where—

> (a)    the court makes an order under subsection (2) in favour of a spouse ("the spouse"),

> (b)    the spouse dies before the payment of the designated benefit has commenced,

the trustees shall, within 3 months of the death of the spouse, provide for the payment to the personal representative of the spouse of an amount equal to the transfer amount calculated in accordance with relevant guidelines.

(10) Subject to subsection (17), where—

> (a)    the court makes an order under subsection (2) in favour of a spouse ("the spouse"), and

> (b)    the spouse dies after payment of the designated benefit has commenced,

the trustees shall, within 3 months of the death of the spouse, provide for the payment to the personal representative of the spouse of an amount equal to the actuarial value, calculated in accordance with relevant guidelines, of the part of the designated benefit which, but for the death of the spouse, would have been payable to the spouse during the lifetime of the member spouse.

(11) Where—

> (a)    the court makes an order under subsection (2) for the benefit of a dependent member of the family ("the person"), and

> (b)    the person dies before payment of the designated benefit has commenced,

the order shall cease to have effect in so far as it relates to that person.

(12) Where—

> (a)    the court makes an order under subsection (2) or (3) in relation to an occupational pension scheme, and

> (b)    the trustees of the scheme concerned have not applied the transfer amount concerned in accordance with subsection (5), (6), (7), (8) or (9), and

> (c)    after the making of the order, the member spouse ceases to be an active member of the scheme,

the trustees shall, within 12 months of the cessation, notify the registrar or clerk of the court concerned and the other spouse of the cessation.

(13) Where the trustees of a scheme apply a transfer amount under subsection (6) or (8), they shall notify the spouse (not being the spouse who is the member spouse) or other person concerned and the registrar or clerk of the court concerned of the application and shall give to that spouse or other person concerned particulars of the scheme or undertaking concerned and of the transfer amount.

(14) Where the court makes an order under subsection (2) or (3) for the payment of a designated benefit or a contingent benefit, as the case may be, the benefit shall be

payable or the transfer amount concerned applied out of the resources of the scheme concerned and, unless otherwise provided for in the order or relevant guidelines, shall be payable in accordance with the rules of the scheme or, as the case may be, applied in accordance with relevant guidelines.

(15) Where the court makes an order under subsection (2), the amount of the retirement benefit payable, in accordance with the rules of the scheme concerned to, or to or in respect of, the member spouse shall be reduced by the amount of the designated benefit payable pursuant to the order.

(16)(a) Where the court makes an order under subsection (3), the amount of the contingent benefit payable, in accordance with the rules of the scheme concerned in respect of the member spouse shall be reduced by an amount equal to the contingent benefit payable pursuant to the order.

(b) Where the court makes an order under subsection (2) and the member spouse concerned dies before payment of the designated benefit concerned has commenced, the amount of the contingent benefit payable in respect of the member spouse in accordance with the rules of the scheme concerned shall be reduced by the amount of the payment made under subsection (7).

(17) Where, pursuant to an order under subsection (2), the trustees of a scheme make a payment or apply a transfer amount under subsection (5), (6), (7), (8), (9) or (10), they shall be discharged from any obligation to make any further payment or apply any transfer amount under any other of those subsections in respect of the benefit payable pursuant to the order.

(18) A person who makes an application under subsection (2) or (3) or an application for an order under section 22(2) in relation to an order under subsection (2) shall give notice thereof to the trustees of the scheme concerned and, in deciding whether to make the order concerned and in determining the provisions of the order, the court shall have regard to any representations made by any person to whom notice of the application has been given under this section or section 40.

(19) An order under subsection (3) shall cease to have effect on the death or remarriage [or registration in a civil partnership][2] of the person in whose favour it was made in so far as it relates to that person.

(20) The court may, in a pension adjustment order or by order made under this subsection after the making of a pension adjustment order, give to the trustees of the scheme concerned such directions as it considers appropriate for the purposes of the pension adjustment order including directions compliance with which occasions non-compliance with the rules of the scheme concerned or the Act of 1990; and a trustee of a scheme shall not be liable in any court or other tribunal for any loss or damage caused by his or her non-compliance with the rules of the scheme or with the Act of 1990 if the non-compliance was occasioned by his or her compliance with a direction of the court under this subsection.

(21) The registrar or clerk of the court concerned shall cause a copy of a pension adjustment order to be served on the trustees of the scheme concerned.

(22)(a) Any costs incurred by the trustees of a scheme under subsection (18) or in complying with a pension adjustment order or a direction under subsection (20) or (25) shall be borne, as the court may determine, by the member spouse or by the other person concerned or by both of them in such proportion as the court may determine and, in the absence of such determination, those costs shall be borne by them equally.

(b) Where a person fails to pay an amount in accordance with paragraph (a) to the trustees of the scheme concerned, the court may, on application to it in that behalf by the trustees, order that the amount be deducted from the amount of any benefit payable to the person under the scheme or pursuant to an order under subsection (2) or (3) and be paid to the trustees.

(23)(a) The court shall not make a pension adjustment order in favour of a spouse who has remarried [or registered in a civil partnership][3].

(b) The court may make a pension adjustment order in addition to or in substitution in whole or in part for an order or orders under section 13, 14, 15 or 16 and, in deciding whether or not to make a pension adjustment order, the court shall have regard to the question whether proper provision, having regard to the circumstances, exists or can be made for the spouse concerned or the dependent member of the family concerned by an order or orders under any of those sections.

(24) Section 54 of the Act of 1990 and any regulations under that section shall apply with any necessary modifications to a scheme if proceedings for the grant of a decree of divorce to which a member spouse is a party have been instituted and shall continue to apply notwithstanding the grant of a decree of divorce in the proceedings.

(25) For the purposes of this Act, the court may, of its own motion, and shall, if so requested by either of the spouses concerned or any other person concerned, direct the trustees of the scheme concerned to provide the spouses or that other person and the court, within a specified period of time—

(a) with a calculation of the value and the amount, determined in accordance with relevant guidelines, of the retirement benefit, or contingent benefit, concerned that is payable (or which, but for the making of the order for the decree of divorce concerned, would have been payable) under the scheme and has accrued at the time of the making of that order, and

(b) with a calculation of the amount of the contingent benefit concerned that is payable (or which, but for the making of the order for the decree of divorce concerned, would have been payable) under the scheme.

(26) An order under this section may restrict to a specified extent or exclude the application of section 22 in relation to the order.

**Notes**

1    Subsection (1) was substituted by the Social Welfare and Pensions Act 2008, s 31.

2    Subsection (19) was amended by the Civil Partnership and Certain Rights and Obligations of Cohabitants Act 2010, s 154(a).

3    Subsection (23)(a) was amended by the Civil Partnership and Certain Rights and Obligations of Cohabitants Act 2010, s 154(b).

## 18      Orders for provision for spouse out of estate of other spouse

(1) Subject to the provisions of this section, where one of the spouses in respect of whom a decree of divorce has been granted dies, the court, on application to it in that behalf by the other spouse ("the applicant") not more than 6 months after representation is first granted under the Act of 1965 in respect of the estate of the deceased spouse, may by order make such provision for the applicant out of the estate of the deceased spouse as it considers appropriate having regard to the rights of any other person having an interest in the matter and specifies in the order if it is satisfied that proper provision in the circumstances was not made for the applicant during the lifetime of the deceased spouse under section 13, 14, 15, 16 or 17 for any reason (other than conduct referred to in subsection (2)(i) of section 20 of the applicant).

(2) The court shall not make an order under this section in favour of a spouse who has remarried [or registered in a civil partnership][1] since the granting of the decree of divorce concerned.

(3) In considering whether to make an order under this section the court shall have regard to all the circumstances of the case including—

(a)    any order under paragraph (c) of section 13(1) or a property adjustment order in favour of the applicant, and

(b)    any devise or bequest made by the deceased spouse to the applicant.

(4) The provision made for the applicant concerned by an order under this section together with any provision made for the applicant by an order referred to in subsection (3)(a) (the value of which for the purposes of this subsection shall be its value on the date of the order) shall not exceed in total the share (if any) of the applicant in the estate of the deceased spouse to which the applicant was entitled or (if the deceased spouse died intestate as to the whole or part of his or her estate) would have been entitled under the Act of 1965 if the marriage had not been dissolved.

(5) Notice of an application under this section shall be given by the applicant to the spouse[, civil partner or former civil partner][2] (if any) of the deceased spouse concerned and to such (if any) other persons as the court may direct and, in deciding whether to make the order concerned and in determining the provisions of the order, the court shall have regard to any representations made by the spouse[, civil partner or former civil partner][2] of the deceased spouse and any other such persons as aforesaid.

(6) The personal representative of a deceased spouse in respect of whom a decree of divorce has been granted shall make a reasonable attempt to ensure that notice of his or her death is brought to the attention of the other spouse concerned and, where an application is made under this section, the personal representative of the deceased spouse shall not, without the leave of the court, distribute any of the estate of that spouse until the court makes or refuses to make an order under this section.

(7) Where the personal representative of a deceased spouse in respect of whom a decree of divorce has been granted gives notice of his or her death to the other spouse concerned ("the spouse") and—

(a)  the spouse intends to apply to the court for an order under this section,

(b)  the spouse has applied for such an order and the application is pending, or

(c)  an order has been made under this section in favour of the spouse,

the spouse shall, not later than one month after the receipt of the notice, notify the personal representative of such intention, application or order, as the case may be, and, if he or she does not do so, the personal representative shall be at liberty to distribute the assets of the deceased spouse, or any part thereof, amongst the parties entitled thereto.

(8) The personal representative shall not be liable to the spouse for the assets or any part thereof so distributed unless, at the time of such distribution, he or she had notice of the intention, application or order aforesaid.

(9) Nothing in subsection (7) or (8) shall prejudice the right of the spouse to follow any such assets into the hands of any person who may have received them.

(10) On granting a decree of divorce or at any time thereafter, the court, on application to it in that behalf by either of the spouses concerned, may, during the lifetime of the other spouse or, as the case may be, the spouse concerned, if it considers it just to do so, make an order that either or both spouses shall not, on the death of either of them, be entitled to apply for an order under this section.

---

**Notes**

1   Subsection (2) was amended by the Civil Partnership and Certain Rights and Obligations of Cohabitants Act 2010, s 155(a).

2   Subsection (5) was amended by the Civil Partnership and Certain Rights and Obligations of Cohabitants Act 2010, s 155(b).

---

## 19   Orders for sale of property

(1) Where the court makes a secured periodical payments of order, a lump sum order or a property adjustment order, thereupon, or at any time thereafter, it may make an order directing the sale of such property as may be specified in the order, being property in which, or in the proceeds of sale of which, either or both of the spouses concerned has or have a beneficial interest, either in possession or reversion.

(2) The jurisdiction conferred on the court by subsection (1) shall not be so exercised as to affect a right to occupy the family home of the spouse concerned that is enjoyed by virtue of an order under this Part.

(3) (a) An order under subsection (1) may contain such consequential or supplementary provisions as the court considers appropriate.

   (b) Without prejudice to the generality of paragraph (a), an order under subsection (1) may contain—

     (i) a provision specifying the manner of sale and some or all of the conditions applying to the sale of the property to which the order relates,

     (ii) a provision requiring any such property to be offered for sale to a person, or a class of persons, specified in the order,

     (iii) a provision directing that the order, or a specified part of it, shall not take effect until the occurrence of a specified event or the expiration of a specified period,

     (iv) a provision requiring the making of a payment or payments (whether periodical payments or lump sum payments) to a specified person or persons out of the proceeds of the sale of the property to which the order relates, and

     (v) a provision specifying the manner in which the proceeds of the sale of the property concerned shall be disposed of between the following persons or such of them as the court considers appropriate, that is to say, the spouses concerned and any other person having an interest therein.

(4) A provision in an order under subsection (1) providing for the making of periodical payments to one of the spouses concerned out of the proceeds of the sale of property shall, on the death or remarriage [or registration in a civil partnership][1] of that spouse, cease to have effect except as respects payments due on the date of the death or remarriage [or civil partnership registration][1].

(5) Where a spouse has a beneficial interest in any property, or in the proceeds of the sale of any property, and a person (not being the other spouse) also has a beneficial interest in that property or those proceeds, then, in considering whether to make an order under this section or section 14 or 15(1)(a) in relation to that property or those proceeds, the court shall give to that person an opportunity to make representations with respect to the making of the order and the contents thereof, and any representations made by such a person shall be deemed to be included among the matters to which the court is required to have regard under section 20 in any relevant proceedings under a provision referred to in that section after the making of those representations.

(6) This section shall not apply in relation to a family home in which, following the grant of a decree of divorce, either of the spouses concerned, having remarried, ordinarily resides with his or her spouse.

**Notes**

1    Subsection (4) was amended by the Civil Partnership and Certain Rights and Obligations of
     Cohabitants Act 2010, s 156.

**20      Provisions relating to certain orders under sections 12 to 18 and 22**

(1) In deciding whether to make an order under section 12, 13, 14, 15(1)(a), 16, 17, 18
or 22 and in determining the provisions of such an order, the court shall ensure that such
provision as the court considers proper having regard to the circumstances exists or will
be made for the spouses and any dependent member of the family concerned.

(2) Without prejudice to the generality of subsection (1), in deciding whether to make
such an order as aforesaid and in determining the provisions of such an order, the court
shall, in particular, have regard to the following matters:

(a)   the income, earning capacity, property and other financial resources which
      each of the spouses concerned has or is likely to have in the foreseeable future,

(b)   the financial needs, obligations and responsibilities which each of the spouses
      has or is likely to have in the foreseeable future (whether in the case of the
      remarriage [or registration in a civil partnership][1] of the spouse or otherwise),

(c)   the standard of living enjoyed by the family concerned before the proceedings
      were instituted or before the spouses commenced to live apart from one
      another, as the case may be,

(d)   the age of each of the spouses, the duration of their marriage and the length of
      time during which the spouses lived with one another,

(e)   any physical or mental disability of either of the spouses,

(f)   the contributions which each of the spouses has made or is likely in the
      foreseeable future to make to the welfare of the family, including any
      contribution made by each of them to the income, earning capacity, property
      and financial resources of the other spouse and any contribution made by either
      of them by looking after the home or caring for the family,

(g)   the effect on the earning capacity of each of the spouses of the marital
      responsibilities assumed by each during the period when they lived with one
      another and, in particular, the degree to which the future earning capacity of a
      spouse is impaired by reason of that spouse having relinquished or foregone the
      opportunity of remunerative activity in order to look after the home or care for
      the family,

(h)   any income or benefits to which either of the spouses is entitled by or under
      statute,

(i)   the conduct of each of the spouses, if that conduct is such that in the opinion of
      the court it would in all the circumstances of the case be unjust to disregard it,

    (j)  the accommodation needs of either of the spouses,

    (k)  the value to each of the spouses of any benefit (for example, a benefit under a pension scheme) which by reason of the decree of divorce concerned, that spouse will forfeit the opportunity or possibility of acquiring,

    (l)  the rights of any person other than the spouses but including a person to whom either spouse is remarried.

(3) In deciding whether to make an order under a provision refined to in subsection (1) and in determining the provisions of such an order, the court shall have regard to the terms of any separation agreement which has been entered into by the spouses and is still in force.

(4) Without prejudice to the generality of subsection (1), in deciding whether to make an order referred to in that subsection in favour of a dependent member of the family concerned and in determining the provisions of such an order, the court shall, in particular, have regard to the following matters:

    (a)  the financial needs of the member,

    (b)  the income, earning capacity (if any), property and other financial resources of the member,

    (c)  any physical or mental disability of the member,

    (d)  any income or benefits to which the member is entitled by or under statute,

    (e)  the manner in which the member was being and in which the spouses concerned anticipated that the member would be educated or trained,

    (f)  the matters specified in paragraphs (a), (b) and (c) of subsection (2) and in subsection (3),

    (g)  the accommodation needs of the member.

(5) The court shall not make an order under a provision referred to in subsection (1) unless it would be in the interests of justice to do so.

---

**Notes**

1   Subsection (2)(b) was amended by the Civil Partnership and Certain Rights and Obligations of Cohabitants Act 2010, s 157.

---

**21**     **Retrospective periodical payments orders**

(1) Where, having regard to all the circumstances of the case, the court considers it appropriate to do so, it may, in a periodical payments order, direct that—

    (a)  the period in respect of which payments under the order shall be made shall begin on such date before the date of the order, not being earlier than the time of the institution of the proceedings concerned for the grant of a decree of divorce, as may be specified in the order,

(b) any payments under the order in respect of a period before the date of the order be paid in one sum and before a specified date, and

(c) there be deducted from any payments referred to in paragraph (b) made to the spouse concerned an amount equal to the amount of such (if any) payments made to that spouse by the other spouse as the court may determine, being payments made during the period between the making of the order for the grant of the decree aforesaid and the institution of the proceedings aforesaid.

(2) The jurisdiction conferred on the court by subsection (1)(b) is without prejudice to the generality of section J3(1)(c).

## 22  Variation, etc, of certain orders under this Part

(1) This section applies to the following orders:

(a) a maintenance pending suit order,

(b) a periodical payments order,

(c) a secured periodical payments order,

(d) a lump sum order if and in so far as it provides for the payment of the lump sum concerned by instalments or requires the payment of any such instalments to be secured,

(e) an order under paragraph (b), (c) or (d) of section 14(1) in so far as such application is not restricted or excluded pursuant to section 14(2),

(f) an order under subparagraph (i) or (ii) of section 15(1)(a),

(g) a financial compensation order,

(h) an order under section 17(2) in so far as such application is not restricted or excluded pursuant to section 17(26),

(i) an order under this section.

(2) Subject to the provisions of this section and section 20 and to any restriction or exclusion pursuant to section 14(2) or 17(26) and without prejudice to section 16(2)(d), the court may, on application to it in that behalf—

(a) by either of the spouses concerned,

(b) in the case of the death of either of the spouses, by any other person who has, in the opinion of the court, a sufficient interest in the matter or by a person on behalf of a dependent member of the family concerned, or

(c) in the case of the remarriage of either of the spouses, by his or her spouse,

if it considers it proper to do so having regard to any change in the circumstances of the case and to any new evidence, by order vary or discharge an order to which this section applies, suspend any provision of such an order or any provision of such an order temporarily, revive the operation of such an order or provision so suspended, further vary an order previously varied under this section or further suspend or revive the operation of an order or provision previously suspended or revived under this section; and, without prejudice to the generality of the foregoing, an order under this section may require the divesting of any property vested in a person under or by virtue of an order to which this section applies.

(3) Without prejudice to the generality of section 12 or 13, that part of an order to which this section applies which provides for the making of payments for the support of a dependent member of the family shall stand discharged if the member ceases to be a dependent member of the family by reason of his or her attainment of the age of 18 years or 23 years, as may be appropriate, and shall be discharged by the court, on application to it under subsection (2), if it is satisfied that the member has for any reason ceased to be a dependent member of the family.

(4) The power of the court under subsection (2) to make an order varying, discharging or suspending an order referred to in subsection (1)(e) shall be subject to any restriction or exclusion specified in that order and shall (subject to the limitation aforesaid) be a power—

    (a)  to vary the settlement to which the order relates in any person's favour or to extinguish or reduce any person's interest under that settlement, and

    (b)  to make such supplemental provision (including a further property adjustment order or a lump sum order) as the court thinks appropriate in consequence of any variation, extinguishment or reduction made pursuant to paragraph (a),

and section 19 shall apply to a case where the court makes such an order as aforesaid under subsection (2) as it applies to a case where the court makes a property adjustment order with any necessary modifications.

(5) The court shall not make an order under subsection (2) in relation to an order referred to in subsection (1)(e) unless it appears to it that the order will not prejudice the interests of any person who—

    (a)  has acquired any right or interest in consequence of the order referred to in subsection (1)(e), and

    (b)  is not a party to the marriage concerned or a dependent member of the family concerned.

(6) This section shall apply, with any necessary modifications, to instruments executed pursuant to orders to which this section applies as it applies to those orders.

(7) Where the court makes an order under subsection (2) in relation to a property adjustment order relating to land, a copy of the order under subsection (2) certified to be a true copy by the registrar or clerk of the court concerned shall, as appropriate, be lodged by him or her in the Land Registry for registration pursuant to section 69(1)(h) of the Registration of Title Act, 1964, in a register maintained under that Act or be registered in the Registry of Deeds.

[(8) Where a property adjustment order lodged under section 14(4) and duly registered pursuant to section 69(1)(h) of the Registration of Title Act 1964 is varied, discharged, suspended or revived by an order under subsection (2) and the second-mentioned order has been duly lodged for registration pursuant to subsection (7), the Property Registration Authority shall—

(a) amend or cancel the entry made in the register, pursuant to section 14(4), under the Registration of Title Act 1964 accordingly, or

(b) note the position in the Registry of Deeds.][1]

---

**Notes**

1  Subsection (8) inserted by Civil Law (Miscellaneous Provisions) Act 2008, s 75(b).

---

**23  Restriction in relation to orders for benefit of dependent members of family**

In deciding whether—

   (a)  to include in an order under section 12 a provision requiring the making of periodical payments for the benefit of a dependent member of the family,

   (b)  to make an order under paragraph (a)(ii), (b)(ii) or (c)(ii) of section 13(1),

   (c)  to make an order under section 22 varying, discharging or suspending a provision referred to in paragraph (a) or an order referred to in paragraph (b),

the court shall not have regard to conduct by the spouse or spouses concerned of the kind specified in subsection (2)(i) of section 20.

**24  Method of making payments under certain orders**

(1) The court may by order provide that a payment under an order to which this section applies shall be made by such method as is specified in the order and be subject to such terms and conditions as it considers appropriate and so specifies.

(2) This section applies to an order under—

   (a)  section 11(2) (b) of the Act of 1964,

   (b)  section 5, 5A or 7 of the Act of 1976,

   (c)  section 7, 8 or 24 of the Act of 1995, and

   (d)  section 12, 13, 19 or 22.

**25  Stay on certain orders the subject of appeal**

Where an appeal is brought from an order under—

   (a)  section 11(2) (b) of the Act of 1964,

   (b)  section 5, 5A or 7 of the Act of 1976,

   (c)  section 7, paragraph (a) or (b) of section 8(1) or section 24 of the Act of 1995, or

   (d)  section 12, paragraph (a) or (b) of section 13(1) or paragraph (a), (b) or (c) of section 22(1),

the operation of the order shall not be stayed unless the court that made the order or to which the appeal is brought directs otherwise.

**26    Orders under Acts of 1976, 1989 and 1995**

(1) Where, while an order ("the first-mentioned order"), being—

   (a)  a maintenance order, an order varying a maintenance order, or an interim order under the Act of 1976,

   (b)  an order under section 14, 15,16, 18 or 22 of the Act of 1989,

   (c)  an order under section 8, 9, 10, 11, 12, 13, 14, 15 or 18 of the Act of 1995,

is in force, an application is made to the court by a spouse to whom the first-mentioned order relates for an order granting a decree of divorce or an order under this Part, the court may by order discharge the first-mentioned order as on and from such date as may be specified in the order.

(2) Where, on the grant of a decree of divorce an order specified in subsection (1) is in force, it shall, unless it is discharged by an order under subsection (1), continue in force as if it were an order made under a corresponding provision of this Act and section 22 shall apply to it accordingly.

**27    Amendment of section 3 of Act of 1976[1]**

---

**Notes**

1    This section amends the Family Law (Maintenance of Spouses and Children) Act 1976, s 3(1); see the amended Act.

---

**28    Transmission of periodical payments through District Court clerk**

Notwithstanding anything in this Act, section 9 of the Act of 1976 shall apply in relation to an order ("the relevant order"), being pending suit order, a maintenance periodical payments order or a secured periodical payments order or any such order as aforesaid as affected by an order under section 22, with the modifications that—

   (a)  the reference in subsection (4) of the said section 9 to the maintenance creditor shall be construed as a reference to the person to whom payments under the relevant order concerned are required to be made,

   (b)  the other references in the said section 9 to the maintenance creditor shall be construed as references to the person on whose application the relevant order was made, and

   (c)  the reference in subsection (3) of the said section 9 to the maintenance debtor shall be construed as a reference to the person to whom payments under the relevant order are required by that order to be made,

and with any other necessary modifications.

## 29 Application of maintenance pending suit and periodical payment orders to certain members of Defence Forces

The reference in section 98(1)*(*h) of the Defence Act, 1954, to an order for payment of alimony shall be construed as including reference to a maintenance pending suit order, a periodical payments order and a secured periodical payments order.

## 30 Amendment of Enforcement of Court Orders Act, 1940

The references in subsections (1) and (7) of section 8 of the Enforcement of Court Orders Act, 1940 (as amended by section 29 of the Act of 1976 and section 22 of the Act of 1995*),* to an order shall be construed as including references to a maintenance pending suit order and a periodical payments order.

PART IV
INCOME TAX, CAPITAL ACQUISITIONS TAX, CAPITAL GAINS TAX, PROBATE TAX
AND STAMP DUTY

## 31 Payments to be made without deduction of income tax

[…][1]

### Notes

1 Section 31 was repealed by the Taxes Consolidation Act 1997, s 1098, Sch 4 with effect from 6 April 1997.

## 32 Income tax treatment of divorced persons

[…][1]

### Notes

1 Section 32 was repealed by the Finance Act 1997, s 5.

## 33 Exemption of certain transfers from stamp duty

[…][1]

### Notes

1 Section 33 was repealed by the Finance Act 1997, s 127(4).

## 34  Exemption of certain transfers from capital acquisitions tax

[...]¹

---

**Notes**

1  Section 34 was repealed by the Finance Act 1997, s 142(3).

---

## 35  Capital gains tax treatment of certain disposals by divorced persons

(1) Notwithstanding the provisions of the Capital Gains Tax Acts, where, by virtue or in consequence of an order made under Part III on or following the granting of a decree of divorce either of the spouses concerned disposes of an asset to the other spouse, both spouses shall be treated for the purpose of those Acts as if the asset was acquired from the spouse making the disposal for a consideration of such amount as would secure that on the disposal neither a gain nor a loss would accrue to the spouse making the disposal:

Provided that this subsection shall not apply if, until the disposal, the asset formed part of the trading stock of a trade carried on by the spouse making the disposal or if the asset is acquired as trading stock for the purposes of a trade carried on by the spouse acquiring the asset.

(2) Where subsection (1) applies in relation to a disposal of an asset by a spouse to the other spouse, then, in relation to a subsequent disposal of the asset (not being a disposal to which subsection (1) applies), the spouse making the disposal shall be treated for the purposes of the Capital Gains Tax Acts as if the other spouse's acquisition or provision of the asset had been his or her acquisition or provision of the asset.

## 36  Abatement and postponement of probate tax on property the subject of an order under section 18

[...]¹

---

**Notes**

1  Section 36 was repealed by the Finance Act 1997, s 143(2).

---

## PART V
### MISCELLANEOUS

## 37  Powers of court in relation to transactions intended to prevent or reduce relief

(1) In this section

**"disposition"** means any disposition of property howsoever made other than a disposition made by a will or codicil;

"**relief**" means the financial or other material benefits conferred by an order under section 12, 13 or 14, paragraph (a) or (b) of section 15(1) or section 16, 17, 18 or 22 (other than an order affecting an order referred to in subsection (1)(e) thereof) and references to defeating a claim for relief are references to

(a) preventing relief being granted to the person concerned, whether for the benefit of the person or a dependent member of the family concerned,

(b) limiting the relief granted, or

(c) frustrating or impeding the enforcement of an order granting relief;

"**reviewable disposition**", in relation to proceedings for the grant of relief brought by a spouse, means a disposition made by the other spouse concerned or any other person but does not include such a disposition made for valuable consideration (other than marriage) to a person who, at the time of the disposition, acted in good faith and without notice of an intention on the part of the respondent to defeat the claim for relief.

(2) (a) The court, on the application of a person ("the applicant") who has instituted proceedings that have not been determined for the grant of relief, may—

    (i) if it is satisfied that the other spouse concerned or any other person, with the intention of defeating the claim for relief, proposes to make any disposition of or to transfer out of the jurisdiction or otherwise deal with any property, make such order as it thinks fit for the purpose of restraining that other spouse or other person from so doing or otherwise for protecting the claim,

    (ii) if it is satisfied that that other spouse or other person has, with that intention, made a reviewable disposition and that, if the disposition were set aside, relief or different relief would be granted to the applicant, make an order setting aside the disposition.

(b) Where relief has been granted by the court and the court is satisfied that the other spouse concerned or another person has, with the intention aforesaid, made a reviewable disposition, it may make an order setting aside the disposition.

(c) An application under paragraph (a) shall be made in the proceedings for the grant of the relief concerned.

(3) Where the court makes an order under paragraph (a) or (b) of subsection (2), it shall include in the order such provisions (if any) as it considers necessary for its implementation (including provisions requiring the making of any payments or the disposal of any property).

(4) Where an application is made under subsection (2) with respect to a disposition that took place less than 3 years before the date of the application or with respect to a disposition or other dealing with property that the other spouse concerned or any other person proposes to make and the court is satisfied—

(a) in case the application is for an order under subsection (2)(a)(i), that the disposition or other dealing concerned would (apart from this section) have the consequence, or

(b)  in case the application is for an order under paragraph (a)(ii) or (b) of subsection (2), that the disposition has had the consequence,

of defeating the applicant's claim for relief, it shall be presumed, unless the contrary is shown, that that other spouse or other person disposed of or otherwise dealt with the property concerned, or, as the case may be, proposes to do so, with the intention of defeating the applicant's claim for relief.

[(5) An application shall not be made for an order setting aside a disposition by reason only of subsection (2)(a)(ii) or (b) after the expiration of 6 years from the date of the disposition.]¹

**Notes**

1  Subsection (5) inserted by Civil Law (Miscellaneous Provisions) Act 2008, s 75(c).

## 38  Jurisdiction of courts and venue

(1) Subject to the provisions of this section, the Circuit Court shall, concurrently with the High Court, have jurisdiction to hear and determine proceedings under this Act and shall, in relation to that jurisdiction, be known as the Circuit Family Court.

(2) Where the rateable valuation of any land to which proceedings in the Circuit Family Court under this Act relate exceeds [€253.95], that Court shall, if an application is made to it in that behalf by any person having an interest in the proceedings, transfer the proceedings to the High Court, but any order made or act done in the course of such proceedings before the transfer shall be valid unless discharged or varied by the High Court by order.

(3) The jurisdiction conferred on the Circuit Family Court by this Act may be exercised by the judge of the circuit in which any of the parties to the proceedings ordinarily resides or carries on any business, profession or occupation.

(4) The Circuit Family Court may, for the purposes of subsection (2) in relation to land that has not been given a rateable valuation or is the subject with other land of a rateable valuation, determine that its rateable valuation would exceed, or would not exceed, [€253.95].

(5) Section 32 of the Act of 1989 shall apply to proceedings under this Act in the Circuit Family Court and sections 33 to 36 of that Act shall apply to proceedings under this Act in that Court and in the High Court.

(6) In proceedings under section 13, 14, 15(1)(a), 16, 17, 18 or 22—

(a)  each of the spouses concerned shall give to the other spouse and to, or to a person acting on behalf of, any dependent member of the family concerned, and

(b)  any dependent member of the family concerned shall give to, or to a person acting on behalf of, any other such member and to each of the spouses concerned, such particulars of his or her property and income as may reasonably be required for the purposes of the proceedings.

(7) Where a person fails or refuses to comply with subsection (6), the court on application to it in that behalf by a person having an interest in the matter, may direct the person to comply with that subsection.

## 39 Exercise of jurisdiction by court in relation to divorce

(1) The court may grant a decree of divorce if, but only if, one of the following requirements is satisfied—

(a) either of the spouses concerned was domiciled in the State on the date of the institution of the proceedings concerned,

(b) either of the spouses was ordinarily resident in the State throughout the period of one year ending on that date.[1]

(2) Where proceedings are pending in a court in respect of an application for the grant of a decree of divorce or in respect of an appeal from the determination of such an application and the court has or had, by virtue of subsection (1), jurisdiction to determine the application, the court shall, notwithstanding section 31(4) of the Act of 1989 or section 39 of the Act of 1995, as the case may be, have jurisdiction to determine an application for the grant of a decree of judicial separation or a decree of nullity in respect of the marriage concerned.

(3) Where proceedings are pending in a court in respect of an application for the grant of a decree of nullity or in respect of an appeal from the determination of such an application and the court has or had, by virtue of section 39 of the Act of 1995, jurisdiction to determine the application, the court shall, notwithstanding subsection (1), have jurisdiction to determine an application for the grant of a decree of divorce in respect of the marriage concerned.

(4) Where proceedings are pending in a court in respect of an application for the grant of a decree of judicial separation or in respect of an appeal from the determination of such an application and the court has or had, by virtue of section 31(4) of the Act of 1989, jurisdiction to determine the application, the court shall, notwithstanding subsection (1), have jurisdiction to determine an application for the grant of a decree of divorce in respect of the marriage concerned.

---

**Notes**

1 See the European Communities (Judgments in Matrimonial Matters and Matters of Parental Responsibility) Regulations 2001 (SI 472/2201), reg 3 regarding the application of s 39(1) and see reg 7 of SI 112/2005.

---

## 40 Notice of proceedings under Act

Notice of any proceedings under this Act shall be given by the person bringing the proceedings to—

(a)  the other spouse concerned or, as the case may be; the spouses concerned, and

(b)  any other person specified by the court.

## 41      Custody of dependent members of family after decree of divorce

Where the court makes an order for the grant of a decree of divorce, it may declare either of the spouses concerned to be unfit to have custody of any dependent member of the family who is a minor and, if it does so and the spouse to whom the declaration relates is a parent of any dependent member of the family who is a minor, that spouse shall not, on the death of the other spouse, be entitled as of right to the custody of that minor.

## 42      Social reports in family law proceedings

Section 47 of the Act of 1995 shall apply to proceedings under this Act.

## 43      Cost of mediation and counselling services

The cost of any mediation services or counselling services provided for a spouse who is or becomes a party to proceedings under this Act, the Act of 1964 or the Act of 1989 or for a dependent member of the family of such a spouse shall be in the discretion of the court concerned.

## 44      Determination of questions between persons formerly engaged to each other in relation to property

Where an agreement to marry is terminated, section 36 of the Act of 1995 shall apply, as if the parties to the agreement were married to each other, to any dispute between them, or claim by one of them, in relation to property in which either or both of them had a beneficial interest while the agreement was in force.

## 45      Amendment of Act of 1989[1]

---

**Notes**

1   Section 45 amends the Judicial Separation and Family Law Reform Act 1989; see the amended Act.

---

## 46      Amendment of Act of 1965

Section 117(6) of the Act of 1965 is hereby amended by the substitution of "6 months" for "twelve months".

## 47      Amendment of Pensions Act, 1990

The Pensions Act, 1990, is hereby amended as follows:

(a)  in subsection (4)(a) (inserted by the Pensions (Amendment) Act, 1996) of section 5, by the substitution of "paragraph (c) or (cc) of section 10(1)" for "section 10(1)(c),",

(b) subsection (4) (inserted by the Pensions (Amendment) Act, 1996) of section 5 shall apply and have effect in relation to section 17 as it applies and has effect in relation to section 12 of the Act of 1995 with the modifications that—

    (i) the reference to the said section 12 shall be construed as a reference to section 17,

    (ii) the reference in paragraph (c) to the Family Law Act, 1995, shall be construed as a reference to the Family Law (Divorce) Act, 1996,

    (iii) the references to subsections (1), (2), (3), (5), (6), (7), (8), (10) and (25) of the said section 12 shall be construed as references to subsections (1), (2), (3), (5), (6), (7), (8), (10) and (25), respectively, of section 17, and

    (iv) the reference to section 2 of the Act of 1995 shall be construed as a reference to section 2,

and

(c) in section 10(1), by the substitution for paragraph (cc) (inserted by the Pensions (Amendment) Act, 1996) of the following paragraph:

"(cc) to issue guidelines or guidance notes generally on the operation of this Act and on the provisions of the Family Law Act, 1995, and the Family Law (Divorce) Act, 1996, relating to pension schemes (within the meaning of section 2 of the Family Law Act, 1995 and section 2 of the Family Law (Divorce) Act, 1996);".

## 48     Amendment of Criminal Damage Act, 1991

Section 1 (3) of the Criminal Damage Act, 1991, is hereby amended—

(a) in paragraph (a), by the insertion after "1976," of the following:

"or a dwelling, within the meaning of section 2(2) of the Family Home Protection Act, 1976, as amended by section 54(1)(a) of the Family Law Act, 1995, in which a person, who is a party to a marriage that has been dissolved under the Family Law (Divorce) Act, 1996, or under the law of a country or jurisdiction other than the State, being a divorce that is entitled to be recognised as valid in the State, ordinarily resided with his or her former spouse, before the dissolution",

and

(b) in paragraph (b), by the substitution of the following subparagraph for subparagraph (i):

"(i) is the spouse of a person who resides, or is entitled to reside, in the home or is a party to a marriage that has been dissolved under the Family Law (Divorce) Act, 1996, or under the law of a country or jurisdiction other than the State, being a divorce that is entitled to be recognised as valid in the State, and".

**49      Amendment of Criminal Evidence Act, 1992**

Section 20 of the Criminal Evidence Act, 1992, is hereby amended in section 20—

(a) by the insertion of the following definition:

> "'decree of divorce' means a decree under section 5 of the Family Law (Divorce) Act, 1996 or any decree that was granted under the law of a country or jurisdiction other than the State and is recognised in the State;", and

(b) by the substitution of the following definition for the definition of former spouse:

> "'former spouse' includes a person who, in respect of his or her marriage to an accused—
>
> (a)   has been granted a decree of judicial separation, or
>
> (b)   has entered into a separation agreement, or
>
> (c)   has been granted a decree of divorce;".

**50      Amendment of Powers of Attorney Act, 1996**

The Powers of Attorney Act, 1996, is hereby amended—

(a) in section 5(7), by the substitution of the following paragraph for paragraph (a):

> "(a)   the marriage is annulled or dissolved either—
>
> (i)    under the law of the State, or
>
> (ii)   under the law of another state and is, by reason of that annulment or divorce, not or no longer a subsisting valid marriage under the law of the State,",

(b) in Part I of the Second Schedule, by the insertion of the following paragraph:

> "2A. The expiry of an enduring power of attorney effected in the circumstances mentioned in section 5(7) shall apply only so far as it relates to an attorney who is the spouse of the donor".

**51      Amendment of Act of 1996**

The references in sections 2 and 3 of the Act of 1996 to a spouse shall be construed as including references to a person who is a party to a marriage that has been dissolved under this Act or under the law of a country or jurisdiction other than the State, being a divorce that is entitled to be recognised as valid in the State.

**52      Amendment of Act of 1995[1]**

---

**Notes**

1   Section 52 amends the Family Law Act 1995, ss 8–12, 15–16, 18, 25, 29, 35–36, 43 and 47; see the amended Act.

---

## 53      Amendment of Maintenance Act, 1994[1]

### Notes

1      Section 53 amends the Maintenance Act 1994, ss 3, 4, and 14; see the amended Act.

# Registration of Births Act 1996

*Number 36 of 1996*

*An Act to amend the Law in relation to the Registration and Re-registration of Births and to provide for Related Matters. [19th December, 1996]¹*

*Be It Enacted by the Oireachtas as Follows:*

---

## Notes

1 This Act, save for subsections (4) and (4A) of s 1, was repealed by the Civil Registration Act 2004.

---

**1**  **Particulars required concerning births registered or reregistered after commencement of Act**

...

[(4) (a)  Where a birth, the registration of which—

   (i) took place on or after 1 October 1997 and before the coming into operation of section 16 and Item 1 of Part 6 of the Schedule to the Social Welfare (Miscellaneous Provisions) Act, 2002, or

   (ii) takes place after the coming into operation of section 16 and Item 1 of Part 6 of the Schedule to the Social Welfare (Miscellaneous Provisions) Act, 2002,

   is being re-registered under any of the enactments mentioned in subsection (2) of this section, the surname of the child shall be—

   (I)  that which has been so registered, or

   (II)  subject to subsection (3) of this section, the surname jointly agreed by the mother and father of the child.

   (b)  Subject to subsection (4A) of this section, a birth which has been re-registered under any of the enactments specified in subsection (2) of this section may not be further re-registered under the enactment concerned.

(4A) Where a birth, the registration of which took place on or after 1 October 1997, has been re-registered under any of the enactments mentioned in subsection (2) of this section before the commencement of section 16 and Item 1 of Part 6 of the Schedule to the Social Welfare (Miscellaneous Provisions) Act, 2002, an tArd-Chláraitheoir may, on the joint application of the mother and father of the child, made in the form for the time being approved by the Minister for that purpose, authorise a second re-registration of the birth under the relevant enactment for the purpose of changing the surname of the child

299

to a surname, subject to subsection (3) of this section, jointly agreed by the mother and father of the child.]¹

**Notes**

1    Subsection 1(4) substituted and subsection 1(4A) inserted by s 16 and Sch, Pt 6 of the Social Welfare (Miscellaneous Provisions) Act 2002.

# Family Law (Miscellaneous Provisions) Act 1997

*Number 18 of 1997*

ARRANGEMENT OF SECTIONS

Section

**Acts Referred To**

| | |
|---|---|
| Domestic Violence Act, 1996 | 1996, No. 1 |
| Family Law Act, 1995 | 1995, No. 26 |
| Marriages (Ireland) Act, 1844 | 1844, c. 81 |
| Powers of Attorney Act, 1966 | 1996, No. 12 |
| Registration of Marriages (Ireland) Act, 1863 | 1863, c. 90 |
| Succession Act, 1965 | 1965, No. 27 |

*An Act to amend the law in relation to notification of intention to marry, the law in relation to barring orders, the law in relation to irrevocable powers of attorney and the law in relation to the distribution of disclaimed estates. [18th may, 1997]*

*Be it enacted by the Oireachtas as follows:*

## 1    Definition

In this Act "**the Act of 1995**" means the Family Law Act, 1995.

## 2    Amendment of Act of 1997[1]

---

**Notes**

1   Section 2 amends the Family Law Act 1995, s 32; see the amended Act.

---

## 3    Validity in law of certain marriages

(1) Where, in relation to a marriage solemnised after the commencement of section 32 (whether before of after the passing of this Act) of the Act of 1995, the notification

provided for in subsection (1) of that section is or was given to a Registrar appointed under section 57 of the Marriages (Ireland) Act, 1844, or section 10 of the Registration of Marriages (Ireland) Act, 1863, or a person authorised by that Registrar to act on his or her behalf and that Registrar is or was not the Registrar (within the meaning of section 32 of the Act of 1995) in relation to that marriage, the marriage shall be and shall be deemed always to have been valid in law if it would have been so valid if the notification had been given to the Registrar (within the meaning aforesaid) in relation to that marriage.

(2) Where, in relation to a marriage, exemption from section 31(1)(a) or 32(1)(a) of the Act of 1995, or both of those provisions, was granted, before the passing of this Act, by a judge of the Circuit Family Court who, in relation to the application concerned, was not the appropriate judge having regard to section 38(4) of the Act of 1995, the marriage shall be and shall be deemed always to have been valid in law if it would have been so valid if the exemption aforesaid had been granted by the judge who, in relation to the application, was the appropriate judge having regard to the said section 38(4).

**4     Amendment of Domestic Violence Act, 1996[1]**

---

**Notes**

1    Section 4 amends the Domestic Violence Act 1996, s 3; see the amended Act.

---

**5     Amendment of Powers of Attorney Act, 1996**

(1) The Powers of Attorney Act 1996, is hereby amended—

   (a)  in section 20, by the substitution of the following subsection for subsection (3):

   "(3)  This section does not apply to a power of attorney that was given otherwise than to secure an interest, or the performance of an obligation, referred to in subsection (1) and was created by an instrument executed before the 1st day of August 1996, but, subject to the foregoing, applies to powers of attorney whenever created.", and

   (b)  by the substitution of the following section for section 25:

   **"Repeals**
   25. Subject to section 20(3), each enactment specified in the Fourth Schedule is hereby repealed to the extent specified in the third column of that Schedule.".

(2) This section shall be deemed to have come into operation upon the commencement of the Powers of Attorney Act, 1996.

**6     Amendment of Succession Act, 1965**

The Succession Act, 1965, is hereby amended by the insertion after section 72 of the following section:

**"Distribution of disclaimed estate**

72A. Where the estate, or part of the estate, as to which a person dies intestate is disclaimed after the passing of the Family Law (Miscellaneous Provisions) Act, 1997 (otherwise than under section 73 of this Act), the estate or part, as the case may be, shall be distributed in accordance with this Part—

  (a)  as if the person disclaiming had died immediately before the death of the intestate, and

  (b)  if that person is not the spouse or a direct lineal ancestor of the intestate, as if that person had died without leaving issue.".

## 7     Short title

This Act may be cited as the Family Law (Miscellaneous Provisions) Act, 1997.[1]

---

### Notes

1   Commencement: 5 May 1997.

---

# Civil Registration Act 2004[1]

*Number 3 of 2004*

## Notes

1   Only the following sections have been commenced:

Part 1, Part 2 (other than section 13(1)(c) and section 13(1)(e), Part 3, Part 5, Part 8, Parts 1, 2 and 5 of the First Schedule (see SI 764/2005) – commencement date 5 December 2005;

Sections 4, 13(1)(e), 27, Part 6, section 65 and the Second Schedule.

ARRANGEMENT OF SECTIONS

## PART 1
### PRELIMINARY AND GENERAL

**Acts Referred to**

## Acts Referred to

| | |
|---|---|
| Army Pensions Acts 1923 to 1980 | |
| Births and Deaths Registration Act (Ireland) 1880 | 1880, c. 13 |
| Births and Deaths Registration Acts 1863 to 1996 | |
| Births, Deaths and Marriages Registration Act 1972 | 1972, No. 25 |
| Capital Acquisitions Tax Consolidation Act 2003 | 2003, No. 1 |
| Civil Service Regulation Acts 1956 to 1996 | |
| Coroners Act 1962 | 1962, No. 9 |
| Data Protection Acts 1988 and 2003 | |
| Defence (Amendment) (No. 2) Act 1960 | 1960, No. 44 |
| Defence Forces (Pensions) Acts 1932 to 1975 | |
| Electoral Act 1992 | 1992, No. 23 |
| Electronic Commerce Act 2000 | 2000, No. 27 |
| Family Law Act 1995 | 1995, No. 26 |
| Family Law (Divorce) Act 1996 | 1996, No. 33 |
| Garda Síochána Act 1989 | 1989, No. 1 |
| Health Act 1947 | 1947, No. 28 |
| Health Act 1970 | 1970, No. 1 |
| Health (Eastern Regional Health Authority) Act 1999 | 1999, No. 13 |
| Housing Act 1966 | 1966, No. 21 |
| Housing Acts 1966 to 2002 | |
| Legitimacy Act 1931 | 1931, No. 13 |
| Legitimacy Declaration Act (Ireland) 1868 | 1868, c. 20 |
| Marriage Act 1835 | 5 & 6 Will 4., c. 54 |
| Marriage Law (Ireland) Amendment Act 1863 | 26 Vict., c. 27 |
| Marriage Law (Ireland) Amendment Act 1873 | 36 & 37 Vict., c. 16 |
| Marriage of Lunatics Act 1811 | 51 Geo 3., c. 37 |
| Marriage (Prohibited Degrees of Relationship) Acts 1907 and 1921 | |
| Marriage (Society of Friends) Act 1860 | 23 & 24 Vict., c. 18 |
| Marriage (Society of Friends) Act 1872 | 35 & 36 Vict., c. 10 |
| Marriages Act 1936 | 1936, No. 47 |
| Marriages Act 1972 | 1972, No. 30 |
| Marriages (Ireland) Act 1844 | 1844, c. 81 |
| Marriages (Ireland) Act 1846 | 9 & 10 Vict., c. 72 |

**Acts Referred to**

| | |
|---|---|
| Matrimonial Causes and Marriage Law (Ireland) Amendment Act 1870 | 33 & 34 Vict., c. 110 |
| Matrimonial Causes and Marriage Law (Ireland) Amendment Act 1871 | 1871, c. 49 |
| Medical Practitioners Act 1978 | 1978, No. 4 |
| Mercantile Marine Act 1955 | 1955, No. 29 |
| Merchant Shipping Act 1894 | 57 & 58 Vict. c. 60 |
| Petty Sessions (Ireland) Act 1851 | 1851, c. 93 |
| Planning and Development Act 2000 | 2000, No. 30 |
| Registration of Births Act 1996 | 1996, No. 36 |
| Registration of Births and Deaths Act 1936 | 1936, No. 34 |
| Registration of Births and Deaths (Ireland) Act 1863 | 1863, c. 11 |
| Registration of Marriages Act 1936 | 1936, No. 35 |
| Registration of Marriages (Ireland) Act 1863 | 1863, c. 90 |
| Road Traffic Act 1961 | 1961, No. 24 |
| Social Welfare (Consolidation) Act 1993 | 1993, No. 27 |
| Stamp Duties Consolidation Act 1999 | 1999, No. 31 |
| Status of Children Act 1987 | 1987, No. 26 |
| Stillbirths Registration Act 1994 | 1994, No. 1 |
| Taxes Consolidation Act 1997 | 1997, No. 39 |
| Vital Statistics and Births, Deaths and Marriages Registration Act 1952 | 1952, No. 8 |

*An Act to Provide for the Reorganisation, Modernisation and Naming of the System (to be known as the Civil Registration Service or, in the Irish Language, An Tseirbhís Um Chlárú Sibhialta) of Registration of Births, Stillbirths, Adoptions, Marriages and Deaths (including Certain Births and Deaths Occurring Outside the State), to Provide for the Extension of the System to Decrees of Divorce and Decrees of Nullity of Marriage and for those Purposes To Revise the Law Relating to the System, to Amend the Law Relating to Marriages and to provide for Related Matters. [27th February, 2004]*

*Be It Enacted by the Oireachtas as Follows:*

## PART 1
### PRELIMINARY AND GENERAL

**1**      **Short title and commencement**

(1) This Act may be cited as the Civil Registration Act 2004.

(2) This Act shall come into operation on such day or days as the Minister may appoint by order or orders either generally or with reference to any particular purpose or provision and different days may be so appointed for different purposes or different provisions, including the application of section 4 to different statutory provisions specified in the Second Schedule.

**2       Interpretation**

(1) In this Act, except where the context otherwise requires—

"**the Act of 1844**" means the Marriages (Ireland) Act 1844;

"**the Act of 1863**" means the Registration of Births and Deaths (Ireland) Act 1863;

["**the Act of 2010**" means the Civil Partnership and Certain Rights and Obligations of Cohabitants Act 2010;][1]

"**the Acts**" means the Births and Deaths Registration Acts 1863 to 1996;

[...][2];

"**Ard-Chláraitheoir**" shall be construed in accordance with section 7;

"**authorised officer**" shall be construed in accordance with section 17(10);

[...][3]

"**birth**" does not include stillbirth;

["**civil partner**" has the meaning assigned to it by the Act of 2010;][1]

["**civil partnership registration**" means registration under section 59D;][1]

"**Civil Registration Service**" shall be construed in accordance with section 8;

["**civil status**" means being single, married, separated, divorced, widowed, in a civil partnership or being a former civil partner in a civil partnership that has ended by death or been dissolved;][1]

"**civil servant**" has the meaning assigned to it by the Civil Service Regulation Acts 1956 to 1996;

["**decree of divorce**" has the meaning assigned to it by the Family Law (Divorce) Act 1996;][1]

["**decree of nullity**—

   (a)  in the case of a decree of nullity of marriage, has the meaning assigned to it by the Family Law (Divorce) Act 1996, and

   (b)  in the case of a decree of nullity of civil partnership, has the meaning assigned to it by the Act of 2010][1];

["**dissolution**" means dissolution of a civil partnership under section 110 of the Act of 2010;][1]

"**event**" means a birth, stillbirth[...][2], marriage, death, decree of [divorce, decree of nullity, civil partnership registration or dissolution][1] occurring or granted anywhere in the State or a birth to which section 26 or 27 applies or a death to which section 38 or 39 applies and includes a birth, stillbirth, [...][2] marriage or death that could have been, but was not, registered in a register formerly maintained under the repealed enactments;

["**Executive**" means the Health Service Executive;][3]

[...]²

**"functions"** includes powers and duties and references to the performance of functions include, as respects powers and duties, references to the exercise of the powers and the carrying out of the duties;

[...]³

**"Minister"** means Minister for Health and Children;

**"Oifig an Ard-Chláraitheora"** shall be construed in accordance with section 12;

**"personal public service number"** has the meaning assigned to it by the Social Welfare (Consolidation) Act 1993;

**"prescribed"** means prescribed by regulations made by the Minister;

**"qualified informant"** in relation to a birth or death, shall be construed in accordance with section 19 or 37, as may be appropriate;

**"registered medical practitioner"**⁴ means a person who is registered or entitled to be registered in the General Register of Medical Practitioners established under section 26 of the Medical Practitioners Act 1978;

**"registrar"**—

(a) in relation to a marriage or intended marriage or the register of marriages, means a registrar within the meaning of section 17,

[(aa) in relation to a civil partnership registration or intended civil partnership registration, or the register of civil partnerships, means a registrar within the meaning of section 17,]¹

(b) in relation to a birth or stillbirth, a newborn child found abandoned or a death or the register of births, the register of stillbirths or the register of deaths, a registrar within the meaning of section 17,

[...]²

(d) in relation to a decree of divorce or the register of decrees of divorce, means the Courts Service[,]¹

[(e) in relation to a decree of nullity of marriage or the register of decrees of nullity of marriage, means the Courts Service,

(f) in relation to a decree of dissolution, or the register of decrees of dissolution, means the Courts Service, and

(g) in relation to a decree of nullity of a civil partnership or the register of decrees of nullity of civil partnerships, means the Courts Service,]¹

and references to a registrar include references to a person authorised by the registrar to act on the registrar's behalf and to the successor of the registrar;

["**registration area**" shall be construed in accordance with section 15(1) and (2A);]³

**"repealed enactments"** means the enactments repealed by section 4;

**"the required particulars"** means—

(a) in relation to a birth or a living new-born child found abandoned, the particulars specified in Part 1 of the First Schedule,

(b)  in relation to a stillbirth, the particulars specified in Part 2 of that Schedule,

[...]²

[...]²

(e)  in relation to a death, the particulars specified in Part 5 of that Schedule;

["**scheme**" means a scheme approved under section 14;]³

"**signature**" includes an electronic signature within the meaning of the Electronic Commerce Act 2000 and cognate words shall be construed accordingly;

"**stillborn child**" means a child who, at birth, weighs not less than 500 grammes or has a gestational age of not less than 24 weeks and shows no sign of life and "stillbirth" shall be construed accordingly;

"**Superintendent Registrar**" shall be construed in accordance with section 17.

(2) For the purposes of this Act there is an impediment to a marriage if—

(a)  the marriage would be void by virtue of the Marriage Act 1835 as amended by the Marriage (Prohibited Degrees of Relationship) Acts 1907 and 1921,

(b)  one of the parties to the marriage is, or both are, already married,

(c)  one or both, of the parties to the intended marriage will be under the age of 18 years on the date of solemnisation of the intended marriage and an exemption from the application of section 31(1)(a) of the Family Law Act 1995 in relation to the marriage was not granted under section 33 of that Act,

(d)  the marriage would be void by virtue of the Marriage of Lunatics Act 1811, [...]¹

(e)  both parties are of the same sex[, or]¹

[(f)  one of the parties to the marriage is, or both are, already party to a subsisting civil partnership.]¹

[(2A) For the purposes of this Act, there is an impediment to a civil partnership registration if—

(a)  the civil partnership would be void by virtue of the Third Schedule,

(b)  one of the parties to the intended civil partnership is, or both are, already party to a subsisting civil partnership,

(c)  one or both of the parties to the intended civil partnership will be under the age of 18 years on the date of the intended civil partnership registration,

(d)  one or both of the parties to the intended civil partnership does not give free and informed consent,

(e)  the parties are not of the same sex, or

(f)  one of the parties to the intended civil partnership is, or both are, married.]¹

(3) In this Act—

(a)  a reference to a birth, stillbirth, [...]² marriage or death includes a reference to such an event that could have been, but was not, registered in a register formerly maintained under the repealed enactments;

(b) a reference to a section, Part or Schedule is a reference to a section, Part or Schedule of or to this Act, unless it is indicated that a reference to some other provision is intended;

(c) a reference to a subsection, paragraph or subparagraph is a reference to the subsection, paragraph or subparagraph of the provision in which the reference occurs unless it is indicated that a reference to some other provision is intended;

(d) a reference to any enactment or instrument made under statute is a reference to that enactment or instrument as amended, adapted or extended at any time by any enactment or instrument made under statute.

**Notes**

1   Definitions of "the Act of 2010", "civil partner", "civil partnership registration", "civil status" and "dissolution", and subsection (2A) inserted by the Civil Partnership and Certain Rights and Obligations of Cohabitants Act 2010, s 7. Definitions of "decrees of divorce" and "decree of nullity" substituted by the Civil Partnership and Certain Rights and Obligations of Cohabitants Act 2010, s 7. Definitions of "event" and "registrar", and subsection (2) amended by the Civil Partnership and Certain Rights and Obligations of Cohabitants Act 2010, s 7.

2   Definitions of "adoption" and "foreign adoption" deleted by the Adoption Act 2010, s 159(a). Definitions of "event" and "the required particulars", and subsection (3)(a) amended by the Adoption Act 2010, s 159(a).

3   Definitions of "registration area" and "scheme" inserted by Health Act 2004, Sch 6. Definitions of "authority" and "health board" deleted by Health Act 2004, Sch 6.

4   See the Medical Practitioners Act 2007, s 108(1) for the construction of references to registered medical practitioner.

## 3        Regulations

(1) The Minister may make regulations—

(a) for any purpose in relation to which regulations are provided for by any of the provisions of this Act,

(b) for prescribing any matter or thing referred to in this Act as prescribed or to be prescribed,

(c) generally for the purpose of giving effect to this Act.

(2) If in any respect any difficulty arises during the period of two years from the commencement of this section in bringing this Act into operation, the Minister may, by regulations made by him or her, do anything which appears to be necessary or expedient for bringing this Act into operation.

(3) A regulation under this section may contain such consequential, supplementary and ancillary provisions as the Minister considers necessary or expedient.

(4) A regulation under this section shall be laid before each House of the Oireachtas as soon as may be after it is made and, if a resolution annulling the regulation is passed by either such House within the next 21 days on which that House has sat after the

regulation is laid before it, the regulation shall be annulled accordingly, but without prejudice to the validity of anything previously done thereunder.

**4        Repeals[1]**

The enactments specified in the Second Schedule are repealed to the extent specified in column 3 of that Schedule.

---

**Notes**

1    Commencement: 5 November 2007 (SI 736/2007).

---

**5        Transitional provisions**

(1) In so far as any order, regulation, rule, agreement, application, decision or reference or order of a court made, approval, consent, notification, notice or direction given or served, requirement imposed, certificate, form or other instrument issued or given, register or index maintained, resolution passed, particulars given, application made or other thing done under an enactment repealed by section 4 could have been made, given, imposed, issued, maintained, passed, served or done under a corresponding provision of this Act, it shall not be invalidated by the repeals effected by section 4 but, except in so far as this Act otherwise provides, shall have effect as if made, given, imposed, issued, maintained, passed, served or done under that corresponding provision.

(2) Where any document refers to an enactment repealed by this Act and provision is made by this Act corresponding to that enactment, then, unless the context otherwise requires, that reference shall be construed as or, as the case may be, as including a reference to the corresponding provision of this Act.

(3) Nothing in this Act affects the validity of a marriage duly solemnised before the commencement of Part 6.

**6        Expenses of Minister and Minister for Finance**

(1) The expenses incurred by the Minister in the administration of this Act shall, to such extent as may be sanctioned by the Minister for Finance, be paid out of moneys provided by the Oireachtas.

(2) The expenses incurred by the Minister for Finance in the administration of this Act shall be paid out of monies provided by the Oireachtas.

PART 2

ADMINISTRATION

**7        Ard-Chláraitheoir**

(1) The office of an tArd-Chláraitheoir provided for by section 4 of the Act of 1863 shall continue in existence after the commencement of this section notwithstanding the repeals effected by this Act, but the office shall be known as an tArd-Chláraitheoir an

tSeirbhís um Chlárú Sibhialta and the person holding the office shall be known as an tArd-Chláraitheoir and is referred to in this Act as an tArd-Chláraitheoir.

(2) An tArd-Chláraitheoir shall be a person appointed to that office by the Minister from among his or her officers.

(3) An tArd-Chláraitheoir shall be a civil servant.

(4) A person appointed to be an tArd-Chláraitheoir shall hold office for a period of 7 years but the Minister may, if he or she thinks fit, continue the appointment (including an appointment previously continued under this subsection) for such further period not exceeding 7 years as he or she considers appropriate.

(5) A person appointed to be an tArd-Chláraitheoir shall, subject to subsection (4), hold office on such terms and conditions as may be determined by the Minister after consultation with the Minister for Finance at the time of the appointment.

(6) (a) The Minister may remove an tArd-Chláraitheoir from office at any time if, in the opinion of the Minister, an tArd-Chláraitheoir is incapable by reason of ill-health of performing his or her functions, or has committed stated misbehaviour or his or her removal from office appears to the Minister to be necessary for the effective performance of the functions of the office.

(b) If an tArd-Chláraitheoir is removed from office under this subsection, the Minister shall cause to be laid before each House of the Oireachtas a statement of the reasons for the removal.

(7) The person who immediately before the commencement of this section held the offices of an tArd-Chláraitheoir shall upon such commencement, be deemed to have been appointed under this section to be an tArd-Chláraitheoir upon terms and conditions equivalent to those upon which he or she held those offices and subsections (4) and (5) do not apply to that person.

(8) The functions of the office of an tArd-Chláraitheoir (being the office provided for by section 52 of the Act of 1844) are transferred to and shall be performed by an tArd-Chláraitheoir.

(9) References in any statute or any instrument made under any statute passed or made before the commencement of this section, or in any other document in existence immediately before such commencement, to the office of an tArd-Chláraitheoir provided for by section 52 of the Act of 1844 shall, upon such commencement, be construed as references to an tArd-Chláraitheoir.

**8    Functions of Ard-Chláraitheoir**

(1) The principal functions of an tArd-Chláraitheoir are—

(a) to maintain, manage and control the system of registration (which shall be known as the Civil Registration Service) established by the repealed enactments of births, stillbirths [...][1], deaths and marriages, wherever occurring in the State, and of births to which section 26 or 27 applies and deaths to which section 38 or 39 applies,

(b) to extend the Civil Registration Service to decrees of divorce, and decrees of nullity [of marriage][2], wherever granted in the State,

[(bb) to extend the Civil Registration Service to civil partnership registration, wherever occurring in the State,

(bbb) to extend the Civil Registration Service to decrees of dissolution and decrees of nullity of civil partnerships, wherever granted in the State,][3]

(c) where appropriate, to modify and adapt the Civil Registration Service so as to provide for changing needs and circumstances (including the use of electronic or other information technology) in relation to the Service,

(d) for the purposes of the Civil Registration Service, where appropriate, to maintain, adapt, modify and enlarge the registers, indexes and other records established and maintained under the repealed enactments,

(e) to establish and maintain registers and indexes for the purposes of the registration of decrees of divorce and decrees of nullity [of marriage][2],

[(ee) to establish and maintain registers and indexes for the purposes of the registration of civil partnerships,

(eee) to establish and maintain registers and indexes for the purpose of the registration of decrees of dissolution of civil partnerships and of decrees of nullity of civil partnerships,][3]

(f) to monitor the operation of this Act,

(g) to make recommendations to the Minister on any measures that are estimated to cost in excess of such amount as may be specified by the Minister from time to time and are, in the opinion of an tArd-Chláraitheoir, necessary to achieve and maintain appropriate standards of efficiency in the Civil Registration Service and, subject to the consent of the Minister, to implement those measures or, instead of or in addition to them, such measures as the Minister may specify in relation to those standards,

(h) to publish guidelines to registrars (within the meaning of section 17) on the operation of this Act,

(i) to initiate and prosecute proceedings in relation to summary offences under this Act or any of the repealed enactments, and

(j) to perform any other functions conferred on him or her by the Minister under subsection (3).

(2) For the purposes of the foregoing and notwithstanding the repeals effected by section 4, the system of registration of births, stillbirths, [deaths and marriages][1] established and maintained under the repealed enactments shall continue in existence after the commencement of that section but may, if and whenever an tArd-Chláraitheoir considers it appropriate to do so, be adapted, modified or enlarged by him or her and, accordingly, the registers, indexes and other records established and maintained under the system shall also continue in existence after such commencement.

(3) The Minister may, by regulations, confer on an tArd-Chláraitheoir such additional functions in relation to the Civil Registration Service as he or she considers appropriate.

(4) An tArd-Chláraitheoir shall be independent in the performance of his or her functions[, including his or her functions under Chapter 1 of Part 10 of the Adoption Act 2010]¹.

(5) An tArd-Chláraitheoir may do all such acts or things as are necessary or expedient for the purpose of the performance of his or her functions[, including his or her functions under Chapter 1 of Part 10 of the Adoption Act 2010]¹.

(6) An tArd-Chláraitheoir may delegate such of his or her functions[, including his or her functions under Chapter 1 of Part 10 of the Adoption Act 2010]¹ as he or she considers appropriate to a member of his or her staff.

---

**Notes**

1   Subsections (1)(a), (2), (4), (5) and (6) were amended by the Adoption Act 2010, s 159(b)

2   Subsections (1)(b) and (1)(e) were amended by the Civil Partnership and Certain Rights and Obligations of Cohabitants Act 2010, s 8.

3   Subsections (1) (bb), (1)(bbb), (1)(ee) and (1)(eee) were inserted by the Civil Partnership and Certain Rights and Obligations of Cohabitants Act 2010, s 8.

---

**9      Ard-Chláraitheoir Cúnta**

(1) There shall stand established the office of an tArd-Chláraitheoir Cúnta an tSeirbhís um Chlárú Sibhialta and the person holding the office is referred to in this Act as an tArd-Chláraitheoir Cúnta.

(2) An tArd-Chláraitheoir Cúnta shall be a person appointed to that office by the Minister from among his or her officers.

(3) An tArd-Chláraitheoir Cúnta shall be a civil servant.

(4) Subject to subsection (5), an tArd-Chláraitheoir Cúnta shall have and may perform such functions as may be determined by the Minister from time to time and shall be subject to the general control and supervision of an tArd-Chláraitheoir.

(5) During a period of absence or incapacity of an tArd-Chláraitheoir or when there is a vacancy in that office, an tArd-Chláraitheoir Cúnta shall have and may perform all the functions of an tArd-Chláraitheoir.

(6) A person appointed to be an tArd-Chláraitheoir Cúnta shall hold office for a period of 7 years but the Minister may, if he or she thinks fit, continue the appointment (including an appointment previously continued under this section) for such further period not exceeding 7 years as he or she considers appropriate.

(7) A person appointed to be an tArd-Chláraitheoir Cúnta shall, subject to subsections (6) and (9), hold office on such terms and conditions as may be determined by the Minister after consultation with the Minister for Finance at the time of the appointment.

(8) (a) The Minister may remove an tArd-Chláraitheoir Cúnta from office at any time if, in the opinion of the Minister, an tArd-Chláraitheoir Cúnta is incapable by reason of ill-health of performing his or her functions or has committed stated misbehaviour or his or her removal from office appears to the Minister to be necessary for the effective performance of the functions of the office.

(b) If an tArd-Chláraitheoir Cúnta is removed from office under this subsection, the Minister shall cause to be laid before each House of the Oireachtas a statement of the reasons for the removal.

(9) If, immediately before the commencement of this section, a person stands appointed under section 10 of the Act of 1863 as assistant to an tArd-Chláraitheoir, he or she shall upon, such commencement, stand appointed to the office of an tArd-Chláraitheoir Cúnta and shall hold that office upon terms and conditions equivalent to those upon which he or she held the office of such assistant and subsections (6) and (7) shall not apply to him or her.

## 10      Staff of Ard-Chláraitheoir

(1) The Minister, after consultation with an tArd-Chláraitheoir and with the consent of the Minister for Finance, may appoint, upon and subject to such terms and conditions as the Minister may determine, after the consultation and with the consent aforesaid, at the time of the appointment, such and so many officers of the Minister to be members of the staff of an tArd-Chláraitheoir as he or she considers necessary, and persons so appointed shall continue to be civil servants.

(2) Persons who were members of the staff of an tArd-Chláraitheoir who is referred to in section 52 of the Act of 1844 or section 4 of the Act of 1863 immediately before the commencement of this section shall, upon such commencement, become and be members of the staff of an tArd-Chláraitheoir upon terms and conditions equivalent to those that applied to their employment immediately before such commencement and shall continue to be civil servants.

## 11      Annual report

(1) An tArd-Chláraitheoir shall, not later than 30 June in each year, beginning with the year 2005, prepare a report in writing (in this section referred to as "the report") on the operation of this Act in the preceding year and shall furnish a copy of it to the Minister.

(2) The report shall, if the Minister so directs, include information in such form and regarding such matters as he or she may specify.

(3) The Minister shall cause copies of the report to be laid before each House of the Oireachtas.

(4) An tArd-Chláraitheoir may prepare such other reports (if any) in writing in relation to matters concerning the Civil Registration Service as the Minister may request or an tArd-Chláraitheoir considers appropriate and furnish copies of them to the Minister.

## 12      Oifig an Ard-Chláraitheora

(1) The office entitled Oifig an Ard-Chláraitheora provided under section 4 of the Act of 1863 shall continue in existence notwithstanding the repeals effected by this Act.

(2) Registers and indexes maintained by an tArd-Chláraitheoir under this Act shall be kept in Oifig an Ard-Chláraitheora or in such other place as an tArd-Chláraitheoir may direct with the approval of the Minister.

(3) An tArd-Chláraitheoir shall, as soon as may be, arrange for the provision of a seal for Oifig an Ard-Chláraitheora which shall be authenticated by the signature of an tArd-Chláraitheoir or a member of his or her staff duly authorised in that behalf by an tArd-Chláraitheoir.

(4) The seal of Oifig an Ard-Chláraitheora shall be judicially noticed and every instrument purporting to be made by Oifig an Ard-Chláraitheora and to be sealed with its seal (purporting to be authenticated in accordance with subsection (3)) shall be received in evidence and be deemed to be such an instrument without further proof unless the contrary is shown.

(5) The functions of the Office entitled Oifig an Ard-Chláraitheora provided under section 52 of the Act of 1844 are transferred to and may be performed by Oifig an Ard-Chláraitheora.

(6) References in any statute or any instrument made under statute passed or made before the commencement of this section or in any document in existence immediately before such commencement to Oifig an Ard-Chláraitheora referred to in subsection (5) shall be construed as references to Oifig an Ard-Chláraitheora.

**13      Registers[1]**

(1) There shall be established, where appropriate, and maintained by an tArd-Chláraitheoir—

   (a)   a register of all births occurring in the State or to which section 26 or 27 applies (which shall be known, and is referred to in this Act, as the register of births),

   (b)   a register of all stillbirths occurring in the State (which shall be known, and is referred to in this Act, as the register of stillbirths),

   (c)   [...][2]

   (d)   a register of all deaths occurring in the State or to which section 38 or 39 applies (which shall be known, and is referred to in this Act as the register of deaths),

   (e)   a register of all marriages taking place in the State (which shall be known, and is referred to in this Act, as the register of marriages),

   (f)   a register of all decrees of divorce (which shall be known, and is referred to in this Act, as the register of [decrees of divorce),][3]

  [(g)   a register of all decrees of nullity of marriage (which shall be known, and is referred to in this Act, as the register of decrees of nullity of marriage),][4]

  [(h)   a register of all civil partnership registrations taking place in the State (which shall be known, and is referred to in this Act, as the register of civil partnerships),

   (i)   a register of all decrees of dissolution (which shall be known, and is referred to in this Act, as the register of decrees of dissolution), and

(j)  a register of all decrees of nullity of civil partnerships (which shall be known, and is referred to in this Act, as the register of decrees of nullity of civil partnerships).]⁵

(2) A register formerly maintained under the repealed enactments shall be deemed, for the purposes of subsection (1) and the other provisions of this Act, to be part of the appropriate register.

(3) A register may be maintained in any legible form or in any other form that is capable of being converted into a legible form and of being used to make a legible copy or reproduction of an entry in the register.

(4) Evidence of an entry in a register and of the facts stated therein may be given by the production of a document purporting to be a legible copy of the entry and to be certified to be a true copy by an tArd-Chláraitheoir, a person authorised in that behalf by an tArd-Chláraitheoir, a Superintendent Registrar, an authorised officer or a registrar.

(5) [...]²

(6) An tArd-Chláraitheoir may give a direction in writing to a registrar (within the meaning of section 17) or other person who holds a marriage register book provided under the repealed enactments to deliver the book or a copy of it to an authority specified in the direction not later than 28 days from the date of the direction.

(7) In subsections (2) to (4), "register" means a register maintained under subsection (1).

---

**Notes**

1  Commencement: s 13(1)(e) commenced by SI 736/2007, with effect from 5 November 2007.

2  Subsections (1)(c) and (5) were deleted by the Adoption Act 2010, s 159(c).

3  Subsection (1)(f) was amended by the Civil Partnership and Certain Rights and Obligations of Cohabitants Act 2010, s 9(a).

4  Subsection (1)(g) was substituted by the Civil Partnership and Certain Rights and Obligations of Cohabitants Act 2010, s 9(b).

5  Subsections (1)(h)-(1)(j) were inserted by the Civil Partnership and Certain Rights and Obligations of Cohabitants Act 2010, s 9(b).

---

## 14    Schemes

[(1) As soon as may be after the appointment of the first Superintendent Registrar of a registration area, he or she shall prepare a scheme in writing for the administration of the Civil Registration Service in that area and shall, after it has been approved by the Executive, submit the scheme to the Minister.]¹

(2) When a scheme or a scheme under subsection (3) is submitted to the Minister, he or she may, after consultation with an tArd-Chláraitheoir, approve of it or refuse to approve of it or request the Superintendent Registrar concerned to make specified amendments, or amendments in relation to specified matters, to the scheme and then re-submit the amended scheme to the Minister for his or her approval.

(3) (a) A scheme may be amended or revoked by a scheme under this subsection prepared by the Superintendent Registrar [of the registration area]² concerned.

(b) A scheme under this subsection shall, after it has been approved by [the Executive]² concerned, be submitted to the Minister.

(4) A scheme or a scheme under subsection (3) shall be subject to the approval of [the Executive]² concerned.

(5) A scheme may contain such incidental, supplementary and consequential provisions as appear to [the Executive]² to be necessary or expedient for the purposes of the scheme.

(6) The Minister may, in consultation with an tArd-Chláraitheoir and [the Executive]², review the operation of a scheme that has been approved by the Minister or a scheme under subsection (3) that has been so approved (except in so far as it revokes another scheme) and may, having regard to the results of the review and after the consultation aforesaid, request the Superintendent Registrar concerned to make specified amendments, or amendments in relation to specified matters, to the scheme or to revoke it and prepare another scheme.

[(7) Without prejudice to the generality of subsection (1), a scheme shall specify in relation to a registration area—

(a) the number of registrars required for the purpose of the performance of the Executive's functions within that area,

(b) the number of other employees required for that purpose,

(c) the locations within that area of the offices of the Executive,

(d) the proposed functions of, and distribution of functions between, the registrars and employees assigned pursuant to the scheme,

(e) particulars of the proposed conditions of employment of the registrars and employees assigned pursuant to the scheme, and

(f) particulars or provisions in relation to any other matter standing specified for the time being by the Minister.]¹

(8) When a scheme or a scheme under subsection (3) is approved by the Minister, it shall have effect in accordance with its terms and the functions of [the Executive in relation to the registration area concerned]² shall be performed in accordance with any relevant provisions of the scheme or the scheme under subsection (3).

(9) A scheme or a scheme under subsection (3) shall come into operation on such day or days as may be specified in it either generally or with reference to any particular purpose or provision and different days may be so specified for different purposes or different provisions.

(10) In this section "registrar" means a registrar within the meaning of section 17.

---

**Notes**

1   Subsections (1) and (7) substituted by s 75 and Part 26 of Schedule 6 of the Health Act 2004.

2    Amended by s 75 and part 26 of Schedule 6 of the Health Act 2004.

## 15    Local registration authorities

[(1) Each functional area of the Health Service Executive shall, subject to subsection (2A), be a registration area for the purposes of this Act.

(2) After consulting with an tArd Chláraitheoir, the Executive shall assign a name to each registration area.

(2A) The Executive may, with the consent of an tArd Chláraitheoir, redefine for the purposes of this Act the boundaries of any of its functional areas, and, if it does so, that functional area as redefined shall be a registration area for those purposes.

(3) Under the overall management, control and supervision of an tArd Chláraitheoir, the Executive shall, in accordance with the provisions of the relevant scheme, manage, control and administer, through the Superintendent Registrar of each registration area, the Civil Registration Service in that area and perform in the area the other functions conferred on it by or under this Act.][1]

(4) An tArd-Chláraitheoir may give a direction in writing to [the Executive][2] in relation to management, control and administration, of the Civil Registration Service in [a registration area][2], and the Executive shall comply with a direction given to it under this subsection.

[(5) The Executive shall, in each year beginning with the year 2005, prepare an estimate in writing of its income and expenditure in the next following year in respect of each registration area and shall submit a copy of it to an tArd Chláraitheoir.][1]

### Notes

1    Subsections (1)–(3) and (5) substituted by s 75 and part 26 of Schedule 6 of the Health Act 2004.

2    Subsection (4) amended by s 75 and part 26 of Schedule 6 of the Health Act 2004.

## 16    Financial provisions relating to authorities[1]

(1) [...][1]

(2) [Accounts of the Executive relating to each scheme][1] shall be audited by the Comptroller and Auditor General.

(3) [...][1]

### Notes

1    Subsections (1) and (3) deleted and subsection (2) amended by s 75 and part 26 of Schedule 6 of the Health Act 2004.

**17      Staff of authorities**

[(1) Subject to the provisions of this section, the Executive, after consulting with an tArd Chláraitheoir, shall—

    (a)  appoint, in respect of each registration area, an employee of the Executive as the chief officer of that area to be known as the Superintendent Registrar,

    (b)  appoint such number of employees of the Executive as registrars of births, stillbirths, [deaths, marriages and civil partnerships]¹ and assign them to each registration area, and

    (c)  assign such number of other employees to each registration area,

as it considers necessary for the performance of its functions.

(2) The appointment and assignment of a registrar under paragraph (b) and the assignment of an employee under paragraph (c) of subsection (1) to a registration area shall be in accordance with the scheme relating to the area.

(3) The Superintendent Registrar of a registration area shall manage, control and administer the Civil Registration Service on behalf of and subject to the control and direction of the Executive in that area and shall perform such other functions in relation to the Civil Registration Service as may from time to time be specified in writing to him or her by the Executive.]²

(4) A registrar shall have and perform [in the registration area to which he or she is assigned]² functions corresponding as nearly as may be to those standing conferred immediately before the commencement of this section on a registrar appointed under the repealed enactments and any other functions conferred on him or her by or under this Act (including [a scheme relating to that area]²).

(5) A registrar or an authorised officer shall, in the performance of his or her functions, be subject to the supervision of the Superintendent Registrar of the [the registration area to which the registar or office is assigned]² and shall comply with any directions given to him or her under subsection (6).

[(6) A Superintendent Registrar of a registration area may give a direction to a registrar or authorised officer assigned to that area.]²

(7) The Minister may, by regulations, confer on registrars such (if any) additional functions as he or she considers appropriate for the purposes of this Act.

(8) Subject to subsection (9), a registrar or other officer appointed after the commencement of this section shall hold office upon such terms and conditions as may be determined by [the Executive]² at the time of the appointment.

[(9) A person holding office under this section (including a Superintendent Registrar and a registrar) may be removed from office by the Executive if, in its opinion, the person is incapable by reason of ill health of performing the functions of the office or has committed stated misbehaviour or his or her removal from office appears to the Executive to be necessary for the effective performance of the functions of the office.]²

[(10)(a) The Executive may appoint any of its employees to be authorised officers either, as may be specified in the instrument of appointment, for the purposes of this Act or for the purposes of specified provisions of this Act and shall assign such officers to a registration area.][2]

(b) An authorised officer, when exercising a power under this Act shall, if so requested by a person affected, produce to the person evidence in writing of his or her appointment as an authorised officer.

(11) A person holding office as a registrar of births, stillbirths, deaths and marriages immediately before the commencement of this section shall, upon such commencement, be deemed to have been appointed under this section as a registrar upon terms and conditions equivalent to those upon which he or she held the office aforesaid immediately before such commencement.

(12) A reference in any statute passed before the commencement of this section or in any instrument made under such a statute to a Superintendent Registrar or a registrar of births, stillbirths, deaths and marriages shall be construed as a reference to a Superintendent Registrar appointed under this section or a registrar, as the case may be, and, accordingly, a function standing vested in Superintendent Registrars or registrars of births, stillbirths, deaths and marriages immediately before such commencement under a provision of such a statute or instrument that continues in force after such commencement shall, upon such commencement, stand vested in Superintendent Registrars appointed under this section or registrars, as the case may be, and may be performed by, such a Superintendent Registrar or by a registrar, as the case may be.

(13) In this section "registrar" means a registrar of births, stillbirths, deaths[, marriages and civil partnerships][3] appointed under this section.

---

**Notes**

1   Subsection (1)(b) was amended by the Civil Partnership and Certain Rights and Obligations of Cohabitants Act 2010, s 10(a).

2   Subsections (1)–(3), (6), (9) and (10)(a) substituted by s 75 and Part 26 of Schedule 6 of the Health Act 2004. Subsections (4), (5) and (8) amended by s 75 and part 26 of Schedule 6 of the Health Act 2004.

3   Subsection (13) was amended by the Civil Partnership and Certain Rights and Obligations of Cohabitants Act 2010, s 10(b).

---

PART 3
REGISTRATION OF BIRTHS AND STILLBIRTHS

**18     "the register" (Part 3)**

In this Part, "the register" means, as the context requires, the register of births or the register of stillbirths and cognate words shall be construed accordingly.

**19      Provision of particulars, and registration, of births**

(1) Subject to the provisions of this Part, when a child is born in the State, it is the duty of—

(a)   the parents or the surviving parent of the child, or

(b)   if the parents are dead or incapable through ill health of complying with this subsection, each other qualified informant, unless he or she reasonably believes that another qualified informant has complied with it in relation to the birth,

not later than 3 months from the date of the birth—

(i)    to attend before any registrar,

(ii)   there, to give to the registrar, to the best of his or her knowledge and belief, the required particulars of the birth, and

(iii)  there, to sign the register in the presence of the registrar.

(2) Where a person complies with subsection (1) in relation to a birth, the other persons referred to in that subsection are discharged from the performance in relation to that birth of the duty imposed by that subsection.

(3) Where, owing to non-compliance with subsection (1), a birth is not registered and, having made reasonable efforts to do so, [the Superintendent Registrar in whose registration area][1] the birth occurred is unable to contact either parent of the child concerned, [the Superintendent Registrar][1] may give a qualified informant a notice in writing requiring the informant—

[(a)   to attend before a registrar in that registration area, at the office of the registrar or such other (if any) convenient place as may be specified by the Superintendent Registrar on or before a day so specified (not being less than 7 days from the date of the notice nor more than 12 months from the date of the birth),][1]

(b)   there, to give to the registrar, to the best of his or her knowledge and belief, the required particulars of the birth, and

(c)   there to sign the register in the presence of the registrar,

and, unless the birth is registered before the date of the attendance aforesaid, the informant shall comply with the requirement.

(4) Where paragraphs (i) to (iii) of subsection (1) or, as the case may be, paragraphs (a) to (c) of subsection (3) have been complied with in relation to a birth, the registrar concerned shall register the birth in such manner as an tArd-Chláraitheoir may direct.

(5) Where, in relation to the birth of a child—

(a)   the parents of the child are dead or incapable through ill health of complying with subsection (1), or

(b)   neither the parents nor another qualified informant can be found after all reasonable efforts to do so have been made,

an tArd-Chláraitheoir may cause the birth to be registered on production to him or her of such evidence as he or she considers adequate for the purpose which, in the case referred to in paragraph (b), shall include, if the place where the birth occurred is known, evidence that the Superintendent Registrar [in whose registration area][1] the birth occurred made all reasonable efforts to find the parents or a qualified informant.

(6) In this section "qualified informant", in relation to the birth of a child, means—

    (a) the parents or the surviving parent of the child,

    (b) a guardian of the child,

    (c) a person present at the birth,

    (d) if the birth occurred in a building used as a dwelling or a part of a building so used, any person who was in the building or part at the time of the birth,

    (e) if the birth occurred in a hospital or other institution or in a building or a part of a building occupied by any other organisation or enterprise the chief officer of the institution, organisation or enterprise (by whatever name called) or a person authorised by the chief officer to perform his or her functions,

    (f) a person having charge of the child, or

    (g) a man who duly makes a request under paragraph (c) or (d) of section 22 (2).

## Notes

1   Amended and subsection (3)(a) substituted by s 75 and part 26 of Schedule 6 of the Health Act 2004.

## 20    Births occurring more than 12 months before registration

(1) A registrar shall not register a birth at a time more than 12 months from the date of the birth without the consent in writing of the Superintendent Registrar [of the registration area to which the registrar is assigned.][1]

(2) The fact of the giving of a consent referred to in subsection (1) to a registrar shall be noted in the register.

## Notes

1   Amended by s 75 and part 26 of Schedule 6 of the Health Act 2004.

## 21    Duty to notify registrar of abandoned new-born children

(1) Where a living new-born child is found abandoned, it is the duty of—

    (a) the person who finds the child, and

    (b) any person in whose charge the child is placed,

not later than 3 months from the date of the finding, to give to a registrar, to the best of his or her knowledge and belief, in such form and manner as may be directed by an tArd-Chláraitheoir, the required particulars of the birth and, thereupon, the registrar shall register the birth in such manner as may be so directed.

(2) Where a person complies with subsection (1) in relation to a child, the other person referred to in that subsection is discharged from the performance in relation to that child of the duty imposed by that subsection.

(3) Where the date of the birth of a child whose birth is required to be registered under this Act is not known and a registered medical practitioner[1] certifies in writing that, in his or her opinion, the birth took place on or about a date specified in the certificate, the registrar concerned may enter that date in the register as the date of the birth of the child.

**Notes**

1    See the Medical Practitioners Act 2007, s 108(1) for the construction of references to registered medical practitioner.

## 22      Registration of father where parents not married

(1) The father of a child who was not married to the mother of the child at the date of his or her birth or at any time during the period of 10 months before such birth shall not be required to give information under this Act about the birth.

(2) Subject to subsection (3), any registrar shall enter in the register the name of a person ("the person") as the father of a child to whom subsection (1) applies—

  (a)  if the mother of the child ("the mother") and the person jointly so request the registrar in writing and give to him or her a declaration in writing of the person that he is the father of the child, or

  (b)  if the mother so requests the registrar in writing and gives to him or her—

      (i)   a declaration in writing of the mother, in a form for the time being standing approved by an tArd-Chláraitheoir, that the person is the father of the child, and

      (ii)  a statutory declaration of the person, in a form for the time being standing approved by an tArd-Chláraitheoir, that he is the father of the child,

    or

  (c)  if the person so requests the registrar in writing and gives to him or her—

      (i)   a declaration in writing of the person, in a form standing approved for the time being by an tArd-Chláraitheoir, that he is the father of the child, and

      (ii)  a statutory declaration of the mother, in a form standing approved for the time being by an tArd-Chláraitheoir, that the person is the father of the child,

    or

  (d)  if the mother or the person so requests the registrar in writing and produces to him or her a document purporting to be a copy of an order made by a court in proceedings referred to in section 45 of the Status of Children Act 1987 and to be certified by or on behalf of the court to be a true copy of the order, finding that the person is the father of the child.

(3) Where, in a case in which the mother of a child to whom sub-section (1) applies ("the mother") was married at the date of the birth of the child or at some time during the period of 10 months ending immediately before such birth, a person would, but for this subsection, fall to be registered under subsection (2) pursuant to a request under paragraph (a), (b) or (c) of that subsection, as the father of the child, the person shall not be so registered unless there is produced to a registrar—

    (a)  a statutory declaration of the person or each person to whom the mother was married at some time during the period aforesaid, in a form standing approved for the time being by an tArd-Chláraitheoir, that he is not the father of the child, or

    (b)  a statutory declaration of the mother, in a form standing approved for the time being by an tArd-Chláraitheoir, that she has been living apart from the person who is or any person who formerly was her husband during the period of 10 months ending immediately before the birth of the child by virtue of a decree of divorce, a decree of divorce a mensa et thoro, a decree of nullity [of marriage][1] or a deed of separation.

(4) Where one of the persons to whom in any particular case sub-section (2)(d) applies makes a request to a registrar under that provision, the registrar shall notify the other person of the request.

(5) When a birth is being registered under this section, the register shall be signed by—

    (a)  the mother of the child concerned if she has made, or joined in the making of, the request concerned under subsection (2), and

    (b)  the person who declares that he is the father of the child, if he has made, or joined in the making of, the request concerned under subsection (2).

(6) This section applies, with any necessary modifications, to stillbirths as it applies to births.

---

**Notes**

1   Subsection 22(3)(b) was amended by the Civil Partnership and Certain Rights and Obligations of Cohabitants Act 2010, s 11.

---

**23     Re-registration of birth to include name of father[1]**

(1) Where the birth of a child whose parents were not married to each other at the date of the birth or at any time during the period of 10 months ending immediately before that date has been registered under this Act or the repealed enactments but no person has been registered as the child's father, then, subject to subsection (2), any registrar shall re-

register the birth in such manner as an tArd-Chláraitheoir may direct and shall enter in the register the name of a person ("the person") as the father of the child—

(a) if the mother of the child and the person jointly so request the registrar in writing and give to him or her a declaration in writing, in a form for the time being standing approved by an tArd-Chláraitheoir, of the person, that he is the father of the child, or

(b) if the mother so requests the registrar in writing and gives to him or her—

    (i) a declaration in writing of the mother, in a form for the time being standing approved by an tArd-Chláraitheoir, that the person is the father of the child, and

    (ii) a statutory declaration of the person, in a form for the time being standing approved by an tArd-Chláraitheoir, that he is the father of the child,

or

(c) if the person so requests the registrar in writing and gives to him or her—

    (i) a declaration in writing of the person, in a form for the time being standing approved by an tArd-Chláraitheoir, that he is the father of the child, and

    (ii) a statutory declaration of the mother, in a form for the time being standing approved by an tArd-Chláraitheoir, that the person is the father of the child,

or

(d) if the mother or the person so requests the registrar in writing and gives to the registrar a document purporting to be a copy of an order made by a court in proceedings referred to in section 45 of the Status of Children Act 1987, and to be certified by or on behalf of the court to be a true copy of the order, finding that the person is the father of the child.

(2) A birth shall not be re-registered under this section without the consent of a Superintendent Registrar [of the registration area to which the registrar is assigned][1].

(3) Where, in a case in which the mother of a child to whom sub-section (1) applies was married at the date of the birth of the child or at some time during the period of 10 months before such date and, but for this subsection, the birth would fall to be re-registered under that subsection pursuant to a request under paragraph (a), (b) or (c) thereof, and a person would fall to be registered under that subsection as the father of the child, the birth shall not be so re-registered and the person shall not be so registered unless there is produced to the registrar concerned—

(a) a statutory declaration of the person to whom the mother was married at that date and of the person or each person to whom she was married at some time during the period aforesaid, in a form standing approved for the time being by an tArd-Chláraitheoir, that he is not the father of the child, or

(b) a statutory declaration of the mother, in a form standing approved for the time being by an tArd-Chláraitheoir, that she has been living apart from the person who is, or the person or each person who was formerly, her husband during a period ending immediately before the date of the birth of the child of more than 10 months by virtue of a decree of divorce, a decree of divorce a mensa et thoro, a decree of nullity [of marriage][2] or a deed of separation.

(4) Where a birth is re-registered under this section, the surname of the child entered in the register shall be—

(a) that which was previously registered, or

(b) a surname determined in accordance with Part 1 or, as may be appropriate, Part 2 of the First Schedule.

(5) A birth which has been re-registered under this section may not be further re-registered save under section 24.

(6) When a birth is being re-registered under this section, the register shall be signed by—

(a) the mother of the child concerned, if she has made, or joined in the making of, the request concerned under subsection (1), and

(b) the person who declares that he is the father of the child, if he has made, or joined in the making of, the request concerned under subsection (1).

(7) When a birth is re-registered under this section, the then existing entry relating to the birth shall be retained in the register.

(8) This section applies, with any necessary modifications, to stillbirths as it applies to births.

---

**Notes**

1  Amended by s 75 and part 26 of Schedule 6 of the Health Act 2004.

2  Subsection (3)(b) was amended by the Civil Partnership and Certain Rights and Obligations of Cohabitants Act 2010, s 12.

---

## 24    Re-registration of births of legitimated persons[1]

(1) Any registrar shall, on application in writing to him or her in that behalf, on production to him or her of such evidence as appears to him or her to be satisfactory and on payment to that registrar of the prescribed fee, re-register the birth of a legitimated person (within the meaning of the Legitimacy Act 1931) whose birth is already registered under this Act or the repealed enactments.

(2) A registrar shall not re-register the birth of a person referred to in subsection (1) if information sufficient for the purpose of the re-registration is not furnished to him or her by both of the parents, or, if one of the parents is dead, by the surviving parent, of the person unless a declaration of the legitimacy of the person has been made under the Legitimacy Declaration Act (Ireland) 1868.

(3) A registrar shall not re-register a birth under this section without the consent of the Superintendent Registrar [of the registration area to which the registrar is assigned][1].

(4) It is the duty of the parents of a legitimated person or, if one of the parents is dead and the re-registration of the birth concerned can be effected on information furnished by the surviving parent, within 3 months of the date of the marriage of the parents, to furnish to the registrar concerned the necessary information with a view to obtaining the re-registration of the birth of that person.

(5) Where the parents of a person whom the registrar concerned believes to have been legitimated under the Legitimacy Declaration Act (Ireland) 1868 fail or either of them fails to comply with subsection (4), the registrar may, by notice in writing served on them, or either of them, require them or, if the notice is served on one only of them, that parent to give to him or her such information concerning the matter as he or she may consider necessary for the purpose of the re-registration of the birth of the person verified in such manner as he or she may direct and for that purpose to attend before the registrar at the office of the registrar or at any other place appointed by the registrar within such time, not being less than 14 days after the receipt of the notice, as may be specified in the notice and a person on whom a notice under this subsection is served shall comply with the requirement it contains.

(6) The failure of the parents of a legitimated person, or of either of them, to furnish information in accordance with this section in respect of the person shall not affect his or her legitimisation.

(7) Where a birth is re-registered under this section, the surname of the child entered in the register shall be—

    (a) that which was previously registered, or

    (b) a surname determined in accordance with Part 1 of the First Schedule.

(8) A birth which has been re-registered under this section may not be further re-registered but the then existing entry relating to the birth shall be retained in the register.

---

**Notes**

1   Amended by s 75 and part 26 of Schedule 6 of the Health Act 2004.

---

**25     Registration, or alteration, of forename of child**

(1) Any registrar shall, on application to him or her in writing, in a form standing approved by an tArd-Chláraitheoir or a form to the like effect, by the parents, the surviving parent or the guardian of a child whose birth has been registered, on production to that registrar of such evidence as appears to him or her to be satisfactory and on payment to that registrar of the prescribed fee—

    (a) if the forename of the child has been registered, change or alter the forename in the entry in the register or add a forename or forenames to the entry, or

    (b) if the forename of the child has not been registered, register the forename of the child.

(2) Where a forename is changed, altered or registered or one or more forenames are added under subsection (1), the then existing entry concerned shall be retained in the register, the change, alteration, registration or addition shall be deemed for all purposes to be and always to have been part of the original entry and the forename or forenames in the register may not be further changed, altered or added to.

## 26 Registration of births outside State of children of Irish citizens domiciled in State

(1) An tArd-Chláraitheoir may, on production to him or her of such evidence as appears to him or her to be satisfactory, cause the birth outside the State (other than a birth to which section 27 applies) of the child of an Irish citizen domiciled in the State to be registered in the register if—

    (a) there was not at the time of the birth a system of registration of births in the place where the birth occurred or such a system that applied to such a child, or

    (b) it is not possible to obtain copies of or extracts from civil records of the birth.

(2) Subsection (1) applies to the stillbirth of a child as it applies to the birth of a child and, accordingly, references in that subsection to birth and births shall be construed as including references to stillbirth and stillbirths, respectively.

## 27 Recording and registration of certain other births occuring outside State[1]

(1) Regulations shall require such persons as may be specified to keep specified records of—

    (a) the birth of a child, whether before or after the commencement of this section, on board an Irish aircraft or an Irish ship,

    (b) the birth of a child of an Irish citizen on board a foreign ship or a foreign aircraft travelling to or from a port, or an airport, as the case may be, in the State, and

    (c) the birth of a child of a member of the Garda Síochána or the Permanent Defence Force outside the State while the member is serving outside the State as such member.

(2) Regulations shall provide for the transmission of copies of records referred to in subsection (1), certified by specified persons to be true copies, to an tArd-Chláraitheoir, and for the making of specified returns in relation to such records to specified persons.

(3) An tArd-Chláraitheoir shall cause to be entered in the register the required particulars relating to births referred to in subsection (1).

(4) Regulations shall provide for the correction of errors in records kept under subsection (1) and for the transmission of copies, certified by specified persons to be true copies, of records corrected under this subsection to an tArd-Chláraitheoir.

(5) On receipt of a corrected record under subsection (4), an tArd-Chláraitheoir shall cause a correct entry that takes account of the corrected record to be entered in the register and the then existing entry relating to the birth concerned shall be retained in the register.

(6) Subsections (1) to (5) apply to the stillbirth of a child as they apply to the birth of a child and, accordingly, references in those subsections to birth or births shall be construed as including references to stillbirth or stillbirths, respectively.

(7) In this section—

**"foreign aircraft"** means an aircraft which is not an Irish aircraft;

**"foreign ship"** means a ship which is not an Irish ship;

**"Irish aircraft"** means an aircraft registered in the State;

**"Irish ship"** has the meaning assigned to it by the Mercantile Marine Act 1955.

**Notes**

1   Commencement: 2 March 2004 (SI 84/2004).

## 28   Registration of stillbirths

(1) Subject to the provisions of this Part, when a child is stillborn—

(a)   the parents or, if one of the parents is dead, the surviving parent of the child, or

(b)   if both of the parents are dead, a relative of either parent,

may, not later than 12 months from the date of the stillbirth—

(i)   attend before any registrar,

(ii)   give to the registrar, to the best of his or her knowledge and belief, the required particulars of the stillbirth and, if it has been obtained, the certificate referred to in subsection (3),

(iii)   after the registrar has entered the required particulars in relation to the stillbirth in the register, sign the register in the presence of the registrar.

(2) Where a person referred to in subsection (1) has taken the steps specified in paragraphs (i) to (iii) of that subsection in relation to a stillbirth, the registrar concerned shall register the stillbirth in the register in such manner as an tArd-Chláraitheoir may direct.

(3) Where a registered medical practitioner has attended the stillbirth of a child, or examined a stillborn child, he or she shall, if so requested by a person referred to in subsection (1), give to him or her a certificate signed by the practitioner stating—

(a)   that he or she attended the stillbirth or, as the case may be, examined the child,

(b)   the estimated weight and gestational age of the child, and

(c)   if the stillbirth occurred in a hospital or other institution or the mother of the child was treated in a hospital or other institution, the name and address of the institution.

(4) Where a stillbirth is not registered during the period of 12 months from the date of the stillbirth, [Superintendent Registrar in whose registration area][1] the stillbirth occurred may—

(a) in case the stillbirth took place, or the mother of the child was treated, in a hospital or other institution, request the institution, and

(b) in case the stillbirth did not take place in a hospital or other institution, but a registered medical practitioner attended the stillbirth or treated the child or a midwife attended the stillbirth, request the practitioner or midwife,

to give to any registrar in that registration area the required particulars of the stillbirth, and the institution or person, as the case may be, shall comply with the request.

(5) Where the required particulars in relation to a stillbirth are given to a registrar pursuant to subsection (1) or (4) and if one has been obtained, the certificate referred to in subsection (3), is given to the registrar pursuant to subsection (1), the registrar shall register the birth in such manner as an tArd-Chláraitheoir may direct.

(6) Where a certificate referred to in subsection (3) is given to a person referred to in that subsection, a duplicate of the certificate may be used for the purpose of the registration of the stillbirth concerned.

(7) If, in the course of his duties, a coroner ascertains that a body is that of a stillborn child, he or she shall notify a registrar in the [registration area][1] in which the body is located of the stillbirth and shall give to the registrar, in as far as he or she can ascertain them, the required particulars in relation to the stillbirth, and the registrar shall register the stillbirth in such manner as an tArd-Chláraitheoir may direct.

**Notes**

1    Amended by s 75 and part 26 of Schedule 6 of the Health Act 2004.

## 29    Registration of stillbirths that occurred before 31 December 1994

Where, in the case of a stillbirth that occurred before 31 December 1994, a parent of the stillborn child or a relative of either parent of the child who has knowledge of the stillbirth gives to any registrar the required particulars in relation to the stillbirth and evidence establishing to the satisfaction of the Superintendent Registrar of the [registration area][1] concerned the occurrence of the stillbirth—

(a) the registrar shall enter the particulars in the register,

(b) the parent or relative shall then sign the register in the presence of the registrar, and

(c) the registrar shall register the stillbirth in such manner as an tArd-Chláraitheoir may direct.

**Notes**

1    Amended by s 75 and part 26 of Schedule 6 of the Health Act 2004.

**30**      **Duty to notify Ard-Chláraitheoir of births and stillbirths**

(1) It shall be the duty of the chief officer (by whatever name called) of a hospital or other institution in which a child is born or stillborn, or a person authorised by the chief officer to perform his or her functions, to give to the [Superintendent Registrar in whose registration area][1] the hospital is situated, as soon as is practicable after the birth or stillbirth and in such manner as an tArd-Chláraitheoir may direct, the required particulars relating to the birth or, as the case may be, the stillbirth.

(2) Where a child is born or stillborn other than in a hospital or other institution—

     (a) in case a registered medical practitioner is present at the birth or stillbirth or examines the child, it shall be the duty of the practitioner, and

     (b) in case a registered medical practitioner is not present, but a midwife is, it shall be the duty of the midwife,

to notify the [Superintendent Registrar in whose registration area][1] the birth or stillbirth occurs of the birth or stillbirth as soon as is practicable after the birth or stillbirth and to do so in the manner directed by an tArd-Chláraitheoir.

---

**Notes**

1    Amended by s 75 and part 26 of Schedule 6 of the Health Act 2004.

---

## PART 4
### REGISTRATION OF ADOPTIONS

[…][1]

---

**Notes**

1    Sections 31–35 repealed by the Adoption Act 2010, s 7(1) and Schedule 1.

---

## PART 5
### REGISTRATION OF DEATHS

**36**      **"the register" (Part 5)**

In this Part, "the register" means the register of deaths, and cognate words shall be construed accordingly.

**37**      **Provision of particulars, and registration, of deaths**

(1) When a death occurs in the State, it is the duty of—

     (a) a relative [or civil partner][1] of the deceased who has knowledge of the required particulars in relation to the death, and (b)　if there is no such relative [or civil partner][1] who can be found or every such relative [or civil partner][1] is incapable through ill health of complying with this subsection, each other qualified informant, unless he or she reasonably believes that another qualified informant has complied with it in relation to the death,

within 3 months from the date of the death to give to any registrar the required particulars of the death in the form standing specified for the time being by an tArd-Chláraitheoir.

(2) Subject to section 40, where, after the expiration of 3 months from the date of the death of a person in the State, the death has not been registered because of non-compliance with subsection (1), the [Superintendent Registrar in whose registration area][2] the death occurred may serve a notice on any qualified informant requiring him or her—

(a)　to attend before a registrar in [that registration area or in the registration area][2] in which the informant ordinarily resides at the office of the registrar or at any other convenient place specified in the notice within such time (not being less than 10 days from the date of the notice) as may be specified in the notice,

(b)　there, to give to the registrar, to the best of his or her knowledge and belief, in a form standing specified by an tArd-Chláraitheoir, the required particulars relating to the death and, if so requested by the registrar, the relevant certificate under section 42, and

(c)　there, to sign the register relating to the death in the presence of the registrar,

and, unless the death is duly registered before the expiration of the time specified in the notice, the informant shall comply with the requirement and, thereupon, the registrar shall register the death in such manner as an tArd-Chláraitheoir may direct.

(3) Where a person complies with subsection (1) in relation to a death, the other persons referred to in that subsection are discharged in relation to that death from the duty imposed by that subsection.

(4) This section applies also to a death that occurred before the commencement of this section and as respects which section 9 of the Births and Deaths Registration Act (Ireland) 1880 was not complied with.

(5) In this section "qualified informant", in relation to a death, means—

(a)　a relative [or civil partner][1] of the deceased who has knowledge of the required particulars concerned,

(b)　a person present at the death,

(c)　any other person who has knowledge of the required particulars,

(d)　if the death occurred in a building used as a dwelling or a part of a building so used, any person who was in the building or part at the time of the death,

(e)　if the death occurred in a hospital or other institution or in a building or a part of a building occupied by any other organisation or enterprise, the chief officer of the institution, organisation or enterprise (by whatever name called) or a person authorised by the chief officer to perform his or her functions,

(f) a person who found the body of the person concerned,

(g) a person who took charge of that body,

(h) the person who procured the disposal of that body, or

(i) any other person who has knowledge of the death.

**Notes**

1 Amended by the Civil Partnership and Certain Rights and Obligations of Cohabitants Act 2010, s 13.

2 Amended by s 75 and part 26 of Schedule 6 of the Health Act 2004.

**38 Registration of deaths occurring outside State of Irish citizens domiciled in State**

An tArd-Chláraitheoir may, on production to him or her of such evidence as appears to him or her to be satisfactory, cause the death outside the State (other than a death to which section 39 applies) of an Irish citizen domiciled in the State to be registered in the register if—

(a) there was not at the time of the death a system of registration of deaths in the place where the death occurred or such a system that applied to such a death, or

(b) it is not possible to obtain copies of or extracts from civil records of the death.

**39 Recording and registration of certain other deaths occurring outside State**

(1) Regulations shall require such persons as may be specified to keep specified records of—

(a) the death of a person on board an Irish aircraft or an Irish ship,

(b) the death of an Irish citizen on board a foreign ship or a foreign aircraft travelling to or from a port, or an airport, as the case may be, in the State, and

(c) the death of a member of the Garda Síochána or the Permanent Defence Force or of the spouse or specified members of the family of such a member outside the State while the member is serving outside the State as such member.

(2) Regulations shall provide for the transmission of copies of records referred to in subsection (1), certified by specified persons to be true copies, to an tArd-Chláraitheoir.

(3) An tArd-Chláraitheoir shall cause to be entered in the register the required particulars relating to deaths to which records referred to in subsection (1) relate.

(4) Regulations shall provide for the correction of errors in records kept under subsection (1) and for the transmission of copies, certified by specified persons to be true copies, of records corrected under this subsection to an tArd-Chláraitheoir.

(5) On receipt of a corrected record under subsection (4), an tArd-Chláraitheoir shall cause a correct entry that takes account of the corrected record to be entered in the

register and the then existing entry relating to the death concerned shall be retained in the register.

(6) In this section—

"**foreign aircraft**" means an aircraft which is not an Irish aircraft;

"**foreign ship**" means a ship which is not an Irish ship;

"**Irish aircraft**" means an aircraft registered in the State;

"**Irish ship**" has the meaning assigned to it by the Mercantile Marine Act 1955.

## 40      Registration after more than 12 months from death

(1) A registrar shall not register a death at a time more than 12 months from the date of the death or the finding of the body concerned without the consent in writing of the Superintendent Registrar [of the registration area to which the registrar is assigned][1].

(2) The fact of the giving of a consent under subsection (1) shall be noted in the register.

### Notes

1    Amended by s 75 and part 26 of Schedule 6 of the Health Act 2004.

## 41      Furnishing of particulars of death by a coroner to registrar

(1) Where, in pursuance of the Coroners Act 1962, a coroner—

(a)  holds an inquest,

(b)  adjourns an inquest at which evidence of identification and medical evidence as to the cause of death has been given, or

(c)  decides, as a result of a post-mortem examination, not to hold an inquest,

he or she shall give the appropriate registrar a certificate containing the required particulars of the death concerned and that registrar shall register the death in such manner as an tArd-Chláraitheoir may direct.

(2) Where a coroner inquires into the circumstances of a death without holding an inquest or causing a post-mortem examination to be made, he or she shall give the appropriate registrar a certificate containing the required particulars of the death and that registrar shall register the death in such manner as an tArd-Chláraitheoir may direct.

(3) Where there is an error in a certificate furnished under subsection (1) or (2) the coroner concerned may give a certificate correcting the error to the registrar concerned, and the registrar shall correct the error in the register.

(4) In this section "appropriate registrar" means a registrar in the [registration area][1] in which the body concerned is lying or was found.

1 Amended by s 75 and part 26 of Schedule 6 of the Health Act 2004.

## 42 Certificate of cause of death

(1) On the death following an illness of a person who was attended during that illness by a registered medical practitioner, the practitioner shall sign and give to a qualified informant (within the meaning of section 37) a certificate stating to the best of his or her knowledge and belief the cause of the death, and the informant shall give the certificate to any registrar together with the form specified in section 37(1) containing the required particulars in relation to the death.

(2) Where a registrar is given a certificate under subsection (1), the registrar shall enter in the register, together with the required particulars—

   (a) the cause of the death concerned stated in the certificate, and

   (b) the name and address of the registered medical practitioner concerned.

## 43 Place of death

(1) Where the body of a dead person is found on land and the place in which the death occurred is not known, the death shall be registered by a registrar in the [registration area]¹ in which the body is found.

(2) Where the body of a dead person is found in a river, lake or waterway or in the sea or any other area of water, the death shall be registered by a registrar in the [registration area]¹ where the body is brought ashore from the area of water in question.

**Notes**

1 Amended by s 75 and part 26 of Schedule 6 of the Health Act 2004.

## 44 Power of coroner to authorise disposal of bodies

(1) A coroner may—

   (a) when he or she has held an inquest on a body, but, subject to paragraph (b), in no other circumstances, if he or she thinks fit, by order authorise—

      (i) a relative of the deceased person, or any other person, who proposes to cause the body to be disposed of, or

      (ii) the undertaker, or any other person, who is in charge of the funeral of the deceased person,

   to dispose of the body before the registration of the death, and

(b)   authorise the disposal of a body, whether it is lying for the time being in or outside his or her district, irrespective of whether he or she has decided that it is, or will become, necessary to hold an inquest on it.

(2) In subsection (1), "disposal", in relation to a body, means disposal by burial, cremation or any other means and cognate words shall be construed accordingly.

PART 6
AMENDMENT OF LAW RELATING TO MARRIAGES

**45      Definitions (Part 6)**

In this Part—

"**body**" means [the Executive][1] or a religious body;

"**marriage registration form**" means a form prescribed under section 48;

"**the register**" means the register of marriages and cognate words shall be construed accordingly;

"**the Register**" means the register maintained under section 53 and cognate words shall be construed accordingly;

"**registered solemniser**" means a person standing registered in the Register;

"**religious body**" means an organised group of people members of which meet regularly for common religious worship.[2]

---

**Notes**

1   Amended by s 75 and part 26 of Schedule 6 of the Health Act 2004.

2   Part 6 commenced 5 November 2007 (SI 736/2007).

---

**46      Notification of marriages**

(1) A marriage solemnised in the State, after the commencement of this section, between persons of any age shall not be valid in law unless the persons concerned—

(a)   (i)   notify any registrar in writing in a form for the time being standing approved by an tArd-Chláraitheoir of their intention to marry not less than 3 months prior to the date on which the marriage is to be solemnised, or

(ii)  are granted an exemption from the application of subparagraph (i) under section 47 and give a copy of the court order granting the exemption to any registrar before the date aforesaid,

and

(b)   attend at the office of that registrar, or at any other convenient place specified by that registrar, at any time during normal business hours not less than 5 days (or such lesser number of days as may be determined by that registrar) before the date aforesaid and make and sign a declaration in his or her presence that there is no impediment to the said marriage.

(2) Except in such circumstances as may be prescribed, a notification referred to in subsection (1)(a)(i) shall be delivered by both of the parties to the intended marriage, in person, to the registrar.[1]

(3) The notification aforesaid shall be accompanied by the prescribed fee and such (if any) other documents and information as may be specified by an tArd-Chláraitheoir.[2]

(4) The requirements specified in subsections (1) and (2) are declared to be substantive requirements for marriage.

(5) When, in relation to an intended marriage, a registrar receives a notification under, or a copy of a court order referred to in, subsection (1) (a) and any other documents or information specified in subsection (3), he or she shall notify in writing of the receipt each of the parties to the intended marriage and the person who is intended to solemnise the marriage.

(6) A notification under subsection (5) shall not be construed as indicating the approval of the registrar concerned of the proposed marriage concerned.

(7) The registrar concerned may require each party to an intended marriage to provide him or her with such evidence relating to that party's forename, surname, address, [civil status][3], age and nationality as may be specified by an tArd-Chláraitheoir.

(8) An tArd-Chláraitheoir may, if so authorised by the Minister, publish, in such form and manner as the Minister may direct, notice of notifications of intended marriages under subsection (1), but a notice under this subsection shall not contain the personal public service number of a party to the intended marriage concerned.

(9) Where, in relation to a marriage solemnised after the commencement of this section, the appropriate notification under section 32(1)(a)(i) of the Family Law Act 1995 was duly given in compliance with that provision on a date before such commencement, the notification shall be deemed to be a notification under subsection (1)(a)(i) duly given in compliance with that provision on that date and the parties to the marriage shall be deemed, for the purposes of this Act, to have complied with subsections (1)(a)(i), (2) and (3).

(10) Where, in relation to a marriage solemnised after the commencement of this section, the parties concerned attended on a date before such commencement at the office of a registrar, or at another convenient place specified by a registrar, and there made and signed a declaration in his or her presence that there is no impediment to the said marriage, the declaration shall be deemed to be a declaration under subsection (1)(b) duly made and signed in compliance with that provision on that date and the parties to the marriage shall be deemed, for those purposes, to have complied with subsection (1)(b).

**Notes**

1   Circumstances prescribed in SI 667/2010, regulations 3–5 and SI 744/2007, regulation 3.

2   Fees prescribed in SI 737/2007, regulation 6.

3   Subsection (7) amended by the Civil Partnership and Certain Right and Obligations of Cohabitants Act 2010, s 14.

---

## 47   Exemption of certain marriages from section 46 (1)(a)(i)

(1) The Circuit Family Court or the High Court may, on application to it in that behalf by both of the parties to an intended marriage, by order exempt the marriage from the application of section 46 (1)(a)(i).

(2) The following provisions shall apply in relation to an application under subsection (1)—

(a)   it may be made informally,

(b)   it may be heard and determined otherwise than in public,

(c)   a court fee shall not be charged in respect of it, and

(d)   it shall not be granted unless the applicants show that its grant is justified by serious reasons and is in their interests.

(3) Where, in relation to a marriage solemnised after the commencement of this section, an order was made under section 33 of the Family Law Act 1995 on a date before such commencement exempting the marriage from the application of section 32(1)(a) of that Act, the order shall be deemed, for the purposes of this Act, to be an order made on that date under subsection (1) exempting the marriage from the application of paragraph (a)(i) of section 46 (1) and to have been given to a registrar, and the parties to the marriage shall be deemed, for those purposes, to have complied with subparagraph (ii) of that paragraph.

(4) The jurisdiction conferred on the Circuit Family Court by this section shall be exercised by a judge of the circuit in which either of the parties to the intended marriage concerned ordinarily resides or carries on any profession, business or occupation or where the place at which the marriage concerned is intended to be solemnised is situate.

## 48   Marriage registration form

(1) Where, in relation to an intended marriage—

(a)   a registrar to whom the notification concerned under, or a copy of the court order concerned referred to in, section 46 was given is satisfied that section 46 has been complied with, or

(b)   a registrar is satisfied that—

(i)   by virtue of subsection (9) of section 46, subsections (1)(a)(i), (2) and (3) of that section are deemed to have been complied with, or

(ii)   by virtue of section 47(3), section 46(1)(a)(ii), is deemed to have been complied with,

and section 46 has been, or is deemed to have been, complied with in all other respects, or

    (c) a registrar is satisfied that, by virtue of subsection (10) of section 46, subsection (1)(b) of that section is deemed to have been complied with, and section 46 has been, or is deemed to have been, complied with in all other respects,

he or she shall complete a marriage registration form in relation to the intended marriage.

(2) In the case of an intended marriage, the registrar aforesaid shall, before the solemnisation of the marriage, give a marriage registration form completed in accordance with subsection (1) to one of the parties to the marriage.

(3) A marriage shall not be solemnised unless one of the parties to the marriage has given the relevant marriage registration form to the person solemnising the marriage, for examination by him or her.

(4) Where a marriage has not been solemnised within the period of 6 months from the date specified in the relevant marriage registration form, but is intended to be solemnised, the parties thereto shall—

    (a) submit to a registrar, as may be appropriate—

        (i) if a notification in relation to the marriage was previously submitted to a registrar pursuant to section 46 (1)(a)(i), another such notification or, if a notification in relation to the marriage was previously submitted to a registrar pursuant to section 32(1)(a)(i) of the Family Law Act 1995, a notification in relation to the marriage pursuant to section 46 (1)(a)(i), or

        (ii) another copy of the relevant order under section 47 or, if an order in relation to the marriage was previously made under section 33 of the Family Law Act 1995, a copy of the order,

    and

    (b) shall comply with paragraph (b) of section 46 (1),

and, upon compliance by the parties with paragraphs (a) and (b), the registrar shall give to one of them another marriage registration form completed by him or her in accordance with subsection (1).

(5) A form, which shall be known as, and is referred to in this Part, as a marriage registration form, may be prescribed for the purposes of this Part.

### 49     Registration of marriages

(1) Immediately after the solemnisation of a marriage, the marriage registration form relating to the marriage shall be signed by—

    (a) each of the parties to the marriage,

    (b) two witnesses to the solemnisation of the marriage, and

    (c) the person who solemnised the marriage.

(2) Either of the parties to a marriage shall give to a registrar, within one month from the date of the marriage, the marriage registration form duly completed in accordance with subsection (1).

(3) A registrar shall, as soon as practicable after he or she receives a marriage registration form under subsection (2), enter the particulars in relation to the marriage concerned specified in the form in the register and register the marriage in such manner as an tArd-Chláraitheoir may direct.

(4) Subject to subsection (5), a registrar shall not register a marriage if he or she has not received the relevant marriage registration form.

(5) Where an tArd-Chláraitheoir is satisfied that the marriage registration form relating to a duly solemnised marriage has been lost, destroyed or damaged, he or she may direct the appropriate registrar—

    (a) to complete another marriage registration form and arrange, insofar as it is practicable to do so, for its signature by the persons referred to in subsection (1), and

    (b) when it has been so signed, to enter the particulars in relation to the marriage specified in the form in the register and to register the marriage in such manner as he or she may direct.

(6) The Minister may provide by regulations for the correction of errors in entries in the register and for the causing of corrected entries to be entered in the register and for the retention of the original entries in the register.

(7) Where an tArd-Chláraitheoir is satisfied that an entry in the register relates to a marriage—

    (a)  (i) that was not exempted under section 33 of the Family Law Act 1995 from the application of section 32(1)(a) of that Act, and

        (ii) in relation to which the said section 32(1)(a) was contravened,

    (b)  (i) that was not exempted under section 47 from the application of section 46 (1)(a)(i), and

        (ii) in relation to which section 46 (1)(a)(i) was contravened,

    or

    (c) in relation to which section 46 (1)(b) was not complied with, he or she—

    (d) shall direct a registrar to cancel the entry and the direction shall be complied with, and

    (e) shall notify the parties concerned of the direction.

(8) Where, in relation to a marriage solemnised in accordance with the rites and ceremonies of the Roman Catholic Church after the commencement of this section, a certificate under section 11 of the Registration of Marriages (Ireland) Act 1863 was procured by a party to the marriage before such commencement, the certificate shall be deemed, for the purposes of this section, to be a marriage registration form duly completed in accordance with subsection (1) and that section shall be deemed, for those purposes, to have been complied with.

(9) Where, in relation to a marriage to which section 11 of the Registration of Marriages (Ireland) Act 1863 applies and which was solemnised before the commencement of this section—

(a) the said section 11 was not complied with, and

(b) a certificate referred to in that section is given to a registrar by one of the parties to the marriage after such commencement,

the said section 11 shall be deemed to have been complied with in relation to the marriage and the registrar may register the marriage in the register in such manner as an tArd-Chláraitheoir may direct.

(10) Where, in relation to a marriage to which section 22 of the Matrimonial Causes and Marriage Law (Ireland) Amendment Act 1871 applies and which was solemnised before the commencement of this section—

(a) the said section 22 was not complied with, and

(b) a certificate referred to in that section is given to a registrar by one of the parties to the marriage after such commencement,

the said section 22 shall be deemed to have been complied with in relation to the marriage and the registrar may register the marriage in the register in such manner as an tArd-Chláraitheoir may direct.

**50    Non-receipt of marriage registration form by registrar**

(1) Where, upon the expiration of 56 days from the date specified in the relevant marriage registration form on which a marriage is intended to be solemnised, the registrar by whom the form was issued has not received the completed marriage registration form, he or she may serve on either of the parties to the marriage a notice, in a form standing approved by an tArd-Chláraitheoir, requiring that party to give, or cause to be given, to him or her, not later than 14 days from the date of the notice, the first-mentioned form duly completed.

(2) If a person fails to comply with a requirement made on him or her under subsection (1), the registrar concerned may serve on him or her a notice, in a form standing approved by an tArd-Chláraitheoir, requiring the person to attend on a date (not being less than 14 days from the date of the notice) specified in the notice at the office of the registrar or at any other convenient place specified in the notice and to give to him or her at that time or not later than 14 days from that date the relevant completed marriage registration form.

**51    Solemnisation of marriages**

(1) A marriage may be solemnised by, and only by, a registered solemniser.

(2) A registered solemniser shall not solemnise a marriage unless—

(a) both parties to the marriage are present,

(b) two persons professing to be 18 years or over are present as witnesses,

[(c) the solemnisation takes place in a place that is open to the public, unless an tArd-Chláraitheoir or a superintendent registrar—

(i) is satisfied on the basis of a certificate of a registered medical practitioner that one or both of the persons to be married is too ill to attend at a place that is open to the public, and

  (ii) gives approval to the solemniser to the solemnisation taking place at another place—

   (I) chosen by the persons to be married, and

   (II) agreed to by the solemniser.]¹

 (d) he or she is satisfied that the parties to the marriage understand the nature of the marriage ceremony and the declarations specified in subsection (4).

(3) A registered solemniser shall not solemnise a marriage except in accordance with a form of ceremony which—

 (a) has been approved by an tArd-Chláraitheoir,

 (b) includes and is in no way inconsistent with the declarations specified in subsection (4), and

 (c) in the case of a registered solemniser who is not a registrar, is recognised by the religious body of which he or she is a member.

(4) The declarations referred to in subsection (3) are—

 (a) a declaration by the parties to the marriage in the presence of—

  (i) each other,

  (ii) the registered solemniser who is solemnising the marriage, and

  (iii) the two witnesses to the solemnisation,

  to the effect that he or she does not know of any impediment to the marriage, and

 (b) a declaration by the parties to the marriage in the presence of—

  (i) each other,

  (ii) the registered solemniser who is solemnising the marriage, and

  (iii) the two witnesses to the solemnisation,

  to the effect that they accept each other as husband and wife.

(5) The requirements specified in subsections (1) to (3) are declared to be substantive requirements for marriage.

(6) (a) If a person, being one of the parties to a marriage, the registered solemniser concerned or one of the witnesses to the solemnisation, does not have a sufficient knowledge of the language of the ceremony to understand the ceremony and that language, the parties to the marriage shall arrange for the translation during the ceremony of the words of the ceremony into a language known to the person by an interpreter (not being a party or a witness to the marriage) present at the ceremony.

 (b) An interpreter who is present at a marriage ceremony pursuant to paragraph (a) shall—

  (i) before the ceremony, sign, in the presence of the registered solemniser, a statement to the effect that the interpreter understands, and is able to converse in, any language in respect of which he or she is to act as interpreter at the ceremony, and give the statement to the registered solemniser, and

    (ii) immediately after the ceremony, give the registered solemniser a certificate written in the language used by the registered solemniser at the ceremony and signed by the interpreter in the presence of the registered solemniser to the effect that the interpreter has faithfully acted as interpreter at the ceremony.

(7) The parties to a marriage solemnised in accordance with this Act shall be taken to be married to each other when both of them have made a declaration in the presence of each other, the registered solemniser and the two witnesses that they accept each other as husband and wife.

(8) This section shall have effect notwithstanding any statutory provision that conflicts with it.

(9) A declaration specified in paragraph (a) of subsection (4) may be made at any time before the declaration under paragraph (b) of that subsection is made, not being a time earlier than 2 days before the day on which the latter declaration is made.

(10) In this section a reference to a registered solemniser, in relation to a marriage which a person is temporarily authorised under section 57 to solemnise, includes a reference to that person.

---

**Notes**

1   Subsection (2)(c) substituted by s 105 and Schedule 1 of the Health Act 2007.

---

**52     Places and times for the solemnisation of marriages**

(1) Notwithstanding any statutory provision that conflicts with this subsection, a marriage may be solemnised only at a place and time chosen by the parties to the marriage with the agreement of the registered solemniser concerned and (if the registered solemniser is a registrar and the place chosen is not the office of a registrar) the approval of the place [the Executive][1], and the question whether to give or withhold such an approval shall be determined by [the Executive][1] by reference to such matters as may be specified by the Minister.

(2) (a) Where a registrar who is a registered solemniser solemnises a marriage at a place other than the office of a registrar, a fee of such amount as [the Executive][1] may determine shall be paid by the parties to the marriage to the registrar.

    (b) Where travel or subsistence expenses are incurred by a registrar who is a registered solemniser in connection with the solemnisation of a marriage by him or her at a place other than his or her office, an amount in respect of the expenses, calculated by reference to a scale drawn up by [the Executive][1], shall be paid to the registrar by the parties to the marriage.

(c) An amount payable under paragraph (a) or (b) may be recovered by the registrar concerned from the parties to the marriage concerned as a simple contract debt in any court of competent jurisdiction.

(3) In this section a reference to a registered solemniser, in relation to a marriage which a person is temporarily authorised under section 57 to solemnise, includes a reference to that person.

[(4) Subsection (1) does not apply in respect of a marriage solemnised in the circumstances described in subparagraph (i) and (ii) of section 51(2)(c).]²

---

**Notes**

1   Amended by section 75 and part 26 of Schedule 6 of the Health Act 2004.

2   Subsection (4) inserted by s 105 and Schedule 1 of the Health Act 2007.

---

## 53      Register of Solemnisers

(1) An tArd-Chláraitheoir shall establish and maintain a register (which shall be known as the Register of Solemnisers and is referred to in this Part as "the Register") of persons empowered, by virtue of their registration in the Register, to solemnise marriages.

(2) The Register shall be open to inspection by members of the public at all reasonable times.

(3) An tArd-Chláraitheoir shall, subject to subsection (4), register a person in respect of whom an application is made under section 54.

(4) An tArd-Chláraitheoir shall refuse to register a person if he or she considers that—

   (a)   the body concerned (not being [the Executive]¹) is not a religious body,

   (b)   the form of marriage ceremony used by the body concerned does not include both of the declarations specified in section 51(4) or is inconsistent with either of them,

   (c)   the form of marriage ceremony used by the body concerned has not been approved by an tArd-Chláraitheoir, or

   (d)   the person is not a fit and proper person to solemnise a marriage.

(5) It shall be the duty of the body on the application of whom a person is registered in the Register to notify an tArd-Chláraitheoir as soon as practicable of—

   (a)   the death, resignation or retirement of the person from the office by virtue of which he or she became so registered, or

   (b)   any change in the information provided in the application, and an tArd-Chláraitheoir shall make such amendments of the Register as he or she considers necessary.

(6) An entry in the Register shall be in such form and contain such particulars as an tArd-Chláraitheoir may determine.

(7) The Minister may provide by regulations for the correction of errors in entries in the Register by causing corrected entries to be entered in the Register and the original entries to be maintained in the Register.

**Notes**

1    Amended by s 75 and part 26 of Schedule 6 of the Health Act 2004.

**54    Application by bodies for registration of persons**

(1) A body may apply to an tArd-Chláraitheoir—

[(a)  in case the body is the Executive, for the registration of a registrar named in the application who is employed by the Executive and is aged 18 years or more.]¹

(b)  in case the body is a religious body, for the registration of a member named in the application who is aged 18 years or more.

(2) An application under subsection (1) shall be in such form and contain particulars in relation to such matters as an tArd-Chláraitheoir may determine.

(3) Where one or more members of a religious body stand registered in the Register, the body shall not make a further application under subsection (1) unless it is satisfied that there is a need for a larger number of its members to be so registered.

**Notes**

1    Amended by s 75 and part 26 of Schedule 6 of the Health Act 2004.

**55    Cancellation of registration**

(1) An tArd-Chláraitheoir may cancel the registration of a person on the ground that—

(a)  the person or the body concerned has requested him or her to cancel it,

(b)  the marriage ceremony used by the body no longer includes both of the declarations specified in section 51(4) or is inconsistent with one or both of them,

(c)  the person—

(i)   has, while registered, been convicted of an offence under this Act,

(ii)  for the purpose of profit or gain has carried on a business of solemnising marriages,

(iii) is not a fit and proper person to solemnise marriages, or

(iv)  for any other reason, should not continue to be registered.

(2) Where an tArd-Chláraitheoir intends to cancel the registration of a person on a ground mentioned in subsection (1)(c), he or she shall, give notice in writing of his or

her intention to the person and the body concerned and shall specify the ground in the notice and the notice shall, if practicable, be of at least 21 days.

(3) After a person receives a notice under subsection (2), he or she shall not solemnise a marriage unless—

    (a)   an tArd-Chláraitheoir notifies the person that he or she has decided not to cancel the registration, or

    (b)   the Minister notifies the person that an appeal under section 56 (2) in respect of his or her registration has been successful,

and, where an tArd-Chláraitheoir gives a notification pursuant to paragraph (a), he or she shall also notify the body concerned of his or her decision.

## 56    Appeals against refusals or cancellations of registration

(1) If an tArd-Chláraitheoir refuses to register a person named in an application by a body under section 54 (1)—

    (a)   an tArd-Chláraitheoir shall notify the person and the body, by notice in writing, of the refusal and of his or her reasons for the refusal, and

    (b)   the person or the body or both of them may appeal against the refusal to the Minister, by notice in writing delivered to the Minister not later than 28 days from the day on which the notice under paragraph (a) is received by the person or the body, as may be appropriate.

(2) If an tArd-Chláraitheoir cancels the registration of a person under section 55 —

    (a)   he or she shall notify the person and the body concerned, by notice in writing, of the cancellation and of his or her reasons for the cancellation, and

    (b)   the person or the body or both of them may appeal against the cancellation to the Minister, by notice in writing delivered to the Minister not later than 28 days from the day on which the notice under paragraph (a) is received by the person or the body, as may be appropriate.

(3) On an appeal under this section, the Minister shall receive and consider such submissions as the parties to the appeal may make to him or her, either orally or in writing, as the Minister may determine.

(4) On an appeal under this section, the Minister shall—

    (a)   notify the person and the body concerned of his or her decision,

    (b)   give an tArd-Chláraitheoir such directions (if any) as he or she considers appropriate.

(5)  (a)   If the Minister dismisses an appeal under this section solely on the ground that the body concerned (not being [the Executive][1]) is not or has ceased to be a religious body, the body may appeal against the dismissal to the Circuit Court.

    (b)   If the Minister dismisses an appeal under this section on any other ground, a party to the appeal may appeal against the dismissal on a point of law to the Circuit Court.

(c) The jurisdiction conferred on the Circuit Court by this subsection shall be exercised—

    (i) in case the appeal is by [the Executive][1] or a religious body, by a judge of the circuit in which [the Executive][1] or the religious body has its principal place of business or its principal office,

    (ii) in case the appeal is by a person (other than [the Executive][1] or a religious body), by a judge of the circuit in which the person ordinarily resides or carries on any profession, business or occupation,

    (iii) in case the appeal is by a person (other than [the Executive][1] or a religious body) and [the Executive][1] or a religious body, by a judge of the circuit in which [the Executive][1] or the body has its principal place of business or its principal office.

**Notes**

1    Amended by s 75 and part 26 of Schedule 6 of the Health Act 2004.

**57**      **Temporary authorisation to solemnise marriage**

(1) An tArd-Chláraitheoir may, on application in writing to him or her by a religious body, grant to a member of the body named in the application who is aged 18 years or more a temporary authorisation to solemnise—

    (a) one or more marriages specified in the authorisation, or

    (b) marriages during a specified period so specified.

(2) An application under subsection (1) shall be in such form and contain such particulars as an tArd-Chláraitheoir may determine.

(3) An authorisation under this section may be made subject to such conditions as are specified therein.

**58**      **Objections**

(1) A person may at any time before the solemnisation of a marriage lodge an objection in writing with any registrar and the objection shall state the reasons for the objection.

[(2) Where an objection under subsection (1) is received by a registrar assigned to a registration area other than the registration area to which is assigned the registrar who, in relation to the marriage concerned, was given the notification referred to in section 46 or a copy of an order referred to in that section—

    (a) the registrar by whom the objection is received shall refer the objection to the Superintendent Registrar of the registration area to which is assigned the registrar who was given the notification or the copy of the court order,

    (b) the Superintendent Registrar to whom the objection is referred shall direct a registrar assigned to his or her registration area to perform the function conferred by this section on the registrar who received the objection,][1]

(c) the registrar who receives the direction shall comply with it, and

(d) references in subsections (3) and (4) and (6) to (8) to the registrar who receives an objection shall be construed as references to the registrar who receives the direction aforesaid, and this section shall apply and have effect accordingly.

(3) If the registrar who receives an objection under subsection (1) is satisfied that the objection relates to a minor error or misdescription in the relevant notification under section 46 which would not constitute an impediment to the marriage, the registrar shall—

(a) notify the parties to the intended marriage of the objection,

(b) make such enquiries as he or she thinks fit,

(c) if the marriage registration form has been given to one of those parties, request its return to the registrar and correct it and the notification and make any necessary corrections to any other records relating to the marriage, and

(d) give the corrected marriage registration form to one of the parties to the marriage.

(4) If the registrar who receives an objection under subsection (1) believes that more than a minor error or misdescription exists in the relevant notification under section 46 and that the possibility of the existence of an impediment to the intended marriage concerned needs to be investigated, he or she shall refer the objection to an tArd-Chláraitheoir for consideration and, pending the decision of an tArd-Chláraitheoir, he or she shall—

(a) notify the parties to the intended marriage that—

    (i) an objection has been lodged and of the grounds on which it is based,

    (ii) the objection is being investigated,

    (iii) the solemnisation of the marriage will not proceed until the investigation is completed,

(b) if the relevant marriage registration form has not been issued, suspend its issue,

(c) if the marriage registration form has been issued, request the party to the marriage to whom it was given to return it to the registrar,

(d) notify the solemniser of the marriage that an objection is being investigated, and

(e) direct him or her not to solemnise the marriage until the investigation is completed, and the solemniser shall comply with the direction.

(5) Where an objection is referred to an tArd-Chláraitheoir pursuant to subsection (4), he or she shall make a decision on the objection as soon as practicable.

(6) In a case referred to in subsection (4), if an tArd-Chláraitheoir decides that no impediment to the intended marriage concerned exists, he or she shall advise the registrar concerned to that effect and the registrar shall—

(a) notify the parties to the marriage that no impediment to the marriage exists,

(b) issue or re-issue the marriage registration form to one of those parties,

(c)  notify the person who lodged the objection that no impediment to the marriage exists.

(7) In a case referred to in subsection (4), if an tArd-Chláraitheoir decides that there is an impediment to the intended marriage, he or she shall advise the registrar concerned to that effect and of the reasons for the decision and the registrar shall—

(a)  notify the parties to the marriage—

(i)  that the solemnisation of the marriage will not proceed, and

(ii)  of the decision of an tArd-Chláraitheoir and of the reasons therefor,

and

(b)  take all reasonable steps to ensure that the solemnisation does not proceed.

(8) If, notwithstanding the steps taken by the registrar concerned pursuant to subsection (7)(b), the marriage concerned is solemnised, the marriage shall not be registered.

(9)  (a)  A party to a proposed marriage may appeal to the Circuit Family Court against the decision of an tArd-Chláraitheoir in relation to the marriage under subsection (7).

(b)  The jurisdiction conferred on the Circuit Family Court by paragraph (a) may be exercised by a judge of the circuit in which either of the parties to the intended marriage concerned ordinarily resides or carries on any profession, business or occupation or where the place at which the marriage concerned had been intended to be solemnised is situated.

(10) A person who has lodged an objection under subsection (1) may withdraw the objection, but an tArd-Chláraitheoir may, if he or she considers it appropriate to do so, investigate, or complete his or her investigation of, the objection and issue any directions to the registrar concerned in relation to the matter that he or she considers necessary.

(11) An objection on the ground that the marriage would be void by virtue of the Marriage of Lunatics Act 1811 shall be accompanied by a certificate of a registered medical practitioner[2] supporting the objection.

---

**Notes**

1   Substituted by s 75 and part 26 of Schedule 6 of the Health Act 2004.

2   See the Medical Practitioners Act 2007, s 108(1) for the construction of references to registered medical practitioner.

---

PART 7

REGISTRATION OF DECREES OF DIVORCE AND DECREES OF NULLITY

**59      Registration of decrees of divorce and decrees of nullity**

(1) When a court grants a decree of divorce, an officer of the Courts Service authorised in that behalf by the Courts Service, shall, as soon as may be, enter or cause to be

entered in the register of decrees of divorce the particulars in relation to the matter specified in Part 6 of the First Schedule.

(2) When a court grants a decree of nullity [of marriage][1], an officer of the Courts Service, authorised in that behalf by the Courts Service, shall, as soon as may be, enter or cause to be entered in the register of decrees of nullity [of marriage][1] the particulars in relation to the matter specified in Part 7 of the First Schedule.

(3) An officer of the Courts Service, authorised in that behalf by the Courts Service, may amend or cancel or cause to be amended or cancelled an entry in a register referred to in subsection (1) or (2).

(4) The Courts Service shall notify an tArd-Chláraitheoir of an amendment or cancellation under subsection (3).

(5) This section shall have effect notwithstanding any statutory provision that conflicts with it.

---

**Notes**

1    Subsection (2) was amended by the Civil Partnership and Certain Rights and Obligations of Cohabitants Act 2010, s 15.

---

## [PART 7A
## REGISTRATION OF CIVIL PARTNERSHIPS

**59A    Definitions (Part 7A)**

In this Part—

**"civil partnership registration form"** means a form prescribed under section 59C;

**"register"** means the register of civil partnerships.

**59B    Notification of civil partnerships**

(1) A civil partnership registered in the State, after the commencement of this section, between persons of any age shall not be valid in law unless the persons concerned—

   (a)   notify any registrar in writing in a form for the time being standing approved by an tArd-Chláraitheoir of their intention to enter into a civil partnership not less than 3 months prior to the date on which the civil partnership is to be registered, and

   (b)   attend at the office of that registrar, or at any other convenient place specified by that registrar, at any time during normal business hours not less than 5 days (or a lesser number of days that may be determined by that registrar) before that date and make and sign a declaration in his or her presence that there is no impediment to the registration of the civil partnership.

(2) Notwithstanding paragraph (a) of subsection (1), the Circuit Court or the High Court may, on application to it by the persons wishing to enter into a civil partnership, order that the registration be exempt from that paragraph if the Court is satisfied, after a

hearing held otherwise than in public, that there are serious reasons for the exemption and that the exemption is in the interests of those persons.

(3) The jurisdiction conferred on the Circuit Court by this section shall be exercised by a judge of the circuit in which either of the parties to the intended civil partnership concerned ordinarily resides or carries on any profession, business or occupation or where the place at which the civil partnership concerned is intended to be registered is situate.

(4) A court fee shall not be charged in respect of an application under subsection (2).

(5) Except in the circumstances that may be prescribed, a notification referred to in paragraph (1)(a) shall be delivered by both of the parties to the intended civil partnership, in person, to the registrar.

(6) The notification shall be accompanied by the prescribed fee and any other documents and information that an tArd-Chláraitheoir may specify.

(7) The requirements specified in subsections (1) and (5) are declared to be substantive requirements for registering a civil partnership.

(8) When, in relation to an intended civil partnership, a registrar receives a notification under paragraph (1)(a) and any other documents or information specified under subsection (6), he or she shall, as soon as reasonably practicable, notify in writing each of the parties to the intended civil partnership and the registrar who is to register the civil partnership of the receipt.

(9) A notification under subsection (8) shall not be construed as indicating the registrar's approval of the proposed civil partnership.

(10) The registrar may require each party to an intended civil partnership to provide him or her with the evidence relating to that party's forename, surname, address, civil status, age and nationality that an tArd-Chláraitheoir may specify.

(11) An tArd-Chláraitheoir may, if so authorised by the Minister, publish, in the form and manner that the Minister may direct, notice of notifications of intended civil partnerships under subsection (1), but a notice under this subsection shall not contain the personal public service number of a party to the intended civil partnership.

## 59C    Civil partnership registration form

(1) A registrar to whom a notification is given under section 59B, or who receives a copy of an exemption order under subsection (2) of that section, who is satisfied that that section has been complied with shall complete a civil partnership registration form for the intended civil partnership.

(2) Before the registration of a civil partnership, the registrar shall give a copy of the civil partnership registration form to one of the parties to the intended civil partnership.

(3) When the parties wish to register a civil partnership, one of them shall give the civil partnership registration form to the registrar who is to register the civil partnership for examination by him or her.

(4) A civil partnership registration form is valid only for a period of 6 months from the date on which it is completed. If the parties do not register the civil partnership during

that period and wish to have their civil partnership registered, they shall again comply with section 59B.

(5) The Minister may prescribe the civil partnership registration form.

## 59D    Civil partnership registration

(1) The parties shall orally make the declarations referred to in subsection (3), and sign the civil partnership registration form in the presence of each other, the registrar and two witnesses professing to be 18 years or over. The declarations shall be made and the signature of the civil partnership registration form shall be in a place that is open to the public, unless an tArd-Chláraitheoir or a superintendent registrar—

(a) is satisfied on the basis of a certificate of a registered medical practitioner that one or both of the parties is too ill to attend at a place that is open to the public, and

(b) gives approval to the registrar that signature of the form take place at another place chosen by the parties and agreed to by the registrar.

(2) The registrar shall be satisfied that the parties understand the nature of the civil partnership and the declarations specified in subsection (3).

(3) Each party to the civil partnership shall make the following declarations:

(a) a declaration that he or she does not know of any impediment to the civil partnership registration;

(b) a declaration of his or her intention to live with and support the other party; and

(c) a declaration that he or she accepts the other party as a civil partner in accordance with the law.

(4) The requirements of subsections (1) to (3) are declared to be substantive requirements for civil partnership registration.

(5) The parties may, before signing the civil partnership registration form, take part in a ceremony in a form approved by an tArd-Chláraitheoir in which the declarations are made in a place open to the public and in the presence of the registrar and the witnesses.

(6) (a) The witnesses shall sign the form after the parties to the civil partnership have done so, and the registrar shall countersign the form.

(b) The parties' civil partnership shall be taken to be registered upon the counter-signature of the registrar.

(c) As soon as practicable after the signatures and counter-signature, the registrar shall give the parties a copy of the form referred to in paragraph (a), enter the particulars in relation to the civil partnership in the register and register the civil partnership in a manner that an tArd-Chláraitheoir may direct.

(7) Where an tArd-Chláraitheoir is satisfied that a duly signed civil partnership registration form has been lost, destroyed or damaged, he or she may direct the appropriate registrar—

(a)  to complete another civil partnership registration form and arrange, insofar as it is practicable to do so, for its signature by the persons referred to in subsection (1), and

(b)  when it has been so signed, to enter the particulars in relation to the civil partnership specified in the form in the register and to register the civil partnership in a manner as an tArd-Chláraitheoir may direct.

(8) The Minister may provide by regulations for the correction of errors in entries in the register and for the causing of corrected entries to be entered in the register and for the retention of the original entries in the register.

(9) Where an tArd-Chláraitheoir is satisfied that an entry in the register relates to a civil partnership in relation to which section 59B(1) was not complied with (other than where there has been an exemption ordered under subsection (2) of that section)—

(a)  an tArd-Chláraitheoir shall direct a registrar to cancel the entry,

(b)  the registrar shall cancel the entry, and

(c)  an tArd-Chláraitheoir shall notify the parties.

**59E    Places and times for registration of civil partnerships**

(1) A civil partnership may be registered only at a place and time chosen by the parties to the civil partnership with the agreement of the registrar and, if the place chosen is not the office of a registrar or a place referred to in section 59D(1)(b), the approval of the place by the Executive, and the question whether to give or withhold the approval, shall be determined by the Executive by reference to the matters that the Minister may specify.

(2) Where a registrar registers a civil partnership at a place other than the office of a registrar, the parties shall pay to the registrar a fee in the amount that the Executive may determine.

(3) When a registrar incurs travel or subsistence expenses in connection with registering a civil partnership at a place other than his or her office, the parties shall pay to the registrar an amount in respect of the expenses, calculated by reference to a scale that the Executive may draw up.

(4) An amount payable under subsection (2) or (3) may be recovered by the registrar from the parties as a simple contract debt in any court of competent jurisdiction.

**59F    Objections**

(1) A person may, at any time before a civil partnership registration, lodge with any registrar an objection in writing that contains the grounds on which the objection is based.

(2) If the registrar who receives an objection under subsection (1) is not assigned to the same registration area as the registrar to whom the notification was given under section 59B (or, where there has been an exemption ordered under subsection (2) of that section, the registrar who is to register the civil partnership)—

(a)  the receiving registrar shall refer the objection to the Superintendent Registrar of the registration area to which the other registrar is assigned,

(b) the Superintendent Registrar shall direct a registrar assigned to that area to perform the function conferred by this section on the receiving registrar,

(c) the registrar who receives the direction shall comply with it, and

(d) references in this section to the registrar who receives an objection shall be construed as references to the registrar who receives the direction and this section shall apply and have effect accordingly.

(3) If the registrar who receives an objection under subsection (1) is satisfied that the objection relates to a minor error or misdescription in the relevant notification under section 59B which would not constitute an impediment to the civil partnership, the registrar shall—

(a) notify the parties to the intended civil partnership registration of the objection,

(b) make the appropriate enquiries,

(c) if the civil partnership registration form has been given to one of the parties, request its return and correct it and the notification and make any necessary corrections to any other records relating to the civil partnership, and

(d) give the corrected civil partnership registration form to one of the parties to the civil partnership.

(4) If the registrar who receives an objection under subsection (1) believes that the possibility of the existence of an impediment to the intended civil partnership registration needs to be investigated, he or she shall refer the objection to an tArd-Chláraitheoir for consideration and, pending the decision of an tArd-Chláraitheoir, he or she shall—

(a) notify the parties to the intended civil partnership registration that—

  (i) an objection has been lodged and the grounds on which it is based,

  (ii) the objection is being investigated, and

  (iii) the civil partnership registration will not proceed until the investigation is completed,

(b) if the civil partnership registration form has not been issued, suspend its issue,

(c) if the civil partnership registration form has been issued, request the party to the intended civil partnership registration to whom it was given to return it to the registrar, and

(d) notify the proposed registrar of the civil partnership, if a different registrar is intended to register the civil partnership, that an objection is being investigated, and direct him or her not to register the civil partnership until the investigation is completed.

(5) A registrar shall comply with a direction under paragraph (4)(d).

(6) Where an objection is referred to an tArd-Chláraitheoir pursuant to subsection (4), he or she shall make a decision on the objection as soon as practicable.

(7) In a case referred to in subsection (4), if an tArd-Chláraitheoir decides that no impediment to the intended civil partnership exists, he or she shall advise the registrar to that effect and the registrar shall—

(a) notify the parties to the civil partnership that no impediment to the civil partnership exists,

(b) issue or re-issue the civil partnership registration form to one of those parties, and

(c) notify the person who lodged the objection that no impediment to the civil partnership exists.

(8) In a case referred to in subsection (4), if an tArd-Chláraitheoir decides that there is an impediment to the intended civil partnership, he or she shall advise the registrar to that effect and of the reasons for the decision and the registrar shall—

(a) notify the parties to the civil partnership—

(i) that the registration of the civil partnership will not proceed, and

(ii) of the decision of an tArd-Chláraitheoir and of the reasons for it, and

(b) take all reasonable steps to ensure that the registration does not proceed.

(9) If, notwithstanding the steps taken by the registrar pursuant to paragraph (8)(b), the civil registration proceeds, the entry in the register is invalid and any person who becomes aware of that entry into the register shall notify an tArd-Chláraitheoir of it.

(10) When an tArd-Chláraitheoir becomes aware of an entry referred to in subsection (9)—

(a) an tArd-Chláraitheoir shall direct a registrar to cancel the entry and notify the parties and the registrar who made the entry of the direction, and

(b) the registrar shall comply with the direction and cancel the entry and ensure that the cancelled entry is retained in the register.

(11) A party to a proposed civil partnership may appeal to the Circuit Court against the decision of an tArd-Chláraitheoir under subsection (8) in relation to the civil partnership.

(12) The jurisdiction conferred on the Circuit Court by subsection (11) may be exercised by a judge of the circuit in which either of the parties to the intended civil partnership ordinarily resides or carries on any profession, business or occupation or the place at which civil partnership concerned had been intended to be registered is situate.

(13) A person who has lodged an objection under subsection (1) may withdraw the objection, but an tArd-Chláraitheoir may, if he or she considers it appropriate to do so, investigate or complete his or her investigation of the objection and issue any directions to the registrar concerned in relation to the matter that he or she considers necessary.

(14) An objection on the ground that the civil partnership would be void by virtue of the incapacity of one or both of the parties to give informed consent shall be accompanied by a certificate supporting the objection made by a registered medical practitioner.

## 59G    Where interpretation required

If a party or a witness to a civil partner-interpretation ship registration does not have sufficient knowledge of the language of the registration to understand the registration documents or the declarations, the parties shall have an interpreter present who shall—

(a) before the parties make the declarations, sign, in the presence of the registrar, a statement to the effect that the interpreter understands and is able to converse in the language in respect of which he or she is to act as interpreter and give the statement to the registrar, and

(b) immediately after those declarations are made, give the registrar a signed certificate written in the language of the registration, to the effect that the interpreter has faithfully acted as interpreter.

## 59H    Effect of registration

The parties to a registered civil partnership shall be taken to be civil partners of each other as soon as the registrar has countersigned the civil partnership form as required by section 59D(6)(a), regardless of whether the registrar has performed the actions required of him or her under section 59D(6)(c), and all duties and benefits that accrue to civil partners under the Act of 2010 or any other law accrue to them.

## 59I    Effect of this Part

This Part shall have effect notwithstanding any statutory provision that conflicts with it.]¹

---

### Notes

1   Part 7A inserted by the Civil Partnership and Certain Rights and Obligations of Cohabitants Act 2010, s 16.

---

[PART 7B
REGISTRATION OF DECREES OF DISSOLUTION OF CIVIL PARTNERSHIP AND
DECREES OF NULLITY OF CIVIL PARTNERSHIP

## 59J    Registration of decrees of dissolution and decrees of nullity of civil partnership

(1) When a court grants a decree of an officer of the Courts Service authorised in that behalf by the Courts Service shall, as soon as may be, enter or cause to be entered in nullity of civil partnership. the register of decrees of dissolution of civil partnership the particulars in relation to the matter set out in Part 6A of the First Schedule.

(2) When a court grants a decree of nullity of civil partnership, an officer of the Courts Service authorised in that behalf by the Courts Service shall, as soon as may be, enter or cause to be entered in the register of decrees of nullity of civil partnership the particulars in relation to the matter set out in Part 7A of the First Schedule.

(3) An officer of the Courts Service authorised in that behalf by the Courts Service may amend or cancel or cause to be amended or cancelled an entry in the register referred to in subsection (1) or (2).

(4) The Courts Service shall notify an tArd-Chláraitheoir of an amendment or cancellation under subsection (3).

(5) This section has effect notwithstanding any statutory provision that conflicts with it.]¹

**Notes**

1   Part 7B inserted by the Civil Partnership and Certain Rights and Obligations of Cohabitants Act 2010, s 17.

PART 8

GENERAL

**60      Appeals**

(1) Where—

    (a)   a registrar fails or refuses to register in the appropriate register specified in section 13 a birth, stillbirth, [death, marriage or civil partnership]¹ or to enter in such a register one or more of the particulars required by this Act to be so entered, and furnished to him or her by a person pursuant to this Act, or

    (b)   an tArd-Chláraitheoir or an authorised officer fails or refuses to comply with a request of a person under section 63,

the registrar, an tArd-Chláraitheoir or the authorised officer, as the case may be, shall notify the qualified informant (within the meaning of Part 3 or 5, as may be appropriate) concerned, the parties to the marriage[, the parties to the civil partnership]² or the person in writing of the reasons for the failure or refusal.

(2) If a person ("the appellant") affected by a failure or refusal by a person under subsection (1) is dissatisfied with it, he or she may appeal against it by lodging a notice of appeal in writing in a form standing approved by an tArd-Chláraitheoir or in a form to the like effect with [the Executive]³, not later than 28 days from the date of his or her receipt of the notification under subsection (1), and the appeal shall be referred [by the Executive to such employee of the Executive]³ (not being the person in relation to whom the appeal is brought) [as the Executive]³ may determine ("the appeals officer"), and the appeals officer shall determine the appeal.

(3) If an appellant is dissatisfied with the decision of an appeals officer under subsection (2), he or she may appeal against it by lodging a notice of appeal in writing in the form standing approved by an tArd-Chláraitheoir or a form to the like effect with an tArd-Chláraitheoir not more than 28 days after his or her receipt of the decision and an tArd-

Chláraitheoir shall determine the appeal and, subject to subsections (6) to (8), the decision shall be final.

(4) The Minister may by regulations make provision in relation to notices of appeal under this section and the procedure to be followed on appeals under this section.

(5) In relation to an appeal under this section, the appeals officer concerned or an tArd-Chláraitheoir, as the case may be—

    (a)  shall notify the parties concerned in writing of his or her decision in relation to the appeal and of the reasons therefor, and

    (b)  may give such directions in relation to the registration or correction concerned to the registrar or authorised officer concerned as he or she considers appropriate, and any such direction shall be complied with by the person to whom it is given.

(6) An appeals officer ("the officer") may revise a decision of another appeals officer under this section if it appears to the officer that the decision was erroneous having regard to evidence first given to the officer, or a fact first made known to the officer, since the date of the decision.

(7) An tArd-Chláraitheoir may revise a decision (including a revised decision under this subsection) of an tArd-Chláraitheoir or an appeals officer if it appears to him or her that the decision was erroneous by reason of a mistake of law or fact.

(8) A person who is dissatisfied with a decision (including a revised decision) of an tArd-Chláraitheoir may appeal against it to the High Court.

(9) A revision under subsection (6) by an appeals officer shall be deemed, for the purpose of subsections (2) to (5) and (7) of this section, to be a decision under subsection (2), and those subsections shall apply and have effect accordingly, with any necessary modifications, in relation to the revision.

(10) A decision or a revision under this section—

    (a)  shall be in writing and be signed by the person by whom it is made, and

    (b)  shall, subject to any appeal under this section, have effect in accordance with its terms.

(11) A document purporting to be a decision or a revision of an tArd-Chláraitheoir or an appeals officer shall be deemed to be such a decision or revision and to have been signed by the person purporting to have signed it unless the contrary is shown and shall be prima facie evidence of the decision or revision and it shall not be necessary to prove that that person was an tArd-Chláraitheoir or, as the case may be, an appeals officer.

---

**Notes**

1   Subsection (1)(a) amended by the Civil Partnership and Certain Rights and Obligations of Cohabitants Act 2010, s 18(a).

2   Subsection (1) amended by the Civil Partnership and Certain Rights and Obligations of Cohabitants Act 2010, s 18(b).

3    Amended by s 75 and part 26 of Schedule 6 of the Health Act 2004.

**61    Searches**

(1) Subject to subsections (3) and (4), a person, following an application in writing, in a form standing approved by an tArd-Chláraitheoir or a form to the like effect, in that behalf to an tArd-Chláraitheoir, a Superintendent Registrar, a registrar or an authorised officer and—

(a)    on payment to him or her of the prescribed fee, may, subject to such conditions (if any) as may stand determined by an tArd-Chláraitheoir, search an index to a register maintained under section 13,

(b)    on payment to him or her of the prescribed fee, be given by him or her—

(i)    a copy, certified by him or her to be a true copy,

(ii)    a copy, or

[(iii)    a certified extract,]¹

of an entry specified by the person in such a register.

(2) Subject to subsections (3) and (4), an tArd-Chláraitheoir, a Superintendent Registrar, a registrar or an authorised officer shall, on application by a person to him or her in that behalf in writing and—

(a)    on payment to him or her of the prescribed fee, search such of the registers maintained under section 13, and the indexes thereto, as are specified in the application, or

(b)    on payment to him or her of the prescribed fee, give the person—

(i)    a copy, certified by him or her to be a true copy,

(ii)    a copy, or

[(iii)    a certified extract,]¹

of an entry specified by the person in any such register.

[(3) This section does not apply to the register of stillbirths or an index to that register or an index kept under—

(a)    section 22 (5) of the Adoption Act 1952, or

(b)    section 86 of the Adoption Act 2010.]²

(4) A copy of an entry referred to in subsection (1) (b) or (2) (b) shall omit any reference to or particulars of a personal public service number and "true copy" in those provisions shall be construed accordingly.

[(5) The Minister may make regulations specifying particulars to be included in a certified extract referred to in subsection (1) or (2).]¹

**Notes**

1   Subparagraphs (1)(b)(iii) and (2)(b)(iii) substituted and section (5) inserted by s 75 and part 26 of Schedule 6 of the Health Act 2004.

2   Subsection (3) substituted by the Adoption Act 2010, s 159(d).

## 62    Search of register of stillbirths

(1) No person other than an tArd-Chláraitheoir or a member of his or her staff authorised by him or her in that behalf may search the register of stillbirths.

(2) A person ("the applicant") shall, on application in writing in that behalf to an tArd-Chláraitheoir, be given by him or her, or a member of his or her staff authorised by him or her in that behalf, a copy of an entry specified by the applicant in the register of stillbirths certified by the person giving it to be a true copy—

    (a)  if—

        (i)  the applicant is the father or mother of the child concerned and furnishes the required particulars relating to the stillbirth to a registrar and makes the application at the same time,

        (ii)  the applicant shows to the satisfaction of an tArd-Chláraitheoir or a member of his or her staff authorised in that behalf by an tArd-Chláraitheoir that he or she is the father or mother of the child, or

        (iii)  in his or her discretion, an tArd-Chláraitheoir, so determines,

    and

    (b)  if the applicant pays the prescribed fee to an tArd-Chláraitheoir.

## 63    Correction of errors at request of persons having an interest

(1) An alteration shall not be made in a register maintained under paragraph (a), (b) or (d) of section 13 (1) otherwise than in accordance with the provisions of this Act.

(2) On the application in that behalf of a person having an interest in the matter to a Superintendent Registrar in writing, he or she may—

    (a)  correct in the manner specified by an tArd-Chláraitheoir a clerical error in any register maintained under section 13, or

    (b)  correct an error of fact in a register specified in the said paragraph (a) or (d) if the person gives to the Superintendent Registrar such evidence as he or she considers to be adequate and a statutory declaration, in a form standing approved by an tArd-Chláraitheoir, of the facts concerned made by—

        (i)  a person required by this Act to give to the registrar the required particulars in relation to the birth, or death, concerned, or

        (ii)  if such a person as aforesaid cannot be found, two credible persons having knowledge of the facts concerned.

(3) Where an error of fact (other than one relating to the cause of death) occurs in the record signed by a coroner of the verdict returned at an inquest held by him or her and the coroner or his or her successor is satisfied by evidence on oath given orally or by statutory declaration of the existence of the error—

(a) he or she may give a certificate to a Superintendent Registrar stating the nature of the error and the relevant facts, and

(b) the officer shall, in such form as an tArd-Chláraitheoir may direct, correct the appropriate entry in the register of deaths and the original entry shall be retained in the register.

(4) On the application in that behalf by a person having an interest in the matter to an tArd-Chláraitheoir in writing a correction or addition to an entry in the register of stillbirths may, if an tArd-Chláraitheoir so directs, be made by but only by a person authorised in that behalf by him or her.

**64      Corrections or cancellations of entries at request of Ard-Chláraitheoir or a registrar**

(1) Where a registrar is satisfied that an entry made by him or her or another registrar in the register of births or the register of deaths contains an error of fact, he or she shall notify the Superintendent Registrar [of the registration area to which the registrar is assigned][1] of the error.

(2) When a Superintendent Registrar of [any registration area][1] receives a notification under subsection (1), the Superintendent Registrar or a registrar [in that registration area][1], if so directed by the Superintendent Registrar, shall by notice in writing given to a qualified informant (within the meaning of Part 3 or 5, as the case may be) in relation to the birth or death concerned ("the person") require him or her—

(a) to attend at the office of a registrar specified by the Superintendent Registrar or at the office of the registrar aforesaid, or at any other convenient place specified in the notice, within such time (not being less than 7 days from the date of the giving of the notice) as may be so specified, and

(b) to give to the registrar a statutory declaration specifying the error and, to the best of his or her knowledge and belief, the relevant facts,

and the person shall also give to the registrar such other information as the Superintendent Registrar or the registrar may reasonably require.

(3) When a person complies with subsection (2), the Superintendent Registrar, or the registrar, concerned may—

(a) correct the error concerned in the register of births or the register of deaths, as the case may be, or

(b) request a direction from an tArd-Chláraitheoir in relation to the matter.

(4) Where, pursuant to subsection (2), the Superintendent Registrar concerned is satisfied that, in relation to the error concerned, neither a person referred to in subsection (2) nor two other credible persons having knowledge of the facts concerned

can be found, he or she may request an tArd-Chláraitheoir to give a direction under subsection (5) in relation to the matter.

(5) When an tArd-Chláraitheoir receives a request under subsection (3) or (4), he or she may, if he or she considers it appropriate to do so, direct the Superintendent Registrar, or the registrar, concerned to make, in such manner as he or she may specify, a correction of the error in the entry concerned in the register, and the direction shall be complied with and the original entry shall be retained in the register.

(6) Where an tArd-Chláraitheoir is satisfied that two or more entries have been made in a register maintained under section 13 in respect of the same event, he or she may direct a Superintendent Registrar, a registrar or an officer of an tArd-Chláraitheoir to cancel such of the entries as he or she may specify, and the direction shall be complied with and the cancelled entry or entries shall be retained in the register.

(7) Where an tArd-Chláraitheoir is satisfied that an entry in the register of marriages relates to—

(a) a marriage, one or both of the parties to which was or were under the age of 18 years at the time of the solemnisation of the marriage,

(b) a marriage, as respects which one or more of the requirements specified in subsections (1) and (2) of section 46 and subsections (1) to (3) of section 51 were not complied with, or

(c) a marriage to which there was an impediment,

an tArd-Chláraitheoir shall—

(i) direct a registrar to cancel the entry and the direction shall be complied with and the cancelled entry shall be retained in the register, and

(ii) notify the parties to the marriage, and the registered solemniser (within the meaning of Part 6), or the person temporarily authorised under section 57, who solemnised the marriage of the direction.

[(8) If an tArd-Chláraitheoir is satisfied that an entry in the register of civil partnerships relates to a civil partnership of a class referred to in subsection (9)—

(a) an tArd-Chláraitheoir shall direct a registrar to cancel the entry and notify the parties to the civil partnership and the registrar who registered it of the direction, and

(b) the registrar shall comply with the direction and ensure that the cancelled entry is retained in the register.

(9) The classes referred to in subsection (8) are:

(a) a civil partnership, as respects which one or more of the requirements specified in subsections (1) and (5) of section 59B were not complied with (other than where there has been an exemption ordered under subsection (2) of that section); and

(b) a civil partnership to which there was an impediment within the meaning of section 2(2A).][2]

**65 Enquiries by Ard-Chláraitheoir[1]**

(1) An tArd-Chláraitheoir may conduct or cause to be conducted such enquiries as he or she considers necessary to ascertain—

(a) whether a birth, stillbirth, [death, marriage or civil partnership][2] required to be registered under this Act or the repealed enactments in the register maintained under paragraph (a), (b), (d) or (e), as may be appropriate, of section 13(1) has occurred and if it has—

(i) whether it has been so registered, and

(ii) if it has been, whether the particulars in relation to it in the entry in the register concerned are correct and complete.

(2) An tArd-Chláraitheoir may, by notice in writing served on a person whom he has reason to believe may be able to provide him or her with information relevant to an inquiry under subsection (1), require the person to provide the information to him or her within such time (not being less than 28 days) from the date of the giving of the notice and in such manner as may be specified in the notice.

(3) If an tArd-Chláraitheoir is satisfied that an event referred to in subsection (1) has occurred and that it has not been registered in the appropriate register referred to in that subsection or, if so registered, that the particulars in the entry in the register concerned in relation to it are incorrect or incomplete, he or she may register the event, or cause it to be registered, in the appropriate register or, as the case may be, correct or complete, or cause to be corrected or completed, the entry aforesaid.

**66 Power of Ard-Chláraitheoir to give information to others**

(1) Notwithstanding anything contained in the Data Protection Acts 1988 to 2003 or any other enactment, an tArd-Chláraitheoir may, after consultation with […][1] the Minister for Social and Family Affairs, give such information as may be prescribed in relation to births, [marriages, civil partnerships, decrees of divorce, decrees of nullity of marriage,

decrees of dissolution or decrees of nullity of civil partnership][2], registered under this Act or under any of the repealed enactments to—

(a) the Minister for Defence for the purpose of—

    (i) the administration of schemes under the Defence Forces (Pensions) Acts 1932 to 1975, or

    (ii) the administration of the Army Pensions Acts 1923 to 1980,

(b) the Minister for the Environment, Heritage and Local Government for the purpose of registration in a register under the Electoral Act 1992,

(c) the Minister for Foreign Affairs for the purpose of—

    (i) determining entitlements to passports, or

    (ii) verifying the identity of persons applying for or holding passports,

(d) the Minister for Justice, Equality and Law Reform for the purpose of determining the immigration or citizenship status of persons,

(e) the Minister for Social and Family Affairs for the purpose of—

    (i) determining entitlement to, or control of, benefit under the Social Welfare (Consolidation) Act 1993, or

    (ii) section 223 of that Act,

(f) the Minister for Transport for the purpose of the grant of driving licences and provisional licences under Part III of the Road Traffic Act 1961,

(g) the Minister for the purpose of the enforcement of regulations under section 31 of the Health Act 1947 and the Minister or [the Executive][3], hospital or other body or agency participating in any cancer screening programme (including any programme of breast or cervical cancer screening) authorised by the Minister, for the purpose of compiling and maintaining a record of the names, addresses and relevant dates of persons who, for public health reasons, may be invited to participate in any such programme,

(h) the Revenue Commissioners for the purpose of the administration of the Taxes Consolidation Act 1997, the Stamp Duties Consolidation Act 1999 and the Capital Acquisitions Tax Consolidation Act 2003,

(i) [the Executive][3] for the purpose of determining entitlement to a service provided for, by or under section 45, [45A][4], 58, 59 or 61 of the Health Act 1970, and

(j) a housing authority (within the meaning of the Housing Act 1966) for the purpose of—

    (i) the determination of entitlement to houses or grants under the Housing Acts 1966 to 2002,

    (ii) [the determination of a rent or other payment under section 31 of the Housing (Miscellaneous Provisions) Act 2009, or][5]

    (iii) the preparation of a housing strategy under the Planning and Development Act 2000.

(2) In this section "information" means personal data (within the meaning of the Data Protection Acts 1988 and 2003) and information extracted from such data.

## Notes

1   Amended by the Social Welfare (Miscellaneous Provisions) Act 2008, s 25.

2   Subsection (1) was amended by the Civil Partnership and Certain Rights and Obligations of Cohabitants Act 2010, s 21.

3   Amended by s 75 and part 26 of Schedule 6 of the Health Act 2004.

4   Subsection (1)(i) amended by the Health Act 2008, s 11.

5   Subsection (1)(j)(ii) substituted by the Housing (Miscellaneous Provisions) Act 2009, s 8 and schedule 2.

## 67      Fees

(1) There shall be payable to an tArd-Chláraitheoir or the Superintendent Registrar, registrar, within the meaning of section 17, or authorised officer, concerned fees of such amounts (if any) as may be prescribed in respect of—

(a)   any performance of such functions of an tArd-Chláraitheoir, a Superintendent Registrar, a registrar, within the meaning of section 17, or an authorised officer as may be prescribed, and

(b)   such other matters as may be prescribed,

and the references aforesaid to registrar, within the meaning of section 17, include references to such a registrar acting as a registered solemniser (within the meaning of Part 6).

(2) A person referred to in subsection (1) may refuse to perform a function (other than a prescribed function) in respect of which a fee is payable under this Act if the fee is not paid to him or her.

(3) A fee under this Act that is due and unpaid may be recovered from the person by whom it is payable by the person to whom it is payable as a simple contract debt in any court of competent jurisdiction.

(4) Amounts received under this Act in respect of fees shall be disposed of in accordance with the directions of the Minister given with the consent of the Minister for Finance.

## 68      Evidence of births, stillbirths and deaths

(1) An entry in the register of births, the register of stillbirths or the register of deaths shall not be evidence of the birth, stillbirth or death unless—

(a)   the entry purports to be signed by the person who gave the required particulars in relation to the birth, stillbirth or death, as the case may be, to the registrar concerned,

(b) that person was a person who, at the time of the making of the entry, was required by this Act or the repealed enactments to give particulars in relation to the event concerned to a registrar, and

(c) the entry was made in accordance with the relevant provisions of this Act or the repealed enactments.

(2) Paragraphs (a) and (b) of subsection (1) do not apply to—

(a) an entry in the register of births made pursuant to section 3 of the Births, Deaths and Marriages Registration Act 1972, or

(b) an entry in the register of deaths made pursuant to that section or section 41.

(3) Where a birth, stillbirth or death is registered more than 12 months from the date of its occurrence, the relevant entry in the register of births, the register of stillbirths or the register of deaths, as the case may be, shall not be evidence of the occurrence unless it purports to have been made with the authority of an tArd-Chláraitheoir or an authorised officer of [the Executive]¹.

---

**Notes**

1   Amended by s 75 and part 26 of Schedule 6 of the Health Act 2004.

---

## 69      Offences

(1) A registrar appointed under section 17 or an officer of the Courts Service or the Adoption Board who, otherwise than in accordance with this Act—

(a) deletes or alters, or permits or procures the deletion or alteration of, information contained in a register or an index to a register, or

(b) keeps, or permits or procures the keeping of, any information (other than information contained in or relating to a register or an index to a register) on a computer on which a register or an index to a register is kept,

is guilty of an offence.

(2) In relation to a computer on which a register or an index to a register is kept, a person (including a person entitled to access information kept on the computer but excluding an tArd-Chláraitheoir, a Superintendent Registrar or a registrar) who, without the consent of an tArd-Chláraitheoir, a Superintendent Registrar or a registrar—

(a) deletes or alters, or permits or procures the deletion or alteration of, information kept on the computer, or

(b) keeps, or permits or procures the keeping of, information (other than information contained in or relating to a register or an index to a register) on the computer whether the keeping is done directly or by adjusting or damaging the computer or its programming or another computer or its programming,

is guilty of an offence.

(3) A person who gives to a registrar particulars or information which he or she knows to be false or misleading is guilty of an offence.

(4) A registrar who, without reasonable cause, fails or refuses to register a birth, stillbirth, marriage[, civil partnership]¹ or death or to include in the relevant entry in the appropriate register any of the particulars required by this Act to be entered in the register in relation to the occurrence and given to him or her by a person required so to do by this Act or the repealed enactments, is guilty of an offence.

(5) A person who is required by this Act to give to a registrar the required particulars relating to a birth, a new born child found abandoned, a stillbirth or a death and who, without reasonable cause, fails or refuses to answer a question put to him or her by a registrar in relation to those particulars is guilty of an offence.

(6) A person who is required by this Act to sign a register in the presence of a registrar and who, without reasonable cause, fails or refuses to do so is guilty of an offence.

(7) A person who is required by this Act (other than section 41) to give a certificate to a registrar and who, without reasonable cause, fails or refuses to do so is guilty of an offence.

(8) A person who, without reasonable cause, fails or refuses to comply with a direction given to him or her under section 13 (6) or a requirement in a notice given to or served on him or her under section 19 (3), 24(5), 37(2), 50(2), 64(2) or 65(2) is guilty of an offence.

(9) A registrar who, without reasonable cause, fails or refuses to give a marriage registration form to one of the parties to an intended marriage in respect of which he or she has received, pursuant to section 46, a notification under subsection (1)(a)(i) of that section or a copy of an order under section 47 granting an exemption from the application of the said subsection (1)(a)(i) is guilty of an offence.

[(9A) A registrar who, without reasonable cause, fails or refuses to give a civil partnership registration form to one of the parties to an intended civil partnership in respect of which he or she has received a notification under section 59B(1)(a), or a copy of an exemption order under section 59B(2), commits an offence.]²

(10) A person who—

    (a)   contravenes subsection (2) or (3) of section 51,

    (b)   not being a registered solemniser (within the meaning of Part 6), or the holder of a temporary authorisation under section 57, conducts a marriage ceremony in such a way as to lead the parties to the marriage to believe that he or she is solemnising a valid marriage,

    (c)   being a registered solemniser (within the meaning aforesaid) or such a holder as aforesaid, solemnises a marriage without a marriage registration form having been given to him or her before the solemnisation for examination by him or her,

    (d)   contravenes paragraph (a) or (b) of section 55(3),

    (e)   solemnises a marriage other than at a place chosen in accordance with section 52,

(f) solemnises or is a party to a marriage in relation to which, to his or her knowledge, subsection (1) or (2) of section 46 is not complied with,

[(fa) registers or is a party to a civil partnership in respect of which, to his or her knowledge, subsection (1) or (5) of section 59B is not complied with, (other than where there has been an exemption ordered under subsection (2) of that section),][3]

(g) being the holder of a temporary authorisation under section 57, solemnises a marriage not specified in the authorisation or solemnises a marriage during a period not so specified,

(h) lodges an objection under section 58 [or 59F][3] that he or she knows to be without foundation,

(i) makes and signs a declaration under section 46 (1)(b)[, or 59B(1)(b)][3] or makes a declaration specified in section 51(4)(a) which he or she knows to be [false or misleading,][3]

(j) not being a registrar, deletes or alters information in relation to the parties to a marriage on a marriage registration form, [or][3]

[(k) not being a registrar, deletes or alters information in relation to the parties to a civil partnership on a civil partnership registration form,][3]

shall be guilty of an offence.

(11) A person who, without reasonable cause, contravenes section 19 (1), 21(1), 24(4), 37(1) or 73(4) is guilty of an offence.

(12) A person who contravenes a provision of regulations under this Act that is stated in the regulations to be a penal provision is guilty of an offence.

(13) In this section "register" means a register maintained under section 13.

---

### Notes

1 Subsection (4) amended by the Civil Partnership and Rights and Obligations of Cohabitants Act 2010, s 22(a).

2 Subsection (9A) inserted by the Civil Partnership and Rights and Obligations of Cohabitants Act 2010, s 22(b).

3 Inserted by the Civil Partnership and Rights and Obligations of Cohabitants Act 2010, s 22(c).

---

## 70 Penalties

(1) A person guilty of an offence under subsection (1), (2) or (3) of section 69 shall be liable—

(a) on summary conviction, to a fine not exceeding €2,000 or imprisonment for a term not exceeding 6 months or both, or

(b) on conviction on indictment, to a fine not exceeding €10,000 or imprisonment for a term not exceeding 5 years or both.

(2) A person guilty of an offence under subsection (4), (5), (6), (7), (8), (9), [(9A),]¹ (10), (11) or (12) of section 69 shall be liable on summary conviction to a fine not exceeding €2,000 or imprisonment for a term not exceeding 6 months or both.

**Notes**

1   Subsection (2) amended by the Civil Partnership and Rights and Obligations of Cohabitants Act 2010, s 23.

## 71     Prosecution of offences

(1) Proceedings for a summary offence under this Act or a regulation thereunder may be brought and prosecuted by an tArd-Chláraitheoir or [the Executive]¹.

(2) Notwithstanding section 10(4) of the Petty Sessions (Ireland) Act 1851, proceedings for a summary offence under this Act or a regulation thereunder may be commenced against a person at any time within 12 months from the date on which evidence that, in the opinion of an tArd-Chláraitheoir or [the Executive]¹ is sufficient to justify the bringing of the proceedings comes to his, her or its notice.

(3) In proceedings for a summary offence under this Act, a document purporting to be signed by an tArd-Chláraitheoir or a person authorised in that behalf by him, her or [the Executive]¹ and to state the date on which evidence referred to in subsection (2) came to his, her or its attention is prima facie evidence of that date and it shall be deemed to have been signed by an tArd-Chláraitheoir or the person authorised as aforesaid and, in case it purports to have been signed by a person so authorised, to have been signed in accordance with the authorisation unless the contrary is shown.

(4) Where an offence under this Act is committed by a body corporate and is proved to have been so committed with the consent or connivance or to be attributable to any neglect on the part of a person, being a director, manager, secretary or other officer of the body corporate, or a person who was purporting to act in any such capacity, that person as well as the body corporate shall be guilty of the offence and be liable to be proceeded against and punished accordingly.

**Notes**

1   Amended by s 75 and part 26 of Schedule 6 of the Health Act 2004.

## 72     Service etc., of documents

Where a notice, certificate or other document is authorised or required by or under this Act to be given or furnished to or served on a person or an application in writing is authorised by this Act to be made to a person, the giving, furnishing, serving or making may be effected in any of the following ways—

(a) where it is addressed to him or her by name, by delivering it to the person,

(b) by leaving it at the address at which the person ordinarily resides or, in a case in which an address for service has been furnished, at that address, or

(c) by sending it by ordinary prepaid post addressed to him or her at the address at which he or she ordinarily resides or, in a case in which an address for service has been furnished, at that address.

## 73    Vital statistics

(1) In this section, vital statistics means statistics in relation to—

(a) births,

(b) stillbirths,

(c) deaths,

(d) marriages,

[(dd) civil partnerships,]¹

(e) decrees of divorce,

(f) decrees of nullity [of marriage]¹, [or]²

[(ff) decrees of dissolution,]¹

[(fff) decrees of nullity of civil partnership,]¹

[(g) any other prescribed matters.]²

(h) [...]²

(2) The Minister may collect, compile, abstract and publish vital statistics.

(3) The Minister may by regulations provide for giving effect to this section and the regulations may, in particular, include—

(a) in the case of any birth, stillbirth, death, marriage, [decree of divorce or decree of nullity of marriage, civil partnership, decree of dissolution, decree of nullity of civil partnership,]³, provisions requiring that specified information relating to the birth, stillbirth, death, marriage, [decree of divorce or decree of nullity of marriage, civil partnership, decree of dissolution, decree of nullity of civil partnership,]³ shall be furnished to the registrar concerned within a specified period,

(b) in the case of any other matter the subject of vital statistics, provision that specified information relating to the matter be furnished to a specified person within a specified period,

(c) provision for the recording of information received pursuant to the regulations and its transmission to the Minister or any other specified person.

(4) A person engaged in receiving information furnished pursuant to regulations under this section or in the collection, compilation, abstraction or publication of vital statistics shall not disclose any such information in a form that identifies, or enables the identification of, a person to whom it relates unless the disclosure is to another person so engaged or a necessary for the purposes of a prosecution under this Act.

(5) Information referred to in subsection (4) may be disclosed to persons engaged in medical or social research or to [medical practitioners employed by the Executive]⁴ if the Minister consents in writing to the disclosure and the disclosure complies with such conditions (if any) as are attached to the consent; and the Minister is hereby authorised to attach such conditions as he or she considers appropriate to a consent under this subsection.

(6) In lieu of acting by his or her own officers for the purposes of this section and the regulations thereunder, the Minister may arrange with any other Minister of the Government—

    (a)  for the collection, compilation, abstraction and publication by officers of that Minister of the Government of any vital statistics, or

    (b)  for the performance by those officers of any other functions provided for by this section or the regulations thereunder.

(7) This section is without prejudice to any other obligation imposed by or under this or any other Act to give information in relation to a birth, stillbirth, death, marriage, [decree of divorce or decree of nullity of marriage, civil partnership, decree of dissolution, decree of nullity of civil partnership,]⁵ or any other matter.

---

**Notes**

1    Subsections (1)(dd), (1)(ff) and (1)(fff) were inserted and subsection (1)(f) was amended by the Civil Partnership and Certain Rights and Obligations of Cohabitants Act 2010, s 24(a).

2    Subsection (1)(f) was amended and subsection (1)(g) was inserted by the Adoption Act 2010, s 159(e). Subsection (1)(h) was deleted by Adoption Act 2010, s 159(e).

3    Amended by the Civil Partnership and Certain Rights and Obligations of Cohabitants Act 2010, s 24(b).

4    Amended by section 75 and part 26 of Schedule 6 of the Health Act 2004.

5    Amended by the Civil Partnership and Certain Rights and Obligations of Cohabitants Act 2010, s 24(c).

---

FIRST SCHEDULE
PARTICULARS TO BE ENTERED IN REGISTERS

Section 19

PART 1
PARTICULARS TO BE ENTERED IN REGISTER OF BIRTHS

Date and place of birth.

Time of birth.

Sex of child.

Forename(s) and surname* of child.

Personal public service number of child.

Forename(s), surname, birth surname, address and occupation of mother.

Former surname(s) (if any) of mother.

Date of birth of mother.

[Civil][1] status of mother.

Personal public service number of mother.

Birth surname of mother's mother.

Forename(s), surname, birth surname, address and occupation of father.

Former surname(s) (if any) of father.

Date of birth of father.

[Civil][1] status of father.

Personal public service number of father.

Birth surname of father's mother.

Forename(s), surname, qualification, address and signature of informant.

Date of registration.

Signature of registrar.

---

**Notes**

1   Amended by the Civil Partnership and Certain Rights and Obligations of Cohabitants Act 2010, s 25(a).

---

## PART 2
### PARTICULARS TO BE ENTERED IN REGISTER OF STILLBIRTHS

Section 28.

Date and place of birth.

Time of birth.

Sex of child.

Weight of child.

Gestational age of child.

Forename(s) and surname* of child.

[...][1]

Forename(s), surname, birth surname, address and occupation of mother.

Former surname(s) (if any) of mother.

Date of birth of mother.

[Civil][2] status of mother.

Personal public service number of mother.

Birth surname of mother's mother.

Forename(s), surname, birth surname, address and occupation of father.

Former surname(s) (if any) of father.

Date of birth of father.

[Civil]² status of father.

Personal public service number of father.

Birth surname of father's mother.

Forename(s), surname, qualification, address and signature of informant.

Date of registration.

Signature of registrar.

**Notes**

1   Amended by the deletion of "personal public service number of child" by s 75 and part 26 of Schedule 6 of the Health Act 2004.

2   Amended by the Civil Partnership and Certain Rights and Obligations of Cohabitants Act 2010, s 25(a).

PART 3

PARTICULARS OF ADOPTIONS WITHIN THE STATE TO BE ENTERED IN REGISTER OF ADOPTIONS

[…]¹

PART 4

PARTICULARS OF FOREIGN ADOPTIONS TO BE ENTERED IN REGISTER OF ADOPTIONS

[…]¹

**Notes**

1   Parts 3 and 4 deleted by the Adoption Act 2010, s 159(f).

PART 5

PARTICULARS OF DEATHS TO BE ENTERED IN REGISTER OF DEATHS

Section 37

Date and place of death.

Place of birth of deceased.

Sex of deceased.

Forename(s), surname, birth surname and address of deceased.

Personal public service number of deceased.

[Civil][1] status of deceased.

Date of birth or age last birthday of deceased.

Profession or occupation of deceased.

[If deceased was married or a civil partner, the profession or occupation of spouse or civil partner.][1]

If deceased was less than 18 years of age on date of death, occupation(s) of his or her parent(s) or guardian(s).

Forename(s) and birth surname of father of deceased.

Forename(s) and birth surname of mother of deceased.

Certificated cause of death, duration of illness and date of certificate under section 42.

Forename, surname, place of business, daytime telephone number and qualification of registered medical practitioner who signed certificate under section 42.

Forename(s), surname, qualification, address and signature of informant.

If an inquest in relation to the death or a post-mortem examination of the body of deceased was held, the forename, surname and place of business of coroner concerned.

Date of registration.

Signature of registrar.

---

**Notes**

1   Amended by the Civil Partnership and Certain Rights and Obligations of Cohabitants Act 2010, s 25(b).

---

PART 6

PARTICULARS OF DECREES OF DIVORCE TO BE ENTERED IN REGISTER OF DECREES OF DIVORCE

Section 59

Court by which the decree was granted.

Year and record number of the proceedings.

Forenames, surnames and birth surnames of the parties to the proceedings.

Personal public service numbers of the parties to the proceedings.

Date and place of marriage.

Date of the decree.

Date of registration.

Forename(s) and surname of officer of Courts Service specified in section 59(1).

[PART 6A
PARTICULARS TO BE ENTERED IN REGISTER OF DISSOLUTIONS

Section 59J

Court by which the decree was granted.

Year and record number of the proceedings.

Forenames, surnames and birth surnames of the parties to the proceedings.

Personal public service numbers of the parties to the proceedings.

Date and place of civil partnership registration.

Date of the decree.

Date of registration of the decree.

Forenames and surname of officer of Courts Service.][1]

**Notes**

1    Part 6A inserted by the Civil Partnership and Certain Rights and Obligations of Cohabitants
     Act 2010, s 25(c).

PART 7
PARTICULARS OF DECREES OF NULLITY OF MARRIAGE TO BE ENTERED IN
REGISTER OF DECREES OF NULLITY [OF MARRIAGE][1]

Section 59

Court by which the decree was granted.

Year and record number of the proceedings.

Forename, surnames and birth surnames of the parties to the proceedings.

Personal public service numbers of the parties to the proceedings.

Date and place of marriage.

Declaration of court.

Date of the decree.

Date of registration.

Forename(s) and surname of officer of Courts Service specified in section 59(2).

* The surname of the child to be entered shall, subject to any linguistic modifications be—

(a) that of the parents of the child as stated in the register of births or of either of them, as may be determined by the person who, pursuant to section 19, gives the required particulars of the birth concerned to the registrar, or

(b) such other name as may be requested by both of the parents or by one of them if the other parent is dead or, after reasonable efforts to do so have been made, cannot be contacted (if an tArd-Chláraitheoir or an officer of an tArd-

Chláraitheoir duly authorised by him or her in that behalf or a Superintendent Registrar is satisfied that the circumstances warrant it and he or she agrees to the request).

* The surname of the child to be entered shall, subject to any linguistic modifications be—

(a) that of the parents of the child as stated in the register of stillbirths or of either of them, as may be determined by the person who, pursuant to section 28, gives the required particulars of the stillbirth concerned to the registrar, or

(b) such other name as may be requested by both of the parents or by one of them if the other parent is dead or, after reasonable efforts to do so have been made, cannot be contacted (if an tArd-Chláraitheoir or an officer of an tArd-Chláraitheoir duly authorised by him or her in that behalf or a Superintendent Registrar is satisfied that the circumstances warrant it and he or she agrees to the request).

---

**Notes**

1    Title amended by the Civil Partnership and Certain Rights and Obligations of Cohabitants Act 2010, s 25(d).

---

[PART 7A

PARTICULARS TO BE ENTERED IN REGISTER OF DECREES OF NULLITY OF CIVIL PARTNERSHIP

Section 59J

Court by which the decree was granted.

Year and record number of the proceedings.

Forenames, surnames and birth surnames of the parties to

the proceedings.

Personal public service numbers of the parties to the proceedings.

Date and place of civil partnership registration.

Declaration of court.

Date of the decree.

Date of registration.

Forenames and surname of officer of Courts Service.][1]

**Notes**

1    Part 7A inserted by the Civil Partnership and Certain Rights and Obligations of Cohabitants
     Act 2010, s 25(e).

SECOND SCHEDULE[1]
ENACTMENTS REPEALED

Section 4

| Session and Chapter or Number and Year (1) | Short Title (2) | Extent of Repeal (3) |
|---|---|---|
| 7 & 8 Vict., c. 81 | Marriages (Ireland) Act 1844 | The whole Act. |
| 9 & 10 Vict., c. 72 | Marriages (Ireland) Act 1846 | The whole Act. |
| 23 & 24 Vict., c. 18 | Marriage (Society of Friends) Act 1860 | The whole Act. |
| 26 Vict., c. 11 | Registration of Births and Deaths (Ireland) Act 1863 | The whole Act. |
| 26 Vict., c. 27 | Marriage Law (Ireland) Amendment Act 1863 | The whole Act. |
| 26 & 27 Vict., c. 90 | Registration of Marriages (Ireland) Act 1863 | The whole Act other than sections 7, 8, 12, 21 and 25. |
| 33 & 34 Vict., c. 110 | Matrimonial Causes and Marriage Law (Ireland) Amendment Act 1870 | Sections 32 to 40 and 42. |
| 34 & 35 Vict., c. 49 | Matrimonial Causes and Marriage Law (Ireland) Amendment Act 1871 | Sections 21 to 29. |
| 35 & 36 Vict., c. 10 | Marriage (Society of Friends) Act 1872 | The whole Act. |
| 36 & 37 Vict., c. 16 | Marriage Law (Ireland) Amendment Act 1873 | The whole Act. |
| 57 & 58 Vict., c. 60 | Merchant Shipping Act 1894 | Section 254. |
| 43 & 44 Vict., c. 13 | Births and Deaths Registration Act (Ireland) 1880 | The whole Act. |
| No. 13 of 1931 | Legitimacy Act 1931 | Section 1(4) and the Schedule. |
| No. 34 of 1936 | Registration of Births and Deaths Act 1936 | The whole Act. |
| No. 35 of 1936 | Registration of Marriages Act 1936 | The whole Act. |

| Session and Chapter or Number and Year (1) | Short Title (2) | Extent of Repeal (3) |
|---|---|---|
| No. 47 of 1936 | Marriages Act 1936 | The whole Act. |
| No. 8 of 1952 | Vital Statistics and Births, Deaths and Marriages Registration Act 1952 | The whole Act. |
| | | [...]² |
| No. 44 of 1960 | Defence (Amendment) (No. 2) Act 1960 | Section 6. |
| No. 9 of 1962 | Coroners Act 1962 | Sections 50 and 51. |
| No. 25 of 1972 | Births, Deaths and Marriages Registration Act 1972 | The whole Act. |
| No. 30 of 1972 | Marriages Act 1972 | The whole Act. |
| No. 26 of 1987 | Status of Children Act 1987 | Section 48. |
| No. 1 of 1989 | Garda Síochána Act 1989 | Section 4. |
| | | [...]² |
| No. 1 of 1994 | Stillbirths Registration Act 1994 | The whole Act. |
| No. 26 of 1995 | Family Law Act 1995 | Section 32; In section 33(1), the words "or section 32(1) (a) or both of those provisions". |
| No. 36 of 1996 | Registration of Births Act 1996 | The whole Act other than subsections (4) and (4A) of section 1. |

**Notes**

1 Commencement: Second Schedule commenced on 5 November 2007 (SI 736/2007).

2 Deleted by the Adoption Act 2010, s 159(g) and schedule 4.

[THIRD SCHEDULE
PROHIBITED DEGREES OF RELATIONSHIP

Section 2

A person may not enter a civil partnership with someone within the prohibited degrees of relationship, as set out in the table below. Relationships within that table should be construed as including relationships in the half-blood (e.g. sibling includes a sibling where there is only one parent in common, etc.), and all the relationships include relationships and former relationships by adoption.

| A man may not enter a civil partnership with his: | A woman may not enter a civil partnership with her: |
| --- | --- |
| Grandfather | Grandmother |
| Grandparent's brother | Grandparent's sister |
| Father | Mother |
| Father's brother | Mother's sister |
| Mother's brother | Father's sister |
| Brother | Sister |
| Nephew | Niece |
| Son | Daughter |
| Grandson | Granddaughter |
| Grandnephew | Grandniece][1] |

**Notes**

1     Third Schedule was inserted by the Civil Partnership and Certain Rights and Obligations of Cohabitants Act 2010, s 26.

# Land and Conveyancing Law Reform Act 2009

*Number 27 of 2009*

---

## Notes

1 Commencement: 1 December 2009 (SI 356/2009).

---

PART 7

CO-OWNERSHIP

### 30 Unilateral severance of a joint tenancy

(1) From the commencement of this Part, any—

    (a) conveyance, or contract for a conveyance, of land held in a joint tenancy, or

    (b) acquisition of another interest in such land,

by a joint tenant without the consent referred to in subsection (2) is void both at law and in equity unless such consent is dispensed with under section 31(2)(e).

(2) In subsection (1) **"consent"** means the prior consent in writing of the other joint tenant or, where there are more than one other, all the other joint tenants.

(3) From the commencement of this Part, registration of a judgment mortgage against the estate or interest in land of a joint tenant does not sever the joint tenancy and if the joint tenancy remains unsevered, the judgment mortgage is extinguished upon the death of the judgment debtor.

(4) Nothing in this section affects the jurisdiction of the court to find that all the joint tenants by mutual agreement or by their conduct have severed the joint tenancy in equity.

### 31 Court orders

(1) Any person having an estate or interest in land which is co-owned whether at law or in equity may apply to the court for an order under this section.

(2) An order under this section includes—

    (a) an order for partition of the land amongst the co-owners,

(b) an order for the taking of an account of incumbrances affecting the land, if any, and the making of inquiries as to the respective priorities of any such incumbrances,

(c) an order for sale of the land and distribution of the proceeds of sale as the court directs,

(d) an order directing that accounting adjustments be made as between the co-owners,

(e) an order dispensing with consent to severance of a joint tenancy as required by section 30 where such consent is being unreasonably withheld,

(f) such other order relating to the land as appears to the court to be just and equitable in the circumstances of the case.

(3) In dealing with an application for an order under subsection (1) the court may—

(a) make an order with or without conditions or other requirements attached to it, or

(b) dismiss the application without making any order, or

(c) combine more than one order under this section.

(4) In this section—

(a) **"person having an estate or interest in land"** includes a mortgagee or other secured creditor, a judgment mortgagee or a trustee,

(b) **"accounting adjustments"** include—

(i) payment of an occupation rent by a co-owner who has enjoyed, or is continuing to enjoy, occupation of the land to the exclusion of any other co-owner,

(ii) compensation to be paid by a co-owner to any other co-owner who has incurred disproportionate expenditure in respect of the land (including its repair or improvement),

(iii) contributions by a co-owner to disproportionate payments made by any other co-owner in respect of the land (including payments in respect of charges, rates, rents, taxes and other outgoings payable in respect of it),

(iv) redistribution of rents and profits received by a coowner disproportionate to his or her interest in the land,

(v) any other adjustment necessary to achieve fairness between the co-owners.

(5) Nothing in this section affects the jurisdiction of the court under the Act of 1976, the Act of 1995 and the Act of 1996.

(6) The equitable jurisdiction of the court to make an order for partition of land which is co-owned whether at law or in equity is abolished.

## 32  Bodies corporate

(1) A body corporate may acquire and hold any property in a joint tenancy in the same manner as if it were an individual.

(2) Where a body corporate and an individual or two or more bodies corporate become entitled to any property in circumstances or by virtue of any instrument which would, if the body or bodies corporate had been an individual or individuals, have created a joint tenancy, they are entitled to the property as joint tenants.

(3) On the dissolution of a body corporate which is a joint tenant of any property, the property devolves on the other surviving joint tenant or joint tenants.

# Civil Partnership and Certain Rights and Obligations of Cohabitants Act 2010

*Number 24 of 2010*

ARRANGEMENT OF SECTIONS

PART 1

PRELIMINARY AND GENERAL

## PART 13
### JURISDICTION AND OTHER RELATED MATTERS

### PART 16
### MISCELLANEOUS

### SCHEDULE
### CONSEQUENTIAL AMENDMENTS TO OTHER ACTS

### PART 1
### CONFLICTS OF INTERESTS PROVISIONS

PART 2
PENSIONS PROVISIONS

PART 3
PROPERTY RIGHTS PROVISIONS

PART 4
REDRESS PROVISIONS

PART 5
MISCELLANEOUS PROVISIONS

**Acts Referred to**

## Acts Referred to

| | |
|---|---|
| Courts of Justice and Court Officers (Superannuation) Act 1961 | 1961, No. 16 |
| Credit Union Act 1997 | 1997, No. 15 |
| Criminal Assets Bureau Act 1996 | 1996, No. 31 |
| Criminal Damage Act 1991 | 1991, No. 31 |
| Criminal Justice Act 1999 | 1999, No. 10 |
| Defence Act 1954 | 1954, No. 18 |
| Defence (Amendment) Act 2007 | 2007, No. 24 |
| Digital Hub Development Agency Act 2003 | 2003, No. 23 |
| Disability Act 2005 | 2005, No. 14 |
| Domestic Violence Act 1996 | 1996, No. 1 |
| Domestic Violence Acts 1996 and 2002 | |
| Electoral Act 1992 | 1992, No. 23 |
| Electricity (Supply) (Amendment) Act 1958 | 1958, No. 35 |
| Electricity (Supply) (Amendment) Act 1970 | 1970, No. 5 |
| Employment Equality Act 1998 | 1998, No. 21 |
| Enforcement of Court Orders Act 1926 | 1926, No. 18 |
| Enforcement of Court Orders Act 1940 | 1940, No. 23 |
| Equal Status Act 2000 | 2000, No. 8 |
| Ethics in Public Office Act 1995 | 1995, No. 22 |
| Family Law (Divorce) Act 1996 | 1996, No. 33 |
| Family Law (Maintenance of Spouses and Children) Act 1976 | 1976, No. 11 |
| Family Law Act 1995 | 1995, No. 26 |
| Farm Tax Act 1985 | 1985, No. 17 |
| Food Safety Authority of Ireland Act 1998 | 1998, No. 29 |
| Garda Síochána (Compensation) Act 1941 | 1941, No. 19 |
| Garda Síochána Act 2005 | 2005, No. 20 |
| Gas (Interim) (Regulation) Act 2002 | 2002, No. 10 |
| Grangegorman Development Agency Act 2005 | 2005, No. 21 |
| Great Southern Railways Company (Superannuation Scheme) Act 1947 | 1947, No. 21 |
| Harbours Act 1946 | 1946, No. 9 |
| Harbours Acts 1946 to 2005 | |
| Health (Amendment) Act 2005 | 2005, No. 3 |
| Health (Miscellaneous Provisions) Act 2001 | 2001, No. 14 |
| Health (Nursing Homes) (Amendment) Act 2007 | 2007, No. 1 |

**Acts Referred to**

| | |
|---|---|
| Health (Nursing Homes) Act 1990 | 1990, No. 23 |
| Health Act 1970 | 1970, No. 1 |
| Health Act 2004 | 2004, No. 42 |
| Housing Act 1988 | 1988, No. 28 |
| Housing (Miscellaneous Provisions) Act 1979 | 1979, No. 27 |
| Housing (Miscellaneous Provisions) Act 2002 | 2002, No. 9 |
| Housing (Private Rented Dwellings) (Amendment) Act 1983 | 1983, No. 22 |
| Housing (Private Rented Dwellings) Act 1982 | 1982, No. 6 |
| Industrial Development (Science Foundation Ireland) Act 2003 | 2003, No. 30 |
| Insurance Act 1989 | 1989, No. 3 |
| Insurance Act 2000 | 2000, No. 42 |
| Investor Compensation Act 1998 | 1998, No. 37 |
| Irish Horse Racing Industry Act 1994 | 1994, No. 18 |
| Judgements (Ireland) Act 1844 | 1844, c. 90 |
| Land Act 1931 | 1931, No. 11 |
| Land Act 1933 | 1933, No. 38 |
| Land Act 1936 | 1936, No. 41 |
| Land Act 1965 | 1965, No. 2 |
| Local Authorities (Higher Education Grants) Act 1968 | 1968, No. 24 |
| Local Authorities (Higher Education Grants) Act 1992 | 1992, No. 19 |
| Local Government (Superannuation) Act 1980 | 1980, No. 8 |
| Local Government Act 1941 | 1941, No. 23 |
| Local Government Act 2001 | 2001, No. 37 |
| Mental Health Act 2001 | 2001, No. 25 |
| Ministerial, Parliamentary and Judicial Offices and Oireachtas Members (Miscellaneous Provisions) Act 2001 | 2001, No. 33 |
| Ministerial and Parliamentary Offices Act 1938 | 1938, No. 38 |
| National Development Finance Agency Act 2002 | 2002, No. 29 |
| National Minimum Wage Act 2000 | 2000, No. 5 |
| National Sports Campus Development Authority Act 2006 | 2006, No. 19 |
| Non-Fatal Offences Against the Person Act 1997 | 1997, No. 26 |
| Occasional Trading Act 1979 | 1979, No. 35 |
| Oireachtas (Allowances to Members) Act 1938 | 1938, No. 34 |
| Oireachtas (Allowances to Members) (Amendment) Act 1968 | 1968, No. 8 |
| Organisation of Working Time Act 1997 | 1997, No. 20 |

## Acts Referred to

| | |
|---|---|
| Partition Act 1868 | 1868, c. 40 |
| Partition Act 1876 | 1876, c. 17 |
| Pensions (Amendment) Act 1996 | 1996, No. 18 |
| Pensions (Amendment) Act 2002 | 2002, No. 18 |
| Pensions Act 1990 | 1990, No. 25 |
| Pharmacy Act 2007 | 2007, No. 20 |
| Pilotage Order Confirmation Act 1927 | 1927, No. 1(P) |
| Planning and Development Act 2000 | 2000, No. 30 |
| Powers of Attorney Act 1996 | 1996, No. 12 |
| Presidential Establishment Act 1938 | 1938, No. 24 |
| Presidential Establishment (Amendment) Act 1991 | 1991, No. 10 |
| Private Security Services Act 2004 | 2004, No. 12 |
| Prosecution of Offences Act 1974 | 1974, No. 22 |
| Railway Safety Act 2005 | 2005, No. 31 |
| Refugee Act 1996 | 1996, No. 17 |
| Registration of Deeds and Title Act 2006 | 2006, No. 12 |
| Registration of Title Act 1964 | 1964, No. 16 |
| Residential Institutions Redress Act 2002 | 2002, No. 13 |
| Residential Tenancies Act 2004 | 2004, No. 27 |
| Sea-Fisheries and Maritime Jurisdiction Act 2006 | 2006, No. 8 |
| Social Welfare (Miscellaneous Provisions) Act 2004 | 2004, No. 9 |
| Social Welfare Acts | |
| Social Welfare and Pensions Act 2007 | 2007, No. 8 |
| Social Welfare and Pensions Act 2008 | 2008, No. 2 |
| Solicitors (Amendment) Act 1994 | 1994, No. 27 |
| Statistics Act 1993 | 1993, No. 21 |
| Statute of Limitations 1957 | 1957, No. 6 |
| Succession Act 1965 | 1965, No. 27 |
| Sustainable Energy Act 2002 | 2002, No. 2 |
| Taxes Consolidation Act 1997 | 1997, No. 39 |
| Transport (Railway Infrastructure) Act 2001 | 2001, No. 55 |
| Trustee Savings Banks Act 1989 | 1989, No. 21 |
| Unfair Dismissals Act 1977 | 1977, No. 10 |
| Valuation Act 2001 | 2001, No. 13 |
| Vocational Education Act 1930 | 1930, No. 29 |

*An Act to provide for the registration of civil partners and for the consequences of that registration, to provide for the rights and obligations of cohabitants and to provide for connected matters.*

*[19th July, 2010]*

*Be it enacted by the Oireachtas as follows:*

## PART 1
### PRELIMINARY AND GENERAL

**1      Short title, commencement and collective citation**

(1) This Act may be cited as the Civil Partnership and Certain Rights and Obligations of Cohabitants Act 2010.

(2) This Act, other than Part 3, shall come into operation on the day or days that the Minister may appoint by order either generally or with reference to a particular purpose or provision and different days may be so appointed for different purposes or different provisions.

(3) Part 3 shall come into operation on the day or days that the Minister may, after consulting with the Minister for Social Protection, appoint by order either generally or with reference to a particular purpose or provision. [1]

---

**Notes**

1    Commencement: 1 January 2011, except for section 5 which was commenced on 23 December 2010 (SI 648/2010).

---

**2      Interpretation**

In this Act—

**"civil partnership registration"** means registration of a civil partnership under section 59D (as inserted by section 16 of this Act) of the Civil Registration Act 2004;

**"Land Registry"** has the meaning assigned to it by the Registration of Title Act 1964;

**"Minister"** means the Minister for Justice and Law Reform;

**"Property Registration Authority"** has the meaning assigned to it by the Registration of Deeds and Title Act 2006;

**"Registry of Deeds"** has the meaning assigned to it by the Registration of Deeds and Title Act 2006.

**3      Civil partners**

For the purposes of this Act a civil partner is either of two persons of the same sex who are—

    (a) parties to a civil partnership registration that has not been dissolved or the subject of a decree of nullity, or

    (b) parties to a legal relationship of a class that is the subject of an order made under section 5 that has not been dissolved or the subject of a decree of nullity.

PART 2

STATUS OF CIVIL PARTNERSHIP

**4**       **Declarations of civil partnership status**

(1) The court may, on application to it in that behalf by either of the civil partners or by any other person who, in the opinion of the court, has a sufficient interest in the matter, make one or more of the following orders in relation to a civil partnership:

    (a) an order declaring that the civil partnership was at its inception a valid civil partnership;

    (b) an order declaring that the civil partnership subsisted on a date specified in the application; and

    (c) an order declaring that the civil partnership did not subsist on a date specified in the application other than the date of its inception.

(2) The court may only make an order under subsection (1) if one of the civil partners—

    (a) is domiciled in the State on the date of the application,

    (b) has been ordinarily resident in the State throughout the period of one year immediately preceding the date of the application, or

    (c) died before the date of the application and—

        (i) was at the time of death domiciled in the State, or

        (ii) had been ordinarily resident in the State throughout the period of one year immediately preceding the date of death.

(3) The other civil partner, the civil partners concerned, or the personal representative within the meaning of the Succession Act 1965 of the civil partner or each civil partner shall be joined in proceedings under this section and the court may order that notice of the proceedings be given to any other person that the court may specify.

(4) Where notice of proceedings under this section is given to a person, the court may, of its own motion or on application to it in that behalf by the person or a party to the proceedings, order that the person be added as a party to the proceedings.

(5) Where a party to proceedings under this section alleges that the civil partnership concerned is void and should be the subject of a decree of nullity of civil partnership, the court may treat the application under subsection (1) as an application for a decree of nullity of civil partnership and proceed to determine the matter accordingly and postpone the determination of the application made under subsection (1).

(6) An order under subsection (1) is binding on the parties to the proceedings concerned and on a person claiming through such a party.

(7) An order under subsection (1) does not prejudice any person if it is subsequently proved to have been obtained by fraud or collusion.

(8) Rules of court may make provision as to the information to be given in an application for an order under subsection (1), including particulars of any previous or pending proceedings in relation to the civil partnership or to the civil partnership status of a civil partner.

(9) The registrar of the court shall notify an tArd-Chláraitheoir of an order under subsection (1).

(10) In this section a reference to a civil partner includes a reference to a person who was a civil partner until the dissolution of the civil partnership or until the civil partnership was annulled by decree of nullity.

**5        Recognition of registered foreign relationships**

(1) The Minister may, by order, declare that a class of legal relationship entered into by two parties of the same sex is entitled to be recognised as a civil partnership if under the law of the jurisdiction in which the legal relationship was entered into—

    (a)  the relationship is exclusive in nature,

    (b)  the relationship is permanent unless the parties dissolve it through the courts,

    (c)  the relationship has been registered under the law of that jurisdiction, and

    (d)  the rights and obligations attendant on the relationship are, in the opinion of the Minister, sufficient to indicate that the relationship would be treated comparably to a civil partnership.

(2) An order under subsection (1) entitles and obliges the parties to the legal relationship to be treated as civil partners under the law of the State from the later of—

    (a)  the day which is 21 days after the date on which the order is made, and

    (b)  the day on which the relationship was registered under the law of the jurisdiction in which it was entered into.

(3) Notwithstanding subsections (1) and (2), an order made under subsection (1) shall not be construed as entitling parties to a legal relationship otherwise recognised by that order to be treated as civil partners under the law of the State if those parties are within the prohibited degrees of relationship set out in the Third Schedule to the Civil Registration Act 2004 (inserted by section 26).

(4) Where an order is made under subsection (1), a dissolution of a legal relationship under the law of the jurisdiction in which it was entered into, or under the law of any other jurisdiction in respect of which a class of legal relationship has been declared by an order made under that subsection to be entitled to be recognised as a civil partnership, shall be recognised as a dissolution and deemed to be a dissolution under section 110, and any former parties to such a relationship shall not be treated as civil partners under the law of the State from the later of—

    (a)  the day which is 21 days after the date on which the order is made, and

    (b)  the day on which the dissolution became effective under the law of the relevant jurisdiction.

(5) Every order made by the Minister under this section shall be laid before each House of the Oireachtas as soon as may be after it is made and, if a resolution annulling the order is passed by either such House within the next 21 days on which that House has sat after the order is laid before it, the order shall be annulled accordingly but without prejudice to the validity of anything previously done under it.[1]

**Notes**

1  This section was commenced on 23 December 2010 (SI 648/2010). See Civil Partnership (Recognition of Foreign Relationships) Order 2010 (SI 649/2010) for the classes of registered foreign relationships to be entitled to be recognised in the State as a civil partnership.

PART 3
REGISTRATION OF CIVIL PARTNERSHIP

**6      Definition, Part 3**

In this Part, "Act of 2004" means the Civil Registration Act 2004.

**7      Amendment of section 2 of Act of 2004**

(1) Section 2(1) of the Act of 2004 is amended—

    (a)  by inserting the following definitions:

    (b)  by substituting the following definition for the definition "decree of divorce":[1]

    (c)  by substituting the following definition for the definition "decree of nullity":[1]

       "'decree of nullity'—

    (d)  in the definition of "event", by substituting "divorce, decree of nullity, civil partnership registration or dissolution" for "divorce or decree of nullity",

    (e)  in the definition of "registrar"—

        (i)    by inserting the following paragraph after paragraph (a):[1]

        (ii)   in paragraph (d), by substituting "," for ", and", and

        (iii)  by substituting the following paragraphs for paragraph (e):[1]

(2) Section 2(2) of the Act of 2004 is amended—

    (a)  in paragraph (d), by substituting "," for ",or",

    (b)  in paragraph (e) by substituting "sex, or" for "sex.", and

    (c)  by inserting the following paragraph after paragraph (e):[1]

(3) Section 2 of the Act of 2004 is amended by inserting the following subsection after subsection (2):[1]

**Notes**

1   See the amended Act.

**8        Amendment of section 8 of Act of 2004**

Section 8(1) of the Act of 2004 is amended—

   (a)   in paragraph (b), by inserting "of marriage" after "nullity",

   (b)   by inserting the following paragraphs after paragraph (b):[1]

   (c)   in paragraph (e), by inserting "of marriage" after "nullity", and

   (d)   by inserting the following paragraphs after paragraph (e):[1]

**Notes**

1   See the amended Act.

**9        Amendment of section 13 of Act of 2004**

Section 13(1) of the Act of 2004 is amended—

   (a)   in paragraph (f), by substituting "decrees of divorce)," for "decrees of divorce), and", and

   (b)   by substituting the following paragraphs for paragraph (g):[1]

**Notes**

1   See the amended Act.

**10       Amendment of section 17 of Act of 2004**

Section 17 of the Act of 2004 is amended—

   (a)   in paragraph (1)(b), by substituting "deaths, marriages and civil partnerships" for "deaths and marriages", and

   (b)   in subsection (13), by substituting ", marriages and civil partnerships" for "and marriages".

**11       Amendment of section 22 of Act of 2004**

Section 22(3)(b) of the Act of 2004 is amended by inserting "of marriage" after "nullity".

## 12 Amendment of section 23 of Act of 2004

Section 23(3)(b) of the Act of 2004 is amended by inserting "of marriage" after "nullity".

## 13 Amendment of section 37 of Act of 2004

Section 37 of the Act of 2004 is amended by inserting "or civil partner" after "relative" wherever it occurs.

## 14 Amendment of section 46 of Act of 2004

Section 46(7) of the Act of 2004 is amended by substituting "civil status" for "marital status".

## 15 Amendment of section 59 of Act of 2004

Section 59(2) of the Act of 2004 is amended by inserting "of marriage" after "nullity" wherever it appears.

## 16 Insertion of new Part 7A of Act of 2004

The Act of 2004 is amended by inserting the following Part after section 59:[1]

**Notes**

1   See the amended Act.

## 17 Insertion of new Part 7B of Act of 2004

The Act of 2004 is amended by inserting the following Part before section 60:[1]

**Notes**

1   See the amended Act.

## 18 Amendment of section 60 of Act of 2004

Section 60(1) of the Act of 2004 is amended—

(a) in paragraph (a), by substituting "death, marriage or civil partnership" for "death or marriage", and

(b) by inserting ", the parties to the civil partnership" before "or the person".

## 19 Amendment of section 64 of Act of 2004

Section 64 of the Act of 2004 is amended by inserting the following subsections after subsection (7):[1]

**Notes**

1   See the amended Act.

**20      Amendment of section 65 of Act of 2004**

Section 65(1)(a) of the Act of 2004 is amended by substituting "death, marriage or civil partnership", for "death or marriage".

**21      Amendment of section 66 of Act of 2004**

Section 66(1) of the Act of 2004 is amended by substituting "marriages, civil partnerships, decrees of divorce, decrees of nullity of marriage, decrees of dissolution or decrees of nullity of civil partnership" for "marriages, decrees of divorce, or decrees of nullity".

**22      Amendment of section 69 of Act of 2004**

Section 69 of the Act of 2004 is amended—

    (a)   in subsection (4), by inserting ", civil partnership" after "marriage",

    (b)   by inserting the following subsection after subsection (9):[1]

    (c)   in subsection (10)—

        (i)    by inserting the following paragraph after paragraph (f):[1]

        (ii)   by inserting in paragraph (h) "or 59F" after "58",

       (iii)   by inserting in paragraph (i) ", or 59B(1)(b)" after "46(1)(b)",

       (iv)   by substituting in paragraph (i), "false or misleading," for "false or misleading, or",

       (v)   by substituting in paragraph (j) "form, or" for "form,", and

      (vi)   by inserting the following paragraph after paragraph (j):[1]

**Notes**

1   See the amended Act.

**23      Amendment of section 70 of Act of 2004**

Section 70(2) of the Act of 2004 is amended by substituting "(9), (9A)," for "(9),".

**24      Amendment of section 73 of Act of 2004**

Section 73 of the Act of 2004 is amended—

    (a)   in subsection (1)—

        (i)    by inserting the following paragraph after paragraph (d):

        (ii)   by inserting "of marriage" after "nullity" in paragraph (f);

   (iii) by inserting the following paragraphs after paragraph (f):[1]

 (b) in paragraph (3)(a), by inserting "of marriage, civil partnership, decree of dissolution, decree of nullity of civil partnership," after "nullity" wherever it appears, and

 (c) in subsection (7), by inserting "of marriage, civil partnership, decree of dissolution, decree of nullity of civil partnership," after "nullity".

 (d) by inserting "of Marriage" at the end of the title to Part 7, and

 (e) by inserting the following Part after Part 7:[1]

---

**Notes**

1 See the amended Act.

---

## 25 Amendment of First Schedule to Act of 2004

The First Schedule to the Act of 2004 is amended—

 (a) by substituting "civil status" for "marital status" wherever it appears,

 (b) in Part 5, by substituting "If deceased was married or a civil partner, the profession or occupation of spouse or civil partner." for "If deceased was married, the profession or occupation of spouse.",

 (c) by inserting the following Part after Part 6:[1]

 (d) by inserting "of Marriage" at the end of the title to Part 7, and

 (e) by inserting the following Part after Part 7:[1]

---

**Notes**

1 See the amended Act.

---

## 26 New Third Schedule to Act of 2004

The Act of 2004 is amended by inserting the following Schedule after the Second Schedule:[1]

---

**Notes**

1 See the amended Act.

---

PART 4
SHARED HOME PROTECTION

**27      Interpretation**

In this Part—

"**conduct**" includes an act and a default or other omission;

"**conveyance**" includes a mortgage, lease, assent, transfer, disclaimer, release, another disposition of property otherwise than by a will or a *donatio mortis causa*, and an enforceable agreement, whether conditional or unconditional, to make one of those conveyances;

"**dwelling**" means a building or part of a building occupied as a separate dwelling and includes—

    (a)  a garden or other land usually occupied with the building that is subsidiary and ancillary to it, is required for amenity or convenience and is not being used or developed primarily for commercial purposes,

    (b)  a structure that is not permanently attached to the ground, and

    (c)  a vehicle or vessel, whether mobile or not, occupied as a separate dwelling;

"**interest**" means any estate, right, title or other interest, legal or equitable;

"**mortgage**" includes an equitable mortgage, a charge on registered land and a chattel mortgage;

"**rent**" includes a conventional rent, a rentcharge within the meaning of section 2(1) of the Statute of Limitations 1957 and a terminable annuity payable in respect of a loan for the purchase of a shared home;

"**shared home**" means—

    (a)  subject to paragraph (b), a dwelling in which the civil partners ordinarily reside; and

    (b)  in relation to a civil partner whose protection is in issue, the dwelling in which that civil partner ordinarily resides or, if he or she has left the other civil partner, in which he or she ordinarily resided before leaving.

**28      Alienation of interest in shared home**

(1) Where a civil partner, without the prior consent in writing of the other civil partner, purports to convey an interest in the shared home to a person except the other civil partner, then, subject to subsections (2), (3), and (8) to (14) and section 29, the purported conveyance is void.

(2) Subsection (1) does not apply to a conveyance if it is made by a civil partner in pursuance of an enforceable agreement made before the civil partners' registration of their civil partnership.

(3) A conveyance is not void by reason only of subsection (1) if—

    (a)  it is made to a purchaser for full value,

    (b)  it is made by a person other than the civil partner to a purchaser for value, or

(c)  its validity depends on the validity of a conveyance in respect of which a condition mentioned in subsection (2) or paragraph (a) or (b) is satisfied.

(4) If any question arises in any proceedings as to whether a conveyance is valid by reason of subsection (2) or (3), the burden of proving the validity is on the person alleging it.

(5) In subsection (3), "full value" means value that amounts or approximates to the value of that for which it is given.

(6) In this section, "purchaser" means a grantee, lessee, assignee, mortgagee, chargeant or other person who in good faith acquires an estate or interest in property.

(7) For the purposes of this section, section 3 of the Conveyancing Act 1882 shall be read as if the words "as such" wherever they appear in paragraph (ii) of subsection (1) of that section were omitted.

(8) Subject to subsection (9), proceedings may only be instituted to have a conveyance declared void by reason only of subsection (1) if they are instituted before the expiration of 6 years from the date of the conveyance.

(9) Proceedings referred to in subsection (8) may be instituted by a civil partner who was in actual occupation of the shared home during the whole period that begins with the date of the conveyance and ends immediately before the institution of the proceedings, even if 6 years have expired from the date of the conveyance.

(10) Subsection (8) is without prejudice to the rights of civil partners to seek redress for contraventions of subsection (1) otherwise than by proceedings referred to in that subsection.

(11) A conveyance is deemed not to be and never to have been void by reason of subsection (1) unless—

(a)  it has been declared void by a court by reason of subsection (1) in proceedings instituted in accordance with subsection (8) on or after the date on which this section commences, or

(b)  subject to the rights of any other person concerned, it is void by reason of subsection (1) and the parties to the conveyance or their successors in title so state in writing before the expiration of 6 years from the date of the conveyance.

(12) A copy of a statement made for the purpose of paragraph (b) of subsection (11) and certified by the parties concerned or their successors in title to be a true copy shall, before the expiration of the 6 years referred to in that paragraph, be lodged by the parties or their successors with the Property Registration Authority for registration in the Land Registry or Registry of Deeds as appropriate.

(13) A person who institutes proceedings to have a conveyance declared void by reason of subsection (1) shall, as soon as may be, cause relevant particulars of the proceedings to be entered as a lis pendens under and in accordance with the Judgements (Ireland) Act 1844 in any form that the rules of court may provide.

(14) A general consent given in writing by a civil partner, after the commencement of this section, to any future conveyance of any interest in a shared home or a former

shared home is deemed, for the purposes of subsection (1), to be a prior consent in writing if the deed for the conveyance is executed after the date of the consent.

## 29  Consent of civil partner

(1) Where the civil partner whose consent is required under section 28 omits or refuses to consent, the court may, subject to this section, dispense with the consent.

(2) The court shall not dispense with the consent unless the court considers that it is unreasonable for the civil partner to withhold consent, taking into account all the circumstances, including—

    (a)  the respective needs and resources of the civil partners, and

    (b)  in a case where the civil partner whose consent is required is offered alternative accommodation, the suitability of that accommodation having regard to the respective degrees of security of tenure in the shared home and the alternative accommodation.

(3) The court shall dispense with the consent of a civil partner whose consent is required if—

    (a)  the civil partner cannot be found after reasonable inquiries, and

    (b)  the court is of the opinion that it would be reasonable to do so.

(4) The court may give the consent on behalf of a civil partner whose consent is required if—

    (a)  a consultant psychiatrist, within the meaning of the Mental Health Act 2001, certifies that the civil partner is incapable of giving consent, and

    (b)  the court is of the opinion that it would be reasonable to do so.

## 30  Conduct leading to loss of shared home

(1) Where it appears to the court, on the application of a civil partner, that the other civil partner is engaging in conduct that might lead to the loss of any interest in the shared home or might render it unsuitable for habitation as a shared home, with the intention of depriving the applicant of his or her residence in the shared home, the court may make any order that it considers proper, directed to the other civil partner or to any other person, for the protection of the shared home in the interest of the applicant.

(2) Where it appears to the court, on the application of a civil partner, that the other civil partner has deprived the applicant of his or her residence in the shared home by conduct that resulted in the loss of any interest in it or rendered it unsuitable for habitation as a shared home, the court may order the other civil partner or any other person to pay to the applicant the amount that the court considers proper to compensate the applicant for their loss or make any other order directed to the other civil partner or to any other person that may appear to the court to be just and equitable.

## 31  Payment of outgoings on shared home

(1) Any payment or tender made or any other thing done by one civil partner in or towards satisfaction of any liability of the other civil partner in respect of rent, mortgage payments or other out-goings affecting the shared home shall be as good as if made or

done by the other civil partner, and shall be treated by the person to whom the payment is made or the thing is done as though it were made or done by the other civil partner.

(2) Nothing in subsection (1) affects any claim by the first-mentioned civil partner against the other to an interest in the shared home by virtue of the payment made or thing done.

**32    Adjournment of proceedings by mortgagee or lessor for possession or sale of shared home**

(1) The court may adjourn proceedings in an action brought by a mortgagee or lessor in relation to non-payment against a civil partner and claiming possession or sale of the shared home if it appears to the court that—

(a) the other civil partner is capable of paying to the mortgagee or lessor the arrears (other than the arrears of principal or interest or rent that do not constitute part of the periodical payments due under the mortgage or lease) of money due under the mortgage or lease within a reasonable time, and future periodical payments falling due under the mortgage or lease, and that the other civil partner desires to pay the arrears and periodical payments, and

(b) it would be just and equitable to do so, in all the circumstances and having regard to the interests of the mortgagee or lessor, the respective interests of the civil partners and the terms of the mortgage or lease.

(2) In considering whether to adjourn the proceedings under this section, and if so, for what period and on what terms, the court shall have regard in particular to whether the other civil partner has been informed, by or on behalf of the mortgagee or lessor or otherwise, of the non-payment of any of the sums in question.

**33    Modification of terms of mortgage or lease as to payment of capital sum**

The court may by order declare, on application by a civil partner, that a term of a mortgage or lease by virtue of which a sum is due, other than periodical payments due under the mortgage or lease, is of no effect for the purpose of proceedings under section 32, if, after the proceedings have been adjourned under that section it appears to the court that—

(a) all arrears (other than the arrears of principal or interest or rent that do not constitute part of the periodical payments due under the mortgage or lease or money due under the mortgage or lease) and periodical payments due as of the date of the order have been paid off, and

(b) the periodical payments subsequently falling due will continue to be paid.

**34    Restriction on disposal of household chattels**

(1) The court may, on the application of a civil partner, by order prohibit, on the terms it may see fit, the other civil partner from disposing of or removing household chattels, if the court is of the opinion that there are reasonable grounds to believe that the other civil partner intends to do so and that it would make it difficult for the applicant to reside in the shared home without undue hardship if the household chattels were disposed of or removed.

(2) Where proceedings for the dissolution of a civil partnership have been instituted by a civil partner, neither civil partner shall sell, lease, pledge, charge or otherwise dispose of or remove any of the household chattels in the shared home until the proceedings have been finally determined, unless—

    (a)  the other civil partner has consented to the disposition or removal, or

    (b)  the court before which the proceedings have been instituted, on application by the civil partner who desires to make the disposition or removal, permits the civil partner to do so, with or without conditions.

(3) Without prejudice to any other civil or criminal liability, a civil partner who contravenes subsection (2) commits an offence and is liable on summary conviction to [a class D fine][1] or to imprisonment for a term not exceeding 6 months or to both.

(4) The court may order, on the application of a civil partner, that the other civil partner provide household chattels or a sum of money to the applicant, so as to place the applicant as nearly as possible in the position that prevailed before—

    (a)  the other civil partner contravened an order under subsection (1) or (2), or

    (b)  the other civil partner sold, leased, pledged, charged or otherwise disposed of or removed the number or proportion of the household chattels in the shared home that made or is likely to make it difficult for the applicant to reside in the shared home without undue hardship.

(5) In proceedings under this section, the court may make an order that appears to it to be proper in the circumstances, directed to a third person who has been informed in writing by a civil partner before the proceedings were taken, with respect to a proposed disposition to the third person by the other civil partner.

(6) For the purposes of this section, "household chattels" means personal property ordinarily used in a household and includes garden effects and domestic animals, but does not include money or any chattels used by either civil partner for business or professional purposes.

---

**Notes**

1    Subsection (3) amended by the Civil Law (Miscellaneous Provisions) Act 2011, s 61(a).

---

**35**    **Joinder of parties**

In any proceedings under or referred to in this Part, each of the civil partners as well as any third person who has or may have an interest in the proceedings may be joined—

    (a)  by service of a third-party notice by an existing party to the proceedings, or

    (b)  by direction of the court.

**36**    **Registration of notice of existence of civil partnership**

(1) A civil partner may lodge with the Property Registration Authority a notice stating that he or she is the civil partner of a person having an interest in property or land.

(2) A notice under subsection (1) shall be registered in the Registry of Deeds or Land Registry, as appropriate.

(3) No stamp duty or fee shall be payable in respect of any such notice.

(4) The fact that notice of a civil partnership has not been registered under subsection (1) shall not give rise to any inference as to the non-existence of a civil partnership.

**37    Restriction of section 59(2) of Registration of Title Act 1964**

Section 59(2) of the Registration of Title Act 1964 (which refers to noting upon the register provisions of any enactment restricting dealings in land) does not apply to this Part.

**38    Creation of joint tenancy in shared home exempt from fees**

No land registration fee, Registry of Deeds fee or court fee shall be payable on any transaction creating a joint tenancy between civil partners in respect of a shared home where the home was immediately prior to such transaction owned by either civil partner or by both civil partners otherwise than as joint tenants.

**39    Offences**

(1) A person commits an offence if he or she—

    (a)  has an interest in premises,

    (b)  is required in writing by or on behalf of a person proposing to acquire the interest to give information necessary to establish if the conveyance of that interest requires a consent under section 28(1), and

    (c)  knowingly gives information that is false or misleading in any material particular.

(2) A person who commits an offence under subsection (1) is liable—

    (a)  on summary conviction, to [a class C fine][1] or to imprisonment for a term not exceeding 12 months, or to both, or

    (b)  on conviction on indictment, to imprisonment for a term not exceeding 5 years.

---

**Notes**

1    Subsection (2)(a) amended by the Civil Law (Miscellaneous Provisions) Act 2011, s 61(b).

---

**40    Protection of certain tenancies**

The Residential Tenancies Act 2004 is amended—

    (a)  in section 3(2)(h) and section 35(4) by inserting ", civil partner within the meaning of the Civil Partnership and Certain Rights and Obligations of Cohabitants Act 2010" after "spouse" wherever it appears, and

(b)   in section 39(3)(a)(i), by inserting "or civil partner within the meaning of the Civil Partnership and Certain Rights and Obligations of Cohabitants Act 2010" after "spouse".

**41      Protection of certain tenancies**

(1) In this section, "Act of 1982" means the Housing (Private Rented Dwellings) Act 1982.

(2) Section 9 of the Act of 1982 is amended in subsection (2) by inserting "or civil partner within the meaning of the Civil Partnership and Certain Rights and Obligations of Cohabitants Act 2010" after "spouse" wherever it appears.

(3) Section 16(1) of the Act of 1982 is amended by inserting "or of the tenant or the tenant's civil partner within the meaning of the Civil Partnership and Certain Rights and Obligations of Cohabitants Act 2010" after "dwelling" where it lastly occurs.

(4) Section 22 of the Act of 1982 is amended by inserting "or civil partner within the meaning of the Civil Partnership and Certain Rights and Obligations of Cohabitants Act 2010" after "spouse" wherever it appears.

**42      Amendment of Civil Legal Aid Act 1995**

Section 28(9)(c)(i) of the Civil Legal Aid Act 1995 is amended by substituting "or proceedings arising out of a dispute between spouses as to the title to or possession of any property, proceedings under Part 4 of the Civil Partnership and Certain Rights and Obligations of Cohabitants Act 2010, or proceedings arising out of a dispute between civil partners within the meaning of that Act as to the title to or possession of any property;" for "or proceedings arising out of a dispute between spouses as to the title to or possession of any property;".

PART 5
MAINTENANCE OF CIVIL PARTNER

**43      Interpretation**

(1) In this Part—

(a)   a maintenance order,

(b)   a variation order,

(c)   an interim order,

(d)   an order under section 48 insofar as it is deemed under that section to be a maintenance order, or

(e)   an order for maintenance pending suit under section 116 or a periodical payments order or secured periodical payments order under Part 12;

**"attachment of earnings order"** means an order under section 53;

**"desertion"** includes conduct on the part of one civil partner that results in the other civil partner, with just cause, leaving and living separately and apart from the first civil partner;

"**earnings**" means any sums payable to a person—

(a) by way of wages or salary (including any fees, bonus, commission, overtime pay or other emoluments payable in addition to wages or salary or payable under a contract of service), and

(b) by way of pension or other like benefit in respect of employment (including an annuity in respect of past services, whether or not rendered to the person paying the annuity, and including periodical payments by way of compensation for the loss, abolition or relinquishment, or diminution in the emoluments, of any office or employment);

"**interim order**" means an order under section 47;

"**maintenance creditor**", in relation to an order under this Part, or to proceedings arising out of the order, means the civil partner who applied for the order;

"**maintenance debtor**" means a person who is required by an order referred to in any of paragraphs (a) to (e) of the definition "antecedent order" to make payments;

"**maintenance order**" means an order under section 45;

"**normal deduction rate**" and "**protected earnings rate**" have the meanings respectively assigned to them in section 53;

"**variation order**" means an order under section 46 varying a maintenance order.

(2) Subject to section 59, the relationship of employer and employee shall be regarded as subsisting between two persons if one of them as a principal and not as a servant or agent pays earnings to the other.

(3) References in this Part to a District Court clerk include references to his or her successor in the office of District Court clerk and to any person acting on his or her behalf.

## 44     Commencement of periodical payments

A periodical payment under an order under this Part shall commence on the date that is specified in the order, which may be before or after the date on which the order is made but not earlier than the date of the application for the order.

## 45     Maintenance order

(1) Subject to subsection (3), where it appears to the court, on application to it by a civil partner, that the other civil partner has failed to provide maintenance for the applicant that is proper in the circumstances, the court may make an order that the other civil partner make to the applicant periodical payments for the support of the applicant, for the period during the lifetime of the applicant, of the amount and at the times that the court may consider proper.

(2) The court shall not make a maintenance order for the support of an applicant where he or she has deserted and continues to desert the other civil partner unless, having regard to all the circumstances, including the conduct of the other civil partner, the court is of the opinion that it would be unjust in all the circumstances not to make a maintenance order.

(3) The court, in deciding whether to make a maintenance order and, if it decides to do so, in determining the amount of any payment, shall have regard to all the circumstances of the case including—

(a)   the income, earning capacity, property and other financial resources of the civil partners, including income or benefits to which either civil partner is entitled by or under statute,

(b)   the financial and other responsibilities of—

(i)   the civil partners towards each other,

(ii)   each civil partner as a parent towards any dependent children, and the needs of any dependent children, including the need for care and attention, and

(iii)   each civil partner towards any former spouse or civil partner, and

(c)   the conduct of each of the civil partners, if that conduct is such that, in the opinion of the court, it would in all the circumstances be unjust to disregard it.

**46      Discharge, variation and termination of maintenance order**

(1) The court may discharge a maintenance order at any time after one year from the time it is made, on the application of the maintenance debtor, where it appears to the court that, having regard to the maintenance debtor's record of payments pursuant to the order and to the other circumstances of the case, the maintenance creditor will not be prejudiced by the discharge.

(2) The court may discharge or vary a maintenance order at any time, on the application of either party, if it thinks it proper to do so having regard to any circumstances not existing when the order was made (including the conduct of each of the civil partners, if that conduct is conduct that the court believes is conduct that it would in all the circumstances be unjust to disregard), or, if it has been varied, when it was last varied, or to any evidence not available to that party when the maintenance order was made or, if it has been varied, when it was last varied.

(3) Notwithstanding subsections (1) and (2), the court shall, on application to it, discharge the part of a maintenance order that provides for the support of a maintenance creditor where it appears to it that the maintenance creditor has deserted and continues to desert the maintenance debtor unless, having regard to all the circumstances (including the conduct of the maintenance debtor) the court is of the opinion that it would be unjust to do so.

**47      Interim order**

On an application to the court for a maintenance order, the court, before deciding whether to make or refuse to make the order, may make an order for the payment to the applicant by the maintenance debtor, for a definite period specified in the order or until the application is adjudicated upon by the court, of a periodical sum that, in the opinion of the court, is proper, if it appears to the court proper to do so having regard to the needs of the applicant and the other circumstances of the case.

**48      Orders in respect of certain agreements between civil partners**

(1) On application by one or both of the civil partners, the court may make an order under this section if it is satisfied that to do so would adequately protect the interests of the civil partners.

(2) An order under this section may make a rule of court a provision in an agreement in writing entered into by the civil partners—

    (a)  by which one civil partner undertakes to make periodical payments towards the maintenance of the other civil partner, or

    (b)  governing the rights and liabilities of the civil partners towards one another in respect of the making or securing of payments (other than payments referred to in paragraph (a)) or the disposition or use of any property.

(3) An order under subsection (2)(a) is deemed to be a maintenance order for the purposes of section 50, Part 6 and section 140.

**49      Preservation of pension entitlements**

(1) On application to it by either of the civil partners in an application under section 48, the court may make an order directing the trustees of a pension scheme of which either or both of the civil partners are members not to regard the separation of the civil partners as a ground for disqualifying either of them for the receipt of a benefit under the scheme that would normally require that the civil partners be residing together at the time when the benefit becomes payable.

(2) The applicant shall give notice of an application under subsection (1) to the trustees of the pension scheme and, in deciding whether to make an order under subsection (1), the court shall have regard to any order made, or proposed to be made, by it in relation to the application by the civil partner or civil partners under section 48 and any representations made by those trustees in relation to the matter.

(3) The court may determine the manner in which the costs incurred by the trustees under subsection (2) or in complying with an order under subsection (1) are to be borne, including by either of the civil partners or by both of them in the proportions that the court may determine.

(4) In this section, "pension scheme" has the meaning assigned to it by section 109.

**50      Transmission of payments through District Court clerk**

(1) Where the court makes a maintenance order, a variation order or an interim order, the court shall—

    (a)  direct that payments under the order be made to the District Court clerk, unless the maintenance creditor requests the court not to do so and the court considers that it would be proper not to do so, and

    (b)  in a case in which the court has not given a direction under paragraph (a), direct, at any time after making the order and on the application of the maintenance creditor, that the payments be made to the District Court clerk.

(2) Where payments to the District Court clerk under this section are in arrear, the District Court clerk shall, if the maintenance creditor so requests in writing, take the steps that he or she considers reasonable in the circumstances to recover the sums in arrear whether by proceedings for an attachment of earnings order or otherwise.

(3) The court, on the application of the maintenance debtor and having afforded the maintenance creditor an opportunity to oppose the application, may discharge a direction under subsection (1),if satisfied that, having regard to the record of the payments made to the District Court clerk and all the other circumstances, it would be proper to do so.

(4) The District Court clerk shall transmit any payments made by virtue of this section to the maintenance creditor.

(5) Nothing in this section affects any right of a person to take proceedings in his or her own name for the recovery of a sum payable, but not paid, to the District Court clerk by virtue of this section.

(6) References in this section to the District Court clerk are references to the District Court clerk in the District Court district that may be determined from time to time by the court concerned.

### 51    Lump sum maintenance orders

(1) The court may, on making a maintenance order under section 45, order the maintenance debtor in addition to, or instead of such an order, to make a lump sum payment or lump sum payments to the maintenance creditor of such amount or amounts and at such time or times as may be specified in the order.

(2) The amount or aggregate amount of a lump sum payment or of lump sum payments to a maintenance creditor under an order under this section shall be—

    (a)  if the order is instead of an order for the making of periodical payments to the maintenance creditor, such amount as the court considers appropriate having regard to the amount of the periodical payments that would have been made, and the periods during which and the times

    (b)  if the first-mentioned order is in addition to an order for the making of periodical payments to the maintenance creditor, such amount as the court considers appropriate having regard to the amount of the periodical payments and the periods during which and the times at which they will be made.

(3) The amount or aggregate amount of a lump sum payment or of lump sum payments provided for in an order of the District Court under this section shall not exceed €6,350.

### 52    Secured orders

The court may, on making a maintenance order under section 45 or at any time after making such an order, on application to it by any person having an interest in the proceedings, order the maintenance debtor concerned to secure it to the maintenance creditor concerned.

## PART 6
## ATTACHMENT OF EARNINGS

**53      Attachment of earnings order**

(1) For the purposes of this Part—

**"attachment of earnings order"** means an order directing that an employer deduct from the maintenance debtor's earnings, at the times specified in the order, periodical deductions of the appropriate amounts specified in the order, having regard to the normal deduction rate and the protected earnings rate;

**"court"** means—

    (a)  the High Court, in respect of an application under this Part made by a person on whose application the High Court has made an antecedent order,

    (b)  the relevant Circuit Court, in respect of an application under this Part made by a person on whose application that court has made an antecedent order, and

    (c)  the District Court, in respect of an application under this Part made by—

        (i)  a person on whose application the District Court has made an antecedent order, or

        (ii)  a District Court clerk to whom payments are required to be made under an antecedent order;

**"employer"** includes a trustee of a pension scheme under which the maintenance debtor is receiving periodical pension benefits;

**"normal deduction rate"** means the rate at which the court considers it reasonable that the earnings to which the attachment of earnings order relates should be applied in satisfying the antecedent order, not exceeding the rate that appears to the court to be necessary for—

    (a)  securing payment of the sums falling due from time to time under the antecedent order, and

    (b)  securing payment within a reasonable period of any sums already due and unpaid under the antecedent order and any costs incurred in proceedings relating to the antecedent order payable by the maintenance debtor;

**"protected earnings rate"** means the rate below which, having regard to the needs of the maintenance debtor, the court considers it proper that the relevant earnings should not be reduced by a payment made in pursuance of the attachment of earnings order.

(2) The court may, on application to it on that behalf, make an attachment of earnings order if it is satisfied that the maintenance debtor is a person to whom earnings fall to be paid and that the order is desirable to secure payments under an antecedent order and any amendments, variations and affirmations of it.

(3) The court that makes an antecedent order, or an order that makes, varies or affirms on appeal an antecedent order, shall make an attachment of earnings order in the same proceedings if it is satisfied of the things mentioned in subsection (2).

(4) A person to whom an attachment of earnings order is directed shall pay the amounts ordered to be deducted—

    (a) in the case of a relevant antecedent order that is an enforceable maintenance order, to the District Court clerk specified in the order for transmission to the maintenance creditor, and

    (b) in any other case, as specified in the order, to the maintenance creditor or to the District Court clerk specified in the order for transmission to the maintenance creditor.

(5) Before deciding whether to make or refuse to make an attachment of earnings order, the court shall give the maintenance debtor an opportunity to make representations, and shall have regard to any representations made, relating to whether the maintenance debtor—

    (a) is a person to whom earnings fall to be paid, and

    (b) would make the payments to which the relevant order relates.

(6) The court shall include in an attachment of earnings order the particulars required so that the person to whom the order is directed may identify the maintenance debtor.

(7) Payments under an attachment of earnings order are in lieu of payments of the like amount under the antecedent order that have not been made and that, but for the attachment of earnings order, would fall to be made under the antecedent order.

**54      Compliance with attachment of earnings order**

(1) The court registrar or court clerk specified in the attachment of earnings order shall cause the order to be served on the person to whom it is directed and on any person who subsequently becomes the maintenance debtor's employer and of whom the registrar or clerk becomes aware.

(2) The service may be effected by leaving the order or a copy of it at the person's residence or place of business in the State, or by sending the order or a copy of it, by registered prepaid post, to that residence or place of business.

(3) A person to whom an attachment of earnings order is directed shall comply with it if it is served on him or her but is not liable for non-compliance before 10 days have elapsed since the service.

(4) If a person to whom an attachment of earnings order is directed is not the maintenance debtor's employer or ceases to be the maintenance debtor's employer, the person shall, within 10 days from the date of service or the date of cesser, give notice of that fact to the court.

(5) The person shall give to the maintenance debtor a statement in writing of the total amount of every deduction made from a maintenance debtor's earnings in compliance with an attachment of earnings order.

**55      Application of sums received by District Court clerk**

Payments made to a District Court clerk under an attachment of earnings order shall, when transmitted by the clerk to the maintenance creditor, be deemed to be payments made by the maintenance debtor so as to discharge—

(a) firstly, any sums payable under the antecedent order, and

(b) secondly, any costs in proceedings relating to the antecedent order payable by the maintenance debtor when the attachment of earnings order was made or last varied.

## 56   Statement as to earnings

(1) In relation to an attachment of earnings order or an application for one, the court may, before or at the hearing or while the order is in force, order—

(a) the maintenance debtor to give to the court, within a specified period, a signed statement in writing specifying—

(i) the name and address of every employer of the maintenance debtor,

(ii) particulars as to the maintenance debtor's earnings and expected earnings, and resources and needs, and

(iii) particulars for enabling the employers to identify the maintenance debtor,

(b) a person appearing to the court to be an employer of the maintenance debtor to give to the court, within a specified period, a statement signed by the person, or on his or her behalf, of specified particulars of the maintenance debtor's earnings and expected earnings.

(2) Notice of an application for an attachment of earnings order served on a maintenance debtor may include a requirement that the maintenance debtor give to the court, within the period and in the manner specified in the notice, a statement in writing of the matters referred to in subsection (1)(a) and of any other matters which are or may be relevant to the determination of the normal deduction rate and the protected earnings rate to be specified in the order.

(3) In any proceedings in relation to an attachment of earnings order, a statement given to the court in compliance with an order under paragraph (a) or (b) of subsection (1) or with a requirement under subsection (2) is admissible as evidence of the facts stated in it and a document purporting to be such a statement is deemed, unless the contrary is shown, to be a statement so given.

## 57   Notification of changes of employment and earnings

Where an attachment of earnings order is in force—

(a) the maintenance debtor shall notify in writing the court that made the order of every occasion on which he or she leaves employment, or becomes employed or re-employed, not later than 10 days after doing so,

(b) the maintenance debtor shall, on any occasion on which he or she becomes employed or re-employed, include in the notification particulars of his or her earnings and expected earnings, and

(c) any person who becomes an employer of the maintenance debtor and who knows that the order is in force and by which court it was made shall, within 10 days of the later of the date of becoming an employer of the maintenance debtor and the date of acquiring the knowledge, notify the court in writing that he or she has become such an employer, and include in the notification a statement of the debtor's earnings and expected earnings.

**58     Power to determine whether particular payments are earnings**

(1) Where an attachment of earnings order is in force, the court that made the order shall, on the application of the maintenance debtor's employer, the maintenance debtor or the person to whom payments are being made under the order, determine whether payments or portions of payments being made to the maintenance debtor that are of a class or description specified in the application are earnings for the purpose of the order.

(2) Where an application is made by the employer under subsection (1), the employer is not liable for non-compliance with the order as respects any payments or portions of payments of the class or description specified by the application that he or she makes while the application, a determination in relation to it or an appeal from the determination is pending.

(3) Subsection (2) does not apply if the employer subsequently withdraws the application or abandons the appeal.

**59     Persons in service of State, local authority, etc**

(1) This section applies when a maintenance debtor is in the service of the State, a local authority within the meaning of the Local Government Act 1941, a harbour authority within the meaning of the Harbours Acts 1946 to 2005, the Health Service Executive, a vocational education committee established by the Vocational Education Act 1930, a committee of agriculture established by the Agriculture Act 1931, or another body if his or her earnings are paid directly out of moneys paid by the Oireachtas or from the Central Fund, or is a member of either House of the Oireachtas.

(2) For the purposes of this Part, the following officers are regarded as being the employers of the maintenance debtor and the earnings paid to the maintenance debtor out of the Central Fund or out of moneys provided by the Oireachtas are regarded as having been paid by them:

(a)   in the case where the maintenance debtor is employed in a department, office, organisation, service, undertaking or other body, its chief officer, or any other officer that may be designated from time to time by the Minister of the Government by whom that body is administered;

(b)   in the case where the maintenance debtor is in the service of an authority or body, its chief officer; and

(c)   in any other case, where the maintenance debtor is paid out of the Central Fund or out of moneys provided by the Oireachtas, the Secretary of the Department of Finance or any other officer that may be designated from time to time by the Minister for Finance.

(3) A question that arises in proceedings for or arising out of an attachment of earnings order as to which body employs a maintenance debtor may be referred to and determined by the Minister for Finance, but he or she is not obliged to consider the reference unless it is made by the court.

(4) A document purporting to contain a determination by the Minister for Finance under subsection (3) and to be signed by an officer of that Minister shall, in any proceedings mentioned in that subsection, be admissible in evidence and be deemed, unless the contrary is shown, to contain an accurate statement of that determination.

## 60 Discharge, variation and lapse of attachment of earnings order

(1) The court that made an attachment of earnings order may, if it thinks fit, on the application of the maintenance creditor, the maintenance debtor or the District Court clerk on whose application the order was made, make an order discharging or varying that order.

(2) The employer on whom an order varying an attachment of earnings order is served shall comply with it but is not liable for noncompliance before 10 days have elapsed since the service.

(3) If an employer affected by an attachment of earnings order ceases to be the maintenance debtor's employer, the order lapses insofar as that employer is concerned, except as respects deductions from earnings paid by the employer after the cesser and payment to the maintenance creditor of deductions from earnings made at any time by that employer.

(4) The lapse of an order under subsection (3) does not prevent its remaining in force for other purposes.

## 61 Cesser of attachment of earnings order

(1) An attachment of earnings order ceases to have effect upon the discharge of the relevant antecedent order, except as regards payments under the attachment of earnings order in respect of any time before the date of the discharge.

(2) The clerk or registrar of the court that made the attachment of earnings order shall give notice of a cesser to the employer.

## 62 Other remedies

(1) Where an attachment of earnings order has been made, any proceedings commenced under section 8(1) of the Enforcement of Court Orders Act 1940 for the enforcement of the relevant antecedent order lapses and any warrant or order issued or made under that subsection ceases to have effect.

(2) An attachment of earnings order ceases to have effect on the making of an order under section 8(1) of the Enforcement of Court Orders Act 1940 for the enforcement of the relevant antecedent order.

## 63 Enforcement

(1) A maintenance creditor who fails to obtain a sum of money due under an attachment of earnings order, or the District Court clerk to whom the sum falls to be paid, may sue for the sum as a simple contract debt in any court of competent jurisdiction, if the failure to obtain the sum is caused by—

    (a) a person failing, without reasonable excuse, to comply with section 54(3) or (4), or 57, or an order under section 56 or 60(2), or

(b)  a person, without reasonable excuse, giving a false or misleading statement under section 56(1) or notification under section 57.

(2) A person who gives to a court a statement pursuant to section 56 or a notification under section 57 that he or she knows to be false or misleading commits an offence and is liable on summary conviction to [a class C fine]¹ or to imprisonment for a term not exceeding six months or to both.

(3) A person who contravenes section 54(5) commits an offence and is liable on summary conviction to [a class E fine]².

**Notes**

1   Subsection (2) amended by the Civil Law (Miscellaneous Provisions) Act 2011, s 61(c)(i).

2   Subsection (3) amended by the Civil Law (Miscellaneous Provisions) Act 2011, s 61(c)(ii).

PART 7
MISCELLANEOUS PROVISIONS RELATING TO PARTS 5 AND 6

**64      Payments without deduction of income tax**

A periodical payment of money pursuant to a maintenance order, a variation order, an interim order, an order under section 48 (insofar as it is deemed to be a maintenance order) or an attachment of earnings order shall be made without deduction of income tax.

**65      Amendment of the Enforcement of Court Orders Act 1940**

The references in sections 8(1) and (7) of the Enforcement of Court Orders Act 1940 (as amended by section 29 of the Family Law (Maintenance of Spouses and Children) Act 1976, section 22 of the Family Law Act 1995 and section 30 of the Family Law (Divorce) Act 1996) to an order shall be construed as including references to an antecedent order.

**66      Property in household allowance**

An allowance made by one civil partner to the other for the purpose of meeting household expenses, and any property or interest in property that was acquired out of the allowance, belong to the civil partners as joint owners, in the absence of any express or implied agreement between them to the contrary.

**67      Voidance of certain provisions of agreements**

An agreement between civil partners is void to the extent to which it would have the effect of excluding or limiting the operation of any provision in Part 5 or Part 6.

PART 8

SUCCESSION

**68      Interpretation**

In this Part, "Act of 1965" means the Succession Act 1965.

**69      Amendment of section 3 of Act of 1965**

Section 3(1) of the Act of 1965 is amended—

    (a)  by inserting the following definition:

"'civil partner' has the meaning assigned to it by the Civil Partnership and Certain Rights and Obligations of Cohabitants Act 2010;",

and

    (b)  by substituting the following for the definition of "legal right":

"'legal right' means—

    (a)  the right of a spouse under section 111 to a share in the estate of a deceased person, and

    (b)  the right of a civil partner under section 111A to a share in the estate of a deceased person;".

**70      Amendment of section 56 of Act of 1965**

Section 56 of the Act of 1965 is amended—

    (a)  by inserting "or civil partner" after "spouse" wherever it appears, and

    (b)  in subsections (9), (10) and (12) by replacing "the spouse's" with "his or her" wherever it appears.

**71      Amendment of section 58 of Act of 1965**

Section 58(6) of the Act of 1965 is amended by inserting "or civil partner" after "spouse".

**72      Amendment of section 67 of Act of 1965**

Section 67 of the Act of 1965 is amended—

    (a)  in subsection (2)(b), by substituting "section 67B(2)" for "subsection (4)", and

    (b)  by repealing subsections (3) and (4).

**73      Insertion of new sections in Act of 1965**

The Act of 1965 is amended by inserting the following after section 67:

"67A Shares of surviving civil partner and issue

(1) If an intestate dies leaving a civil surviving civil partner and no issue, the civil partner shall take the whole estate.

(2) If an intestate dies leaving a civil partner and issue—

    (a)  subject to subsections (3) to (7), the civil partner shall take two-thirds of the estate; and

425

(b)   the remainder shall be distributed among the issue in accordance with section 67B(2).

(3) The court may, on the application by or on behalf of a child of an intestate who dies leaving a civil partner and one or more children, order that provision be made for that child out of the intestate's estate only if the court is of the opinion that it would be unjust not to make the order, after considering all the circumstances, including—

(a)   the extent to which the intestate has made provision for that child during the intestate's lifetime,

(b)   the age and reasonable financial requirements of that child,

(c)   the intestate's financial situation, and

(d)   the intestate's obligations to the civil partner.

(4) The court, in ordering provision of an amount under subsection (3) shall ensure that—

(a)   the amount to which any issue of the intestate is entitled shall not be less than that to which he or she would have been entitled had no such order been made, and

(b)   the amount provided shall not be greater than the amount to which the applicant would have been entitled had the intestate died leaving neither spouse nor civil partner.

(5) Rules of court shall provide for the conduct of proceedings under this section in a summary manner.

(6) The costs in the proceedings shall be at the discretion of the court.

(7) An order under this section shall not be made except on an application made within 6 months from the first taking out of representation of the deceased's estate.

67B Share of issue where no surviving spouse or surviving civil partner

(1) If an intestate dies leaving issue and no spouse or civil partner, the estate shall be distributed among the issue in accordance with sub-section (2).

(2) If all the issue are in equal degree of relationship to the deceased the distribution shall be in equal shares among them; if they are not, it shall be per stirpes.".

## 74      Amendment of section 68 of Act of 1965

Section 68 of the Act of 1965 is amended by inserting "nor civil partner" after "spouse".

## 75      Amendment of section 69 of Act of 1965

Section 69 of the Act of 1965 is amended by inserting "nor civil partner" after "spouse" wherever it appears.

## 76      Amendment of section 70 of Act of 1965

Section 70 of the Act of 1965 is amended by inserting "nor civil partner" after "spouse".

**77        Amendment of section 82 of Act of 1965**

Section 82(1) of the Act of 1965 is amended by inserting "or civil partner" after "spouse" wherever it appears.

**78        Amendment of section 83 of Act of 1965**

Section 83 of the Act of 1965 is amended by inserting "or civil partner" after "spouse".

**79        Amendment of section 85 of Act of 1965**

Section 85(1) of the Act of 1965 is amended by inserting "or entry into a civil partnership" after "marriage" wherever it appears.

**80        Amendment of section 109 of Act of 1965**

Section 109(1) of the Act of 1965 is amended by inserting "or civil partner" after "spouse" wherever it appears.

**81        Insertion of section 111A in Act of 1965**

The Act of 1965 is amended by inserting the following section after section 111:

"111A Right of surviving civil partner

(1) If the testator leaves a civil partner surviving civil and no children, the civil partner shall have a right to one-half of the estate.

(2) Subject to section 117(3A), if the testator leaves a civil partner and children, the civil partner shall have a right to one-third of the estate.".

**82        Amendment of section 112 of Act of 1965**

Section 112 of the Act of 1965 is amended by inserting "or the right of a civil partner under section 111A" after "section 111".

**83        Insertion of section 113A in Act of 1965**

The Act of 1965 is amended by inserting the following section after section 113:

"113A Renunciation of legal right

The legal right of a civil partner may be renounced in an ante-civil-partnership-registration contract made in writing between the parties to an intended civil partnership or may be renounced in writing by the civil partner after registration and during the lifetime of the testator.".

**84        Amendment of section 114 of Act of 1965**

Section 114 of the Act of 1965 is amended by inserting "or civil partner" after "spouse" wherever it appears.

**85        Amendment of section 115 of Act of 1965**

Section 115 of the Act of 1965 is amended—

    (a)  by inserting "or civil partner" after "spouse" wherever it appears, and

    (b)  in subsection (5), by inserting "or civil partner's" after "spouse's".

## 86 Amendment of section 117 of Act of 1965

Section 117 of the Act of 1965 is amended by inserting the following subsection after subsection (3):

> "(3A) An order under this section shall not affect the legal right of a surviving civil partner unless the court, after consideration of all the circumstances, including the testator's financial circumstances and his or her obligations to the surviving civil partner, is of the opinion that it would be unjust not to make the order.".

## 87 Amendment of section 120 of Act of 1965

Section 120 of the Act of 1965 is amended—

(a) by inserting the following subsection after subsection (2):

> "(2A) A deceased's civil partner who has deserted the deceased is precluded from taking any share in the deceased's estate as a legal right or on intestacy if the desertion continued up to the death for two years or more.",

(b) by inserting the following subsection after subsection (3):

> "(3A) A civil partner who was guilty of conduct which justified the deceased in separating and living apart from him or her is deemed to be guilty of desertion within the meaning of subsection (2A).",

(c) in subsection (4), by inserting "or civil partner" after "spouse".

## 88 Amendment of section 121 of Act of 1965

Section 121 of the Act of 1965 is amended in subsections (2), (5) and (7) by inserting "or civil partner" after "spouse" wherever it appears.

## 89 Amendment of section 45 of Statute of Limitations 1957

Section 45(1) of the Statute of Limitations 1957, as inserted by the Succession Act 1965, is amended by inserting "or section 111A" after "section 111".

PART 9
DOMESTIC VIOLENCE

## 90 Interpretation

In this Part, "Act of 1996" means the Domestic Violence Act 1996.

## 91 Amendment of section 1 of Act of 1996

Section 1(1) of the Act of 1996 is amended by inserting the following definitions:[1]

---

**Notes**

1 See the amended Act.

---

## 92 Amendment of definition of "the applicant" in section 2 of Act of 1996

The definition "the applicant" in section 2(1)(a) of the Act of 1996 is amended by inserting the following subparagraph after subparagraph (i):[1]

### Notes

1 See the amended Act.

## 93 Amendment of section 3 of Act of 1996

Section 3(1) of the Act of 1996 is amended by inserting the following paragraph after paragraph (a):[1]

### Notes

1 See the amended Act.

## 94 Insertion of section 8A of Act of 1996

The Act of 1996 is amended by inserting the following section after section 8:[1]

### Notes

1 See the amended Act.

## 95 Amendment of section 9 of Act of 1996

Section 9(2) of the Act of 1996 is amended by inserting the following paragraph after paragraph (c):[1]

### Notes

1 See the amended Act.

## 96 Amendment of section 13 of Act of 1996

Section 13(2) of the Act of 1996 is amended by inserting "or any annulment or dissolution proceedings under the Act of 2010," after "matrimonial cause or matter".

PART 10

MISCELLANEOUS CONSEQUENCES OF CIVIL PARTNERSHIP REGISTRATION

**97      Ethics and conflict of interests**

(1) For the purposes of determining matters concerning ethics and conflicts of interests under any rule of law or enactment—

(a)  with respect to a person, a reference to a "connected person" or a "connected relative" of that person shall be construed as including the person's civil partner and the child of the person's civil partner who is ordinarily resident with the person and the civil partner, and

(b)  a declaration that must be made in relation to a spouse of a person shall also be made in relation to a civil partner of a person.

(2) Without limiting the generality of subsection (1), the Acts specified in Part 1 of the Schedule are amended as indicated in that Schedule.

**98      Amendment of Mental Health Act 2001**

(1) In this section, "Act of 2001" means the Mental Health Act 2001.

(2) Section 2(1) of the Act of 2001 is amended by inserting the following definition:

"'civil partner' means a civil partner within the meaning of the Civil Partnership and Certain Rights and Obligations of Cohabitants Act 2010;".

(3) Section 9 of the Act of 2001 is amended—

(a)  in paragraph (1)(a), by inserting "or civil partner" after "spouse",

(b)  in paragraphs (2)(b) and (f), by inserting "or civil partner" after "spouse", and

(c)  in subsection (8), by inserting the following definition:

"'civil partner' in relation to a person, does not include a civil partner of the person who is living separately and apart from the person or in respect of whom an application or order has been made under the Domestic Violence Acts 1996 and 2002 as amended by the Civil Partnership and Certain Rights and Obligations of Cohabitants Act 2010;".

(4) Section 10(3)(c) of the Act of 2001 is amended by inserting ", a civil partner" after "spouse".

(5) Section 14(3)(a) of the Act of 2001 is amended by inserting ", a civil partner" after "spouse".

(6) Section 24(1) of the Act of 2001 is amended by inserting ", civil partner" after "spouse".

**99      Pensions**

(1) A benefit under a pension scheme that is provided for the spouse of a person is deemed to provide equally for the civil partner of a person.

(2) Without limiting the generality of subsection (1), the Acts specified in Part 2 of the Schedule are amended as indicated in that Schedule.

(3) In this section "pension scheme" has the meaning assigned to it by section 109.

**100    Amendment of the Pensions Act 1990**

The Pensions Act 1990 is amended—

(a) in section 65(1) (substituted by section 22(1) of the Social Welfare (Miscellaneous Provisions) Act 2004), by deleting the definition of "marital status" and inserting the following definition:

"'civil status' means civil status within the meaning of the Civil Registration Act 2004 as amended by the Civil Partnership and Certain Rights and Obligations of Cohabitants Act 2010;",

(b) in section 66(2)(a)(ii) (substituted by section 22(1) of the Social Welfare (Miscellaneous Provisions) Act 2004), by substituting "civil status" for "marital status" in subparagraph (a)(ii),

(c) in section 66(2)(b) (substituted by section 22(1) of the Social Welfare (Miscellaneous Provisions) Act 2004), by substituting "civil status" for "marital status" wherever it appears,

(d) in section 67(1)(b) (substituted by section 22(1) of the Social Welfare (Miscellaneous Provisions) Act 2004), by substituting "civil status" for "marital status" wherever it appears,

(e) in section 72 (substituted by section 22(1) of the Social Welfare (Miscellaneous Provisions) Act 2004), by substituting "civil status" for "marital status" wherever it appears, and

(f) in section 75(1) (substituted by section 22(1) of the Social Welfare (Miscellaneous Provisions) Act 2004), by substituting "civil status" for "marital status".

**101    Amendment of Criminal Damage Act 1991**

Section 1 of the Criminal Damage Act 1991 (as amended by the Family Law (Divorce) Act 1996) is amended by inserting the following subsection after subsection (3):

"(3A) A reference to any property belonging to another, however expressed, shall be construed as a reference to a shared home as respects an offence under section 2, 3(a) or 4(a) if—

(a) the property is either a shared home or a dwelling, within the meaning of section 27 of the Civil Partnership and Certain Rights and Obligations of Cohabitants Act 2010, in which a person who was a civil partner in a civil partnership that has been dissolved under that Act ordinarily resided with his or her former civil partner before the dissolution, and

(b) the person charged—

(i) is the civil partner, or was the civil partner until the dissolution of their civil partnership, of a person who resides, or is entitled to reside, in the home, and

(ii) is the subject of a protection order or barring order or is excluded from the home pursuant to an order under the Domestic Violence

Act 1996 as amended by Part 9 of the Civil Partnership and Certain Rights and Obligations of Cohabitants Act 2010 or another order of a court.".

## 102    Amendment of Employment Equality Act 1998

(1) In this section, "Act of 1998" means the Employment Equality Act 1998.

(2) Section 2(1) of the Act of 1998 is amended—

    (a)  by inserting the following definition:

"'civil status' means being single, married, separated, divorced, widowed, in a civil partnership within the meaning of the Civil Partnership and Certain Rights and Obligations of Cohabitants Act 2010 or being a former civil partner in a civil partnership that has ended by death or been dissolved;";

    (b)  by deleting the definition "marital status"; and

    (c)  by inserting, in paragraphs (a) and (b) of the definition "member of the family", "or civil partner within the meaning of the Civil Partnership and Certain Rights and Obligations of Cohabitants Act 2010" after "spouse" wherever it appears.

(3) The Act of 1998 is amended by substituting "civil status" for "marital status" wherever it appears.

## 103    Amendment of Equal Status Act 2000

(1) In this section, "Act of 2000" means the Equal Status Act 2000.

(2) Section 2(1) of the Act of 2000 is amended—

    (a)  by inserting the following definition:

"'civil status' means being single, married, separated, divorced, widowed, in a civil partnership within the meaning of the Civil Partnership and Certain Rights and Obligations of Cohabitants Act 2010 or being a former civil partner in a civil partnership that has ended by death or been dissolved;",

    (b)  by deleting the definition "marital status", and

    (c)  by inserting, in the definition "near relative", "or civil partner within the meaning of the Civil Partnership and Certain Rights and Obligations of Cohabitants Act 2010" after "spouse".

(3) The Act of 2000 is amended by substituting "civil status" for "marital status" wherever it appears.

## 104    Amendment of Powers of Attorney Act 1996

(1) In this section, "Act of 1996" means the Powers of Attorney Act 1996.

(2) Section 5 of the Act of 1996 is amended—

    (a)  by inserting, in subsection (4)(b), "or civil partner within the meaning of the Civil Partnership and Certain Rights and Obligations of Cohabitants Act 2010" after "spouse", and

(b)  by inserting the following subsection after subsection (7):

"(7A) An enduring power in favour of a civil partner within the meaning of the Civil Partnership and Certain Rights and Obligations of Cohabitants Act 2010 shall, unless the power provides otherwise, be invalidated or, as the case may be, cease to be in force if subsequently—

   (a)  a decree of nullity or a decree of dissolution of the civil partnership is granted or recognised under the law of the State,

   (b)  a written agreement to separate is entered into between the civil partners, or

   (c)  a protection order, interim barring order, barring order or safety order is made against the attorney on the application of the donor, or vice versa.".

(3) Section 6(7)(b)(iii)(II) of the Act of 1996 is amended by inserting "or civil partner within the meaning of the Civil Partnership and Certain Rights and Obligations of Cohabitants Act 2010" after "spouse".

(4) The First Schedule to the Act of 1996 is amended by inserting the following paragraph after paragraph 3(1)(a):

"(aa) the donor's civil partner, within the meaning of the Civil Partnership and Certain Rights and Obligations of Cohabitants Act 2010;".

(5) Part I of the Second Schedule to the Act of 1996 is amended by inserting the following paragraph after paragraph 2A (inserted by the Family Law (Divorce) Act 1996):

"2B. The expiry of an enduring power of attorney effected in the circumstances mentioned in section 5(7A) shall apply only so far as it relates to an attorney who is the civil partner of the donor.".

(6) Part II of the Second Schedule to the Act of 1996 is amended by inserting the following paragraph after paragraph 3:

"4. The expiry of an enduring power of attorney effected in the circumstances mentioned in section 5(7A) shall apply only so far as it relates to an attorney who is the civil partner of the donor.".

**105     Amendment of Civil Liability Act 1961**

Paragraph (a) of the definition "dependant" in section 47(1) (as amended by section 1(1) of the Civil Liability (Amendment) Act 1996) of the Civil Liability Act 1961 is amended by inserting ", civil partner within the meaning of the Civil Partnership and Certain Rights and Obligations of Cohabitants Act 2010" after "spouse".

**106     Determination of questions between civil partners in relation to property**

(1) Either civil partner may apply to the court in a summary manner to determine a question arising between them as to the title to or possession of property.

(2) The court may, on application to it under subsection (1)—

   (a)  make the order it considers proper with respect to the property in dispute (including an order that the property be sold or partitioned), and as to the costs consequent on the application, and

(b)  direct the inquiries, and give the other directions, it considers proper in relation to the application.

(3) A civil partner or a child of a deceased person who was a civil partner before death may make an application under subsection (1) when he or she is of the view that the conditions specified in subsection (4) are present.

(4) The conditions for an application under subsection (3) are:

(a)  the applicant claims that the other civil partner has possessed or controlled—

    (i)  money to which, or a share of which, the applicant was beneficially entitled whether because it represented the proceeds of sale of property to which, or to an interest in which, the applicant was beneficially entitled or for any other reason, or

    (ii)  property other than money to which, or to an interest in which, the applicant was beneficially entitled;

and

(b)  the money or the property has ceased to be in the possession or under the control of the other civil partner or the applicant does not know whether it is still in the possession or under the control of the other civil partner.

(5) If the court is satisfied on an application under subsections (1) and (3) of the matters specified in subsection (6), the court may make an order under subsection (2) in relation to the application and may, in addition to or in lieu of that order, make an order requiring the other civil partner to pay to the applicant—

(a)  a sum in respect of the money to which the application relates, or the applicant's proper share of it, or

(b)  a sum in respect of the value of the property other than money, or the applicant's proper share of it.

(6) For the purposes of subsection (5), the court must be satisfied that—

(a)  the other civil partner possesses or controls, or has possessed or controlled, money or other property referred to in subsection (4)(a)(i) or (ii), and

(b)  the other civil partner has not made to the applicant a payment or disposition other than a testamentary disposition that would have been appropriate in the circumstances.

(7) A person (other than the applicant or the other civil partner) who is a party to proceedings under this section shall be treated as a stakeholder only, for the purposes of costs or any other matter.

(8) In this section, references to a civil partner include references to—

(a)  a personal representative of a deceased civil partner, and

(b)  either of the parties to a void civil partnership, whether or not it has been the subject of a decree of nullity granted under section 107.

PART 11
NULLITY OF CIVIL PARTNERSHIP

**107    Grant of decree of nullity**

On application to it in that behalf by either of the civil partners or by another person who, in the opinion of the court, has sufficient standing in the matter, the court may grant a decree of nullity if satisfied that at the time the civil partners registered in a civil partnership—

(a)  either or both of the parties lacked the capacity to become the civil partner of the other for any reason, including—

(i)   either or both of the parties was under the age of eighteen years,

(ii)  either or both of the parties was already a party to a valid marriage, and

(iii) either or both of the parties was already registered in a relationship with another person which was entitled to be recognised as a civil partnership in the State in accordance with section 5 and which had not been dissolved,

(b)  the formalities for the registration of the civil partnership were not observed,

(c)  either or both of the parties did not give free and informed consent to the civil partnership registration for any reason, including—

(i)   the consent was given under duress,

(ii)  the consent was given under undue influence,

(iii) the party or parties did not intend, at the time of the registration, to accept the other as a civil partner in accordance with the law, and

(iv)  either or both of the parties was unable to give informed consent, as attested by a consultant psychiatrist within the meaning of section 2(1) of the Mental Health Act 2001,

(d)  the parties were within the prohibited degrees of relationship within the meaning of the Third Schedule to the Civil Registration Act 2004 (as inserted by section 26 of this Act), or

(e)  the parties were not of the same sex.

**108    Effect of decree of nullity**

(1) Where the court grants a decree of nullity, the civil partnership is declared not to have existed and either civil partner may register in a new civil partnership or marry.

(2) The rights of a person who relied on the existence of a civil partnership which is subsequently the subject of a decree of nullity are not prejudiced by that decree.

PART 12
DISSOLUTION OF CIVIL PARTNERSHIP

**109    Definitions, etc**

(1) In this Part—

"**court**" shall be construed in accordance with section 140;

"**decree of dissolution**" means a decree under section 110;

"**decree of nullity**" means a decree granted by a court under section 107 declaring a civil partnership to be void;

"**financial compensation order**" means an order under section 120;

"**lump sum order**" means an order under section 117(1)(c);

"**maintenance pending suit order**" means an order under section 116;

"**member**" in relation to a pension scheme, means a person who, having been admitted to membership of the scheme under its rules, remains entitled to any benefit under the scheme;

"**pension adjustment order**" means an order under sections 121 to 126;

"**pension scheme**" means—

    (a)  an occupational pension scheme within the meaning of the Pensions Act 1990,

    (b)  an annuity contract approved by the Revenue Commissioners under section 784 of the Taxes Consolidation Act 1997, or a contract so approved under section 785 of that Act,

    (c)  a trust scheme, or part of a trust scheme, approved under section 784(4) or 785(5) of the Taxes Consolidation Act 1997,

    (d)  a policy or contract of assurance approved by the Revenue Commissioners under Chapter 1 of Part 30 of the Taxes Consolidation Act 1997, or

    (e)  another scheme or arrangement, including a personal pension plan and a scheme or arrangement established by or pursuant to statute or instrument made under statute other than under the Social Welfare Acts, that provides or is intended to provide either or both of the following:

        (i)  benefits for a person who is a member of the scheme or arrangement upon retirement at normal pensionable age or upon earlier or later retirement or upon leaving or upon the ceasing of the relevant employment, and

        (ii)  benefits for the widow, widower or dependants of the person referred to in subparagraph (i), for his or her civil partner or the person that was his or her civil partner until the death of the person referred to in subparagraph (i) or for any other persons, on the death of that person;

"**periodical payments order**" means an order under section 117(1)(a);

"**property adjustment order**" means an order under section 118;

"**secured periodical payments order**" means an order under section 117(1)(b);

"**shared home**" has the meaning assigned to it in Part 4, with the modification that the references to a civil partner in that Part shall be construed as references to a civil partner within the meaning of this Part;

"**trustees**", in relation to a scheme that is established under a trust, means the trustees of the scheme and, in relation to a pension scheme not established under a trust, means the persons who administer the scheme.

(2) In this Part, where the context so requires—

(a) a reference to a civil partnership includes a reference to a civil partnership that has been dissolved under this Part,

(b) a reference to a registration in a new civil partnership includes a reference to a registration in a civil partnership that takes place after a civil partnership that has been dissolved under this Part, and

(c) a reference to a civil partner includes a reference to a person who was a civil partner in a civil partnership that has been dissolved under this Part.

## 110    Grant of decree of dissolution

Subject to the provisions of this Part, the court may, on application to it in that behalf by either of the civil partners, grant a decree of dissolution in respect of a civil partnership if it is satisfied that—

(a) at the date of the institution of the proceedings, the civil partners have lived apart from one another for a period of, or periods amounting to, at least two years during the previous three years, and

(b) provision that the court considers proper having regard to the circumstances exists or will be made for the civil partners.

## 111    Adjournment of proceedings to assist reconciliation, mediation or agreements on terms of dissolution

(1) The court may adjourn or further adjourn proceedings under section 110 at any time for the purpose of enabling the civil partners to attempt, if they both so wish, with or without the assistance of a third party—

(a) to reconcile, or

(b) to reach agreement on some or all of the terms of the proposed dissolution.

(2) Either or both of the civil partners may at any time request that the hearing of proceedings adjourned under subsection (1) be resumed as soon as may be and, if that request is made, the court shall, subject to any other power of the court to adjourn proceedings, resume the hearing.

(3) The powers conferred by this section are additional to any other power of the court to adjourn proceedings.

(4) The court may, at its discretion when adjourning proceedings under this section, advise the civil partners to seek the assistance of a mediator or other third party in relation to the civil partners' proposed reconciliation or reaching of an agreement between them on some or all of the terms of the proposed dissolution.

## 112    Non-admissibility as evidence of certain communications

The following are not admissible as evidence in any court:

(a) an oral or written communication between either of the civil partners and a third party, whether or not made in the presence or with the knowledge of the other civil partner, for the purpose of—

      (i)   seeking assistance to effect a reconciliation, or

     (ii)  reaching agreement between them on some or all of the terms of a dissolution;

  and

  (b)  any record of such a communication, made or caused to be made by either of the civil partners concerned or the third party.

## 113    Effect of decree of dissolution

Where the court grants a decree of dissolution, the civil partnership is thereby dissolved and either civil partner may register in a new civil partnership or marry.

## 114    Interpretation

An order made under any of sections 115 to 128 that refers to a civil partner shall be construed as including a person who was a civil partner until the dissolution of the civil partnership under this Part.

## 115    Preliminary orders in proceedings for dissolution

Where an application is made to the court for the grant of a decree of dissolution, the court, before deciding whether to grant or refuse to grant the decree may, in the same proceedings and without the institution of proceedings under any other Act, if it appears to the court to be proper to do so, make one or more of the following orders:

  (a)  a safety order, a barring order, an interim barring order or a protection order under the Domestic Violence Acts 1996 and 2002, as amended by Part 9 of this Act; and

  (b)  an order under section 30 or section 34.

## 116    Maintenance pending suit orders

(1) Where an application is made to the court for the grant of a decree of dissolution, the court may make an order requiring either of the civil partners to make to the other periodical payments or lump sum payments for support that the court considers proper and specifies in the order.

(2) Periodical payments ordered under subsection (1) may be for the period beginning not earlier than the date of the application and ending not later than the date of its determination that the court specifies in the order.

## 117    Periodical payments and lump sum orders

(1) On granting a decree of dissolution or at any other time after granting the decree, the court, on application to it in that behalf by either of the civil partners may, during the lifetime of either of the civil partners, make one or more of the following orders:

  (a)  an order that either of the civil partners make to the other the periodical payments in the amounts, during the period and at the times that may be specified in the order;

(b) an order that either of the civil partners secure to the other, to the satisfaction of the court, the periodical payments of the amounts, during the period and at the times that may be specified in the order; and

(c) an order that either of the civil partners make to the other a lump sum payment or lump sum payments of the amount or amounts and at the time or times that may be specified in the order.

(2) The court may order a civil partner to pay a lump sum to the other civil partner to meet any liabilities or expenses reasonably incurred by the other civil partner in maintaining himself or herself before the making of an application by the other civil partner for an order under subsection (1).

(3) An order under this section for the payment of a lump sum may provide for the payment of the lump sum by instalments of the amounts that may be specified in the order and may require the payment of the instalments to be secured to the satisfaction of the court.

(4) The period specified in an order under subsection (1)(a) or (b) shall begin not earlier than the date of the application for the order and shall end not later than the death of the first civil partner to die.

(5) An order made under subsection (1)(a) or (b) ceases to have effect on the date of entry into a new civil partnership or marriage of the civil partner in whose favour the order was made, except as respects payments due under it on that date.

(6) The court shall not make an order under this section in favour of a civil partner who has entered into a new civil partnership or has married.

(7) The court that makes an order under subsection (1)(a) shall, in the same proceedings, make an attachment of earnings order under Part 6 to secure payments under the order if it is satisfied, after taking into consideration any representations on the matter made to it by the civil partner ordered to make payments under that subsection, that—

(a) the order is desirable to secure payments under an order under subsection (1)(a) and any variations and affirmations of that order, and

(b) the person against whom the attachment of earnings order is made is a person to whom earnings fall to be paid.

## 118    Property adjustment orders

(1) On granting a decree of dissolution or at any other time after the decree is granted, the court, on application to it in that behalf by either of the civil partners may, during the lifetime of either of the civil partners, make one or more of the following orders:

(a) an order transferring specified property in which a civil partner has an interest either in possession or reversion from that civil partner to the other;

(b) an order settling specified property in which a civil partner has an interest either in possession or reversion for the benefit of the other, to the satisfaction of the court;

(c) an order varying an ante-registration or post-registration settlement made by the civil partners, including one made by will or codicil, for the benefit of one of the civil partners; and

(d) an order extinguishing or reducing the interest of either of the civil partners under such a settlement.

(2) An order under subsection (1)(b), (c) or (d) may restrict to a specified extent or may exclude the application of section 131 in relation to the order.

(3) If, after the grant of the decree of dissolution, either of the civil partners registers in a new civil partnership or marries, the court shall not make an order under subsection (1) in favour of that civil partner.

(4) The registrar or clerk of the court that makes an order under subsection (1) in relation to land shall lodge with the Property Registration Authority a copy of the order certified to be a true copy for registration in the Registry of Deeds or Land Registry, as appropriate.

(5) Where a property adjustment order lodged under subsection (4) and registered pursuant to section 69(1)(h) of the Registration of Title Act 1964 or in the Registry of Deeds has been complied with, the Property Registration Authority shall, on being satisfied that the order has been complied with—

(a) cancel the entry made in the register under the Registration of Title Act 1964, or

(b) note compliance with the order in the Registry of Deeds.

(6) The court may order a person other than the person directed by an order under subsection (1) to execute a deed or instrument in the name of the person who had been directed to do so if—

(a) that person refuses or neglects to comply with the direction, or

(b) the court considers it necessary to do so for another reason.

(7) A deed executed by a person in the name of another person pursuant to an order under subsection (6) is as valid as if it had been executed by the person who had been originally directed to do so.

(8) The court may determine the manner in which the costs incurred in complying with an order under this section are to be borne, including by one or the other of the civil partners or by both of them in the proportions that the court may determine.

(9) This section does not apply in relation to a shared or family home in which, following the grant of a decree of dissolution, either of the civil partners resides with a new civil partner or spouse.

**119    Miscellaneous ancillary orders**

(1) On granting a decree of dissolution or at any other time after it is granted, the court, on application to it in that behalf by either of the civil partners may, during the lifetime of either of the civil partners, make one or more of the following orders:

(a) an order providing for the conferral on one civil partner, either for life or for another specified definite or contingent period that the court may specify, of the right to occupy the shared home to the exclusion of the other civil partner;

(b) an order directing the sale of the shared home subject to the conditions that the court considers proper and providing for the disposition of the proceeds of the sale between the civil partners and any other person with an interest in it;

(c) an order under section 30, 33, 34 or 106;

(d) an order under the Domestic Violence Acts 1996 and 2002 as amended by Part 9; and

(e) an order for the partition of property or under the Partition Act 1868 and the Partition Act 1876.

(2) The court, in exercising its jurisdiction under subsection (1)(a) or (b) shall have regard to the welfare of the civil partners and, in particular, shall take into consideration—

(a) that, where a decree of dissolution is granted, it is not possible for the civil partners to reside together, and

(b) that proper and secure accommodation should, where practicable, be provided for a civil partner who is wholly or mainly dependent on the other civil partner.

(3) Subsections (1)(a) and (b) do not apply in relation to a shared or family home in which, following the grant of a decree of dissolution, either of the civil partners resides with a new civil partner or spouse.

## 120    Financial compensation orders

(1) If the court is of the view that one of the reasons set out in subsection (2) exists, the court, on application to it in that behalf by either of the civil partners, during the lifetime of either of the civil partners, may make, on granting a decree of dissolution or at any time after granting it, one or more of the following orders:

(a) an order requiring the other civil partner to effect a policy of life insurance for the benefit of the applicant civil partner;

(b) an order requiring the other civil partner to assign to the applicant the whole or a specified part of the interest in a policy of life insurance that he or she has effected or that both of the civil partners have effected; and

(c) an order requiring the other civil partner to make or to continue to make to the person by whom a policy of life insurance is or was issued the payments which he or she or both of the civil partners is or are required to make under the terms of the policy.

(2) The reasons referred to in subsection (1) are:

(a) the financial security of the applicant can be provided for if the order is made; and

(b) the forfeiture by the applicant of the opportunity of acquiring a benefit (for example a benefit under a pension scheme) by reason of the decree of dissolution can be compensated wholly or partly by making the order.

(3) The court may make an order under subsection (1) in addition to or in substitution in whole or in part for orders under sections 117, 118, 119 or 121 and, in deciding whether or not to make the order, the court shall have regard to whether proper provision, having regard to the circumstances, exists, or can be made, for the civil partner concerned by orders under those sections.

(4) An order made under subsection (1) ceases to have effect on the entry into a new civil partnership, marriage or death of the applicant.

(5) The court shall not make an order under this section in favour of a civil partner who has entered into a new civil partnership or has married.

(6) An order under section 131 in relation to an order made under subsection (1)(a) or (b) may make the provision that the court considers appropriate in relation to the disposal of—

(a) an amount representing any accumulated value of the insurance policy effected pursuant to the order under subsection (1)(a),or

(b) the interest or part of the interest to which the order under subsection (1)(b) relates.

**121    Pension adjustment orders**

(1) In this section and sections 122 to 126—

**"Act of 1990"** means the Pensions Act 1990;

**"active member"** in relation to a scheme, means a member of the scheme who is in reckonable service;

**"actuarial value"** means the equivalent cash value of a benefit (including, where appropriate, provision for any revaluation of the benefit) under a scheme calculated by reference to appropriate financial assumptions and making due allowance for the probability of survival to normal pensionable age and beyond in accordance with normal life expectancy on the assumption that the member, at the effective date of calculation, is in a normal state of health having regard to his or her age;

**"approved arrangement"**, in relation to the trustees of a scheme, means an arrangement whereby the trustees, on behalf of the person for whom the arrangement is made, effect policies or contracts of insurance that are approved of by the Revenue Commissioners with, and make the appropriate payments under the policies or contracts to, one or more undertakings;

**"contingent benefit"** means a benefit payable under a scheme, other than a payment under section 123(4), to or for the benefit of the surviving civil partner, any dependants of the member civil partner or the personal representative of the member civil partner, if the member civil partner dies while in relevant employment and before attaining any normal pensionable age provided for under the rules of the scheme;

**"defined contribution scheme"** has the meaning assigned to it by section 2(1) (as amended by section 29(1)(a)(ii) of the Social Welfare and Pensions Act 2008) of the Act of 1990;

**"designated benefit"** in relation to a pension adjustment order, means an amount determined by the trustees of a scheme, in accordance with relevant guidelines and by reference to the period and the percentage of the retirement benefit specified in an order under subsection (2);

**"member civil partner"** in relation to a scheme, means a civil partner who is a member of the scheme;

**"normal pensionable age"** means the earliest age at which a member of a scheme is entitled to receive benefits under the rules of the scheme on retirement from relevant employment, disregarding any rules providing for early retirement on grounds of ill health or otherwise;

**"occupational pension scheme"** has the meaning assigned to it by section 2(1) of the Act of 1990;

**"reckonable service"** means service in relevant employment during membership in any scheme;

**"relevant guidelines"** means any relevant guidelines for the time being in force under section 10(1)(c)or(cc) (as amended by section 5 of the Pensions (Amendment) Act 1996, section 47(c) of the Family Law (Divorce) Act 1996, section 13(b) of the Pensions (Amendment) Act 2002 and section 37 of the Social Welfare and Pensions Act 2007) of the Act of 1990;

**"relevant employment"** in relation to a scheme, means any employment, or any period treated as employment, or any period of self-employment to which a scheme applies;

**"retirement benefit"**, in relation to a scheme, means all benefits, other than contingent benefits, payable under the scheme;

**"rules"**, in relation to a scheme, means the provisions of the scheme by whatever name called;

**"scheme"** means a pension scheme;

**"transfer amount"** shall be construed in accordance with subsection (4);

**"undertaking"** has the same meaning as "'insurance undertaking' or 'undertaking'" in section 2(1) (as inserted by section 3(1) of the Insurance Act 2000) of the Insurance Act 1989.

(2) On granting a decree of dissolution or at any other time after it is granted, the court, on application to it in that behalf by either of the civil partners, may, during the lifetime of a member civil partner, make an order providing for the payment, in accordance with this section and sections 122 to 126, to the other civil partner of a benefit consisting of the part of the benefit that is payable (or that, but for the making of the decree, would have been payable) under the scheme and has accrued at the time of the making of the decree, or of the part of that part that the court considers appropriate.

(3) The order under subsection (2) shall specify—

   (a) the period of reckonable service of the member civil partner prior to the granting of the decree to be taken into account, and

   (b) the percentage of the retirement benefit accrued during the period to be paid to the other civil partner.

(4) Where the court makes an order under subsection (2) in favour of a civil partner and payment of the designated benefit concerned has not commenced, the civil partner is entitled to the application in accordance with section 123(1) of an amount of money from the scheme (in this subsection referred to as a "transfer amount") equal to the value of the designated benefit as determined by the trustees of the scheme in accordance with relevant guidelines.

(5) On granting a decree of dissolution or at any time within one year after it is granted, the court, on application to it in that behalf by either of the civil partners, may make an order providing for the payment, on the death of the member civil partner, to the other civil partner of that part of a contingent benefit that is payable (or that, but for the making of the decree, would have been payable) under the scheme, or of the part of that part, that the court considers appropriate.

(6) The court shall not make an order under this section in favour of a civil partner who has registered in a new civil partnership or has married.

(7) The court may make an order under this section in addition to or in substitution in whole or in part for an order under section 117, 118, 119 or 120 and, in deciding whether or not to make a pension adjustment order, the court shall have regard to the question whether proper provision, having regard to the circumstances, exists or can be made for the civil partner who is not a member under those sections.

(8) An order under this section may restrict to a specified extent or exclude the application of section 131 in relation to the order.

## 122    Procedural provisions respecting pension adjustment orders

(1) A person who makes an application under section 121(2) or (5) or an application for an order under section 131(2) in relation to an order under section 121(2) shall give notice of the application to the trustees of the scheme. The court shall, in deciding whether to make the order and in determining the provisions of the order, have regard to representations made by the persons to whom notice has been given under this section or section 141.

(2) An order referred to in subsection (1) ceases to have effect on the entry into a new civil partnership, marriage or death of the applicant.

(3) The court may, in making an order referred to in subsection (1), give to the trustees of the scheme any directions that it considers appropriate, including a direction that would require the trustees not to comply with the rules of the scheme or the Act of 1990.

(4) The registrar or clerk of the court that makes an order referred to in subsection (1) shall cause a copy of the order to be served on the trustees of the scheme.

## 123 Rules respecting payments under schemes

(1) Subject to section 124(4), the trustees of a scheme in respect of which an order has been made under section 121(2) shall, where the conditions set out in subsection (2) are present, apply, in accordance with relevant guidelines, the transfer amount calculated in accordance with those guidelines—

(a) if the trustees and the civil partner so agree, in providing a benefit for or in respect of the civil partner that is of the same actuarial value as the transfer amount, or

(b) in making a payment, at the option of the civil partner—

    (i) to another occupational pension scheme whose trustees agree to accept the payment, or

    (ii) to discharge another payment falling to be made by the trustees under any such other approved arrangement.

(2) The conditions referred to in subsection (1) are:

(a) the court has made an order under section 121(2) in favour of the civil partner;

(b) payment of the designated benefit has not commenced;

(c) the civil partner has applied to the trustees in that behalf; and

(d) the civil partner furnishes the information that the trustees require.

(3) Subject to section 124(4), trustees of a defined contribution scheme in respect of which an order has been made under section 121(2) may, if the civil partner has not made an application under subsections (1) and (2), apply in accordance with relevant guidelines the transfer amount calculated in accordance with those guidelines to make a payment, at their option—

(a) to another occupational pension scheme whose trustees agree to accept the payment, or

(b) to discharge another payment falling to be made by the trustees under any such other approved arrangement.

(4) Subject to section 124(4), the trustees of a scheme in respect of which an order has been made under section 121(2) shall, within 3 months of the death of a member civil partner who dies before the payment of the designated benefit has commenced, provide for the payment to the other civil partner of an amount that is equal to the transfer amount calculated in accordance with relevant guidelines.

(5) Subject to section 124(4), the trustees of a scheme in respect of which an order has been made under section 121(2) may, if the member civil partner ceases to be a member otherwise than on death, apply, in accordance with relevant guidelines, the transfer amount under the scheme, at their option—

(a) if the trustees and the other civil partner so agree, in providing a benefit for or in respect of that civil partner that is of the same actuarial value as the transfer amount, or

(b)  in making a payment, either—

>  (i)  to another occupational pension scheme whose trustees agree to accept the payment, or
>
>  (ii)  to discharge another payment falling to be made by the trustees under any such other approved arrangement.

(6) Subject to section 124(4), the trustees of a scheme in respect of which an order has been made under section 121(2) shall, within 3 months of the death of the civil partner who is not the member and who dies before payment of the designated benefit has commenced, provide for the payment to the personal representative of that civil partner of an amount that is equal to the transfer amount calculated in accordance with relevant guidelines.

(7) Subject to section 124(4), the trustees of a scheme in respect of which an order has been made under section 121(2) shall, within 3 months of the death of the civil partner who is not the member and who dies after payment of the designated benefit has commenced, provide for the payment to the personal representative of that civil partner of an amount that is equal to the actuarial value, calculated in accordance with relevant guidelines, of the part of the designated benefit that, but for the death of that civil partner, would have been payable to him or her during his or her lifetime.

(8) The trustees of a scheme in respect of which an order has been made under section 121(2) or (5) shall, within 12 months of the member civil partner's ceasing to be a member, notify the registrar or clerk of the court and the other civil partner of the cessation, if the trustees have not applied the transfer amount in accordance with any of subsections (1) to (6).

(9) The trustees of a scheme who apply a transfer amount under subsection (3) or (5) shall notify the civil partner who is not the member and the registrar or clerk of the court, giving particulars to that civil partner of the scheme and the transfer amount.

**124  Payments further to orders under section 121**

(1) A benefit payable pursuant to an order made under section 121(2), or a contingent benefit payable pursuant to an order made under section 121(5), is payable out of the resources of the scheme and, unless the order or relevant guidelines provide otherwise, in accordance with the rules of the scheme and those guidelines.

(2) The amount of retirement benefit payable to the member civil partner, or the amount of contingent benefit payable to or in respect of the member civil partner, in accordance with the rules of the relevant scheme shall be reduced by the designated benefit or contingent benefit payable pursuant to an order made under section 121(2) or (5), as the case may be, to the other civil partner.

(3) The amount of contingent benefit payable in accordance with the rules of the scheme in respect of a member civil partner who dies before the payment of the designated benefit payable pursuant to an order under section 121(2) has commenced shall be reduced by the amount of the payment made under section 123(4).

(4) Trustees who make a payment or apply a transfer amount under any of subsections (1) to (7) of section 123 are discharged from any obligation to make further payment or

apply another transfer amount under any of those subsections in respect of the benefit payable pursuant to the order made under section 121(2).

(5) A trustee is not liable for any loss or damage caused by complying with a direction referred to in section 122(3) rather than the rules of the scheme or the Act of 1990.

### 125 Costs

(1) The court may determine the manner in which the costs incurred by the trustees of a scheme further to an order under section 121 are to be borne, including by one or the other of the civil partners or by both of them in the proportions that the court may determine, and in default of a determination, the civil partners shall bear those costs equally.

(2) The court may, on application to it by the trustees, order that an amount ordered to be paid by a civil partner under subsection (1) that has not been paid be deducted from any benefits payable to the civil partner—

    (a) pursuant to an order made under section 121, if the civil partner is the beneficiary of the order; and

    (b) pursuant to the scheme, if the civil partner is the member civil partner.

### 126 Other provisions for orders under section 121

(1) Section 54 of the Act of 1990 and regulations made under that section apply with any necessary modifications to a scheme if proceedings for the grant of a decree of dissolution to which a member civil partner is a party have been instituted, and continue to apply notwithstanding the grant of the decree of dissolution.

(2) For the purposes of this section and sections 121 to 125, the court may, of its own motion, and shall, if so requested by either of the civil partners or another concerned person, direct the trustees of the scheme to provide the civil partners or the other person and the court, within a specified period—

    (a) with a calculation of the value and amount, determined in accordance with relevant guidelines, of the retirement benefit or contingent benefit that is payable or that, but for the making of the order for the decree of dissolution, would have been payable under the scheme and has accrued at the time of making the order, and

    (b) with a calculation of the amount of the contingent benefit that is payable or that, but for the making of the order for the decree of dissolution concerned, would have been payable, under the scheme.

### 127 Applications for provision from estate of deceased civil partner

(1) A civil partner may, after the death of his or her civil partner but not more than 6 months after representation is first granted under the Succession Act 1965 in respect of that civil partner's estate, apply for an order under this section for provision out of the estate.

(2) The court may by order make the provision for the applicant that the court considers appropriate having regard to the rights of any other person having an interest in the

matter, if the court is satisfied that proper provision in the circumstances was not made for the applicant during the lifetime of the deceased for any reason other than conduct by the applicant that, in the opinion of the court, it would in all the circumstances be unjust to disregard.

(3) The court shall not make an order under this section in favour of a civil partner who has registered in a new civil partnership, or has married, since the granting of the decree of dissolution.

(4) In considering whether to make an order under this section, the court shall have regard to all the circumstances of the case, including—

    (a)  any order made under section 117(1)(c) or a property adjustment order made under section 118 in favour of the applicant, and

    (b)  any devise or bequest made by the deceased in favour of the applicant.

(5) The total value for the applicant of the provision made by an order referred to in subsection (4)(a) on the date on which that order was made and an order made under this section shall not exceed any share of the applicant in the estate of the deceased civil partner to which the applicant was entitled or, if the deceased civil partner died intestate as to the whole or part of his or her estate, would have been entitled, if the civil partnership had not been dissolved, under the Succession Act 1965 as amended by Part 8.

(6) The applicant shall give notice of an application under this section to any spouse or other civil partner of the deceased and to any other persons that the court may direct and, in deciding whether to make the order and in determining the provisions of the order, the court shall have regard to any representations made by any of those persons.

(7) The personal representative of a deceased civil partner in respect of whom a decree of dissolution has been granted shall make a reasonable attempt to ensure that notice of the death is brought to the attention of the other civil partner concerned and, where an application is made under this section, that personal representative shall not, without leave of the court, distribute any of the estate of the deceased civil partner until the court makes or refuses to make an order under this section.

(8) A civil partner shall notify the personal representative of the deceased civil partner not later than one month after receipt of the notice referred to in subsection (7) if the other civil partner—

    (a)  intends to apply for an order under this section,

    (b)  has applied for an order under this section and the application is pending, or

    (c)  has successfully obtained an order under this section.

(9) If the civil partner does not notify the personal representative as required by subsection (8), the personal representative may distribute the assets of the deceased civil partner or any part of them amongst the persons entitled to them and is not liable to the civil partner for that distribution.

(10) Nothing in this section prejudices the rights of the civil partner to follow assets into the hands of a person who has received them.

(11) On granting a decree of dissolution or at any other time after it is granted, the court, on application to it in that behalf by either of the civil partners, may make an order that either or both of the civil partners may not, on the death of either of them, apply for an order under this section, if the court considers it just to do so.

(12) In this section, "civil partner" means a civil partner whose civil partnership has been dissolved.

## 128    Orders for sale of property

(1) The court may make an order directing the sale of property specified in the order if—

- (a)  the property is property in which, or in the proceeds of sale of which, either or both of the civil partners has a beneficial interest, either in possession or reversion, and

- (b)  the court makes or has made a secured periodical payments order, a lump sum order or a property adjustment order.

(2) The court shall not exercise its jurisdiction under subsection (1) in a way that would affect a civil partner's right to occupy the shared home by virtue of an order under this Act.

(3) An order under subsection (1) may contain the consequential and supplementary provisions that the court considers appropriate, including provisions—

- (a)  specifying the manner of sale and some or all of the conditions applying to the sale of the property,

- (b)  requiring the property to be offered for sale to a person or class of persons specified in the order,

- (c)  directing that the order, or a specified part of it, not take effect until the occurrence of a specified event or the expiration of a specified period,

- (d)  requiring the making of a payment or payments, whether periodically or in a lump sum, to a specified person out of the proceeds of the sale of the property, and

- (e)  specifying the manner in which the proceeds of the sale of the property are to be disposed of between the civil partners and other persons.

(4) A provision in an order under subsection (1) requiring the making of periodical payments to one of the civil partners out of the proceeds of the sale ceases to have effect on the registration in a new civil partnership, marriage or death of that civil partner, except as respects payments due under it on the date of the registration, marriage or death.

(5) The court shall, in considering whether to make an order under this section or section 118 or 119 with respect to a property in which a civil partner has a beneficial interest or in the proceeds of sale of which the civil partner has a beneficial interest, give to a person who also has a beneficial interest in the property or proceeds an opportunity to make representations with respect to the making and contents of the order.

(6) The representations made under subsection (5) are deemed to be included in section 129 as matters to which the court is required to have regard in proceedings under a provision referred to in that section.

(7) This section does not apply in relation to a shared or family home in which, following the grant of a decree of dissolution, either of the civil partners resides with a new civil partner or spouse.

**129 Provisions relating to certain orders**

(1) In deciding whether to make an order under section 116, 117, 118, 119(1)(a) or (b), 120, 121 to 126, 127 or 131, and in determining the provisions of the order, the court shall ensure that the provision that the court considers proper having regard to the circumstances exists or will be made for the civil partners.

(2) In deciding whether to make an order referred to in subsection (1) and in determining the provisions of the order, the court shall, in particular, have regard to the following matters:

(a) the income, earning capacity, property and other financial resources that each of the civil partners has or is likely to have in the foreseeable future;

(b) the financial needs, obligations and responsibilities that each of the civil partners has or is likely to have in the foreseeable future, whether in the case of the registration of a new civil partnership or marriage or otherwise;

(c) the standard of living enjoyed by the civil partners before the proceedings were instituted or before they commenced to live apart;

(d) the age of the civil partners, the duration of their civil partnership and the length of time during which the civil partners lived with each other after registration of their civil partnership;

(e) any physical or mental disability of either of the civil partners;

(f) the contributions that each of the civil partners has made or is likely to make in the foreseeable future to the welfare of the civil partners, including any contribution made by each of them to the income, earning capacity, property and financial resources of the other, and any contribution made by either of them by looking after the shared home;

(g) the effect on the earning capacity of each of the civil partners of the civil partnership responsibilities assumed by each during the period when they lived with one another after the registration of their civil partnership and the degree to which the future earning capacity of a civil partner is impaired by reason of that civil partner having relinquished or foregone the opportunity of remunerative activity in order to look after the shared home;

(h) any income or benefits to which either of the civil partners is entitled by or under statute;

(i) the conduct of each of the civil partners, if that conduct is such that, in the opinion of the court, it would in all the circumstances be unjust to disregard;

(j) the accommodation needs of both of the civil partners;

(k)  the value to each of the civil partners of any benefit (for example, a benefit under a pension scheme) which, by reason of the decree of dissolution, a civil partner will forfeit the opportunity or possibility of acquiring; and

(l)  the rights of any person other than the civil partners but including a person with whom either civil partner is registered in a new civil partnership or to whom the civil partner is married, or any child to whom either of the civil partners owes an obligation of support.

(3) In deciding whether to make an order under a provision referred to in subsection (1) and in determining the provisions of the order, the court shall have regard to the terms of any separation agreement that the parties have entered into and that is still in force.

(4) The court shall not make an order under a provision referred to in subsection (1) unless it would be in the interests of justice to do so.

## 130    Retrospective periodical payment orders

The court may, if, having regard to all the circumstances of the case, it considers it appropriate to do so, in a periodical payments order, direct that—

(a)  the period in respect of which payments under the order are to be made begins on a specified date that is before the date of the order but after the date of the institution of the proceedings for the grant of the decree of dissolution,

(b)  without prejudice to section 117(1)(c), any payments under the order in respect of the period before the date of the order be paid in one sum and before a specified date, and

(c)  the civil partner making the payments referred to in paragraph (b) deduct a specified amount equal to any payment made by that civil partner to the other civil partner during the period between the making of the order for the grant of the decree of dissolution and the institution of the proceedings.

## 131    Variations etc., of certain orders

(1) This section applies to the following orders:

(a)  a maintenance pending suit order;

(b)  a periodical payments order;

(c)  a secured periodical payments order;

(d)  a lump sum order if and insofar as it provides for the payment of the lump sum by instalments or requires the payment of instalments to be secured;

(e)  an order under section 118(1)(b), (c) or (d) to the extent that the application of this section is not restricted or excluded pursuant to section 118(2);

(f)  an order under section 119(1)(a) or (b);

(g)  a financial compensation order;

(h)  an order under section 121(2), to the extent that the application of this section is not restricted or excluded pursuant to section 121(8); and

(i)  an order under this section.

(2) Any of the following persons may apply under this section with respect to an order referred to in subsection (1):

(a) either of the civil partners concerned;

(b) in the case of the death of a civil partner, another person who has, in the opinion of the court, sufficient interest in the matter; and

(c) in the case of the registration of a new civil partnership or the marriage of either of the civil partners, his or her new civil partner or spouse.

(3) Subject to this section and section 129 and to any restriction or exclusion pursuant to section 118(2) or 121(8), and without prejudice to section 120(6), the court may, on application under subsection (2) and if it considers it proper to do so, having regard to any change in the circumstances of the case and to any new evidence, by order—

(a) vary or discharge the order,

(b) suspend any provision of the order,

(c) suspend temporarily any provision of the order,

(d) revive the operation of a suspended provision,

(e) further vary an order previously varied under this section, and

(f) further suspend or revive the operation of a provision previously suspended or revived under this section.

(4) An order under this section may require the divesting of property vested in a person under an order referred to in subsection (1).

(5) The court's power under subsection (3) to vary, discharge or suspend an order referred to in subsection (1)(e) is subject to any restriction or exclusion specified in that order and is a power—

(a) to vary the settlement to which that order relates in any person's favour or to extinguish or reduce any person's interest under that settlement; and

(b) to make the supplemental provision, including a further property adjustment order or a lump sum order, that the court thinks appropriate in consequence of any variation, extinguishment or reduction made under paragraph (a).

(6) Section 128 applies, with the necessary modifications, to a case where the court makes an order under subsection (5) as it applies to a case where the court makes a property adjustment order.

(7) The court shall not make an order under subsection (5) if it appears to the court that the order could prejudice the rights of a person who is not a civil partner concerned and has acquired a right or interest in consequence of the order referred to in subsection (1)(e).

(8) This section applies, with any necessary modifications, to instruments executed pursuant to orders referred to in subsection (1) as it applies to those orders.

(9) The registrar or clerk of the court shall, as appropriate, lodge a copy of an order made under subsection (3) in relation to a property adjustment order relating to land,

which he or she has certified to be a true copy, with the Property Registration Authority for registration in the Registry of Deeds or Land Registry, as appropriate.

(10) Where a property adjustment order lodged under section 118(4) and duly registered pursuant to section 69(1)(h) of the Registration of Title Act 1964 is varied, discharged, suspended or revived by an order under subsection (3) and the second-mentioned order has been duly lodged for registration pursuant to subsection (9), the Property Registration Authority shall—

(a) amend or cancel accordingly the entry made in the register, pursuant to section 118(4), under the Registration of Title Act 1964, or

(b) note the position in the Registry of Deeds.

**132     Method of making payments under certain orders**

(1) This section applies to an order under section 45, 47, 116, 117, 128 or 131.

(2) The court may by order provide that a payment under an order referred to in subsection (1) be made by the method specified in the order and be subject to the specified terms and conditions that the court considers appropriate.

**133     Stay on certain orders being appealed**

The operation of an order being appealed shall not be stayed unless the court that made the order or to which the appeal is brought directs otherwise, in the case of an appeal brought from an order under section 45, 47, 116, 117(1)(a) or (b) or 131(1)(a), (b) or (c).

**134     Transmission of periodical payments through District Court clerk**

Notwithstanding anything in this Part, section 50 applies in relation to a maintenance pending suit order, a periodical payments order or a secured periodical payments order, or one of those orders affected by an order under section 131, with all necessary modifications, including—

(a) the reference in section 50(4) to the maintenance creditor shall be construed as a reference to the person to whom payments under the relevant order are required to be made;

(b) the other references in section 50 to the maintenance creditor shall be construed as references to the person on whose application the relevant order was made; and

(c) the references in section 50(3) to the maintenance debtor shall be construed as a reference to the person by whom payments under the relevant order are required to be made.

**135     Application of maintenance pending suit and periodical payment orders to certain members of Defence Forces**

(1) The reference in section 98(1)(h) of the Defence Act 1954 to an order for payment of alimony shall be construed as including a reference to a maintenance pending suit order, periodical payments order or secured periodical payments order made under this Act.

(2) The references in section 99 of the Defence Act 1954 to a wife shall be construed as including a reference to a civil partner within the meaning of the Civil Partnership and Certain Rights and Obligations of Cohabitants Act 2010.

**136    Amendment of Enforcement of Court Orders Act 1940**

The references in subsections (1) and (7) of section 8 of the Enforcement of Court Orders Act 1940 to an order shall be construed as including references to a maintenance order, a variation order, a maintenance pending suit order and a periodical payments order made under this Act.

**137    Powers of court in relation to transactions intended to prevent or reduce relief**

(1) In this section—

**"disposition"** means a disposition of property, other than a disposition by will or codicil;

**"relief"** means the financial or other material benefits conferred by an order under section 116, 117, 118, 119(1)(a), (b) or (c), 120, 121 to 126, 127, or 131 (other than an order affecting an order referred to in section 131(1)(e)), and references to defeating a claim for relief are references to—

    (a)  preventing the relief being granted to the person concerned,

    (b)  limiting the relief granted, or

    (c)  frustrating or impeding the enforcement of an order granting relief;

**"reviewable disposition"**, in relation to proceedings for the grant of relief brought by a civil partner, means a disposition made by the other civil partner or another person, but does not include a disposition made for valuable consideration (other than on registration in a new civil partnership or marriage) to a person who, at the time of the disposition, acted in good faith and without notice of an intention on the part of the other civil partner to defeat the claim for relief.

(2) The court, on application made by a person who makes it during the proceedings instituted for the grant of relief, may—

    (a)  if satisfied that the other civil partner concerned or another person, with the intention of defeating the claim for relief, proposes to make a disposition of or transfer out of the jurisdiction or otherwise deal with property, make the order that it thinks fit for the purpose of restraining the other civil partner or person from doing so or otherwise for protecting the claim, or

    (b)  if satisfied that the other civil partner or person has, with that intention, made a reviewable disposition and that, if the disposition were set aside, relief or different relief would be granted to the applicant,

make an order setting aside the disposition.

(3) Where the court has granted relief and the court is satisfied that the other civil partner or person has, with the intention referred to in subsection (2)(a), made a reviewable disposition, it may make an order setting aside the disposition.

(4) A court that makes an order under subsection (2) or (3) shall include in the order any provisions that it considers necessary for the implementation of the order, including provisions requiring the making of any payments or the disposal of any property.

(5) In proceedings on an application made under subsection (2) or (3) with respect to a disposition that took place less than 3 years before the date of the application or with respect to a disposition or other dealing with property that is proposed to be made, there is a presumption, unless the contrary is shown, that the other civil partner or person disposed of or otherwise dealt with the property or proposes to do so with the intention of defeating the applicant's claim for relief if—

(a) in a case referred to in subsection (2)(a), the disposition or other dealing would, apart from this section, have that consequence, or

(b) in any other case, the disposition has had that consequence.

(6) An application shall not be made for an order setting aside a disposition by reason only of subsection (2)(b) or (3) after the expiration of 6 years from the date of the disposition.

**138 Cost of mediation and counseling services**

The costs of mediation services or counselling services provided for a civil partner who is or becomes party to proceedings under this Part are in the discretion of the court.

PART 13
JURISDICTION AND OTHER RELATED MATTERS

**139 Definitions**

In this Part—

"**Circuit Court**" means the Circuit Court when it is exercising its jurisdiction to hear and determine civil partnership law proceedings or transferring civil partnership law proceedings to the High Court;

"**civil partner**" includes, where the context requires, a person who was a civil partner in a partnership that has been dissolved;

"**civil partnership law proceedings**" in relation to a court, means proceedings before a court of competent jurisdiction—

(a) under this Act, with the exception of Part 15,

(b) under the Domestic Violence Act 1996 as amended by Part 9, or

(c) between civil partners under the Partition Act 1868 and the Partition Act 1876, where the fact that they are civil partners of each other is of relevance to the proceedings.

**140 Jurisdiction and venue**

(1) Subject to the other provisions of this section, the Circuit Court has concurrent jurisdiction with the High Court to hear and determine civil partnership law proceedings.

(2) The District Court, and the Circuit Court on appeal from the District Court, have concurrent jurisdiction with the High Court to hear and determine proceedings under sections 45, 46, 47 and 50 except that—

(a) they do not have jurisdiction to make an order under one of those sections for the payment of a periodical sum at a rate greater than 500 per week for support of a civil partner,

(b) they do not have jurisdiction to make an order or direction under one of those sections in a matter in relation to which the High Court has made an order or direction under that section, and

(c) the District Court does not have jurisdiction to make an order or direction under one of those sections in a matter in relation to which the Circuit Court has made an order or direction otherwise than on appeal from the District Court.

(3) The court shall only exercise its jurisdiction in civil partnership law proceedings if a party to the proceedings—

(a) is domiciled in the State on the date on which the proceedings are commenced, or

(b) is ordinarily resident in the State throughout the one-year period that ends on that date.

(4) The jurisdiction conferred on the Circuit Court may be exercised by the judge of the circuit in which a party to the civil partnership law proceedings ordinarily resides or carries on a business, profession or occupation.

(5) The Circuit Court shall transfer proceedings to the High Court, on application to it by a party to the proceedings, if land to which the proceedings relate—

(a) has a rateable valuation that exceeds €254, or

(b) has not been given a rateable valuation or is the subject with other land of a rateable valuation, if the Circuit Court determines that the rateable valuation would exceed €254.

(6) An order made or act done in the course of the proceedings before a transfer under subsection (5) is valid unless discharged or varied by the High Court.

(7) The District Court and the Circuit Court shall transfer to the High Court proceedings under Part 4 in which the value of household chattels exceeding €6,350 is at issue, on application to it by a party to the proceedings.

(8) An order made or act done in the course of the proceedings before a transfer under subsection (7) is valid unless discharged or varied by the High Court.

(9) If a civil partner is a person of unsound mind and there is a committee of the civil partner's estate, the jurisdiction under this section in proceedings under Part 4 may, subject to subsections (5) to (8), be exercised by the court that has appointed the committee.

(10) Subject to subsection (9), the District Court has all the jurisdiction of the High Court to hear and determine—

   (a)  civil partnership law proceedings under Part 4 if—

       (i)  the rateable valuation does not exceed €25, or

      (ii)  the land has not been given a rateable valuation or the land is the subject with other land of a rateable valuation, if the District Court determines that the rateable valuation would not exceed that amount,

   and

   (b)  a question arising out of section 34 where the value of the household chattels intended to be disposed of or removed or actually disposed of or removed does not exceed €6,350 or where the chattels are or immediately before the disposal or removal were in a shared home if—

       (i)  the rateable valuation of the shared home does not exceed €25, or

      (ii)  the shared home has not been given a rateable valuation or the shared home is the subject with other land of a rateable valuation, if the District Court determines that the rateable valuation would exceed that amount.

## 141    Notice of civil partnership law proceedings

A person bringing civil partnership law proceedings shall give notice of them to—

   (a)  the other civil partner or the civil partners concerned, and

   (b)  another person if the court so specifies.

## 142    Particulars of property

(1) In civil partnership law proceedings under section 45, 46, 47, 50, 117, 118, 119(1)(a) or (b), 120, 121 to 126, 127 or 131, each of the civil partners shall give to the other the particulars of his or her property or income that may be reasonably required for the purposes of the proceedings.

(2) The court may direct a person who fails or refuses to comply with subsection (1) to comply with it.

## 143    Hearing of proceedings

The Circuit Court shall sit to hear and determine civil partnership law proceedings in a different place or at different times or on different days from those on which the ordinary sittings of the Circuit Court are held.

## 144    Conduct of proceedings

(1) Civil partnership law proceedings shall be as informal as is practicable and consistent with the administration of justice.

(2) A judge sitting to hear and determine civil partnership law proceedings, and a barrister or solicitor appearing in the proceedings, shall not wear a wig or a gown.

## 145    Privacy

Subject to the provisions of section 40 of the Civil Liability and Courts Act 2004, civil partnership law proceedings shall be heard otherwise than in public.

**146    Costs**

The costs in civil partnership law proceedings are at the discretion of the court.

**147    Rules of court**

Rules of court shall provide for the documentation required for the commencement of civil partnership law proceedings in a summary manner.

PART 14

OTHER CONSEQUENTIAL AMENDMENTS, ETC.

**148    Application and amendment of Pensions Act 1990**

(1) Section 5(4) of the Pensions Act 1990 (as amended by the Pensions (Amendment) Act 1996 and the Family Law (Divorce) Act 1996) applies and has effect in relation to sections 121 to 126 and 187 to 192 as it applies and has effect by virtue of section 47 of the Family Law (Divorce) Act 1996 in relation to section 17 of that Act, with the following modifications:

  (a)  a reference to section 12 of the Family Law Act 1995 or section 17 of the Family Law (Divorce) Act 1996 is to be construed as a reference to sections 121 to 126 and sections 187 to 192;

  (b)  the reference in paragraph (c) to the Family Law Act 1995 or the Family Law (Divorce) Act 1996 is to be construed as a reference to the Civil Partnership and Certain Rights and Obligations of Cohabitants Act 2010;

  (c)  the references to subsections (1), (2), (3), (5), (6), (7), (8), (10) and (25) of section 12 of the Family Law Act 1995 and section 17 of the Family Law (Divorce) Act 1996 are to be construed as references to sections 121(1), (2) and (5), 123(1), (2), (3), (4), (5) and (7) and 126(2),or sections 187(1), (2) and (5), 189(1), (2), (3), (4), (5) and (7) and 192, as the case may be, of the Civil Partnership and Certain Rights and Obligations of Cohabitants Act 2010, respectively; and

  (d)  the reference to section 2 of the Family Law Act 1995 or the Family Law (Divorce) Act 1996 is to be construed as a reference to section 109 or 187.

(2) Subsection 10(1)(cc) (as amended by section 5 of the Pensions (Amendment) Act 1996 and section 47(c) of the Family Law (Divorce) Act 1996) of the Pensions Act 1990, is amended by substituting "and on the provisions of the Family Law Act 1995, the Family Law (Divorce) Act 1996 and the Civil Partnership and Certain Rights and Obligations of Cohabitants Act 2010, relating to pension schemes (within the meaning of section 2 of the Family Law Act 1995, section 2 of the Family Law (Divorce) Act 1996 and section 109 and 187 of the Civil Partnership and Certain Rights and Obligations of Cohabitants Act 2010)"for "and on the provisions of the Family Law Act 1995, and the Family Law (Divorce) Act 1996, relating to pension schemes (within the meaning of section 2 of the Family Law Act 1995 and section 2 of the Family Law (Divorce) Act 1996)".

## 149    Definition

In this section and sections 150 to 157, "Act of 1996" means the Family Law (Divorce) Act 1996.

## 150    Amendment of section 2 of Act of 1996

Section 2(1) of the Act of 1996 is amended by inserting the following definitions:[1]

---

**Notes**

1    See the amended Act.

---

## 151    Amendment of section 13 of Act of 1996

Section 13(5) of the Act of 1996 is amended—

    (a)  in paragraph (a)—

        (i)  by inserting "or registration in a civil partnership", after "upon the remarriage", and

        (ii)  by inserting "or civil partnership registration" after "date of the remarriage",

    and

    (b)  in paragraph (b) by inserting "or registers in a civil partnership" after "remarries".

## 152    Amendment of section 14 of Act of 1996

Section 14(3) of the Act of 1996 is amended by inserting "or registers in a civil partnership" after "remarries".

## 153    Amendment of section 16 of Act of 1996

Section 16(2) of the Act of 1996 is amended—

    (a)  in paragraph (b), by inserting ", registration in a civil partnership" before "or death", and

    (b)  in paragraph (c), by inserting "or registered in a civil partnership" after "remarried".

## 154    Amendment of section 17 of Act of 1996

Section 17 of the Act of 1996 is amended—

    (a)  in subsection (19) by inserting "or registration in a civil partnership" after "remarriage", and

    (b)  in subsection (23)(a) by inserting "or registered in a civil partnership" after "remarried".

## 155    Amendment of section 18 of Act of 1996

Section 18 of the Act of 1996 is amended—

- (a) in subsection (2) by inserting "or registered in a civil partnership" after "remarried", and

- (b) in subsection (5) by inserting ", civil partner or former civil partner" after "the spouse" wherever it appears.

## 156    Amendment of section 19 of Act of 1996

Section 19(4) of the Act of 1996 is amended—

- (a) by inserting "or registration in a civil partnership" before "of that spouse", and

- (b) by inserting "or civil partnership registration" after "remarriage" at the end.

## 157    Amendment of section 20 of Act of 1996

Section 20(2)(b) of the Act of 1996 is amended by inserting "or registration in a civil partnership" after "remarriage".

## 158    Definition

In this section and sections 159 to 167, "Act of 1995" means the Family Law Act 1995.

## 159    Amendment of section 2 of Act of 1995

Section 2(1) of the Act of 1995 is amended by inserting the following definitions:[1]

---

**Notes**

1   See the amended Act.

---

## 160    Amendment of section 8 of Act of 1995

Section 8(5) of the Act of 1995 is amended—

- (a) in paragraph (a)—

  - (i) by inserting "or registration in a civil partnership" before "of the spouse", and

  - (ii) by inserting "or civil partnership registration" after "date of the remarriage",

and

- (b) in paragraph (b), by inserting "or registers in a civil partnership" after "remarries".

## 161    Amendment of section 9 of Act of 1995

Section 9(3) of the Act of 1995 is amended by inserting "or registers in a civil partnership" after "remarries".

**162     Amendment of section 11 of Act of 1995**

Section 11(2) of the Act of 1995 is amended—

(a)   in paragraph (b) by inserting ", registration in a civil partnership" before "or death", and

(b)   in paragraph (c) by inserting "or registered in a civil partnership" after "remarried".

**163     Amendment of section 12 of Act of 1995**

Section 12 of the Act of 1995 is amended—

(a)   in subsection (19) by inserting "or registration in a civil partnership" after "remarriage", and

(b)   in subsection (23)(a) by inserting "or registered in a civil partnership" after "remarried".

**164     Amendment of section 15 of Act of 1995**

Section 15(4) of the Act of 1995 is amended—

(a)   by inserting "or registration in a civil partnership" before "of that spouse", and

(b)   by inserting "or civil partnership registration" after "remarriage" in the last line.

**165     Amendment of section 15A of Act of 1995**

Section 15A(2) (inserted by section 52(g) of the Family Law (Divorce) Act 1996) of the Act of 1995 is amended by inserting "or registered in a civil partnership" after "remarried".

**166     Amendment of section 23 of Act of 1995**

Section 23 of the Act of 1995 is amended—

(a)   in subsection (2)(d)—

   (i)    by substituting "Where a person" for "Where a spouse",

   (ii)   by inserting "or registered in a civil partnership" after "remarried", and

   (iii)  by substituting "of that person" for "of that spouse" wherever it appears,

(b)   in subsection (5), by inserting "or registration in a civil partnership" after "the remarriage", and

(c)   in subsection (6)—

   (i)    in paragraph (b), by inserting "or registration in a civil partnership" after "remarriage" wherever it appears, and

   (ii)   in paragraph (c), by inserting "or registers in a civil partnership" after "remarries".

**167     Amendment of section 25 of Act of 1995**

(1) Section 25(2) of the Act of 1995 is amended by inserting "or registered in a civil partnership" after "remarried".

(2) Section 25(6) of the Act of 1995 is amended—

    (a)  by inserting ", or civil partner (if any)" after "spouse (if any)", and

    (b)  by inserting "or civil partner" after "representation made by the spouse".

### 168    Property rights

The Acts specified in Part 3 of the Schedule are amended as indicated in that Schedule.

### 169    Redress provisions

The Acts specified in Part 4 of the Schedule are amended as indicated in that Schedule.

### 170    Other miscellaneous provisions

The Acts specified in Part 5 of the Schedule are amended as indicated in that Schedule.

PART 15

COHABITANTS

### 171    Definitions

In this Part—

"cohabitant" has the meaning assigned to it in section 172;

"court" means the High Court, the Circuit Court or the District Court;

"dependent child", in relation to a cohabitant or a couple of cohabitants, means any child of whom both the cohabitants are the parents and who is—

    (a)  under the age of 18 years, or

    (b)  18 years of age or over and is—

        (i)  receiving full-time education or instruction at any university, college, school or other educational establishment and is under the age of 23 years, or

        (ii)  incapable of taking care of his or her own needs because of a mental or physical disability.

### 172    Cohabitant and qualified cohabitant

(1) For the purposes of this Part, a cohabitant is one of 2 adults (whether of the same or the opposite sex) who live together as a couple in an intimate and committed relationship and who are not related to each other within the prohibited degrees of relationship or married to each other or civil partners of each other.

(2) In determining whether or not 2 adults are cohabitants, the court shall take into account all the circumstances of the relationship and in particular shall have regard to the following:

    (a)  the duration of the relationship;

    (b)  the basis on which the couple live together;

    (c)  the degree of financial dependence of either adult on the other and any agreements in respect of their finances;

    (d)  the degree and nature of any financial arrangements between the adults including any joint purchase of an estate or interest in land or joint acquisition of personal property;

    (e)  whether there are one or more dependent children;

    (f)  whether one of the adults cares for and supports the children of the other; and

    (g)  the degree to which the adults present themselves to others as a couple.

(3) For the avoidance of doubt a relationship does not cease to be an intimate relationship for the purpose of this section merely because it is no longer sexual in nature.

(4) For the purposes of this section, 2 adults are within a prohibited degree of relationship if—

    (a)  they would be prohibited from marrying each other in the State, or

    (b)  they are in a relationship referred to in the Third Schedule to the Civil Registration Act 2004 inserted by section 26 of this Act.

(5) For the purposes of this Part, a qualified cohabitant means an adult who was in a relationship of cohabitation with another adult and who, immediately before the time that that relationship ended, whether through death or otherwise, was living with the other adult as a couple for a period—

    (a)  of 2 years or more, in the case where they are the parents of one or more dependent children, and

    (b)  of 5 years or more, in any other case.

(6) Notwithstanding subsection (5), an adult who would otherwise be a qualified cohabitant is not a qualified cohabitant if—

    (a)  one or both of the adults is or was, at any time during the relationship concerned, an adult who was married to someone else, and

    (b)  at the time the relationship concerned ends, each adult who is or was married has not lived apart from his or her spouse for a period or periods of at least 4 years during the previous 5 years.

## 173    Application for redress in respect of economically dependent qualified cohabitant

(1) A qualified cohabitant may, subject to any agreement under section 202, apply to the court, on notice to the other cohabitant, for an order under sections 174, 175 and 187 or any of them.

(2) If the qualified cohabitant satisfies the court that he or she is financially dependent on the other cohabitant and that the financial dependence arises from the relationship or the ending of the relationship, the court may, if satisfied that it is just and equitable to do so in all the circumstances, make the order concerned.

(3) In determining whether or not it is just and equitable to make an order in all the circumstances, the court shall have regard to—

(a)  the financial circumstances, needs and obligations of each qualified cohabitant existing as at the date of the application or which are likely to arise in the future,

(b)  subject to subsection (5), the rights and entitlements of any spouse or former spouse,

(c)  the rights and entitlements of any civil partner or former civil partner,

(d)  the rights and entitlements of any dependent child or of any child of a previous relationship of either cohabitant,

(e)  the duration of the parties' relationship, the basis on which the parties entered into the relationship and the degree of commitment of the parties to one another,

(f)  the contributions that each of the cohabitants made or is likely to make in the foreseeable future to the welfare of the cohabitants or either of them including any contribution made by each of them to the income, earning capacity or property and financial resources of the other,

(g)  any contributions made by either of them in looking after the home,

(h)  the effect on the earning capacity of each of the cohabitants of the responsibilities assumed by each of them during the period they lived together as a couple and the degree to which the future earning capacity of a qualified cohabitant is impaired by reason of that qualified cohabitant having relinquished or foregone the opportunity of remunerative activity in order to look after the home,

(i)  any physical or mental disability of the qualified cohabitant, and

(j)  the conduct of each of the cohabitants, if the conduct is such that, in the opinion of the court, it would be unjust to disregard it.

(4) The court may order that notice be given to any other person that it specifies and may hear the other person on the terms and in respect of the matters it thinks fit in the interests of justice before making an order referred to in this section.

(5) The court shall not make an order referred to in this section in favour of a qualified cohabitant that would affect any right of any person to whom the other cohabitant is or was married.

(6) The court may, on the application of the qualified cohabitant or the other cohabitant, if it considers it proper to do so having regard to any change in the circumstances of the case and to any new evidence, including any change in the circumstances occasioned by a variation by another order of the court made in favour of a person to whom the other cohabitant is or was married, by order—

(a)  vary or discharge an order under section 175 or 187,

(b)  suspend any provision of such an order,

(c)  suspend temporarily any provision of such an order,

(d)  revive the operation of a suspended provision,

(e)  further vary an order previously varied under this section, or

(f)  further suspend or revive the operation of a provision previously suspended or revived under this section.

(7) Where the court makes an order under section 174, 175(1)(c) or 187 in favour of a qualified cohabitant, the court may, in the same proceedings or at any later date, on the application of either of the qualified cohabitants concerned, order that either or both of them shall not, on the death of the other, be entitled to apply for an order under section 194.

(8) If the order under section 174, 175(1)(c) or 187 referred to in subsection (7) has been made but not yet executed at the time that the order is made under subsection (7), the order under subsection (7) shall not take effect until the execution of that other order.

## 174    Property adjustment orders

(1) An order under this section may provide for one or more of the following matters:

(a)  the transfer by either of the cohabitants to or for the benefit of the other, of specified property in which the cohabitant has an interest either in possession or reversion;

(b)  the settlement to the satisfaction of the court of specified property in which the cohabitant has an interest either in possession or reversion, for the benefit of the other cohabitant or of a dependent child;

(c)  the variation for the benefit of either of the cohabitants or of a dependent child of an agreement referred to in section 202 (subject to section 202(4)) or another settlement (including one made by will or codicil) made on the cohabitants; and

(d)  the extinguishment or reduction of the interest of either of the cohabitants under an agreement referred to in section 202 (subject to section 202(4)).

(2) Before making an order under this section, the court shall have regard to whether in all the circumstances it would be practicable for the financial needs of the qualified cohabitant to be met by an order made under section 175 or 187, having regard to all the circumstances, including the likelihood of a future change of circumstances of either of the qualified cohabitants.

## 175    Compensatory maintenance orders

(1) The court, on application to it in that behalf by the qualified cohabitant, may, during the lifetime of either of the cohabitants, make one or more of the following orders:

(a)  an order that either of the cohabitants make to the other the periodical payments in the amounts, during the period and at the times that may be specified in the order;

(b)  an order that either of the cohabitants secure to the other, to the satisfaction of the court, the periodical payments of the amounts, during the period and at the times that may be specified in the order; and

(c)  an order that either of the cohabitants make to the other a lump sum payment or lump sum payments of the amount or amounts and at the time or times that may be specified in the order.

(2) The court may order a qualified cohabitant to pay a lump sum to the other qualified cohabitant to meet any liabilities or expenses reasonably incurred by the other qualified cohabitant in maintaining himself or herself before the making of an application by the other qualified cohabitant for an order under subsection (1).

(3) An order under this section for the payment of a lump sum may provide for the payment of the lump sum by instalments of the amounts that may be specified in the order and may require the payment of the instalments to be secured to the satisfaction of the court.

(4) The period specified in an order under subsection (1)(a) or (b) shall begin not earlier than the date of the application for the order and shall end not later than the date of death of the first qualified cohabitant to die.

(5) An order made under subsection (1)(a) or (b) ceases to have effect on the marriage or registration in a civil partnership, or in a legal relationship that is the subject of an order under section 5, of the qualified cohabitant in whose favour the order was made, except as respects payments due under it on the date of the marriage or registration.

(6) The court shall not make an order under this section in favour of a qualified cohabitant who has married or registered in a civil partnership, or in a legal relationship that is the subject of an order under section 5.

(7) The court that makes an order under subsection (1)(a) shall, in the same proceedings, make an attachment of earnings order under section 176 to secure payments under the order if it is satisfied, after taking into consideration any representations on the matter made to it by the qualified cohabitant ordered to make payments under that subsection, that—

(a)  the order is desirable to secure payments under an order under subsection (1)(a) and any variations and affirmations of that order, and

(b)  the person against whom the attachment of earnings order is made is a person to whom earnings fall to be paid.

## 176    Attachment of earnings order

(1) For the purposes of this section and sections 177 to 186—

"**antecedent order**" means an order under section 175;

"**attachment of earnings order**" means an order directing that an employer deduct from the maintenance debtor's earnings, at the times specified in the order, periodical deductions of the appropriate amounts specified in the order, having regard to the normal deduction rate and the protected earnings rate;

"**employer**" includes a trustee of a pension scheme under which the maintenance debtor is receiving periodical pension benefits;

"**maintenance creditor**" in relation to an attachment of earnings order, means the qualified cohabitant who applied for the order;

"**maintenance debtor**" means a qualified cohabitant who is required by an antecedent order to make payments;

"**normal deduction rate**" means the rate at which the court considers it reasonable that the earnings to which the attachment of earnings order relates should be applied in satisfying an antecedent order, not exceeding the rate that appears to the court to be necessary for—

(a) securing payment of the sums falling due from time to time under the antecedent order, and

(b) securing payment within a reasonable period of any sums already due and unpaid under the antecedent order and any costs incurred in proceedings relating to the antecedent order payable by the maintenance debtor;

"**protected earnings rate**" means the rate below which, having regard to the needs of the maintenance debtor, the court considers it proper that the relevant earnings should not be reduced by a payment made in pursuance of the attachment of earnings order.

(2) The court may, on application to it in that behalf, make an attachment of earnings order if it is satisfied that the maintenance debtor is a person to whom earnings fall to be paid and that the order is desirable to secure payments under the antecedent order and any amendments, variations and affirmations of it.

(3) The court that makes an antecedent order, or an order that makes, varies or affirms on appeal an antecedent order, shall make an attachment of earnings order in the same proceedings if it is satisfied of the things mentioned in subsection (2).

(4) A person to whom an attachment of earnings order is directed shall pay the amounts ordered to be deducted to the maintenance creditor or to the District Court clerk specified in the order for transmission to the maintenance creditor.

(5) Before deciding whether to make or refuse to make an attachment of earnings order, the court shall give the maintenance debtor an opportunity to make representations, and shall have regard to any representations made, relating to whether the maintenance debtor—

(a) is a person to whom earnings fall to be paid, and

(b) would make the payments to which the relevant order relates.

(6) The court shall include in an attachment of earnings order the particulars required so that the person to whom the order is directed may identify the maintenance debtor.

(7) Payments under an attachment of earnings order are in lieu of payments of the like amount under the antecedent order that have not been made and that, but for the attachment of earnings order, would fall to be made under the antecedent order.

## 177    Compliance with attachment of earnings order

(1) The court registrar or court clerk specified in the attachment of earnings order shall cause the order to be served on the person to whom it is directed and on any person who subsequently becomes the maintenance debtor's employer and of whom the registrar or clerk becomes aware.

(2) The service may be effected by leaving the order or a copy of it at the person's residence or place of business in the State, or by sending the order or a copy of it, by registered prepaid post, to that residence or place of business.

(3) A person to whom an attachment of earnings order is directed shall comply with it if it is served on him or her but is not liable for non-compliance before 10 days have elapsed since the service.

(4) If a person to whom an attachment of earnings order is directed is not the maintenance debtor's employer or ceases to be the maintenance debtor's employer, the person shall, within 10 days from the service or the date of cesser, give notice of that fact to the court.

(5) The person shall give to the maintenance debtor a statement in writing of the total amount of every deduction made from a maintenance debtor's earnings in compliance with an attachment of earnings order.

## 178 Application of sums received by clerk

Payments made to a court clerk under an attachment of earnings order shall, when transmitted by the clerk to the maintenance creditor, be deemed to be payments made by the maintenance debtor so as to discharge—

(a) firstly, any sums payable under the antecedent order, and

(b) secondly, any costs in proceedings relating to the antecedent order payable by the maintenance debtor when the attachment of earnings order was made or last varied.

## 179 Statement as to earnings

(1) In relation to an attachment of earnings order or an application for one, the court may, before or at the hearing or while the order is in force, order—

(a) the maintenance debtor to give to the court, within a specified period, a signed statement in writing specifying—

(i) the name and address of every employer of the maintenance debtor,

(ii) particulars as to the debtor's earnings and expected earnings, and resources and needs, and

(iii) particulars for enabling the employers to identify the maintenance debtor,

(b) a person appearing to the court to be an employer of the maintenance debtor to give to the court, within a specified period, a statement signed by the person, or on his or her behalf, of specified particulars of the debtor's earnings and expected earnings.

(2) Notice of an application for an attachment of earnings order served on a maintenance debtor may include a requirement that the maintenance debtor give to the court, within the period and in the manner specified in the notice, a statement in writing of the matters referred to in subsection (1)(a) and of any other matters which are or may be relevant to the determination of the normal deduction rate and the protected earnings rate to be specified in the order.

(3) In any proceedings in relation to an attachment of earnings order, a statement given to the court in compliance with an order under paragraph (a) or (b) of subsection (1) or with a requirement under subsection (2) is admissible as evidence of the facts stated in it and a document purporting to be such a statement is deemed, unless the contrary is shown, to be a statement so given.

### 180    Notification of changes of employment and earnings

Where an attachment of earnings order is in force—

(a) the maintenance debtor shall notify in writing the court that made the order of every occasion on which he or she leaves employment, or becomes employed or reemployed, not later than 10 days after doing so,

(b) the maintenance debtor shall, on any occasion on which he or she becomes employed or re-employed, include in the notification particulars of his or her earnings and expected earnings, and

(c) any person who becomes an employer of the maintenance debtor and who knows that the order is in force and by which court it was made shall, within 10 days of the later of the date of becoming an employer of the maintenance debtor and the date of acquiring the knowledge, notify the court in writing that he or she has become an employer, and include in the notification a statement of the debtor's earnings and expected earnings.

### 181    Power to determine whether particular payments are earnings

(1) Where an attachment of earnings order is in force, the court that made the order shall, on the application of the maintenance debtor's employer, the maintenance debtor or the person to whom payments are being made under the order, determine whether payments or portions of payments being made to the maintenance debtor that are of a class or description specified in the application are earnings for the purpose of the order.

(2) Where an application is made by the employer under subsection (1), the employer is not liable for non-compliance with the order as respects any payments or portions of payments of the class or description specified by the application that he or she makes while the application, a determination in relation to it or an appeal from the determination is pending.

(3) Subsection (2) does not apply if the employer subsequently withdraws the application or abandons the appeal.

### 182    Persons in service of State, local authority, etc

(1) This section applies when a maintenance debtor is in the service of the State, a local authority within the meaning of the Local Government Act 1941, a harbour authority within the meaning of the Harbours Acts 1946 to 2005, the Health Service Executive, a vocational education committee established by the Vocational Education Act 1930, a committee of agriculture established by the Agriculture Act 1931, or another body if his or her earnings are paid directly out of moneys paid by the Oireachtas or from the Central Fund, or is a member of either House of the Oireachtas.

(2) For the purposes of sections 176 to 186, the following officers are regarded as being the employers of the maintenance debtor and the earnings paid to the maintenance debtor out of the Central Fund or out of moneys provided by the Oireachtas are regarded as having been paid by them:

(a) in the case where the maintenance debtor is employed in a department, office, organisation, service, undertaking or other body, its chief officer, or any other officer that may be designated from time to time by the Minister of the Government by whom that body is administered;

(b) in the case where the maintenance debtor is in the service of an authority or body, its chief officer; and

(c) in any other case, where the maintenance debtor is paid out of the Central Fund or out of moneys provided by the Oireachtas, the Secretary of the Department of Finance or any other officer that may be designated from time to time by the Minister for Finance.

(3) A question that arises in proceedings for or arising out of an attachment of earnings order as to which body employs a maintenance debtor may be referred to and determined by the Minister for Finance, but he or she is not obliged to consider the reference unless it is made by the court.

(4) A document purporting to contain a determination by the Minister for Finance under subsection (3) and to be signed by an officer of that Minister shall, in any proceedings mentioned in that subsection, be admissible in evidence and be deemed, unless the contrary is shown, to contain an accurate statement of that determination.

**183    Discharge, variations and lapse of attachment of earnings order**

(1) The court that made an attachment of earnings order may, if it thinks fit, on the application of the maintenance creditor, the maintenance debtor or the clerk on whose application the order was made, make an order discharging or varying that order.

(2) The employer on whom an order varying an attachment of earnings order is served shall comply with it but is not liable for noncompliance before 10 days have elapsed since the service.

(3) If an employer affected by an attachment of earnings order ceases to be the maintenance debtor's employer, the order lapses insofar as that employer is concerned, except as respects deductions from earnings paid by the employer after the cesser and payment to the maintenance creditor of deductions from earnings made at any time by that employer.

(4) The lapse of an order under subsection (3) does not prevent its remaining in force for other purposes.

**184    Cesser of attachment of earnings order**

(1) An attachment of earnings order ceases to have effect upon the discharge of the relevant antecedent order, except as regards payments under the attachment of earnings order in respect of any time before the date of the discharge.

(2) The clerk or registrar of the court that made the attachment of earnings order shall give notice of a cesser to the employer.

## 185    Other remedies

(1) Where an attachment of earnings order has been made, any proceedings commenced under subsection (1) of section 8 of the Enforcement of Court Orders Act 1940 for the enforcement of the relevant antecedent order lapses and any warrant or order issued or made under that subsection ceases to have effect.

(2) An attachment of earnings order ceases to have effect on the making of an order under section 8 of the Enforcement of Court Orders Act 1940 for the enforcement of the relevant antecedent order.

## 186    Enforcement

(1) A maintenance creditor who fails to obtain a sum of money due under an attachment of earnings order, or the clerk to whom the sum falls to be paid, may sue for the sum as a simple contract debt in any court of competent jurisdiction, if the failure to obtain the sum is caused by—

(a) a person failing, without reasonable excuse, to comply with section 177(3) or (4), or 180, or an order under section 179 or 183(2), or

(b) a person, without reasonable excuse, giving a false or misleading statement under section 179(1) or notification under section 180.

(2) A person who gives to a court a statement pursuant to section 179 or a notification under section 180 that he or she knows to be false or misleading commits an offence and is liable on summary conviction to [a class C fine]¹ or to imprisonment for a term not exceeding six months or to both.

(3) A person who contravenes section 177(3) commits an offence and is liable on summary conviction to [a class E fine]².

---

### Notes

1   Subsection (2) amended by the Civil Law (Miscellaneous Provisions) Act 2011, s 61(d)(i).

2   Subsection (3) amended by the Civil Law (Miscellaneous Provisions) Act 2011, s 61(d)(ii).

---

## 187    Pension adjustment orders

(1) In this section and sections 188 to 192—

"**Act of 1990**" means the Pensions Act 1990;

"**active member**" in relation to a scheme, means a member of the scheme who is in reckonable service;

"**actuarial value**" means the equivalent cash value of a benefit (including, where appropriate, provision for any revaluation of the benefit) under a scheme calculated by reference to appropriate financial assumptions and making due allowance for the probability of survival to normal pensionable age and beyond in accordance with normal life expectancy on the assumption that the member, at the effective date of calculation, is in a normal state of health having regard to his or her age;

"**approved arrangement**", in relation to the trustees of a scheme, means an arrangement whereby the trustees, on behalf of the person for whom the arrangement is made, effect policies or contracts of insurance that are approved of by the Revenue Commissioners with, and make the appropriate payments under the policies or contracts to, one or more undertakings;

"**contingent benefit**" means a benefit payable under a scheme, other than a payment under section 189(4), to or for the benefit of the surviving qualified cohabitant (if the scheme so permits) or to or for the benefit of, any dependants of the member qualified cohabitant or the personal representative of the member qualified cohabitant, if the member qualified cohabitant dies while in relevant employment and before attaining any normal pensionable age provided for under the rules of the scheme;

"**defined contribution scheme**" has the meaning assigned to it by section 2(1) (as amended by section 29(1)(a)(ii) of the Social Welfare and Pensions Act 2008) of the Act of 1990;

"**designated benefit**" in relation to a pension adjustment order, means an amount determined by the trustees of a scheme, in accordance with relevant guidelines and by reference to the period and the percentage of the retirement benefit specified in an order under subsection (2);

"**member qualified cohabitant**" in relation to a scheme, means a qualified cohabitant who is a member of the scheme;

"**normal pensionable age**" means the earliest age at which a member of a scheme is entitled to receive benefits under the rules of the scheme on retirement from relevant employment, disregarding any rules providing for early retirement on grounds of ill health or otherwise;

"**occupational pension scheme**" has the meaning assigned to it by section 2(1) of the Act of 1990;

"**reckonable service**" means service in relevant employment during membership in any scheme;

"**relevant guidelines**" means any relevant guidelines for the time being in force under section 10(1)(c)or(cc) (as amended by section 5 of the Pensions (Amendment) Act 1996, section 47(c) of the Family Law (Divorce) Act 1996, section 13(b) of the Pensions (Amendment) Act 2002 and section 37 of the Social Welfare and Pensions Act 2007) of the Act of 1990;

"**relevant employment**" in relation to a scheme, means any employment, or any period treated as employment, or any period of self-employment to which a scheme applies;

"**retirement benefit**", in relation to a scheme, means all benefits, other than contingent benefits, payable under the scheme;

"**rules**", in relation to a scheme, means the provisions of the scheme by whatever name called;

**"scheme"** means—

(a) an occupational pension scheme within the meaning of the Pensions Act 1990,

(b) an annuity contract approved by the Revenue Commissioners under section 784 of the Taxes Consolidation Act 1997, or a contract so approved under section 785 of that Act,

(c) a trust scheme, or part of a trust scheme, approved under section 784(4) or 785(5) of that Act,

(d) a policy or contract of assurance approved by the Revenue Commissioners under Chapter 1 of Part 30 of the Taxes Consolidation Act 1997, or

(e) another scheme or arrangement, including a personal pension plan and a scheme or arrangement established by or pursuant to statute or instrument made under statute other than under the Social Welfare Acts, that provides or is intended to provide either or both of the following:

  (i) benefits for a person who is a member of the scheme or arrangement upon retirement at normal pensionable age or upon earlier or later retirement or upon leaving or upon the ceasing of the relevant employment, and

  (ii) benefits for the widow, widower or dependants of the person referred to in subparagraph (i), for his or her civil partner or the person that was his or her civil partner until the death of the person referred to in subparagraph (i), for his or her qualified cohabitant or the person that was his or her qualified cohabitant until the death of the person referred to in subparagraph (i) or for any other persons, on the death of that person;

**"transfer amount"** shall be construed in accordance with subsection (4);

**"undertaking"** has the same meaning as "'insurance undertaking' or 'undertaking'" in section 2(1) (as inserted by section 3(1) of the Insurance Act 2000) of the Insurance Act 1989.

(2) The court, on application to it in that behalf by either of the qualified cohabitants, may, during the lifetime of a member qualified cohabitant, make an order providing for the payment, in accordance with this section and sections 188 to 192, to the other qualified cohabitant of a benefit consisting of the part of the benefit that is payable under the scheme and has accrued at the time of the making of the order, or of the part of that part, that the court considers appropriate.

(3) The order under subsection (2) shall specify—

(a) the period of reckonable service of the member qualified cohabitant to be taken into account, and

(b) the percentage of the retirement benefit accrued during the period to be paid to the other qualified cohabitant.

(4) Where the court makes an order under subsection (2) in favour of a qualified cohabitant and payment of the designated benefit concerned has not commenced, the qualified cohabitant is entitled to the application in accordance with section 189(1) of an amount of money from the scheme (in this subsection referred to as a "transfer amount")

equal to the value of the designated benefit as determined by the trustees of the scheme in accordance with relevant guidelines.

(5) The court, on application to it in that behalf by either of the qualified cohabitants, may make an order providing for the payment, on the death of the member qualified cohabitant, to the other qualified cohabitant of that part of a contingent benefit that is payable under the scheme, or of the part of that part, that the court considers appropriate.

(6) In deciding whether or not to make a pension adjustment order, the court shall have regard to whether proper provision, having regard to the circumstances, exists or can be made for the qualified cohabitant who is not a member under section 175.

### 188  Procedural provisions respecting pension adjustment orders

(1) A person who makes an application under section 187(2) or (5) shall give notice of the application to the trustees of the scheme. The court shall, in deciding whether to make the order and in determining the provisions of the order, have regard to representations made by the persons to whom notice has been given under this section.

(2) An order referred to in subsection (1) ceases to have effect on the entry into a civil partnership, marriage or death of the person in whose favour the order was made.

(3) The court may, in making an order referred to in subsection (1), give to the trustees of the scheme any directions that it considers appropriate, including a direction that would require the trustees not to comply with the rules of the scheme or the Act of 1990.

(4) Notwithstanding subsection (3), a direction given under that subsection shall not permit a payment under section 187(5) unless the scheme concerned expressly provides for payments of contingent benefits to cohabitants.

(5) The registrar or clerk of the court that makes an order referred to in subsection (1) shall cause a copy of the order to be served on the trustees of the scheme.

### 189  Rules respecting payments under schemes

(1) Subject to section 190(4), the trustees of a scheme in respect of which an order has been made under section 187(2) shall, where the conditions set out in subsection (2) are present, apply, in accordance with relevant guidelines, the transfer amount calculated in accordance with those guidelines—

    (a)  if the trustees and the qualified cohabitant so agree, in providing a benefit for or in respect of the qualified cohabitant that is of the same actuarial value as the transfer amount, or

    (b)  in making a payment, at the option of the qualified cohabitant—

        (i)  to another occupational pension scheme whose trustees agree to accept the payment, or

        (ii)  to discharge another payment falling to be made by the trustees under any such other approved arrangement.

(2) The conditions referred to in subsection (1) are—

    (a)  the court has made an order under section 187(2) in favour of the qualified cohabitant;

(b)  payment of the designated benefit has not commenced;

(c)  the qualified cohabitant has applied to the trustees in that behalf; and

(d)  the qualified cohabitant furnishes the information that the trustees require.

(3) Subject to section 190(4), trustees of a defined contribution scheme in respect of which an order has been made under section 187(2) may, if the qualified cohabitant has not made an application under subsections (1) and (2), apply in accordance with relevant guidelines the transfer amount calculated in accordance with those guidelines to make a payment, at their option—

(a)  to another occupational pension scheme whose trustees agree to accept the payment, or

(b)  to discharge another payment falling to be made by the trustees under any such other approved arrangement.

(4) Subject to section 190(4), the trustees of a scheme in respect of which an order has been made under section 187(2) shall, within 3 months of the death of a member qualified cohabitant who dies before the payment of the designated benefit has commenced, provide for the payment to the other qualified cohabitant of an amount that is equal to the transfer amount calculated in accordance with relevant guidelines.

(5) Subject to section 190(4), the trustees of a scheme in respect of which an order has been made under section 187(2) may, if the member qualified cohabitant ceases to be a member otherwise than on death, apply, in accordance with relevant guidelines, the transfer amount under the scheme, at their option—

(a)  if the trustees and the other qualified cohabitant so agree, in providing a benefit for or in respect of that qualified cohabitant that is of the same actuarial value as the transfer amount, or

(b)  in making a payment, either—

(i)  to another occupational pension scheme whose trustees agree to accept the payment, or

(ii)  to discharge another payment falling to be made by the trustees under any such other approved arrangement.

(6) Subject to section 190(4), the trustees of a scheme in respect of which an order has been made under section 187(2) shall, within 3 months of the death of the qualified cohabitant who is not the member and who dies before payment of the designated benefit has commenced, provide for the payment to the personal representative of that qualified cohabitant of an amount that is equal to the transfer amount calculated in accordance with relevant guidelines.

(7) Subject to section 190(4), the trustees of a scheme in respect of which an order has been made under section 187(2) shall, within 3 months of the death of the qualified cohabitant who is not the member and who dies after payment of the designated benefit has commenced, provide for the payment to the personal representative of that qualified cohabitant of an amount that is equal to the actuarial value, calculated in accordance with relevant guidelines, of the part of the designated benefit that, but for the death of

that qualified cohabitant, would have been payable to him or her during his or her lifetime.

(8) The trustees of a scheme in respect of which an order has been made under section 187(2) or (5) shall, within 12 months of the member qualified cohabitant's ceasing to be a member, notify the registrar or clerk of the court and the other qualified cohabitant of the cessation, if the trustees have not applied the transfer amount in accordance with any of subsections (1) to (6).

(9) The trustees of a scheme who apply a transfer amount under subsection (3) or (5) shall notify the qualified cohabitant who is not the member and the registrar or clerk of the court, giving particulars to that qualified cohabitant of the scheme and the transfer amount.

### 190 Payments further to orders under section 187

(1) A benefit payable pursuant to an order made under section 187(2), or a contingent benefit payable pursuant to an order made under section 187(5), is payable out of the resources of the scheme and, unless the order or relevant guidelines provide otherwise, in accordance with the rules of the scheme and those guidelines.

(2) The amount of retirement benefit payable to the member qualified cohabitant, or the amount of contingent benefit payable to or in respect of the member qualified cohabitant, in accordance with the rules of the relevant scheme shall be reduced by the designated benefit or contingent benefit payable pursuant to an order made under section 187(2) or (5), as the case may be, to the other qualified cohabitant.

(3) The amount of contingent benefit payable in accordance with the rules of the scheme in respect of a member qualified cohabitant who dies before the payment of the designated benefit payable pursuant to an order under section 187(2) has commenced shall be reduced by the amount of the payment made under section 189(4).

(4) Trustees who make a payment or apply a transfer amount under any of subsections (1) to (7) of section 189 are discharged from any obligation to make further payment or apply another transfer amount under any of those subsections in respect of the benefit payable pursuant to the order made under section 187(2).

(5) A trustee is not liable for any loss or damage caused by complying with a direction referred to in section 188(3) rather than the rules of the scheme or the Act of 1990.

### 191 Costs

(1) The court may determine the manner in which the costs incurred by the trustees of a scheme further to an order under section 187 are to be borne, including by one or the other of the qualified cohabitants or by both of them in the proportions that the court may determine, and in default of a determination, the qualified cohabitants shall bear those costs equally.

(2) The court may, on application to it by the trustees, order that an amount ordered to be paid by a qualified cohabitant under subsection (1) that has not been paid be deducted from any benefits payable to the qualified cohabitant—

(a) pursuant to an order made under section 187, if the qualified cohabitant is the beneficiary of the order; and

(b) pursuant to the scheme, if the qualified cohabitant is the member qualified cohabitant.

## 192    Value of benefit calculation

For the purposes of this section and sections 187 to 191, the court may, of its own motion, and shall, if so requested by either of the qualified cohabitants or another concerned person, direct the trustees of the scheme to provide the qualified cohabitants or the other person and the court, within a specified period of time—

(a) with a calculation of the value and amount, determined in accordance with relevant guidelines, of the retirement benefit or contingent benefit that is payable or that would have been payable under the scheme and has accrued at the time of making the order, and

(b) with a calculation of the amount of the contingent benefit that is payable or that would have been payable, under the scheme.

## 193    Mediation and other alternatives to proceedings

(1) The court may adjourn or further adjourn proceedings under section 173 at any time for the purpose of enabling the cohabitants to attempt, if they both so wish, with or without the assistance of a third party—

(a) to reconcile, or

(b) to reach agreement on some or all of the terms of a possible settlement between them.

(2) Either or both of the cohabitants may at any time request that the hearing of proceedings adjourned under subsection (1) be resumed as soon as may be and, if a request is made, the court shall, subject to any other power of the court to adjourn proceedings, resume the hearing.

(3) The powers conferred by this section are additional to any other power of the court to adjourn proceedings.

(4) The court may, at its discretion when adjourning proceedings under this section, advise the cohabitants to seek the assistance of a mediator or other third party in relation to the cohabitants' proposed reconciliation or reaching of an agreement between them on some or all of the terms of a possible settlement.

## 194    Application for provision from estate of deceased cohabitant

(1) A qualified cohabitant may, after the death of his or her cohabitant but not more than 6 months after representation is first granted under the Succession Act 1965 in respect of that cohabitant's estate, apply for an order under this section for provision out of the net estate.

(2) Notwithstanding subsection (1), a qualified cohabitant shall not apply for an order under this section where the relationship concerned ended 2 years or more before the death of the deceased, unless the applicant—

    (a) was in receipt of periodical payments from the deceased, whether under an order made under section 175 or pursuant to a cohabitants' agreement or otherwise,

    (b) had, not later than 2 years after that relationship ended, made an application for an order under section 174, 175 or 187 and either—

        (i) the proceedings were pending at the time of the death, or

        (ii) any such order made by the court had not yet been executed,

    or

    (c) had, not later than 2 years after the relationship ended, made an application for an order under section 174, 175 or 187, the order was made, an application under section 173(6) was subsequently made in respect of that order and either—

        (i) the proceedings in respect of that application were pending at the time of the death, or

        (ii) any such order made by the court under section 173(6) in favour of the qualified cohabitant who is the applicant under this section had not yet been executed.

(3) The court may by order make the provision for the applicant that the court considers appropriate having regard to the rights of any other person having an interest in the matter, if the court is satisfied that proper provision in the circumstances was not made for the applicant during the lifetime of the deceased for any reason other than conduct by the applicant that, in the opinion of the court, it would in all the circumstances be unjust to disregard.

(4) In considering whether to make an order under this section, the court shall have regard to all the circumstances of the case, including—

    (a) an order made under section 173(6), 174, 175 or 187 in favour of the applicant,

    (b) a devise or bequest made by the deceased in favour of the applicant,

    (c) the interests of the beneficiaries of the estate, and

    (d) the factors set out in section 173(3).

(5) The court shall not make an order under this section where the relationship concerned ended before the death of the deceased and—

    (a) the court is not satisfied that the applicant is financially dependent on the deceased within the meaning of section 173(2), or

    (b) the applicant has married or registered in a civil partnership, or in a legal relationship of a class that is the subject of an order under section 5.

(6) The applicant shall give notice of an application under this section to the personal representative of the deceased, any spouse or civil partner of the deceased and to any other persons that the court may direct and, in deciding whether to make the order and in determining the provisions of the order, the court shall have regard to any representations made by any of those persons.

(7) The total value for the applicant of the provision made by an order referred to in subsection (4)(a) on the date on which that order was made and an order made under this section shall not exceed any share of the applicant in the estate of the deceased qualified cohabitant to which the applicant would have been entitled if the qualified cohabitants had been spouses or civil partners of each other.

(8) If the qualified cohabitant does not notify the personal representative as required by subsection (6), the personal representative may distribute the assets of the deceased qualified cohabitant or any part of them amongst the persons entitled to them and is not liable to the qualified cohabitant for that distribution.

(9) Nothing in this section prejudices the rights of the qualified cohabitant to follow assets into the hands of a person who has received them.

(10) An order under this section shall not affect the legal right of a surviving spouse.

(11) For the purposes of this section, "net estate", with respect to the estate of a person, means the estate that remains after provision for the satisfaction of—

    (a)   other liabilities of the estate having priority over the rights referred to in paragraphs (b) and (c),

    (b)   any rights, under the Succession Act 1965, of any surviving spouse of the person, and

    (c)   any rights, under the Succession Act 1965, of any surviving civil partner of the person.

## 195    Limitation period

Proceedings under this Part other than proceedings under sections 173(6) and 194, shall, save in exceptional circumstances, be instituted within 2 years of the time that the relationship between the cohabitants ends, whether through death or otherwise.

## 196    Jurisdiction and venue

(1) Subject to the other provisions of this section, the Circuit Court has concurrent jurisdiction with the High Court to hear and determine applications for orders for redress referred to in section 173 and orders for provision from the estates of deceased cohabitants under section 194.

(2) The District Court, and the Circuit Court on appeal from the District Court, have concurrent jurisdiction with the High Court to hear and determine applications for orders for redress referred to in section 173 and orders for provision from the estates of deceased cohabitants under section 194, except that—

    (a)   they do not have jurisdiction to make such an order for periodical payments at a rate greater than €500 per week,

    (b)   they do not have jurisdiction to make such an order in a matter in relation to which the High Court has made such an order, and

    (c)   the District Court does not have jurisdiction to make such an order in a matter in relation to which the Circuit Court has made such an order otherwise than on appeal from the District Court.

(3) The court shall only exercise its jurisdiction to hear and determine an application for an order for redress referred to in section 173 if both of the cohabitants concerned were ordinarily resident in the State throughout the one-year period prior to the end of their relationship, and either of the cohabitants—

(a) is domiciled in the State on the date on which the application is made, or

(b) is ordinarily resident in the State throughout the one-year period that ends on that date.

(4) The court shall only exercise its jurisdiction to hear and determine an application for an order for provision from the estate of a deceased cohabitant under section 194 if—

(a) in the case where the relationship concerned ended before the death of the deceased, each of the cohabitants concerned was ordinarily resident in the State throughout the one-year period prior to the end of their relationship and—

(i) each of the cohabitants concerned was ordinarily resident in the State throughout the one-year period that ended on the date of the death of the deceased,

(ii) on the date of the death of the deceased, the applicant was in receipt of periodical payments from the deceased, whether under an order made under section 175 or pursuant to a cohabitants' agreement or otherwise,

(iii) the applicant had, not later than 2 years after that relationship ended, made an application for an order under section 174, 175 or 187 and either—

(I) the proceedings were pending at the time of the death, or

(II) any such order made by the court had not yet been executed,

or

(iv) the applicant had, not later than 2 years after the relationship ended, made an application for an order under section 174, 175 or 187, the order was made, an application under section 173(6) was subsequently made in respect of that order and either—

(I) the proceedings were pending at the time of the death, or

(II) any such order made by the court under section 173(6) in favour of the applicant had not yet been executed,

and

(b) in any other case, each of the cohabitants concerned was ordinarily resident in the State throughout the one-year period that ended on the date of the death of the deceased.

(5) The jurisdiction conferred on the Circuit Court may be exercised by the judge of the circuit in which a party to the application ordinarily resides or carries on a business, profession or occupation.

(6) The Circuit Court shall transfer, to the High Court, proceedings on applications for orders for redress referred to in section 173, on application to it by a party to the application for the order concerned, if land to which the proceedings relate—

(a)  has a rateable valuation that exceeds €254, or

(b)  has not been given a rateable valuation or is the subject with other land of a rateable valuation, if the Circuit Court determines that the rateable valuation would exceed €254.

(7) An order made or act done in the course of the proceedings before a transfer under subsection (6) is valid unless discharged or varied by the High Court.

## 197    Particulars of property

(1) In proceedings under this Part, each of the qualified cohabitants shall give to the other the particulars of his or her property or income that may be reasonably required for the purposes of the proceedings.

(2) The court may direct a person who fails or refuses to comply with subsection (1) to comply with it.

(3) A qualified cohabitant who fails or refuses to comply with subsection (1) or a direction under subsection (2) commits an offence and is liable on summary conviction to [a class C fine][1], or to imprisonment for a term not exceeding 6 months, or to both.

### Notes

1    Subsection (3) amended by the Civil Law (Miscellaneous Provisions) Act 2011, s 61(e).

## 198    Conduct of proceedings

(1) Proceedings under this Part shall be as informal as is practicable and consistent with the administration of justice.

(2) A judge sitting to hear and determine proceedings under this Part, and a barrister or solicitor appearing in the proceedings, shall not wear a wig or a gown.

## 199    Privacy

Subject to the provisions of section 40 of the Civil Liability and Courts Act 2004, proceedings under this Part shall be heard otherwise than in public.

## 200    Costs

The costs in proceedings under this Part are at the discretion of the court.

## 201    Rules of court

(1) Rules of court shall provide for the documentation required for the commencement of proceedings under this Part in a summary manner.

(2) Rules of court may make provision, in cases where one or both of the parties to an application under section 175 or 187, or to an application to vary an order under one of those sections, is or was married, for—

(a)  the adjournment of those proceedings or any proceedings for the financial support of the person to whom the party is or was married,

(b) the postponement of an order made under any of the proceedings referred to in paragraph (a), or

(c) any other procedure reasonably required in order to ensure that that party's financial circumstances are taken into account in the proceedings.

**202    Validity of certain agreements between cohabitants**

(1) Notwithstanding any enactment or rule of law, cohabitants may enter into a cohabitants' agreement to provide for financial matters during the relationship or when the relationship ends, whether through death or otherwise.

(2) A cohabitants' agreement is valid only if—

    (a) the cohabitants—

        (i) have each received independent legal advice before entering into it, or

        (ii) have received legal advice together and have waived in writing the right to independent legal advice,

    (b) the agreement is in writing and signed by both cohabitants, and

    (c) the general law of contract is complied with.

(3) Subject to subsection (4), a cohabitants' agreement may provide that neither cohabitant may apply for an order for redress referred to in section 173, or an order for provision from the estate of his or her cohabitant under section 194.

(4) The court may vary or set aside a cohabitants' agreement in exceptional circumstances, where its enforceability would cause serious injustice.

(5) An agreement that meets the other criteria of this section shall be deemed to be a cohabitants' agreement under this section even if entered into before the cohabitation has commenced.

**203    Amendment of section 39 of Residential Tenancies Act 2004**

Section 39(3)(a)(ii) of the Residential Tenancies Act 2004 is amended by substituting "was the tenant's cohabitant within the meaning of section 172 of the Civil Partnership and Certain Rights and Obligations of Cohabitants Act 2010 and lived with the tenant" for "cohabited with the tenant as husband and wife".

**204    Amendment of section 47 of Civil Liability Act 1961**

The definition of "dependant" in section 47(1) (as substituted by section 1 of the Civil Liability (Amendment) Act 1996) of the Civil Liability Act 1961 is amended by substituting the following for paragraph (c):

    "(c) a person who was not married to or a civil partner of the deceased but who, until the date of the deceased's death, had been living with the deceased as the deceased's cohabitant within the meaning of section 172 of the Civil Partnership and Certain Rights and Obligations of Cohabitants Act 2010 for a continuous period of not less than three years,".

**205     Amendment of Powers of Attorney Act 1996**

Paragraph 3(1) of the First Schedule of the Powers of Attorney Act 1996 is amended—

    (a)  in subparagraph (h) by substituting "blood;" for "blood.", and

    (b)  by inserting the following:

        "(i) the donor's qualified cohabitant, within the meaning of section 172 of the Civil Partnership and Certain Rights and Obligations of Cohabitants Act 2010.".

**206     Transitional provision — redress orders**

An order for redress referred to in section 173 shall only be made if the application for it is made with respect to a relationship that ends, whether by death or otherwise, after the commencement of this section but the time during which two persons lived as a couple before the commencement date is included for the purposes of calculating whether they are qualified cohabitants within the meaning of this Part.

**207     Transitional provision — agreements**

Nothing in section 202(2) prevents a court from enforcing an agreement entered into between two persons before the commencement of this Part.

PART 16

MISCELLANEOUS

**208     Saver in relation to rights of others**

In making an order under this Act and in particular in making a maintenance order, lump sum order, property adjustment order, pension adjustment order or order for provision from the estate of a deceased person, the court shall have regard to the rights of any other person with an interest in the matter, including a spouse or former spouse and a civil partner or former civil partner.

SCHEDULE
CONSEQUENTIAL AMENDMENTS TO OTHER ACTS

Section 97

PART 1
CONFLICTS OF INTERESTS PROVISIONS

| Item | Act | Provision | Amendment |
|------|-----|-----------|-----------|
| 1 | Companies Act 1963 | Section 193(1) | substitute "himself or herself and to his or her spouse or civil partner within the meaning of the Civil Partnership and Certain Rights and Obligations of Cohabitants Act 2010" for "himself and to his spouse" |
| 2 | Companies Act 1963 | Section 301A(4)(a) (inserted by section 147 of Companies Act 1990) | insert "civil partner within the meaning of the Civil Partnership and Certain Rights and Obligations of Cohabitants Act 2010" after "spouse" |
| 3 | Companies Act 1963 | Section 315(1)(c) (substituted by section 170 of Companies Act 1990) | insert ", civil partner within the meaning of the Civil Partnership and Certain Rights and Obligations of Cohabitants Act 2010" after "spouse" |
| 4 | Housing (Private Rented Dwellings) (Amendment) Act 1983 | Section 14(5) | (a) substitute "he or she or his or her spouse or civil partner within the meaning of the Civil Partnership and Certain Rights and Obligations of Cohabitants Act 2010" for "he or his spouse" wherever it appears; (b) substitute "any" for "either" in paragraph (b) |
| 5 | Farm Tax Act 1985 | Paragraph 14(2) of the Schedule | insert "or civil partner within the meaning of the Civil Partnership and Certain Rights and Obligations of Cohabitants Act 2010" after "spouse" wherever it appears |
| 6 | Building Societies Act 1989 | Section 52 | insert "or civil partner within the meaning of the Civil Partnership and Certain Rights and Obligations of Cohabitants Act 2010" after "spouse" wherever it appears |

| Item | Act | Provision | Amendment |
|------|-----|-----------|-----------|
| 7 | Building Societies Act 1989 | Section 87(2)(e) | insert "or civil partner within the meaning of the Civil Partnership and Certain Rights and Obligations of Cohabitants Act 2010" after "spouse" and "his spouse" wherever either of these expressions appear |
| 8 | Trustee Savings Banks Act 1989 | Section 21(5) | insert "or civil partner within the meaning of the Civil Partnership and Certain Rights and Obligations of Cohabitants Act 2010" after "trustee's spouse" |
| 9 | Companies Act 1990 | Section 72 | (a) delete "family and corporate" from the shoulder note; (b) substitute "his or her spouse or civil partner within the meaning of the Civil Partnership and Certain Rights and Obligations of Cohabitants Act 2010" for "his spouse" in section 72(1) |
| 10 | Companies Act 1990 | Section 187 | insert ", civil partner within the meaning of the Civil Partnership and Certain Rights and Obligations of Cohabitants Act 2010" after "spouse" wherever it appears |
| 11 | Ethics in Public Office Act 1995 | Section 2(1) | insert the following definition: "'civil partner', in relation to a person, means a civil partner within the meaning of the Civil Partnership and Certain Rights and Obligations of Cohabitants Act 2010 but does not include a civil partner who is living separately and apart from the person;" |
| 12 | Ethics in Public Office Act 1995 | Section 13(5) | insert "or civil partner" after "spouse" wherever it appears |
| 13 | Ethics in Public Office Act 1995 | Section 15(2)(b) | insert "or civil partner" after "spouse" |
| 14 | Ethics in Public Office Act 1995 | Section 15(2)(ii) | insert "or civil partner" after "relative" |
| 15 | Ethics in Public Office Act 1995 | Section 15(4)(a)(ii) | insert "or civil partner" after "spouse" |

| Item | Act | Provision | Amendment |
|---|---|---|---|
| 16 | Ethics in Public Office Act 1995 | Section 16(1)(a) | (a) insert "or civil partner" after "actual knowledge of his or her spouse" in subparagraph (ii); (b) substitute "spouse or civil partner or child a substantial benefit" for "spouse or child a substantial benefit" |
| 17 | Ethics in Public Office Act 1995 | Section 17(1)(a) | (a) insert "or civil partner" after "actual knowledge of his or her spouse" in subparagraph (ii); (b) substitute "spouse or civil partner or child a substantial benefit" for "spouse or child a substantial benefit" |
| 18 | Ethics in Public Office Act 1995 | Section 18(1)(a) | (a) insert "or civil partner" after "actual knowledge of his or her spouse" in subparagraph (ii); (b) substitute "spouse or civil partner or child a substantial benefit" for "spouse or child a substantial benefit" |
| 19 | Ethics in Public Office Act 1995 | Section 19(3)(a)(i) | (a) insert "or civil partner" after "actual knowledge of his or her spouse"; (b) substitute "spouse or civil partner or child a substantial benefit" for "spouse or child a substantial benefit" |
| 20 | Ethics in Public Office Act 1995 | Section 29(2) | (a) substitute "applies or of the spouse or civil partner of such a person" for "applies or of the spouse of such a person" in paragraph (a); (b) substitute "an interest of his or her spouse or civil partner" for "an interest of his or her spouse" in paragraph (c)(i) |
| 21 | Ethics in Public Office Act 1995 | Section 30 | substitute "that his or her spouse or civil partner or a child" for "that his or her spouse or a child" |

| Item | Act | Provision | Amendment |
|------|-----|-----------|-----------|
| 22 | Ethics in Public Office Act 1995 | Paragraph 1 of the Second Schedule | (a) in subparagraph (4), substitute "private home of the person or of his or her spouse or civil partner," for "private home of the person or of his or her spouse,"; (b) in subparagraph (5) substitute "relative or civil partner or friend of the person or of his or her spouse or civil partner" for "relative or friend of the person or of his or her spouse" wherever it appears; (c) in subparagraph (6)(b), substitute "relative or civil partner or friend of the person or of his or her spouse or civil partner" for "relative or friend of the person or of his or her spouse" |
| 23 | Credit Union Act 1997 | Section 35(10) | insert "or a civil partner within the meaning of the Civil Partnership and Certain Rights and Obligations of Cohabitants Act 2010," after "spouse" |
| 24 | Credit Union Act 1997 | Section 114(2)(b) | insert ", civil partner within the meaning of the Civil Partnership and Certain Rights and Obligations of Cohabitants Act 2010," after "spouse" |
| 25 | Food Safety Authority of Ireland Act 1998 | Paragraph (f) of definition of "interests" in section 41(7) | insert "or civil partner within the meaning of the Civil Partnership and Certain Rights and Obligations of Cohabitants Act 2010" after "spouse" |
| 26 | Planning and Development Act 2000 | Section 148 | insert "or civil partner within the meaning of the Civil Partnership and Certain Rights and Obligations of Cohabitants Act 2010" after "spouse" wherever it appears |
| 27 | Aviation Regulation Act 2001 | Paragraph (d) of definition of "interests" in section 17(7) | insert "or civil partner within the meaning of the Civil Partnership and Certain Rights and Obligations of Cohabitants Act 2010" after "spouse" |
| 28 | Local Government Act 2001 | Definition of "connected person" in section 166(1) | substitute "spouse or civil partner within the meaning of the Civil Partnership and Certain Rights and Obligations of Cohabitants Act 2010 of the person" for "spouse of the person" |

| Item | Act | Provision | Amendment |
|------|-----|-----------|-----------|
| 29 | Local Government Act 2001 | Section 175"(g)(i) | substitute "relative or friend of the person or of his or her spouse or civil partner within the meaning of the Civil Partnership and Certain Rights and Obligations of Cohabitants Act 2010 or of a child of the person or his or her spouse for purely personal reasons only" for "relative or friend of the person or of his or her spouse or of a child of the person or his or her spouse for purely personal reasons only" |
| 30 | Transport (Railway Infrastructure) Act 2001 | Section 29(2) | insert "or civil partner within the meaning of the Civil Partnership and Certain Rights and Obligations of Cohabitants Act 2010" after "connected relative" wherever it appears |
| 31 | Valuation Act 2001 | Paragraph 13 of Schedule 2 | (a) insert "or civil partner within the meaning of the Civil Partnership and Certain Rights and Obligations of Cohabitants Act 2010" after "spouse" in subparagraph (2) wherever it appears; (b) substitute the following for the definition of "relative" in subparagraph (10): "'relative', in relation to a person, means a brother, sister, parent, spouse, or civil partner within the meaning of the Civil Partnership and Certain Rights and Obligations of Cohabitants Act 2010, of the person or a child of the person or of the spouse."; (c) insert the following subparagraph after subparagraph (11): "(12) For the purposes of subparagraphs (2) and (9) of this paragraph, 'civil partner' in relation to a person, does not include a civil partner who is living separately and apart from the person.". |
| 32 | Gas (Interim) (Regulation) Act 2002 | Paragraph (c) of definition of "interests" in section 9(7) | insert "or civil partner within the meaning of the Civil Partnership and Certain Rights and Obligations of Cohabitants Act 2010" after "spouse" |

| Item | Act | Provision | Amendment |
|------|-----|-----------|-----------|
| 33 | National Development Finance Agency Act 2002 | Section 17(10)(a) | insert "or civil partner within the meaning of the Civil Partnership and Certain Rights and Obligations of Cohabitants Act 2010" after "spouse" |
| 34 | Sustainable Energy Act 2002 | Section 18(2) | insert "or civil partner within the meaning of the Civil Partnership and Certain Rights and Obligations of Cohabitants Act 2010" after "connected relative" wherever it appears |
| 35 | Digital Hub Development Agency Act 2003 | Paragraph (e) of definition of "interests" in section 24(5) | insert "or civil partner within the meaning of the Civil Partnership and Certain Rights and Obligations of Cohabitants Act 2010" after "spouse" |
| 36 | Industrial Development (Science Foundation Ireland) Act 2003 | Section 16(2) | insert "or civil partner within the meaning of the Civil Partnership and Certain Rights and Obligations of Cohabitants Act 2010" after "connected relative" wherever it appears |
| 37 | Private Security Services Act 2004 | Section 17(2) | insert "or civil partner within the meaning of the Civil Partnership and Certain Rights and Obligations of Cohabitants Act 2010" after "connected relative" wherever it appears |
| 38 | Grangegorman Development Agency Act 2005 | Paragraph (e) of definition of "interests" in section 28(5) | insert "or civil partner within the meaning of the Civil Partnership and Certain Rights and Obligations of Cohabitants Act 2010" after "spouse" |
| 39 | Railway Safety Act 2005 | Section 20(2) | insert "or civil partner within the meaning of the Civil Partnership and Certain Rights and Obligations of Cohabitants Act 2010" after "connected relative" wherever it appears |
| 40 | National Sports Campus Development Authority Act 2006 | Section 16(2) | (a) insert "or civil partner within the meaning of the Civil Partnership and Certain Rights and Obligations of Cohabitants Act 2010" after "connected relative" wherever it appears; (b) substitute "any" for "either" in paragraph (a) |

| Item | Act | Provision | Amendment |
|---|---|---|---|
| 41 | Registration of Deeds and Title Act 2006 | Section 14(2) | insert "or civil partner within the meaning of the Civil Partnership and Certain Rights and Obligations of Cohabitants Act 2010" after "connected relative" wherever it appears |
| 42 | Sea-Fisheries and Maritime Jurisdiction Act 2006 | Section 57(2) | insert "or civil partner within the meaning of the Civil Partnership and Certain Rights and Obligations of Cohabitants Act 2010" after "connected relative" wherever it appears |
| 43 | Consumer Protection Act 2007 | Section 25(2) | (a) insert "or civil partner within the meaning of the Civil Partnership and Certain Rights and Obligations of Cohabitants Act 2010" after "connected relative" wherever it appears; (b) substitute "any" for "either" in paragraph (a) of section 25(2) |
| 44 | Pharmacy Act 2007 | Definition of "beneficial interest" in section 63(5)(a) | insert "or civil partner within the meaning of the Civil Partnership and Certain Rights and Obligations of Cohabitants Act 2010" after "spouse" |
| 45 | Pharmacy Act 2007 | Subparagraph 9(3) of Schedule 1 | Substitute "or civil partner within the meaning of the Civil Partnership and Certain Rights and Obligations of Cohabitants Act 2010 of that member or a nominee of any of them" for "of that member or a nominee of either of them" |
| 46 | Pharmacy Act 2007 | Subparagraph 10(3) of Schedule 1 | Substitute "or civil partner within the meaning of the Civil Partnership and Certain Rights and Obligations of Cohabitants Act 2010 of the employee or any of them" for "of the employee or either of them" |

Section 99

PART 2
PENSIONS PROVISIONS

| Item | Act | Provision | Amendment |
|---|---|---|---|
| 1 | Pilotage Order Confirmation Act 1927 | Schedule | substitute "surviving spouse, or surviving civil partner within the meaning of the Civil Partnership and Certain Rights and Obligations of Cohabitants Act 2010," for "widow" wherever it appears |
| 2 | Ministerial and Parliamentary Offices Act 1938 | Section 20 (substituted by section 15 of the Ministerial, Parliamentary and Judicial Offices and Oireachtas Members (Miscellaneous Provisions) Act 2001) | (a) insert "or surviving civil partner" after "surviving spouse" wherever it appears; (b) insert "or surviving civil partner's" after "surviving spouse's" wherever it appears; (c) insert "or civil partner" after "spouse" wherever it appears; (d) in subsection (3), insert "or enters into a new civil partnership" after "remarries"; |
| | | | (e) in subsection (9), insert the following definition: "'civil partner' has the meaning assigned to it in the Civil Partnership and Certain Rights and Obligations of Cohabitants Act 2010." |
| 3 | Ministerial and Parliamentary Offices Act 1938 | Section 20C (inserted by section 16 of the Ministerial, Parliamentary and Judicial Offices and Oireachtas Members (Miscellaneous Provisions) Act 2001) | (a) in subsection (1), substitute "spouse's pension or surviving civil partner's (within the meaning of the Civil Partnership and Certain Rights and Obligations of Cohabitants Act 2010) pension that has ceased to be payable because that person has married, remarried or entered into a civil partnership" for "spouse's pension that has ceased to be payable because that person has remarried"; (b) inserting "or civil partnership" after "marriage" |

491

| Item | Act | Provision | Amendment |
|------|-----|-----------|-----------|
| 4 | Ministerial and Parliamentary Offices Act 1938 | Section 21(4) | substitute "surviving spouses' pensions, surviving civil partners' pensions" for "widows' pensions" |
| 5 | Oireachtas (Allowances to Members) Act 1938 | Section 6A(6)(a)(i) (inserted by section 1 of the Oireachtas (Allowances to Members) (Amendment) Act 1968) | substitute "surviving spouses or surviving civil partners, within the meaning of the Civil Partnership and Certain Rights and Obligations of Cohabitants Act 2010" for "widows" |
| 6 | Presidential Establishment Act 1938 | Section 4(1) (substituted by section 3 of the Presidential Establishment (Amendment) Act 1991) | insert ", or surviving civil partner within the meaning of the Civil Partnership and Certain Rights and Obligations of Cohabitants Act 2010," after "widower" |
| 7 | Presidential Establishment Act 1938 | Section 4(2) (substituted by section 3 of the Presidential Establishment (Amendment) Act 1991) | substitute "married, remarried or entered into a civil partnership within the meaning of the Civil Partnership and Certain Rights and Obligations of Cohabitants Act 2010 after the death of the spouse or civil partner" for "remarried after the death of the spouse" |
| 8 | Presidential Establishment Act 1938 | Section 4(3) (substituted by section 3 of the Presidential Establishment (Amendment) Act 1991) | substitute "spouse or civil partner until, in case the person marries, remarries or enters into a civil partnership, such marriage, remarriage or entry into a civil partnership, or, in case the person does not marry, remarry or enter into a civil partnership," for "spouse until, in case the person remarries, such remarriage or, in case the person does not remarry," |
| 9 | Garda Síochána (Compensation) Act 1941 | Section 12 | substitute "surviving spouse or surviving civil partner within the meaning of the Civil Partnership and Certain Rights and Obligations of Cohabitants Act 2010" for "widow" wherever it appears |

| Item | Act | Provision | Amendment |
|---|---|---|---|
| 10 | Central Bank Act 1942 | Definition of "superannuation benefit" in section 33AG(8) (inserted by section 26 of the Central Bank and Financial Services Authority of Ireland Act 2003) | insert "or civil partner within the meaning of the Civil Partnership and Certain Rights and Obligations of Cohabitants Act 2010" after "spouse" |
| 11 | Central Bank Act 1942 | Paragraph 5(1) of Schedule 7 (inserted by section 22 of the Central Bank and Financial Services Authority of Ireland Act 2004) | insert "or civil partner within the meaning of the Civil Partnership and Certain Rights and Obligations of Cohabitants Act 2010" after "spouse" |
| 12 | Harbours Act 1946 | Section 151(9) | substitute "surviving spouse or surviving civil partner within the meaning of the Civil Partnership and Certain Rights and Obligations of Cohabitants Act 2010" for "widow" |
| 13 | Great Southern Railways Company (Superannuation Scheme) Act 1947 | Schedule | (a) substitute "surviving spouse, or surviving civil partner within the meaning of the Civil Partnership and Certain Rights and Obligations of Cohabitants Act 2010," for "widow" wherever it appears other than in paragraph 23(a)(ii); (b) in paragraph 23(a)(ii), substitute "surviving spouse or surviving civil partner within the meaning of the Civil Partnership and Certain Rights and Obligations of Cohabitants Act 2010," for "widower or widow" |
| 14 | Electricity (Supply) (Amendment) Act 1958 | Section 15(1) | substitute "to that person's spouse or civil partner within the meaning of the Civil Partnership and Certain Rights and Obligations of Cohabitants Act 2010" for ", if the person making the surrender is a man, to his wife." |

| Item | Act | Provision | Amendment |
|------|-----|-----------|-----------|
| 15 | Electricity (Supply) (Amendment) Act 1958 | | substitute "the dependant or wife, or civil partner within the meaning of the Civil Partnership and Certain Rights and Obligations of Cohabitants Act 2010," for "the wife or dependant" |
| 16 | Courts of Justice and Court Officers (Superannuation) Act 1961 | | substitute "spouse or civil partner within the meaning of the Civil Partnership and Certain Rights and Obligations of Cohabitants Act 2010" for "wife" wherever it appears |
| 17 | Companies Act 1963 | | substitute "his or her surviving spouse or surviving civil partner, within the meaning of the Civil Partnership and Certain Rights and Obligations of Cohabitants Act 2010, or dependants" for "his widow or dependants" |
| 18 | Electricity (Supply) (Amendment) Act 1970 | | substitute "spouse, civil partner within the meaning of the Civil Partnership and Certain Rights and Obligations of Cohabitants Act 2010 or a dependent" for "wife or a dependent" |
| 19 | Local Government (Superannuation) Act 1980 | | substitute "surviving spouses or surviving civil partners, within the meaning of the Civil Partnership and Certain Rights and Obligations of Cohabitants Act 2010" for "widows" |
| 20 | Courts (Supplemental Provisions) (Amendment) Act 1991 | Section 4(2) | insert ", civil partner within the meaning of the Civil Partnership and Certain Rights and Obligations of Cohabitants Act 2010," after "spouse" |
| 21 | Courts (Supplemental Provisions) (Amendment) Act 1991 | Section 7(1) | insert ", civil partner within the meaning of the Civil Partnership and Certain Rights and Obligations of Cohabitants Act 2010" after "spouse" |

| Item | Act | Provision | Amendment |
|------|-----|-----------|-----------|
| 22 | Air Navigation and Transport (Amendment) Act 1998 | Section 32(12) | insert ", civil partner within the meaning of the Civil Partnership and Certain Rights and Obligations of Cohabitants Act 2010," after "spouse" wherever it appears |
| 23 | Garda Síochána Act 2005 | Section 122(1)(i) | insert "or civil partners within the meaning of the Civil Partnership and Certain Rights and Obligations of Cohabitants Act 2010" after "spouses" |

Section 168

## PART 3
### PROPERTY RIGHTS PROVISIONS

| Item | Act | Provision | Amendment |
|---|---|---|---|
| 1 | Land Act 1931 | Section 35(3)(a) | substitute "spouse, civil partner within the meaning of the Civil Partnership and Certain Rights and Obligations of Cohabitants Act 2010" for "husband" |
| 2 | Land Act 1933 | Section 29(1) | insert "or the civil partner within the meaning of the Civil Partnership and Certain Rights and Obligations of Cohabitants Act 2010" after "husband" |
| 3 | Land Act 1936 | Section 16(2)(b) | insert "or the civil partner within the meaning of the Civil Partnership and Certain Rights and Obligations of Cohabitants Act 2010" after "husband" wherever it appears |
| 4 | Companies Act 1963 | Section 289(3) | insert "or civil partner within the meaning of the Civil Partnership and Certain Rights and Obligations of Cohabitants Act 2010" after "spouse" |
| 5 | Companies Act 1963 | Section 300A(1)(b) (inserted by section 146 of the Companies Act 1990) | insert "or civil partner within the meaning of the Civil Partnership and Certain Rights and Obligations of Cohabitants Act 2010" after "spouse" |
| 6 | Land Act 1965 | Section 6(3) | (a) insert "or who is a civil partner within the meaning of the Civil Partnership and Certain Rights and Obligations of Cohabitants Act 2010 whose civil partner (not being interested jointly or in common in the land) is alive on that date," after "on that date"; (b) insert "or civil partner" after "spouse" in paragraph (a); (c) insert "or civil partner" after "spouse" in paragraph (b) wherever it appears |
| 7 | Land Act 1965 | Section 6(4) | (a) substitute "unmarried," for "unmarried or"; (b) insert "or is a surviving civil partner" after "widow"; (c) insert "or civil partner" after "spouse" |

| Item | Act | Provision | Amendment |
|---|---|---|---|
| 8 | Agricultural Credit Act 1978 | Section 31(2)(a)(i)(II) | insert "or civil partner within the meaning of the Civil Partnership and Certain Rights and Obligations of Cohabitants Act 2010" after "husband" |
| 9 | Housing (Miscellaneous Provisions) Act 1979 | Section 4(5) (inserted by section 25 of the Housing Act 1988) | (a) substitute "marriage or civil partnership within the meaning of the Civil Partnership and Certain Rights and Obligations of Cohabitants Act 2010" for "marriage" in paragraph (a)(i); (b) substitute "separated from his or her spouse or civil partner" for "separated from his spouse" in paragraph (a) (ii); (c) add "or civil partner" after "spouse" in paragraph (c) |
| 10 | Housing (Miscellaneous Provisions) Act 1979 | Section 11(3)(b) | insert "or civil partner within the meaning of the Civil Partnership and Certain Rights and Obligations of Cohabitants Act 2010" after "spouse" |
| 11 | Occasional Trading Act 1979 | Section 2(2)(j) | insert ", civil partner within the meaning of the Civil Partnership and Certain Rights and Obligations of Cohabitants Act 2010" after "spouse" |
| 12 | Abattoirs Act 1988 | Section 13(2) | insert "or civil partner within the meaning of the Civil Partnership and Certain Rights and Obligations of Cohabitants Act 2010" after "spouse" |
| 13 | Abattoirs Act 1988 | Section 28(2) | insert "or civil partner within the meaning of the Civil Partnership and Certain Rights and Obligations of Cohabitants Act 2010" after "spouse" |
| 14 | Bankruptcy Act 1988 | Section 61(5) | (a) insert "or shared home within the meaning of the Civil Partnership and Certain Rights and Obligations of Cohabitants Act 2010" after "family home" wherever it appears; (b) insert "or civil partner within the meaning of the Civil Partnership and Certain Rights and Obligations of Cohabitants Act 2010" after "spouse" |
| 15 | Housing Act 1988 | Section 3(2)(e) | insert "or civil partner within the meaning of the Civil Partnership and Certain Rights and Obligations of Cohabitants Act 2010" after "spouse" |

| Item | Act | Provision | Amendment |
|------|-----|-----------|-----------|
| 16 | Housing Act 1988 | Section 4 | insert "or civil partner within the meaning of the Civil Partnership and Certain Rights and Obligations of Cohabitants Act 2010" after "spouse" wherever it appears |
| 17 | Central Bank Act 1989 | Paragraph (a) of the definition of "connected person" in section 53 | insert "or civil partner within the meaning of the Civil Partnership and Certain Rights and Obligations of Cohabitants Act 2010" after "spouse" |
| 18 | Companies Act 1990 | Section 26(1)(a) (substituted by section 76 of the Company Law Enforcement Act 2001) | insert ", civil partner within the meaning of the Civil Partnership and Certain Rights and Obligations of Cohabitants Act 2010," after "spouse" wherever it appears |
| 19 | Companies Act 1990 | Section 64 | insert "or civil partner within the meaning of the Civil Partnership and Certain Rights and Obligations of Cohabitants Act 2010" after "spouse" wherever it appears |
| 20 | Irish Horseracing Industry Act 1994 | Section 48(21)(a)(i) | insert "or civil partner within the meaning of the Civil Partnership and Certain Rights and Obligations of Cohabitants Act 2010" after "spouse" |
| 21 | Consumer Credit Act 1995 | Section 45(3) | insert the following paragraph after paragraph (a): "(aa) for the purposes of the Civil Partnership and Certain Rights and Obligations of Cohabitants Act 2010, send any written communication connected with the agreement to the consumer's civil partner, or" |
| 22 | Investor Compensation Act 1998 | Paragraph (d) of definition of "excluded investor" in section 2(1) | insert ", a civil partner within the meaning of the Civil Partnership and Certain Rights and Obligations of Cohabitants Act 2010" after "relative" |

Section 169

## PART 4
### REDRESS PROVISIONS

| Item | Act | Provision | Amendment |
|---|---|---|---|
| 1 | Garda Síochána (Compensation) Act 1941 | Section 3(a) | substitute "surviving spouse or surviving civil partner within the meaning of the Civil Partnership and Certain Rights and Obligations of Cohabitants Act 2010" for "widow" |
| 2 | Civil Liability Act 1961 | Definition of "dependant" in section 47(1) (substituted by section 1 of the Civil Liability (Amendment) Act 1996) | (a) insert ", civil partner within the meaning of the Civil Partnership and Certain Rights and Obligations of Cohabitants Act 2010" after "spouse"; (b) delete "or" at the end of paragraph (b); (c) insert the following paragraph after paragraph (b): "(ba) a person whose civil partnership with the deceased has been dissolved by a decree of dissolution that was granted under the Civil Partnership and Certain Rights and Obligations of Cohabitants Act 2010 or under the law of a country or jurisdiction other than the State and is recognised in the State, or" |
| 3 | Residential Institutions Redress Act 2002 | Section 9(1) and (2) | substitute "the children, spouse or civil partner within the meaning of the Civil Partnership and Certain Rights and Obligations of Cohabitants Act 2010" for "the children or spouse" wherever it appears |

| Item | Act | Provision | Amendment |
|------|-----|-----------|-----------|
| 4 | Air Navigation and Transport (International Conventions) Act 2004 | Definition of "dependant" in section 7(1) | (a) insert ", or civil partner within the meaning of the Civil Partnership and Certain Rights and Obligations of Cohabitants Act 2010" after "husband"; (b) insert the following paragraph after paragraph (b): "(ba) a person whose civil partnership with the deceased— (i) has been dissolved by a decree of dissolution that was granted under the Civil Partnership and Certain Rights and Obligations of Cohabitants Act 2010,or (ii) has been dissolved in accordance with the law of a country or jurisdiction (other than the State), but only if the dissolution is recognised in the State;" |
| 5 | Commission to Inquire into Child Abuse (Amendment) Act 2005 | Section 27(1) | insert "or the civil partner within the meaning of the Civil Partnership and Certain Rights and Obligations of Cohabitants Act 2010" after "relative" |

Section 170

## PART 5
### MISCELLANEOUS PROVISIONS

| Item | Act | Provision | Amendment |
|------|-----|-----------|-----------|
| 1 | Enforcement of Court Orders Act 1926 | Section 13(1) | insert ", or the civil partner within the meaning of the Civil Partnership and Certain Rights and Obligations of Cohabitants Act 2010," after "husband" |
| 2 | Aliens Act 1935 | Section 5(4) | insert ", or the civil partner to whom an order made under section 5 of the Civil Partnership and Certain Rights and Obligations of Cohabitants Act 2010 applies," after "spouse" wherever it appears |
| 3 | Defence Act 1954 | Section 161(4)(a)(ii) (inserted by section 18(c)of the Defence (Amendment) Act 2007) | insert "or the civil partner within the meaning of the Civil Partnership and Certain Rights and Obligations of Cohabitants Act 2010" after "family" |

| Item | Act | Provision | Amendment |
|---|---|---|---|
| 4 | Local Authorities (Higher Education Grants) Act 1968 | Section 2(1A)(a)(iii) (inserted by section 3 of the Local Authorities (Higher Education Grants) Act 1992) | insert "or civil partners within the meaning of the Civil Partnership and Certain Rights and Obligations of Cohabitants Act 2010" after "spouses" |
| 5 | Health Act 1970 | Section 45(2) (inserted by section 1 of the Health (Amendment) Act 2005), section 58(2) (inserted by section 5 of the Health (Amendment) Act 2005), section 1(1)(b) of the Health (Miscellaneous Provisions) Act 2001, section 68(3) | insert "or civil partner within the meaning of the Civil Partnership and Certain Rights and Obligations of Cohabitants Act 2010" after "spouse", wherever it appears |
| 6 | Prosecution of Offences Act 1974 | Section 6(2)(a)(ii) | insert "or the civil partner within the meaning of the Civil Partnership and Certain Rights and Obligations of Cohabitants Act 2010" after "family" |
| 7 | Unfair Dismissals Act 1977 | Section 2(1)(c) | insert ", civil partner within the meaning of the Civil Partnership and Certain Rights and Obligations of Cohabitants Act 2010" after "spouse" |
| 8 | Bankruptcy Act 1988 | Section 45(1) | substitute "spouse or civil partner within the meaning of the Civil Partnership and Certain Rights and Obligations of Cohabitants Act 2010" for "wife" |

| Item | Act | Provision | Amendment |
|------|-----|-----------|-----------|
| 9 | Bankruptcy Act 1988 | Section 59 | (a) insert "or civil partnership within the meaning of the Civil Partnership and Certain Rights and Obligations of Cohabitants Act 2010" after "marriage" in subsection (1); (b) insert the following subsection after subsection (2): "(2A) A covenant or contract made by any person (in this section called the settlor) in consideration of his or her entry into civil partnership within the meaning of the Civil Partnership and Certain Rights and Obligations of Cohabitants Act 2010, either for the future payment of money for the benefit of the settlor's civil partner, or for the future settlement, on or for the settlor's civil partner, of property wherein the settlor had not at the date of the registration of the civil partnership any estate or interest, whether vested or contingent, in possession or remainder, shall, if the settlor is adjudicated bankrupt and the covenant or contract has not been executed at the date of the adjudication, be void as against the Official Assignee, except so far as it enables the civil partner entitled under the covenant or contract to claim for dividend in the settlor's bankruptcy under or in respect of the covenant or contract, but any such claim to dividend shall be postponed until all the claims of the other creditors for valuable consideration in money or money's worth have been satisfied." |
| 10 | Health (Nursing Homes) Act 1990 | Section 2(1) | insert "or civil partner within the meaning of the Civil Partnership and Certain Rights and Obligations of Cohabitants Act 2010" before "or of a parent" |

| Item | Act | Provision | Amendment |
|---|---|---|---|
| 11 | Health (Nursing Homes) Act 1990 | Section 7B (substituted by section 3 of the Health (Nursing Homes) (Amendment) Act 2007) | (a) insert "or civil partner within the meaning of the Civil Partnership and Certain Rights and Obligations of Cohabitants Act 2010" after "spouse" wherever it appears; (b) insert "civil partner, or a" before "married or cohabiting person" in subsection (4); (c) substitute "applicant and his or her civil partner or spouse" for "married couple" in subsection (4) |
| 12 | Electoral Act 1992 | Section 12(2) | insert "or the civil partner within the meaning of the Civil Partnership and Certain Rights and Obligations of Cohabitants Act 2010" after "spouse" |
| 13 | Statistics Act 1993 | Section 27(1)(a) | replace "spouse or" with "spouse, civil partner within the meaning of the Civil Partnership and Certain Rights and Obligations of Cohabitants Act 2010,or a" |
| 14 | Solicitors (Amendment) Act 1994 | Section 32(4) | insert ", civil partner within the meaning of the Civil Partnership and Certain Rights and Obligations of Cohabitants Act 2010" after "spouse" |
| 15 | Criminal Assets Bureau Act 1996 | Sections 11(1), 13(1) and 15(1) | insert "or the civil partner within the meaning of the Civil Partnership and Certain Rights and Obligations of Cohabitants Act 2010" after "family" wherever it appears |
| 16 | Refugee Act 1996 | Section 18(3)(a) | insert "or the civil partner within the meaning of the Civil Partnership and Certain Rights and Obligations of Cohabitants Act 2010" after "family" |
| 17 | Non-Fatal Offences Against the Person Act 1997 | Sections 9(1) and 11(1) | insert "or the civil partner within the meaning of the Civil Partnership and Certain Rights and Obligations of Cohabitants Act 2010" after "family" wherever it appears |
| 18 | Organisation of Working Time Act 1997 | Section 3(2)(b) | (a) insert "or is employed by the person's civil partner within the meaning of the Civil Partnership and Certain Rights and Obligations of Cohabitants Act 2010" after "household" in subparagraph (i); (b) insert "or civil partner" after "relative" in subparagraph (ii) |

| Item | Act | Provision | Amendment |
|------|-----|-----------|-----------|
| 19 | Criminal Justice Act 1999 | Section 41(1)(a) | insert "or his or her civil partner within the meaning of the Civil Partnership and Certain Rights and Obligations of Cohabitants Act 2010" after "family" |
| 20 | National Minimum Wage Act 2000 | Section 5(a) | insert ", civil partner within the meaning of the Civil Partnership and Certain Rights and Obligations of Cohabitants Act 2010" after "spouse" |
| 21 | Housing (Miscellaneous Provisions) Act 2002 | Section 13(2)(a) | substitute ", civil status within the meaning of the Civil Partnership and Certain Rights and Obligations of Cohabitants Act 2010" for "marital status" |
| 22 | Health Act 2004 | Sections 46(3)(a) and 46(4) | insert "or civil partner within the meaning of the Civil Partnership and Certain Rights and Obligations of Cohabitants Act 2010" after "relative" wherever it appears |
| 23 | Disability Act 2005 | Section 9(2)(a) | insert ", civil partner within the meaning of the Civil Partnership and Certain Rights and Obligations of Cohabitants Act 2010" after "spouse" |
| 24 | Registration of Deeds and Title Act 2006 | Definition of "deed" in section 32(1) | (a) insert "or under section 36 of the Civil Partnership and Certain Rights and Obligations of Cohabitants Act 2010" after "Act 1976" in paragraph (j); (b) insert "or under section 28(12) of the Civil Partnership and Certain Rights and Obligations of Cohabitants Act 2010" after "Act 1976" in paragraph (k) |

# Part 2: Other Statutes

# Partition Act 1868

[...]¹

---

## Notes

1    Repealed by the Land and Conveyancing Law Reform Act 2009, Schedule 2.

---

# Partition Act 1876

[...][1]

---

**Notes**

1    Repealed by the Land and Conveyancing Law Reform Act 2009, Schedule 2.

---

# Bunreacht na hÉireann 1937

## THE FAMILY

**ARTICLE 41**

1.  1°  The State recognises the Family as the natural primary and fundamental unit group of Society, and as a moral institution possessing inalienable and imprescriptible rights, antecedent and superior to all positive law.

    2°  The State, therefore, guarantees to protect the Family in its constitution and authority, as the necessary basis of social order and as indispensable to the welfare of the Nation and the State.

2.  1°  In particular, the State recognises that by her life within the home, woman gives to the State a support without which the common good cannot be achieved.

    2°  The State shall, therefore, endeavour to ensure that mothers shall not be obliged by economic necessity to engage in labour to the neglect of their duties in the home.

3.  1°  The State pledges itself to guard with special care the institution of Marriage, on which the Family is founded, and to protect it against attack.

    2°  A Court designated by law may grant a dissolution of marriage where, but only where, it is satisfied that

    i.  at the date of the institution of the proceedings, the spouses have lived apart from one another for a period of, or periods amounting to, at least four years during the five years,

    ii.  there is no reasonable prospect of a reconciliation between the spouses,

    iii.  such provision as the Court considers proper having regard to the circumstances exists or will be made for the spouses, any children of either or both of them and any other person prescribed by law, and

    iv.  any further conditions prescribed by law are complied with.

    3°  No person whose marriage has been dissolved under the civil law of any other State but is a subsisting valid marriage under the law for the time being in force within the jurisdiction of the Government and Parliament established by this Constitution shall be capable of contracting a valid marriage within that jurisdiction during the lifetime of the other party to the marriage so dissolved.[1]

---

**Notes**

1   Article 41 was amended by the Fifteenth Amendment to the Constitution Act 1995, which was signed on 17 June 1996, and provided for the dissolution of marriage in certain specified circumstances.

---

EDUCATION

## ARTICLE 42

1. The State acknowledges that the primary and natural educator of the child is the Family and guarantees to respect the inalienable right and duty of parents to provide, according to their means, for the religious and moral, intellectual, physical and social education of their children.

2. Parents shall be free to provide this education in their homes or in private schools or in schools recognised or established by the State.

3.    1°   The State shall not oblige parents in violation of their conscience and lawful preference to send their children to schools established by the State, or to any particular type of school designated by the State.

     2°   The State shall, however, as guardian of the common good, require in view of actual conditions that the children receive a certain minimum education, moral, intellectual and social.

4. The State shall provide for free primary education and shall endeavour to supplement and give reasonable aid to private and corporate educational initiative, and, when the public good requires it, provide other educational facilities or institutions with due regard, however, for the rights of parents, especially in the matter of religious and moral formation.

5. In exceptional cases, where the parents for physical or moral reasons fail in their duty towards their children, the State as guardian of the common good, by appropriate means shall endeavour to supply the place of the parents, but always with due regard for the natural and imprescriptible rights of the child.

# Taxes Consolidation Act 1997

*Number 39 of 1997*

ARRANGEMENT OF SECTIONS

## PART 44
### MARRIED, SEPARATED AND DIVORCED PERSONS

*CHAPTER 1*
*INCOME TAX*

*CHAPTER 2*
*CAPITAL GAINS TAX*

## PART 44A
### TAX TREATMENT OF CIVIL PARTNERSHIPS

*CHAPTER 1*
*INCOME TAX*

1031C. Assessment of nominated civil partner in respect of income of both civil partners.

1031D. Election for assessment under section 1031C.

1031E. Special provisions relating to year of registration of civil partnership.

1031F. Repayment of tax in case of certain civil partners.

1031G. Special provisions relating to tax on individual's civil partner's income.

1031H. Application for separate assessments.

1031I. Method of apportioning reliefs and charging tax in cases of separate assessments.

1031J. Maintenance of civil partners living apart.

1031K. Dissolution or annulment of civil partnerships: adaptation of provisions relating to civil partners.

CHAPTER 2
CAPITAL GAINS TAX

1031L. Interpretation (Chapter 2).

1031M. Civil partners.

1031N. Application of section 1031G for purposes of capital gains tax.

1031O. Transfers of assets where civil partnership dissolved.

PART 44B
TAX TREATMENT OF COHABITANTS

CHAPTER 1
INCOME TAX

1031P. Interpretation (Chapter 1).

1031Q. Maintenance where relationship between cohabitants ends.

CHAPTER 2
CAPITAL GAINS TAX

1031R. Transfers of assets where relationship between cohabitants ends.

PART 44
MARRIED, SEPARATED AND DIVORCED PERSONS
CHAPTER 1
INCOME TAX

**1015    Interpretation (Chapter 1)**

(1) In this Chapter, "**the inspector**", in relation to a notice, means any inspector who might reasonably be considered by the person giving notice to be likely to be concerned with the subject matter of the notice or who declares himself or herself ready to accept the notice.

(2) A wife shall be treated for income tax purposes as living with her husband unless either—

    (a) they are separated under an order of a court of competent jurisdiction or by deed of separation, or

    (b) they are in fact separated in such circumstances that the separation is likely to be permanent.

(3) (a) In this Chapter, references to the income of a wife include references to any sum which apart from this Chapter would be included in computing her total income, and this Chapter shall apply in relation to any such sum notwithstanding that some enactment (including, except in so far as the contrary is expressly provided, an enactment passed after the passing of this Act) requires that that sum should not be treated as income of any person other than her.

    (b) In the Income Tax Acts, a reference to a person who has duly elected to be assessed to tax in accordance with a particular section includes a reference to a person who is deemed to have elected to be assessed to tax in accordance with that section, and any reference to a person who is assessed to tax in accordance with section 1017 for a year of assessment includes a reference to a case where the person and his or her spouse are assessed to tax for that year in accordance with section 1023.

(4) Any notice required to be served under any section in this Chapter may be served by post.

**1016    Assessment as single persons**

(1) Subject to subsection (2), in any case in which a wife is treated as living with her husband, income tax shall be assessed, charged and recovered, except as is otherwise provided by the Income Tax Acts, on the income of the husband and on the income of the wife as if they were not married.

(2) Where an election under section 1018 has effect in relation to a husband and wife for a year of assessment, this section shall not apply in relation to that husband and wife for that year of assessment.

**1017    Assessment of husband in respect of income of both spouses**

(1) Where in the case of a husband and wife an election under section 1018 to be assessed to tax in accordance with this section has effect for a year of assessment—

    (a) the husband shall be assessed and charged to income tax, not only in respect of his total income (if any) for that year, but also in respect of his wife's total income (if any) for any part of that year of assessment during which she is living with him, and for this purpose and for the purposes of the Income Tax Acts that last-mentioned income shall be deemed to be his income,

    (b) the question whether there is any income of the wife chargeable to tax for any year of assessment and, if so, what is to be taken to be the amount of that income for tax purposes shall not be affected by this section, and

(c) any tax to be assessed in respect of any income which under this section is deemed to be income of a woman's husband shall, instead of being assessed on her, or on her trustees, guardian or committee, or on her executors or administrators, be assessable on him or, in the appropriate cases, on his executors or administrators.

(2) Any relief from income tax authorised by any provision of the Income Tax Acts to be granted to a husband by reference to the income or profits or gains or losses of his wife or by reference to any payment made by her shall be granted to a husband for a year of assessment only if he is assessed to tax for that year in accordance with this section.

## 1018    Election for assessment under section 1017

(1) A husband and his wife, where the wife is living with the husband, may at any time during a year of assessment, by notice in writing given to the inspector, jointly elect to be assessed to income tax for that year of assessment in accordance with section 1017 and, where such election is made, the income of the husband and the income of the wife shall be assessed to tax for that year in accordance with that section.

(2) Where an election is made under subsection (1) in respect of a year of assessment, the election shall have effect for that year and for each subsequent year of assessment.

(3) Notwithstanding subsections (1) and (2), either the husband or the wife may, in relation to a year of assessment, by notice in writing given to the inspector before the end of the year, withdraw the election in respect of that year and, on the giving of that notice, the election shall not have effect for that year or for any subsequent year of assessment.

(4) (a) A husband and his wife, where the wife is living with the husband and where an election under subsection (1) has not been made by them for a year of assessment (or for any prior year of assessment) shall be deemed to have duly elected to be assessed to tax in accordance with section 1017 for that year unless before the end of that year either of them gives notice in writing to the inspector that he or she wishes to be assessed to tax for that year as a single person in accordance with section 1016.

(b) Where a husband or his wife has duly given notice under paragraph (a), that paragraph shall not apply in relation to that husband and wife for the year of assessment for which the notice was given or for any subsequent year of assessment until the year of assessment in which the notice is withdrawn, by the person who gave it, by further notice in writing to the inspector.

## 1019    Assessment of wife in respect of income of both spouses

(1) In this section—

**"the basis year"**, in relation to a husband and wife, means the year of marriage or, if earlier, the latest year of assessment preceding that year of marriage for which details of the total incomes of both the husband and the wife are available to the inspector at the time they first elect, or are first deemed to have duly elected, to be assessed to tax in accordance with section 1017;

**"year of marriage"**, in relation to a husband and wife, means the year of assessment in which their marriage took place.

(2) Subsection (3) shall apply for a year of assessment where, in the case of a husband and wife who are living together—

(a) (i) an election (including an election deemed to have been duly made) by the husband and wife to be assessed to income tax in accordance with section 1017 has effect in relation to the year of assessment, and

(ii) the husband and the wife by notice in writing jointly given to the inspector before [1 April]¹ in the year of assessment elect that the wife should be assessed to income tax in accordance with section 1017,

or

(b) (i) the year of marriage is the year 1993–94 or a subsequent year of assessment,

(ii) not having made an election under section 1018(1) to be assessed to income tax in accordance with section 1017, the husband and wife have been deemed for that year of assessment, in accordance with section 1018(4), to have duly made such an election, but have not made an election in accordance with paragraph (a)(ii) for that year, and

(iii) the inspector, to the best of his or her knowledge and belief, considers that the total income of the wife for the basis year exceeded the total income of her husband for that basis year.

(3) Where this subsection applies for a year of assessment, the wife shall be assessed to income tax in accordance with section 1017 for that year, and accordingly references in section 1017 or in any other provision of the Income Tax Acts, however expressed—

(a) to a husband being assessed, assessed and charged or chargeable to income tax for a year of assessment in respect of his own total income (if any) and his wife's total income (if any), and

(b) to income of a wife being deemed for income tax purposes to be that of her husband,

shall, subject to this section and the modifications set out in subsection (6) and any other necessary modifications, be construed respectively for that year of assessment as references—

(i) to a wife being assessed, assessed and charged or chargeable to income tax in respect of her own total income (if any) and her husband's total income (if any), and

(ii) to the income of a husband being deemed for income tax purposes to be that of his wife.

(4) (a) Where in accordance with subsection (3) a wife is by virtue of subsection (2)(b) to be assessed and charged to income tax in respect of her total income (if any) and her husband's total income (if any) for a year of assessment—

(i) in the absence of a notice given in accordance with subsection (1) or (4)(a) of section 1018 or an application made under section 1023, the wife shall be so assessed and charged for each subsequent year of assessment, and

(ii) any such charge shall apply and continue to apply notwithstanding that her husband's total income for the basis year may have exceeded her total income for that year.

(b) Where a notice under section 1018(4)(a) or an application under section 1023 is withdrawn and, but for the giving of such a notice or the making of such an application in the first instance, a wife would have been assessed to income tax in respect of her own total income (if any) and the total income (if any) of her husband for the year of assessment in which the notice was given or the application was made, as may be appropriate, then, in the absence of an election made in accordance with section 1018(1) (not being such an election deemed to have been duly made in accordance with section 1018(4)), the wife shall be so assessed to income tax for the year of assessment in which that notice or application is withdrawn and for each subsequent year of assessment.

(5) Where an election is made in accordance with subsection (2)(a)(ii) for a year of assessment, the election shall have effect for that year and each subsequent year of assessment unless it is withdrawn by further notice in writing given jointly by the husband and the wife to the inspector before [1 April][1] in a year of assessment and the election shall not then have effect for the year for which the further notice is given or for any subsequent year of assessment.

(6) For the purposes of the other provisions of this section and as the circumstances may require—

(a) a reference in the Income Tax Acts, however expressed, to an individual or a claimant, being a man, a married man or a husband shall be construed respectively as a reference to a woman, a married woman or a wife, and a reference in those Acts, however expressed, to a woman, a married woman or a wife shall be construed respectively as a reference to a man, a married man or a husband, and

(b) any provision of the Income Tax Acts shall, in so far as it may relate to the treatment of any husband and wife for the purposes of those Acts, be construed so as to give effect to this section.

---

**Notes**

1   Substituted by Finance Act 2001, s 77(2) and Schedule 2.

---

**1020   Special provisions relating to year of marriage**

(1) In this section—

["income tax month" means—

(a) in relation to a period prior to 6 December 2001, a month beginning on the 6th day of a month and ending on the 5th day of the next month,

(b) the period beginning on 6 December 2001 and ending on 31 December 2001, and

(c) thereafter, a calendar month;]¹

**"year of marriage"**, in relation to a husband and wife, means the year of assessment in which their marriage took place.

(2) Section 1018 shall not apply in relation to a husband and his wife for the year of marriage.

(3) Where, on making a claim in that behalf, a husband and his wife prove that the amount equal to the aggregate of the income tax paid and payable by the husband on his total income for the year of marriage and the income tax paid and payable by his wife on her total income for the year of marriage is in excess of the income tax which would have been payable by the husband on his total income and the total income of his wife for the year of marriage if—

(a) he had been charged to income tax for the year of marriage in accordance with section 1017, and

(b) he and his wife had been married to each other throughout the year of marriage,

they shall be entitled, subject to subsection (4), to repayment of income tax of an amount determined by the formula—

$$A \times \frac{B}{[12]^2}$$

where—

A is the amount of the aforementioned excess, and

B is the number of income tax months in the period between the date on which the marriage took place and the end of the year of marriage, part of an income tax month being treated for this purpose as an income tax month in a case where the period consists of part of an income tax month or of one or more income tax months and part of an income tax month.²

(4) Any repayment of income tax under subsection (3) shall be allocated to the husband and to the wife concerned in proportion to the amounts of income tax paid and payable by them, having regard to subsection (2), on their respective total incomes for the year of marriage.

(5) Any claim for a repayment of income tax under subsection (3) shall be made in writing to the inspector after the end of the year of marriage and shall be made by the husband and wife concerned jointly.

(6) (a) Subsections (1) and (2) of section 459 and section 460 shall apply to a repayment of income tax under this section as they apply to any allowance,

deduction, relief or reduction under the provisions specified in the Table to section 458.

(b) Subsections (3) and (4) of section 459 and paragraph 8 of Schedule 28 shall, with any necessary modifications, apply in relation to a repayment of tax under this section.

**Notes**

1    Definition of "income tax" substituted by Finance Act 2001, s 77(2) and Schedule 2.

2    Subsection (3) amended by Finance Act 2001, s 77(2).

## 1021    Repayment of tax in case of certain husbands and wives

(1) This section shall apply for a year of assessment in the case of a husband and wife one of whom is assessed to income tax for the year of assessment in accordance with section 1017 and to whom section 1023 does not apply for that year.

(2) Where for a year of assessment this section applies in the case of a husband and wife, any repayment of income tax to be made in respect of the aggregate of the net tax deducted or paid under any provision of the Tax Acts [...]¹ in respect of the total income (if any) of the husband and of the total income (if any) of the wife shall be allocated to the husband and the wife concerned in proportion to the net amounts of tax so deducted or paid in respect of their respective total incomes; but this subsection shall not apply where a repayment, which but for this subsection would not be made to a spouse, is less than [€25]¹.

(3) Notwithstanding subsection (2), where the inspector, having regard to all the circumstances of a case, is satisfied that a repayment or a greater part of a repayment of income tax arises by reason of some allowance or relief which, if sections 1023 and 1024 had applied for the year of assessment, would have been allowed to one spouse only, the inspector may make the repayment to the husband and the wife in such proportions as the inspector considers just and reasonable.

**Notes**

1    Subsection (2) amended by Finance Act 2000, s 69(2) and Schedule 2, Part 2 and further amended by s 240 and Schedule 5 of the Finance Act 2001 consequent on the changeover to euro.

## 1022    Special provisions relating to tax on wife's income

[(1) Where—

(a) an assessment to income tax (in this section referred to as "the original assessment") has been made for any year of assessment on a man, or on a man's trustee, guardian or committee, or on a man's executors or administrators,

(b) the Revenue Commissioners are of the opinion that, if an application for separate assessment under section 1023 had been in force with respect to that year of assessment, an assessment in respect of or of part of the same income would have been made on, or on the trustee, guardian or committee of, or on the executors or administrators of, a woman who is the man's wife or was his wife in that year of assessment, and

(c) the whole or part of the amount payable under the original assessment has remained unpaid at the expiration of 28 days from the time when it became due,

the Revenue Commissioners may give to that woman, or, if she is dead, to her executors or administrators, or, if an assessment referred to in paragraph (b) could in the circumstances referred to in that paragraph have been made on her trustee, guardian or committee, to her or to her trustee, guardian or committee, a notice stating—

(i) particulars of the original assessment and of the amount remaining unpaid under that assessment, and

(ii) to the best of their judgment, particulars of the assessment (in this subsection referred to as the "last mentioned assessment") which would have been so made,

and requiring the person to whom the notice is given to pay [the lesser of—

(A) the amount which would have been payable under the last-mentioned assessment if it conformed with those particulars, and

(B) the amount remaining unpaid under the original assessment.][1]

(2) The same consequences as respects—

(a) the imposition of a liability to pay, and the recovery of, the tax with or without interest,

(b) priority for the tax in bankruptcy or in the administration of the estate of a deceased person,

(c) appeals to the Appeal Commissioners, the rehearing of such appeals and the stating of cases for the opinion of the High Court, and

(d) the ultimate incidence of the liability imposed,

shall follow on the giving of a notice under subsection (1) [to the spouse or to the spouse's representative, or to the spouse's executors or administrators, as would have followed on the making on the spouse, or on the spouse's representative, or on the spouse's executors or administrators][2], as the case may be, of an assessment referred to in subsection (1)(b), being an assessment which—

(i) was made on the day of the giving of the notice,

(ii) charged the same amount of tax as is required to be paid by the notice,

(iii)  fell to be made and was made by the authority who made the original assessment, and

(iv)  was made by that authority to the best of that authority's judgment,

and the provisions of the Income Tax Acts relating to the matters specified in paragraphs (a) to (d) shall, with the necessary modifications, apply accordingly.

(3) Where a notice is given under subsection (1), tax up to the amount required to be paid by the notice shall cease to be recoverable under the original assessment and, where the tax charged by the original assessment carried interest under section 1080, such adjustment shall be made of the amount payable under that section in relation to that assessment and such repayment shall be made of any amounts previously paid under that section in relation to that assessment as are necessary to secure that the total sum, if any, paid or payable under that section in relation to that assessment is the same as it would have been if the amount which ceases to be recoverable had never been charged.

(4) Where the amount payable under a notice under subsection (1) is reduced as the result of an appeal or of a case stated for the opinion of the High Court—

(a)  the Revenue Commissioners shall, if having regard to that result they are satisfied that the original assessment was excessive, cause such relief to be given by means of repayment or otherwise as appears to them to be just; but

(b)  subject to any relief so given, a sum equal to the reduction in the amount payable under the notice shall again become recoverable under the original assessment.

(5) The Revenue Commissioners and the inspector or other proper officer shall have the like powers of obtaining information with a view to the giving of, and otherwise in connection with, a notice under subsection (1) as they would have had with a view to the making of, and otherwise in connection with, an assessment referred to in subsection (1)(b) if the necessary conditions had been fulfilled for the making of such an assessment.

[(6) Where a husband or a wife dies (in this subsection and subsections (7) and (8) referred to as the 'deceased spouse') and at any time before the death the husband and wife were living together, then the other spouse or, if the other spouse is dead, the executors or administrators of the other spouse may, not later than 2 months from the date of the grant of probate or letters of administration in respect of the deceased spouse's estate or, with the consent of the deceased spouse's executors or administrators, at any later date, give to the deceased spouse's executors or administrators and to the inspector a notice in writing declaring that, to the extent permitted by this section, the other spouse or the executors or administrators of the other spouse disclaim responsibility for unpaid income tax in respect of all income of the deceased spouse for any year of assessment or part of a year of assessment, being a year of assessment or a part of a year of assessment for which any income of the deceased spouse was deemed to be the income of the other spouse and in respect of which the other spouse was assessed to tax under section 1017 or under that section as modified by section 1019.][3]

(7) A notice given to the inspector pursuant to subsection (6) shall be deemed not to be a valid notice unless it specifies the names and addresses of [the deceased spouse's executors or administrators][4].

(8) Where a notice under subsection (6) has been given to [a deceased spouse's executors or administrators][5] and to the inspector—

(a) it shall be the duty of the Revenue Commissioners and the Appeal Commissioners to exercise such powers as they may then or thereafter be entitled to exercise under subsections (1) to (5) in connection with any assessment made on or before the date when the giving of that notice is completed, being an assessment in respect of any of the income to which that notice relates, and

(b) the assessments (if any) to tax which may be made after that date shall, in all respects and in particular as respects the persons assessable and the tax payable, be the assessments which would have been made if—

(i) an application for separate assessment under section 1023 had been in force in respect of the year of assessment in question, and

(ii) all assessments previously made had been made accordingly.

[(9) The Revenue Commissioners may nominate in writing any of their officers to perform any acts and discharge any functions authorised by this section to be performed or authorised by the Revenue Commissioners.][6]

## Notes

1 Subsection (1) substituted by s 29(1)(a) of the Finance Act 2000. Section 29(2) provides as follows:

(a) Paragraphs (a) to (e) of subsection (1) shall apply as respects assessments made on or after 10 February 2000.

(b) Paragraph (f) of subsection (1) shall apply as respects assessments made before, on or after 10 February 2000.

2 Subsection (2) amended by s 29(1)(b) of the Finance Act 2000.

3 Subsection (6) substituted by s 29(1)(c) of the Finance Act 2000.

4 Subsection (7) amended by s 29(1)(d) of the Finance Act 2000.

5 Subsection (8) amended by s 29(1)(e) of the Finance Act 2000.

6 Subsection (9) inserted by s 29(1)(f) of the Finance Act 2000.

## 1023    Application for separate assessments

(1) In this section and in section 1024, "personal reliefs" means relief under any of the provisions specified in the Table to section 458, apart from relief under sections [461A][1], 462 and 463.

(2) Where an election by a husband and wife to be assessed to income tax in accordance with section 1017 has effect in relation to a year of assessment and, in relation to that

year of assessment, an application is made for the purpose under this section in such manner and form as may be prescribed by the Revenue Commissioners, either by the husband or by the wife, income tax for that year shall be assessed, charged and recovered on the income of the husband and on the income of the wife as if they were not married and the provisions of the Income Tax Acts with respect to the assessment, charge and recovery of tax shall, except where otherwise provided by those Acts, apply as if they were not married except that—

(a)  the total deductions from total income [and reliefs]¹ allowed to the husband and wife by means of personal reliefs shall be the same as if the application had not had effect with respect to that year,

(b)  the total tax payable by the husband and wife for that year shall be the same as the total tax which would have been payable by them if the application had not had effect with respect to that year, and

(c)  section 1024 shall apply.

(3) An application under this section in respect of a year of assessment may be made—

(a)  in the case of persons marrying during the course of that year, before the [1 April]² in the following year, and

(b)  in any other case, within 6 months before [1 April]² in that year.

(4) Where an application is made under subsection (2), that subsection shall apply not only for the year of assessment for which the application was made, but also for each subsequent year of assessment; but, in relation to a subsequent year of assessment, the person who made the application may, by notice in writing given to the inspector before [1 April]² in that year, withdraw that election and, on the giving of that notice, subsection (2) shall not apply for the year of assessment in relation to which the notice was given or any subsequent year of assessment.

(5) A return of the total incomes of the husband and of the wife may be made for the purposes of this section either by the husband or by the wife but, if the Revenue Commissioners are not satisfied with any such return, they may require a return to be made by the wife or by the husband, as the case may be.

(6) The Revenue Commissioners may by notice require returns for the purposes of this section to be made at any time.

---

**Notes**

1    Subsections (1) and (2) amended by Schedule 1 of the Finance Act 2000.

2    Subsections (3) and (4) amended by Finance Act, s 77(2) and Schedule 2.

---

**1024   Method of apportioning reliefs and charging tax in cases of separate assessments**

(1) This section shall apply where pursuant to an application under section 1023 a husband and wife are assessed to tax for a year of assessment in accordance with that section.

(2)  (a)  Subject to subsection (3), the benefit flowing from the personal reliefs for a year of assessment may be given either by means of reduction of the amount of the tax to be paid or by repayment of any excess of tax which has been paid, or by both of those means, as the case requires, and shall be allocated to the husband and the wife, in so far as it flows from—

   [(i)    relief under sections 244 and 372AR, in the proportions in which they incurred the expenditure giving rise to the relief;]¹

   (ii)    relief under sections 461, 464, 465 (other than [subsection (3)]²) and 468, in the proportions of one-half and one-half;

   (iii)   relief in respect of a child under [section 465(3)]³ and relief in respect of a dependent relative under section 466, to the husband or to the wife according as he or she maintains the child or dependent relative;

   (iv)    relief under section 467, in the proportions in which they bear the cost of employing the person in respect of whom the relief is given;

   (v)    relief under section 469, in the proportions in which they bore the expenditure giving rise to the relief;

   [(vi)   relief under sections 470, 470A [,470B]⁴ and 473, to the husband or to the wife according as he or she made the payment giving rise to the relief;]

   (vii)   relief under section 471, in the proportions in which they incurred the expenditure giving rise to the relief;

   [(viii)  relief under sections 472, 472A and 472B relief to the husband or to the wife according as the emoluments from which the deduction under those sections is granted as the emoluments of the husband or of the wife;]⁵

   [(viiia)  relief under section 472C, to the husband or the wife according as he or she is entitled to the relief under the said section;]⁶

   (ix)    relief under sections 473A [, 476]⁷, 477, 478 and 479, in the proportions in which they incurred the expenditure giving rise to the relief;

   (x)    relief under section 481, in the proportions in which they made the relevant investment giving rise to the relief

   [(xa)   relief under section 848A(7), to the husband and wife according as he or she made the relevant donation giving rise to the relief;]⁸

   (xi)   relief under Part 16, in the proportions in which they subscribed for the eligible shares giving rise to the relief;

   (xii)   relief under paragraphs 12 and 20 of Schedule 32, in the proportions in which they incurred the expenditure giving rise to the relief.

   (b)  Any reduction of income tax to be made under section 187(4)(b) or 188(5) for a year of assessment shall be allocated to the husband and to the wife in proportion to the amounts of income tax which but for section 187(4)(b) or 188(5) would have been payable by the husband and by the wife for that year.

[(c) Subject to subsection (4), section 15 shall apply for the year of assessment in relation to each of the spouses concerned.]⁹

(3) Where the amount of relief allocated to the husband under subsection (2)(a) exceeds the income tax chargeable on his income for the year of assessment, the balance shall be applied to reduce the income tax chargeable on the income of the wife for that year, and where the amount of relief allocated to the wife under that paragraph exceeds the income tax chargeable on her income for the year of assessment, the balance shall be applied to reduce the income tax chargeable on the income of the husband for that year.

[(4) Where the part of the taxable income of a spouse chargeable to tax in accordance with subsection (2)(c) at the standard rate is less than that of the other spouse and is less than the part of taxable income specified in column (1) of Part 2 of the Table to section 15 (in this subsection referred to as "the appropriate part") in respect of which the first-mentioned spouse is so chargeable to tax at that rate, the part of taxable income of the other spouse which by virtue of that subsection is to be charged to tax at that rate shall be increased by the amount by which the taxable income of the first-mentioned spouse chargeable to tax at that rate is less than the appropriate part.]¹⁰

**Notes**

1 Subsection 2(a)(i) substituted by schedule 2 of the Finance Act 2002.

2 Subsection 2(a)(ii) amended by schedule 6 of the Finance Act 2002.

3 Subsection 2(a)(iii) amended by schedule 6 of the Finance Act 2002.

4 Subsection 2(a)(vi) substituted by Finance Act 2001, s 20(b) and subsequently amended by Health Insurance (Miscellaneous Provisions) Act 2009, s 24.

5 Subsection 2(a)(viii) substituted by schedule 1 of the Finance Act 2000.

6 Subsection 2(a)(viiia) inserted by s 11 of the Finance Act, 2001.

7 Subsection 2(a)(ix) amended by s 21(2) of the Finance Act 2000 and schedule 6 of the Finance Act 2002.

8 Subsection 2(a)(xa) inserted by schedule 6 of the Finance Act 2002.

9 Subsection 2(c) substituted by s 3 of the Finance Act 2000.

10 Subsection (4) substituted by s 3 of the Finance Act 2000.

**1025    Maintenance in case of separated spouses**

(1) In this section—

**"maintenance arrangement"** means an order of a court, rule of court, deed of separation, trust, covenant, agreement, arrangement or any other act giving rise to a legally enforceable obligation and made or done in consideration or in consequence of—

(a)  the dissolution or annulment of a marriage, or

(b)  such separation of the parties to a marriage as is referred to in section 1015(2), and a maintenance arrangement relates to the marriage in consideration or in consequence of the dissolution or annulment of which, or of the separation of the parties to which, the maintenance arrangement was made or arises;

"**payment**" means a payment or part of a payment, as the case may be;

a reference to a child of a person includes a child in respect of whom the person was at any time before the making of the maintenance arrangement concerned entitled to [relief under section 465]¹.

(2) (a) This section shall apply to payments made directly or indirectly by a party to a marriage under or pursuant to a maintenance arrangement relating to the marriage for the benefit of his or her child, or for the benefit of the other party to the marriage, being payments—

    (i) which are made at a time when the wife is not living with the husband,

    (ii) the making of which is legally enforceable, and

    (iii) which are annual or periodical;

but this section shall not apply to such payments made under a maintenance arrangement made before the 8th day of June, 1983, unless and until such time as one of the following events occurs, or the earlier of such events occurs where both occur—

    (I) the maintenance arrangement is replaced by another maintenance arrangement or is varied, and

    (II) both parties to the marriage to which the maintenance arrangement relates, by notice in writing to the inspector, jointly elect that this section shall apply,

and where such an event occurs in either of those circumstances, this section shall apply to all such payments made after the date on which the event occurs.

(b) For the purposes of this section and of section 1026 but subject to paragraph (c), a payment, whether conditional or not, which is made directly or indirectly by a party to a marriage under or pursuant to a maintenance arrangement relating to the marriage (other than a payment of which the amount, or the method of calculating the amount, is specified in the maintenance arrangement and from which, or from the consideration for which, neither a child of the party to the marriage making the payment nor the other party to the marriage derives any benefit) shall be deemed to be made for the benefit of the other party to the marriage.

(c) Where the payment, in accordance with the maintenance arrangement, is made or directed to be made for the use and benefit of a child of the party to the marriage making the payment, or for the maintenance, support, education or other benefit of such a child, or in trust for such a child, and the amount or the method of calculating the amount of such payment so made or directed to be made is specified in the maintenance arrangement, that payment shall be deemed to be made for the benefit of such child, and not for the benefit of any other person.

(3) Notwithstanding anything in the Income Tax Acts but subject to section 1026, as respects any payment to which this section applies made directly or indirectly by one party to the marriage to which the maintenance arrangement concerned relates for the benefit of the other party to the marriage—

(a) the person making the payment shall not be entitled on making the payment to deduct and retain out of the payment any sum representing any amount of income tax on the payment,

(b) the payment shall be deemed for the purposes of the Income Tax Acts to be profits or gains arising to the other party to the marriage, and income tax shall be charged on that other party under Case IV of Schedule D in respect of those profits or gains, and

(c) the party to the marriage by whom the payment is made, having made a claim in that behalf in the manner prescribed by the Income Tax Acts, shall be entitled for the purposes of the Income Tax Acts to deduct the payment in computing his or her total income for the year of assessment in which the payment is made.

(4) Notwithstanding anything in the Income Tax Acts, as respects any payment to which this section applies made directly or indirectly by a party to the marriage to which the maintenance arrangement concerned relates for the benefit of his or her child—

(a) the person making the payment shall not be entitled on making the payment to deduct and retain out of the payment any sum representing any amount of income tax on the payment,

(b) the payment shall be deemed for the purposes of the Income Tax Acts not to be income of the child,

(c) the total income for any year of assessment of the party to the marriage who makes the payment shall be computed for the purposes of the Income Tax Acts as if the payment had not been made, and

(d) for the purposes of [section 465(5)]², the payment shall be deemed to be an amount expended on the maintenance of the child by the party to the marriage who makes the payment and, notwithstanding that the payment is made to the other party to the marriage to be applied for or towards the maintenance of the child and is so applied, it shall be deemed for the purposes of that section not to be an amount expended by that other party on the maintenance of the child.

(5) (a) Subsections (1) and (2) of section 459 and section 460 shall apply to a deduction under subsection (3)(c) as they apply to any allowance, deduction, relief or reduction under the provisions specified in the Table to section 458.

(b) Subsections (3) and (4) of section 459 and paragraph 8 of Schedule 28 shall, with any necessary modifications, apply in relation to a deduction under subsection (3)(c).³

### 1026   Separated and divorced persons: adaptation of provisions relating to married persons[1]

(1) Where a payment to which section 1025 applies is made in a year of assessment by a party to a marriage (being a marriage which has not been dissolved or annulled) and both parties to the marriage are resident in the State for that year, section 1018 shall apply in relation to the parties to the marriage for that year of assessment as if—

    (a)   in subsection (1) of that section ", where the wife is living with the husband," were deleted, and

    (b)   subsection (4) of that section were deleted.

(2) Where by virtue of subsection (1) the parties to a marriage elect as provided for in section 1018(1), then, as respects any year of assessment for which the election has effect—

    (a)   subject to subsection (1) and paragraphs (b) and (c), the Income Tax Acts shall apply in the case of the parties to the marriage as they apply in the case of a husband and wife who have elected under section 1018(1) and whose election has effect for that year of assessment,

    (b)   the total income or incomes of the parties to the marriage shall be computed for the purposes of the Income Tax Acts as if any payments to which section 1025 applies made in that year of assessment by one party to the marriage for the benefit of the other party to the marriage had not been made, and

    (c)   income tax shall be assessed, charged and recovered on the total income or incomes of the parties to the marriage as if an application under section 1023 had been made by one of the parties and that application had effect for that year of assessment.

(3) Notwithstanding subsection (1), where a payment to which section 1025 applies is made in a year of assessment by a spouse who is a party to a marriage, that has been dissolved, for the benefit of the other spouse, and—

    (a)   the dissolution was under either—

        (i)   section 5 of the Family Law (Divorce) Act, 1996, or

        (ii)   the law of a country or jurisdiction other than the State, being a divorce that is entitled to be recognised as valid in the State,

    (b)   both spouses are resident in the State for tax purposes for that year of assessment, and

    (c)   neither spouse has entered into another marriage [or a civil partnership][2], then, subsections (1) and (2) shall, with any necessary modifications, apply in relation to the spouses for that year of assessment as if their marriage had not been dissolved.

**Notes**

1　See also the Social Welfare Consolidation Act 2005, s 37

2　Section 1026(3)(c) amended by the Finance (No 3) Act 2011, Sch 1.

**1027　Payments pursuant to certain orders under Judicial Separation and Family Law Reform Act, 1989, Family Law Act, 1995, and Family Law (Divorce) Act, 1996, to be made without deduction of income tax**

Payment of money pursuant to—

    (a)　an order under Part II of the Judicial Separation and Family Law Reform Act, 1989,

    (b)　an order under the Family Law Act, 1995 (other than section 12 of that Act), and

    (c)　an order under the Family Law (Divorce) Act, 1996 (other than section 17 of that Act),

shall be made without deduction of income tax.

CHAPTER 2

CAPITAL GAINS TAX

**1028　Married persons**

(1) Subject to this section, the amount of capital gains tax on chargeable gains accruing to a married woman in a year of assessment or part of a year of assessment during which she is a married woman living with her husband shall be assessed and charged on the husband and not otherwise; but this subsection shall not affect the amount of capital gains tax chargeable on the husband apart from this subsection or result in the additional amount of capital gains tax charged on the husband by virtue of this subsection being different from the amount which would otherwise have remained chargeable on the married woman.

(2)　(a)　Subject to paragraph (b), subsection (1) shall not apply in relation to a husband and wife in any year of assessment where, before [1 April]¹ in the year following that year of assessment, an application is made by either the husband or wife that subsection (1) shall not apply, and such an application duly made shall have effect not only as respects the year of assessment for which it is made but also for any subsequent year of assessment.

    (b)　Where the applicant gives, for any subsequent year of assessment, a notice withdrawing an application under paragraph (a), that application shall not have effect with respect to the year for which the notice is given or any subsequent year; but such notice of withdrawal shall not be valid unless it is given before [1

April]¹ in the year following the year of assessment for which the notice is given.

(3) In the case of a woman who during a year of assessment or part of a year of assessment is a married woman living with her husband, any allowable loss which under section 31 would be deductible from the chargeable gains accruing in that year of assessment to the one spouse but for an insufficiency of chargeable gains shall for the purposes of that section be deductible from chargeable gains accruing in that year of assessment to the other spouse; but this subsection shall not apply in relation to losses accruing in a year of assessment to either spouse where an application that this subsection shall not apply is made by the husband or the wife before [1 April]¹ in the year following that year of assessment.

(4) [...]²

(5) Where in any year of assessment in which or in part of which the married woman is a married woman living with her husband, the husband disposes of an asset to the wife, or the wife disposes of an asset to the husband, both shall be treated as if the asset was acquired from the spouse making the disposal for a consideration of such amount as would secure that on the disposal neither a gain nor a loss would accrue to the spouse making the disposal; but this subsection shall not apply if until the disposal the asset formed part of trading stock of a trade carried on by the spouse making the disposal, or if the asset is acquired as trading stock for the purposes of a trade carried on by the spouse acquiring the asset.

(6) Subsection (5) shall apply notwithstanding section 596 or any other provision of the Capital Gains Tax Acts fixing the amount of the consideration deemed to be given on a disposal or acquisition.

[(6A) Subsection (5) shall not apply where the spouse who acquired the asset could not be taxed in the State for the year of assessment in which the acquisition took place, in respect of a gain on a subsequent disposal in that year by that spouse of the asset, if that spouse had made such a disposal and a gain accrued on the disposal.]³

(7) Where subsection (5) is applied in relation to a disposal of an asset by a husband to his wife, or by his wife to him, then, in relation to a subsequent disposal of the asset (not within that subsection), the spouse making the disposal shall be treated for the purposes of the Capital Gains Tax Acts as if the other spouse's acquisition or provision of the asset had been his or her acquisition or provision of the asset.

(8) An application or notice of withdrawal under this section shall be in such form and made in such manner as may be prescribed.

---

**Notes**

1   Subsections (2) and (3) amended by Finance Act 2001, s 77(2) and Schedule 2.

2   Subsection (4) deleted by s 75 of the Finance Act 1998.

3   Subsection (6A) inserted by Finance 2006, s 75(1)(a).

---

**1029  Application of section 1022 for purposes of capital gains tax**

Section 1022 shall apply with any necessary modifications in relation to capital gains tax as it applies in relation to income tax.

**1030  Separated spouses: transfers of assets**

(1) In this section, "spouse" shall be construed in accordance with section 2(2)(c) of the Family Law Act, 1995.[1]

(2) Notwithstanding any other provision of the Capital Gains Tax Acts, where by virtue or in consequence of—

    (a)  an order made under Part II of the Family Law Act, 1995, on or following the granting of a decree of judicial separation within the meaning of that Act,

    (b)  an order made under Part II of the Judicial Separation and Family Law Reform Act, 1989, on or following the granting of a decree of judicial separation where such order is treated, by virtue of section 3 of the Family Law Act, 1995, as if made under the corresponding provision of the Family Law Act, 1995,

    (c)  a deed of separation [...],[2]

    [(d)  a relief order (within the meaning of the Family Law Act, 1995) made following the dissolution of a marriage or following the legal separation of spouses, or][3]

    [(e)  an order or other determination to like effect, which is analogous to an order referred to in paragraph (d), of a court under the law of a territory other than the State made under or in consequence of the dissolution of a marriage or the legal separation of spouses, being a dissolution or legal separation that is entitled to be recognised as valid in the State,][4]

either of the spouses concerned disposes of an asset to the other spouse, then, subject to subsection (3), both spouses shall be treated for the purposes of the Capital Gains Tax Acts as if the asset was acquired from the spouse making the disposal for a consideration of such amount as would secure that on the disposal neither a gain nor a loss would accrue to the spouse making the disposal.

[(2A) Subsection (2) shall not apply where the spouse who acquired the asset could not be taxed in the State for the year of assessment in which the acquisition took place, in respect of a gain on a subsequent disposal in that year by that spouse of the asset, if that spouse had made such a disposal and a gain accrued on the disposal.][5]

(3) Subsection (2) shall not apply if until the disposal the asset formed part of the trading stock of a trade carried on by the spouse making the disposal or if the asset is acquired as trading stock for the purposes of a trade carried on by the spouse acquiring the asset.

(4) Where subsection (2) applies in relation to a disposal of an asset by a spouse to the other spouse, then, in relation to a subsequent disposal of the asset (not being a disposal to which subsection (2) applies), the spouse making the disposal shall be treated for the purposes of the Capital Gains Tax Acts as if the other spouse's acquisition or provision of the asset had been his or her acquisition or provision of the asset.

**Notes**

1   Note – s 88(2) of the Finance Act 2000 provides that subsection (1) will apply to disposals made after 10 February 2000.

2   Subsection (2)(c) amended by s 88 of the Finance Act 2000.

3   Subsection (2)(d) substituted by s 88 of the Finance Act 2000.

4   Subsection (2)(e) inserted by s 88 of the Finance Act 2000.

5   Subsection (2A) inserted by the Finance Act 2006, s 75(1)(b).

---

**1031    Divorced persons: transfers of assets**

(1) In this section, "spouse" shall be construed in accordance with section 2(2)(c) of the Family Law (Divorce) Act, 1996.

(2) Notwithstanding any other provision of the Capital Gains Tax Acts, where by virtue or in consequence of an order made under Part III of the Family Law (Divorce) Act, 1996, on or following the granting of a decree of divorce, either of the spouses concerned disposes of an asset to the other spouse, then, subject to subsection (3), both spouses shall be treated for the purpose of the Capital Gains Tax Acts as if the asset was acquired from the spouse making the disposal for a consideration of such amount as would secure that on the disposal neither a gain nor a loss would accrue to the spouse making the disposal.

[(2A) Subsection (2) shall not apply where the spouse who acquired the asset could not be taxed in the State for the year of assessment in which the acquisition took place, in respect of a gain on a subsequent disposal in that year by that spouse of the asset, if that spouse had made such a disposal and a gain accrued on the disposal.][1]

(3) Subsection (2) shall not apply if until the disposal the asset formed part of the trading stock of a trade carried on by the spouse making the disposal or if the asset is acquired as trading stock for the purposes of a trade carried on by the spouse acquiring the asset.

(4) Where subsection (2) applies in relation to a disposal of an asset by a spouse to the other spouse, then, in relation to a subsequent disposal of the asset (not being a disposal to which subsection (2) applies), the spouse making the disposal shall be treated for the purposes of the Capital Gains Tax Acts as if the other spouse's acquisition or provision of the asset had been his or her acquisition or provision of the asset.

---

**Notes**

1   Subsection (2A) inserted by FA 2006, s 75(1)(c).

---

[Part 44A
Tax Treatment of Civil Partnerships
*Chapter 1*
*Income Tax*

## 1031A  Interpretation (Chapter 1)

(1) In this Chapter—

"**inspector**", in relation to a notice, means any inspector who might reasonably be considered by the individual giving notice to be likely to be concerned with the subject matter of the notice or who declares himself or herself ready to accept the notice;

"**nominated civil partner**", in relation to a civil partnership, means the civil partner who is nominated for the purposes of this Chapter in accordance with section 1031D;

"**other civil partner**", in relation to a civil partnership, means the civil partner who is not the nominated civil partner.

(2) A civil partner shall be treated for income tax purposes as living with his or her civil partner unless they are in fact living separately and apart in circumstances where reconciliation is unlikely.

(3) (a)  In this Chapter, references to the income of the other civil partner include references to any sum which apart from this Chapter would be included in computing that civil partner's total income, and this Chapter shall apply in relation to any such sum notwithstanding that an enactment (including, except in so far as the contrary is expressly provided, an enactment passed after 1 January 2011) requires that that sum should not be treated as income of any individual other than that civil partner.

(b)  In the Income Tax Acts, a reference to an individual who has duly elected to be assessed to tax in accordance with a particular section includes a reference to an individual who is deemed to have elected to be assessed to tax in accordance with that section, and any reference to an individual who is assessed to tax in accordance with section 1031C for a year of assessment includes a reference to a case where the individual and his or her civil partner are assessed to tax for that year in accordance with section 1031H.

(4) Any notice required to be served under any section in this Chapter may be served by post.

## 1031B  Assessment as single persons

(1) Subject to subsection (2), in any case in which civil partners are treated as living together, income tax shall be assessed, charged and recovered, except as is otherwise provided by the Income Tax Acts, on the income of each civil partner as if they were not in a civil partnership.

(2) Where an election under section 1031D has effect in relation to 2 individuals who are civil partners of each other for a year of assessment, this section shall not apply in relation to those civil partners for that year of assessment.

**1031C  Assessment of nominated civil partner in respect of income of both civil partners**

(1) Where an election under section 1031D to be assessed to tax in accordance with this section has effect for a year of assessment—

(a)  the nominated civil partner shall be assessed and charged to income tax, not only in respect of his or her total income (if any) for that year but also in respect of the other civil partner's total income (if any) for any part of that year of assessment during which they are living together, and for those purposes and for the purposes of the Income Tax Acts, that last-mentioned income shall be deemed to be the income of the nominated civil partner,

(b)  the question of whether there is any income of the other civil partner chargeable to tax for any year of assessment and, if so, what is to be taken to be the amount of that income for tax purposes shall not be affected by this section, and

(c)  any tax to be assessed in respect of any income which under this section is deemed to be income of the nominated civil partner shall, instead of being assessed on the other civil partner, or on his or her trustees, guardian or committee, or on his or her executors or administrators, be assessable on the nominated civil partner or, in the appropriate cases, on his or her executors or administrators.

(2) Any relief from income tax authorised by any provision of the Income Tax Acts to be granted to the nominated civil partner by reference to the income or profits or gains or losses of the other civil partner or by reference to any payment made by the other civil partner shall be granted to the nominated civil partner for a year of assessment only if the nominated civil partner is assessed to tax for that year in accordance with this section.

**1031D  Election for assessment under section 1031C**

(1) (a)  An individual and his or her civil partner who are living together may, at any time during a year of assessment, by notice in writing given to the inspector, jointly—

(i)  elect to be assessed to income tax for that year of assessment in accordance with section 1031C, and

(ii)  nominate which of them is to be the nominated civil partner for the purposes of this Chapter.

(b)  If the notice under paragraph (a) does not nominate one of the civil partners to be the nominated civil partner, the Revenue Commissioners shall deem one of the civil partners to be the nominated civil partner.

(c)  Where an election is made under paragraph (a), the income of the nominated civil partner and the income of the other civil partner shall be assessed to tax for that year in accordance with section 1031C.

(2) Where an election is made under subsection (1) for a year of assessment, the election shall have effect for that year and for each subsequent year of assessment.

(3) Notwithstanding subsections (1) and (2), either civil partner may, for a year of assessment, by notice in writing given to the inspector before the end of the year, withdraw the election for that year and, on the giving of that notice, the election shall not have effect for that year or for any subsequent year of assessment.

(4) (a) Where an individual and his or her civil partner are living together and an election under subsection (1) has not been made by them for a year of assessment (or for any prior year of assessment), the civil partners shall be deemed to have duly elected to be assessed to tax in accordance with section 1031C for that year and the Revenue Commissioners shall deem one of the civil partners to be the nominated civil partner, unless before the end of that year either of them gives notice in writing to the inspector that he or she wishes to be assessed to tax for that year as a single person in accordance with section 1031B.

(b) Where a civil partner has duly given notice under paragraph (a), that paragraph shall not apply in relation to the civil partners concerned for the year of assessment for which the notice was given or for any subsequent year of assessment until the year of assessment in which the notice is withdrawn, by the civil partner who gave it, by further notice in writing to the inspector.

**1031E  Special provisions relating to year of registration of civil partnership**

(1) In this section—

"**income tax month**" means a calendar month;

"**year of registration**", in relation to 2 individuals who are civil partners of each other, means—

(a) in the case of civil partners whose civil partnership was registered in the State, the year of assessment in which their civil partnership was registered, and

(b) in the case of civil partners whose legal relationship, entered into in another jurisdiction, is recognised pursuant to an order made under section 5 of the Civil Partnership and Certain Rights and Obligations of Cohabitants Act 2010, the year of assessment in which falls the day on which, by virtue of subsection (2) of that section, the civil partners are to be treated as civil partners under the law of the State,

and 'registered' in relation to a civil partnership shall be construed accordingly.

(2) Section 1031D shall not apply in relation to civil partners for the year of registration.

(3) Where, on making a claim in that behalf, 2 individuals who are civil partners of each other prove that the amount equal to the aggregate of the income tax paid and payable by each of them on his or her total income for the year of registration is in excess of the income tax which would have been payable by one of the civil partners on his or her total income and the total income of his or her civil partner for the year of registration if—

(a) the civil partner had been charged to income tax as the nominated civil partner for the year of registration in accordance with section 1031C, and

(b) the civil partners had been civil partners of each other throughout the year of registration,

they shall be entitled, subject to subsection (4), to repayment of income tax of an amount determined by the formula—

$$\frac{A \times B}{12}$$

where—

A  is the amount of the excess, and

B  is the number of income tax months in the period between the date on which the civil partnership was registered and the end of the year of registration, part of an income tax month being treated for this purpose as an income tax month in a case where the period consists of part of an income tax month or of one or more income tax months and part of an income tax month.

(4) Any repayment of income tax under subsection (3) shall be allocated to the civil partners concerned in proportion to the amounts of income tax paid and payable by them, having regard to subsection (2), on their respective total incomes for the year of registration.

(5) Any claim for a repayment of income tax under subsection (3) shall be made in writing to the inspector after the end of the year of registration and shall be made by both civil partners concerned jointly.

(6) (a) Subsections (1) and (2) of section 459 and section 460 shall apply to a repayment of income tax under this section as they apply to any allowance, deduction, relief or reduction under the provisions specified in the Table to section 458.

(b) Subsections (3) and (4) of section 459 and paragraph 8 of Schedule 28 shall, with any necessary modifications, apply in relation to a repayment of tax under this section.

## 1031F  Repayment of tax in case of certain civil partners

(1) This section shall apply for a year of assessment in the case of civil partners who are assessed to income tax for the year of assessment in accordance with section 1031C and to whom section 1031H does not apply for that year.

(2) Where for a year of assessment this section applies in the case of civil partners, any repayment of income tax to be made in respect of the aggregate of the net tax deducted or paid under any provision of the Tax Acts in respect of the total income (if any) of the nominated civil partner and of the total income (if any) of the other civil partner shall be allocated to the civil partners concerned in proportion to the net amounts of tax so deducted or paid in respect of their respective total incomes; but this subsection shall not

apply where a repayment, which but for this subsection would not be made to the other civil partner, is less than €25.

(3) Notwithstanding subsection (2), where the inspector, having regard to all the circumstances of a case, is satisfied that a repayment or a greater part of a repayment of income tax arises by reason of some allowance or relief which, if sections 1031H and 1031I had applied for the year of assessment, would have been allowed to one civil partner only, the inspector may make the repayment to the nominated civil partner and the other civil partner in such proportions as the inspector considers just and reasonable.

**1031G  Special provisions relating to tax on individual's civil partner's income**

(1) Where—

    (a) an assessment to income tax (in this section referred to as the 'original assessment') has been made for any year of assessment on an individual, or on an individual's trustee, guardian or committee (in this section referred to as the 'representative'), or on an individual's executors or administrators,

    (b) the Revenue Commissioners are of the opinion that, if an application for separate assessment under section 1031H had been in force with respect to that year of assessment, an assessment in respect of or of part of the same income would have been made on, or on the representative of, or on the executors or administrators of, an individual who is the civil partner of the individual referred to in paragraph (a) or who was the civil partner of the individual referred to in paragraph (a) (in this subsection and in subsection (2) referred to as the 'other civil partner') in that year of assessment, and

    (c) the whole or part of the amount payable under the original assessment has remained unpaid at the expiration of 28 days from the time when it became due,

the Revenue Commissioners may give to the other civil partner, or, if the other civil partner is dead, to the other civil partner's executors or administrators, or, if an assessment referred to in paragraph (b) could in the circumstances referred to in that paragraph have been made on the other civil partner's representative, to the other civil partner, or to the other civil partner's executors or administrators, a notice stating—

    (i) particulars of the original assessment and of the amount remaining unpaid under that assessment, and

    (ii) to the best of their judgement, particulars of the assessment (in this subsection referred to as the 'last-mentioned assessment') which would have been so made,

and requiring the other civil partner to whom the notice is given to pay the lesser of—

    (i) the amount which would have been payable under the last-mentioned assessment if it conformed with those particulars, and

    (ii) the amount remaining unpaid under the original assessment.

(2) The same consequences as respects—

    (a) the imposition of a liability to pay, and the recovery of, the tax with or without interest,

(b) priority for the tax in bankruptcy or in the administration of the estate of a deceased individual,

(c) appeals to the Appeal Commissioners, the rehearing of such appeals and the stating of cases for the opinion of the High Court, and

(d) the ultimate incidence of the liability imposed,

shall follow on the giving of a notice under subsection (1) to the other civil partner or to the other civil partner's representative, or to the other civil partner's executors or administrators, as would have followed on the making on the other civil partner, or on the other civil partner's representative, or on the other civil partner's executors or administrators, as the case may be, of an assessment referred to in subsection (1)(b), being an assessment which—

(i) was made on the day of the giving of the notice,

(ii) charged the same amount of tax as is required to be paid by the notice,

(iii) fell to be made and was made by the authority who made the original assessment, and

(iv) was made by that authority to the best of that authority's judgment,

and the provisions of the Income Tax Acts relating to the matters specified in paragraphs (a) to (d) shall, with the necessary modifications, apply accordingly.

(3) Where a notice is given under subsection (1), tax up to the amount required to be paid by the notice shall cease to be recoverable under the original assessment and, where the tax charged by the original assessment carried interest under section 1080, such adjustment shall be made of the amount payable under that section in relation to that assessment and such repayment shall be made of any amounts previously paid under that section in relation to that assessment as are necessary to secure that the total sum, if any, paid or payable under that section in relation to that assessment is the same as it would have been if the amount which ceases to be recoverable had never been charged.

(4) Where the amount payable under a notice under subsection (1) is reduced as the result of an appeal or of a case stated for the opinion of the High Court—

(a) the Revenue Commissioners shall, if having regard to that result they are satisfied that the original assessment was excessive, cause such relief to be given by means of repayment or otherwise as appears to them to be just, but

(b) subject to any relief given, a sum equal to the reduction in the amount payable under the notice concerned shall again become recoverable under the original assessment.

(5) The Revenue Commissioners and the inspector or other proper officer shall have the like powers of obtaining information with a view to the giving of, and otherwise in connection with, a notice under subsection (1) as they would have had with a view to the making of, and otherwise in connection with, an assessment referred to in subsection (1)(b) if the necessary conditions had been fulfilled for the making of such an assessment.

(6) Where a civil partner dies (in this subsection and subsections (7) and (8) referred to as the 'deceased civil partner') and, at any time before the death, the deceased civil partner and his or her civil partner were living together, then the surviving civil partner or his or her executors or administrators (if he or she is also deceased) may, not later than 2 months from the date of the grant of probate or letters of administration in respect of the deceased civil partner's estate or, with the consent of the deceased civil partner's executors or administrators, at any later date, give to the deceased civil partner's executors or administrators and to the inspector a notice in writing declaring that, to the extent permitted by this section, the surviving civil partner, or his or her executors or administrators, as the case may be, disclaim responsibility for unpaid income tax in respect of all income of the deceased civil partner for any year of assessment or part of a year of assessment, being a year of assessment or a part of a year of assessment for which any income of the deceased civil partner was deemed to be the income of the surviving civil partner and in respect of which the surviving civil partner was assessed to tax under section 1031C.

(7) A notice given to the inspector pursuant to subsection (6) shall be deemed not to be a valid notice unless it specifies the names and addresses of the deceased civil partner's executors or administrators.

(8) Where a notice under subsection (6) has been given to a deceased civil partner's executors or administrators and to the inspector—

    (a) it shall be the duty of the Revenue Commissioners and the Appeal Commissioners to exercise such powers as they may then or thereafter be entitled to exercise under subsections (1) to (5) in connection with any assessment made on or before the date when the giving of that notice is completed, being an assessment in respect of any of the income to which that notice relates, and

    (b) the assessments (if any) to tax which may be made after that date shall, in all respects and in particular as respects the civil partners assessable and the tax payable, be the assessments which would have been made if—

        (i) an application for separate assessment under section 1031H had been in force in respect of the year of assessment in question, and

        (ii) all assessments previously made had been made accordingly.

(9) The Revenue Commissioners may nominate in writing any of their officers to perform any acts and discharge any functions authorised by this section to be performed or discharged by the Revenue Commissioners.

**1031H   Application for separate assessments**

(1) In this section and in section 1031I, 'personal reliefs' means relief under any of the provisions specified in the Table to section 458, apart from relief under sections 461A, 462 and 463.

(2) Where an election by civil partners to be assessed to income tax in accordance with section 1031C has effect for a year of assessment and, for that year of assessment, an application is made for the purpose under this section in such manner and form as may

be prescribed by the Revenue Commissioners, by either civil partner, income tax for that year shall be assessed, charged and recovered on the income of each civil partner as if they were not civil partners of each other and the provisions of the Income Tax Acts with respect to the assessment, charge and recovery of tax shall, except where otherwise provided by those Acts, apply as if they were not civil partners of each other except that—

    (a)  the total deductions from total income and reliefs allowed to the civil partners by means of personal reliefs shall be the same as if the application had not had effect for that year,

    (b)  the total tax payable by the civil partners for that year shall be the same as the total tax which would have been payable by them if the application had not had effect for that year, and

    (c)  section 1031I shall apply.

(3) An application under this section for a year of assessment may be made—

    (a)  before 1 April in the following year—

        (i)  in the case of individuals whose civil partnership was registered in the State during the course of that year of assessment, and

        (ii)  in the case of civil partners whose legal relationship, entered into in another jurisdiction, is recognised pursuant to an order made under section 5 of the Civil Partnership and Certain Rights and Obligations of Cohabitants Act 2010, if the date on which the civil partners are to be treated as civil partners under the law of the State, by virtue of subsection (2) of that section, falls during the course of that year,

    and

    (b)  in any other case, within 6 months before 1 April in that year.

(4) Where an application is made under subsection (2), that subsection shall apply not only for the year of assessment for which the application was made, but also for each subsequent year of assessment; but, in relation to a subsequent year of assessment, the civil partner who made the application may, by notice in writing given to the inspector before 1 April in that year, withdraw that election and, on the giving of that notice, subsection (2) shall not apply for the year of assessment in relation to which the notice was given or any subsequent year of assessment.

(5) A return of the total incomes of both civil partners may be made for the purposes of this section by either civil partner concerned but, if the Revenue Commissioners are not satisfied with any such return, they may require a return to be made by the civil partner who did not make the return.

(6) The Revenue Commissioners may by notice require returns for the purposes of this section to be made at any time.

**1031I Method of apportioning reliefs and charging tax in cases of separate assessments**

(1) This section shall apply where pursuant to an application under section 1031H, civil partners are assessed to tax for a year of assessment in accordance with that section.

(2) (a) Subject to subsection (3), the benefit flowing from the personal reliefs for a year of assessment may be given either by means of reduction of the amount of the tax to be paid or by repayment of any excess of tax which has been paid, or by both of those means, as the case requires, and shall be allocated to the civil partners—

    (i) in so far as it flows from relief under sections 244 and 372AR, in the proportions in which they incurred the expenditure giving rise to the relief,

    (ii) in so far as it flows from relief under sections 461, 464, 465 (other than subsection (3)) and 468, in the proportions of one-half and one-half,

    (iii) in so far as it flows from relief in respect of a child under section 465(3) and relief in respect of a dependent relative under section 466, to the civil partner who maintains the child or dependent relative,

    (iv) in so far as it flows from relief under section 467, in the proportions in which each civil partner bears the cost of employing the individual in respect of whom the relief is given,

    (v) in so far as it flows from relief under section 469, in the proportions in which each civil partner incurred the expenditure giving rise to the relief,

    (vi) in so far as it flows from relief under sections 470, 470B and 473, to either civil partner according as he or she made the payment giving rise to the relief,

    (vii) in so far as it flows from relief under section 471, in the proportions in which each civil partner incurred the expenditure giving rise to the relief,

    (viii) in so far as it flows from relief under sections 472, 472A and 472B, to either civil partner according as the emoluments from which relief under those sections is granted are emoluments of that civil partner,

    (ix) in so far as it flows from relief under sections 473A, 476 and 477, in the proportions in which each civil partner incurred the expenditure giving rise to the relief,

    (x) in so far as it flows from relief under section 481, in the proportions in which each civil partner made the relevant investment giving rise to the relief,

    (xi) in so far as it flows from relief under section 848A(7), to each civil partner according as he or she made the relevant donation giving rise to the relief,

    (xii) in so far as it flows from relief under Part 16, in the proportions in which each civil partner subscribed for the eligible shares giving rise to the relief, and

(xiii) in so far as it flows from relief under paragraphs 12 and 20 of Schedule 32, in the proportions in which each civil partner incurred the expenditure giving rise to the relief.

(b) Any reduction of income tax to be made under section 188(5) for a year of assessment shall be allocated to each civil partner in proportion to the amounts of income tax which but for section 188(5) would have been payable by both civil partners for that year.

(c) Subject to subsection (4), Part 1 of the Table to section 15 shall apply to each of the civil partners concerned.

(3) Where the amount of relief allocated to a civil partner under subsection (2)(a) exceeds the income tax chargeable on his or her income for the year of assessment, the balance shall be applied to reduce the income tax chargeable on the income of his or her civil partner for that year, and where the amount of relief allocated to that civil partner under that paragraph exceeds the income tax chargeable on his or her income for the year of assessment, the balance shall be applied to reduce the income tax chargeable on the income of the first-mentioned civil partner for that year.

(4) Where the part of the taxable income of a civil partner chargeable to tax in accordance with subsection (2)(c) at the standard rate is less than that of his or her civil partner and is less than the part of taxable income specified in column (1) of Part 1 of the Table to section 15 (in this subsection referred to as the 'appropriate part') in respect of which the first-mentioned civil partner is so chargeable to tax at that rate, the part of taxable income of the civil partner other than the first-mentioned civil partner which by virtue of subsection (2)(c) is to be charged to tax at the standard rate shall be increased, to an amount not exceeding the part of taxable income specified in column (1) of Part 3 of the Table to section 15 in respect of which an individual to whom that Part applies is so chargeable at that rate, by the amount by which the taxable income of the first-mentioned civil partner chargeable to tax at the standard rate is less than the appropriate part.

## 1031J  Maintenance of civil partners living apart

(1) In this section—

"**maintenance arrangement**" means an order of a court under Part 5 or 12 of the Civil Partnership and Certain Rights and Obligations of Cohabitants Act 2010 giving rise to a legally enforceable obligation;

"**payment**" means a payment or part of a payment, as the case may be.

(2) (a) This section shall apply to payments made directly or indirectly by a civil partner under or pursuant to a maintenance arrangement.

(b) For the purposes of this section and of section 1031K, a payment, whether conditional or not, which is made directly or indirectly by a civil partner or former civil partner under or pursuant to a maintenance arrangement shall be deemed to be made for the benefit of his or her civil partner or former civil partner.

(3) Notwithstanding anything in the Income Tax Acts but subject to section 1031K, as respects any payment to which this section applies made directly or indirectly by one civil partner or former civil partner under or pursuant to a maintenance arrangement for the benefit of his or her civil partner or former civil partner—

   (a)   the individual making the payment—

   (i)   shall not be entitled on making the payment to deduct and retain out of the payment any sum representing any amount of income tax on the payment, and

   (ii)   shall, if he or she makes a claim in that behalf in the manner prescribed by the Income Tax Acts, be entitled, for the purposes of those Acts, to deduct the payment in computing his or her total income for the year of assessment for which the payment is made,

   and

   (b)   the payment shall be deemed for the purposes of the Income Tax Acts to be profits or gains arising to the individual receiving the payment, and income tax shall be charged on that individual under Case IV of Schedule D in respect of those profits or gains.

(4) (a)   Subsections (1) and (2) of section 459 and section 460 shall apply to a deduction under subsection (3)(a)(ii) as they apply to any allowance, deduction, relief or reduction under the provisions specified in the Table to section 458.

   (b)   Subsections (3) and (4) of section 459 and paragraph 8 of Schedule 28 shall, with any necessary modifications, apply in relation to a deduction under subsection (3)(a)(ii).

## 1031K Dissolution or annulment of civil partnerships: adaptation of provisions relating to civil partners

(1) Where a payment to which section 1031J applies is made in a year of assessment by a civil partner (whose civil partnership has not been dissolved or annulled) and both civil partners concerned are resident in the State for that year, section 1031D shall apply in relation to those civil partners for that year of assessment as if—

   (a)   the words 'who are living together' in subsection (1)(a) of that section were deleted, and

   (b)   subsection (4) of that section were deleted.

(2) Where by virtue of subsection (1) both civil partners elect as provided for in section 1031D(1), then, for any year of assessment for which the election has effect—

   (a)   subject to subsection (1) and paragraphs (b) and (c), the Income Tax Acts shall apply in the case of the civil partners as they apply in the case of civil partners who have elected under section 1031D(1) and whose election has effect for that year of assessment,

   (b)   the total income or incomes of the civil partners shall be computed for the purposes of the Income Tax Acts as if any payments to which section 1031J applies made in that year of assessment by one civil partner for the benefit of his or her civil partner had not been made, and

(c) income tax shall be assessed, charged and recovered on the total income or incomes of the civil partners as if an application under section 1031H had been made by one of the civil partners and that application had effect for that year of assessment.

(3) Notwithstanding subsection (1), where a payment to which section 1031J applies is made in a year of assessment by a civil partner whose civil partnership has been dissolved, for the benefit of the other civil partner, and—

(a) the dissolution was a dissolution under section 110 of the Civil Partnership and Certain Rights and Obligations of Cohabitants Act 2010, or deemed to be such a dissolution under section 5(4) of that Act,

(b) both civil partners are resident in the State for tax purposes for that year of assessment, and

(c) neither civil partner has entered into another civil partnership or a marriage,

then, subsections (1) and (2) shall, with any necessary modifications, apply in relation to the civil partners for that year of assessment as if their civil partnership had not been dissolved.

CHAPTER 2<br>CAPITAL GAINS TAX

### 1031L   Interpretation (Chapter 2)

(1) In this Chapter—

"**inspector**", in relation to a notice, means any inspector who might reasonably be considered by the individual giving notice to be likely to be concerned with the subject matter of the notice or who declares himself or herself ready to accept the notice;

"**nominated civil partner**", in relation to a civil partnership, means the civil partner who is nominated for the purposes of this Chapter in accordance with section 1031M;

"**other civil partner**", in relation to a civil partnership, means the civil partner who is not the nominated civil partner.

(2) In the Capital Gains Tax Acts, a reference to an individual who has been duly nominated to be the nominated civil partner in accordance with section 1031M includes a reference to an individual who is deemed to be the nominated civil partner in accordance with that section.

(3) Any notice required to be served under any section in this Chapter may be served by post.

### 1031M  Civil partners

(1) (a) An individual and his or her civil partner who are living together, may, for a year of assessment, by notice in writing given to the inspector on or before 1 April in the year following that year of assessment, jointly nominate which of them is to be the nominated civil partner for the purposes of this Chapter.

(b) If the notice under paragraph (a) is not given on or before the date mentioned in that paragraph, the Revenue Commissioners shall deem one of the civil partners to be the nominated civil partner.

(2) Subject to this section, the amount of capital gains tax on chargeable gains accruing to civil partners in a year of assessment or part of a year of assessment during which they are living together shall be assessed and charged on the civil partner who is the nominated civil partner and not otherwise; but this subsection shall not affect the amount of capital gains tax chargeable on the nominated civil partner apart from this subsection or result in the additional amount of capital gains tax charged on the nominated civil partner by virtue of this subsection being different from the amount which would otherwise have remained chargeable on the other civil partner.

(3) (a) Subject to paragraph (b), subsection (2) shall not apply in relation to a civil partner in any year of assessment where, on or before 1 April in the year following that year of assessment, an application is made by either civil partner that subsection (2) shall not apply, and such an application duly made shall have effect not only as respects the year of assessment for which it is made but also for any subsequent year of assessment.

(b) Where the applicant gives, for any subsequent year of assessment, a notice withdrawing an application under paragraph (a), that application shall not have effect with respect to the year for which the notice is given or any subsequent year; but such notice of withdrawal shall not be valid unless it is given before 1 April in the year following the year of assessment for which the notice is given.

(4) In the case of a civil partner who during a year of assessment or part of a year of assessment is a civil partner living with his or her civil partner, any allowable loss which under section 31 would be deductible from the chargeable gains accruing in that year of assessment to one civil partner but for an insufficiency of chargeable gains shall for the purposes of that section be deductible from chargeable gains accruing in that year of assessment to the other civil partner; but this subsection shall not apply in relation to losses accruing in a year of assessment to either civil partner where an application that this subsection shall not apply is made by either of them before 1 April in the year following that year of assessment.

(5) Where, in any year of assessment in which or in part of which a civil partner is living with his or her civil partner, either civil partner disposes of an asset to his or her civil partner, both civil partners shall be treated as if the asset was acquired from the civil partner making the disposal for a consideration of such amount as would secure that on the disposal neither a gain nor a loss would accrue to the civil partner making the disposal; but this subsection shall not apply if until the disposal the asset formed part of trading stock of a trade carried on by the civil partner making the disposal, or if the asset is acquired as trading stock for the purposes of a trade carried on by the civil partner acquiring the asset.

(6) Subsection (5) shall apply notwithstanding section 596 or any other provision of the Capital Gains Tax Acts fixing the amount of the consideration deemed to be given on a disposal or acquisition.

(7) Subsection (5) shall not apply where the civil partner who acquired the asset could not be taxed in the State for the year of assessment in which the acquisition took place, in respect of a gain on a subsequent disposal in that year by that civil partner of the asset, if that civil partner had made such a disposal and a gain accrued on the disposal.

(8) Where subsection (5) is applied in relation to a disposal of an asset by a civil partner to his or her civil partner, then, in relation to a subsequent disposal of the asset (not within that subsection), the civil partner making the disposal shall be treated for the purposes of the Capital Gains Tax Acts as if the acquisition or provision of the asset by his or her civil partner had been his or her own acquisition or provision of the asset.

(9) An application or notice of withdrawal under this section shall be in such form and made in such manner as may be prescribed by the Revenue Commissioners.

## 1031N  Application of section 1031G for purposes of capital gains tax

Section 1031G shall apply with any necessary modifications in relation to capital gains tax as it applies in relation to income tax.

## 1031O  Transfers of assets where civil partnership dissolved

(1) Notwithstanding any other provision of the Capital Gains Tax Acts, where by virtue or in consequence of an order made under Part 12 of the Civil Partnership and Certain Rights and Obligations of Cohabitants Act 2010, on or following the granting of a decree of dissolution or a dissolution deemed under section 5(4) of that Act to be a dissolution under section 110 of that Act, either of the civil partners concerned disposes of an asset to his or her civil partner, then, subject to subsection (3), both civil partners shall be treated for the purpose of the Capital Gains Tax Acts as if the asset was acquired from the civil partner making the disposal for a consideration of such amount as would secure that on the disposal neither a gain nor a loss would accrue to the civil partner making the disposal.

(2) Subsection (1) shall not apply where the civil partner who acquired the asset could not be taxed in the State for the year of assessment in which the acquisition took place, in respect of a gain on a subsequent disposal in that year by that civil partner of the asset, if that civil partner had made such a disposal and a gain accrued on the disposal.

(3) Subsection (1) shall not apply if until the disposal the asset formed part of the trading stock of a trade carried on by the civil partner making the disposal or if the asset is acquired as trading stock for the purposes of a trade carried on by the civil partner acquiring the asset.

(4) Where subsection (1) applies in relation to a disposal of an asset by a civil partner to his or her civil partner, then, in relation to a subsequent disposal of the asset (not being a disposal to which subsection (1) applies), the civil partner making the disposal shall be treated for the purposes of the Capital Gains Tax Acts as if the acquisition or provision of the asset by his or her civil partner had been his or her own acquisition or provision of the asset.

PART 44B

TAX TREATMENT OF COHABITANTS
*CHAPTER 1*
*INCOME TAX*

**1031P   Interpretation (Chapter 1)**

In this Part—

**"cohabitant"** has the same meaning as in section 172 of the Civil Partnership and Certain Rights and Obligations of Cohabitants Act 2010;

**"inspector"**, in relation to a notice, means any inspector who might reasonably be considered by the individual giving notice to be likely to be concerned with the subject matter of the notice or who declares himself or herself ready to accept the notice;

**"qualified cohabitant"** has the same meaning as in section 172 of the Civil Partnership and Certain Rights and Obligations of Cohabitants Act 2010.

**1031Q   Maintenance where relationship between cohabitants ends**

(1) In this section—

**"maintenance arrangement"** means an order of a court under section 175 of the Civil Partnership and Certain Rights and Obligations of Cohabitants Act 2010 giving rise to a legally enforceable obligation;

**"payment"** means a payment or part of a payment, as the case may be.

(2) (a)  This section applies to payments made directly or indirectly by a qualified cohabitant under or pursuant to a maintenance arrangement.

(b)  For the purposes of this section a payment, whether conditional or not, which is made directly or indirectly by a qualified cohabitant under or pursuant to a maintenance arrangement shall be deemed to be made for the benefit of the other qualified cohabitant.

(3) Notwithstanding anything in the Income Tax Acts, as respects any payment to which this section applies made directly or indirectly by an individual under or pursuant to a maintenance arrangement for the benefit of a qualified cohabitant—

(a)  the individual making the payment—

(i)  shall not be entitled on making the payment to deduct and retain out of the payment any sum representing any amount of income tax on the payment, and

(ii)  shall, if he or she makes a claim in that behalf in the manner prescribed by the Income Tax Acts, be entitled, for the purposes of those Acts, to deduct the payment in computing his or her total income for the year of assessment in which the payment is made,

and

(b)  the payment shall be deemed for the purposes of the Income Tax Acts to be profits or gains arising to the qualified cohabitant, and income tax shall be charged on that qualified cohabitant under Case IV of Schedule D in respect of those profits or gains.

(4) (a) Subsections (1) and (2) of section 459 and section 460 shall apply to a deduction under subsection (3)(a)(ii) as they apply to any allowance, deduction, relief or reduction under the provisions specified in the Table to section 458.

(b) Subsections (3) and (4) of section 459 and paragraph 8 of Schedule 28 shall, with any necessary modifications, apply in relation to a deduction under subsection (3)(a)(ii).

CHAPTER 2

CAPITAL GAINS TAX

**1031R Transfers of assets where relationship between cohabitants ends**

(1) Notwithstanding any other provision of the Capital Gains Tax Acts, where by virtue or in consequence of an order made under section 174 of the Civil Partnership and Certain Rights and Obligations of Cohabitants Act 2010, on or following the ending of a relationship between cohabitants, either of the cohabitants concerned disposes of an asset to the other cohabitant, then, subject to subsections (2) and (3), both cohabitants shall be treated for the purposes of the Capital Gains Tax Acts as if the asset was acquired from the cohabitant making the disposal for a consideration of such amount as would secure that on the disposal neither a gain nor a loss would accrue to the cohabitant making the disposal.

(2) Subsection (1) shall not apply where the cohabitant who acquired the asset could not be taxed in the State for the year of assessment in which the acquisition took place, in respect of a gain on a subsequent disposal in that year by that cohabitant of the asset, if that cohabitant had made such a disposal and a gain accrued on the disposal.

(3) Subsection (1) shall not apply if until the disposal the asset formed part of the trading stock of a trade carried on by the cohabitant making the disposal or if the asset is acquired as trading stock for the purposes of a trade carried on by the cohabitant acquiring the asset.

(4) Where subsection (1) applies in relation to a disposal of an asset by a cohabitant to the other cohabitant, then, in relation to a subsequent disposal of the asset (not being a disposal to which subsection (1) applies), the cohabitant making the disposal shall be treated for the purposes of the Capital Gains Tax Acts as if the other cohabitant's acquisition or provision of the asset had been the acquisition or provision of the asset by the cohabitant who made the disposal.

(2) (a) In each provision of the Taxes Consolidation Act 1997 set out in column (2) of Schedule 1 —

(i) if no words are set out in column (3) of that Schedule, the words which are set out opposite the entry in column (4) of that Schedule are to be inserted as indicated in that provision, and

(ii) in any other case, the words in that provision which are set out in column (3) of that Schedule are to be deleted and the words which are set out opposite the entry in column (4) of that Schedule are to be inserted.

(b) Where words are mentioned more than once in a provision of the Taxes Consolidation Act 1997 set out in column (2) of Schedule 1, then any deletion or insertion, or any case of both deletion and insertion provided for by paragraph (a) in relation to the provision, shall apply as respects those words to each mention of those words in that provision.][1]

**Notes**

1  Parts 44A and 44B inserted by the Finance (No 3) Act 2011, s 1(1).

# Jurisdiction of Courts and Enforcement of Judgments Act 1998

*Number 52 of 1998*

ARRANGEMENT OF SECTIONS

## PART I
### PRELIMINARY AND GENERAL

## PART II
### THE 1968 CONVENTION AND THE ACCESSION CONVENTIONS

## PART III
### THE LUGANO CONVENTION

## PART IV
### AMENDMENTS AND REPEALS

21.  "Act of 1994".

22.  Amendment of Act of 1994.

23.  Repeals.

### SCHEDULE
TEXT NOT REPRODUCED HERE

### Acts Referred to

| | |
|---|---|
| Building Societies Act, 1989 | 1989, No. 17 |
| Central Bank Acts, 1942 to 1998 | |
| Courts (Supplemental Provisions) Acts, 1961 to 1998 | |
| Defence Act, 1954 | 1954, No. 18 |
| European Communities Act, 1972 | 1972, No. 27 |
| Enforcement of Court Orders Act, 1940 | 1940, No. 23 |
| Family Law Act, 1995 | 1995, No. 26 |
| Family Law (Divorce) Act, 1996 | 1996, No. 33 |
| Family Law (Maintenance of Spouses and Children) Act, 1976 | 1976, No. 11 |
| Jurisdiction of Courts and Enforcement of Judgments Act, 1993 | 1993, No. 9 |
| Jurisdiction of Courts and Enforcement of Judgments Acts, 1988 and 1993 | |
| Jurisdiction of Courts and Enforcement of Judgments (European Communities) Act, 1988 | 1988, No. 3 |
| Maintenance Act, 1994 | 1994, No. 28 |
| Status of Children Act, 1987 | 1987, No. 26 |
| Trustee Savings Banks Act, 1989 | 1989, No 21 |

*An Act to consolidate the Jurisdiction of Courts and Enforcement of Judgments Acts, 1988 and 1993, to give the force of law to the Convention signed at Brussels on the 29th day of November, 1996 on the Accession of the Republic of Austria, The Republic of Finland and the Kingdom of Sweden to the Convention on Jurisdiction and the Enforcement of Judgments in Civil and Commercial Matters and to the Protocol on its Interpretation by the Court of Justice of the European Communities with the Adjustments made to them by the Convention on the Accession of the Kingdom of Denmark, of Ireland and of the United Kingdom of Great Britain and Northern Ireland, By the Convention on the Accession of the Hellenic Republic and by the Convention on the Accession of the Kingdom of Spain and the Portuguese Republic and to provide for related matters. [23rd December, 1998]*

*Be it enacted by the Oireachtas as follows:*

## PART I
### PRELIMINARY AND GENERAL

**1      Short title and commencement**

(1) This Act may be cited as the Jurisdiction of Courts and Enforcement of Judgments Act, 1998.

(2) This Act shall come into operation on such day or days as, by order or orders made by the Minister, may be fixed either generally or with reference to any particular purpose or provision, and different days may be so fixed for different purposes and different provisions.

**2      Interpretation**

(1) In this Act, unless the context otherwise requires—

**"the Accession Conventions"** means the 1978 Accession Convention, the 1982 Accession Convention, the 1989 Accession Convention and the 1996 Accession Convention;

**"the 1978 Accession Convention"** means the Convention on the accession to the 1968 Convention and the 1971 Protocol of the State, Denmark and the United Kingdom, signed at Luxembourg on the 9th day of October, 1978;

**"the 1982 Accession Convention"** means the Convention on the accession to the 1968 Convention and the 1971 Protocol (as amended in each case by the 1978 Accession Convention) of the Hellenic Republic, signed at Luxembourg on the 25th day of October, 1982;

**"the 1989 Accession Convention"** means the Convention on the accession to the 1968 Convention and the 1971 Protocol (as amended in each case by the 1978 Accession Convention and the 1982 Accession Convention) of the Kingdom of Spain and the Portuguese Republic, signed at San Sebastian on the 26th day of May, 1989;

**"the 1996 Accession Convention"** means the Convention on the accession to the 1968 Convention and the 1971 Protocol (as amended in each case by the 1978 Accession Convention, the 1982 Accession Convention and the 1989 Accession Convention) of the Republic of Austria, the Republic of Finland and the Kingdom of Sweden, signed at Brussels on the 29th day of November, 1996;

**"the 1968 Convention"** means the Convention on jurisdiction and the enforcement of judgments in civil and commercial matters (including the protocol annexed to that Convention), signed at Brussels on the 27th day of September, 1968;

**"court"** includes a tribunal;

**"the European Communities"** has the same meaning as in section 1 of the European Communities Act, 1972;

**"the European Court"** means the Court of Justice of the European Communities;

**"the Lugano Convention"** means the Convention on jurisdiction and the enforcement of judgments in civil and commercial matters, signed at Lugano on the 16th day of September, 1988, and includes Protocol 1;

"**the Minister**" means the Minister for Justice, Equality and Law Reform;

"**the 1971 Protocol**" means the Protocol on the interpretation of the 1968 Convention by the European Court, signed at Luxembourg on the 3rd day of June, 1971;

"**Protocol 1**" means the protocol on certain questions of jurisdiction, procedure and enforcement, signed at Lugano on the 16th day of September, 1988.

(2) In this Act, unless the context otherwise requires, a reference to, or to any provision of, the 1968 Convention or the 1971 Protocol is to the 1968 Convention, the 1971 Protocol or the provision, as amended by—

    (a)  the 1978 Accession Convention,

    (b)  the 1982 Accession Convention,

    (c)  the 1989 Accession Convention, and

    (d)  the 1996 Accession Convention in so far as it is in force between the State and a state respecting which it has entered into force in accordance with Article 16 of that Convention.

(3) In this Act—

    (a)  a reference to a section, a Part or a Schedule is to a section or a Part of, or a Schedule to, this Act unless it is indicated that a reference to some other enactment is intended,

    (b)  a reference to a subsection or paragraph is to the subsection or paragraph of the provision in which the reference occurs unless it is indicated that a reference to some other provision is intended, and

    (c)  a reference to an enactment is to that enactment as amended or modified by any other enactment including this Act.

(4) The collective citation "the Courts (Supplemental Provisions) Acts, 1961 to 1998" shall include sections 7 to 10, 13, 14 and 16 of this Act, and those Acts and those sections shall be construed together as one Act.

**3      Texts of Conventions and Protocols**

(1) For convenience of reference, the following texts are set out in the Schedules:

    (a)  in the First Schedule, the 1968 Convention as amended by—

        (i)   Titles II and III of the 1978 Accession Convention,

        (ii)  Titles II and III of the 1982 Accession Convention,

        (iii)  Titles II and III of, and Annex 1 to, the 1989 Accession Convention, and

        (iv)  Titles II and III of the 1996 Accession Convention;

    (b)  in the Second Schedule, the 1971 Protocol as amended by—

        (i)   Title IV of the 1978 Accession Convention,

        (ii)  Title IV of the 1982 Accession Convention,

        (iii)  Title IV of the 1989 Accession Convention, and

        (iv)  Title IV of the 1996 Accession Convention;

(c)  in the Third Schedule, Titles V and VI of the 1978 Accession Convention as amended by the 1989 Accession Convention;

(d)  in the Fourth Schedule, Titles V and VI of the 1982 Accession Convention;

(e)  in the Fifth Schedule, Titles VI and VII of the 1989 Accession Convention;

(f)  in the Sixth Schedule, Titles V and VI of the 1996 Accession Convention;

(g)  in the Seventh Schedule, the Lugano Convention;

(h)  in the Eighth Schedule, Protocol 1.

(2) The texts set out in the Schedules are prepared from—

(a)  in the case of the First Schedule and the Second Schedule, the authentic texts, in the English and Irish languages, referred to in Articles 37 and 41 of the 1978 Accession Convention, Article 17 of the 1982 Accession Convention, Article 34 of the 1989 Accession Convention and Article 18 of the 1996 Accession Convention, and

(b)  in the case of the remaining Schedules, the authentic texts, in the English language, referred to in the Articles mentioned in paragraph (a) and in Article 68 of the Lugano Convention.

## PART II
### THE 1968 CONVENTION AND THE ACCESSION CONVENTIONS

**4        Interpretation of this Part**

(1) In this Part, unless the context otherwise requires—

**"Contracting State"** means a state—

(a)  which is—

(i)  one of the original parties to the 1968 Convention (Belgium, the Federal Republic of Germany, France, Italy, Luxembourg and the Netherlands), or

(ii)  one of the parties acceding to the 1968 Convention under any of the Accession Conventions (the State, Denmark, the United Kingdom, the Hellenic Republic, the Kingdom of Spain, the Portuguese Republic, the Republic of Austria, the Republic of Finland and the Kingdom of Sweden), and

(b)  respecting which—

(i)  the 1978 Accession Convention has entered into force in accordance with Article 39 of that Convention,

(ii)  the 1982 Accession Convention has entered into force in accordance with Article 15 of that Convention,

(iii)  the 1989 Accession Convention has entered into force in accordance with Article 32 of that Convention, or

(iv)  the 1996 Accession Convention has entered into force in accordance with Article 16 of that Convention, as the case may be;

"**the Conventions**" means the 1968 Convention, the 1971 Protocol and the Accession Conventions;

"enforceable maintenance order" means—

(a) a maintenance order respecting all of which an enforcement order has been made, or

(b) if an enforcement order has been made respecting only part of a maintenance order, the maintenance order to the extent to which it is so ordered to be enforced;

"**enforcement order**" means an order for the recognition or enforcement of all or part of a judgment where the order—

(a) is made by the Master of the High Court under section 7, or

(b) is made or varied on appeal from a decision of the Master of the High Court under section 7 or from a decision of the High Court relating to the Master's decision;

"**judgment**" means a judgment or order (by whatever name called) that is a judgment for the purposes of the 1968 Convention, and, except in sections 10, 12 and 14, includes—

(a) an instrument or settlement referred to in Title IV of the 1968 Convention, and

(b) an arrangement relating to maintenance obligations concluded with or authenticated by an administrative authority, as referred to in Article 10 of the 1996 Accession Convention;

"**maintenance**" means maintenance within the meaning of the Conventions;

"**maintenance creditor**" means, in relation to a maintenance order, the person entitled to the payments for which the order provides;

"**maintenance debtor**" means, in relation to a maintenance order, the person liable to make payments under the order;

"**maintenance order**" means a judgment relating to maintenance.

(2) The Minister for Foreign Affairs may, by order, declare—

(a) that any state specified in the order is a Contracting State, or

(b) that a declaration has been made pursuant to Article IV of the 1968 Convention, or a communication has been made pursuant to Article VI of that Convention, to the Secretary General of the Council of the European Communities.

(3) The text of a declaration or communication referred to in subsection (2)(b) shall be set out in the order declaring that the declaration or communication has been made.

(4) An order that is in force under subsection (2) is—

(a) if made under subsection (2)(a), evidence that any state to which the declaration relates is a Contracting State, and

(b) if made under subsection (2)(b), evidence that the declaration pursuant to Article IV or the communication pursuant to Article VI was made and evidence of its contents.

(5) The Minister for Foreign Affairs may, by order, amend or revoke an order made under subsection (2) or this subsection.

**5        Conventions to have force of law**

The Conventions shall have the force of law in the State and judicial notice shall be taken of them.

**6        Interpretation of Conventions**

(1) Judicial notice shall be taken of—

(a) a ruling or decision of, or expression of opinion by, the European Court on any question about the meaning or effect of a provision of the Conventions, and

(b) the reports listed in subsection (2).

(2) When interpreting a provision of the Conventions, a court may consider the following reports (which are reproduced in the Official Journal of the European Communities) and shall give them the weight that is appropriate in the circumstances:

(a) the reports by Mr. P. Jenard on the 1968 Convention and the 1971 Protocol[1];

(b) the report by Professor Peter Schlosser on the 1978 Accession Convention[2];

(c) the report by Professor Demetrios Evrigenis and Professor K. D. Kerameus on the accession of the Hellenic Republic to the 1968 Convention and the 1971 Protocol[3];

(d) the report by Mr. Almeida Cruz, Mr. Desantes Real and Mr. P. Jenard on the 1989 Accession Convention[4].

---

**Notes**

1   OJ No. C59 of 5. 3. 1979, p. 1.

2   OJ No. C59 of 5. 3. 1979, p. 71.

3   OJ No. C298 of 24. 11. 1986, p. 1.

4   OJ No. C189 of 28. 7. 1990, p. 35.

---

**7        Applications for recognition and enforcement of Community judgments**

(1) An application under the Conventions for the recognition or enforcement in the State of a judgment shall—

(a) be made to the Master of the High Court, and

(b) be determined by the Master by order in accordance with the Conventions.

(2) An order made by the Master of the High Court under subsection (1) may include an order for the recognition or enforcement of only part of a judgment.

**8      Enforcement of Community judgments by the High Court**

(1) Subject to section 10 (4) and to the restrictions on enforcement contained in Article 39 of the 1968 Convention, if an enforcement order has been made respecting a judgment—

(a)  the judgment shall, to the extent to which its enforcement is authorised by the enforcement order, be of the same force and effect as a judgment of the High Court, and

(b)  the High Court has the same powers respecting enforcement of the judgment, and proceedings may be taken on the judgment, as if it were a judgment of that Court.

(2) Subject to subsections (3) and (6), subsection (1) shall apply only to a judgment other than a maintenance order.

(3) On application by the maintenance creditor under an enforceable maintenance order, the Master of the High Court may, by order, declare that the following shall be regarded as being payable under a judgment referred to in subsection (1):

(a)  sums which were payable under the maintenance order as periodic payments but were not paid before the relevant enforcement order was made;

(b)  a lump sum (not being a sum referred to in paragraph (a)) which is payable under the enforceable maintenance order.

(4) A declaration shall not be made under subsection (3) unless the Master of the High Court considers that by doing so the enforceable maintenance order would be more effectively enforced respecting any sums or sum referred to in that subsection.

(5) If a declaration is made under subsection (3), the sums or sum to which the declaration relates shall be deemed, for the purposes of this Part, to be payable under a judgment referred to in subsection (1) and not otherwise.

(6) A maintenance order shall be regarded as a judgment referred to in subsection (1) if the District Court does not have jurisdiction to enforce the order under section 9(7).

**9      Enforcement of Community maintenance orders by the District Court**

(1) Subject to section 10(4) and to the restrictions on enforcement contained in Article 39 of the 1968 Convention, the District Court shall have jurisdiction to enforce an enforceable maintenance order.

(2) An enforceable maintenance order shall, from the date on which the maintenance order was made, be deemed for the purposes of—

(a)  subsection (1),

(b)  section 98(1) of the Defence Act, 1954, and

(c)  subject to the 1968 Convention, the variation or discharge of that order under section 6 of the Family Law (Maintenance of Spouses and Children) Act, 1976, as amended by the Status of Children Act, 1987, to be an order made by the District Court under section 5 or section 5A or 21A (inserted by the Status of

Children Act, 1987) of the Family Law (Maintenance of Spouses and Children) Act, 1976, as may be appropriate.

(3) Subsections (1) and (2) shall apply even though an amount payable under the enforceable maintenance order exceeds the maximum amount the District Court has jurisdiction to award under the appropriate enactment mentioned in subsection (2).

(4) Where an enforceable maintenance order is varied by a court in a Contracting State other than the State and an enforcement order has been made respecting all or part of the enforceable maintenance order as so varied, or respecting all or part of the order effecting the variation, the enforceable maintenance order shall, from the date on which the variation takes effect, be enforceable in the State only as so varied.

(5) Where an enforceable maintenance order is revoked by a court in a Contracting State other than the State and an enforcement order has been made respecting the order effecting the revocation, the enforceable maintenance order shall, from the date on which the revocation takes effect, cease to be enforceable in the State except in relation to any sums under the order that were payable, but were not paid, on or before that date.

(6) Subject to section 8(3) to (5) of this Act, the following shall be regarded as being payable pursuant to an order made under section 5 or section 5A or 21A (inserted by the Status of Children Act, 1987) of the Family Law (Maintenance of Spouses and Children) Act, 1976:

(a) any sums that were payable under an enforceable maintenance order but were not paid before the date of the making of the relevant enforcement order;

(b) any costs of or incidental to the application for the enforcement order that are payable under section 10(2) of this Act.

(7) The jurisdiction vested in the District Court by this section may be exercised by the judge of that Court for the time being assigned to—

(a) if the maintenance debtor under an enforceable maintenance order resides in the State, the district court district in which the debtor resides or carries on any profession, business or occupation, or

(b) if the maintenance debtor under an enforceable maintenance order does not reside in the State but is in the employment of an individual residing or having a place of business in the State or of a corporation or association having its seat in the State, the district court district in which that individual resides or that corporation or association has its seat.

(8) Despite anything to the contrary in an enforceable maintenance order, the maintenance debtor shall pay any sum payable under that order to—

(a) in the case referred to in subsection (7)(a), the district court clerk for the district court [area]¹ in which the debtor for the time being resides, or

(b) in a case referred to in subsection (7)(b), a district court clerk specified by the District Court, for transmission to the maintenance creditor under the order or, if a public authority has been authorised by the creditor to receive that sum, to that authority.

(9) If a sum payable under an enforceable maintenance order is not duly paid and if the maintenance creditor under the order so requests in writing, the district court clerk concerned shall make an application respecting that sum under—

    (a)   section 10 (which relates to the attachment of certain earnings) of the Family Law (Maintenance of Spouses and Children) Act, 1976, or

    (b)   section 8 (which relates to the enforcement of certain maintenance orders) of the Enforcement of Court Orders Act, 1940.

(10) For the purposes of subsection (9)(b), a reference in section 8 of the Enforcement of Court Orders Act, 1940 (other than in subsections (4) and (5) of that section) to an applicant shall be construed as a reference to the district court clerk.

(11) Nothing in this section shall affect the right of a maintenance creditor under an enforceable maintenance order to institute proceedings for the recovery of a sum payable to a district court clerk under subsection (8).

(12) Section 8(7) of the Enforcement of Court Orders Act, 1940, does not apply to proceedings for the enforcement of an enforceable maintenance order.

(13) The maintenance debtor under an enforceable maintenance order shall give notice to the district court clerk for the district court area in which the debtor has been residing of any change of address.

(14) A person who, without reasonable excuse, contravenes subsection (13) shall be guilty of an offence and shall be liable on summary conviction to a fine not exceeding [€1,269.74].

(15) If there are two or more district court clerks for a district court area, a reference in this section to a district court clerk shall be construed as a reference to any of those clerks.

(16) For the purposes of this section, the Dublin Metropolitan [District]¹ shall be deemed to be a district court area.

---

**Notes**

1   Section 9(8)(a) and (16) were amended by the Courts and Court Officers Act 2002, s 37.

---

**10     Provisions in enforcement orders for payment of interest on judgments and payment of costs**

(1) Where, on application for an enforcement order respecting a judgment, it is shown—

    (a)   that the judgment provides for the payment of a sum of money, and

    (b)   that, in accordance with the law of the Contracting State in which the judgment was given, interest on that sum is recoverable under the judgment at a particular rate or rates and from a particular date or time,

the enforcement order, if made, shall provide that the person liable to pay that sum shall also be liable to pay that interest, apart from any interest on costs recoverable under subsection (2), in accordance with the particulars noted in the order, and the interest shall be recoverable by the applicant as though it were part of that sum.

(2) An enforcement order may, at the discretion of the court concerned or the Master of the High Court, as may be appropriate provide for the payment to the applicant by the respondent of the reasonable costs of or incidental to the application for the enforcement order.

(3) A person required by an enforcement order to pay costs shall be liable to pay interest on the costs as if they were the subject of an order for the payment of costs made by the High Court on the date the enforcement order was made.

(4) Interest shall be payable on a sum referred to in subsection (1) only as provided for in this section.

**11      Currency of payments under Community maintenance orders**

(1) An amount payable in the State under a maintenance order by virtue of an enforcement order shall be paid in the currency of the State.

(2) If the amount referred to in subsection (1) is stated in the maintenance order in a currency other than that of the State, the payment shall be made on the basis of the exchange rate prevailing, on the date the enforcement order is made, between the currency of the State and the other currency.

(3) For the purposes of this section, a certificate purporting to be signed by an officer of an authorised institution and to state the exchange rate prevailing on a specified date between a specified currency and the currency of the State shall be admissible as evidence of the facts stated in the certificate.

(4) In this section, "**authorised institution**" means any of the following:

   (a)   a body licensed under the Central Bank Acts, 1942 to 1998, or authorised under regulations made under the European Communities Act, 1972, to carry on banking business;

   (b)   a building society incorporated or deemed to be incorporated under section 10 of the Building Societies Act, 1989;

   (c)   a society licensed under section 10 of the Trustee Savings Banks Act, 1989, to carry on the business of a trustee savings bank;

   (d)   An Post;

   (e)   [...][1]

   (f)   [...][2]

---

**Notes**

1   Section 11(4)(e) was repealed by the ACC Bank Act 2001.

2   Section 11(4)(f) was repealed by the ICC Bank Act 2000, s 7, Sch 7.

---

**12      Proof and admissibility of certain judgments, documents and related translations**

(1) For the purposes of the Conventions—

   (a)  a document that is duly authenticated and purports to be a copy of a judgment given by a court of a Contracting State other than the State shall, without further proof, be deemed to be a true copy of the judgment, unless the contrary is shown, and

   (b)  the original or any copy of a document mentioned in Article 46.2 or 47 of the 1968 Convention shall be admissible as evidence of any matter to which the document relates.

(2) A document purporting to be a copy of a judgment given by a court of a Contracting State, shall, for the purposes of this Act, be regarded as being duly authenticated if it purports—

   (a)  to bear the seal of that court, or

   (b)  to be certified by a judge or officer of that court to be a true copy of a judgment given by that court.

(3) A document shall be admissible as evidence of a translation if—

   (a)  it purports to be the translation of—

     (i)  a judgment given by a court of a Contracting State other than the State,

     (ii)  a document mentioned in Article 46.2, 47 or 50 of the 1968 Convention, or

     (iii)  a document containing a settlement referred to in Article 51 of the 1968 Convention or containing an arrangement referred to in Article 10 of the 1996 Accession Convention, and

   (b)  it is certified as correct by a person competent to do so.

**13      Provisional, including protective, measures**

(1) On application pursuant to Article 24 of the 1968 Convention, the High Court may grant any provisional, including protective, measures of any kind that the Court has power to grant in proceedings that, apart from this Act, are within its jurisdiction, if—

   (a)  proceedings have been or are to be commenced in a Contracting State other than the State, and

   (b)  the subject matter of the proceedings is within the scope of the 1968 Convention as determined by Article 1 (whether or not that Convention has effect in relation to the proceedings).

(2) On an application under subsection (1), the High Court may refuse to grant the measures sought if, in its opinion, the fact that, apart from this section, that Court does not have jurisdiction in relation to the subject matter of the proceedings makes it inexpedient for it to grant those measures.

(3) Subject to Article 39 of the 1968 Convention, an application to the Master of the High Court for an enforcement order respecting a judgment may include an application

for any protective measures the High Court has power to grant in proceedings that, apart from this Act, are within its jurisdiction.

(4) Where an enforcement order is made, the Master of the High Court shall grant any protective measures referred to in subsection (3) that are sought in the application for the enforcement order.

**14      Provision of certain documents by courts in the State to interested parties**

If a judgment is given by a court in the State, the registrar or clerk of that court shall, at the request of an interested party and subject to any conditions that may be specified by rules of court, give to the interested party—

   (a)  a duly authenticated copy of the judgment,

   (b)  a certificate signed by the registrar or clerk of the court stating—

      (i)  the nature of the proceedings,

     (ii)  the grounds, pursuant to the 1968 Convention, on which the court assumed jurisdiction,

    (iii)  the date on which the time for lodging an appeal against the judgment will expire or, if it has expired, the date on which it expired,

    (iv)  whether notice of appeal against, or, if the judgment was given in default of appearance, notice to set aside, the judgment has been entered,

     (v)  if the judgment is for the payment of a sum of money, the rate of interest, if any, payable on the sum and the date from which interest is payable, and

    (vi)  any other particulars that may be specified by rules of court, and

   (c)  if the judgment was given in default of appearance, the original or a copy, certified by the registrar or clerk of the court to be a true copy, of a document establishing that notice of the institution of proceedings was served on the person in default.

**15      Domicile for purposes of 1968 Convention and this Part**

(1) In order to determine for the purposes of the 1968 Convention and this Part whether an individual is domiciled in the State, in a place in the State or in a state other than a Contracting State, the following provisions shall apply:

   (a)  Part I of the Ninth Schedule, in relation to the text in the English language of the 1968 Convention;

   (b)  Part II of the Ninth Schedule, in relation to the text in the Irish language of the 1968 Convention.

(2) The seat of a corporation or association shall be treated as its domicile and in order to determine for the purposes of Article 53 of the 1968 Convention and this Part whether a corporation or association has its seat in the State, in a place in the State or in a state other than a Contracting State, the following provisions shall apply:

   (a)  Part III of the Ninth Schedule, in relation to the text in the English language of the 1968 Convention;

(b)  Part IV of the Ninth Schedule, in relation to the text in the Irish language of the 1968 Convention.

(3) In order to determine for the purposes of the 1968 Convention and this Part whether a trust is domiciled in the State the following provisions shall apply:

(a)  Part V of the Ninth Schedule, in relation to the text in the English language of the 1968 Convention;

(b)  Part VI of the Ninth Schedule, in relation to the text in the Irish language of the 1968 Convention.

(4) In this section—

"association" means an unincorporated body of persons;

"corporation" means a body corporate.

**16      Venue for certain proceedings in Circuit Court or District Court**

(1) Subject to Title II of the 1968 Convention, the jurisdiction of the Circuit Court respecting proceedings that may be instituted in the State by virtue of Article 2, 8.1, 11, 14 or 16(1)(b) of that Convention shall be exercised by the judge of that Court for the time being assigned to the circuit where the defendant, or one of the defendants, ordinarily resides or carries on any profession, business or occupation.

(2) Subsection (1) shall apply where, apart from that subsection, the Circuit Court's jurisdiction would be determined by reference to the place where the defendant resides or carries on business.

(3) The jurisdiction of the Circuit Court or District Court respecting proceedings that may be instituted in the State by virtue of Article 14 of the 1968 Convention by a plaintiff domiciled in the State may be exercised as follows:

(a)  in the case of the Circuit Court, by the judge of the Circuit Court for the time being assigned to the circuit where the plaintiff or one of the plaintiffs ordinarily resides or carries on any profession, business or occupation;

(b)  in the case of the District Court, by the judge of the District Court for the time being assigned to the district court district in which the plaintiff or one of the plaintiffs ordinarily resides or carries on any profession, business or occupation.

PART III
THE LUGANO CONVENTION

**17      Interpretation of this Part**

(1) For the purposes of this Part, unless the context otherwise requires—

"**Contracting State**" means a state respecting which the Lugano Convention has entered into force in accordance with Article 61 or 62 of that Convention;

"**enforceable maintenance order**" means—

(a)  a maintenance order respecting all of which an enforcement order has been made, or

(b)  if an enforcement order has been made respecting only part of a maintenance order, the maintenance order to the extent to which it is so ordered to be enforced;

**"enforcement order"** means an order for the recognition or enforcement of all or part of a judgment where the order—

(a)  is made by the Master of the High Court under section 7 as applied by this section, or

(b)  is made or varied on appeal from a decision of the Master of the High Court under section 7 as applied by this Part or from a decision of the High Court relating to the Master's decision;

**"judgment"** means a judgment or order (by whatever name called) that is a judgment for the purposes of the Lugano Convention, and, except in sections 10, 12 and 14 as applied by this Part, includes an instrument or settlement referred to in Title IV of that Convention;

**"maintenance"** means maintenance within the meaning of the Lugano Convention;

**"maintenance creditor"** means, in relation to a maintenance order, the person entitled to the payments for which the order provides;

**"maintenance debtor"** means, in relation to a maintenance order, the person liable to make payments under the order;

**"maintenance order"** means a judgment relating to maintenance.

(2) The Minister for Foreign Affairs may, by order, declare—

(a)  that any state specified in the order is a Contracting State, or (b) that—

(i)  a denunciation has been made pursuant to Article 64 of the Lugano Convention,

(ii)  a declaration has been made pursuant to Article Ia, Ib, or IV of Protocol 1, or

(iii)  a communication has been made pursuant to Article 63 of the Lugano Convention or Article VI of Protocol 1.

(3) The text of a denunciation, declaration or communication referred to in subsection (2)(b) shall be set out in the order declaring that the denunciation, declaration or communication has been made.

(4) An order that is in force under subsection (2) shall be—

(a)  if made under subsection (2)(a), evidence that any state to which the declaration relates is a Contracting State, and

(b)  if made under subsection (2)(b), evidence that the denunciation, declaration or communication, the text of which is set out in the order, was made and evidence of its contents.

(5) The Minister for Foreign Affairs may, by order, amend or revoke an order made under subsection (2) or this subsection.

(6) The definition of "judgment" in subsection (1) shall not be construed to limit the effect of Article 54b of the Lugano Convention.

## 18     Convention to have force of law

The Lugano Convention shall have the force of law in the State and judicial notice shall be taken of it.

## 19     Interpretation of Convention

(1) Judicial notice shall be taken of relevant decisions delivered by courts of other Contracting States concerning the provisions of the Lugano Convention, and a court shall, when interpreting and applying those provisions, pay due account to the principles laid down in those decisions.

(2) Judicial notice shall be taken of the report prepared by Mr. P. Jenard and Mr. G. Möller on the Lugano Convention[1], and, when interpreting any provision of that Convention, a court may consider that report and shall give it the weight that is appropriate in the circumstances.

### Notes

1   OJ No. C189 of 28. 7. 1990, p. 57.

## 20     Application of certain provisions of Part II

(1) Sections 7 to 16 apply in relation to the application of the Lugano Convention in the State pursuant to section 18 as they apply in relation to the application, pursuant to section 5, of the Conventions (as defined in section 4) with—

(a)   the modifications set out in subsection (2), and

(b)   any other necessary modifications.

(2) For the purposes of subsection (1),

(a)   a reference in sections 7 to 16 to a numbered Article or Title of the 1968 Convention shall be construed as a reference to the corresponding Article or Title of the Lugano Convention,

(b)   a reference in sections 7 to 16 to an instrument or settlement shall be construed as a reference to an instrument or settlement referred to in Title IV of the Lugano Convention, and

(c)   a reference in sections 7 to 16 to a term defined in section 17 shall be construed in accordance with that section.

PART IV
AMENDMENTS AND REPEALS

## 21.     "Act of 1994"

In this Part, "the Act of 1994" means the Maintenance Act, 1994.

## 22     Amendment of Act of 1994

(1) Section 3 (1) of the Act of 1994 is hereby amended by the substitution of the following definition for the definitions of "the Act of 1988" and "the Act of 1993":

> "'the Act of 1998' means the Jurisdiction of Courts and Enforcement of Judgments Act, 1998;".

(2) Section 4 (2) of the Act of 1994 (as amended by section 45 (b) of the Family Law Act, 1995, and section 53 (b) of the Family Law (Divorce) Act, 1996) is hereby amended by the substitution of the following paragraph for paragraph (a):

> "(a) For the purposes of section 8 of the Enforcement of Court Orders Act, 1940, the Act of 1976, the Act of 1995, the Act of 1996, the Act of 1998 and this Act, the Central Authority shall have authority to act on behalf of a maintenance creditor or of a claimant, as defined in section 13 (1), and references in those enactments to a maintenance creditor or to such a claimant shall be construed as including references to the Central Authority.".

(3) Section 5 of the Act of 1994 is hereby amended by the substitution of "Jurisdiction of Courts and Enforcement of Judgments Act, 1998" for "Jurisdiction of Courts and Enforcement of Judgments Acts, 1988 and 1993".

(4) Section 6 of the Act of 1994 is hereby amended—

> (a) in subsection (1) by the substitution of the following definitions for the definitions of "**the Brussels Convention**", and "**the Lugano Convention**" respectively:
>
> "'the Brussels Convention' means—
>
> (a)   the 1968 Convention, and
>
> (b)   the Accession Conventions,
>
> as defined in the Act of 1998, and a reference to an Article of the Brussels Convention shall be construed as including a reference to the corresponding Article of the Lugano Convention;",
>
> "'**the Lugano Convention**' has the meaning assigned to it by the Act of 1998;",
>
> (b) in subsection (1) in the definition of "**reciprocating jurisdiction**", by the substitution of "**the Act of 1998**" for "**the Acts of 1988 and 1993**", and
>
> (c) in subsection (2)(a), by the substitution of "**the Act of 1998**" for "**the Acts of 1988 and 1993**".

(5) Section 7(1) of the Act of 1994 is hereby amended by the substitution of "in accordance with section 7 of the Act of 1998" for "in accordance with section 5 of the Act of 1988".

(6) Section 14 of the Act of 1994 is hereby amended—

> (a) in subsection (1), by the substitution of the following for paragraph (a):
>
> > "(a) if the request is accompanied by an order of a court in a Contracting State (as defined in the Act of 1998), transmit the request to the Master of

the High Court for determination in accordance with section 7 of the Act of 1998 and Part II of this Act, and the other provisions of the Act of 1998 shall apply accordingly, with any necessary modifications,",

(b) in subsection (2), by the substitution of the following for paragraphs (a) and (b):

"(a) the order of the District Court shall be deemed to be an enforceable maintenance order as defined in the Act of 1998, and (b) sections 8, 9 and 10 of that Act shall apply in relation to that order, with any necessary modifications.", and

(c) by the insertion of the following subsection after subsection (9):

"(9A) In subsections (1) (a) and (9) a reference to an order of, or made by, a court shall be construed as including a reference to—

(a) an instrument or settlement within the meaning of the Brussels Convention as defined in Part II, and

(b) an arrangement relating to maintenance obligations concluded with or authenticated by an administrative authority, as referred to in Article 10 of the 1996 Accession Convention as defined in section 2 of the Act of 1998.".

(7) Section 20(1) of the Act of 1994 is hereby amended by the substitution of "the Act of 1998" for "the Act of 1988".

## 23     Repeals

The following are hereby repealed:

(a) the Jurisdiction of Courts and Enforcement of Judgments (European Communities) Act, 1988;

(b) the Jurisdiction of Courts and Enforcement of Judgments Act, 1993;

(c) sections 7(7) and 9 to 12 of the Act of 1994.

---

**Notes**

Schedules not reproduced here.

---

# European Convention on Human Rights Act 2003

*Number 20 of 2003*

**Act Referred to**

| Human Rights Commission Act 2000 | 2000, No. 9 |
| --- | --- |

*An Act to Enable Further Effect to be given, Subject to the Constitution, to Certain*
*Provisions of the Convention For the Protection of Human Rights and Fundamental*

569

*Freedoms done at Rome on the 4th Day of November 1950 and Certain Protocols Thereto, to Amend the Human Rights Commission Act 2000 and to Provide for Related Matters. [30th June, 2003]*

*Be it enacted by the Oireachtas as follows:*

---

**Notes**

1   Commencement: 30 December 2003.

---

## 1        Interpretation

(1) In this Act unless the context otherwise requires—

'the Convention' means the Convention for the Protection of Human Rights and Fundamental Freedoms done at Rome on the 4th day of November, 1950 (the text of which, in the English language, is, for convenience of reference, set out in Schedule 1 to this Act), as amended by Protocol No. 11 done at Strasbourg on the 11th day of May, 1994;

'Convention provisions' means, subject to any derogation which the State may make pursuant to Article 15 of the Convention, Articles 2 to 14 of the Convention and the following protocols thereto as construed in accordance with Articles 16 to 18 of the Convention:

   (a)   the Protocol to the Convention done at Paris on the 20th day of March, 1952;

   (b)   Protocol No. 4 to the Convention securing certain rights and freedoms other than those already included in the Convention and in the First Protocol thereto done at Strasbourg on the 16th day of September, 1963;

   (c)   Protocol No. 6 to the Convention concerning the abolition of the death penalty done at Strasbourg on the 28th day of April, 1983;

   (d)   Protocol No. 7 to the Convention done at Strasbourg on the 22nd day of November, 1984;

(the texts of which protocols, in the English language, are, for convenience of reference, set out in Schedules 2, 3, 4 and 5 respectively, to this Act);

'declaration of incompatibility' means a declaration under section 5;

'European Court of Human Rights' shall be construed in accordance with section 4;

'functions' includes powers and duties and references to the performance of functions includes, as respects powers and duties, references to the exercise of the powers and the performance of the duties;

'Minister' means the Minister for Justice, Equality and Law Reform;

'organ of the State' includes a tribunal or any other body (other than the President or the Oireachtas or either House of the Oireachtas or a Committee of either such House or a

Joint Committee of both such Houses or a court) which is established by law or through which any of the legislative, executive or judicial powers of the State are exercised;

'rule of law' includes common law;

'statutory provision' means any provision of an Act of the Oireachtas or of any order, regulation, rule, licence, bye-law or other like document made, issued or otherwise created thereunder or any statute, order, regulation, rule, licence, bye-law or other like document made, issued or otherwise created under a statute which continued in force by virtue of Article 50 of the Constitution.

(2) In this Act—

  (a)  a reference to any enactment shall, unless the context otherwise requires, be construed as a reference to that enactment as amended or extended by or under any subsequent enactment including this Act,

  (b)  a reference to a section is a reference to a section of this Act unless it is indicated that reference to some other enactment is intended,

  (c)  a reference to a subsection, paragraph or subparagraph is a reference to a subsection, paragraph or subparagraph of the provision in which the reference occurs unless it is indicated that reference to some other provision is intended.

**2  Interpretation of laws**

(1) In interpreting and applying any statutory provision or rule of law, a court shall, in so far as is possible, subject to the rules of law relating to such interpretation and application, do so in a manner compatible with the State's obligations under the Convention provisions.

(2) This section applies to any statutory provision or rule of law in force immediately before the passing of this Act or any such pro-vision coming into force thereafter.

**3  Performance of certain functions in a manner compatible with Convention provisions**

(1) Subject to any statutory provision (other than this Act) or rule of law, every organ of the State shall perform its functions in a manner compatible with the State's obligations under the Convention provisions.

(2) A person who has suffered injury, loss or damage as a result of a contravention of subsection (1), may, if no other remedy in damages is available, institute proceedings to recover damages in respect of the contravention in the High Court (or, subject to subsection (3), in the Circuit Court) and the Court may award to the person such damages (if any) as it considers appropriate.

(3) The damages recoverable under this section in the Circuit Court shall not exceed the amount standing prescribed, for the time being by law, as the limit of that Court's jurisdiction in tort.

(4) Nothing in this section shall be construed as creating a criminal offence.

  (5)  (a)  Proceedings under this section shall not be brought in respect of any contravention of subsection (1) which arose more than 1 year before the commencement of the proceedings.

(b)  The period referred to in paragraph (a) may be extended by order made by the Court if it considers it appropriate to do so in the interests of justice.

## 4        Interpretation of Convention provisions

Judicial notice shall be taken of the Convention provisions and of—

(a)  any declaration, decision, advisory opinion or judgment of the European Court of Human Rights established under the Convention on any question in respect of which that Court has jurisdiction,

(b)  any decision or opinion of the European Commission of Human Rights so established on any question in respect of which it had jurisdiction,

(c)  any decision of the Committee of Ministers established under the Statute of the Council of Europe on any question in respect of which it has jurisdiction,

and a court shall, when interpreting and applying the Convention provisions, take due account of the principles laid down by those declarations, decisions, advisory opinions, opinions and judgments.

## 5        Declaration of incompatibility

(1) In any proceedings, the High Court, or the Supreme Court when exercising its appellate jurisdiction, may, having regard to the provisions of section 2, on application to it in that behalf by a party, or of its own motion, and where no other legal remedy is adequate and available, make a declaration (referred to in this Act as 'a declaration of incompatibility') that a statutory provision or rule of law is incompatible with the State's obligations under the Convention provisions.

(2) A declaration of incompatibility—

(a)  shall not affect the validity, continuing operation or enforcement of the statutory provision or rule of law in respect of which it is made, and

(b)  shall not prevent a party to the proceedings concerned from making submissions or representations in relation to matters to which the declaration relates in any proceedings before the European Court of Human Rights.

(3) The Taoiseach shall cause a copy of any order containing a declaration of incompatibility to be laid before each House of the Oireachtas within the next 21 days on which that House has sat after the making of the order.

(4) Where—

(a)  a declaration of incompatibility is made,

(b)  a party to the proceedings concerned makes an application in writing to the Attorney General for compensation in respect of an injury or loss or damage suffered by him or her as a result of the incompatibility concerned, and

(c)  the Government, in their discretion, consider that it may be appropriate to make an *ex gratia* payment of compensation to that party ('a payment'),

the Government may request an adviser appointed by them to advise them as to the amount of such compensation (if any) and may, in their discretion, make a payment of the amount aforesaid or of such other amount as they consider appropriate in the circumstances.

(5) In advising the Government on the amount of compensation for the purposes of subsection (4), an adviser shall take appropriate account of the principles and practice applied by the European Court of Human Rights in relation to affording just satisfaction to an injured party under Article 41 of the Convention.

**6     Notice of proceedings under Act**

(1) Before a court decides whether to make a declaration of incompatibility the Attorney General and the Human Rights Commission shall be given notice of the proceedings in accordance with rules of court.

(2) The Attorney General shall thereupon be entitled to appear in the proceedings and to become a party thereto as regards the issue of the declaration of incompatibility.

**7     Amendment of Human Rights Commission Act 2000**

The Human Rights Commission Act 2000 is hereby amended in section 11, by the substitution in subsection (3)(b) for 'such force;' of:

> 'such force, and
>
> > (c)   the rights, liberties and freedoms conferred on, or guaranteed to, persons by the Convention provisions within the meaning of the European Convention on Human Rights Act 2003;'.

**8     Expenses**

The expenses incurred by the Minister for [Public Expenditure and Reform][1] in the administration of this Act shall be paid out of moneys provided by the Oireachtas and the expenses incurred by any other Minister of the Government in the administration of this Act shall, to such extent as may be sanctioned by the Minister for Finance, be paid out of moneys provided by the Oireachtas.

**Notes**

1     Section 8 amended by SI 418/2011.

**9     Short title and commencement**

(1) This Act may be cited as the European Convention on Human Rights Act 2003.

(2) This Act shall come into operation on such day not later than 6 months after its passing as the Minister may appoint by order.

SCHEDULE 1

CONVENTION FOR THE PROTECTION OF HUMAN RIGHTS AND FUNDAMENTAL FREEDOMS

*Rome, 4.XI.1950*

THE GOVERNMENTS SIGNATORY HERETO, being members of the Council of Europe,

Considering the Universal Declaration of Human Rights proclaimed by the General Assembly of the United Nations on 10th December 1948;

Considering that this Declaration aims at securing the universal and effective recognition and observance of the Rights therein declared;

Considering that the aim of the Council of Europe is the achievement of greater unity between its members and that one of the methods by which that aim is to be pursued is the maintenance and further realisation of human rights and fundamental freedoms;

Reaffirming their profound belief in those fundamental freedoms which are the foundation of justice and peace in the world and are best maintained on the one hand by an effective political democracy and on the other by a common understanding and observance of the human rights upon which they depend;

Being resolved, as the governments of European countries which are like-minded and have a common heritage of political traditions, ideals, freedom and the rule of law, to take the first steps for the collective enforcement of certain of the rights stated in the Universal Declaration,

Have agreed as follows:

*Article 1[1]*
*Obligation to respect human rights*

The High Contracting Parties shall secure to everyone within their jurisdiction the rights and freedoms defined in Section I of this Convention.


SECTION I[1]

RIGHTS AND FREEDOMS

*Article 2[1]*
*Right to life*

1 Everyone's right to life shall be protected by law. No one shall be deprived of his life intentionally save in the execution of a sentence of a court following his conviction of a crime for which this penalty is provided by law.

2 Deprivation of life shall not be regarded as inflicted in contravention of this article when it results from the use of force which is no more than absolutely necessary:

    a  in defence of any person from unlawful violence;

    b  in order to effect a lawful arrest or to prevent the escape of a person lawfully detained;

    c  in action lawfully taken for the purpose of quelling a riot or insurrection.

---

1.    Heading added according to the provisions of Protocol No. 11 (ETS No 155).

*Article 3[1]*
*Prohibition of torture*

No one shall be subjected to torture or to inhuman or degrading treatment or punishment.

*Article 4[1]*
*Prohibition of slavery and forced labour*

1 No one shall be held in slavery or servitude.

2 No one shall be required to perform forced or compulsory labour.

3 For the purpose of this article the term 'forced or compulsory labour' shall not include:

    a  any work required to be done in the ordinary course of detention imposed according to the provisions of Article 5 of this Convention or during conditional release from such detention;

    b  any service of a military character or, in case of conscientious objectors in countries where they are recognised, service exacted instead of compulsory military service;

    c  any service exacted in case of an emergency or calamity threatening the life or well-being of the community;

    d  any work or service which forms part of normal civic obligations.

*Article 5[1]*
*Right to liberty and security*

1 Everyone has the right to liberty and security of person. No one shall be deprived of his liberty save in the following cases and in accordance with a procedure prescribed by law:

    a  the lawful detention of a person after conviction by a competent court;

    b  the lawful arrest or detention of a person for non-compliance with the lawful order of a court or in order to secure the fulfilment of any obligation prescribed by law;

    c  the lawful arrest or detention of a person effected for the purpose of bringing him before the competent legal authority on reasonable suspicion of having committed an offence or when it is reasonably considered necessary to prevent his committing an offence or fleeing after having done so;

    d  the detention of a minor by lawful order for the purpose of educational supervision or his lawful detention for the purpose of bringing him before the competent legal authority;

    e  the lawful detention of persons for the prevention of the spreading of infectious diseases, of persons of unsound mind, alcoholics or drug addicts or vagrants;

---

1.    Heading added according to the provisions of Protocol No. 11 (ETS No 155).

f the lawful arrest or detention of a person to prevent his effecting an unauthorised entry into the country or of a person against whom action is being taken with a view to deportation or extradition.

2 Everyone who is arrested shall be informed promptly, in a language which he understands, of the reasons for his arrest and of any charge against him.

3 Everyone arrested or detained in accordance with the provisions of paragraph 1.c of this article shall be brought promptly before a judge or other officer authorised by law to exercise judicial power and shall be entitled to trial within a reasonable time or to release pending trial. Release may be conditioned by guarantees to appear for trial.

4 Everyone who is deprived of his liberty by arrest or detention shall be entitled to take proceedings by which the lawfulness of his detention shall be decided speedily by a court and his release ordered if the detention is not lawful.

5 Everyone who has been the victim of arrest or detention in contravention of the provisions of this article shall have an enforceable right to compensation.

*Article 6[1]*
*Right to a fair trial*

1 In the determination of his civil rights and obligations or of any criminal charge against him, everyone is entitled to a fair and public hearing within a reasonable time by an independent and impartial tribunal established by law. Judgment shall be pronounced publicly but the press and public may be excluded from all or part of the trial in the interests of morals, public order or national security in a democratic society, where the interests of juveniles or the protection of the private life of the parties so require, or to the extent strictly necessary in the opinion of the court in special circumstances where publicity would prejudice the interests of justice.

2 Everyone charged with a criminal offence shall be presumed innocent until proved guilty according to law.

3 Everyone charged with a criminal offence has the following minimum rights:

a  to be informed promptly, in a language which he understands Sch. 1 and in detail, of the nature and cause of the accusation against him;

b  to have adequate time and facilities for the preparation of his defence;

c  to defend himself in person or through legal assistance of his own choosing or, if he has not sufficient means to pay for legal assistance, to be given it free when the interests of justice so require;

d  to examine or have examined witnesses against him and to obtain the attendance and examination of witnesses on his behalf under the same conditions as witnesses against him;

e  to have the free assistance of an interpreter if he cannot understand or speak the language used in court.

---

1    Heading added according to the provisions of Protocol No. 11 (ETS No. 155).

*Article 7[1]*
*No punishment without law*

1 No one shall be held guilty of any criminal offence on account of any act or omission which did not constitute a criminal offence under national or international law at the time when it was committed. Nor shall a heavier penalty be imposed than the one that was applicable at the time the criminal offence was committed.

2 This article shall not prejudice the trial and punishment of any person for any act or omission which, at the time when it was committed, was criminal according to the general principles of law recognised by civilised nations.

*Article 8[1]*
*Right to respect for private and family life*

1 Everyone has the right to respect for his private and family life, his home and his correspondence.

2 There shall be no interference by a public authority with the exercise of this right except such as is in accordance with the law and is necessary in a democratic society in the interests of national security, public safety or the economic well-being of the country, for the prevention of disorder or crime, for the protection of health or morals, or for the protection of the rights and freedoms of others.

*Article 9[1]*
*Freedom of thought, conscience and religion*

1 Everyone has the right to freedom of thought, conscience and religion; this right includes freedom to change his religion or belief and freedom, either alone or in community with others and in public or private, to manifest his religion or belief, in worship, teaching, practice and observance.

2 Freedom to manifest one's religion or beliefs shall be subject only to such limitations as are prescribed by law and are necessary in a democratic society in the interests of public safety, for the protection of public order, health or morals, or for the protection of the rights and freedoms of others.

*Article 10[1]*
*Freedom of expression*

1 Everyone has the right to freedom of expression. This right shall include freedom to hold opinions and to receive and impart information and ideas without interference by public authority and regardless of frontiers. This article shall not prevent States from requiring the licensing of broadcasting, television or cinema enterprises.

2 The exercise of these freedoms, since it carries with it duties and responsibilities, may be subject to such formalities, conditions, restrictions or penalties as are prescribed by law and are necessary in a democratic society, in the interests of national security, territorial integrity or public safety, for the prevention of disorder or crime, for the protection of health or morals, for the protection of the reputation or rights of others, for preventing the disclosure of information received in confidence, or for maintaining the authority and impartiality of the judiciary.

---

1    Heading added according to the provisions of Protocol No. 11 (ETS No. 155).

*Article 11[1]*
*Freedom of assembly and association*

1 Everyone has the right to freedom of peaceful assembly and to freedom of association with others, including the right to form and to join trade unions for the protection of his interests.

2 No restrictions shall be placed on the exercise of these rights other than such as are prescribed by law and are necessary in a democratic society in the interests of national security or public safety, for the prevention of disorder or crime, for the protection of health or morals or for the protection of the rights and freedoms of others. This article shall not prevent the imposition of lawful restrictions on the exercise of these rights by members of the armed forces, of the police or of the administration of the State.

*Article 12[1]*
*Right to marry*

Men and women of marriageable age have the right to marry and to found a family, according to the national laws governing the exercise of this right.

*Article 13[1]*
*Right to an effective remedy*

Everyone whose rights and freedoms as set forth in this Convention are violated shall have an effective remedy before a national authority notwithstanding that the violation has been committed by persons acting in an official capacity.

*Article 14[1]*
*Prohibition of discrimination*

The enjoyment of the rights and freedoms set forth in this Convention shall be secured without discrimination on any ground such as sex, race, colour, language, religion, political or other opinion, national or social origin, association with a national minority, property, birth or other status.

*Article 15[1]*
*Derogation in time of emergency*

1 In time of war or other public emergency threatening the life of the nation any High Contracting Party may take measures derogating from its obligations under this Convention to the extent strictly required by the exigencies of the situation, provided that such measures are not inconsistent with its other obligations under international law.

2 No derogation from Article 2, except in respect of deaths resulting from lawful acts of war, or from Articles 3, 4 (paragraph 1) and 7 shall be made under this provision.

3 Any High Contracting Party availing itself of this right of derogation shall keep the Secretary General of the Council of Europe fully informed of the measures which it has taken and the reasons therefor. It shall also inform the Secretary General of the Council of Europe when such measures have ceased to operate and the provisions of the Convention are again being fully executed.

---

1     Heading added according to the provisions of Protocol No. 11 (ETS No. 155).

*Article 16[1]*
*Restrictions on political activity of aliens*

Nothing in Articles 10, 11 and 14 shall be regarded as preventing the High Contracting Parties from imposing restrictions on the political activity of aliens.

*Article 17[1]*
*Prohibition of abuse of rights*

Nothing in this Convention may be interpreted as implying for any State, group or person any right to engage in any activity or perform any act aimed at the destruction of any of the rights and freedoms set forth herein or at their limitation to a greater extent than is provided for in the Convention.

*Article 18[1]*
*Limitation on use of restrictions on rights*

The restrictions permitted under this Convention to the said rights and freedoms shall not be applied for any purpose other than those for which they have been prescribed.

## SECTION II
## EUROPEAN COURT OF HUMAN RIGHTS

*Article 19*
*Establishment of the Court*

To ensure the observance of the engagements undertaken by the High Contracting Parties in the Convention and the Protocols thereto, there shall be set up a European Court of Human Rights, hereinafter referred to as 'the Court'. It shall function on a permanent basis.

*Article 20*
*Number of judges*

The Court shall consist of a number of judges equal to that of the High Contracting Parties.

*Article 21*
*Criteria for office*

1 The judges shall be of high moral character and must either possess the qualifications required for appointment to high judicial office or be jurisconsults of recognised competence.

2 The judges shall sit on the Court in their individual capacity.

3 During their term of office the judges shall not engage in any activity which is incompatible with their independence, impartiality or with the demands of a full-time office; all questions arising from the application of this paragraph shall be decided by the Court.

---

1    Heading added according to the provisions of Protocol No. 11 (ETS No. 155).

*Article 22*
*Election of judges*

1 The judges shall be elected by the Parliamentary Assembly with respect to each High Contracting Party by a majority of votes cast from a list of three candidates nominated by the High Contracting Party.

2 The same procedure shall be followed to complete the Court in the event of the accession of new High Contracting Parties and in filling casual vacancies.

*Article 23*
*Terms of office*

1 The judges shall be elected for a period of six years. They may be re-elected. However, the terms of office of one-half of the judges elected at the first election shall expire at the end of three years.

2 The judges whose terms of office are to expire at the end of the Sch. 1 initial period of three years shall be chosen by lot by the Secretary General of the Council of Europe immediately after their election.

3 In order to ensure that, as far as possible, the terms of office of one-half of the judges are renewed every three years, the Parliamentary Assembly may decide, before proceeding to any subsequent election, that the term or terms of office of one or more judges to be elected shall be for a period other than six years but not more than nine and not less than three years.

4 In cases where more than one term of office is involved and where the Parliamentary Assembly applies the preceding paragraph, the allocation of the terms of office shall be effected by a drawing of lots by the Secretary General of the Council of Europe immediately after the election.

5 A judge elected to replace a judge whose term of office has not expired shall hold office for the remainder of his predecessor's term.

6 The terms of office of judges shall expire when they reach the age of 70.

7 The judges shall hold office until replaced. They shall, however, continue to deal with such cases as they already have under consideration.

*Article 24*
*Dismissal*

No judge may be dismissed from his office unless the other judges decide by a majority of two-thirds that he has ceased to fulfil the required conditions.

*Article 25*
*Registry and legal secretaries*

The Court shall have a registry, the functions and organisation of which shall be laid down in the rules of the Court. The Court shall be assisted by legal secretaries.

*Article 26*
*Plenary Court*

The plenary Court shall

    a   elect its President and one or two Vice-Presidents for a period of three years; they may be re-elected;

b set up Chambers, constituted for a fixed period of time;

c elect the Presidents of the Chambers of the Court; they may be re-elected;

d adopt the rules of the Court, and

e elect the Registrar and one or more Deputy Registrars.

*Article 27*
*Committees, Chambers and Grand Chamber*

1 To consider cases brought before it, the Court shall sit in commit-tees of three judges, in Chambers of seven judges and in a Grand Chamber of seventeen judges. The Court's Chambers shall set up committees for a fixed period of time.

2 There shall sit as an *ex officio* member of the Chamber and the Grand Chamber the judge elected in respect of the State Party concerned or, if there is none or if he is unable to sit, a person of its choice who shall sit in the capacity of judge.

3 The Grand Chamber shall also include the President of the Court, the Vice-Presidents, the Presidents of the Chambers and other judges chosen in accordance with the rules of the Court. When a case is referred to the Grand Chamber under Article 43, no judge from the Chamber which rendered the judgment shall sit in the Grand Chamber, with the exception of the President of the Chamber and the judge who sat in respect of the State Party concerned.

*Article 28*
*Declarations of inadmissibility by committees*

A committee may, by a unanimous vote, declare inadmissible or strike out of its list of cases an application submitted under Article 34 where such a decision can be taken without further examination. The decision shall be final.

*Article 29*
*Decisions by Chambers on admissibility and merits*

1 If no decision is taken under Article 28, a Chamber shall decide on the admissibility and merits of individual applications submitted under Article 34.

2 A Chamber shall decide on the admissibility and merits of inter-State applications submitted under Article 33.

3 The decision on admissibility shall be taken separately unless the Court, in exceptional cases, decides otherwise.

*Article 30*
*Relinquishment of jurisdiction to the Grand Chamber*

Where a case pending before a Chamber raises a serious question affecting the interpretation of the Convention or the protocols thereto, or where the resolution of a question before the Chamber might have a result inconsistent with a judgment previously delivered by the Court, the Chamber may, at any time before it has rendered its judgment, relinquish jurisdiction in favour of the Grand Chamber, unless one of the parties to the case objects.

*Article 31*
*Powers of the Grand Chamber*

The Grand Chamber shall

    a  determine applications submitted either under Article 33 or Article 34 when a Chamber has relinquished jurisdiction under Article 30 or when the case has been referred to it under Article 43; and

    b  consider requests for advisory opinions submitted under Article 47.

*Article 32*
*Jurisdiction of the Court*

1 The jurisdiction of the Court shall extend to all matters concerning the interpretation and application of the Convention and the protocols thereto which are referred to it as provided in Articles 33, 34 and 47.

2 In the event of dispute as to whether the Court has jurisdiction, the Court shall decide.

*Article 33*
*Inter-State cases*

Any High Contracting Party may refer to the Court any alleged breach of the provisions of the Convention and the protocols thereto by another High Contracting Party.

*Article 34*
*Individual applications*

The Court may receive applications from any person, non-governmental organisation or group of individuals claiming to be the victim of a violation by one of the High Contracting Parties of the rights set forth in the Convention or the protocols thereto. The High Contracting Parties undertake not to hinder in any way the effective exercise of this right.

*Article 35*
*Admissibility criteria*

1 The Court may only deal with the matter after all domestic remedies have been exhausted, according to the generally recognised rules of international law, and within a period of six months from the date on which the final decision was taken.

2 The Court shall not deal with any application submitted under Article 34 that

    a  is anonymous; or

    b  is substantially the same as a matter that has already been examined by the Court or has already been submitted to another procedure of international investigation or settlement and contains no relevant new information.

3 The Court shall declare inadmissible any individual application submitted under Article 34 which it considers incompatible with the provisions of the Convention or the protocols thereto, manifestly ill-founded, or an abuse of the right of application.

4 The Court shall reject any application which it considers inadmissible under this Article. It may do so at any stage of the proceedings.

*Article 36*
*Third party intervention*

1 In all cases before a Chamber of the Grand Chamber, a High Contracting Party one of whose nationals is an applicant shall have the right to submit written comments and to take part in hearings.

2 The President of the Court may, in the interest of the proper administration of justice, invite any High Contracting Party which is not a party to the proceedings or any person concerned who is not the applicant to submit written comments or take part in hearings.

*Article 37*
*Striking out applications*

1 The Court may at any stage of the proceedings decide to strike an application out of its list of cases where the circumstances lead to the conclusion that

    a  the applicant does not intend to pursue his application; or

    b  the matter has been resolved; or

    c  for any other reason established by the Court, it is no longer justified to continue the examination of the application.

However, the Court shall continue the examination of the application if respect for human rights as defined in the Convention and the protocols thereto so requires.

2 The Court may decide to restore an application to its list of cases if it considers that the circumstances justify such a course.

*Article 38*
*Examination of the case and friendly settlement proceedings*

1 If the Court declares the application admissible, it shall

    a  pursue the examination of the case, together with the representatives of the parties, and if need be, undertake an investigation, for the effective conduct of which the States concerned shall furnish all necessary facilities;

    b  place itself at the disposal of the parties concerned with a view to securing a friendly settlement of the matter on the basis of respect for human rights as defined in the Convention and the protocols thereto.

2 Proceedings conducted under paragraph 1.b shall be confidential.

*Article 39*
*Finding of a friendly settlement*

If a friendly settlement is effected, the Court shall strike the case out of its list by means of a decision which shall be confined to a brief statement of the facts and of the solution reached.

*Article 40*
*Public hearings and access to documents*

1 Hearings shall be in public unless the Court in exceptional circumstances decides otherwise.

2 Documents deposited with the Registrar shall be accessible to the public unless the President of the Court decides otherwise.

## Article 41
### Just satisfaction

If the Court finds that there has been a violation of the Convention or the protocols thereto, and if the internal law of the High Contracting Party concerned allows only partial reparation to be made, the Court shall, if necessary, afford just satisfaction to the injured party.

## Article 42
### Judgments of Chambers

Judgments of Chambers shall become final in accordance with the provisions of Article 44, paragraph 2.

## Article 43
### Referral to the Grand Chamber

1 Within a period of three months from the date of the judgment of the Chamber, any party to the case may, in exceptional cases, request that the case be referred to the Grand Chamber.

2 A panel of five judges of the Grand Chamber shall accept the request if the case raises a serious question affecting the interpretation or application of the Convention or the protocols thereto, or a serious issue of general importance.

3 If the panel accepts the request, the Grand Chamber shall decide the case by means of a judgment.

## Article 44
### Final judgments

1 The judgment of the Grand Chamber shall be final.

2 The judgment of a Chamber shall become final

    a when the parties declare that they will not request that the case be referred to the Grand Chamber; or

    b three months after the date of the judgment, if reference of the case to the Grand Chamber has not been requested; or

    c when the panel of the Grand Chamber rejects the request to refer under Article 43.

3 The final judgment shall be published.

## Article 45
### Reasons for judgments and decisions

1 Reasons shall be given for judgments as well as for decisions declaring applications admissible or inadmissible.

2 If a judgment does not represent, in whole or in part, the unanimous opinion of the judges, any judge shall be entitled to deliver a separate opinion.

## Article 46
### Binding force and execution of judgments

1 The High Contracting Parties undertake to abide by the final judgment of the Court in any case to which they are parties.

2 The final judgment of the Court shall be transmitted to the Committee of Ministers, which shall supervise its execution.

## Article 47
### Advisory opinions

1 The Court may, at the request of the Committee of Ministers, give advisory opinions on legal questions concerning the interpretation of the Convention and the protocols thereto.

2 Such opinions shall not deal with any question relating to the content or scope of the rights or freedoms defined in Section I of the Convention and the protocols thereto, or with any other question which the Court or the Committee of Ministers might have to consider in consequence of any such proceedings as could be instituted in accordance with the Convention.

3 Decisions of the Committee of Ministers to request an advisory opinion of the Court shall require a majority vote of the representatives entitled to sit on the Committee.

## Article 48
### Advisory jurisdiction of the Court

The Court shall decide whether a request for an advisory opinion submitted by the Committee of Ministers is within its competence as defined in Article 47.

## Article 49
### Reasons for advisory opinions

1 Reasons shall be given for advisory opinions of the Court.

2 If the advisory opinion does not represent, in whole or in part, the unanimous opinion of the judges, any judge shall be entitled to deliver a separate opinion.

3 Advisory opinions of the Court shall be communicated to the Committee of Ministers.

## Article 50
### Expenditure on the Court

The expenditure on the Court shall be borne by the Council of Europe.

## Article 51
### Privileges and immunities of judges

The judges shall be entitled, during the exercise of their functions, to the privileges and immunities provided for in Article 40 of the Statute of the Council of Europe and in the agreements made thereunder.

SECTION III[1],[2]

MISCELLANEOUS PROVISIONS

*Article 52*

*Inquiries by the Secretary General*

On receipt of a request from the Secretary General of the Council of Europe any High Contracting Party shall furnish an explanation of the manner in which its internal law ensures the effective implementation of any of the provisions of the Convention.

*Article 53[1]*

*Safeguard for existing human rights*

Nothing in this Convention shall be construed as limiting or derogating from any of the human rights and fundamental freedoms which may be ensured under the laws of any High Contracting Party or under any other agreement to which it is a Party.

*Article 54[1]*

*Powers of the Committee of Ministers*

Nothing in this Convention shall prejudice the powers conferred on the Committee of Ministers by the Statute of the Council of Europe.

*Article 55[1]*

*Exclusion of other means of dispute settlement*

The High Contracting Parties agree that, except by special agreement, they will not avail themselves of treaties, conventions or declarations in force between them for the purpose of submitting, by way of petition, a dispute arising out of the interpretation or application of this Convention to a means of settlement other than those provided for in this Convention.

*Article 56[1]*

*Territorial application*

1 Any State may at the time of its ratification or at any time there-after declare by notification addressed to the Secretary General of the Council of Europe that the present Convention shall, subject to paragraph 4 of this Article, extend to all or any of the territories for whose international relations it is responsible.

2 The Convention shall extend to the territory or territories named in the notification as from the thirtieth day after the receipt of this notification by the Secretary General of the Council of Europe.

3 The provisions of this Convention shall be applied in such territories with due regard, however, to local requirements.

4 Any State which has made a declaration in accordance with paragraph 1 of this article may at any time thereafter declare on behalf of one or more of the territories to which the declaration relates that it accepts the competence of the Court to receive applications

---

1      Heading added according to the provisions of Protocol No. 11 (ETS No. 155).

2      The articles of this section are renumbered according to the Provisions of Protocol No. 11 (ETS No 155).

from individuals, non-governmental organisations or groups of individuals as provided by Article 34 of the Convention.

## Article 57[1]
### Reservations

1 Any State may, when signing this Convention or when depositing its instrument of ratification, make a reservation in respect of any particular provision of the Convention to the extent that any law then in force in its territory is not in conformity with the provision. Reservations of a general character shall not be permitted under this article.

2 Any reservation made under this article shall contain a brief statement of the law concerned.

## Article 58[1]
### Denunciation

1 A High Contracting Party may denounce the present Convention only after the expiry of five years from the date on which it became a party to it and after six months' notice contained in a notification addressed to the Secretary General of the Council of Europe, who shall inform the other High Contracting Parties.

2 Such a denunciation shall not have the effect of releasing the High Contracting Party concerned from its obligations under this Convention in respect of any act which, being capable of constituting a violation of such obligations, may have been performed by it before the date at which the denunciation became effective.

3 Any High Contracting Party which shall cease to be a member of the Council of Europe shall cease to be a Party to this Convention under the same conditions.

4[2] The Convention may be denounced in accordance with the pro-visions of the preceding paragraphs in respect of any territory to which it has been declared to extend under the terms of Article 56.

## Article 59[1]
### Signature and ratification

1 This Convention shall be open to the signature of the members of the Council of Europe. It shall be ratified. Ratifications shall be deposited with the Secretary General of the Council of Europe.

2 The present Convention shall come into force after the deposit of ten instruments of ratification.

3 As regards any signatory ratifying subsequently, the Convention shall come into force at the date of the deposit of its instrument of ratification.

4 The Secretary General of the Council of Europe shall notify all the members of the Council of Europe of the entry into force of the Convention, the names of the High Contracting Parties who have ratified it, and the deposit of all instruments of ratification which may be effected subsequently.

---

1    Heading added according to the provisions of Protocol No. 11 (ETS No. 155).
2    Text amended according to the provisions of Protocol No. 11 (ETS No. 155).

Done at Rome this 4th day of November 1950, in English and French, both texts being equally authentic, in a single copy which shall remain deposited in the archives of the Council of Europe. The Secretary General shall transmit certified copies to each of the signatories.

SCHEDULE 2

PROTOCOL TO THE CONVENTION FOR THE PROTECTION OF HUMAN RIGHTS AND FUNDAMENTAL FREEDOMS[1]

*Paris, 20.III.1952*

THE GOVERNMENTS SIGNATORY HERETO, being members of the Council of Europe,

Being resolved to take steps to ensure the collective enforcement of certain rights and freedoms other than those already included in Section I of the Convention for the Protection of Human Rights and Fundamental Freedoms signed at Rome on 4 November 1950 (hereinafter referred to as 'the Convention'),

Have agreed as follows:

*Article 1*

*Protection of property*

Every natural or legal person is entitled to the peaceful enjoyment of his possessions. No one shall be deprived of his possessions except in the public interest and subject to the conditions provided for by law and by the general principles of international law.

The preceding provisions shall not, however, in any way impair the right of a State to enforce such laws as it deems necessary to control the use of property in accordance with the general interest or to secure the payment of taxes or other contributions or penalties.

*Article 2*

*Right to education*

No person shall be denied the right to education. In the exercise of any functions which it assumes in relation to education and to teaching, the State shall respect the right of parents to ensure such education and teaching in conformity with their own religious and philosophical convictions.

*Article 3*

*Right to free elections*

The High Contracting Parties undertake to hold free elections at reasonable intervals by secret ballot, under conditions which will ensure the free expression of the opinion of the people in the choice of the legislature.

---

1    Headings of articles added and text amended according to the provisions of Protocol No. 11 (ETS No. 155).

*Article 4[1]*
*Sch 2 Territorial application*

Any High Contracting Party may at the time of signature or ratification or at any time thereafter communicate to the Secretary General of the Council of Europe a declaration stating the extent to which it undertakes that the provisions of the present Protocol shall apply to such of the territories for the international relations of which it is responsible as are named therein.

Any High Contracting Party which has communicated a declaration in virtue of the preceding paragraph may from time to time communicate a further declaration modifying the terms of any former declaration or terminating the application of the provisions of this Protocol in respect of any territory.

A declaration made in accordance with this article shall be deemed to have been made in accordance with paragraph 1 of Article 56 of the Convention.

*Article 5*
*Relationship to the Convention*

As between the High Contracting Parties the provisions of Articles 1, 2, 3 and 4 of this Protocol shall be regarded as additional articles to the Convention and all the provisions of the Convention shall apply accordingly.

*Article 6*
*Signature and ratification*

This Protocol shall be open for signature by the members of the Council of Europe, who are the signatories of the Convention; it shall be ratified at the same time as or after the ratification of the Convention. It shall enter into force after the deposit of ten instruments of ratification. As regards any signatory ratifying subsequently, the Protocol shall enter into force at the date of the deposit of its instrument of ratification.

The instruments of ratification shall be deposited with the Secretary General of the Council of Europe, who will notify all members of the names of those who have ratified.

Done at Paris on the 20th day of March 1952, in English and French, both texts being equally authentic, in a single copy which shall remain deposited in the archives of the Council of Europe. The Secretary General shall transmit certified copies to each of the signatory governments.

---

1    Text amended according to the provisions of Protocol No. 11 (ETS No. 155).

SCHEDULE 3

PROTOCOL NO. 4 TO THE CONVENTION FOR THE PROTECTION OF HUMAN
RIGHTS AND FUNDAMENTAL FREEDOMS SECURING CERTAIN RIGHTS AND
FREEDOMS OTHER THAN THOSE ALREADY INCLUDED IN THE CONVENTION
AND IN THE FIRST PROTOCOL THERETO[1]

*Strasbourg, 16.IX.1963*

THE GOVERNMENTS SIGNATORY HERETO, being members of the Council of
Europe,

Being resolved to take steps to ensure the collective enforcement of certain rights and
freedoms other than those already included in Section 1 of the Convention for the
Protection of Human Rights and Fundamental Freedoms signed at Rome on 4th
November 1950 (hereinafter referred to as the 'Convention') and in Articles 1 to 3 of the
First Protocol to the Convention signed at Paris on 20th March 1952,

Have agreed as follows:

*Article 1*
*Prohibition of imprisonment for debt*

No one shall be deprived of his liberty merely on the ground of inability to fulfil a
contractual obligation.

*Article 2*
*Freedom of movement*

1 Everyone lawfully within the territory of a State shall, within that territory, have the
right to liberty of movement and freedom to choose his residence.

2 Everyone shall be free to leave any country, including his own.

3 No restrictions shall be placed on the exercise of these rights other than such as are in
accordance with law and are necessary in a democratic society in the interests of
national security or public safety, for the maintenance of ordre public, for the prevention
of crime, for the protection of health or morals, or for the protection of the rights and
freedoms of others.

4 The rights set forth in paragraph 1 may also be subject, in particular areas, to
restrictions imposed in accordance with law and justified by the public interest in a
democratic society.

*Article 3*
*Prohibition of expulsion of nationals*

1 No one shall be expelled, by means either of an individual or of a collective measure,
from the territory of the State of which he is a national.

2 No one shall be deprived of the right to enter the territory of the state of which he is a
national.

---

1      Headings of articles added and text amended according to the provisions of Protocol No. 11 (ETS
       No. 155).

*Article 4*
*Prohibition of collective expulsion of aliens*

Collective expulsion of aliens is prohibited.

*Article 5*
*Territorial application*

1 Any High Contracting Party may, at the time of signature or ratification of this Protocol, or at any time thereafter, communicate to the Secretary General of the Council of Europe a declaration stating the extent to which it undertakes that the provisions of this Protocol shall apply to such of the territories for the inter-national relations of which it is responsible as are named therein.

2 Any High Contracting Party which has communicated a declaration in virtue of the preceding paragraph may, from time to time, communicate a further declaration modifying the terms of any former declaration or terminating the application of the pro-visions of this Protocol in respect of any territory.

3[1] A declaration made in accordance with this article shall be deemed to have been made in accordance with paragraph 1 of Article 56 of the Convention.

4 The territory of any State to which this Protocol applies by virtue of ratification or acceptance by that State, and each territory to which this Protocol is applied by virtue of a declaration by that State under this article, shall be treated as separate territories for the purpose of the references in Articles 2 and 3 to the territory of a State.

5[2] Any State which has made a declaration in accordance with paragraph 1 or 2 of this Article may at any time thereafter declare on behalf of one or more of the territories to which the declaration relates that it accepts the competence of the Court to receive applications from individuals, non-governmental organisations or groups of individuals as provided in Article 34 of the Convention in respect of all or any of Articles 1 to 4 of this Protocol.

*Article 6[2]*
*Relationship to the Convention*

As between the High Contracting Parties the provisions of Articles 1 to 5 of this Protocol shall be regarded as additional articles to the Convention, and all the provisions of the Convention shall apply accordingly.

*Article 7*
*Signature and ratification*

1 This Protocol shall be open for signature by the members of the Council of Europe who are the signatories of the Convention; it shall be ratified at the same time as or after the ratification of the Convention. It shall enter into force after the deposit of five instruments of ratification. As regards any signatory ratifying subsequently, the Protocol shall enter into force at the date of the deposit of its instrument of ratification.

---

1    Text amended according to the provisions of Protocol No. 11 (ETS No. 155).
2    Text added according to the provisions of Protocol No. 11 (ETS No. 155).

2 The instruments of ratification shall be deposited with the Secretary General of the Council of Europe, who will notify all members of the names of those who have ratified.

In witness whereof the undersigned, being duly authorised thereto, have signed this Protocol.

Done at Strasbourg, this 16th day of September 1963, in English and in French, both texts being equally authoritative, in a single copy which shall remain deposited in the archives of the Council of Europe. The Secretary General shall transmit certified copies to each of the signatory states.

SCHEDULE 4

PROTOCOL NO. 6 TO THE CONVENTION FOR THE PROTECTION OF HUMAN RIGHTS AND FUNDAMENTAL FREEDOMS CONCERNING THE ABOLITION OF THE DEATH PENALTY[1]

*Strasbourg, 28.IV.1983*

THE MEMBER STATES OF THE COUNCIL OF EUROPE, signatory to this Protocol to the Convention for the Protection of Human Rights and Fundamental Freedoms, signed at Rome on 4 November 1950 (hereinafter referred to as 'the Convention'),

Considering that the evolution that has occurred in several member States of the Council of Europe expresses a general tendency in favour of abolition of the death penalty;

Have agreed as follows:

*Article 1*
*Abolition of the death penalty*

The death penalty shall be abolished. No one shall be condemned to such penalty or executed.

*Article 2*
*Death penalty in time of war*

A State may make provision in its law for the death penalty in respect of acts committed in time of war or of imminent threat of war; such penalty shall be applied only in the instances laid down in the law and in accordance with its provisions. The State shall communicate to the Secretary General of the Council of Europe the relevant provisions of that law.

*Article 3*
*Prohibition of derogations*

No derogation from the provisions of this Protocol shall be made under Article 15 of the Convention.

*Article 4[2]*
*Prohibition of reservations*

No reservation may be made under Article 57 of the Convention in respect of the provisions of this Protocol.

---

1    Headings of articles added and text amended according to the provisions of Protocol No. 11 (ETS No. 155).

2    Text amended according to the provisions of Protocol No. 11 (ETS No. 155).

*Article 5*
*Territorial application*

1 Any State may at the time of signature or when depositing its instrument of ratification, acceptance or approval, specify the territory or territories to which this Protocol shall apply.

2 Any State may at any later date, by a declaration addressed to the Secretary General of the Council of Europe, extend the application of this Protocol to any other territory specified in the declaration. In respect of such territory the Protocol shall enter into force on the first day of the month following the date of receipt of such declaration by the Secretary General.

3 Any declaration made under the two preceding paragraphs may, in respect of any territory specified in such declaration, be with-drawn by a notification addressed to the Secretary General. The withdrawal shall become effective on the first day of the month following the date of receipt of such notification by the Secretary General.

*Article 6*
*Relationship to the Convention*

As between the States Parties the provisions of Articles 1 and 5 of this Protocol shall be regarded as additional articles to the Convention and all the provisions of the Convention shall apply accordingly.

*Article 7*
*Signature and ratification*

The Protocol shall be open for signature by the member States of the Council of Europe, signatories to the Convention. It shall be subject to ratification, acceptance or approval. A member State of the Council of Europe may not ratify, accept or approve this Protocol unless it has, simultaneously or previously, ratified the Convention. Instruments of ratification, acceptance or approval shall be deposited with the Secretary General of the Council of Europe.

*Article 8*
*Entry into force*

1 This Protocol shall enter into force on the first day of the month following the date on which five member States of the Council of Europe have expressed their consent to be bound by the Protocol in accordance with the provisions of Article 7.

2 In respect of any member State which subsequently expresses its consent to be bound by it, the Protocol shall enter into force on the first day of the month following the date of the deposit of the instrument of ratification, acceptance or approval.

*Article 9*
*Depositary functions*

The Secretary General of the Council of Europe shall notify the member States of the Council of:

    a  any signature;

    b  the deposit of any instrument of ratification, acceptance or approval;

c any date of entry into force of this Protocol in accordance with Articles 5 and 8;

d any other act, notification or communication relating to this Protocol.

In witness whereof the undersigned, being duly authorised thereto, have signed this Protocol.

Done at Strasbourg, this 28th day of April 1983, in English and in French, both texts being equally authentic, in a single copy which shall be deposited in the archives of the Council of Europe. The Secretary General of the Council of Europe shall transmit certified copies to each member State of the Council of Europe.

SCHEDULE 5
PROTOCOL No. 7 TO THE CONVENTION FOR THE PROTECTION OF HUMAN RIGHTS AND FUNDAMENTAL FREEDOMS[1]

*Strasbourg, 22.XI.1984*

The member States of the Council of Europe signatory hereto,

Being resolved to take further steps to ensure the collective enforcement of certain rights and freedoms by means of the Convention for the Protection of Human Rights and Fundamental Freedoms signed at Rome on 4 November 1950 (hereinafter referred to as 'the Convention'),

Have agreed as follows:

## Article 1
### Procedural safeguards relating to expulsion of aliens

1 An alien lawfully resident in the territory of a State shall not be expelled therefrom except in pursuance of a decision reached in accordance with law and shall be allowed:

a to submit reasons against his expulsion,

b to have his case reviewed, and

c to be represented for these purposes before the competent authority or a person or persons designated by that authority.

2 An alien may be expelled before the exercise of his rights under paragraph 1.a, b and c of this Article, when such expulsion is necessary in the interests of public order or is grounded on reasons of national security.

## Article 2
### Right of appeal in criminal matters

1 Everyone convicted of a criminal offence by a tribunal shall have the right to have his conviction or sentence reviewed by a higher tribunal. The exercise of this right, including the grounds on which it may be exercised, shall be governed by law.

2 This right may be subject to exceptions in regard to offences of a minor character, as prescribed by law, or in cases in which the person concerned was tried in the first instance by the highest tribunal or was convicted following an appeal against acquittal.

---

1    Headings of articles added and text amended according to the provisions of Protocol No. 11 (ETS No. 155).

### Article 3
### Compensation for wrongful conviction

When a person has by a final decision been convicted of a criminal offence and when subsequently his conviction has been reversed, or he has been pardoned, on the ground that a new or newly discovered fact shows conclusively that there has been a miscarriage of justice, Sch. 5 the person who has suffered punishment as a result of such conviction shall be compensated according to the law or the practice of the State concerned, unless it is proved that the non-disclosure of the unknown fact in time is wholly or partly attributable to him.

### Article 4
### Right not to be tried or punished twice

1 No one shall be liable to be tried or punished again in criminal proceedings under the jurisdiction of the same State for an offence for which he has already been finally acquitted or convicted in accordance with the law and penal procedure of that State.

2 The provisions of the preceding paragraph shall not prevent the reopening of the case in accordance with the law and penal procedure of the State concerned, if there is evidence of new or newly discovered facts, or if there has been a fundamental defect in the previous proceedings, which could affect the outcome of the case.

3 No derogation from this Article shall be made under Article 15 of the Convention.

### Article 5
### Equality between spouses

Spouses shall enjoy equality of rights and responsibilities of a private law character between them, and in their relations with their children, as to marriage, during marriage and in the event of its dissolution. This Article shall not prevent States from taking such measures as are necessary in the interests of the children.

### Article 6
### Territorial application

1 Any State may at the time of signature or when depositing its instrument of ratification, acceptance or approval, specify the territory or territories to which the Protocol shall apply and state the extent to which it undertakes that the provisions of this Protocol shall apply to such territory or territories.

2 Any State may at any later date, by a declaration addressed to the Secretary General of the Council of Europe, extend the application of this Protocol to any other territory specified in the declaration. In respect of such territory the Protocol shall enter into force on the first day of the month following the expiration of a period of two months after the date of receipt by the Secretary General of such declaration.

3 Any declaration made under the two preceding paragraphs may, in respect of any territory specified in such declaration, be with-drawn or modified by a notification addressed to the Secretary General. The withdrawal or modification shall become effective on the first day of the month following the expiration of a period of two months after the date of receipt of such notification by the Secretary General.

4[1] A declaration made in accordance with this Article shall be deemed to have been made in accordance with paragraph 1 of Article 56 of the Convention.

5 The territory of any State to which this Protocol applies by virtue of ratification, acceptance or approval by that State, and each territory to which this Protocol is applied by virtue of a declaration by that State under this Article, may be treated as separate territories for the purpose of the reference in Article 1 to the territory of a State.

6[2] Any State which has made a declaration in accordance with paragraph 1 or 2 of this Article may at any time thereafter declare on behalf of one or more of the territories to which the declaration relates that it accepts the competence of the Court to receive applications from individuals, non-governmental organisations or groups of individuals as provided in Article 34 of the Convention in respect of Articles 1 to 5 of this Protocol.

## Article 7[2]
### Relationship to the Convention

As between the States Parties, the provisions of Articles 1 to 6 of this Protocol shall be regarded as additional Articles to the Convention, and all the provisions of the Convention shall apply accordingly.

## Article 8
### Signature and ratification

This Protocol shall be open for signature by member States of the Council of Europe which have signed the Convention. It is subject to ratification, acceptance or approval. A member State of the Council of Europe may not ratify, accept or approve this Protocol without previously or simultaneously ratifying the Convention. Instruments of ratification, acceptance or approval shall be deposited with the Secretary General of the Council of Europe.

## Article 9
### Entry into force

1 This Protocol shall enter into force on the first day of the month following the expiration of a period of two months after the date on which seven member States of the Council of Europe have expressed their consent to be bound by the Protocol in accordance with the provisions of Article 8.

2 In respect of any member State which subsequently expresses its consent to be bound by it, the Protocol shall enter into force on the first day of the month following the expiration of a period of two months after the date of the deposit of the instrument of ratification, acceptance or approval.

---

1    Text amended according to the provisions of Protocol No. 11 (ETS No. 155).
2    Text added according to the provisions of Protocol No. 11 (ETS No. 155).

*Article 10*
*Depositary functions*

The Secretary General of the Council of Europe shall notify all the member States of the Council of Europe of:

    a  any signature;

    b  the deposit of any instrument of ratification, acceptance or approval;

    c  any date of entry into force of this Protocol in accordance with Articles 6 and 9;

    d  any other act, notification or declaration relating to this Protocol.

In witness whereof the undersigned, being duly authorised thereto, have signed this Protocol.

Done at Strasbourg, this 22nd day of November 1984, in English and French, both texts being equally authentic, in a single copy which shall be deposited in the archives of the Council of Europe. The Secretary General of the Council of Europe shall transmit certified copies to each member State of the Council of Europe.

# Part 3: Court Rules

# Circuit Court Rules 2001

*S.I. No. 510 of 2001[1]*

---

**Notes**

1    Commencement: 3 December 2001.

---

## ORDER 59[1]

### FAMILY LAW

---

**Notes**

1    Commencement: 20 September 2005.

---

### Rule 1 — Appointment of registered father as guardian

(1) This Rule provides for a special procedure for the determination of an application by the father to be appointed as guardian of an infant where—

    (a)   the mother consents in writing to the appointment of the father as guardian, and

    (b)   the father is registered as the father in a Register maintained under the Civil Registration Act 2004.

(2) Every application under this Rule shall be brought in the County where the applicant or the infant to whom the application relates ordinarily resides or carries on any profession, business or occupation.

(3) All proceedings under this Rule shall be instituted by the issue, out of the Office, of an originating Motion.

(4) All applications made with the consent in writing of the mother pursuant to section 6A of the Guardianship of Infants Act 1964 (as inserted by section 12 of the Status of Children Act 1987) shall be brought in accordance with Form 37E of the Schedule of Forms annexed hereto or such modification thereof as may be appropriate and shall be dated and shall bear the name, address and description of the applicant and shall be signed by his solicitor, if any, or if none, by himself.

(5) On the issue of an originating Motion, a copy thereof shall be filed and the County Registrar shall thereupon enter the same and cause the same to be listed on the return date mentioned therein. It shall not be necessary in the first instance to give notice of the application to the mother save that, in cases where the mother has not completed a Statutory Declaration in Form 37F of the Schedule of Forms annexed hereto or a suitable modification thereof or in the absence of the appearance of the mother in Court on the return date, the Judge may in his discretion adjourn the said application and may

direct that notice thereof be served upon the mother and may give such further or other directions as to the hearing of the said application as may to him seem appropriate in the circumstances of the case.

(6) Every application under this Rule shall be heard on oral evidence. It will be necessary for the applicant to produce suitable evidence of the consent in writing of the mother, and a certified copy of the entry in the Register maintained under the Civil Registration Act 2004, showing that the applicant is registered as the father of the infant to whom the application relates.

(7) Every application under this Rule shall be heard otherwise than in public.

## Rule 2 — Declaration of Parentage

(1) Every application under this Rule shall be brought in the County where any party to the application ordinarily resides or carries on any profession, business or occupation, or, where no party to the proceedings ordinarily resides or carries on any profession, business or occupation in the State, before the Dublin Circuit.

(2) All proceedings under this Rule shall be instituted by the issue, out of the Office of the County Registrar, of a Family Law Civil Bill.

(3) Every Family Law Civil Bill containing an application made pursuant to Section 35 of the Status of Children Act 1987, shall be brought in accordance with Form 2N of the Schedule of Forms annexed hereto or such modification thereof as may be appropriate and shall be dated and shall bear the name, address and description of the applicant and shall be signed by his Solicitor, if any, or if none, by himself, save that where the applicant is under eighteen years of age on the date of the institution of proceedings, the Family Law Civil Bill shall bear the name, address and description of the next friend of the applicant and shall be signed by the Solicitor of the next friend, if any, or if none, by the next friend. Every Family Law Civil Bill issued pursuant to this Rule shall contain the following information where applicable, and where not applicable, that fact shall be stated—

(a) the address within the State where every party to the proceedings resides or carries on any profession, business or occupation;

(b) the date of birth of the applicant;

(c) the place of birth of the applicant;

(d) if the place of birth of the applicant is not within the State, the reasons for seeking the declaration from the Court;

(e) the name and address of the person named as the father of the applicant;

(f) whether the person named as the father of the applicant is or is not alive;

(g) the name and address of the person named as the mother of the applicant;

(h) whether the person named as the mother of the applicant is or is not alive;

(i) in respect of each person named as father or mother, a brief statement of the grounds upon which it is alleged that the said person is the father or mother of the applicant.

(4) Any person or persons named as father or mother of the applicant shall be named as respondents to the proceedings, unless he or she is the next friend of the applicant for the purpose of the said application. If any person who would otherwise be named as respondent is not alive or is not available for service of proceedings within the jurisdiction, then the application may be made in the first instance without service on that person. In every case the Court may direct that notice of any proceedings under this Rule shall be given to such person or persons as the Court thinks fit and the Court may, either of its own motion or on the application of that person or any party to the proceedings, order that that person shall be added as a party to those proceedings. Such notice shall be given by service upon such person to be notified of a true copy of Family Law Civil Bill and of notice of the making of the order directing the giving of such notice.

(5) On the issue of a Family Law Civil Bill pursuant to this Rule, a copy thereof shall be filed and the County Registrar shall thereon enter the same.

(6) Every Family Law Civil Bill issued pursuant to this Rule shall be served in the manner prescribed by Order 11 on the respondent (or party directed to be notified as aforesaid) at his last known place of residence. An affidavit of service of every Family Law Civil Bill shall be sworn and shall be filed in the Office. Where it is difficult or impossible to serve any such respondent or other person within the jurisdiction, the Court or the County Registrar may make an Order for substituted service or for service outside the jurisdiction of the said Family Law Civil Bill or notice thereof or for both substituted service and service outside the jurisdiction.

(7) If the respondent or any person served with notice of the said Family Law Civil Bill or any person who has been made a party to the said proceedings wishes to dispute, wholly or in part, the claim of the applicant or any of the information set out on the Family Law Civil Bill, he shall, within ten days of the service on him of the said Civil Bill or within such further time as the Court may allow, serve upon the applicant or his Solicitor a Defence in Form 6A in the Schedule of Forms hereto or such modification thereof as may be appropriate. A true copy of such Defence shall be filed at the Office and served on every other party to the said proceedings within two days after the service thereof upon the applicant or his Solicitor. If default is made in serving and/or filing any Defence, the Court may on application made by Motion on notice to the party in default give judgment on the Civil Bill or direct that the application proceed on the footing that the matters set out in the Civil Bill be deemed to be admitted by the party in default, upon the Court being satisfied that the said party in default was served with notice of the said application at least four clear days prior to the hearing thereof.

(8) On the return date fixed therefor, or on any adjourned date, the Court may give such direction or directions as it may deem expedient relating to the said application and to the hearing thereof, including but not limited to the giving of particulars, the provision of information, the sending of papers to the Attorney General, the adding of the Attorney General or any other person as a party to the proceedings, the notification of the application to any person, and any other matter in relation to which applications or directions are provided by Part VI of the Status of Children Act 1987.

(9) Save where the Court otherwise directs, every proceeding under this Rule shall be heard on oral evidence. On the hearing of every proceeding the Court may direct that the whole or any part thereof shall be heard otherwise than in public, and an application for a direction under this Rule shall be so heard unless the Court otherwise directs.

(10) Every application made pursuant to section 35 (v) (for a direction that papers be sent to the Attorney General) or section 35 (vii) (ordering that a person be added as a party to the proceedings) of the Status of Children Act 1987, and every application for judgment pursuant to sub-rule (7) shall, without prejudice to the power of the Court to act of its own motion, be made by Motion on notice to such parties as are affected thereby, which notice shall be served at least four clear days before the hearing of such Motion. Service by post shall be deemed to have been effected on the second day following the day of posting.

(11) Any declaration made under this Rule shall be made in Form 37G of the Schedule of Forms annexed hereto or such modification thereof as may be appropriate. A copy of every declaration made under this Rule shall be furnished by the County Registrar to An tArd-Chláraitheóir within ten days of the making of such declaration.

### Rule 3 — Blood Tests where Parentage is in Issue

(1) Every application made pursuant to Section 38 of the Status of Children Act 1987, for a direction for the use of blood tests shall, without prejudice to the power of the Court to make a direction of its own motion, be made by Motion on Notice in accordance with Form 37H of the Schedule of Forms annexed hereto or such modification thereof as may be appropriate. Such notice of motion shall be headed up with the title of the proceedings in which the application is brought and shall specify the name of the person whose parentage is in dispute and shall set out the full name and address and date of birth of each person from whom it is proposed that a blood sample be taken.

(2) The notice of motion shall be served on every person from whom it is proposed that a blood sample be taken at least four clear days before the date fixed for the hearing thereof. Service by post shall be deemed to have been effected on the second day after the day of posting.

(3) Every said application shall be heard on oral evidence, unless the Court otherwise allows or directs.

(4) Every direction under section 38(1) shall be in Form 37I of the Schedule of Forms annexed hereto.

(5) Where blood samples have been tested pursuant to section 40 of the Act, no party to the proceedings shall, unless the Court otherwise directs, be entitled to call as a witness the person under whose control the blood samples were tested or any person by whom anything necessary for the purpose of enabling these tests to be carried out was done, unless within fourteen days after receiving a copy of the report he serves a notice in Form 37J of the Schedule of Forms annexed hereto or such modification thereof as may be appropriate on the other parties to the proceedings or on such of them as the Court may direct, of his intention to call that person as a witness.

**Rule 4 —**

**Guardianship of Infants Act 1964**

**Family Law (Maintenance of Spouses and Children) Act 1976**

**Family Home Protection Act 1976**

**Judicial Separation and Family Law Reform Act 1989**

**Family Law Act 1995**

**Family Law (Divorce) Act 1996**

**Children Act 1997**

## Introduction

(1) In this Rule

"the 1996 Act" means the Family Law (Divorce) Act 1996 (No. 33 of 1996) and

"the 1995 Act" means the Family Law Act 1995 (No. 26 of 1995) and

"the 1989 Act" means the Judicial Separation and Family Law Reform Act 1989 (No. 6 of 1989) and

"the 1964 Act" means the Guardianship of Infants Act 1964 (No. 7 of 1964),

"the 1997 Act" means the Children Act 1997 (No. 40 of 1997),

"the First 1976 Act" means the Family Law (Maintenance of Spouses and Children) Act 1976 (No. 11 of 1976) and

"the Second 1976 Act" means the Family Home Protection Act 1976 (No. 27 of 1976).

## Venue

(2) Any proceedings under this Rule shall be brought in the county where any party to the proceedings ordinarily resides or carries on any profession, business or occupation.

## Commencement

(3) (a)  All proceedings for divorce, judicial separation, relief after foreign divorce or separation outside the State, nullity, declarations of marital status, the determination of property issues between spouses pursuant to section 36 of the 1995 Act/formerly engaged couples pursuant to section 44 of the 1996 Act, relief pursuant to section 25 of the 1995 Act, section 18 of the 1996 Act or section 15A of the 1995 Act, relief pursuant to the 1964 Act, relief pursuant to the 1997 Act, relief pursuant to the First 1976 Act or relief pursuant to the Second 1976 Act under this Rule shall be instituted by the issuing out of the office of the County Registrar for the appropriate county of the appropriate Family Law Civil Bill in accordance with Form 2N of the Schedule of Forms annexed hereto with such modifications thereto as may be appropriate in the format and manner hereinafter provided save that no Family Law Civil Bill for relief after foreign divorce or separation outside the State shall be issued until requirements set down in sub-rule (4)(b) of this Rule have been complied with.

Upon issue, the Family Law Civil Bill shall be served in a manner provided for hereunder.

(b) No proceedings for a relief order after foreign divorce or separation outside the State shall issue without the leave of the appropriate Court in accordance with section 23(3) of the 1995 Act. Such application for leave to issue proceedings shall be made ex parte by way of ex parte docket grounded upon the Affidavit of the Applicant or another appropriate person. The aforementioned Affidavit shall exhibit a draft of the Family Law Civil Bill for relief after divorce or separation outside the State which the Applicant seeks leave to issue as well as the foreign divorce or separation decree, shall set forth fully the reasons why relief is being sought and shall make specific averment to the fact that, to the knowledge, information and belief of the Applicant, the jurisdictional requirements of section 27 of the 1995 Act are complied with in the particular case, specifying the particular basis of jurisdiction being relied upon.

## Form of Proceedings

(4) Every Family Law Civil Bill shall be in numbered paragraphs setting out the relief sought and the grounds relied upon in support of the application. The Civil Bill shall be in accordance with the form set out in Form 2N herein or such modification thereof as may be appropriate, subject to the requirements hereinafter set out.

(a) A Family Law Civil Bill for a Decree of Divorce shall, in all cases, include the following details—

  (i) the date and place of marriage of the parties;

  (ii) the length of time the parties have lived apart, including the date upon which the parties commenced living apart, and the addresses of both of the parties during that time, where known;

  (iii) details of any previous matrimonial relief sought and/or obtained and details of any previous separation agreement entered into between the parties (where appropriate a certified copy of any relevant court order and/or deed of separation/separation agreement should be annexed to the Civil Bill);

  (iv) the names and ages and dates of birth of any dependent children of the marriage;

  (v) details of the family home(s) and/or other residences of the parties including, if relevant, details of any former family home/residence to include details of the manner of occupation/ownership thereof;

  (vi) where reference is made in the Civil Bill to any immovable property, whether it is registered or unregistered land and a description of the land/premises so referred to;

  (vii) the basis of jurisdiction under the 1996 Act;

  (viii) the occupation(s) of each party;

  (ix) the grounds relied upon for the relief sought;

  (x) each section of the 1996 Act under which relief is sought.

(b) A Family Law Civil Bill for a Decree of Judicial Separation shall, in all cases, include the following details:

   (i) the date and place of marriage of the parties;

   (ii) the names and ages and dates of birth of any dependent children of the marriage;

   (iii) details of the family home(s) and/or other residence of the parties including, if relevant, details of any former family home/residence to include details of the manner of occupation/ownership thereof;

   (iv) where reference is made in the Civil Bill to any immovable property, whether it is registered or unregistered land and a description of the land/ premises so referred to;

   (v) the basis of jurisdiction under the Act;

   (vi) the occupation(s) of each party;

   (vii) the grounds relied upon for the decree and any other relief sought;

   (viii) each section of the Act under which relief is sought including whether or not an Order pursuant to section 54(3) of the 1995 Act is sought.

(c) A Family Law Civil Bill for relief after foreign divorce or separation outside the State pursuant to section 23 of the 1995 Act shall, in all cases, include the following details—

   (i) the date and place of marriage and divorce/separation of the parties (a certified copy of the decree absolute or final decree of divorce/separation together with, where appropriate, an authenticated translation thereof shall be annexed to the Family Law Civil Bill);

   (ii) financial and property and custodial/access arrangements operating ancillary to the said decree, whether such arrangements were made by agreement or by Order of the Court or otherwise and whether such arrangements were made contemporaneous to the decree or at another time and the extent of compliance therewith;

   (iii) the names and ages and dates of birth of any dependent children of the marriage;

   (iv) the family home and/or other residence of the parties including, if relevant, details of any former family home/residence to include details of the manner of occupation/ownership thereof;

   (v) where reference is made in the Civil Bill to any immovable property within the State, whether it is registered or unregistered land and a description of the land/premises so referred to;

   (vi) the basis of jurisdiction under section 27 of the 1995 Act;

   (vii) the present marital status and occupation(s) of each party;

   (viii) the grounds relied upon for the relief sought;

   (ix) each section of the 1995 Act under which relief is sought;

   (x) details relevant to the matters referred to in section 26 of the 1995 Act.

(d) A Family Law Civil Bill for nullity shall, in all cases, include the following details—

    (i) the date and place of marriage of the parties;

    (ii) the domicile of the spouses on the date of the marriage and on the date of the institution of proceedings and, where either spouse has died prior to the institution of proceedings, the domicile of the said spouse at the date of death;

    (iii) whether or not the spouses or either of them has been ordinarily resident in the State throughout the period of one year prior to the date of institution of proceedings and, where either spouse has died prior to the institution of proceedings, whether or not the said spouse was ordinarily resident in the State throughout the period of one year prior to his death;

    (iv) the address and description of each party;

    (v) the number of children of the marriage;

    (vi) the grounds upon which decree and any other relief is sought;

    (vii) the relief sought (including whether or not a declaration relating to the custody of a dependent member of the family pursuant to section 46 of the 1995 Act is being sought) and the issues to be tried.

(e) A Family Law Civil Bill for Declaration of Marital Status shall, in all cases, include the following details—

    (i) the nature of the Applicant's reason for seeking such a declaration;

    (ii) full details of the marriage/divorce/annulment/legal separation in respect of which the declaration is sought including the date and place of such marriage/divorce/annulment/legal separation (where possible, a certified copy of the marriage certificate/decree of divorce/annulment/legal separation should be annexed to the Civil Bill);

    (iii) the manner in which the jurisdictional requirements of section 29(2) of the 1995 Act are satisfied;

    (iv) particulars of any previous or pending proceedings in relation to any marriage concerned or to the matrimonial status of a party to any such marriage in accordance with section 30 of the 1995 Act;

    (v) the relief being sought;

    (vi) any other relevant facts.

(f) A Family Law Civil Bill for the determination of property issues between spouses, pursuant to section 36 of the 1995 Act or between formerly engaged persons, pursuant to section 44 of the 1996 Act, shall, in all cases, include the following—

    (i) the description, nature and extent of the disputed property or monies;

    (ii) the state of knowledge of the Applicant spouse in relation to possession and control of the disputed property or monies at all relevant times;

    (iii) the nature and extent of the interest being claimed by the Applicant in the property or monies and the basis upon which such a claim is made;

(iv) the nature and extent of any claim for relief being made and the basis upon which any such claim for relief is being made;

(v) where reference is made in the Civil Bill to any immovable property, whether it is registered or unregistered land and a description of the land/ premises so referred to;

(vi) the manner in which it is claimed that the Respondent spouse has failed, neglected or refused to make to the Applicant spouse such appropriate payment or disposition in all of the circumstances and details of any payment or disposition made;

(vii) that the time limits referred to at section 36(7) of the 1995 Act have been complied with;

(viii) any other relevant matters.

(g) A Family Law Civil Bill for relief pursuant to section 18 of the 1996 Act or section 15A or section 25 of the 1995 Act shall, in all cases include the following details—

(i) the date and place of marriage and the date of any decree of divorce/ judicial separation and the marriage certificate and a certified copy of the decree of divorce/separation shall be annexed to the Civil Bill (with authenticated translations, where appropriate);

(ii) details of previous matrimonial relief obtained by the Applicant and in particular lump sum maintenance orders and property adjustment orders, if any;

(iii) details of any benefits previously received from or on behalf of the deceased spouse whether by way of agreement or otherwise and details of any benefits accruing to the Applicant under the terms of the Will of the deceased spouse or otherwise;

(iv) the date of death of the deceased spouse, the date on which representation was first granted in respect of the estate of the said spouse and, if applicable, the date upon which notice of the death of the deceased spouse was given to the Applicant spouse and the date upon which the Applicant spouse notified the personal representative of his/her intention to apply for relief pursuant to section 18(7) of the 1996 Act and section 15A(7) of the 1995 Act;

(v) the nature and extent of any claim for relief being made and the basis upon which any such claim for relief is being made;

(vi) the marital status of the deceased spouse at the date of death and the marital status of the Applicant at the date of the application and whether the Applicant has remarried since the dissolution of the marriage between the Applicant and the deceased spouse;

(vii) details of all dependents of the deceased spouse at the date of death and of all dependents of the Applicant at the date of the application together with details of any other interested persons;

     (viii)  that no order pursuant to section 18(10) of the 1996 Act or section 15A(10) of the 1995 Act has previously been made;

     (ix)  details of the value of the estate of the deceased spouse, where known;

     (x)  any other relevant facts.

Applications pursuant to section 15A(6) or section 25(7) of the 1995 Act or section 18(6) of the 1996 Act by the personal representative in relation to the distribution of the estate shall be by motion, grounded on affidavit, on notice to the applicant spouse and such other persons as the Court shall direct.

(h)  A Family Law Civil Bill for relief under the 1964 Act or the 1997 Act shall in all cases contain the following details—

     (i)  the precise reliefs being sought;

     (ii)  whether the Applicant is the mother or the father or some other relative of the infant;

     (iii)  whether the Respondent is the mother or the father or some other relative of the infant;

     (iv)  details of the guardians of the infant;

     (v)  the residential address and occupation of the Applicant and the Respondent;

     (vi)  the grounds upon which the application is being made;

     (vii)  the date of birth and place of residence of the infant together with all other relevant details relating to the infant;

     (viii)  any other relevant information.

(i)  A Family Law Civil Bill for relief under the First 1976 Act shall in all cases contain the following details—

     (i)  the precise reliefs being sought and the persons in respect of whom they are being sought;

     (ii)  the residential address and occupation of the Applicant and the Respondent;

     (iii)  the relationship between the Applicant and the Respondent and the persons in respect of whom the application is being made;

     (iv)  date of marriage (if applicable) including details of the date and place of marriage;

     (v)  names and dates of birth of all children concerned in the application together with their places of residence;

     (vi)  the nature of the failure to maintain being asserted;

     (vii)  any relevant change of circumstances (if applicable);

     (viii)  any other relevant circumstances.

(j)  A Family Law Civil Bill for relief under the Second 1976 Act shall in all cases contain the following details—

     (i)  the address and description of the family home;

     (ii)  the date and place of marriage of the parties;

  (iii)  the residential address and occupation of the Applicant and the Respondent (if known);

  (iv)  the relief being sought and the facts intended to be relied upon;

  (v)  the rateable valuation of the premises;

  (vi)  any other relevant circumstances.

(5) All Family Law Civil Bills shall be dated and shall bear the name, address and description of the Applicant and an address for service of proceedings, and shall be signed by the party's Solicitor, if any, or, where the Applicant does not have a Solicitor, by that party personally. The address to which a Respondent should apply in order to receive information in relation to legal aid shall also be included in such Civil Bills.

**Issuing and Entry**

(6) On the issuing of a Family Law Civil Bill the original thereof shall be filed, together with the appropriate certificate (pursuant to section 5 of the 1989 Act or section 6 of the 1996 Act), an Affidavit of Means in the intended action sworn by the Applicant in compliance with sub-rules (17) and (18) hereof and, in all circumstances where there are dependent children, an Affidavit of Welfare in the intended action in compliance with sub-rule (19) hereof, and the County Registrar shall thereupon enter same.

**Service**

(7)  (a)  All Family Law Civil Bills shall be served by registered post on the Respondent at his last-known address or alternatively shall be served personally on the Respondent by any person over the age of eighteen years together with the appropriate certificate in the form set out in Form 37D of the Schedule of Forms annexed hereto (pursuant to section 5 of the 1989 Act or section 6 of the 1996 Act), an Affidavit of Means in compliance with sub-rules (17) and (18) hereof in the form set out in Form 37A of the Schedule of Forms annexed hereto or such modification thereof as may be appropriate and in all cases where there are dependent children, an Affidavit of Welfare in compliance with Rule 19 hereof in the form set out in Form 37B of the Schedule of Forms annexed hereto. Where relief pursuant to section 12 and/or section 13 of the 1995 Act or section 17 of the 1996 Act is sought, notice thereof in accordance with Form 37C of the Schedule of Forms annexed hereto shall also be served on the trustees of the pension scheme in question by registered post at their registered office or other appropriate address and an Affidavit of such Service sworn and filed within fourteen days of service of the Civil Bill. Service shall be endorsed upon all Family Law Civil Bills in accordance with the provisions of Order 11 Rule 21 of these Rules. All other pleadings may be served by ordinary pre-paid post.

  (b)  In all cases in which a declaration of marital status under Section 29 of the 1995 Act is sought, the Family Law Civil Bill shall, in addition to the provisions of sub-rule (8)(a) hereof, be served upon the parties to the marriage or, where no longer living, their personal representatives (all of whom shall be parties to the proceedings) and to such other persons as the Court may direct, including the Attorney General, in accordance with the provisions as to service of Family Law Civil Bills hereinbefore set out in respect of the Respondent to proceedings which said persons (excepting the Attorney General) may be made parties to the application in accordance with section 29(6) of the 1995 Act. The Attorney General shall, however, be entitled to interplead in such proceedings.

(c) Where relief is sought pursuant to sections 15A or 25 of the 1995 Act or section 18 of the 1996 Act, the Family Law Civil Bill shall be served in accordance with these Rules on the personal representative of the deceased and on the spouse (if any) of the deceased and on such other person or persons as the Court shall direct.

(d) Where, in any application pursuant to this Rule, it is appropriate to direct an Order to any third person who is not a party to the proceedings, the Court may if it thinks fit adjourn the matter and direct the Applicant or the Respondent to notify the third person against whom an Order is sought of the fact that an Order is sought against him and of the adjourned date, so that this said third person may appear and be heard in relation to the making of the said Order. Alternatively, the Court may, when making an Order directed to any third person, provide, in the said Order, that the said third person should have liberty to apply to the Court on notice to the Applicant and the Respondent to set aside the Order made insofar as it is directed against or relates to the said third person.

**Appearance**

(8) If a Respondent intends to contest the application, or any part thereof, he/she shall enter an Appearance in the Office within 10 days of the service upon him/her of the Family Law Civil Bill together with the appropriate certificate in the form set out in Form 37D of the Schedule of Forms annexed hereto (pursuant to section 6 of the 1989 Act and section 7 of the 1996 Act), and shall serve a copy of the Appearance and appropriate certificate on the Applicant's Solicitors or, where appropriate, on the Applicant. The Appearance shall bear an address for service of any interlocutory applications and shall be signed by the Respondent's Solicitor or, if the Respondent does not have a Solicitor, by the Respondent personally.

**Defence**

(9) (a) A Respondent shall at the same time as entering an Appearance, or within 10 clear days from the date of service of the Appearance, or such further time as may be agreed between the parties or allowed by the Court, file and serve a Defence, together with an Affidavit of Means in compliance with sub-rules (17) and (18) hereof and, in all cases where there are dependent children, an Affidavit of Welfare in compliance with sub-rule (19) hereof on the Applicant, or the Applicant's Solicitor, if any, and on the County Registrar in the forms set out in Forms 37A and 37B of the Schedule of Forms annexed hereto or such modification thereof as may be appropriate. Where relief pursuant to section 12 and/or section 13 of the 1995 Act or section 17 of the 1996 Act is sought by

way of Counterclaim, notice thereof in accordance with Form 37C of the Schedule of Forms annexed hereto shall also be served on the trustees of the pension scheme in question by registered post at their registered office and a Affidavit of such Service sworn and filed within 7 days of service of the Defence and Counterclaim.

(b) No Appearance or Defence shall be entered after the time specified in these Rules without the leave of the Court or of the County Registrar or the agreement of the parties, and no Defence shall be entered unless the Respondent has previously entered an Appearance as required by these Rules.

(c) Whether or not a Defence is filed and served in any proceedings, the Respondent shall, where appropriate, in any event be obliged to file and serve an Affidavit of Means and a Welfare Statement in accordance with these Rules of Court within 20 days after the service of the Family Law Civil Bill upon him/her subject to sub-rule (36).

(d) Without prejudice to the entitlement of the Court to permit representations in relation to the making or refusal of an attachment of earnings order at the hearing of the action, such representations for the purposes of section 8(6)(b) of the 1995 Act or section 13(6)(b) of the 1996 Act or section 10(3)(a) of the First 1976 Act may be included in the Defence.

**Motions for Judgment**

[(10)(a) In any case in which a Respondent has made default in entering an Appearance or filing a Defence, as the case may be, the Applicant may, subject to the provisions of the following sub-rules of this Rule, at any time after such default, on notice to be served on the Respondent and, where relief pursuant to section 12 and/or 13 of the 1995 Act and section 17 of the 1996 Act is sought, on the trustees of the pension scheme concerned, not less than fourteen days before the hearing, apply to the Court for judgment in default of Appearance or Defence. Such application, save in the case of motions returnable in the Dublin Circuit, shall be returnable initially before the County Registrar in accordance with sub-rule (38)(5).]¹

(b) No notice of motion for Judgment in default of defence shall be served unless the Applicant has at least fourteen days prior to the service of such notice written to the Respondent giving him notice of his/her intention to serve a notice of motion for Judgment in default of defence and at the same time consenting to the late filing of a Defence within fourteen days from the date of the letter.

(c) If no defence is delivered within the said period the Applicant shall be at liberty to serve a notice of motion for Judgment in default of defence which shall be returnable to a date not less than fourteen clear days from the date of the service of the notice, such notice of motion to be filed not later than six days before the return date.

(d)  If in any case the Applicant can establish special reasons for making it necessary to serve a notice of motion for Judgment in default of appearance/defence in the cases provided for by this Rule with greater urgency than in accordance with the provisions hereinbefore contained, he may apply ex parte to the Court for an Order giving him liberty to serve a notice of motion for Judgment in default of appearance/defence giving not less than four clear days' notice to the Respondent, or in the alternative the Judge may deem good the service of a notice of motion giving not less than four clear days' notice to the Respondent.

(e)  Upon the hearing of such application the Court may, on proof of such default as aforesaid, and upon hearing such evidence, oral or otherwise, as may be adduced, give judgment upon the Applicant's claim endorsed upon the Family Law Civil Bill, or may give leave to the Respondent to defend the whole or part of the claim upon such terms as he or she may consider just.

(f)  Upon the hearing of an application for judgment under this Rule the Court may make such order as to costs as the Court considers just.

(g)  In any case in which the parties are agreed in respect of all of the reliefs being sought and a Defence in accordance with sub-rule (9) has been filed and served by the Respondent which reflects this agreement, the Applicant or the Respondent may, subject to the provisions of the following sub-rules of this Rule, at any time after such Defence has been filed and served, on notice to be served on the other party and, where relief pursuant to section 12 and/or 13 of the 1995 Act and section 17 of the 1996 Act is sought, on the trustees of the pension scheme concerned, not less than fourteen clear days before the hearing, apply to the Court for judgment, the application to be by way of motion on notice.

(h)  Upon the hearing of such application the Court may, upon hearing such evidence, oral or otherwise, as may be adduced

   (i)  give judgment in the terms agreed between the parties or

   (ii) give such directions in relation to the service of a Notice of Trial/Notice to fix a date for Trial as to the Court appears just.

(i)  Upon the hearing of an application for judgment under this Rule the Court may make such order as to costs as the Court considers just.

**Notice of Trial / Notice to fix a date for Trial**

[(11) Subject to sub-rule (10)(h) and (i) and sub-rule (38)(14)(g), when a Defence has been duly entered and served, the Applicant may serve a notice of trial or a notice to fix a date for trial, as appropriate, in accordance with Forms 15A and 15B of the Schedule of Forms.][1]

**Notice of Trial (Circuits other than Dublin Circuit)**

(12) This sub-rule shall not apply to the Dublin Circuit. Not less than ten days' notice of trial shall be served upon the Respondent and all other necessary parties and, where

relief is sought under sections 12 and/or 13 of the 1995 Act or section 17 of the 1996 Act, upon the trustees of the pension scheme in question, and shall be for the Sittings next ensuing after the expiration of the time mentioned in the said notice, and same shall be filed at the Office not later than seven days before the opening of such Sittings. Such notice of trial and filing thereof shall operate to set down the action or matter (including counterclaim if any) for hearing at the next ensuing Sittings.

**Notice to fix a date for Trial (Dublin Circuit)**

[(13) This rule shall apply only to the Dublin Circuit. A party desiring to give notice to fix a date for trial in accordance with sub-rule (11) or sub-rule (14) shall lodge with the Office a notice to fix a date for trial in the Form 15B of the Schedule of Forms. On receipt of such notice, duly completed, from the Office, that party shall serve a copy of the completed notice setting out the date upon which a date for hearing will be fixed by the County Registrar on all of the other parties and, where relief is sought under sections 12 and/or 13 of the 1995 Act or section 17 of the 1996 Act, on the trustees of the pension scheme in question. At least ten days' notice to fix a date for trial shall be given. The service of notice to fix a date for a trial, as duly completed in the Office, on all necessary parties shall operate to set down the action (including a counterclaim if any) for hearing upon such date as may be fixed by the County Registrar.][3]

**Service by Respondent**

(14) Where the Applicant has failed to serve a notice of trial or notice to fix a date for trial, as appropriate, within ten days after the service and entry of the Defence, the Respondent may do so and may file the same in accordance with these Rules.

**Joinder**

(15) The Court, if it considers it desirable, may order that two or more actions be tried together, and on such terms as to costs as the Court shall deem just.

**Affidavits of Representation**

(16)(a)   Save where the Court shall otherwise direct, any notice party, including the trustees of a pension scheme, who wishes to make representations to the Court pursuant to section 12(18) and/or section 13(2) of the 1995 Act or section 17(18) of the 1996 Act shall make such representations by Affidavit of Representation to be filed and served on all parties to the proceedings within 28 days of service upon them of notice of the application for relief under section 12 and/or 13 of the 1995 Act or section 17 of the 1996 Act in accordance with sub-rules (7) and (9) or within such time or in such manner as the Court may direct.

(b)   Without prejudice to the entitlement of the Court to permit representations by persons having a beneficial interest in property (not being the other spouse) pursuant to section 15(5) of the 1995 Act and section 19(5) of the 1996 Act or by interested persons pursuant to section 15A(5) or section 25(6) of the 1995 Act and section 18(5) of the 1996 Act at the hearing of the action, such representations may be made by way of Affidavit of Representation to be filed and served on all parties to the proceedings as directed by the Court.

**Affidavit of Means**

(17) Without prejudice to the right of each party to make application to the Court for an Order of Discovery pursuant to these Rules and without prejudice to the jurisdiction of the Court pursuant to section 12(25) of the 1995 Act and section 17(25) of the 1996 Act, in any case where financial relief under the Acts is sought, the parties shall file Affidavits of Means in accordance with sub-rules (6) and (9) in respect of which the following rules shall be applicable—

[(a) in all cases where a Defence and/or Counterclaim has been filed (save for a Defence pursuant to Order 59 Rule 4(10)(g) each party shall, unless the other party dispenses in writing with the requirement of vouching, vouch his Affidavit of Means, in the manner specified in Form 37L, within 28 days of the date of filing of the Respondent's Affidavit of Means or 21 days before the date fixed for a case progression hearing, whichever be the earlier;

(b) in all cases where a Defence has not been filed and a case progression hearing has been listed, each party shall vouch his Affidavit of Means within such time as the County Registrar shall direct;][1]

[(c) in the event of a party failing to file, serve, or properly vouch the items referred to in, their Affidavits of Means as required by these Rules—

(i) the Court, on application by notice of motion, and, in accordance with section 34(1) and the Second Schedule of the Courts and Court Officers Act 1995, the County Registrar, on application by notice of motion or in the course of case progression, may make an Order enlarging the time within which the party in default must file or serve an Affidavit of Means and/or vouch (in such manner or on such terms as the Court, or the County Registrar as the case may be, directs) the items referred to in any Affidavit of Means or may make an Order for Discovery, or

(ii) the Court may make such other Orders as the Court deems appropriate and necessary (including an Order that such party shall not be entitled to pursue or defend as appropriate a claim for any ancillary reliefs under the Acts save as permitted by the Court upon such terms as the Court may determine are appropriate and/or adjourning the proceedings for a specified period of time to enable compliance) and furthermore and/or in the alternative relief pursuant to section 38(8) of the 1995 Act or section 38(7) of the 1996 Act may be sought in accordance with sub-rule (23).][2]

(18) The Affidavit of Means shall set out in schedule form details of the party's income, assets, debts, expenditure and other liabilities wherever situated and from whatever source and, to the best of the deponent's knowledge, information and belief the income, assets, debts, expenditure and other liabilities wherever situated and from whatever source of any dependent member of the family and shall be in accordance with the form set out in Form 37A herein or such modification thereof as may be appropriate. Where

relief pursuant to section 12 of the 1995 Act is sought, the Affidavit of Means shall also state to the best of the deponent's knowledge, information and belief, the nature of the scheme, the benefits payable thereunder, the normal pensionable age and the period of reckonable service of the member spouse and where information relating to the pension scheme has been obtained from the trustees of the scheme under the Pensions Acts 1990 to 2002, such information should be exhibited in the Affidavit of Means and where such information has not been obtained a specific averment shall be included in the Affidavit of Means as to why such information has not been obtained.

**Affidavit of Welfare**

(19) An Affidavit of Welfare shall be in the form set out in Form 37B. In circumstances in which the Respondent agrees with the facts as averred to in the Affidavit of Welfare filed and served by the Applicant, the Respondent may file and serve an Affidavit of Welfare in the alternative form provided for in Form 37B herein. In circumstances in which the Respondent disagrees with the Affidavit of Welfare filed and served by the Applicant, a separate Affidavit of Welfare, including the schedule provided for in the form set out in Form 37B shall be sworn, filed and served by the Respondent in accordance with sub-rule (9).

**Counterclaims**

(20) Save where otherwise directed by the Court, a Counterclaim, if any, brought by a Respondent shall be included in and served with the Defence, in accordance with the provisions of these Rules relating thereto, and shall, in particular, set out in numbered paragraphs

    (a)  in the case of an application for a decree of divorce—

        (i)  the facts specified at sub-rule (4)(a) hereof in like manner as in the Family Law Civil Bill;

        (ii)  outline the ground(s) for a decree of divorce, if sought;

        (iii)  specify any ground upon which the Respondent intends to rely in support of any ancillary relief claimed; and

        (iv)  the relief sought pursuant to the 1996 Act;

    (b)  in the case of an application for a decree of judicial separation

        (i)  the facts specified at sub-rule (4)(b) hereof in like manner as in the Family Law Civil Bill;

        (ii)  outline the ground(s) for a decree of judicial separation, if sought;

        (iii)  specify any additional ground upon which the Respondent intends to rely in support of any ancillary relief claimed; and

        (iv)  the relief sought pursuant to the 1995 Act;

    (c)  in the case of an application for relief after divorce or separation outside the State

        (i)  the facts specified at sub-rule (4)(c) hereof in like manner as in the Family Law Civil Bill;

    (ii)  specify any additional ground upon which the Respondent intends to rely in support of any ancillary relief claimed; and

    (iii)  the relief sought pursuant to the 1995 Act;

(d)  in the case of an application for a decree of nullity

    (i)  outline the ground(s) for a decree of nullity, if sought;

    (ii)  specify any additional ground upon which the Respondent intends to rely in support of any relief claimed; and

    (iii)  the relief sought (including whether or not a declaration relating to the custody of a dependent member of the family pursuant to section 46 of the 1995 Act is being sought) and any additional issues to be tried;

(e)  in the case of an application for a Declaration of Marital Status

    (i)  the facts specified at sub-rule (4)(e) hereof in like manner as in the Family Law Civil Bill;

    (ii)  specify any additional ground upon which the Respondent intends to rely in support of any relief claimed; and

    (iii)  the relief sought pursuant to the 1995 Act;

(f)  in the case of an application for the determination of property issues between spouses, pursuant to section 36 of the 1995 Act/formerly engaged person pursuant to section 44 of the 1996 Act

    (i)  the facts specified at sub-rule (4)(f) hereof in like manner as in the Family Law Civil Bill;

    (ii)  specify any additional ground upon which the Respondent intends to rely in support of any relief claimed; and

    (iii)  the relief sought pursuant to the 1995 Act;

(g)  in the case of an application for relief under the 1964 Act or the 1997 Act

    (i)  the facts specified at sub-rule (4)(h) hereof in like manner as in the Family Law Civil Bill;

    (ii)  specify any additional ground upon which the Respondent intends to rely in support of any relief claimed; and

    (iii)  the relief sought pursuant to the 1964 and/or the 1997 Act;

(h)  in the case of an application for relief under the First 1976 Act

    (i)  the facts specified at sub-rule (4)(i) hereof in like manner as in the Family Law Civil Bill;

    (ii)  specify any additional ground upon which the Respondent intends to rely in support of any relief claimed; and

    (iii)  the relief sought pursuant to the First 1976 Act;

(i)  in the case of an application for relief under the Second 1976 Act

    (i)  the facts specified at sub-rule (4)(j) hereof in like manner as in the Family Law Civil Bill;

    (ii)  specify any additional ground upon which the Respondent intends to rely in support of any relief claimed; and

      (iii)   the relief sought pursuant to the Second 1976 Act.

**Evidence**

(21) Save where the Court otherwise directs and subject to sub-rule (25), every Application under this Rule shall be heard on oral evidence, such hearings to be held in camera.

(22) Notwithstanding the provisions of sub-rule (21), where relief pursuant to section 12 of the 1995 Act or section 17 of the 1996 Act is sought by the Applicant or the Respondent, evidence of the actuarial value of a benefit under the scheme (as defined in section 12(1) of the 1995 Act and section 17(1) of the 1996 Act) may be by Affidavit filed on behalf of the Applicant/Respondent, such Affidavit to be sworn by an appropriate person and served on all parties to the proceedings and filed at least 14 days in advance of the hearing and subject to the right of the Respondent/Applicant to serve Notice of Cross-examination in relation to same. Where one of the parties has adduced evidence of the actuarial value of a benefit by Affidavit as provided for herein and the other party intends to adduce similar or contra oral evidence, notice of such intention shall be served by the disputing party upon all other parties at least 10 days in advance of the hearing.

**Interim and Interlocutory Applications**

(23)(a)   An application for Preliminary Orders pursuant to section 6 of the 1995 Act or section 11 of the 1996 Act or for maintenance pending suit/relief pursuant to section 7 or section 24 of the 1995 Act or section 12 of the 1996 Act or for information pursuant to section 12(25) of the 1995 Act or section 17(25) of the 1996 Act or for relief pursuant to section 35 of the 1995 Act or section 37 of the 1996 Act or for relief pursuant to section 38(8) of the 1995 Act or section 38(7) of the 1996 Act or for a report pursuant to section 47 of the 1995 Act or section 42 of the 1995 Act or for any other interlocutory relief shall be by Notice of Motion to be served upon the parties to the proceedings and, in the case of applications pursuant to section 12(25) of the 1995 Act or section 17(25) of the 1996 Act, upon the trustees of the pension scheme concerned.

    (b)   Prior to any interlocutory application for discovery or for information pursuant to section 12(25) of the 1995 Act or section 17(25) of the 1996 Act being made, the information being sought shall be requested in writing voluntarily at least 14 days prior to the issuing of the motion for the relief concerned and upon failure to make such a request, the judge may adjourn the motion or strike out the motion or make such other order, including an order as to costs, as to the Court may appear appropriate.

    (c)   An application for alimony pending suit in nullity proceedings shall be by Notice of Motion grounded upon Affidavit setting out the assets, liabilities, income, debts and expenditure of the Applicant for alimony and, in so far as same is known to the Applicant, the assets, liabilities, income, debts, and expenditure of the Respondent to the said Motion. In every case in which the Respondent wishes to defend such an application for alimony, the Respondent shall file a replying Affidavit setting out details of his assets, liabilities, income, debts and expenditure.

(d)   Applications for the appointment of medical and/or psychiatric inspectors in respect of the Applicant and/or the Respondent shall be made by Motion on Notice to the other party and such Motion shall be issued not later than 14 days after the elapsing of the times for the entry of an Appearance and delivery of a Defence save with the leave of the Court or the County Registrar. Where medical and/or psychiatric inspectors are appointed by the Court or the County Registrar, the solicitors for the parties shall attend with the parties on the appointed day at the place in which the inspection is to take place for the purpose of identifying the parties to the County Registrar or his/her nominee. In any circumstances in which a party is unrepresented, appropriate photographic proof of identity must be produced sufficient to satisfy the County Registrar or his/her nominee of the identity of the party concerned. No inspection shall be carried out unless the procedures contained herein are satisfied. Upon completion of the inspection, a report thereof shall be sent by the inspector directly to the County Registrar for the County in which the proceedings have issued.

(e)   In any case where the Court is satisfied that the delay caused by proceeding by Motion on Notice under this Rule would or might entail serious harm or mischief, the Court may make an Order ex parte as it shall consider just. Urgent applications under this sub-rule may be made to a Judge at any time or place approved by him, by arrangement with the County Registrar for the County in question.

(f)   Interim and interlocutory applications shall where appropriate be made to the County Registrar in accordance with the Second Schedule to the Court and Court Officers Act 1995 and Orders 18 and 19 of the Rules of the Circuit Court.

(24) If on the date for hearing of any Application under this Rule the matter is not dealt with by the Court for any reason, and, in particular, on foot of an adjournment sought by either party, the other party, whether consenting to the adjournment or not, may apply for, and the Court may grant, such interim or interlocutory relief as to it shall seem appropriate without the necessity of service of a Notice of Motion.

(25) Any interim or interlocutory application shall be heard on Affidavit, unless the Court otherwise directs, save that the Deponent of any Affidavit must be available to the Court to give oral evidence or to be cross-examined as to the Court shall seem appropriate, save that a Motion for Discovery and a Motion in the course of nullity proceedings for the appointment of medical/psychiatric inspectors shall be heard on a Notice of Motion only. Where any oral evidence is heard by the Court in the course of such applications ex parte, a note of such evidence shall be prepared by the applicant or the applicant's solicitor and approved by the Judge and shall be served upon the respondent forthwith together with a copy of the Order made (if any), unless otherwise directed by the Court.

**Further relief and applications on behalf of dependent persons**

(26)(a)   Where either party or a person on behalf of a dependent member of the family wishes at any time after the hearing of the Application to seek further relief as provided for in the Act or to vary or discharge an Order previously made by the Court that party shall issue a Notice of Motion to re-enter or to vary or discharge as the case may be grounded upon an Affidavit seeking such relief. Such Motions shall be subject to the provisions of sub-rules (7), (16), (17), (18), (21) and (22), as appropriate.

(b)   Where a person on behalf of a dependent member of the family wishes to make application for ancillary reliefs at the hearing of the action, such application shall be by way of Notice of Motion to be served on all other parties to the proceedings setting out the reliefs sought grounded on Affidavit which said Motion shall be listed for hearing on the same date as the hearing of the action contemporaneously therewith. Such Motions shall be subject to the provisions of sub-rules (7), (16), (17), (18), (21) and (22), as appropriate.

(27) Where any party to proceedings for a declaration under section 29 of the 1995 Act alleges that the marriage in question was void or voidable and the Court decides to treat the application as one for annulment of the marriage, the provisions of these Rules in relation to the procedures applicable to decrees of nullity may be adapted in such manner as the Court shall direct.

**Relief under section 33 of the 1995 Act**

(28) Applications under section 33 of the 1995 Act for an order or orders exempting the marriage from the application of section 31(1)(a) or section 32(1)(a) of the 1995 Act may be made ex parte by the parties where both are over the age of 18 years, by the legal guardians of the parties to the intended marriage where both are under the age of 18 years or, where one of the parties is over the age of 18 years, by that party and the legal guardian or guardians of the other party, and further, where deemed appropriate by the Court, a guardian or guardians ad litem may be appointed by the Court to represent either or both of the parties. Such applications may be grounded upon Affidavit or upon oral evidence given by or on behalf of the parties, as the Court may direct, which evidence shall set out the reasons justifying the exemption and the basis upon which it is claimed that the application is in the interests of the parties to the intended marriage.

**Applications under section 8 of the First 1976 Act**

(29) Applications pursuant to section 8 of the First 1976 Act may be made by way of originating Notice of Motion, grounded upon affidavit.

(30) For the purposes of sub-rule (29), the notice of motion shall be entitled in the matter of the Act (as amended) and shall state the relief sought (including whether or not relief pursuant to section 8B of the First 1976 Act, as inserted by section 43 of the 1995 Act is sought); state the name and place of residence or address for service of the applicant; the date upon which it is proposed to apply to the Court for relief and shall be filed in the Office of the County Registrar for the County in which the application is

being brought in accordance with sub-rule (3) (hereinafter referred to as "the appropriate Office").

(31) For the purposes of sub-rule (29), without prejudice to the jurisdiction of the Court to make an Order for substituted service, the Motion shall be served by registered post on the Respondent at his last-known address or alternatively shall be served personally on the Respondent by any person over the age of eighteen years. Where relief pursuant to section 8B of the First 1976 Act is sought, the motion shall be served upon the trustees of the pension scheme also. There must be at least ten clear days between the service of the notice and the day named therein for the hearing of the motion.

(32)(a) Subject to the right of the Court to give such directions as it considers appropriate or convenient, evidence at the hearing of the motion under sub-rule (29) shall be by affidavit.

(b) Any affidavit to be used in support of the motion shall be filed in the Office of the appropriate County Registrar and a copy of any such affidavit shall be served with the notice. Any affidavit to be used in opposition to the application shall be filed in the Office of the appropriate County Registrar and served upon the applicant and, where relief pursuant to section 8B of the First 1976 Act is sought, upon the trustees of the pension scheme by the respondent following the service on him of the applicant's affidavit and any affidavit of representations to be used by the trustees of the pension scheme shall be filed in the appropriate Office and served upon the applicant and the respondent.

[(33) The plaintiff in proceedings wherein it is sought to have a conveyance declared void pursuant to the provisions of section 3 of the Family Home Protection Act 1976 (as amended by section 54 of the Family Law Act 1995)(which said proceedings shall be instituted by way of Equity Civil Bill seeking declaratory relief) shall forthwith and without delay following the institution of such proceedings cause relevant particulars of the proceedings to be entered as a lis pendens upon the property and/or premises in question under and in accordance with section 121 of the Land and Conveyancing Law Reform Act 2009.][4]

**Costs**

(34)(a) The costs as between party and party may be measured by the Judge, and if not so measured shall be taxed, in default of agreement by the parties, by the County Registrar according to such scale of costs as may be prescribed. Any party aggrieved by such taxation may appeal to the Court and have the costs reviewed by it.

(b) Where necessary, the Court may make an order determining who shall bear any costs incurred by trustees of a pension scheme pursuant to section 12(22) of the 1995 Act or section 17(22) of the 1996 Act and in making such determination the Court shall have regard, inter alia, to the representations made by the trustees pursuant to sub-rule (16), if any.

## General

(35) The Court may, upon such terms (if any) as it may think reasonable, enlarge or abridge any of the times fixed by these Rules for taking any step or doing any act in any proceeding, and may also, upon such terms as to costs or otherwise as it shall think fit, declare any step taken or act done to be sufficient, even though not taken or done within the time or in the manner prescribed by these Rules.

## Certificates

(36) The Certificates required by Sections 5 or 6 of the 1989 Act and Sections 6 or 7 of the 1996 Act shall be in accordance with Form 37D of the Schedule of Forms annexed hereto.

## Service of orders by the registrar of the Court

(37) In all circumstances in which the registrar of the Court and/or the County Registrar is required to serve or lodge a copy of an order upon any person(s) or body such service or lodgment shall be satisfied by the service of a certified copy of the said order by registered post to the said person(s) or body.

## [Case Progression

(38) (1) This sub-rule shall apply to proceedings in which relief is being sought under any of the Acts referred to in this Rule.

(2) In this rule, "case progression" means the preparation of proceedings for trial in accordance with the procedure under this sub-rule.

(3) The purpose of case progression is to ensure that proceedings are prepared for trial in a manner which is just, expeditious and likely to minimise the costs of the proceedings and that the time and other resources of the' court are employed optimally.

(4) (a) The County Registrar shall cause the proceedings to be listed before him for a case progression hearing on a date which is not later than 70 days after filing by the Respondent of his Defence, his Affidavit of Means and, where required by this Rule, his Affidavit of Welfare. The County Registrar shall issue a Summons, in Form 37L of the Schedule of Forms, to each of the parties to attend such hearing, to which shall be attached the case progression questionnaire referred to in paragraph (23). In fixing the date on which the proceedings are listed before him for case progression, the County Registrar shall allow the parties sufficient time to vouch the items referred to in their respective Affidavits of Means within the time prescribed by sub-rule (17) and to complete the case progression questionnaire within the time prescribed by paragraph (23).

(b) Where a pension adjustment order is sought by either party, the Notice to the Trustees shall be served, the Affidavit of Service in respect of same shall be filed and a copy of such Notice and Affidavit shall be served on the other party prior to the case progression hearing.

(5) Save in the case of motions for judgment in default of Appearance or Defence returnable in the Dublin Circuit, any motion for judgment in default of Appearance or

Defence in proceedings not already subject to case progression under this sub-rule, any matter remitted or transferred from the High Court and any motion for re-entry of proceedings shall be returnable initially before the County Registrar.

(6) On the initial return date for a motion for judgment in default of Appearance or Defence returned before the County Registrar in accordance with paragraph (5), the County Registrar shall—

    (a) in any case where he is satisfied, having made such inquiries as he may consider necessary, that the motion is not contested or that the parties are agreed in respect of all of the reliefs being sought, transfer the motion to the appropriate Court Motions List for such date as the County Registrar shall appoint;

    (b) in any case where he is satisfied, having made such inquiries as he may consider necessary, that the motion is contested, appoint ~ elate for a case progression hearing before him in the proceedings, and where he considers it appropriate, issue a Summons in Form 37L to any party to attend such hearing.

(7) Where the County Registrar has appointed a date for a case progression hearing under sub-paragraph (b) of paragraph (6), the County Registrar may make such order as he shall deem fit enlarging the time for the entry of an Appearance, or the delivery and filing of a Defence, or the service and filing of an Affidavit of Means or Affidavit of Welfare, or for the doing of any other act or taking of any other step in the proceedings.

(8) On—

    (a) receipt of proceedings remitted or transferred from the High Court, or

    (b) re-entry of proceedings by a party,

the County Registrar shall appoint a date for a case progression hearing before him in the proceedings, and where he considers it appropriate, shall issue a Summons in Form 37L to any party to attend such hearing.

(9) In the Dublin Circuit, where a motion for judgment in default of Appearance or Defence is contested in proceedings not already subject to case progression under this sub-rule, the motion shall, save where the Court otherwise directs, be remitted to the County Registrar for case progression, in which event the County Registrar shall proceed in like manner as provided for in paragraph (8).

(10) The Court may direct that proceedings which are before it (including proceedings on foot of an appeal from an order of the District Court and proceedings sent forward from the District Court) shall be subject to case progression, in which event the County Registrar shall proceed in like manner as provided for in paragraph (8).

(11) Any applicant, and any respondent who has filed an Appearance, may apply to the County Registrar for case progression, in which event the County Registrar shall proceed in like manner as provided for in paragraph (8).

(12) Where a case progression hearing has been listed before the County Registrar the County Registrar may give directions as to the vouching of the items referred to in the parties respective Affidavits of Means where there is a dispute between the parties in

relation to the vouching of any particular item or the adequacy of the said vouching. The County Registrar may fix a date by which such directions are to be complied with.

(13)(a) Each County Registrar shall maintain a record which may be in electronic form, of all proceedings at case progression hearings before him.

 (b) Such record shall for the proceedings concerned include particulars of—

    (i) the date of issue of the summons to attend the hearing;

    (ii) the date of each hearing and any adjournment thereof;

    (iii) where the hearing is adjourned; the reason for the adjournment;

    (iv) the name of the County Registrar conducting the hearing;

    (v) the names of counsel, solicitor and any parties attending; or

    (vi) the orders made or directions given at the hearing or any adjournment thereof.

 (c) A copy of the record shall be placed on the Court file and a further copy of same shall be made available to a party to the proceedings at his request.

(14) At the case progression hearing the County Registrar—

 (a) shall establish what steps remain to be taken to prepare the case for trial, fix a timetable for the completion of preparation of the case for trial, and for

 (b) may make orders or give directions with respect to pleadings, the exchange of between the parties of statements of issues, the identifying of issues in dispute between the parties, particulars, discovery, interrogatories, inspection of documents, inspection of real or personal property, commissions and examination of witnesses, or otherwise, which may be necessary or expedient;

 (c) may list the proceedings before the Court for the purpose of an application pursuant to Section 47 of the 1995 Act or, after consultation with the appropriate County Registrar, cause the proceedings to be listed at the next sitting of the Court at any venue within the Circuit for that purpose;

 (d) may, save in respect of any issue affecting a dependent child, receive and record on behalf of the Court undertakings to the Court from a party to the proceedings having effect pending the trial of the proceedings or until further order made by the Court;

 (e) may adjourn the case progression hearing to enable any order made or any direction given to be complied with or any other act to be done or step to be taken in the proceedings;

 (f) may make inquiries of the parties so as to ascertain the likely length of the trial and the arrangements, if any, for witnesses, information and communications technology (including video conferencing) and any other arrangements which require to be made for the trial;

 (g) may fix the time and mode 'of trial, and may fix a date for trial and may also give directions as to the service of a notice of trial or a notice to fix a date for trial;

(h)  may make any orders and give any directions in respect of arrangements for the trial as he considers necessary;

(i)  may direct any expert witnesses to consult with each other within such time as the County Registrar shall specify for the purposes of—

   (a)  identifying the issues in respect of which they intend to give evidence,

   (b)  where possible, reaching agreement on the evidence that they intend to give in respect of those issues, and

   (c)  considering any matter which the County Registrar or the Judge may direct them to consider,

and require that such witnesses record in a memorandum (0 be jointly submitted by them to the County Registrar and delivered by them to the parties, particulars of the outcome of their consultations, within such time as the County Registrar shall specify:

provided that any such outcome shall not be in any way binding on the parties;

(15) Any order made or direction given at a case progression hearing shall be issued within twenty one days of that hearing.

(16) The County Registrar may adjourn a case progression hearing from time to time and from place to place as may be appropriate, for the purposes of allowing any steps directed by the County Registrar or matters agreed to be done to be carried out, or so as to resume a case progression hearing after a matter has been referred to the Court by way of a Motion, or pursuant to sub-rule (38)(17)(a) for any other reason, to enable the County Registrar to ensure that the proceedings are prepared for trial in the manner referred to in paragraph (3).

(17)(a)  Where the County Registrar concludes that there has been undue delay or default in -complying with any order made or direction given by the Court or by him, or with any requirement of these Rules, he may list the matter for hearing at the next sitting of the Court or, after consultation with the appropriate County Registrar, cause the matter to be listed at the next sitting of the Court at any venue within the Circuit.

(b)  Where the County Registrar so concludes, he shall furnish a Report to the Court setting out the delay or default concerned. Such report shall be in Form 37M of the Schedule of Forms.

(18) The solicitors appearing for each of the parties or, where a party is not represented by a solicitor, the party himself, shall attend the case progression hearing and any adjournment thereof. Where the County Registrar considers it necessary or desirable, he may direct that a party attend the hearing notwithstanding the fact that the party may be represented by a solicitor.

(19) Each representative of a party attending the case progression hearing shall ensure that he is sufficiently familiar with the proceedings and has authority from the party he represents to deal with any matters that are likely to be dealt with.

(20) Where a party is represented by counsel such counsel may attend the case progression hearing, but the fees of counsel for either party for attending the case

progression hearing will be allowed in the taxation and measurement of costs only where the County Registrar so certifies.

(21)(a) The County Registrar may award costs incurred in connection with the case progression hearing as between party and party.

(b) The County Registrar may tax and measure any such costs, and may, where the Court so directs, tax and measure any solicitor and client costs incurred in connection with a case progression hearing.

(22) Where it appears to the County Registrar that a case progression hearing cannot conveniently proceed, or it appears to the Court that a case progression hearing could not conveniently proceed by reason of the failure of a party to be prepared for such hearing or, by reason of the default of any party in complying with any order or direction of the County Registrar, the County Registrar or, as the case may be, the Court, may award costs against such party, or may disallow the costs of such party, as the case may be.

(23) Each party shall lodge with the County Registrar and serve on the other party not later than seven days before the date fixed for the case progression hearing a case progression questionnaire, duly completed, in Form 37N of the Schedule of Forms. Where the County Registrar directs, a party shall revise or update a case progression questionnaire within such time as is directed by the County Registrar.

(24) The Circuit Court Judge or the County Registrar may, on any occasion when proceedings are listed before him (including for mention or in any callover) direct the updating and vouching of Affidavits of Means, and/or expert reports, where necessary, to such date as is directed.][5]

---

**Notes**

1   Rule 4(10)(a), (11) and (17)(a) and (b) substituted by SI 358/2008, r 3.

2   Rule 4(17)(c) inserted by SI 538/2008, r 3.

3   Rule 4(13) substituted by SI 189/2008, r 3.

4   Rule 4(33) substituted by SI 155/2010, r 3.

5   Rule 4(38) inserted by SI 358/2008, r 3.

---

**Rule 5 — Domestic Violence**

(1) In this Rule "the Act" means the Domestic Violence Act 1996 (No. 1 of 1996).

**Venue**

(2) In accordance with section 14 of the Act, an application under this Rule shall be brought in the county where the applicant in the proceedings ordinarily resides (subject to section 14(2) of the Act) or where the place in relation to which the application for a Barring Order is made is situate save that, where the application is made by the Health Service Executive pursuant to section 6 of the Act, the application shall be brought in the county where any party on whose behalf the application is made ordinarily resides or

where the place in relation to which the application for a Barring Order is made is situate.

## Forms

(3) An application for the making, varying or discharging of a Barring Order or Safety Order shall be instituted by the issuing of a Domestic Violence Civil Bill in the form specified at Form 20 of the Schedule of Forms annexed hereto or such modification thereof as may be appropriate in the circumstances.

## Interim orders

(4) An application for a Protection Order may be made by Motion on Notice or by ex parte application after the institution of proceedings for a Barring Order or Safety Order and an application for an interim Barring Order may be made by Motion on Notice or by ex parte application after the institution of proceedings for a Barring Order and such applications shall be grounded upon an affidavit to be sworn by the applicant or such other person as may be appropriate. An application for the discharge or variation of a Protection Order or interim Barring Order made pursuant to this Rule shall be by Motion on Notice or by ex parte application and shall be grounded upon an affidavit to be sworn by the respondent or such other person as may be appropriate. Urgent applications under this Rule may be made to a Judge at any time or place approved by him or her, by arrangement with the County Registrar. Where interim relief of any nature is granted following an ex parte application, the applicant shall forthwith cause a Notice of Motion to issue in respect of the reliefs which are being sought and/or affirming the ex parte Orders which have been made, such Motion to be returnable before the Court not later than 8 days following the granting of the ex parte relief and to be served upon the respondent in accordance with the provisions of sub-rule (8), unless otherwise directed by the Court. Save where otherwise directed by the Court, all ex parte Orders obtained shall lapse upon the expiration of 8 days following the making thereof.

## Entry

(5) Every Domestic Violence Civil Bill under sub-rule (3) shall be entered in the Office before service and a date for the hearing of same or a date upon which a date for hearing shall be fixed by the Court shall be obtained.

## Dates

(6) Every Domestic Violence Civil Bill under sub-rule (3) shall state the date upon which the application shall be listed for hearing or shall state the date upon which a date for hearing shall be fixed by the Court. For the purpose of obtaining an expeditious hearing of such application, the same may be set down for hearing at any sitting of the Court within the Circuit.

## Signature

(7) Every Domestic Violence Civil Bill under sub-rule (3) and every Notice of Motion and every ex parte docket shall be dated and bear the name, address and description of the applicant and shall be signed by the applicant or by the applicant's solicitor.

**Service**

(8) Every Domestic Violence Civil Bill under sub-rule (3) and every Notice of Motion under sub-rule (4) shall be served at least four clear days before the date scheduled for the hearing thereof, either personally in accordance with the provisions of Order 11, or alternatively, by leaving a true copy of the same at the respondent's residence. In the event that there is no Summons Server assigned to the relevant area any person over the age of eighteen years shall be deemed to be an authorised person for the purpose of the service of such Domestic Violence Civil Bill or Notice of Motion. An Affidavit of Service of every Domestic Violence Civil Bill under sub-rule (3) and every Motion on Notice under sub-rule (4) shall be sworn and shall be handed in at the hearing of the application or Motion.

**Evidence**

(9) Save by special leave of the Court, all applications made ex parte or by Motion on Notice for an interim Barring Order or Protection Order or for the variation or discharge of same pursuant to sub-rule (4) shall be heard on affidavit evidence only and where, by leave of the Court, any oral evidence is heard by the Court in the course of such applications ex parte, a note of such evidence shall be prepared by the applicant or the applicant's solicitor or the Health Service Executive or the solicitor for the Health Service Executive and approved by the Judge, unless otherwise directed by the Court. Save by special leave of the Court, all applications for a Barring Order or Safety Order and all applications for a variation or discharge of any Barring Order or Safety Order pursuant to sub-rule (4) shall be heard on oral evidence.

**Joinder**

(10) Any application for a Barring Order or Safety Order may be joined together with any other application on the same Notice or application.

**Service**

(11) On the making, varying or discharging of a Barring Order, a Safety Order, an interim Barring Order or a Protection Order, the County Registrar shall cause a copy of the Order in question to be given or sent as soon as practicable to the applicant, to the respondent, to the Health Service Executive where application was made by the Health Service Executive pursuant to section 6 of the Act, to the member of the Garda Síochána in charge of the Garda Síochána station for the area in which is situate the place in relation to which the application for the Barring Order or interim Barring Order was made or the member of the Garda Síochána in charge of the Garda Síochána station for the area in which the person for whose benefit the safety order or protection order was made resides or such other area as the Court shall deem appropriate and to such other persons as are specified in section 11 of the Act. Where an interim Barring Order or Protection Order is made ex parte, the copy Order sent to the respondent spouse shall have enclosed therewith a copy of the affidavit upon which the application was grounded and a copy of the approved note of any oral evidence heard in the course of such application, unless otherwise ordered by the Court.

**Stamp duty**

(12) No stamp duty shall be payable in respect of any applications brought under the Act.

**Rule 6**    **Section 40, Civil Liability and Courts Act 2004 (No. 31 of 2004) Admission to proceedings for the purposes of section 40 of the Civil Liability and Courts Act 2004**

(1) A person (hereinafter referred to as "the recorder") referred to in section 40(3)(a) of the Civil Liability and Courts Act 2004 intending to attend any proceedings to which a relevant enactment (as defined in section 40(2) of the said Act) relates for the purpose of the preparation and publication of a report of such proceedings in accordance with section 40(3) shall, prior to or at the commencement of the hearing of the proceedings, identify himself or herself to the Court and apply for such direction as the Court may give under section 40(3) of the said Act.

(2) On any such application, the Court—

     (a) if satisfied that the recorder is a person referred to in section 40(3)(a) of the said Act and that the recorder intends to attend the proceedings for the purpose of the preparation and publication of a report of proceedings to which a relevant enactment relates, and

     (b) having heard any submission made by or on behalf of any party to the proceedings, may allow the recorder to attend the proceedings subject to such directions as the court may give in that regard.

(3) Where a party, being the applicant or the respondent or other party in the proceedings, wishes to be accompanied in court in any proceedings to which a relevant enactment relates by another person (hereinafter referred to as "the accompanying person") in accordance with section 40(5) of the said Act, the party to the proceedings shall complete Form 37K and

     (a) where the other party or parties to the proceedings have agreed to the accompanying person, the party making such application shall lodge Form 37K, duly completed, with the County Registrar prior to or at the commencement of the hearing in the proceedings, and shall apply to the Court at that hearing to approve the accompanying of the party concerned by the accompanying person and for such directions as the Court may give under section 40(5) of the said Act;

     (b) Save in ex parte applications, where the other party or parties have not agreed to the accompanying of the party by the accompanying person, the party seeking to be so accompanied shall, by motion (to which Form 37K, duly completed, shall be appended) on notice to the other party or parties returnable not later than fourteen days prior to the date fixed for the hearing of such proceedings, unless the Court otherwise directs, apply to the Court to approve the accompanying of the party concerned by the accompanying person and for such directions as the Court may give under section 40(5) of the said Act;

(c) In ex parte applications, subject to the filing of Form 37K in accordance with sub-rule (a) above, the approval of any accompanying person shall be at the discretion of the Court.

On any such application, the Court may approve the accompaniment of the party concerned by the accompanying person, subject to such directions as the Court may give, or may refuse such approval.

(4) The Court may, of its own motion or on the application of any party or person, vary or modify any directions given under sub-rule (2) or sub-rule (3) during the course of any proceedings.

**Disclosure of documents, information or evidence for the purposes of section 40 of the Civil Liability and Courts Act 2004**

(5) An application by a party for an order for the disclosure to any third party of documents, information or evidence connected with or arising in the course of proceedings under a relevant enactment (as defined in section 40(2) of the Civil Liability and Courts Act 2004) for the purposes set out in section 40(8) of the said Act shall be made by motion to the Court on notice to the other party or parties, grounded upon an affidavit sworn by or on behalf of the moving party.

# [ORDER 59A

## CIVIL PARTNERSHIP AND CERTAIN RIGHTS AND OBLIGATIONS OF COHABITANTS ACT 2010

### Rule 1

In this Order:

**"the Act"** means the Civil Partnership and Certain Rights and Obligations of Cohabitants Act 2010;

**"the Act of 2004"** means the Civil Registration Act 2004;

**"civil partnership law proceedings"** has the same meaning as in section 139 of the Act;

**"cohabitation proceedings"** means proceedings under Part 15 of the Act, and

reference to registration of a civil partnership includes, in the case of a civil partnership recognised by virtue of section 5 of the Act, registration of a legal relationship as referred to in that section.

### Venue

### Rule 2

Any proceedings under this Order shall be brought in the county where any party to the proceedings ordinarily resides or carries on any profession, business or occupation.

**Commencement of civil partnership or cohabitation proceedings**

**Rule 3**

(1) All proceedings for the following reliefs in civil partnership law proceedings under this Order shall be instituted by the issuing out of the Office for the appropriate county of the appropriate Civil Partnership Civil Bill in accordance with Form 2S of the Schedule of Forms with such modifications as may be appropriate in the format and manner provided:

- (a) an order under section 4(1) of the Act including where such relief is sought by virtue of an order made under section 5 of the Act;
- (b) an order on an application by a civil partner to have a conveyance declared void, under section 28 of the Act, or for relief under section 34 of the Act;
- (c) an order under section 29(1) of the Act to the Court to dispense with the consent of a civil partner required under section 28 of the Act or section 29(4) of the Act to give the consent required under section 28 of the Act on behalf of a civil partner;
- (d) relief under section 30(1) of the Act or section 30(2) of the Act;
- (e) relief under Part 5 of the Act;
- (f) an order on an application by a civil partner or a child of a deceased person who was a civil partner before death under section 106 of the Act to determine a question arising between civil partners as to the title to or possession of property;
- (g) a decree of nullity of civil partnership under section 107 of the Act;
- (h) a decree of dissolution in respect of a civil partnership under section 110 of the Act;
- (i) an order for provision out of the estate of a deceased civil partner under section 127 of the Act;
- (j) an order directing the sale of property under section 128 of the Act;
- (k) subject to rule 23, an order setting aside a disposition under section 137 of the Act.

(2) Cohabitation proceedings for any one or more orders under sections 174, 175, 187 and 194 of the Act shall be instituted by the issuing out of the Office for the appropriate county of the appropriate Cohabitation Civil Bill in accordance with Form 2T of the Schedule of Forms with such modifications as may be appropriate.

(3) Upon issue, the Civil Partnership Civil Bill or Cohabitation Civil Bill shall be served in a manner provided for in this Order.

**Form of Proceedings**

**Rule 4**

(1) Every Civil Partnership Civil Bill and every Cohabitation Civil Bill shall be in numbered paragraphs setting out the relief sought and the grounds relied upon in support of the application.

(2) A Civil Partnership Civil Bill for a Decree of Dissolution shall, in all cases, include the following details—

    (a)  the date and place of registration of the civil partnership;

    (b)  the length of time the parties have lived apart, including the date upon which the parties commenced living apart, and the addresses of both of the parties during that time, where known;

    (c)  the ages of the civil partners, the duration of their civil partnership and the length of time during which the civil partners lived with each other after registration of their civil partnership;

    (d)  any physical or mental disability of either of the civil partners;

    (e)  full particulars of any children of the Applicant or Respondent civil partner or to whom either of the civil partners owes an obligation of support and stating whether and if so what provision has been made for each and any such child;

    (f)  whether any possibility of a reconciliation between the Applicant and Respondent exists and if so on what basis the same might take place;

    (g)  details of any previous civil partnership relief sought and/or obtained and details of any previous separation agreement entered into between the parties (and where appropriate, a certified copy of any relevant court order and/or agreement should be annexed to the Civil Bill);

    (h)  details of any previous matrimonial or family law relief sought and/or obtained and details of any previous separation agreement entered into by either party with any other person (and where appropriate a certified copy of any relevant court order and/or deed of separation/separation agreement should be annexed to the Civil Bill);

    (i)  details of the shared home(s) and/or other residences of the parties including, if relevant, details of any former shared home/residence to include details of the manner of occupation/ownership thereof;

    (j)  where reference is made in the Civil Bill to any immovable property, whether it is registered or unregistered land and a description of the land/premises so referred to;

    (k)  the basis of jurisdiction under section 140 of the Act;

    (l)  the occupation(s) of each party;

    (m)  the grounds relied upon for the relief sought;

    (n)  each section of the Act under which relief is sought;

(o) any other matter which will assist the Court for the purposes set out in section 129(2) of the Act.

(3) A Civil Partnership Civil Bill for nullity shall, in all cases, include such of the particulars mentioned in sub-rule (2) as are appropriate and the following details—

(a) the date and place of registration of the civil partnership;

(b) the domicile of the civil partners on the date of the civil partnership and on the date of the institution of proceedings and, where either civil partner has died prior to the institution of proceedings, the domicile of the said civil partner at the date of death;

(c) whether or not the civil partners or either of them has been ordinarily resident in the State throughout the period of one year prior to the date of institution of proceedings and, where either civil partner has died prior to the institution of proceedings, whether or not the said deceased civil partner was ordinarily resident in the State throughout the period of one year prior to his or her death;

(d) the address and description of each party;

(e) the number of dependent children of each of the civil partners;

(f) the grounds upon which the decree and any other relief is sought;

(g) the relief sought and the issues to be tried.

(4) A Civil Partnership Civil Bill for the determination of property issues between civil partners pursuant to section 106 of the Act shall, in all cases, include such of the particulars mentioned in sub-rule (2) as are appropriate and the following details—

(a) the description, nature and extent of the money or other property to which the application relates;

(b) the state of knowledge of the Applicant civil partner in relation to possession and control of the money or other property to which the application relates at all relevant times;

(c) the nature and extent of the interest being claimed by the Applicant in the property or monies and the basis upon which such a claim is made;

(d) the nature and extent of any claim for relief being made and the basis upon which any such claim for relief is being made;

(e) where reference is made in the Civil Bill to any immovable property, whether it is registered or unregistered land and a description of the land/premises so referred to;

(f) the manner in which it is claimed that the Respondent civil partner has failed, neglected or refused to make to the Applicant civil partner such appropriate payment or disposition in all of the circumstances and details of any payment or disposition made;

(g) any other relevant matters.

(5) A Civil Partnership Civil Bill for relief pursuant to section 127 of the Act shall, in all cases, include such of the particulars mentioned in sub-rule (2) as are appropriate and the following details—

(a) the date and place of the registration of the civil partnership and the date of any decree of dissolution and the civil partnership registration form and a certified copy of any decree of dissolution shall be annexed to the Civil Bill (with authenticated translations, where appropriate);

(b) details of previous civil partnership relief obtained by the Applicant and in particular lump sum maintenance orders and property adjustment orders, if any;

(c) details of any benefits previously received from or on behalf of the deceased civil partner whether by way of agreement or otherwise and details of any benefits accruing to the Applicant under the terms of the will of the deceased civil partner or otherwise;

(d) the date of death of the deceased civil partner, the date on which representation was first granted in respect of the estate of the said civil partner and, if applicable, the date upon which notice of the death of the deceased civil partner was given to the Applicant civil partner and the date upon which the Applicant civil partner notified the personal representative of his/her intention to apply for relief pursuant to section 127(8) of the Act;

(e) the nature and extent of any claim for relief being made and the basis upon which any such claim for relief is being made;

(f) the civil partnership or marital status of the deceased civil partner at the date of death and the civil partnership or marital status of the Applicant at the date of the application and whether the Applicant has entered into a new civil partnership or a marriage since the dissolution of the civil partnership between the Applicant and the deceased civil partner;

(g) details of all dependants of the deceased civil partner at the date of death and of all dependants of the Applicant at the date of the application together with details of any other interested persons;

(h) that no order pursuant to section 127(11) of the Act has previously been made;

(i) details of the value of the estate of the deceased civil partner, where known;

(j) any other relevant facts.

(6) Applications pursuant to section 127(7) of the Act by the personal representative in relation to the distribution of the estate shall be by motion, grounded on affidavit, on notice to the Applicant civil partner and such other persons as the Court shall direct.

(7) A Civil Partnership Civil Bill for relief under section 4 of the Act, shall include such of the particulars mentioned in sub-rule (2) as are appropriate and:

(a) the nature of the Applicant's reason for seeking the relief sought under section 4 of the Act;

(b)  full details of the registration of the civil partnership and/or dissolution of the civil partnership in respect of which the declaration is sought including the date and place of such civil partnership was registered and/or dissolved (and, where appropriate, a certified copy of the civil partnership registration form and/or decree of dissolution should be exhibited to the affidavit);

(c)  where a declaration is sought under section 4 by virtue of an order made under section 5 of the Act, a certified copy of the instrument of registration or of dissolution (with, where appropriate, an authenticated translation thereof, exhibited to the affidavit);

(d)  particulars of any previous or pending proceeding(s) in relation to any civil partnership concerned or relating to the civil partnership or matrimonial status of a party to the civil partnership concerned;

(e)  the rights of any person other than the civil partners concerned which may be affected by the relief sought, including a person with whom either civil partner is registered in a new civil partnership or to whom either civil partner is married, or any child of either civil partner or to whom either of the civil partners owes an obligation of support.

(8) A Civil Partnership Civil Bill for relief under Part 4 of the Act shall in all cases contain such of the particulars mentioned in sub-rule (2) as are appropriate and the following details—

(a)  the address and description of the shared home;

(b)  the date and place of registration of the civil partnership of the parties;

(c)  the residential address and occupation of the Applicant and the Respondent (if known);

(d)  the relief being sought and the facts intended to be relied upon;

(e)  the rateable valuation of the premises;

(f)  any other relevant circumstances.

(9) A Civil Partnership Civil Bill for relief under Part 5 of the Act shall, in all cases, contain such of the particulars mentioned in sub-rule (2) as are appropriate and the following details—

(a)  the precise reliefs being sought and the persons in respect of whom they are being sought;

(b)  the residential address and occupation of the Applicant and the Respondent (if known);

(c)  the date and place of registration of the civil partnership of the parties;

(d)  full particulars of any children of the Applicant or Respondent civil partner or to whom either of the civil partners owes an obligation of support and stating whether and if so what provision has been made for each and any such child;

(e)  the nature of the failure to maintain being asserted;

(f)  any relevant change of circumstances (if applicable);

(g)  any other relevant circumstances.

(10) A Cohabitation Civil Bill shall contain such of the following particulars mentioned in this sub-rule as are appropriate—

(a)  particulars of the duration of the relationship between the parties and of the duration of their cohabitation;

(b)  particulars of the basis on which the parties live together;

(c)  the degree of financial dependence of either party on the other and any agreements in respect of their finances;

(d)  particulars of the degree and nature of any financial arrangements between the parties including any joint purchase of an estate or interest in land or joint acquisition of personal property;

(e)  whether there are one or more dependent children of either or both parties;

(f)  whether one of the parties cares for and supports any child of the other;

(g)  the degree to which the parties present themselves to others as a couple;

(h)  any physical or mental disability of either of the parties;

(i)  full particulars of any children of the Applicant or Respondent and of any child of a previous relationship of either party and stating whether and if so what provision has been made for each and any such child;

(j)  details of any previous matrimonial, family law or civil partnership relief obtained by either of the parties (and where appropriate a certified copy of any relevant Court order and/or agreement should be exhibited to the affidavit);

(k)  where each party is domiciled at the date of the application commencing the proceeding or where each party has been ordinarily resident for the year preceding the date of such application;

(l)  details of the place(s) where the parties have lived together during their relationship;

(m)  where reference is made in the Cohabitation Civil Bill to any immovable property whether it is registered or unregistered land and a description of the lands/premises so referred to;

(n)  any other matter which will assist the Court for the purposes set out in section 173(3) of the Act.

(11) In the case of an application for provision out of the estate of a deceased cohabitant under section 194 of the Act, the Cohabitation Civil Bill shall include such of the particulars mentioned in sub-rule (10) as are appropriate and:

(a)  details of any previous cohabitation reliefs obtained by the Applicant;

(b)  details of any benefit received from or on behalf of the deceased cohabitant whether by way of agreement or otherwise and details of any benefits accruing to the Applicant under the terms of the will of the deceased cohabitant or otherwise;

(c) the date of death of the deceased cohabitant, the date upon which representation was first granted in respect of the estate of the said cohabitant and the date upon which the Applicant notified the personal representative of an intention to apply for relief pursuant to section 194(6) of the Act;

(d) the civil partnership or marital status of the deceased cohabitant at the date of death and the civil partnership or marital status of the Applicant at the date of the application;

(e) details of the dependants of the deceased cohabitant at the date of death, of the dependants of the Applicant at the date of the application, and of any other interested persons;

(f) details of whether any order has previously been made under section 173(7) of the Act;

(g) details of the value of the estate of the deceased cohabitant where known.

**Rule 5**

All Civil Partnership Civil Bills and Cohabitation Civil Bills shall be dated and shall bear the name, address and description of the Applicant and an address for service of proceedings, and shall be signed by the party's Solicitor, if any, or, where the Applicant does not have a Solicitor, by that party personally. The address to which a Respondent should apply in order to receive information in relation to legal aid shall also be included in such Civil Bills.

**Issuing and Entry**

**Rule 6**

On the issuing of a Civil Partnership Civil Bill or Cohabitation Civil Bill a copy thereof shall be filed, together with an Affidavit of Means, in the intended action sworn by the Applicant in compliance with rules 17 and 18 and the County Registrar shall thereupon enter same.

**Service**

**Rule 7**

(1) All Civil Partnership Civil Bills and all Cohabitation Civil Bills shall be served. In any case in which financial relief is sought, an Affidavit of Means in compliance with rules 17 and 18 in the form set out in Form 51 of the Schedule of Forms or such modification thereof as may be appropriate shall be served with the Civil Bill. Where relief pursuant to section 121 of the Act or section 187 of the Act is sought, notice thereof in accordance with Form 51A of the Schedule of Forms shall also be served on the trustees of the pension scheme in question in accordance with Order 11, rule 17, and an Affidavit of such service sworn and filed within fourteen days of service of the Civil Bill. All other pleadings in proceedings begun in accordance with this rule may be served in accordance with Order 11, rule 17 and shall be deemed to have been served on the second day after the day of posting.

(2) Where relief is sought pursuant to section 127 of the Act, the Civil Partnership Civil Bill shall be served in accordance with these Rules on the personal representative of the deceased, and on the civil partner or spouse (if any) of the deceased and on such other person or persons as the Court shall direct. Where relief is sought pursuant to section 194 of the Act, the Cohabitation Civil Bill shall be served in accordance with these Rules on the personal representative of the deceased, and on the civil partner or spouse (if any) of the deceased and on such other person or persons as the Court shall direct.

(3) Where, in any application pursuant to this Order, it is appropriate to direct an order to any third person who is not a party to the proceedings, the Court may if it thinks fit adjourn the matter and direct the Applicant or the Respondent to notify the third person against whom an order is sought of the fact that an order is sought against him and of the adjourned date, so that this said third person may appear and be heard in relation to the making of the said order. Alternatively, the Court may, when making an order directed to any third person, provide, in the said order, that the said third person should have liberty to apply to the Court on notice to the Applicant and the Respondent to set aside the order made insofar as it is directed against or relates to the said third person.

**Appearance**

**Rule 8**

If a Respondent intends to contest the application, or any part thereof, he/she shall enter an Appearance in the Office within 10 days of the service upon him/her of the Civil Partnership Civil Bill or, as the case may be, the Cohabitation Civil Bill, and shall serve a copy of the Appearance and appropriate certificate on the Applicant's Solicitors or, where appropriate, on the Applicant. The Appearance shall bear an address for service of any interlocutory applications and shall be signed by the Respondent's Solicitor or, if the Respondent does not have a Solicitor, by the Respondent personally.

**Defence**

**Rule 9**

(1) A Respondent shall at the same time as entering an Appearance, or within 10 clear days from the date of service of the Appearance, or such further time as may be agreed between the parties or allowed by the Court, file and serve a Defence, together with an Affidavit of Means (where required) in compliance with rules 17 and 18, on the Applicant, or the Applicant's Solicitor, if any, and on the County Registrar in the form set out in Form 51 or such modification thereof as may be appropriate. Where relief pursuant to section 121 or section 187 of the Act is sought by way of Counterclaim, notice thereof in accordance with Form 51A of the Schedule of Forms shall also be served on the trustees of the pension scheme in question and a Affidavit of such service sworn and filed within seven days of service of the Defence and Counterclaim.

(2) No Appearance or Defence shall be entered after the time specified in these Rules without the leave of the Court or of the County Registrar or the agreement of the parties, and no Defence shall be entered unless the Respondent has previously entered an Appearance as required by these Rules.

(3) Whether or not a Defence is filed and served in any proceedings, the Respondent shall, where appropriate, in any event be obliged to file and serve an Affidavit of Means within 20 days after the service of the Civil Partnership Civil Bill or, as the case may be, the Cohabitation Civil Bill, upon him/her.

(4) Without prejudice to the entitlement of the Court to permit representations in relation to the making or refusal of an attachment of earnings order at the hearing of the action, such representations for the purposes of section 117(7) or section 175(7) of the Act may be included in the Defence.

**Motions for Judgment**

**Rule 10**

(1) In any case in which a Respondent has made default in entering an Appearance or filing a Defence, as the case may be, the Applicant may, subject to the provisions of this rule, at any time after such default, on notice to be served on the Respondent and, where relief pursuant to section 121 or section 187 of the Act is sought, on the trustees of the pension scheme concerned, not less than fourteen days before the hearing, apply to the Court for judgment in default of Appearance or Defence. Such application, save in the case of motions returnable in the Dublin Circuit, shall be returnable initially before the County Registrar in accordance with Order 59, rule 4(38)(5) as applied to civil partnership law proceedings and cohabitation proceedings.

(2) No notice of motion for judgment in default of defence shall be served unless the Applicant has at least fourteen days prior to the service of such notice written to the Respondent giving him notice of his/her intention to serve a notice of motion for Judgment in default of defence and at the same time consenting to the late filing of a Defence within fourteen days from the date of the letter.

(3) If no Defence is delivered within the said period the Applicant shall be at liberty to serve a notice of motion for Judgment in default of Defence which shall be returnable to a date not less than 14 clear days from the date of the service of the notice, such notice of motion to be filed not later than six days before the return date.

(4) If in any case the Applicant can establish special reasons for making it necessary to serve a notice of motion for Judgment in default of Appearance/Defence in the cases provided for by this Rule with greater urgency than in accordance with the provisions hereinbefore contained, he may apply ex parte to the Court for an Order giving him liberty to serve a notice of motion for Judgment in default of Appearance/Defence giving not less than four clear days' notice to the Respondent, or in the alternative the Judge may deem good the service of a notice of motion giving not less than four clear days' notice to the Respondent.

(5) Upon the hearing of such application the Court may, on proof of such default as aforesaid, and upon hearing such evidence, oral or otherwise, as may be adduced, give judgment upon the Applicant's claim endorsed upon the Civil Partnership Civil Bill or, as the case may be, the Cohabitation Civil Bill, or may give leave to the Respondent to defend the whole or part of the claim upon such terms as he or she may consider just.

(6) In any case in which the parties are agreed in respect of all of the reliefs being sought and a Defence in accordance with rule 9 has been filed and served by the Respondent which reflects this agreement, the Applicant or the Respondent may, subject to the provisions of the following sub-rules, at any time after such Defence has been filed and served, on notice to be served on the other party and, where relief pursuant to section 121 or section 187 of the Act is sought, on the trustees of the pension scheme concerned, not less than 14 clear days before the hearing, apply to the Court for judgment, the application to be by way of motion on notice.

(7) Upon the hearing of such application the Court may, upon hearing such evidence, oral or otherwise, as may be adduced—

   (i)   give judgment in the terms agreed between the parties, or

   (ii)   give such directions in relation to the service of a Notice of Trial/Notice to fix a date for Trial as to the Court appears just.

(8) Upon the hearing of an application for judgment under this Rule the Court may make such order as to costs as the Court considers just.

### Notice of Trial / Notice to fix a date for Trial

### Rule 11

Subject to rule 10(7) and (8) and to Order 59, rule 4(38)(14)(g) as applied to civil partnership law proceedings and cohabitation proceedings, when a Defence has been duly entered and served, the Applicant may serve a notice of trial or a notice to fix a date for trial, as appropriate, in accordance with Forms 15A and 15B.

### Notice of Trial (Circuits other than Dublin Circuit)

### Rule 12

This Rule shall not apply to the Dublin Circuit. Not less than ten days' notice of trial shall be served upon the Respondent and all other necessary parties. Where relief is sought under section 121 or section 187 of the Act, notice of trial shall also be served upon the trustees of the pension scheme in question. The notice of trial shall be filed at the Office not later than seven days after it is served. Service and filing of the notice of trial shall operate to set down the action or matter (including counterclaim if any) for hearing at the next ensuing Sittings. The service of notice to fix a date for a trial, as duly completed in the Office, on all necessary parties shall operate to set down the action (including a counterclaim if any) for hearing, to be listed before the County Registrar for allocation of a date for the hearing.

### Notice to fix a date for Trial (Dublin Circuit)

### Rule 13

This rule shall apply only to the Dublin Circuit. A party desiring to give notice to fix a date for trial in accordance with rule 11 or rule 14 shall lodge with the Office a notice to fix a date for trial in the Form 15B of the Schedule of Forms. On receipt of such notice, duly completed, from the Office, that party shall serve a copy of the completed notice setting out the date upon which a date for hearing will be fixed by the County Registrar on all of the other parties and, where relief is sought under section 121 or section 187 of the Act, on the trustees of the pension scheme in question. At least ten days' notice to fix a date for trial shall be given. The service of notice to fix a date for a trial, as duly completed in the Office, on all necessary parties shall operate to set down the action (including a counterclaim if any) for hearing upon such date as may be fixed by the County Registrar.

**Service by Respondent**

**Rule 14**

Where the Applicant has failed to serve a notice of trial or notice to fix a date for trial, as appropriate, within ten days after the service and entry of the Defence, the Respondent may do so and may file the same in accordance with these Rules.

**Joinder**

**Rule 15**

The Court, if it considers it desirable, may order that two or more actions be tried together, and on such terms as to costs as the Court shall deem just.

**Affidavits of Representation**

**Rule 16**

(1) Save where the Court shall otherwise direct, any notice party, including the trustees of a pension scheme, who wishes to make representations to the Court pursuant to section 122 or, as the case may be, section 188, of the Act shall make such representations by Affidavit of Representation to be filed and served on all parties to the proceedings within 28 days of service upon them of notice of the application for relief under section 121 or, as the case may be, section 187, of the Act in accordance with rules 7 and 9 or within such time or in such manner as the Court may direct.

(2) Without prejudice to the entitlement of the Court to permit representations by persons having a beneficial interest in property (not being the other civil partner) pursuant to section 128(5) of the Act or by interested persons pursuant to section 127(6) or section 194(6) of the Act at the hearing of the action, such representations may be made by way of Affidavit of Representation to be filed and served on all parties to the proceedings as directed by the Court.

**Affidavit of Means**

**Rule 17**

(1) Without prejudice to:

   (a) the right of each party to request and/or make application to direct the delivery of further particulars or information;

   (b) the right of each party to make application to the Court for an Order of Discovery; and

   (c) the jurisdiction of the Court pursuant to section 142 and section 197 of the Act, in any case where financial relief under the Act is sought, the parties shall file Affidavits of Means in accordance with rules 6 and 9 in respect of which the following sub-rules shall apply.

(2) In all cases where a Defence and/or Counterclaim has been filed (save for a Defence pursuant to rule 10(6)) each party shall, unless the other party dispenses in writing with the requirement of vouching, vouch his Affidavit of Means, in the manner specified in Form 51C, within 28 days of the date of filing of the Respondent's Affidavit of Means or 21 days before the date fixed for a case progression hearing, whichever is earlier.

(3) In all cases where a Defence has not been filed and a case progression hearing has been listed, each party shall vouch his Affidavit of Means within such time as the County Registrar shall direct.

(4) In the event of a party failing to file, serve, or properly vouch the items referred to in, their Affidavits of Means as required by these Rules—

    (i)  the Court, on application by notice of motion, and, in accordance with section 34(1) and the Second Schedule of the Courts and Court Officers Act 1995, the County Registrar, on application by notice of motion or in the course of case progression, may make an Order enlarging the time within which the party in default must file or serve an Affidavit of Means and/or vouch (in such manner or on such terms as the Court or the County Registrar, as the case may be, directs) the items referred to in any Affidavit of Means or may make an Order for Discovery, or

    (ii)  the Court may make such other order as the Court deems appropriate and necessary (including an order that such party shall not be entitled to pursue or defend as appropriate a claim for any ancillary reliefs under the Act save as permitted by the Court upon such terms as the Court may determine are appropriate and/or adjourning the proceedings for a specified period of time to enable compliance) and furthermore or in the alternative an order pursuant to section 142(2) of the Act or, as the case may be, section 197(2) of the Act, may be sought in accordance with rule 23.

### Rule 18

The Affidavit of Means shall set out in schedule form details of the party's income, assets, property, financial resources, debts, liabilities, financial obligations and financial responsibilities wherever situated and from whatever source and, to the best of the deponent's knowledge, information and belief the income, assets, property, financial resources, debts, liabilities, financial obligations and financial responsibilities wherever situated and from whatever source of any dependent child of the party and shall be in accordance with the form set out in Form 51 or such modification thereof as may be appropriate.

### Rule 19

Where relief pursuant to section 121 or section 187 of the Act is sought, the Affidavit of Means shall also state to the best of the deponent's knowledge, information and belief, the nature of the scheme, the benefits payable thereunder, the normal pensionable age and the period of reckonable service of the member civil partner and where information relating to the pension scheme has been obtained from the trustees of the scheme under the Pensions Acts 1990 to 2009, such information should be exhibited in the Affidavit of Means and where such information has not been obtained a specific averment shall be included in the Affidavit of Means as to why such information has not been obtained.

**Counterclaims**

**Rule 20**

(1) Save where otherwise directed by the Court, a Counterclaim, if any, brought by a Respondent shall be included in and served with the Defence, in accordance with the provisions of these Rules relating thereto, and shall, in particular, set out in numbered paragraphs the matters set out in the following sub-rules, where relevant.

(2) In the case of an application for a decree of dissolution, the Counterclaim shall set out in like manner as in the Civil Partnership Civil Bill the facts specified at rule 4(2) in like manner as in the Civil Partnership Civil Bill, and the following:

    (a) the ground(s) for a decree of dissolution, if sought;

    (b) any ground upon which the Respondent intends to rely in support of any ancillary relief claimed; and

    (c) the relief sought pursuant to the Act.

(3) In the case of an application for a decree of nullity, the Counterclaim shall set out in like manner as in the Civil Partnership Civil Bill such of the facts specified at rule 4(3) as are appropriate and the following:

    (a) the ground(s) for a decree of nullity;

    (b) any additional ground upon which the Respondent intends to rely in support of any relief claimed; and

    (c) the relief sought and any additional issues to be tried.

(4) In the case of an application for the determination of property issues between civil partners, pursuant to section 106 of the Act, the Counterclaim shall set out in like manner as in the Civil Partnership Civil Bill such of the facts specified at rule 4(4) as are appropriate and the following:

    (a) any additional ground upon which the Respondent intends to rely in support of any relief claimed; and

    (b) the relief sought pursuant to the Act.

(5) In the case of an application for relief under section 4 of the Act, the Counterclaim shall set out in like manner as in the Civil Partnership Civil Bill such of the facts specified at rule 4(7) as are appropriate and the following:

    (a) any additional ground upon which the Respondent intends to rely in support of any relief claimed; and

    (b) the relief sought pursuant to the Act.

(6) In the case of an application for relief under Part 4 of the Act, the Counterclaim shall set out in like manner as in the Civil Partnership Civil Bill such of the facts specified at rule 4(8) as are appropriate and the following:

   (a)  any additional ground upon which the Respondent intends to rely in support of any relief claimed; and

   (b)  the relief sought pursuant to Part 4 of the Act.

(7) In the case of an application for relief under Part 5 of the Act, the Counterclaim shall set out in like manner as in the Civil Partnership Civil Bill such of the facts specified at rule 4(9) as are appropriate and the following:

   (a)  any additional ground upon which the Respondent intends to rely in support of any relief claimed; and

   (b)  the relief sought pursuant to Part 5 of the Act.

(8) In the case of an application for relief under Part 15 of the Act, the Counterclaim shall set out in like manner as in the Cohabitation Civil Bill such of the facts specified at rule 4(10) as are appropriate and the following:

   (a)  any additional ground upon which the Respondent intends to rely in support of any relief claimed; and

   (b)  the relief sought pursuant to Part 15 of the Act.

**Evidence**

**Rule 21**

Save where the Court otherwise directs and subject to rule 25, every Application under this Order shall be heard on oral evidence, such hearings to be held in camera.

**Rule 22**

Notwithstanding the provisions of rule 21, where relief pursuant to section 121 or section 187 of the Act is sought by the Applicant or the Respondent, evidence of the actuarial value of a benefit under the scheme may be by Affidavit filed on behalf of the Applicant/Respondent, such Affidavit to be sworn by an appropriate person and served on all parties to the proceedings and filed at least 14 days in advance of the hearing and subject to the right of the Respondent/Applicant to serve Notice of Cross-examination in relation to same. Where one of the parties has adduced evidence of the actuarial value of a benefit by Affidavit as provided for herein and the other party intends to adduce similar or contra oral evidence, notice of such intention shall be served by the disputing party upon all other parties at least 10 days in advance of the hearing.

**Interim and Interlocutory Applications**

**Rule 23**

(1) The following applications shall be by Notice of Motion to be served upon the parties to the proceedings and, in the case of applications pursuant to section 126(2) or section 192 of the Act, upon the trustees of the pension scheme concerned:

   (a)  an application for an Interim Order pursuant to section 47 of the Act;

(b) an application for a Preliminary Order pursuant to section 115 of the Act;

(c) an application for maintenance pending suit/relief pursuant to section 116 of the Act;

(d) an application for information pursuant to section 126(2) of the Act;

(e) an application for relief pursuant to section 137 of the Act, where that is not the primary relief sought in the proceedings;

(f) an application for relief pursuant to section 142(2) of the Act;

(g) an application for relief pursuant to section 197(2) of the Act;

(h) an application for any other interlocutory relief.

(2) Prior to any interlocutory application for discovery or application pursuant to section 142(2) or section 197(2) of the Act being made, the information being sought shall be requested in writing voluntarily at least 14 days prior to the issuing of the motion for the relief concerned and upon failure to make such a request, the judge may adjourn the motion or strike out the motion or make such other order, including an order as to costs, as to the Court may appear appropriate.

(3) Where an application for a decree of nullity involves an allegation that either or both of the parties was unable to give informed consent, the attestation to that effect mentioned in section 107(c)(iv) of the Act shall in the first instance be given by the consultant psychiatrist by way of Affidavit. Where any such attestation is disputed by the opposing party then, without prejudice to the right of that party to cross-examine and/or to adduce expert evidence, application may be made for the appointment of psychiatric inspectors in respect of the Applicant and/or the Respondent by Motion on Notice to the other party.

(4) In any application for a decree of nullity, application may be made for the appointment of medical and/or psychiatric inspectors in respect of the Applicant and/or the Respondent by Motion on Notice to the other party.

(5) A Motion mentioned in sub-rule (3) or (4) shall be issued not later than 14 days after the elapsing of the times for the entry of an Appearance and delivery of a Defence save with the leave of the Court or the County Registrar. Where medical and/or psychiatric inspectors are appointed by the Court or the County Registrar, the solicitors for the parties shall attend with the parties on the appointed day at the place in which the inspection is to take place for the purpose of identifying the parties to the County Registrar or his/her nominee. In any circumstances in which a party is unrepresented, appropriate photographic proof of identity must be produced sufficient to satisfy the County Registrar or his/her nominee of the identity of the party concerned. No inspection shall be carried out unless the procedures contained herein are satisfied. Upon completion of the inspection, a report thereof shall be sent by the inspector directly to the County Registrar for the County in which the proceedings have issued.

(6) In any case where the Court is satisfied that the delay caused by proceeding by Motion on Notice under this rule would or might entail serious harm or mischief, the Court may make an Order ex parte as it shall consider just. Urgent applications under

this sub-rule may be made to a Judge at any time or place approved by him, by arrangement with the County Registrar for the County in question.

(7) Interim and interlocutory applications shall where appropriate be made to the County Registrar in accordance with the Second Schedule to the Court and Court Officers Act 1995 and Orders 18 and 19.

### Rule 24

If on the date for hearing of any Application under this rule the matter is not dealt with by the Court for any reason, and, in particular, on foot of an adjournment sought by either party, the other party, whether consenting to the adjournment or not, may apply for, and the Court may grant, such interim or interlocutory relief as to it shall seem appropriate without the necessity of service of a Notice of Motion.

### Rule 25

Any interim or interlocutory application shall be heard on Affidavit, unless the Court otherwise directs, save that the Deponent of any Affidavit must be available to the Court to give oral evidence or to be cross-examined as to the Court shall seem appropriate, save that a Motion for Discovery and a Motion in the course of nullity proceedings for the appointment of medical/psychiatric inspectors shall be heard on a Notice of Motion only. Where any oral evidence is heard by the Court in the course of such applications ex parte, a note of such evidence shall be prepared by the Applicant or the Applicant's solicitor and approved by the Judge and shall be served upon the Respondent forthwith together with a copy of the Order made (if any), unless otherwise directed by the Court.

### Further relief and applications on behalf of dependent persons

### Rule 26

(1) Where either party or a person on behalf of a dependent child of a civil partner or deceased civil partner wishes at any time after the hearing of the Application to seek further relief as provided for in the Act or to vary or discharge an order previously made by the Court that party shall issue a Notice of Motion to re-enter or to vary or discharge as the case may be grounded upon an Affidavit seeking such relief. Such Motions shall be subject to the provisions of rules 7, 16, 17, 18, 19, 21 and 22, as appropriate.

(2) Where a person on behalf of a dependent child of a civil partner or deceased civil partner wishes to make application for ancillary reliefs at the hearing of the action, such application shall be by way of Notice of Motion to be served on all other parties to the proceedings setting out the reliefs sought grounded on Affidavit which said Motion shall be listed for hearing on the same date as the hearing of the action contemporaneously therewith. Such Motions shall be subject to the provisions of rules 7, 16, 17, 18, 19, 21 and 22, as appropriate.

### Rule 27

Where any party to proceedings for a declaration under section 4 of the Act alleges that the civil partnership in question was void or voidable and the Court decides to treat the application as one for a decree of nullity of the civil partnership, the provisions of this

Order in relation to the procedures applicable to decrees of nullity may be adapted in such manner as the Court shall direct.

**Relief under section 59B(2) of the Act of 2004**

**Rule 28**

Applications under section 59B(2) of the Act of 2004 for an order exempting the civil partnership from the application of section 59B(1)(a) of the Act of 2004 may be made ex parte by the parties. Such application may be grounded upon Affidavit or upon oral evidence given by or on behalf of the parties, as the Court may direct, which evidence shall set out the reasons justifying the exemption and the basis upon which it is claimed that the application is in the interests of the parties to the intended civil partnership.

**Applications under section 48 of the Act**

**Rule 29**

Applications pursuant to section 48 of the Act may be made by way of originating Notice of Motion, grounded upon affidavit.

**Rule 30**

For the purposes of rule 29, the notice of motion shall be entitled in the matter of the Act and shall state the relief sought (including whether or not relief pursuant to section 49 of the Act, is sought); state the name and place of residence or address for service of the Applicant; the date upon which it is proposed to apply to the Court for relief and shall be filed in the Office for the County in which the application is being brought in accordance with rule 3 (hereinafter referred to as "the appropriate Office").

**Rule 31**

For the purposes of rule 29, without prejudice to the jurisdiction of the Court to make an Order for substituted service, the Motion shall be served by registered post on the Respondent at his last-known address or alternatively shall be served personally on the Respondent by any person over the age of eighteen years. Where relief pursuant to section 49 of the Act is sought, the motion shall, in addition to being served on the Respondent, be served upon the trustees of the pension scheme. There must be at least ten clear days between the service of the notice and the day named therein for the hearing of the motion.

**Rule 32**

(1) Subject to the right of the Court to give such directions as it considers appropriate or convenient, evidence at the hearing of the motion under rule 29 shall be by affidavit.

(2) Any affidavit to be used in support of the motion shall be filed in the Office and a copy of any such affidavit shall be served with the notice. Any affidavit to be used in opposition to the application shall be filed in the Office and served upon the Applicant and, where relief pursuant to section 49 of the Act is sought, upon the trustees of the pension scheme by the Respondent following the service on him of the Applicant's affidavit and any affidavit of representations to be used by the trustees of the pension

scheme shall be filed in the appropriate Office and served upon the Applicant and the Respondent.

**Miscellaneous**

**Rule 33**

The plaintiff in proceedings wherein it is sought to have a conveyance declared void pursuant to the provisions of section 28 of the Act shall without delay following the institution of such proceedings cause relevant particulars of the proceedings to be entered as a lis pendens upon the property and/or premises in question under and in accordance with section 121 of the Land and Conveyancing Law Reform Act 2009.

**Rule 34**

A statement as to earnings for the purposes of section 56(1) or section 179(1) of the Act shall be in Form 51B in the Schedule of Forms with the necessary modifications. Such a statement by a maintenance debtor shall be verified on affidavit or on oath at the hearing of the application. Such a statement by an employer need not be verified on affidavit unless so required by the maintenance creditor.

**Rule 35**

(1) Civil partnership law proceedings for relief under the Domestic Violence Acts 1996 to 2002 (as amended by Part 9 of the Act) shall be brought, heard and determined in accordance with Order 59, rule 5.

(2) Civil partnership law proceedings for relief between civil partners under the Partition Act 1868 and the Partition Act 1876, where the fact that they are civil partners of each other is of relevance to the proceedings, shall be brought, heard and determined in accordance with Order 46.

**Costs**

**Rule 36**

(1) The costs as between party and party may be measured by the Judge, and if not so measured shall be taxed, in default of agreement by the parties, by the County Registrar according to such scale of costs as may be prescribed. Any party aggrieved by such taxation may appeal to the Court and have the costs reviewed by it.

(2) Where necessary, the Court may make an order determining who shall bear any costs incurred by trustees of a pension scheme pursuant to section 49, section 125 or section 191 of the Act and in making such determination the Court shall have regard, inter alia, to the representations made by the trustees pursuant to rule 16, if any.

**General**

**Rule 37**

The Court may, upon such terms (if any) as it may think reasonable, enlarge or abridge any of the times fixed by these Rules for taking any step or doing any act in any proceeding, and may also, upon such terms as to costs or otherwise as it shall think fit, declare any step taken or act done to be sufficient, even though not taken or done within the time or in the manner prescribed by these Rules.

### Service of orders by the registrar of the Court

### Rule 38

In all circumstances in which the registrar of the Court and/or the County Registrar is required to serve or lodge a copy of an order upon any person(s) or body such service or lodgment shall be satisfied by the service of a certified copy of the said order by registered post to the said person(s) or body.

### Case Progression

### Rule 39

Order 59, rule 4(38) shall apply, with the necessary modifications, to civil partnership law proceedings and to cohabitation proceedings and the Forms 37L, 37M and 37N modified accordingly shall be used in case progression in civil partnership law proceedings and in cohabitation proceedings.][1]

---

**Notes**

1    Order 59A inserted by SI 385/2011, r 2.

---

## FAMILY LAW

## FORMS

### Form 2N
### Family Law Civil Bill

Circuit [Family]¹ Court _____Circuit County of _____

IN THE MATTER OF THE GUARDIANSHIP OF INFANTS ACT, 1964

OR

IN THE MATTER OF PART VI OF THE STATUS OF CHILDREN ACT, 1987

OR

IN THE MATTER OF THE FAMILY LAW (MAINTENANCE OF SPOUSES AND CHILDREN) ACT, 1976

OR

IN THE MATTER OF THE FAMILY HOME PROTECTION ACT, 1976

OR

IN THE MATTER OF THE JUDICIAL SEPARATION AND FAMILY LAW REFORM ACT, 1989 AND IN THE MATTER OF THE FAMILY LAW ACT, 1995

OR

IN THE MATTER OF THE FAMILY LAW ACT, 1995

OR

IN THE MATTER OF THE FAMILY LAW (DIVORCE) ACT, 1996

BETWEEN ............................................................................................. Applicant

AND ...................................................................................................... Respondent

You are hereby required within ten days after the service of this Civil Bill upon you to enter or cause to be entered with the County Registrar, at his Office at _____, an Appearance to answer the claim of _____ of _____, the Applicant herein.

And take notice that unless you do enter an Appearance, you will be held to have admitted the said claim, and the Applicant may proceed therein and judgment may be given against you in your absence without further notice.

And further take notice that, if you intend to defend the proceeding on any grounds, you must not only enter an Appearance, but also, within ten days after Appearance, deliver a statement in writing showing the nature and grounds of your Defence.

The Appearance may be entered by posting same to the said Office and by giving copies thereof to the Applicant or his Solicitor by post and the Defence may be delivered by posting same to the Applicant or his Solicitor.

Dated this day of _____ .

Signed _____

         Applicant/Solicitors for the Applicant


To: _____

         The Respondent/Solicitor for the Respondent

## INDORSEMENT OF CLAIM

[Here insert details of the Applicant's claim and the grounds upon which relief is being sought as required by these Rules including the basis upon which jurisdiction is claimed]


THE APPLICANT CLAIMS:

[Insert reliefs sought by the Applicant]


_____

Applicant/Solicitors for the Applicant

                _____

## Form 2O
## Domestic Violence Civil Bill

Circuit [Family][1] Court _____Circuit County of _____

## IN THE MATTER OF THE DOMESTIC VIOLENCE ACT, 1996

BETWEEN .................................................................................................. Applicant

AND .................................................................................................. Respondent

You are hereby required within ten days after the service of this Civil Bill upon you to enter or cause to be entered with the County Registrar, at his Office at _____, an Appearance to answer the claim of _____ of _____, the Applicant herein.

And take notice that unless you do enter an Appearance, you will be held to have admitted the said claim, and the Applicant may proceed therein and judgment may be given against you in your absence without further notice.

And further take notice that, if you intend to defend the proceeding on any grounds, you must not only enter an Appearance, but also, within ten days after Appearance, deliver a statement in writing showing the nature and grounds of your Defence.

The Appearance may be entered by posting same to the said Office and by giving copies thereof to the Applicant or his Solicitor by post and the Defence may be delivered by posting same to the Applicant or his Solicitor.

Dated the day of_____

Signed _____

    Applicant/Solicitors for the Applicant


To: _____

    The Respondent/Solicitor for the Respondent

## INDORSEMENT OF CLAIM

[Here insert details of the Applicant's claim and the grounds upon which relief is being sought as required by these Rules including the basis upon which jurisdiction is claimed]

THE APPLICANT CLAIMS:

[Insert reliefs sought by the Applicant]

    ...............................................................
    Applicant/Solicitors for the Applicant

    _____

**[Form 2S**
**The Circuit Court**

CIRCUIT COUNTY OF

CIVIL PARTNERSHIP CIVIL BILL

CIVIL PARTNERSHIP AND CERTAIN RIGHTS AND OBLIGATIONS OF
COHABITANTS ACT 2010

BETWEEN..................................................................................................Applicant

AND.......................................................................................................Respondent

You are hereby required within ten days after the service of this Civil Bill upon you to enter or cause to be entered with the County Registrar, at his Office at_____, an Appearance to answer the claim of _____ of _____, the Applicant herein.

And take notice that unless you do enter an Appearance, you will be held to have admitted the said claim, and the Applicant may proceed therein and judgment may be given against you in your absence without further notice.

And further take notice that, if you intend to defend the proceeding on any grounds, you must not only enter an Appearance, but also, within ten days after Appearance, deliver a statement in writing showing the nature and grounds of your Defence.

The Appearance may be entered by posting same to the said Office and by giving copies thereof to the Applicant or his Solicitor by post and the Defence may be delivered by posting same to the Applicant or his Solicitor.

Dated this _____ day of_____

Signed _____

Applicant/Solicitors for the Applicant

To: _____

The Respondent/Solicitor for the Respondent

## INDORSEMENT OF CLAIM

[Here insert details of the Applicants claim and the grounds upon which relief is being sought as required by these Rules including the basis upon which jurisdiction is claimed]

THE APPLICANT CLAIMS:

[Insert reliefs sought by the Applicant]

_____

Applicant/Solicitors for the Applicant][2]

_____

**[Form 2T
An Chúirt Chuarda
The Circuit Court**

CIRCUIT COUNTY OF

COHABITATION CIVIL BILL

CIVIL PARTNERSHIP AND CERTAIN RIGHTS AND OBLIGATIONS OF
COHABITANTS ACT 2010

BETWEEN ........................................................................................ Applicant

AND ............................................................................................. Respondent

You are hereby required within ten days after the service of this Civil Bill upon you to enter or cause to be entered with the County Registrar, at his Office at..............., an Appearance to answer the claim of _____ of _____, the Applicant herein.

And take notice that unless you do enter an Appearance, you will be held to have admitted the said claim, and the Applicant may proceed therein and judgment may be given against you in your absence without further notice.

And further take notice that, if you intend to defend the proceeding on any grounds, you must not only enter an Appearance, but also, within ten days after Appearance, deliver a statement in writing showing the nature and grounds of your Defence.

The Appearance may be entered by posting same to the said Office and by giving copies thereof to the Applicant or his Solicitor by post and the Defence may be delivered by posting same to the Applicant or his Solicitor.

Dated this_____ day of _____

Signed_____

Applicant/Solicitors for the Applicant

To:_____

The Respondent/Solicitor for the Respondent

## INDORSEMENT OF CLAIM

[Here insert details of the Applicants claim and the grounds upon which relief is being sought as required by these Rules including the basis upon which jurisdiction is claimed]

THE APPLICANT CLAIMS:

[Insert reliefs sought by the Applicant]

_____

Applicant/Solicitors for the Applicant][2]

## Form No 5A

Circuit Family Court _____Circuit County of _____

IN THE MATTER OF COUNCIL REGULATION (EC) NO 2201/2003 AND IN THE MATTER OF [INSERT ANY OTHER APPLICABLE LEGISLATION]

BETWEEN........................................................................................ AB Applicant

AND ............................................................................................. CD Respondent

### APPEARANCE

1. To the County Registrar

At _____

I request you will enter an Appearance herein on behalf of the Respondent to the proceedings served upon him on, without prejudice and solely for the purpose of contesting the jurisdiction of this Honourable Court to hear and determine the within proceedings.

Dated this day of

Signed:_____

        Respondent/Solicitors for the Respondent

2. To the Applicant/Solicitors for the Applicant

The Appearance mentioned above was this day [lodged by hand]* [sent by post]* and the said Respondent intends to contest the jurisdiction of this Honourable Court to hear and determine the within proceedings.

Dated this day of _____


Signed: _____

        Respondent/Solicitors for the Respondent

delete as appropriate

_____

# Form No 37A

Circuit [Family]¹ Court _____Circuit County of _____

IN THE MATTER OF THE FAMILY LAW (MAINTENANCE OF SPOUSES AND CHILDREN) ACT, 1976

OR

IN THE MATTER OF THE JUDICIAL SEPARATION AND FAMILY LAW REFORM ACT, 1989 AND IN THE MATTER OF THE FAMILY LAW ACT, 1995

OR

IN THE MATTER OF THE FAMILY LAW (DIVORCE) ACT, 1996 AND IN THE MATTER OF AN INTENDED ACTION (IF APPROPRIATE)

BETWEEN .......................................................................................... [Applicant]¹

AND ................................................................................................ [Respondent]¹

## AFFIDAVIT OF MEANS

I, [Insert name of Deponent]

[Insert occupation of Deponent]

of [Insert address of Deponent]

being aged 18 years and upwards MAKE OATH and say as follows:

1. I say that I am the [Applicant/Respondent]¹ [delete as appropriate] in the above entitled proceedings and I make this Affidavit from facts within my own knowledge save where otherwise appears and where so appearing I believe the same to be true.

2. I say that I have set out in the First Schedule hereto all the assets to which I am legally or beneficially entitled and the manner in which such property is held.

3. I say that I have set out in the Second Schedule hereto all income which I receive and the sources of such income.

4. I say that I have set out in the Third Schedule hereto all my debts and liabilities and the persons to whom such debts and liabilities are due.

5. I say that my weekly outgoings amount to the sum of and I say that the details of such outgoings have been set out in the Fourth Schedule hereto.

6. I say that to the best of my knowledge, information and belief, all pension information known to me relevant to the within proceedings is set out in the Fifth Schedule hereto.

*First Schedule*

[Insert list of assets]

*Second Schedule*

[Insert details of income]

*Third Schedule*
[Insert list of debts and liabilities]
*Fourth Schedule*
[Insert list of Weekly Expenditure]
Fifth Schedule
[Insert details of pension]
SWORN etc.

## Form No 37B

Circuit [Family]¹ Court _____Circuit County of _____

IN THE MATTER OF THE JUDICIAL SEPARATION AND FAMILY LAW
REFORM ACT, 1989 AND IN THE MATTER OF THE FAMILY LAW ACT, 1995

OR

IN THE MATTER OF THE FAMILY LAW (DIVORCE) ACT, 1996 AND IN THE
MATTER OF AN INTENDED ACTION (IF APPROPRIATE)

BETWEEN ...................................................................................... [Applicant]¹

AND ............................................................................................. [Respondent]¹

### AFFIDAVIT OF WELFARE

I, [Insert name of Deponent]

[Insert occupation of Deponent]

of [Insert address of Deponent]

being aged 18 years and upwards MAKE OATH and say as follows:

1. I say that I am the [Applicant/Respondent]¹ [delete as appropriate] in the above entitled proceedings and I make this Affidavit from facts within my own knowledge save where otherwise appears and where so appearing I believe the same to be true.

2. I say and believe that the facts set out in the Schedule hereto are true.

[In circumstances in which the [Respondent]¹ does not dispute the facts as deposed to by the Applicant in his/her Affidavit of Welfare, the following averment shall be included, replacing Paragraph 2 hereof, and in such circumstances, the Schedule shall not be completed by the [Respondent]¹:

2. I say that I am fully in agreement with the facts as averred to by the [Applicant]¹ in his/her Affidavit of Welfare sworn herein on the day of and I say and believe that the facts set out in the Schedule thereto are true.]

SCHEDULE

*Part I — Details of Children*

1. Details of children born to the [Applicant]¹ and the [Respondent]¹ or adopted by both the [Applicant]¹ and the [Respondent]¹:

| Forenames | Surname | Date of Birth |
|---|---|---|

2. Details of other children of the family or to which the parties or either of them are in loco parentis

| Forenames | Surname | Date of Birth | Relationship to [Applicant/ Respondent]¹ |
|---|---|---|---|

*Part II — Arrangements for the children of the family*

1. Home Details:

   (a)  The address or addresses at which the children now live

   (b)  Give details of number of living rooms, bedrooms etc. at the address(es) in (a) above

   (c)  Is the house rented or owned and, if so, name the tenant(s) or owner(s)?

   (d)  Is the rent or mortgage being regularly paid and, if so, by whom?

   (e)  Give names of all other persons living with the children either on a full-time or parttime basis and state their relationship to the children, if any.

   (f)  Will there be any change in these arrangements and, if so, give details.

*Part III — Education and training details*

   (a)  Give names of the school, college or place of training attended by each child.

   (b)  Do the children have any special education needs? If so, please specify.

   (c)  Is the school, college or place of training fee-paying? If so, give details.

*Part IV — Childcare details*

   (a)  Which parent looks after the children from day to day? If responsibility is shared, please give details.

   (b)  Give details of work commitments of both parents.

   (c)  Does someone look after the children when the parent is not there? If yes, give details.

   (d)  Who looks after the children during school holidays?

   (e)  Will there be any change in these arrangements? If yes, give details.

*Part V — Maintenance*

   (a)  Does [Applicant/Respondent][1] pay towards the upkeep of the children? If yes, give details.

      Please specify any other source of maintenance.

   (b)  Is the maintenance referred to (a) above paid under court order? If yes, give details.

   (c)  Has maintenance for the children been agreed? If yes, give details.

   (d)  If not, will you be applying for a maintenance order from the court?

*Part VI — Details of contact with children*

   (a)  Do the children see the [Applicant/Respondent][1]? Please give details.

   (b)  Do the children stay overnight and/or have holiday visits with the [Applicant/ Respondent][1]. Please give details.

   (c)  Will there be any change to these arrangements?

*Part VII — Details of Health*

(a)  Are the children generally in good health? Please give details of any serious disability or chronic illness suffered by any of the children.

(b)  Do the children or any of them have any special health needs? Please give details of the care needed and how it is to be provided.

(c)  Are the [Applicant][1] and the [Respondent][1] generally in good health? In not, please give details.

*Part VIII — Details of care and other Court Proceedings*

(a)  Are the children or any of them in the care of a Health Board or under the supervision of a Social Worker or Probation Officer? If so, please specify.

(b)  Are there or have there been any proceedings in any Court involving the children or any of them? If so, please specify. All relevant Court Orders relating to the children or any of them should be annexed hereto.

SWORN etc.

## Form No 37C

Circuit [Family]¹ Court _____Circuit County of _____

IN THE MATTER OF THE JUDICIAL SEPARATION AND FAMILY LAW
REFORM ACT, 1989 AND IN THE MATTER OF THE FAMILY LAW ACT, 1995

OR

IN THE MATTER OF THE FAMILY LAW (DIVORCE) ACT, 1996

BETWEEN.........................................................................................[Applicant]¹

AND ..............................................................................................[Respondent]¹

### NOTICE TO TRUSTEES

TAKE NOTICE that relief has been claimed by the [Applicant/Respondent]¹ in the above entitled proceedings pursuant to Section(s) 12 and/or 13 of the Family Law Act, 1995 OR pursuant to Section 17 of the Family Law (Divorce) Act, 1996, and in particular in relation to [here insert pension details against which relief is claimed]....

..................................................................................................................................

and that the hearing of the Action will take place on the day of....................................

at the Circuit Court sitting at.........................................................................................

at o'clock in the forenoon. (or, if appropriate, "in relation to which claim you will be advised of the date for trial in due course")

Dated this day of .................................................

Signed .................................................

Solicitors for the

[Applicant/Respondent] or

[Applicant/Respondent] in person

To: The County Registrar

And

To: The Trustees of the relevant pension scheme(s)

And

To: [Applicant/Respondent]/Solicitors for the [Applicant]/Solicitors for the [Respondent]

## Form No 37D

Circuit [Family]¹ Court _____Circuit County of _____

IN THE MATTER OF THE JUDICIAL SEPARATION AND FAMILY LAW REFORM ACT, 1989 AND IN THE MATTER OF THE FAMILY LAW ACT, 1995

OR

IN THE MATTER OF THE FAMILY LAW (DIVORCE) ACT, 1996 AND IN THE MATTER OF AN INTENDED ACTION (IF APPROPRIATE)

BETWEEN .......................................................................................... [Applicant]¹

AND .......................................................................................... [Respondent]¹

CERTIFICATION PURSUANT TO SECTION 5 OR SECTION 6 OF THE JUDICIAL SEPARATION AND FAMILY LAW REFORM ACT, 1989 OR SECTION 6 OR SECTION 7 OF THE FAMILY LAW (DIVORCE) ACT, 1996

[Solicitors for the [Applicant/Respondent]¹ (as appropriate) to certify that the [Applicant/Respondent]¹ (as appropriate) has been fully advised in relation to alternative forms of matrimonial dispute resolution to include marriage guidance counselling, mediation, separation agreements and other forms of matrimonial litigation]

Dated this day of ...................................................

Signed ................................................................
Solicitors for the
[Applicant/Respondent]¹


(delete as appropriate)

_____

## Form No 37E

Circuit Court _____Circuit County of _____

IN THE MATTER OF SECTION 6A OF THE GUARDIANSHIP OF INFANTS ACT, 1964

APPLICATION BY FATHER TO BE APPOINTED GUARDIAN WITH WRITTEN CONSENT OF MOTHER

[NOTE: This form is for use where the applicant's name already appears on the Births Register as father of the child and the mother consents in writing to the applicant's appointment as guardian.]

NAME OF APPLICANT:......................................................................................

ADDRESS OF APPLICANT: .............................................................................

.................................................................................................................................

NAME OF INFANT: .........................................................................................

ADDRESS OF INFANT: ....................................................................................

.................................................................................................................................

TAKE NOTICE that the applicant intends to apply to this Court sitting at ................

in the County of ............................... on the day of for an Order

pursuant to section 6A of the Guardianship of Infants Act, 1964, as inserted by section 12 of the Status of Children Act, 1987, to be appointed as guardian of the above named infant.

The applicant will rely upon proof of the following matters in support of his application:

1. That he is the father of the infant named above and that he is registered as such father in a Register maintained under the Births and Deaths Registration Acts, 1863 to 1987;

[NOTE: It will be necessary to produce at the hearing a recent Birth Certificate which shows the applicant as father.]

2. That the mother of the said infant is .........................................................................

and resides at .................................................................................................................

3. That the mother has consented in writing to the appointment of the applicant as guardian as aforesaid;

[NOTE: It will be necessary to produce at the hearing the written consent of the mother. Form 37F provides a means for her to give written consent. If the mother does not appear at the hearing, the Judge may adjourn the application to enable notice to be served on her.]

4. That the applicant understands and is willing to take on the responsibilities and duties involved in acting as guardian of the said infant jointly with the mother and undertakes to exercise the said duties and the said responsibilities in the best interests of the said infant.

Dated this day of .

Signed ...................................................................

Applicant/Solicitor for the Applicant

To: The County Registrar

## Form No 37F

Circuit [Family] Court _____Circuit County of _____

IN THE MATTER OF THE GUARDIANSHIP OF INFANTS ACT, 1964 AS
AMENDED BY THE STATUS OF CHILDREN ACT, 1987

STATUTORY DECLARATION OF MOTHER

I, [Here insert name of mother], ............................................................ do solemnly and
sincerely declare that:—

1. I reside at [insert address]

2. I am the mother of ................................................. who was born on the day of

3. I hereby consent to the appointment of

the father of the said infant, as guardian of the said infant;

OR

I beg to refer to my written consent to the appointment of............................................,
the father of the above named infant, as guardian of the said infant, upon which marked
with the letter "A" I have signed my name prior to the making of this Declaration.

4. I understand and acknowledge that as guardian of the said infant, the said father will
be entitled to act jointly with me as guardian of the said infant and will exercise the
duties and responsibilities of looking after the best interests of the said ...........................
until he or she reaches the age of eighteen years.

I make this solemn Declaration conscientiously believing the same to be true and by
virtue of the Statutory Declarations Act, 1938.


Signed ................................................................
Mother of the infant


DECLARED BEFORE ME BY
who is personally known to me (or who is identified to me by

who is personally known to me) at .................................................this day of

PEACE COMMISSIONER/COMMISSIONER FOR OATHS/NOTARY PUBLIC/
PRACTISING SOLICITOR

_____

# Form No 37G

Circuit [Family][1] Court _____Circuit County of _____

IN THE MATTER OF PART VI OF THE STATUS OF CHILDREN ACT, 1987

DECLARATION

BETWEEN ......................................................................................... [Applicant][1]

(applying by ................................................................. Next Friend, if appropriate)

AND ............................................................................................. [Respondent][1]

TAKE NOTICE that whereas the application of the above named applicant pursuant to Part VI of the Status of Children Act, 1987, came before this Court and was determined on the day of,

NOW IT IS HEREBY DECLARED that:

1. ...................................... of.............................................................................

in the County of.............................is the father of the above named applicant; and/or

2. ................................................ of................................................................

in the County of............................. is the mother of the above named applicant; and/or

3. ................................................ of................................................................ .

and ............................................. of................................................................ .

are the parents of the above named applicant; and

4. The above named applicant of            in the County of .....................................

was born on the day of .................. ......................................................................... .

Which said Declaration is made this .................... day of .................... by His Honour Judge

sitting at The Courthouse,.............. ..............in the County of .....................................

SEALED with the Seal of this Court by

County Registrar, this day of .................................

Signed ...............................................................

County Registrar

To: The Applicant

## Form No 37H

Circuit [Family][1] Court _____Circuit County of _____

IN THE MATTER OF PART VII OF THE STATUS OF CHILDREN ACT, 1987

NOTICE OF MOTION FOR THE TAKING OF BLOOD SAMPLE

BETWEEN.....................................................................................[Applicant][1]

(applying by ................................................................ Next Friend, if appropriate)

AND.........................................................................................[Respondent][1]

TAKE NOTICE that at ..................... o'clock on the .............................day of,

an application will be made to the Court sitting at ......................................................

on behalf of the above named [Applicant/Respondent][1] (delete as appropriate) for an Order directing that blood tests be carried out in respect of the persons whose names are set out below for the purpose of ascertaining the parentage of (name of person whose parentage is in dispute)

Name Address Age

    1.

    2.

    3.

Dated this day of ..........................................................................................................


Signed ................................................................

[Applicant/Respondent][1]/Solicitor for the

[Applicant]/Solicitor for the [Respondent][1]


To: The County Registrar

And

To: All other parties

_____

## Form No 37I

Circuit [Family]¹ Court _____Circuit County of _____

### IN THE MATTER OF PART VII OF THE STATUS OF CHILDREN ACT, 1987
### DIRECTION FOR THE TAKING OF BLOOD SAMPLE

BETWEEN ........................................................................................ [Applicant]¹

(applying by ................................................................. Next Friend, if appropriate)

AND ............................................................................................ [Respondent]¹

IT IS HEREBY DIRECTED that

be appointed to take blood samples from the following persons:

Name Address Age

    1.

    2.

    3.

for the purpose of ascertaining the parentage of (name of person whose parentage is in dispute) ......................................................................................................... .

and such appointee is hereby directed to furnish the results of such tests to the parties hereto and to this Honourable Court at the earliest possible opportunity.

IT IS FURTHERMORE DIRECTED that the costs of the said tests be paid by (insert details).

BY THE COURT

County Registrar

_____

## Form No 37J

Circuit [Family]¹ Court _____ Circuit County of _____

IN THE MATTER OF PART VII OF THE STATUS OF CHILDREN ACT, 1987
NOTICE OF INTENTION TO CALL AS A WITNESS THE PERSON UNDER
WHOSE CONTROL BLOOD TESTS WERE TESTED OR OTHER PERSONS
INVOLVED IN THE BLOOD TESTING PROCESS

BETWEEN...........................................................................................[Applicant]¹

(applying by ...................................................... Next Friend, if appropriate)

AND.................................................................................................[Respondent]¹

TAKE NOTICE that......................................................................Applicant/Respondent,
intends to call (insert name of witness).

as a witness at the hearing of the action herein, the report in respect of such tests having
been received by the Applicant/Respondent on ........................ the day of .

Signed ...............................................................

        [Applicant/Respondent]¹/Solicitor for the
        [Applicant]¹/Solicitor for the [Respondent]¹

To: All other parties

and

To: The County Registrar

**[Form No 37K
Order 59 Rule 6**

Circuit Family Court _____Circuit County of _____

IN THE MATTER OF THE ACT 19 (OR ACTS, AS THE CASE MAY BE) AND IN
THE MATTER OF SECTION 40(5) OF THE CIVIL LIABILITY AND COURTS
ACT, 2004

BETWEEN ................................................................................................AB Applicant

AND ................................................................................................CD Respondent

REQUEST FOR THE COURT'S PERMISSION TO BE ACCOMPANIED BY A PERSON AT
THE HEARING OF PROCEEDINGS

1. Name of party applying to be accompanied at hearing:

2. Named and address of person who it is proposed will accompany the Applicant/
Respondent/other party (delete as appropriate):

3. Relationship or connection of person referred to in 2. to Applicant/Respondent/other
party (delete as appropriate):

4. I have/have not previously obtained the permission of the Court to be accompanied in
these proceedings. (If permission has previously been granted, give details of the
accompanying person at that time):

Dated this day of _____20 _____

Signed: _____
            Applicant/Respondent/Other Party][3]

_____

## [Form No 37L
## The Circuit Family Court

Circuit _____                    County of 20.. No ....

BETWEEN................................................................................. AB Applicant

AND ...................................................................................... CD Respondent

## SUMMONS TO ATTEND CASE PROGRESSION HEARING

Take Notice that these proceedings will appear in the County Registrar's List on the .... day of ............ 20...... at .................. for the purposes of a case progression hearing, at which

*[You and your solicitor are required to attend]

* [You are required to attend].

** [TAKE NOTICE that, unless the other party dispenses in writing with the requirement of vouching, you are required to vouch all items in your Affidavit of Means within 28 days of the date of filing of the Respondent's Affidavit of Means or 21 days before the date mentioned above for the case progression hearing, whichever be the earlier.]

AND FURTHER TAKE NOTICE, that if you seek a pension adjustment order in your proceedings, you shall in advance of the above date for the case progression hearing (i) serve on the Trustees of the relevant Pension Scheme concerned and file a Notice, (ii) file an Affidavit of Service in respect of the service of the said Notice and (iii) serve on the other party a copy of such Notice and Affidavit of Service (see Order 59, Rule 4(38)(4)(c) of the Circuit Court Rules).

AND FURTHER TAKE NOTICE that each party shall complete and file in the Circuit Court Office a Case Progression Questionnaire, a copy of which is attached, at least seven days in advance of the date fixed for the case progression hearing.

All items in the Affidavit of Means of the parties shall be properly vouched to the other party. Such vouching shall, where relevant, include, but is not limited to, the following:

    (i)   Statements including credit cards statements from each and every bank or other financial institution at which an account has been maintained or funds otherwise held by, to the order or for the benefit of the party concerned, whether in that party's name or otherwise, for a period of one year prior to the date of the Respondent's Affidavit of Means;

    (ii)  Detailed particulars of the assets and liabilities of each party (including benefits accruing and liabilities arising under any contingency) in existence at the commencement of, or acquired or incurred during the period of one year prior to the date of the Respondent's Affidavit of Means;

    (iii) Copies of any guarantees/indemnities given by or existing in favour of either party;

(iv)   Copies of all tax returns returned by the party concerned for the last complete tax year ending in the period of one year prior to the date of the Respondent's Affidavit of Means and for any subsequent complete tax year, and of assessments to tax made upon the party concerned for that tax year or those tax years, together with supporting documentation and balancing statements;

(v)   P60s for the party concerned for the last complete tax year ending in the period of one year prior to the date of the Respondent's Affidavit of Means and for any subsequent complete tax year together with pay slips for any subsequent period showing the pattern of income during that subsequent period and up to the date of vouching and any deductions at source therefrom;

(vi)   Sets of full annual accounts for the last complete year of trading ending in the period of one year prior to the date of the Respondent's Affidavit of Means (audited where required by law together with, where such accounts are required by law to be audited but audited accounts have not been produced for that period, the most recent audited accounts) of any company, partnership, profession or business in which any party has a shareholding or interest, save for a company which is publicly quoted in a recognised exchange, or as otherwise directed County Registrar;

(vii)   Detailed particulars of any grants, subsidies, payments from any public fund or agency, or similar benefits for a one year period;

(viii)   Detailed particulars of any pension and insurance/assurance policies or their equivalent;

(ix)   Detailed particulars of any settlement, trust or other instrument of equivalent effect of which the party concerned is settlor, eficiary or a potential beneficiary;

(x)   Detailed particulars of any benefits received under any of instruments mentioned at (ix);

(xi)   Vouching shall be for a one year period unless otherwise by the Court or by the County Registrar, or agreed between the parties.

Any application in relation to the vouching done or to be done by either party may be made to the County Registrar at the case progression hearing.

Dated_____.

(Signed)_____

County Registrar

To:_____

      (applicant/Solicitor for the Applicant)

And to: _____

      (Respondent/Solicitor for the Respondent)

* Insert as appropriate

** Insert where a Defence has been filed: see Order 59, Rule 4(17)(a) of the Circuit Court Rules.][4]

## [Form No 37M
## The Circuit Family Court

REPORT OF COUNTY REGISTRAR PURSUANT TO ORDER 59, RULE 4(38)(11)
IN RESPECT OF DELAY OR DEFAULT

[Set out in detail delay or default including all relevant dates]

I hereby report to the Honourable Court accordingly


(Signed)_____
County Registrar][4]

# [Form No 37N

Circuit                                        County of 20__ No ____

BETWEEN ...................................................................................................AB Applicant

AND ...................................................................................................CD Respondent

### CASE PROGRESSION QUESTIONNAIRE
### (FAMILY LAW PROCEEDINGS)
### THE COMPLETED QUESTIONNAIRE MUST BE SERVED ON THE OTHER
### PARTY AND FILED AT LEAST SEVEN DAYS BEFORE THE DATE FIXED FOR
### THE CASE PROGRESSION HEARING

| Information to be supplied | Applicant's reply | Respondent's reply |
|---|---|---|
| 1. Is the [divorce] [judicial separation]*, apart from other issues, being contested— | | |
| 2 Are the parties agreed as to the arrangements which should be made for custody of the dependent child/children—<br><br>If so, what are the arrangements—<br><br>If not, what are the respective positions<br><br>of the parties— | | |
| 3. Are the parties agreed as to the arrangements which should be made for access to the dependent child/children—<br><br>If so what are the arrangements—<br><br>If not, what are the respective positions of the parties— | | |
| 4. Are further pleadings necessary— | | |
| 5. Have both parties filed their Affidavits of Means— | | |
| 6. Have both parties vouched their Affidavits of Means— | | |
| 7. Are the parties satisfied with the disclosure and vouching in the Affidavits of Means filed—<br><br>If not, what are the alleged deficiencies—<br><br>In particular, what vouchers are outstanding— | | |

| Information to be supplied | Applicant's reply | Respondent's reply |
|---|---|---|
| 8. Do the parties envisage or intend to apply that disclosure/vouching for a greater period than 12 months will be required— <br><br> If so, what disclosure is required, and over what period— | | |
| 9. Have both parties files their Affidavits of Welfare (where applicable)— | | |
| 10. Have the parties <br><br> (a) exchanged statements of the issues— <br><br> (b) identified the issues in dispute between them— | | |
| 11. Has inter partes discovery been made— <br><br> If not, will an order be required— | | |
| 12. Do the parties envisage that third party discovery will be required— <br><br> If so, against whom— | | |
| 13. Are pension adjustment orders being sought— <br><br> Note: H so, a Notice to the Trustees of the relevant Pension Scheme must be served, copies of such Notice and an Affidavit of Service thereof on the trustees served on the other party, and the Affidavit of Service filed before the case progression hearing. | | |
| 14. Have particulars of property income been furnished in accordance with [s. 38(7) of the Family Law Act 1995] [Section 38(6) of the Family Law (Divorce) Act 1996]*— | | |
| 15.(1) expert witness being retained by the parties to give evidence in the case— <br><br> (in particular, each party should indicate whether they intend to retain an accountant to give evidence in relation to the income, assets or liabilities of one or both parties.) | | |

| Information to be supplied | Applicant's reply | Respondent's reply |
|---|---|---|
| 16. Have the parties obtained, or considered retaining. any joint expert in respect of any of the matters referred to at 14— | | |
| 17. Identify (a) the expert, <br><br> (b) the expert's professional standing. <br><br> (c) the financial, medical, valuation or other subject matter in respect of which such expert witness will be giving evidence and <br><br> (d) if the expert is jointly retained. | | |
| 18. What period is required for each expert to have completed his/her investigations and to have reported thereon— | | |
| 19. Is it agreed that the reports of each expert witness intended be called will be exchanged between the parties— | | |
| 20. Can expert witnesses discuss the issues and identity matters in dispute— | | |
| 21. Will any social report(s) be sought under s 47 of the Family Law Act 1995— <br><br> If so, what period is required for such report(s) to be completed— | | |
| 22. Is the trial of any preliminary issue necessary and, if so, indicate the nature of such issue, the estimated duration of any such hearing, and the likely effect on the outcome of the substantive proceedings. | | |
| 23. Are there any other matters which should be brought to the attention of the Court— | | |

* Delete if not applicable

Signed_____

Applicant/Solicitor for the Applicant

Respondent/Solicitor for the Respondent][4]

**[Form 51
An Chúirt Chuarda
The Circuit Court**

CIRCUIT COUNTY OF

IN THE MATTER OF THE CIVIL PARTNERSHIP AND CERTAIN RIGHTS AND
OBLIGATIONS OF COHABITANTS ACT 2010

BETWEEN...............................................................................................Applicant

AND........................................................................................................Respondent

AFFIDAVIT OF MEANS

I, [Insert name of Deponent], .................... [Insert occupation of Deponent],
........................ of [Insert address of Deponent] ............................ being aged 18 years
and upwards MAKE OATH and say as follows:—

1. I say that I am the Applicant/Respondent [delete as appropriate] in the above entitled
proceedings and I make this Affidavit from facts within my own knowledge save where
otherwise appears and where so appearing I believe the same to be true.

2. I say that I have set out in the First Schedule hereto all the assets, property and
financial resources to which I am legally or beneficially entitled and the manner in
which such property is held.

3. I say that I have set out in the Second Schedule hereto all income which I receive and
the sources of such income.

4. I say that I have set out in the Third Schedule hereto all my debts, liabilities, financial
obligations and financial responsibilities and the persons to whom such debts and
liabilities are due.

5. I say that my weekly outgoings amount to the sum of ......... and I say that the details
of such outgoings have been set out in the Fourth Schedule hereto.

6. I say that to the best of my knowledge, information and belief, all pension information
known to me relevant to the within proceedings is set out in the Fifth Schedule hereto.

FIRST SCHEDULE

[Insert list of assets]

SECOND SCHEDULE

[Insert details of income]

THIRD SCHEDULE

[Insert list of debts and liabilities]

FOURTH SCHEDULE

[Insert list of Weekly Expenditure]

FIFTH SCHEDULE

[Insert details of pension]

SWORN etc.][5]

**[Form 51A**
**An Chúirt Chuarda**
**The Circuit Court**

CIRCUIT COUNTY OF
IN THE MATTER OF CIVIL PARTNERSHIP AND CERTAIN RIGHTS AND
OBLIGATIONS OF COHABITANTS ACT 2010

BETWEEN ................................................................................................... Applicant

AND ................................................................................................... Respondent

NOTICE TO TRUSTEES

TAKE NOTICE that relief has been claimed by the Applicant/Respondent in the above entitled proceedings pursuant to section 121 [or, as the case may be, section 187] of the Civil Partnership and certain Rights and Obligations of Cohabitants Act 2010, and in particular in relation to [here insert pension details against which relief is claimed]............ and that the hearing of the Action will take place on the..... day of.......... at the Circuit Court sitting at..................... at.... o'clock in the forenoon. (or, if appropriate, "in relation to which claim you will be advised of the date for trial in due course")

Dated this .......... day of ...............................

Signed...............................................

Solicitors for the Applicant/Respondent or Applicant/Respondent in person
To: The County Registrar
And To: The Trustees of the relevant pension scheme(s)
And To: Applicant/Respondent/Solicitors for the Applicant/Solicitors for the Respondent][5]

**[Form 51B**
**An Chúirt Chuarda**
**The Circuit Court**

CIRCUIT COUNTY OF

IN THE MATTER OF CIVIL PARTNERSHIP AND CERTAIN RIGHTS AND
OBLIGATIONS OF COHABITANTS ACT 2010

BETWEEN..................................................................Applicant /Maintenance Creditor

AND.......................................................................Respondent /Maintenance Debtor

IN THE MATTER OF SECTION *56(1) **179(1) OF THE CIVIL PARTNERSHIP
AND CERTAIN RIGHTS AND OBLIGATIONS OF COHABITANTS ACT 2010

## STATEMENT AS TO EARNINGS

I,...................., ............... [insert occupation], of.............., aged 18 years and upwards say
as follows:—

1. I am the respondent/maintenance debtor [delete as appropriate] in the above entitled
proceedings.

2. I have set out in the First Schedule the name and address of every employer by whom
I am employed, together with particulars enabling each such employer to identify me,
and particulars of my earnings and expected earnings from each such employment and
other sources, my resources and needs.

## FIRST SCHEDULE

†Name and address of Employer(s)................................................................................

(or trustee of a pension scheme under...........................................................................

 which the maintenance debtor is................................................................................

receiving periodical pension benefits) .........................................................................

Commencement date......................................................................................................

Nature of work ..............................................................................................................

Place of work ................................................................................................................

Weekly earnings.............................................................................................................

Expected changes to weekly earnings...........................................................................

Employee/contractor identification...............................................................................

number/code (if any)......................................................................................................

P.P.S. number................................................................................................................

‡Income from any other sources .................................................................

Nature of income ..............................................................................................

Source ..............................................................................................................

Identification/account number/code (if any) ................................................

Weekly income..................................................................................................

‡Financial resources ........................................................................................

Nature of resource ...........................................................................................

Location (e.g. bank account) ..........................................................................

Gross value ......................................................................................................

Needs

[Here set out full details of regular personal outings].

Dated: 20

Signed ............................................

\*       For civil partnership proceeding

\*\*      For cohabitation proceedings

†       Repeat for each separate employer, pension provider, or for income as self-employed

‡       Repeat for each separate income source or, as the case may be, resource

OR

I,...................., ............... [insert occupation], of.............., aged 18 years and upwards say as follows:—

1. I am the employer of the maintenance debtor in the above entitled proceedings (or a trustee of a pension scheme under which the maintenance debtor is receiving periodical pension benefits).

2. I certify the following particulars of the maintenance debtor:

## FIRST SCHEDULE

Name and address of Employer(s) ..................................................................

(or trustees)....................................................................................................

Commencement date ......................................................................................

Nature of work................................................................................................

Place of work...................................................................................................

Weekly earnings ..............................................................................................

Expected changes to weekly earnings..........................................................................

Employee/contractor identification number/code (if any)............................................

of the maintenance debtor........................................................................................

P.P.S. number of the maintenance debtor ..................................................................

Dated: ...................................20............

Signed ................................................

\*      For civil partnership proceedings \*\*For cohabitation proceedings][5]

---

## Notes

1    Forms 2N, 2O, 37A, 37B, 37C, 37D, 37G, 37H, 37I and 37J amended by SI 358/2008.

2    Forms 2S and 2T inserted by SI 385/2011.

3    Form 37K inserted by SI 527/2005, to take effect from 20 September 2005.

4    Forms 37L, 37M and 37N inserted by SI 358/2008.

5    Forms 51, 51A and 51B inserted by SI 385/2011.

# Circuit Court Rules (Recording Of Proceedings) 2008

*SI 354/2008*

1. These Rules, which may be cited as the Circuit Court Rules (Recording of Proceedings) 2008, shall come into operation on the 1 day of October 2008.

2. These Rules shall be construed together with the Circuit Court Rules 2001 to 2008.

3. The Circuit Court Rules are amended:

    (a)  by the insertion in the Interpretation of Terms provisions of the following:

> "25. The "Courts Service" means the Courts Service established by the Courts Service Act 1998";

    (b)  by the substitution for rule 1 of Order 58 of the following:

> "1. In this Order:
>
> "the Act" means the Local Elections (Petitions and Disqualifications) Act 1974 (No.8 of 1974);
>
> "Local Election" has the meaning assigned to it by Section 1(1) of the Act;
>
> "record", and "transcript writer" each has the same meaning as in Order 67A.";

    (c)  by the substitution for rule 7 of Order 58 of the following:

> "7. A record shall be made of the hearing of every proceeding under the Act by a person appointed by the Courts Service.";

    (d)  by the substitution for rule 12 of Order 58 of the following:

> "12. (1) The person responsible for the storage or custody of the record of the proceedings shall, at the Court's or the County Registrar's request, make available the record or any part thereof to the Court or the County Registrar, in such manner as is required.
>
> (2) The transcript writer shall furnish to the Court or the County Registrar at the County Registrar's request a transcript of the whole of the record of the proceedings or of such part thereof as the Court or the County Registrar may require. The transcript shall be typewritten or printed and certified by the transcript writer to be a complete and correct transcript of the whole of such record, or of the part required.
>
> (3) The record shall contain the evidence, any objection taken in the course thereof, and the judgment of the Judge but shall not unless otherwise ordered by the Judge include any part of the speeches of Solicitor or Counsel.
>
> (4) A party interested in an appeal may obtain from the County Registrar the whole or of any part of the transcript prepared for the purposes of the appeal, upon payment of the proper charges.";

(d) by the insertion, immediately following Order 67, of the following:

"Order 67A

Recording of Proceedings

1. In this Order,

"record" means a contemporaneous record of the proceedings concerned made by anyone or more means, including, without limitation

(a) any shorthand or other note, whether written, typed or printed, and

(b) any sound recording or other recording, capable of being reproduced in legible, audible or visual form, approved by the court;

"transcript writer" means any person (including a body corporate acting by its employee or contractor) appointed by the Courts Service to make a transcript of the record."

2. Subject to rule 3 and to rule 7 of Order 58, at the trial or hearing of any cause or action, any party may, with the Court's permission and subject to and in accordance with any direction of the Court, make or cause to be made a record of the proceedings, which record shall include

(a) the oral evidence;

(b) in the case of an action tried by a Judge and jury, the Judge's charge arid directions to the jury, and the submissions and requisitions made to the judge and his ruling thereon;

(c) in any case tried by a Judge without a jury, the Judge's judgment (unless it be a written judgment).

3. The record of any criminal proceedings shall be made or caused to be made by a person appointed by the Courts Service, and such record shall include all submissions made by counsel in the course of the trial including opening and closing speeches to the jury and any submissions made in mitigation of sentence.

4. At the hearing of any proceedings before the County Registrar any party may, with the County Registrar's permission, and subject to any order or direction of the County Registrar, make or cause to be made a record of the proceedings in such case, which record shall include

(a) any oral evidence;

(b) any speech or submissions by counselor solicitor;

(c) the County Registrar's judgment or ruling (unless it be a written judgment or ruling).

5. The party making or causing to be made a record in a case referred to in rule 2 or rule 4 shall pay the cost of the production of the record and, where any transcript is required, the cost of the production of such transcript and the said payment shall be borne by the said party unless the Judge or the County Registrar (as the case may be) shall after the trial or

hearing certify that in his opinion it was expedient that the proceedings or any part thereof should have been so recorded, or, as the case may be, a transcript produced. If such certificate is given, the cost occasioned by the making of the record (and, where certified, any cost arising from the production of a transcript of or from the record) to which the certificate relates shall be part of the costs in the cause.

6. The Judge shall have power during the course or at the conclusion of the trial or hearing, to direct that a transcript of the record or any part thereof be furnished to him at the public expense or be furnished to any party applying therefor at the expense of that party.

7. Unless:

(a)    otherwise permitted by and in accordance with this Order, or

(b)    otherwise permitted by the Court and, in that event, subject to and in accordance with any direction of the Court,

no person, other than the Courts Service or a person authorised by it on its behalf, shall make any record of proceedings otherwise than by written or shorthand notes.".

## Explanatory Note

(This note is not part of the Instrument and does not purport to be a legal interpretation.) These rules are intended to facilitate the introduction of digital and other non-manual means of recording proceedings in addition to shorthand recording in criminal and civil proceedings.

# Rules of the Superior Courts 1986

*SI 15/1986*

## ORDER 70

## MATRIMONIAL CAUSES AND MATTERS

### I. Petition

1. Proceedings in matrimonial causes and matters shall be commenced by filing a petition, which shall be addressed to the High Court and which shall be in the Form No. 1 Appendix L. (The forms hereinafter referred to in this Order are the forms set forth in said Appendix).

2. Every petition by which such proceedings shall be commenced shall state the domicile of the parties at the respective dates of the marriage and of the petition, the place of the marriage, the address and description of each party, and the number of children of the marriage.

3. Every petition shall be accompanied by an affidavit made by the petitioner, verifying the facts of which he or she has personal knowledge, and deposing as to belief in the truth of the other facts alleged in the petition and such affidavit shall be filed with the petition.

4. In cases where the petitioner is seeking a decree of nullity of marriage [...][1], the petitioner's affidavit filed with his or her petition, shall further state that no collusion or connivance exists between the petitioner and the other party to the marriage or alleged marriage, and in cases where the petitioner is seeking a decree for restitution of conjugal rights the affidavit filed with the petition, shall further state sufficient facts to show that a written demand for cohabitation and restitution of conjugal rights has been made by the petitioner upon the party to be cited, and that after a reasonable opportunity for compliance therewith, such cohabitation and restitution of conjugal rights has been withheld.

### II. Citation

5. Every petitioner who files a petition and affidavit shall forthwith extract a citation, under seal of the Court, for service on each respondent in the cause.

6. Every citation shall be in the Form No. 2, and the party extracting the same, or his solicitor, shall take it up, together with a praecipe and get the citation signed. The praecipe shall contain the registered place of business of the solicitor depositing same, or if there be no solicitor, an address for service within the jurisdiction where notices, pleadings, orders, warrants, and other documents may be left for such party.

### III. Service

7. Citations shall be served personally when that can be done.

8. Service of a citation shall be effected by personally delivering a true copy of the citation to the party cited, and producing the original, if required.

9. To every person served with a citation shall be delivered, together with the copy of the citation, a certified copy of the petition under seal of the Court.

10. In cases where personal service cannot be effected, application may be made by motion to the Court to substitute some other mode of service.

11. After service has been effected the citation, with a certificate of service in the Form No. 3 indorsed thereon, shall be forthwith filed in the Central Office.

12. When it is ordered that a citation shall be advertised, the newspapers containing the advertisement shall be filed in the Central Office with the citation.

13. Rules 7 to 12, so far as they relate to the service of citations, shall apply to the service of all other documents requiring personal service.

14. A petitioner may not proceed, after having extracted a citation, until an appearance shall have been entered by or on behalf of the respondents, or it shall be shown by affidavit, filed in the Central Office, that they have been duly cited and have not appeared.

15. The citation referred to in the affidavit of service shall be annexed to such affidavits, and marked by the person before whom the same is sworn. The affidavit of service of a citation shall be in the Form No. 4.

## IV. Appearance

16. All appearances to citations shall be entered in the Central Office in a book provided for that purpose, and shall be in the Form No. 5.

17. An appearance may be entered at any time before a proceeding has been taken in default, or afterwards by leave of the Court, and every appearance shall contain the registered place of business of the solicitor entering same, or, if there be no solicitor, an address for service as prescribed by rule 6.

18. If a party cited wishes to raise any question as to the jurisdiction of the Court; he shall enter an appearance under protest, and within eight days file in the Central Office his act on petition in extension of such protest, and on the same day deliver a copy thereof to the petitioner, or to his solicitor. After the entry of an absolute appearance to the citation, a party cited cannot raise any objection as to jurisdiction.

## V. Intervener

19. Application for leave to intervene in any cause shall be made to the Court, by motion, supported by affidavit, and every party intervening shall join in the proceedings at the stage in which he finds them, unless it is otherwise ordered by the Court but the Court may give liberty to a party intervening to plead, as if he was a party to the proceedings originally.

## VI. Answer

20. Each respondent who has entered an appearance may within twenty-eight days after service of the citation on him file in the Central Office an answer to the petition, in the Form No. 6.

21. Each respondent shall on the day he files an answer deliver a copy thereof to the petitioner, or to his solicitor.

22. Every answer which contains matter other than a simple denial of the facts stated in the petition, shall be accompanied by an affidavit made by the respondent, verifying such other or additional matter, so far as he has personal knowledge thereof, and deposing as to his belief in the truth of the rest of such other or additional matter, and such affidavit shall be filed with the answer.

23. In cases involving a decree of nullity of marriage [...][1], the respondent who is husband or wife of the petitioner, shall in the affidavit filed with the answer, further state that there is not any collusion or connivance between the deponent and the petitioner.

## VII. Further pleadings

24. Within fourteen days from the filing and delivery of the answer the petitioner may file a reply thereto, and no further pleading shall be allowed without leave of the Court.

25. A copy of every reply and subsequent pleading shall on the day the same is filed be delivered to the opposite parties or to their solicitors.

## VIII. General rules as to pleadings

26. Either party desiring to alter or amend any pleading shall apply to the Master by motion on notice for permission to do so, unless the alteration or amendment be merely verbal, or in the nature of a clerical error, in which case the application may be made ex parte.

27. When a petition, answer, or other pleading has been ordered to be altered or amended, the time for filing and delivering a copy of the next pleading shall be reckoned from the time of the order having been complied with.

28. A copy of every pleading showing the alterations and amendments made therein shall be delivered to the opposite parties on the day such alterations and amendments are made in the pleading filed in the Central Office; and the opposite parties, if they have already pleaded, shall be at liberty to amend such pleading within four days after such delivery, or such further time as may be allowed for the purpose.

29. If either party in the cause fail to file or deliver a copy of the answer, reply, or other pleading, or to alter or amend the same, or to deliver a copy of any altered or amended pleading, within the time allowed for the purpose, the party to whom the copy of such answer, reply, or other pleading or altered or amended pleading, ought to have been delivered, shall not be bound to receive it, and such answer, reply, or other pleading, shall not be filed, or be treated or considered as having been filed, or be altered or amended, unless by order of the Court. The expense of obtaining such order shall fall on the party applying for it, unless the Court shall otherwise direct.

30. Applications for further particulars of matters pleaded shall be made to the Court by motion on notice.

31. No pleading in any matrimonial cause or matter except the petition by which the proceedings shall be commenced shall be filed, delivered, or amended in the Long vacation unless directed by the Court, but every such petition may be delivered in the Long vacation without any order.

## IX. Medical inspection

32. (1) In proceedings for nullity on the ground of impotence or incapacity, the petitioner shall, after the filing of the last pleading or, if no appearance has been entered or answer filed, after the expiration of the time allowed for entering an appearance or filing an answer (as the case may be), apply to the Master to determine whether medical inspectors should be appointed to examine the parties.

(2) Upon such application the Master may appoint two medical inspectors to examine the parties and report to the Court the result of such examination.

(3) At the hearing of any such proceedings the Court may appoint a medical inspector or two medical inspectors to examine any party who has not been examined or to examine further any party who has been examined, and to report to the Court the result of such examination.

(4) In proceedings for nullity on the ground that the marriage has not been consummated owing to the wilful refusal of the respondent to do so, either party may, after the filing of the last pleading, apply to the Master for the appointment of medical inspectors to examine the parties and to report to the Court the result of such examination. Upon such application the Master shall appoint two medical inspectors and either of the parties shall be at liberty to submit himself for examination to one or both of the inspectors so appointed.

(5) The party on whose application medical inspectors have been appointed as aforesaid shall cause notice of the time and place of the examination to be given to the other party.(6) Every examination shall be held at the consulting rooms of one of the medical inspectors so appointed as aforesaid or at some other convenient place to be specified in the order appointing them.

(7) A Registrar shall attend at the place fixed for the examination and call upon the solicitors for the parties to identify the parties to be examined. When the parties have been identified, the Registrar shall certify such identification in the Form No. 8, and shall administer an oath in the Form No. 9 to the medical inspectors who shall sign the same. The certificate of identification and oath shall be filed by the Registrar in the Central Office.

(8) Every report made under this rule shall be sent by prepaid registered post by the medical inspectors to the Master at the Four Courts, Dublin, and thereupon shall be filed in the Central Office, and either party shall be entitled to obtain a copy thereof upon payment of the prescribed fee.

## X. Trial or hearing

33. No cause shall be called on for trial or hearing until after the expiration of ten days from the day when the application to settle the mode of trial shall have been heard, unless by consent or by special order.

34. Any respondent in the cause, after entering an appearance, without filing an answer to the petition in the principal cause, may be heard in respect of any question as to costs.

35. The Court may, on the trial or hearing of any cause, order an adjournment to such time and subject to such conditions as to costs and otherwise as it shall think fit.

## XI. Evidence taken by affidavit

36. When the Court has directed that all or any of the facts set forth in the pleadings be proved by affidavits, such affidavits shall be filed in the Central Office within eight days from the time when such direction was given, unless the Court shall otherwise direct.

37. Counter-affidavits as to any facts to be proved by affidavit may be filed within eight days from the filing of the affidavits which they are intended to answer.

38. Copies of all affidavits shall on the day when the same are filed be delivered to the other parties to be heard on the trial or hearing of the cause, or to their solicitors.

39. Affidavits in reply to counter-affidavits shall not be filed without permission of the Court.

40. The Court may, on the application of any party, order the attendance for cross-examination of any person making an affidavit.

## XII. Proceedings by petition

41. Any party to a cause who has entered an appearance may apply on motion to the Court to be heard on his petition touching any collateral questions which may arise in a suit.

42. The party to whom leave has been given to be heard on his petition shall within eight days file his act on petition in the Central Office, and on the same day deliver a copy thereof to such parties in the cause as are required to answer thereto.

43. Each party to whom a copy of an act on petition is delivered shall within eight days after receiving the same file his answer thereto in the Central Office, and on the same day deliver a copy thereof to the opposite party, and the same course shall be pursued with respect to any subsequent pleading. But no pleading after the reply shall be allowed without leave of the Court.

44. The parties to the act on petition respectively, within eight days from that on which the last pleading is filed, shall (unless any different mode of proof shall be directed by the Court) file in the Central Office such affidavit and other proofs as may be necessary in support of their several averments.

45. After the time for filing affidavits and proofs has expired, unless any different mode of proof shall have been directed by the Court, the party filing the act on petition shall set down the petition for hearing; and in the event of his failing to do so within a month any party who has filed an answer thereto may set the same down for hearing, and the petition will be heard by the Court without a jury.

46. The order directing any different mode of proof mentioned in rules 44 and 45 shall provide for the hearing of the petition.

## XIII. Alimony

47. The wife, being the petitioner in a cause, may apply for alimony pending suit by motion on notice supported by affidavit at any time after the citation has been duly served on the husband or after order made by the Court to dispense with such service, provided the factum of marriage between the parties is established by affidavit previously filed.

48. The wife, being the respondent in a cause after having entered an appearance may also apply by motion on notice supported by affidavit for alimony pending suit.

49. The husband shall within eight days after the service of the notice of motion and copy of the affidavit in support thereof file an affidavit in answer and give notice of the filing thereof to the wife.

50. The husband, being respondent in the cause, shall enter an appearance before he can file an affidavit in answer to an application for alimony.

51. If the wife is not satisfied with the sufficiency of the husband's affidavit in answer, she may apply to the Court by motion to order him to give a further and fuller affidavit in answer or to order his attendance on the hearing of the motion for the purpose of being examined thereon.

52. In case the affidavit in answer of the husband alleges that the wife has property of her own, she may within eight days after notice of filing thereof, file an affidavit in reply to that allegation, but the husband shall not be at liberty to file an affidavit by way of rejoinder without permission of the Court.

53. If no affidavit in answer is filed by the husband the wife may proceed with the motion or may apply to the Court by motion to order his attendance at the hearing thereof for the purpose of being examined thereon.

54. A wife who has obtained a final decree [...][1] may apply to the Court by motion for an allotment of permanent alimony, provided that she shall eight days at least before making such application give notice thereof to the husband or his solicitor.

55. A wife may at any time after alimony has been allotted to her, whether alimony pending suit [...][1], apply by motion for an increase of the alimony allotted by reason of the increased faculties of the husband or by the reduction of her own faculties, or a husband may apply by motion for a diminution of the alimony allotted by reason of reduced faculties or of the wife's increased faculties, and the course of proceeding in such cases shall be the same as required by this Order in respect of the original application for alimony and the allotment thereof so far as the same are applicable.

56. Permanent alimony shall, unless otherwise ordered, commence and be computed from the date of the final decree of the Court.

57. Alimony pending suit [...][1] shall be paid to the wife or to some person to be nominated in writing by her and approved of by the Court as trustee on her behalf.

## XIV. Restitution of conjugal rights

58. At any time after the commencement of proceedings for restitution of conjugal rights the respondent may apply to the Court for an order to stay the proceedings in the cause by reason that he is willing to resume or to return to cohabitation with the petitioner.

## XV. Guardians of infants

59. An infant may elect any one or more of his next-of-kin as guardian, for the purpose of proceeding on his behalf as petitioner, respondent, or intervener in a cause.

60. The necessary instrument of election shall be filed in the Central Office before the guardian elected can be permitted to extract a citation or to enter an appearance on behalf of the infant.

61. Where an infant has not elected a guardian as aforesaid, the Court shall assign a guardian to the infant for such suit.

## XVI. Attachment and Sequestration

62. In all matrimonial causes and matters, orders of attachment and orders of sequestration are to be prepared by the party at whose instance the order for the issue thereof has been obtained or the party applying for the issue thereof and taken to the Central Office with an attested copy of the order if made and a praecipe for the order and when approved or signed by the Master or the Registrar shall be sealed and it shall not be necessary for the Judge to seal such orders.

63. Any person in custody under an order of attachment may apply for his discharge to the Court.

## XVII. Notices

64. All notices required by this Order or by the practice of the Court, shall be signed by the party, or by his solicitor.

## XVIII. Service of pleadings, notices, &c

65. It shall be sufficient to leave all pleadings, notices and other documents, which by this Order are required to be given or delivered to the opposite parties in the cause, or to their solicitors, and personal services of which is not expressly required, at the registered place of business or address for service furnished as aforesaid by the petitioner and respondent respectively.

66. Where it is necessary to give notice of any motion to be made to the Court, such notice shall be served on the opposite parties who have entered an appearance two clear days previously to the hearing of such motion, and a copy of the notice so served shall be filed in the Central Office, but no proof of the service of the notice will be required, unless by direction of the Court.

67. If an order be obtained on motion without due notice to the opposite parties, such order shall be rescinded on the application of the parties upon whom the notice should have been served; and the expense of and arising from the rescinding of such order shall fall on the party who obtained it, unless the Court shall otherwise direct.

68. When it is necessary to serve personally any judgement or order, the original judgement or order, or an attested copy thereof, shall be produced to the party served, and annexed to the affidavit of service.

## XIX. Change of solicitor

69. A party may obtain an order to change his or her solicitor, upon application to the Master.

70. In case the former solicitor neglects to file his bill of costs for taxation at the time required by the order served upon him, the party may, with the sanction of the Court, proceed in the cause by the new solicitor, without previous payment of such costs.

## XX. Motion papers

71. Motion papers are to set forth the style and object of, and the names and descriptions of the parties to, the cause or proceeding before the Court; the proceedings already had in the cause, and the dates of the same; the prayer of the party on whose behalf the motion is made, and briefly the circumstances on which it is founded.

72. If the motion papers tendered are deficient in any of the above particulars, the same shall not be received without permission of the Master.

73. The motion paper and the affidavit in support thereof and all original documents referred to in such affidavits shall be filed and left in the Central Office.

74. All bills of cost for business in matrimonial causes and matters shall be taxed by the Taxing Master.

75. After directions have been given as to the mode of hearing of trial of a cause, or in an earlier stage of a cause, where special circumstances are shown, the Court may, on the application by motion of a wife who is a petitioner or who has entered an appearance (unless the husband shall prove that the wife has sufficient separate estate or show other good reason) make an order directing him to pay her costs of the cause up to the date of such application, and her further costs de die in diem up to the trial or hearing, and directing the Taxing Master to tax such costs and at the time of such taxation (if directions as to the mode of hearing or trial have been given before such taxation) to ascertain and certify what is a sufficient sum of money to be paid into Court or what is a sufficient security to be given by the husband to cover the costs of the wife of and incidental to the hearing or trial of the cause.

76. In all cases in which the Court at the hearing of a cause condemns any party to the suit in costs, the solicitor of the party to whom such costs are to be paid may forthwith lodge his bill of costs and obtain an appointment for the taxation, provided that such taxation shall not take place before the time allowed for moving for a new trial shall have expired.

77. When the Taxing Master shall have signed his certificate of taxation or as to security, it may be lodged by the party obtaining the same in the Central Office, and the Master shall at once issue an order for payment of the amount or giving of security within seven days, and this order shall be served on the party liable or his solicitor, but unless by leave of the Court no sequestration to enforce such payment shall be issued.

78. When on the hearing or trial of a cause the decision of the Court or the verdict of the jury is against the wife, no costs of the wife of and incidental to such hearing or trial shall be allowed as against the husband, except such as shall be applied for, and ordered to be allowed by the Court at the time of such hearing or trial.

79. Where a party served with a citation does not appear within the time limited for appearance, upon the filing by the petitioner of a proper affidavit of service, the cause may proceed as if such party had appeared, but any pleadings or motions required to be

served on such party shall be filed with the proper officer in the Central Office in lieu of service.

---

**Notes**

1   Amended by SI 97/1990.

---

# [ORDER 70A

## FAMILY LAW PROCEEDINGS

Rule: 1:

(1) In this Order family law proceedings shall include:

(a)   Any proceeding pursuant to section 36 of the Family Law Act, 1995 or to that section as applied by section 44 of the Family Law (Divorce) Act, 1996.

(b)   An application pursuant to section 3 of the Adoption Act, 1974 or pursuant to section 3 of the Adoption Act, 1988.

(c)   An application pursuant to section 3(8) of the Family Home Protection Act, 1976.

(d)   Any application pursuant to section 6 of the Family Law Act, 1981.

(e)   Any proceeding pursuant to the Guardianship of Infants Act, 1964, the Family Law (Maintenance of Spouses and Children) Act, 1976 or pursuant to the Domestic Violence Act, 1996 which has been instituted and maintained in the High Court pursuant to Article 34.3.1 of the Constitution.

(f)   An application for a decree of judicial separation pursuant to section 3 of the Judicial Separation and Family Law Reform Act, 1989 and any preliminary or ancillary application relating thereto under Part II of the Family Law Act, 1995.

(g)   Any proceeding transferred to the High Court pursuant to section 31(3) of the Judicial Separation and Family Law Reform Act, 1989.

(h)   An application for a decree of divorce pursuant to section 5 of the Family Law (Divorce) Act, 1996 and any preliminary or ancillary application relating thereto under Part III thereof.

(i)   An application to institute proceedings for relief subsequent to a divorce or separation outside the State pursuant to section 23 of the Family Law Act, 1995.

(j)   An application pursuant to section 15(A) or section 25 of the Family Law Act, 1995 or pursuant to section 18 of the Family Law (Divorce) Act, 1996.

(k)   An application for a declaration as to marital status under Part IV of the Family Law Act, 1995.

(2) In this Order—

"the 1989 Act" means the Judicial Separation and Family Law Reform Act, 1989,

"the 1995 Act" means the Family Law Act, 1995,

"the 1996 Act" means the Family Law (Divorce) Act, 1996,

"the Acts" means all or any of the Acts referred to in rule 1(1).

**Commencement**

Rule 2: All family law proceedings other than an Application under rule 16 of this Order shall be commenced by a special summons which shall be a family law summons and shall be entitled:

The High Court

Family Law

In the matter of the _____ Act, 20____ (as the case may be)

Between............................................................................................ A. the Applicant

and............................................................................................ C.B the Respondent.

Rule 3: The endorsement of claim shall be entitled "Special Endorsement of Claim" and shall state specifically, with all necessary particulars, the relief sought and each section of the Act or Acts under which the relief is sought and the grounds upon which it is sought.

Rule 4: In any proceeding pursuant to rule 1(1) above an affidavit verifying such proceeding or in reply thereto shall contain the following, where applicable:

   (a)  In the case of an application for a judicial separation or a decree of divorce

      (1)  The date and place of the marriage of the parties.

      (2)  The length of time the parties have lived apart and the address of both of the parties during that time, where known.

      (3)  Full particulars of any children of the applicant or respondent stating whether each or any of them is or are a dependent child of the family and stating whether and if so what provision has been made for each and any such dependent child of the applicant or respondent as the case may be.

      (4)  Whether any possibility of a reconciliation between the applicant and respondent exists and if so on what basis the same might take place.

      (5)  Details of any previous matrimonial relief sought and/or obtained and details of any previous separation agreement entered into between the parties. (Where appropriate a certified copy of any relevant Court order and/or Deed of Separation/Separation Agreement should be exhibited with the affidavit).

      (6)  Where each party is domiciled at the date of the application commencing the proceeding or where each party has been ordinarily resident for the year preceding the date of such application.

    (7)  Details of the family home/s and/or other residences of the parties including, if relevant, details of any former family homes/residences which should include details of the manner of occupation and ownership thereof.

    (8)  Where reference is made in the summons to any immovable property whether it is registered or unregistered land and a description of the lands/ premises so referred to.

(b)  In the case of an application for relief after a foreign divorce or separation outside the State, such of the particulars at (a) above as are appropriate and

    (1)  The date and place of marriage and divorce/ separation of the parties. (Where appropriate, a certified copy of the decree absolute or final decree of divorce/separation, (together with, where appropriate, an authenticated translation thereof) should be exhibited with the affidavit).

    (2)  Particulars of the financial, property and custodial/access arrangements operating ancillary to the said decree, and whether such arrangements were made by agreement or by order of the Court or otherwise, and whether such agreements were made contemporaneously with the decree or at another time and the extent of compliance therewith.

    (3)  The present marital status and occupation of each party.

    (4)  All details relevant to the matters referred to in section 26 of the 1995 Act.

(c)  In the case of an application for a declaration as to marital status, such of the particulars at (a) above as are appropriate together with

    (1)  The nature of the applicant's reason for seeking such a declaration.

    (2)  Full details of the marriage/divorce/annulment/ legal separation in respect of which the declaration is sought including the date and place of such a marriage/divorce/annulment/legal separation. (Where appropriate a certified copy of the marriage certificate/decree of divorce/ annulment/ legal separation should be exhibited with the affidavit).

    (3)  The manner in which the jurisdictional requirements of section 29(2) of the 1995 Act are satisfied.

    (4)  Particulars of any previous or pending proceeding in relation to any marriage concerned or relating to the matrimonial status of a party to any such marriage in accordance with section 30 of the 1995 Act.

(d)  In the case of an application for the determination of property issues between spouses pursuant to section 36 of the 1995 Act or that section as applied by section 44 of the 1996 Act to engaged persons, such particulars of (a) above as are appropriate and

    (1)  The description, nature and extent of the disputed property or monies.

    (2)  The state of knowledge of the applicant's spouse in relation to possession or control of the disputed properties or monies at all relevant times.

(3)   The nature and extent of the interest being claimed by the applicant in the property or monies and the basis upon which such claim is made.

(4)   The nature and extent of any claim for relief being made and the basis upon which any such claim is made.

(5)   The manner in which it is claimed that the respondent has failed, neglected or refused to make to the applicant such appropriate payment or disposition in all of the circumstances and details of any payment or disposition actually made.

(6)   Sufficient particulars to show that the time limits referred to at section 36(7) of the 1995 Act have been complied with.

(e)   In the case of an application for relief out of the estate of a deceased spouse pursuant to section 15(A) or section 25 of the 1995 Act or section 18 of the 1996 Act, such of the particulars at (a) above as are appropriate and

(1)   The date and place of the marriage and date of any decree of divorce/ judicial separation. (The marriage certificate and a certified copy of the decree of divorce/separation shall be exhibited with the affidavit (with authenticated translations where appropriate)).

(2)   Details of any previous matrimonial relief's obtained by the applicant and in particular lump sum maintenance orders and property adjustment orders, if any.

(3)   Details of any benefits received from or on behalf of the deceased spouse whether by way of agreement or otherwise and details of any benefits accruing to the applicant under the terms of the will of the deceased spouse or otherwise.

(4)   The date of death of the deceased spouse, the date upon which representation was first granted in respect of the estate of the said spouse and, if applicable, the date upon which notice of the death of the deceased spouse was given to the applicant spouse and the date upon which the applicant spouse notified the personal representative of an intention to apply for relief pursuant to section 18(7) of the 1996 Act and section 15(A)(7) of the 1995 Act, as the case may be.

(5)   The marital status of the deceased spouse at the date of death and the marital status of the applicant at the date of the application and whether the applicant has remarried since the dissolution of the marriage between the applicant and the deceased spouse.

(6)   Details of the dependants of the deceased spouse at the date of death and of all the dependants of the applicant at the date of the application together with details of any other interested persons.

(7)   A Vermont as to whether any order pursuant to section 18(10) of the 1996 Act or section 15(A)(10) of the 1995 Act has previously been made.

(8)   Details of the value of the estate of the deceased spouse where known.

Rule 5: Any such affidavit filed under rule 4 shall, where appropriate, also exhibit the certificate required under section 5 or, as the case may be, section 6 of the 1989 Act or under section 6, or as the case may be, section 7 of the 1996 Act which shall be in Form Nos. 1, 2, 3 or 4 respectively as set out in the Schedule hereto.

**Affidavit of means**

Rule 6:

(1) Without prejudice to the right of any party to seek particulars of any matter from the other party to any proceeding or to the right of such party to make application to the Court for an order of discovery and without prejudice to the jurisdiction of the Court pursuant to section 12(25) of the 1995 Act or section 17(25) of the 1996 Act, in any case where financial relief under either of the Acts is sought each party shall file and serve an Affidavit of Means in the proceeding.

(2) The Affidavit of Means shall be in Form No. 5 as set out in the Schedule hereto.

(3) An Affidavit of Means of the applicant shall be served with the verifying affidavit grounding such proceeding and the Affidavit of Means of any respondent or any other party shall be served with the replying affidavit in the proceeding unless otherwise ordered by the Master or the Court. Subsequent to the service of an Affidavit of Means either party may request the other party to vouch all or any of the items referred to therein within 21 days of the said request.

(4) In the event of a party failing properly to comply with the provisions in relation to the filing and serving of an Affidavit of Means as herein before provided for or failing properly to vouch the matters set out therein, the Court may, on application by notice of motion, grant an order for discovery and/or make any such order as the Court deems appropriate and necessary, including an order that such party shall not be entitled to pursue or defend as appropriate such claim for any ancillary relief under the Act save as permitted by the Court and upon such terms as the Court may determine are appropriate or the Court may adjourn the proceeding for a specified period of time to enable compliance with any such previous request or order of the Court.

**Affidavit of welfare**

Rule 7: In any case in which there is a dependant child or children of the spouses or either of them an Affidavit of Welfare shall be filed and served on behalf of the applicant and shall be in Form No. 6 as set out in the Schedule hereto. In a case in which the respondent agrees with the facts as averred to in the Affidavit of Welfare filed and served by the applicant, the respondent may file and serve an Affidavit of Welfare in the alternative form provided in Form No. 3 of the Schedule hereto. In a case in which the respondent disagrees with all or any of the Affidavit of Welfare served and filed by an applicant, a separate Affidavit of Welfare in the said Form No. 6 herein shall be sworn, filed and served by the respondent within 21 days from the date of service of the applicant's Affidavit of Welfare.

**Ex parte application to seek relief under section 23 of the 1995 Act**

Rule 8:

(1) An applicant for relief under section 23 of the 1995 Act may issue but not serve a special summons and shall as soon as may be after the issue of such summons apply ex

parte to the Court for leave to make the application for the relief claimed in the summons.

(2) The applicant shall by affidavit verify the requirements specified in section 27 of the 1995 Act and shall set forth the substantial grounds relied upon for seeking relief.

(3) The Court may upon such application, if appropriate, grant or refuse such application or may, in circumstances which seem appropriate, adjourn the application to allow the applicant to put further evidence before the Court on any relevant matter.

(4) If upon application made to it the Court shall grant leave to make the application for the relief claimed in the summons, the applicant may thereupon proceed to serve the summons in the manner provided for by these rules and the matter shall thereupon proceed in accordance with the provisions of this Order.

**Interim and interlocutory relief**

Rule 9:

(1) An application for:

    (a)  a preliminary order pursuant to section 6 of the 1995 Act; or

    (b)  a preliminary order pursuant to section 11 of the 1996 Act: or

    (c)  maintenance pending suit pursuant to section 7 of the 1995 Act; or

    (d)  maintenance pending relief pursuant to section 24 of the 1995 Act; or

    (e)  maintenance pending suit pursuant to section 12 of the 1996 Act; or

    (f)  calculations pursuant to section 12(25) of the 1995 Act; or

    (g)  calculations pursuant to section 17(25) of the 1996 Act; or

    (h)  relief pursuant to section 35 of the 1995 Act; or

    (i)  relief pursuant to section 37 of the 1996 Act; or

    (j)  relief pursuant to section 38(8) of the 1995 Act: or

    (k)  relief pursuant to section 38(7) of the 1996 Act; or

    (l)  a report pursuant to section 47 of the 1995 Act; or

    (m)  a report pursuant to section 42 of the 1996 Act; or

for any other interlocutory relief, shall be by notice of motion to the Court. Such notice shall be served upon the other party or parties to the proceeding 14 clear days before the return date and shall, where appropriate, be grounded upon the affidavit or affidavits of the parties concerned.

(2) An application may be made ex parte to the Court in any case in which interim relief of an urgent and immediate nature is required by the applicant and the Court may in any case, where it is satisfied that it is appropriate, grant such relief or make such order as appears proper in the circumstances.

(3) Any interim or interlocutory application shall be heard on affidavit unless the Court otherwise directs. Where any oral evidence is heard by the Court in the course of any such application ex parte, a note of such evidence shall be prepared by the applicant or the applicant's solicitor and approved by the Court and shall be served upon the

respondent forthwith together with a copy of the order made, if any, unless otherwise directed by the Court.

## Notice to Trustees

Rule 10: An applicant who seeks an order under Part II of the 1995 Act or under Part III of the 1996 Act affecting a pension in any way shall give notice to the trustees thereof in the Form No. 7 as set out in the Schedule hereto informing them of the application and of the right to make representations in relation thereto to the Court.

## Motion for Directions

Rule 11:

(1) An applicant or respondent may, at any stage, bring a motion for directions to the Court:

(a) Where there are any dependant children who are sui juris and whose welfare or position is or is likely to be affected by the determination of the proceeding or of any issue in the proceeding;

(b) Where an order is sought concerning the sale of any property in respect of which any other party has or may have an interest;

(c) Where an order of any type is sought which will affect the rules of a pension scheme or require non-compliance therewith; or

(d) Where an application is brought seeking provision out of the estate of a deceased spouse,

or in any other case in which it is appropriate. Such notice of motion shall be grounded upon the affidavit of the applicant which shall, in particular, identify the party or parties whose interests are or are likely to be affected by the determination of the proceeding or any issue in the proceeding and who ought to be put on notice of the said proceeding and given an opportunity of being heard.

(2) The Court may, upon such motion or of its own motion, make such order or give such direction pursuant to section 40 of the 1995 Act or section 40 of the 1996 Act as appears appropriate and may, where any order affecting the rules of a pension scheme is sought, direct that further notice be given to the trustees of such pension scheme in accordance with the Form No. 7 set out in the Schedule hereto or in such variation thereof as the Court may direct, as appropriate.

(3) Save where the Court shall otherwise direct, a notice party who wishes to make representations to the Court shall make such representations by affidavit which shall be filed and served on all parties to the proceeding within 28 days of service upon them of the notice of application for relief or within such further time as the Court may direct.

Rule 12: The Court may, at any stage, direct that the parties to any proceeding exchange pleadings in relation to all or any of the issues arising in the proceeding between the parties or between the parties or any of them and any third party on such terms as appear appropriate and may give such directions in relation to the matter as appear necessary.

## Hearing

Rule 13:

(1) Save where the Court otherwise directs, the hearing of any interim or interlocutory application brought under the Acts shall be on the affidavits of the parties subject to the right of the parties to seek to cross examine the opposing party on their affidavit. Any party may serve a notice to cross examine in relation to the deponent of any affidavit served on him.

(2) Save where the Court otherwise directs the hearing of any application under the Acts shall be on the oral evidence of the parties.

(3) Where relief is sought by the applicant or the respondent pursuant to section 12 of the 1995 Act or section 17 of the 1996 Act, evidence of the actuarial value of the benefit under the scheme shall be by affidavit filed on behalf of the applicant or respondent as the case may be. Such affidavit on behalf of an applicant shall be sworn and served on all parties to the proceeding and filed at least 28 days in advance of the hearing and subject to the right to serve notice of cross examination in relation to the affidavit. When one of the parties has adduced evidence of the actuarial value of the benefit by such affidavit as provided herein which the other party intends to dispute, he shall do so by affidavit which shall be filed at least 14 days in advance of the hearing, subject to the right to serve notice of cross examination in relation to same.

Rule 15:

(1) Where any action or proceeding is pending in the High Court which might have been commenced in the Circuit Court or the District Court any party to such action or proceeding may apply to the High Court that the action be remitted or transferred to the Circuit Court or the District Court (as the case may be) and if the High Court should, in the exercise of its discretion, consider such an order to be in the interests of justice it shall remit or transfer such action or proceeding to the Circuit Court or the District Court (as the case may be) to be prosecuted before the Judge assigned to such Circuit or (as the case may require) the Judge assigned to such District as may appear to the Court suitable and convenient, upon such terms and subject to such conditions as to costs or otherwise as may appear just.

(2) An application under this rule to remit or transfer an action or proceeding may be made at any time after an appearance has been entered.

Rule 16: The provisions of Order 49, rules 1, 2, 3 and 6 shall apply to any proceeding commenced under rule 2 above.

Rule 17: Any respondent in family law proceedings may counterclaim by way of a replying affidavit and such affidavit shall clearly set out the relief claimed and the grounds upon which it is claimed in like manner as if he were an applicant and subject to the provisions of this order.

Rule 18: In any proceeding which has been transferred to the High Court pursuant to section 31(3) of the 1989 Act, the applicant and the respondent shall each within fourteen days from the making of the order or such further time as the Master may allow, file in the Central Office an affidavit or supplemental affidavits as shall appear necessary to conform to the requirements of this order as if the proceeding had commenced in the High Court, together with a certified copy of the order transferring the same and the proceeding shall thereupon be listed for hearing.

Rule 19: An application by either spouse or on behalf of a dependent member pursuant to section 18 of the 1995 Act or section 22 of the 1996 Act shall be made to the Court by motion in the proceeding on notice to the party concerned and shall be supported by an affidavit verifying the same and shall set out fully how, when and in what respect circumstances have changed or what new evidence exists as a result of which the Court should vary or discharge or otherwise modify in any respect an order to which the section applies.

Rule 20: An application pursuant to section 35 of the 1995 Act or pursuant to section 37 of the 1996 Act may, at any time, be made to the Court by motion on notice in the proceeding to the party concerned and shall be supported by an affidavit verifying the facts alleged in relation to the disposition complained of and shall specify the relief claimed and the way in which the disposition is said to be intended to defeat the relief claimed or to affect it in any way and the Court may make such order upon such motion as appears proper in the circumstances and may, if necessary, adjourn the motion in order to give notice of the application to any party affected by the disposition complained of or the disposal of the property concerned.

Rule 21: An application pursuant to section 8 the 1989 Act, for the rescission of a grant of a decree of judicial separation shall be preceded by a notice of re-entry which shall have been given at least one month before the date of the application and shall be grounded on an affidavit sworn by each of the spouses seeking such rescission which shall specify the nature and extent of the reconciliation including whether they have resumed cohabiting as husband and wife and shall also specify such necessary ancillary orders (if any) as they require the Court to make or to consider making in the circumstances.

**Subsequent Ancillary Relief**

Rule 22: Subsequent to the grant of a decree of judicial separation or of a decree of divorce any party who seeks any or any further ancillary relief under Part II of the 1995 Act or under Part III of the 1996 Act shall do so by notice of motion in the proceeding. Such notice shall be served on any party concerned and shall be grounded on the affidavit of the moving party.

**Service of Orders**

Rule 23: In all cases in which the Registrar of the Court is required to serve or lodge a copy of an order upon any person or persons or body such service or lodgement may be effected by the service of a certified copy of the said order by registered post to the said person or persons or body.

**Adoption**

Rule 24:

(1) In any proceeding pursuant to section 3 of the Adoption Act, 1974 and upon the service of a summons on An Bord Uchtála, the Board shall take the following steps:

(a) It shall cause the person who has agreed to the placing of the child, the subject matter of the application for adoption, to be informed of the following matters:

    (i) the fact of the institution of the proceeding under section 3 of the Adoption Act, 1974 without revealing to such person the name or identity of the applicants;

    (ii) the fact that such person is entitled to be heard and represented upon the hearing of the summons.

(b) It shall ascertain from such person the following information:

    (i) whether such person wishes to be heard and to be represented at the hearing of such summons;

    (ii) whether such person has available to him/her advice and is in a position from his/her own resources to be represented by solicitor or solicitor and counsel at the hearing of such summons;

    (iii) the address at which such person may be informed of the proceeding and in particular of the date of any hearing at which such person will be heard and represented.

(2) Upon the completion of the steps provided for in sub rule (1) the Board shall apply by Motion on Notice to the applicants to the Court for directions. Such application shall, in the first instance, be made on affidavit and in the event that it has been possible to communicate with the person involved such affidavits shall include an affidavit by the servant or officer of the Board who has actually spoken to and had communication with such person. Such person shall not be identified in the body of the affidavit but the name and address present and future of such person shall be set out in a sealed envelope exhibited in such affidavit. Such exhibit shall be opened by the Judge only and unless by special direction of the Court the name, address and identity of such person shall not be revealed to any of the other parties in the suit.

(3) Upon the hearing of such motion for directions the Court may give such direction as it shall think fit for the hearing of the action and in particular may:

(a) provide, if necessary, for the representation of such person;

(b) fix a date for the hearing in camera of the evidence and submissions on behalf of the applicants in the absence of such person but in the presence of the solicitor or solicitor and counsel representing such person;

(c) fix a separate date for the hearing in camera of the evidence and submissions by and on behalf of such person in the absence of the applicants but in the presence of the solicitor or solicitor and counsel for the applicants.

(4) If it is satisfied upon the affidavits supporting such motion or upon such further evidence, oral or otherwise, as may be adduced on behalf of the Board that it is not possible to ascertain the whereabouts of the person who has placed the child for adoption and that it is not possible to communicate with such person the Court may proceed to hear and determine the application without further notice to such person.

Rule 25:

(1) In an application brought pursuant to section 3(1)(a) of the Adoption Act, 1988, the Health Board shall serve a copy of the summons on the applicants and shall verify by affidavit the reasons why it considers it proper to make the application.

(2) In any proceeding brought pursuant to section 3(1)(b) of the Adoption Act, 1988 the applicants shall serve a copy of the summons on the relevant Health Board and thereupon the Health Board shall verify by affidavit its reasons for (as the case may be):

    (i) declining to apply to the Court, or

    (ii) failing to apply to the Court and failing to serve the notice required by section 3(1)(b)(i) of the Act.

Such affidavit shall be sworn by the Chief Executive Officer or by a Deputy Chief Executive Officer of the Board.

(3) In an application brought under sub rule (1) or (2) above, the provisions of rule 24 relating to the steps to be taken by An Bord Uchtála shall apply mutatis mutandis to a Health Board in relation to the parents alleged to have failed in their duty to the child or children concerned.

Rule 26:

(1) In an application to Court pursuant to section 6A or section 11(4) of the Guardianship of Infants Act, 1964 (as inserted by sections 12 of the Status of Children Act, 1987, respectively) where an infant is in the care of prospective adoptive parents under the Adoption Acts, 1952 and 1988, the following procedure shall be followed:

    (i) Upon the service of a summons on An Bord Uchtála, the Board shall take the following steps:

        (a) It shall cause the prospective adoptive parents to be informed of the following matters:

            (i) the fact of the institution of the proceeding under section 6A or section 11(4) of the Guardianship of Infants Act, 1964 without revealing to such parents the name or identity of the applicant or of the natural mother;

            (ii) the fact that such parents are entitled to be heard and represented upon the hearing of the summons.

        (b) It shall ascertain from such parents the following information:

            (i) whether they wish to be heard and to be represented at the hearing of such summons;

            (ii) whether they have available to them advice and are in a position from their own resources to be represented by solicitor or solicitor and counsel at the hearing of such summons;

            (iii) the address at which they may be informed of the proceeding and in particular of the date of any hearing at which they will be heard and represented.

(2) Upon the completion of the steps provided for in sub rule (1) the Board shall apply by Motion on Notice to the father to the Court for directions. Such application shall, in the first instance, be made on affidavit and such affidavits shall include an affidavit by the person who has actually spoken to and had communication with such parents. Such parents shall not be identified in the body of the affidavit but their names and addressees present and future shall be set out in a sealed envelope exhibited in such affidavit. Such exhibit shall be opened by the Judge only and unless by special direction of the Court the name, address and identity of such person shall not be revealed to any of the other parties in the suit.

(3) Upon the hearing of such motion for directions the Court may give such directions as it shall think fit for the trial of the action and in particular may:

(a)  provide, if necessary, for the representation of such parents and of the father and mother of the child;

(b)  fix a date for the hearing in camera of the evidence and submissions on behalf of the applicant and the natural mother in the absence of such parents but in the presence of the solicitor or solicitor and counsel representing such parents;

(c)  fix a separate date for the hearing in camera of the evidence and submissions by and on behalf of such parents in the absence of the applicant and the natural mother but in the presence of the solicitor or the solicitor and counsel for the applicant and the natural mother.

Rule 27:

An application to Court pursuant to section 6A(3) of the Guardianship of Infants Act, 1964 (as inserted by section 12 of the Status of Children Act, 1987) shall be by Motion on Notice to the mother and not by summons and shall be entitled in a similar manner as in rule 2 and shall be grounded on the affidavit of the father seeking to be appointed guardian. Such affidavit shall afford proof of the paternity of the said infant and shall exhibit the written consent of the mother to the appointment of the father as guardian (such consent having been witnessed by a registered medical practitioner or a solicitor) and a true copy of the Birth Certificate of the infant in respect of whom the father wishes to be appointed guardian. The Court may require such proof of paternity of an infant as it thinks fit.

Rule 28: The provisions of Order 119 rules 2 and 3, solely insofar as they relate to the wearing of a wig and gown, shall not apply to any cause, action or proceeding under Order 70 or Order 70A.[1]

**Admission to proceedings for the purposes of section 40 of the Civil Liability and Courts Act 2004**

Rule 29:

(1) A person referred to in section 40(3)(a) of the Civil Liability and Courts Act 2004 intending to attend any proceedings to which a relevant enactment (as defined in section 40(2) of the said Act) relates for the purpose of the preparation and publication of a report of such proceedings in accordance with section 40(3) shall, prior to or at the commencement of the hearing of the proceedings, identify himself or herself to the

Court and apply for such directions as the Court may give under section 40(3) of the said Act.

(2) On any such application, the Court

    (a)  if satisfied that the applicant is a person referred to in section 40(3)(a) of the Civil Liability and Courts Act 2004 and that the applicant intends to attend the proceedings for the purpose of the preparation and publication of a report of proceedings to which a relevant enactment relates, and

    (b)  having heard any submission made by or on behalf of any party to the proceedings,

may allow the applicant to attend the proceedings subject to such directions as the Court may give in that regard.

(3) Where a party (in this sub-rule referred to as the "applicant") wishes to be accompanied in court in any proceedings to which a relevant enactment relates by another person (in this sub-rule referred to as "the other person") in accordance with section 40(5) of the Civil Liability and Courts Act 2004, the applicant shall complete Form No. 8 and

    (a)  where the other party or parties have agreed to the accompanying of the applicant by the other person, the applicant shall lodge Form No. 8, duly completed, with the Registrar of the Court prior to or at the commencement of the hearing in the proceedings, and shall apply to the Court at that hearing to approve the accompanying of the applicant by the other person and for such directions as the Court may give under section 40(5) of the said Act, or

    (b)  where the other party or parties have not agreed to the accompanying of the applicant by the other person, the applicant shall, by motion (to which Form No. 8, duly completed, shall be appended) on notice to the other party or parties returnable not later than seven days prior to the date fixed for the hearing in such proceedings, unless the Court otherwise directs, apply to the Court to approve the accompanying of the party by the other person and for such directions as the Court may give under section 40(5) of the said Act.

On any such application, the Court may approve the accompaniment of the applicant at the proceedings by the other person, subject to such directions as the Court may give, or may refuse such approval.

(4) The Court may, of its own motion or on the application of any party or person, vary or modify any directions given under sub-rule (2) or sub-rule (3) during the course of any proceedings.[2]

**Disclosure of documents, information or evidence for the purposes of section 40 of the Civil Liability and Courts Act 2004**

Rule 30:

An application by a party for an order for the disclosure to any third party of documents, information or evidence connected with or arising in the course of proceedings under a relevant enactment (as defined in section 40(2) of the Civil Liability and Courts Act 2004) for the purposes set out in section 40(8) of the said Act of 2004 shall be made by motion to the Court on notice to the opposing party or parties, grounded upon an affidavit sworn by or on behalf of the moving party.²]³

---

### Notes

1 Rule 28 was amended by SI 327/2000.
2 Rule 29 and 30 were inserted by SI 247/2005.
3 Order 70A inserted by SI 97/1990 and substituted by SI 343/1997.

---

## [ORDER 70B

## CIVIL PARTNERSHIP AND CERTAIN RIGHTS AND OBLIGATIONS OF COHABITANTS ACT 2010

### I PRELIMINARY

1. In this Order:

the "**Act**" means the Civil Partnership and Certain Rights and Obligations of Cohabitants Act 2010;

the "**Act of 2004**" means the Civil Registration Act 2004;

"**civil partnership law proceedings**" has the same meaning as in section 139 of the Act;

"**cohabitation proceedings**" means proceedings under Part 15 of the Act;

reference to registration of a civil partnership includes, in the case of a civil partnership recognised by virtue of section 5 of the Act, registration of a legal relationship as referred to in that section.

### II CIVIL PARTNERSHIP LAW PROCEEDINGS

### Commencement of civil partnership law proceedings

2. (1) Civil partnership law proceedings for any one or more of the following reliefs shall be commenced by special summons, which shall be a civil partnership summons:

    (a)  an order under section 4(1) of the Act including where such relief is sought by virtue of an order made under section 5 of the Act;

    (b)  an order on an application by a civil partner to have a conveyance declared void, under section 28 of the Act, or for relief under section 34 of the Act;

    (c)  an order under section 29(1) of the Act dispensing with the consent of a civil partner required under section 28 of the Act or an order under section 29(4) of the Act to give the consent required under section 28 of the Act on behalf of a civil partner;

    (d)  relief under section 30(1) of the Act or section 30(2) of the Act;

    (e)  a maintenance order under section 45 of the Act;

(f) an order on an application by a civil partner or a child of a deceased person who was a civil partner before death under section 106 of the Act determining a question arising between civil partners as to the title to or possession of property;

(g) a decree of nullity of civil partnership under section 107 of the Act;

(h) a decree of dissolution in respect of a civil partnership under section 110 of the Act;

(i) an order for provision out of the estate of a deceased civil partner under section 127 of the Act;

(j) an order directing the sale of property under section 128 of the Act;

(k) subject to rule 15, an order setting aside a disposition under section 137 of the Act;

(l) relief between civil partners under the Partition Act 1868 and the Partition Act 1876, where the fact that they are civil partners of each other is of relevance to the proceedings.

(2) The following civil partnership law proceedings shall be commenced by originating notice of motion:

(a) an application to the Court pursuant to section 48 of the Act, which shall be grounded on the affidavits of both civil partners, to one of which is exhibited the agreement concerned, and in which each civil partner verifies that he or she has taken, or has the opportunity to take, independent legal advice in relation to the agreement, provided that where relief under section 48 of the Act is sought in addition to other relief under the Act, such relief may be sought in any special summons, without the necessity to bring an originating motion separately;

(b) an application to the Court pursuant to section 127(7) of the Act by the personal representative of a deceased civil partner for leave to distribute the estate.

(3) All civil partnership law proceedings shall be entitled:

"THE HIGH COURT

CIVIL PARTNERSHIP

In the matter of section of the Civil Partnership and Certain Rights and Obligations of Cohabitants Act 2010 (or as the case may be)

Between/

A.B., Applicant

and

C.D., Respondent"

(4) The endorsement of claim shall be entitled "Special Endorsement of Claim" and shall state specifically, with all necessary particulars, the relief sought and each section of the Act under which the relief is sought and the grounds upon which it is sought.

3. (1) Civil partnership law proceedings for relief under the Domestic Violence Acts 1996 to 2002 (as amended by Part 9 of the Act) which have been instituted and maintained in the High Court pursuant to Article 34.3.1 of the Constitution shall be brought, heard and determined in accordance with Order 70A, with such modifications as are necessary.

(2) An application to the Court pursuant to section 59B(2) of the Act of 2004 (as inserted by section 16 of the Act) shall be commenced by originating notice of motion, which shall be grounded on the affidavit of one or both intending civil partners setting out and proving the reasons for the exemption sought from the requirement of section 59B(1)(a) and why the exemption is in the interests of the intending civil partners.

### Verification of claim

4. (1) In any proceedings pursuant to rule 2(1), an affidavit verifying the proceedings or in reply thereto (in this rule, the "affidavit") shall contain one or more the particulars set out in this rule, where applicable.

(2) In the case of an application for a decree of dissolution of a civil partnership, the affidavit shall include:

   (a)  the date and place of the registration of the civil partnership of the parties;

   (b)  the length of time the parties have lived apart and the address of each of the parties during that time, where known;

   (c)  the age of the civil partners, the duration of their civil partnership and the length of time during which the civil partners lived with each other after registration of their civil partnership;

   (d)  any physical or mental disability of either of the civil partners;

   (e)  full particulars of any children of the applicant or respondent or to whom either of the civil partners owes an obligation of support and stating whether and if so what provision has been made for each and any such child;

   (f)  whether any possibility of a reconciliation between the applicant and respondent exists and if so on what basis the same might take place;

   (g)  details of any previous civil partnership law relief sought and/or obtained and details of any previous separation agreement entered into between the parties (and where appropriate, a certified copy of any relevant Court order and/or agreement should be exhibited to the affidavit);

   (h)  details of any previous matrimonial or family law relief obtained by either of the parties (and where appropriate a certified copy of any relevant Court order and/or agreement should be exhibited to the affidavit);

   (i)  where each party is domiciled at the date of the application commencing the proceeding or where each party has been ordinarily resident for the year preceding the date of such application;

   (j)  details of the shared home(s) and/or other residences of the parties including, if relevant, details of any former shared homes/residences which should include details of the manner of occupation and ownership thereof;

  (k)  where reference is made in the civil partnership summons to any immovable property, whether it is registered or unregistered land and a description of the lands/premises so referred to;

  (l)  any other matter which is relevant for the purposes of section 129(2) of the Act.

(3) In the case of an application for a decree of nullity under section 107 of the Act, the affidavit shall include such of the particulars mentioned in sub-rule (2) as are appropriate and:

  (a)  particulars of the grounds set out in section 107 of the Act on which such a decree might be granted and of each of the facts alleged to support such grounds;

  (b)  where the application involves an allegation that either or both of the parties was unable to give informed consent, the attestation to that effect mentioned in section 107(c)(iv) of the Act shall in the first instance be given by the consultant psychiatrist by affidavit, and where any such attestation is disputed by the opposing party then, without prejudice to the right of that party to cross-examine and/or to adduce expert evidence, application may be made to the Master for the appointment of a psychiatric inspector in respect of the party concerned;

  (c)  in any other appropriate case, the Master may appoint a medical and/or psychiatric inspector in respect of either party.

(4) In the case of an application for relief under section 4 of the Act, the affidavit shall include such of the particulars mentioned in sub-rule (2) as are appropriate and:

  (a)  the nature of the applicants reason for seeking the relief sought under section 4 of the Act;

  (b)  full details of the registration of the civil partnership and/or dissolution of the civil partnership in respect of which the declaration is sought including the date and place of the registration and/or the dissolution of the civil partnership (and, where appropriate, a certified copy of the civil partnership registration form and/ or decree of dissolution should be exhibited to the affidavit);

  (c)  where a declaration is sought under section 4 by virtue of an order made under section 5 of the Act, a certified copy of the instrument of registration or of dissolution, with, where appropriate, an authenticated translation thereof, should be exhibited to the affidavit;

  (d)  particulars of any previous or pending proceeding in relation to any civil partnership concerned or relating to the civil partnership or matrimonial status of a party to the civil partnership concerned;

  (e)  the rights of any person other than the civil partners concerned which may be affected by the relief sought, including a person with whom either civil partner is registered in a new civil partnership or to whom either civil partner is married, or any child of either civil partner or to whom either of the civil partners owes an obligation of support.

(5) In the case of an application for relief under section 106 of the Act, the affidavit shall include such of the particulars mentioned in sub-rule (2) as are appropriate and:

    (a)  the description, nature and extent of the money or other property to which the application relates;

    (b)  the state of knowledge of the applicant civil partner or deceased parent in relation to the possession or control of the money or other property to which the application relates at all relevant times;

    (c)  the nature and extent of the interest being claimed by the applicant in the money or other property to which the application relates and the basis upon which such claim is made;

    (d)  the nature and extent of any claim for relief being made and the basis upon which any such claim is made;

    (e)  particulars of any relevant payment or disposition made by the respondent civil partner or deceased parent civil partner;

    (f)  the rights of any person other than the civil partners concerned which may be affected by the relief sought, including a person with whom either civil partner is registered in a new civil partnership or to whom either civil partner is married, or any child of either civil partner or to whom either of the civil partners owes an obligation of support.

(6) In the case of an application for provision out of the estate of a deceased civil partner under section 127 of the Act, the affidavit shall include such of the particulars mentioned in sub-rule (2) as are appropriate and:

    (a)  the date and place of the registration of the civil partnership and of any dissolution of the civil partnership (and, where appropriate, a certified copy of the civil partnership registration form and/ or decree of dissolution should be exhibited to the affidavit);

    (b)  details of any previous civil partnership law reliefs obtained by the applicant and in particular any lump sum maintenance orders, financial compensation orders and property adjustment orders;

    (c)  details of any benefit received from or on behalf of the deceased civil partner whether by way of agreement or otherwise and details of any benefits accruing to the applicant under the terms of the will of the deceased civil partner or otherwise;

    (d)  the date of death of the deceased civil partner, the date upon which representation was first granted in respect of the estate of the said civil partner and, if applicable, the date upon which notice of death of the deceased civil partner was given to the applicant under section 127(7) of the Act and the date upon which the applicant notified the personal representative of an intention to apply for relief pursuant to section 127(8) of the Act;

    (e)  the civil partnership or marital status of the deceased civil partner at the date of death and the civil partnership or marital status of the applicant at the date of the application and whether the applicant has entered another civil partnership or a marriage since the dissolution of the civil partnership between the applicant and the deceased civil partner;

(f)  details of the dependants of the deceased civil partner at the date of death, of the dependants of the applicant at the date of the application, and of any other interested persons;

(g)  An averment as to whether any order has previously been made under section 127(11) of the Act;

(h)  details of the value of the estate of the deceased civil partner where known.

(7) In the case of an application for relief between civil partners under the Partition Act 1868 and the Partition Act 1876, where the fact that they are civil partners of each other is of relevance to the proceedings, the affidavit shall include such of the particulars mentioned in sub-rule (2) as are appropriate and:

(a)  the description, nature and extent of the money or other property to which the application relates;

(b)  the nature and extent of any claim for relief being made and the basis upon which any such claim is made;

(c)  the rights of any person other than the civil partners concerned which may be affected by the relief sought, including a person with whom either civil partner is registered in a new civil partnership or to whom either civil partner is married, or any child of either civil partner or to whom either of the civil partners owes an obligation of support.

**Affidavit of Means**

5. (1) Without prejudice to:

(a)  the right of any party to seek particulars of any matter from the other party to any proceeding, or

(b)  the right of any party to apply to the Court for an order of discovery, or

(c)  the jurisdiction of the Court under section 142 of the Act,

in any case where financial relief under the Act is sought each party shall file and serve an Affidavit of Means in the proceeding.

(2) The Affidavit of Means shall be in Form No. 1 in Appendix II.

(3) An Affidavit of Means of the applicant shall be served with the verifying affidavit grounding the proceeding and the Affidavit of Means of any respondent or any other party shall be served with the replying affidavit in the proceeding unless otherwise ordered by the Master or the Court. Subsequent to the service of an Affidavit of Means either party may request the other party to vouch all or any of the items referred to therein within 21 days of the said request.

(4) In the event of a party failing properly to comply with the provisions in relation to the filing and serving of an Affidavit of Means or failing properly to vouch the matters set out therein, the Court may, on application by notice of motion, grant an order for discovery and/or make any such order as the Court deems appropriate and necessary,

including an order that such party shall not be entitled to pursue or defend as appropriate such claim for any ancillary relief under the Act save as permitted by the Court and upon such terms as the Court may determine are appropriate or the Court may adjourn the proceeding for a specified period of time to enable compliance with any such previous request or order of the Court.

**Interim, interlocutory, ancillary or consequential relief**

6. (1) An application to the Court for any interim or interlocutory relief, including for any of the following reliefs, shall be by notice of motion to the Court:

    (a)  an order under section 30 or section 34 of the Act;

    (b)  an order under section 46 of the Act discharging or varying a maintenance order;

    (c)  an interim maintenance order under section 47 of the Act;

    (d)  an order under section 50(3) of the Act to discharge a direction for the transmission of maintenance payments;

    (e)  an order under section 52 of the Act to secure a maintenance order;

    (f)  an order under section 53(2) of the Act for an attachment of earnings order;

    (g)  a determination under section 58 of the Act;

    (h)  an order under section 60 of the Act discharging or varying an attachment of earnings order;

    (i)  a safety order, a barring order, an interim barring order or a protection order under the Domestic Violence Acts 1996 and 2002, as amended by Part 9 of the Act, or an order under section 30 or section 34 of the Act pending application for a decree of dissolution;

    (j)  an order under section 116 of the Act requiring a civil partner to make periodical payments or lump sum payments for support pending application for a decree of dissolution.

(2) An application to the Court for any subsequent ancillary or consequential relief after a decree of dissolution has been made, including for any of the following reliefs, shall be by notice of motion to the Court:

    (a)  an order under section 117 of the Act requiring a civil partner to make and/or secure periodical payments or lump sum payments for support and/or an attachment of earnings order in respect of any such payments following the making of a decree of dissolution;

    (b)  a property adjustment order under section 118 of the Act following the making of a decree of dissolution;

    (c)  an ancillary order under section 119 of the Act following the making of a decree of dissolution;

    (d)  a financial compensation order under section 120 of the Act following the making of a decree of dissolution;

(e)  a pension adjustment order under section 121 of the Act following the making of a decree of dissolution;

(f)  an order under section 127(11) of the Act;

(g)  subject to rule 14, an order under section 131(2) of the Act discharging or varying an order mentioned in section 131(1) of the Act.

(3) An application for the appointment of a medical and/or psychiatric inspector in respect of a party shall be by motion on notice and on the hearing of the motion, the Master may, on such terms as he considers appropriate, appoint a suitably qualified person to examine a party and to report to the Court on such matters as are directed.

(4) A copy of the notice of motion under sub-rule (1), (2) or (3) shall be served upon the other party or parties to the proceeding 14 clear days before the return date and shall, where appropriate, be grounded upon the affidavit of the moving party.

(5) An application to which sub-rule (1) applies may be made ex parte to the Court in any case in which interim relief of an urgent and immediate nature is required by the applicant and the Court may in any case, where it is satisfied that it is appropriate, grant such relief or make such order as appears proper in the circumstances.

(6) A statement as to earnings for the purposes of paragraph (a) or paragraph (b) of section 56(1) of the Act shall be in Form No. 2 or 3 as appropriate in Appendix II. Such a statement by a maintenance debtor shall be verified on affidavit or on oath at the hearing of the application. Such a statement by an employer need not be verified on affidavit unless so required by the maintenance creditor.

(7) Any application to which this rule applies shall be heard on affidavit unless the Court otherwise directs. Where any oral evidence is heard by the Court in the course of any application ex parte, a note of such evidence shall be prepared by the applicant or the applicants solicitor and approved by the Court and shall be served upon the respondent forthwith together with a copy of the order made, if any, unless otherwise directed by the Court.

(8) An application by an interested civil partner for an adjournment of proceedings against another civil partner under section 32 of the Act or for relief under section 33 of the Act shall be by motion in the proceedings against the other civil partner on notice to each of the parties to those proceedings seeking to be joined to those proceedings (if the applicant has not been served with a third party notice in those proceedings) and specifying any order sought under section 32 or section 33 of the Act.

**Notice to Trustees**

7. (1) An applicant who seeks an order under the Act affecting a pension in any way shall give notice to the trustees of the pension scheme concerned in the Form No. 4 in Appendix II informing them of the application.

(2) A calculation provided by such trustees in accordance with section 126(2) of the Act shall be certified by a person duly authorised in that behalf by the trustees, but need not be verified on affidavit unless so required by one of the parties.

(3) The trustees may, if they consider it necessary, file an Affidavit of Representations.

**Motion for Directions**

8. (1) An applicant or respondent may, at any stage, bring a motion for directions to the Court:

    (a)  where there are any dependent children of either civil partner who are sui juris and whose welfare or position is or is likely to be affected by the determination of the proceeding or of any issue in the proceedings;

    (b)  where an order is sought concerning the sale of any property in respect of which any other party has or may have an interest;

    (c)  where an order of any type is sought which will affect the rules of a pension scheme or require non-compliance therewith; or

    (d)  where an application is brought seeking provision out of the estate of a deceased civil partner,

or where the Court in any other case directs.

(2) The notice of motion for directions shall be grounded upon the affidavit of the moving party which shall, in particular, identify the party or person whose interests are or are likely to be affected by the determination of the proceeding or any issue in the proceeding and who ought to be put on notice of the said proceeding and given an opportunity of being heard.

(3) The Court may, upon such motion or of its own motion, make such order or give such direction pursuant to section 141 of the Act as appears appropriate and may, where any order affecting the rules of a pension scheme is sought, direct that further notice be given to the trustees of such pension scheme in accordance with the Form No. 4 in Appendix II or in such variation thereof as the Court may direct, as appropriate.

(4) Save where the Court shall otherwise direct, a notice party who wishes to make representations to the Court shall make such representations by affidavit which shall be filed and served on all parties to the proceeding within 28 days of service upon them of the notice of application for relief or within such further time as the Court may direct.

9. The Court may, at any stage, direct that the parties to any proceeding exchange pleadings in relation to all or any of the issues arising in the proceeding between the parties or between the parties or any of them and any third party on such terms as appears appropriate and may give such directions in relation to the matter as appear necessary.

**Hearing**

10. (1) Save where the Court otherwise directs, the hearing of any interim or interlocutory application brought under the Act shall be on the affidavits of the parties subject to the right of the parties to seek to cross examine the opposing party on their affidavit. Any party may serve a notice to cross examine in relation to the deponent of any affidavit served on him.

(2) Save where the court otherwise directs the hearing of any application under the Act shall be on the oral evidence of the parties.

(3) Where relief is sought by the applicant or the respondent pursuant to section 121 of the Act (or under section 48 of the Act where the agreement involves a pension adjustment), any evidence of the actuarial value of the benefit under the scheme considered necessary in addition to the calculation supplied under section 126(2) of the Act shall be by affidavit filed on behalf of the applicant or respondent as the case may be. Such affidavit on behalf of a moving party shall be sworn and served on all parties to the proceeding and filed at least 28 days in advance of the hearing and subject to the right to serve notice of cross examination in relation to the affidavit. When one of the parties has adduced evidence of the actuarial value of the benefit by such affidavit which the other party intends to dispute, he shall do so by affidavit which shall be filed at least 14 days in advance of the hearing, subject to the right to serve notice of cross examination in relation to same.

11. Where any relief is sought which has not been specifically claimed, the Court may adjourn the proceedings to allow such amendments to the civil partnership summons as may be necessary and upon such terms and conditions as it seems fit.

12. An application to remit or transfer civil partnership law proceedings pending before the Court to the Circuit Court or the District Court under section 25 of The Courts of Justice Act 1924 and section 11 of the Courts of Justice Act 1936 may be made by motion on notice at any time after an appearance has been entered.

13. In any civil partnership law proceeding which has been transferred to the High Court pursuant to section 140(5) or section 140(7) of the Act, the applicant and the respondent shall each within fourteen days from the making of the order or such further time as the Master may allow, file in the Central Office an affidavit or supplemental affidavits as shall appear necessary to conform to the requirements of this Order as if the proceeding had commenced in the High Court, together with certified copy of the order transferring the same and the proceeding shall thereupon be listed for hearing.

14. An application under section 131 of the Act shall be made to the Court by motion in the proceeding on notice to the party concerned and shall be supported by an affidavit verifying the same and shall set out fully how, when and in what respect circumstances have changed or what new evidence exists as a result of which the Court should vary or discharge or otherwise modify in any respect an order to which the section applies.

15. Where civil partnership law proceedings seeking other relief are in being between the parties, an application under section 137 of the Act may, at any time, be made to the Court by motion on notice in the proceeding to the party concerned and shall be supported by an affidavit verifying the facts alleged in relation to the disposition complained of and shall specify the relief claimed and the way in which the disposition is said to be intended to defeat the relief claimed or to affect it in any way and the Court may make such order upon such motion as appears proper in the circumstances and may, if necessary, adjourn the motion in order to give notice of the application to any party affected by the disposition complained of or the disposal of the property concerned.

III COHABITATION PROCEEDINGS

**Commencement of cohabitation proceedings**

16. (1) Proceedings under Part 15 of the Act, including any proceedings transferred to the High Court under section 196(6) of the Act, shall be known as "cohabitation proceedings" and this rule and rules 17 to 19 inclusive shall apply to all such proceedings.

(2) Cohabitation proceedings for any one or more orders under sections 174, 175, 187 and 194 of the Act shall be commenced by special summons, which shall be a cohabitation summons.

(3) All cohabitation proceedings shall be entitled:

"THE HIGH COURT

COHABITATION

In the matter of section of the Civil Partnership and Certain Rights and Obligations of Cohabitants Act 2010 (or as the case may be)

Between/

A.B., Applicant

and

C.D., Respondent"

(4) The endorsement of claim shall be entitled "Special Endorsement of Claim" and shall state specifically, with all necessary particulars, the relief sought and each section of the Act under which the relief is sought and the grounds upon which it is sought.

(5) The provisions of rule 5 and rules 7-14 inclusive shall apply mutatis mutandis in cohabitation proceedings and in particular shall apply in such proceedings as if reference in any of those rules to a "civil partner" were reference to a "cohabitant" and as if the reference in any of those rules to a provision of the Act mentioned in column (1) of the table to this sub-rule were a reference to the provision of the Act in column (2) of that table immediately opposite.

| Column (1) | Column (2) |
|---|---|
| **Provision of the Act in civil partnership law proceedings** | **Corresponding provision of the Act in cohabitation proceedings** |
| section 56(1) | section 179(1) |
| section 121 | section 187 |
| section 126(2) | section 192 |
| section 131 | section 173(6) |
| section 140(5) | section 196(6) |
| section 142 | section 197 |

**Verification of claim**

17. (1) In any proceedings pursuant to rule 16(2), an affidavit verifying the proceedings or in reply thereto (in this rule, the "affidavit") shall contain one or more of the particulars set out in this rule, where applicable.

(2) In any such proceedings, the affidavit shall include:

(a) particulars of the duration of the relationship between the parties and of the duration of their cohabitation;

(b) particulars of the basis on which the parties live or lived together;

(c) the degree of financial dependence of either party on the other and any agreements in respect of their finances;

(d) particulars of the degree and nature of any financial arrangements between the parties including any joint purchase of an estate or interest in land or joint acquisition of personal property;

(e) whether there are one or more dependent children of either or both parties;

(f) whether one of the parties cares for and supports any child of the other;

(g) the degree to which the parties present themselves to others as a couple;

(h) any physical or mental disability of either of the parties;

(i) full particulars of any children of the applicant or respondent and of any child of a previous relationship of either party and stating whether and if so what provision has been made for each and any such child;

(j) details of any previous matrimonial, family law or civil partnership law relief obtained by either of the parties (and where appropriate a certified copy of any relevant Court order and/or agreement should be exhibited to with the affidavit);

(k) where each party is domiciled at the date of the application commencing the proceeding or where each party has been ordinarily resident for the year preceding the date of such application;

(l) details of the place(s) where the parties have lived together during their relationship;

(m) where reference is made in the cohabitation summons to any immovable property, whether it is registered or unregistered land and a description of the lands/premises so referred to;

(n) any other matter which is relevant for the purposes of section 173(3) of the Act.

(3) In the case of an application for provision out of the estate of a deceased cohabitant under section 194 of the Act, the affidavit shall include such of the particulars mentioned in sub-rule (2) as are appropriate and:

(a) details of any previous cohabitation reliefs obtained by the applicant;

(b) details of any benefit received from or on behalf of the deceased cohabitant whether by way of agreement or otherwise and details of any benefits accruing to the applicant under the terms of the will of the deceased cohabitant or otherwise;

(c) the date of death of the deceased cohabitant, the date upon which representation was first granted in respect of the estate of the said cohabitant and the date upon which the applicant notified the personal representative of an intention to apply for relief pursuant to section 194(6) of the Act;

(d) the civil partnership or marital status of the deceased cohabitant at the date of death and the civil partnership or marital status of the applicant at the date of the application;

(e) details of the dependants of the deceased cohabitant at the date of death, of the dependants of the applicant at the date of the application, and of any other interested persons;

(f) an averment as to whether any order has previously been made under section 173(7) of the Act;

(g) details of the value of the estate of the deceased cohabitant where known.

### Interim, interlocutory, ancillary or consequential relief

18. (1) An application to the Court in cohabitation proceedings for any interim or interlocutory relief, including for any of the following reliefs, shall be by notice of motion to the Court:

(a) subject to rule 21, an order under section 173(6) of the Act discharging or varying an order under section 175 or section 187 of the Act, or suspending or reviving any provision of such an order;

(b) an order under section 175(2) of the Act;

(c) an order under section 175(3) of the Act to secure a maintenance order;

(d) an order under section 176 of the Act for an attachment of earnings order;

(e) an order under section 183 of the Act discharging or varying an attachment of earnings order.

(2) A copy of the notice of motion under sub-rule (1) shall be served upon the other party or parties to the proceeding 14 clear days before the return date and shall, where appropriate, be grounded upon the affidavit of the moving party.

(3) An application to which sub-rule (1) applies may be made ex parte to the Court in any case in which interim relief of an urgent and immediate nature is required by the applicant and the Court may in any case, where it is satisfied that it is appropriate, grant such relief or make such order as appears proper in the circumstances.

(4) A statement as to earnings for the purposes of paragraph (a) or (b) of section 179(1) or section 179(1) of the Act shall be in Form No. 2 or 3 as appropriate in Appendix II. Such a statement by a maintenance debtor shall be verified on affidavit or on oath at the hearing of the application. Such a statement by an employer need not be verified on affidavit unless so required by the maintenance creditor.

(5) Any application to which this rule applies shall be heard on affidavit unless the Court otherwise directs. Where any oral evidence is heard by the Court in the course of any application ex parte, a note of such evidence shall be prepared by the applicant or the applicants solicitor and approved by the Court and shall be served upon the respondent forthwith together with a copy of the order made, if any, unless otherwise directed by the Court.

19. An application under section 173(6) of the Act shall be made to the Court by motion in the proceeding on notice to the party concerned and shall be supported by an affidavit verifying the same and shall set out fully how, when and in what respect circumstances have changed or what new evidence exists as a result of which the Court should vary or discharge or otherwise modify in any respect an order to which section 173(6) of the Act applies.

## IV MISCELLANEOUS

20. The provisions of Order 49, rules 1, 2, 3 and 6 shall apply to any proceeding commenced under rule 2 or rule 16.

21. Any respondent in civil partnership law proceedings or cohabitation proceedings may counterclaim by way of a replying affidavit and such affidavit shall clearly set out the relief claimed and the grounds upon which it is claimed in like manner as if he were an applicant and subject to the provisions of this Order.

22. In all cases in which the Registrar of the Court is required to serve or lodge a copy of an order upon or with any person or persons or body such service or lodgement may be effected by the service of a certified copy of the said order by registered post upon the said person or persons or body.

23. The provision of Order 119 rules 2 and 3 shall not apply to any cause, action or proceeding under this Order.][1]

**Notes**

1    Order 70B inserted by SI 348/2011.

## Schedule of Forms

### Form No 1

THE HIGH COURT

FAMILY LAW

IN THE MATTER OF THE JUDICIAL SEPARATION AND FAMILY LAW
REFORM ACT, 1989 AND IN THE MATTER OF THE FAMILY LAW ACT, 1995

BETWEEN..................................................................................... A.B. Applicant

and............................................................................................. C.D. Respondent

### CERTIFICATE PURSUANT TO SECTION 5 OF THE JUDICIAL SEPARATION AND FAMILY LAW REFORM ACT, 1989

I, _____, the Solicitor acting for the above Applicant do hereby certify as
follows:-

1. I have discussed with the Applicant the possibility of reconciliation with the
   Respondent and I have given the Applicant the names and addresses of persons
   qualified to help effect a reconciliation between spouses who have become
   estranged.

2. I have discussed with the Applicant the possibility of engaging in mediation to
   help effect a separation on an agreed basis with the Respondent and I have
   given the Applicant the names and addresses of persons and organisations
   qualified to provide a mediation service.

3. I have discussed with the Applicant the possibility of effecting a separation by
   the negotiation and conclusion of a Separation Deed or written Separation
   Agreement with the Respondent.

Dated the day of_____, 20___.

Signed: _____

Solicitor

Address:

---

## Form No 2

### THE HIGH COURT
### FAMILY LAW
### IN THE MATTER OF THE JUDICIAL SEPARATION AND FAMILY LAW REFORM ACT, 1989 AND IN THE MATTER OF THE FAMILY LAW ACT, 1995

BETWEEN ..................................................................................................A.B. Applicant

and .............................................................................................................C.D. Respondent

### CERTIFICATE PURSUANT TO SECTION 6 OF THE JUDICIAL SEPARATION AND FAMILY LAW REFORM ACT, 1989

I, _____, the Solicitor acting for the above Respondent do hereby certify as follows:

1. I have discussed with the Respondent the possibility of reconciliation with the Applicant and I have given the Respondent the names and addresses of persons qualified to help effect a reconciliation between spouses who have become estranged.

2. I have discussed with the Respondent the possibility of engaging in mediation to help effect a separation on an agreed basis with the Applicant and I have given the Respondent the names and addresses of persons and organisations qualified to provide a mediation service.

3. I have discussed with the Respondent the possibility of effecting a separation by the negotiation and conclusion of a Separation Deed or written Separation Agreement with the Applicant.

Dated the day of_____, 20___.

Signed: _____

Solicitor

Address:

## Form No. 3

### THE HIGH COURT
### FAMILY LAW
### IN THE MATTER OF THE FAMILY LAW (DIVORCE) ACT, 1996

BETWEEN.......................................................................................... A.B. Applicant

and................................................................................................... C.D. Respondent

### CERTIFICATE PURSUANT TO SECTION 6 OF THE FAMILY LAW (DIVORCE) ACT, 1996

I, _____, the Solicitor acting for the above Applicant do hereby certify as follows:

1. I have discussed with the Applicant the possibility of reconciliation with the Respondent and I have given the Applicant the names and addresses of persons qualified to help effect a reconciliation between spouses who have become estranged.

   [The following paragraphs to be inserted where appropriate].

2. I have discussed with the Applicant the possibility of engaging in mediation to help effect a separation on an agreed basis (the spouses the parties hereto not being separated) or a divorce on the basis agreed between the Applicant with the Respondent and I have given the Applicant the names and addresses of persons and organisations qualified to provide a mediation service for spouses who have become estranged.

3. I have discussed with the Applicant the possibility of effecting a separation by the negotiation and conclusion of a Separation Deed or written Separation Agreement with the Respondent.

4. I have ensured that the Applicant is aware of judicial separation as an alternative to divorce, no decree of judicial separation in relation to the Applicant and the Respondent being in force.

Dated the day of_____, 20___.

Signed: _____

Solicitor

Address:

**Form No. 4**

THE HIGH COURT
FAMILY LAW
IN THE MATTER OF THE FAMILY LAW (DIVORCE) ACT, 1996

BETWEEN ...................................................................................A.B. Applicant

and ................................................................................C.D. Respondent

## CERTIFICATE PURSUANT TO SECTION 7 OF THE FAMILY LAW (DIVORCE) ACT, 1996

I, _____, the Solicitor acting for the above Respondent do hereby certify as follows:

1. I have discussed with the Respondent the possibility of reconciliation with the Applicant and I have given the Respondent the names and addresses of persons qualified to help effect a reconciliation between spouses who have become estranged.

   [The following paragraphs to be inserted where appropriate].

2. I have discussed with the Respondent the possibility of engaging in mediation to help effect a separation on an agreed basis (the spouses the parties hereto not being separated) or a divorce on the basis agreed between the Respondent with the Applicant and I have given the Respondent the names and addresses of persons and organisations qualified to provide a mediation service for spouses who have become estranged.

3. I have discussed with the Respondent the possibility of effecting a separation by the negotiation and conclusion of a Separation Deed or written Separation Agreement with the Applicant.

4. I have ensured that the Respondent is aware of judicial separation as an alternative to divorce, no decree of judicial separation in relation to the Respondent and the Applicant being in force.

Dated the day of_____, 20___.

Signed: _____

Solicitor

Address:

_____

## Form No 5

### THE HIGH COURT
### FAMILY LAW
[INSERT AS APPROPRIATE]
### IN THE MATTER OF THE JUDICIAL SEPARATION AND FAMILY LAW REFORM ACT, 1989
### IN THE MATTER OF THE FAMILY LAW ACT, 1995
### IN THE MATTER OF THE FAMILY LAW (DIVORCE) ACT, 1996

BETWEEN.................................................................................... A.B. Applicant

and .............................................................................................. C.D. Respondent

AFFIDAVIT OF MEANS

I, _____,[insert occupation], of,_____, aged 18 years and upwards
MAKE OATH
And say as follows;_

1. I say that I am the Applicant/Respondent [DELETE AS APPROPRIATE] in the above entitled proceedings and I make this Affidavit from facts within my own knowledge save where otherwise appears and where so appearing I believe the same to be true.

2. I say that I have set out in the First Schedule hereto all the assets to which I am legally or beneficially entitled and the manner in which such property is held.

3. I say that I have set out in the Second Schedule hereto all income which I receive and the source(s) of such income.

4. I say that I have set out in the Third Schedule hereto all my debts and/or liabilities and the persons to whom such debts and liabilities are due.

5. I say that my weekly out goings amount to the sum of €___ and I say that the details of such out goings have been set out in the Fourth Schedule hereto.

6. I say that to the best of my knowledge, information and belief, all pension information known to me relevant to the within proceedings is set out in the Fifth Schedule hereto. [Where information has been obtained from the trustees of the pension scheme concerned under the Pensions Act, 1990, such information should be exhibited and where such information has not been obtained, the Deponent should depose to the reason(s) why such information has not been obtained].

FIRST SCHEDULE

[Here set out in numbered paragraphs alt assets whether held in the Applicant/ Respondent's sole name or jointly with another, whether held legally or beneficially, the

726

manner in which the assets are held, whether they are subject to a mortgage or other charge or lien and such further and other details as are appropriate].

## SECOND SCHEDULE

[Here set out in numbered paragraphs all income from whatever source(s)].

## THIRD SCHEDULE

[Here set out in numbered paragraphs all debts and/or liabilities and the persons/institutions to which such debts and/or liabilities are due].

## FOURTH SCHEDULE

[Here set out full details of weekly personal out goings].

## FIFTH SCHEDULE

[Here full details of nature of pension scheme, benefits payable thereunder, normal pensionable age and period of reckonable service should be listed to the best of the Deponent's knowledge, information and belief].

SWORN etc.

---

## Form No 6

THE HIGH COURT

FAMILY LAW

[INSERT AS APPROPRIATE]

IN THE MATTER OF THE JUDICIAL SEPARATION AND FAMILY LAW
REFORMACT, 1989

IN THE MATTER OF THE FAMILY LAW ACT, 1995

IN THE MATTER OF THE FAMILY LAW (DIVORCE) ACT, 1996

BETWEEN....................................................................................... A.B. Applicant

and............................................................................................... C.D. Respondent

AFFIDAVIT OF WELFARE

I, _____, [insert occupation], of, _____, aged 18 years and upwards
MAKE OATH

and say as follows;

1.  I say that I am the Applicant/Respondent [DELETE AS APPROPRIATE] in
    the above entitled proceedings and I make this Affidavit from facts within my
    own knowledge save where otherwise appears and where so appearing I believe
    the same to be true.

2.  I say and believe that the facts set out in the Schedule hereto are true.

    [In circumstances in which the Respondent does not dispute the facts deposed
    to by the Applicant in his/her Affidavit of Welfare, the following averment
    shall be included, replacing paragraph 2 hereof, and in such circumstances, the
    Schedule shall not be completed by the Respondent:

2.  I say that I am fully in agreement with the facts as averred to by the Applicant
    in his/her Affidavit of Welfare sworn herein on the _____day of
    _____20___ and I say and believe that the facts set out in the Schedule
    hereto are true].

### SCHEDULE

*Part 1*
*Details of the children*

1.  Details of children born to the Applicant and the Respondent or adopted by
    both the Applicant and the Respondent.

    Forenames _____ Surname _____ Date of Birth

2.  Details of other children of the family or to which the parents or either of them
    are in loco parentis

    Forenames _____Surname _____Date of Birth _____
    Relationship to Applicant/Respondent

*Part II*
*Arrangements for the children of the family*

3.  Home details

    (a)  The address or addresses at which the children now live.

    (b)  Give details of the number of living rooms, bedrooms, etc., at the addresses in (a) above.

    (c)  Is the house rented or owned and, if so, name the tenant(s) or owner(s).

    (d)  Is the rent or mortgage being regularly paid and, if so, by whom?

    (e)  Give the name of all other persons living with the children either on a fulltime or part-time basis and state their relationship to the children, if any.

    (f)  Will there be any change in these arrangements and, if so, give details.

*Part III*
*Education and Training Details*

    (a)  Give the names of the school, college or place of training attended by each child.

    (b)  Do the children have any special educational needs. If so, please specify.

    (c)  Is the school, college or place of training fee paying. If so, give details of how much the fees are per term/year. Are fees regularly paid and, if so, by whom?

    (d)  Will there by any change in these circumstances? If so, give details.

*Part IV*
*Childcare Details*

    (a)  Which parent looks after the children from day to day? If responsibility is shared, please give details.

    (b)  Give details of work commitments of both parents.

    (c)  Does someone look after the children when the parent is not there? If yes, give details.

    (d)  Who looks after the children during school holidays?

    (e)  Will there be any change in these arrangements? If yes, give details.

*Part V*
*Maintenance*

    (a)  Does the Applicant/Respondent pay towards the upkeep of the children? If yes, give details. Please specify any other source of maintenance.

    (b)  Is the maintenance referred to at (a) above paid under court order? If yes, give details.

    (c)  Has maintenance for the children been agreed? If yes, give details.

    (d)  If not, will you be applying for a maintenance order from the Court?

*Part VI*
*Details of Contact with the Children*

    (a)  Do the children see the Applicant/Respondent? Please give details.

(b) Do the children stay overnight and/or have holiday visits with the Applicant/Respondent? Please give details.

(c) Will there be any change to these arrangements? Please give details.

*Part VII*
*Details of Health*

(a) Are the children generally in good health? Please give details of any serious disability or chronic illness suffered by any of the children.

(b) Do the children or any of them have any special health needs? Please give details of the care needed and how it is to be provided.

(c) Are the Applicant or Respondent generally in good health? If not, please give details.

*Part VIII*
*Details of Care and Other Court Proceedings*

(a) Are the children or any of them in the care of a health board or under the supervision of a social worker or probation officer? If so, please specify.

(b) Are there or have there been any proceeding in any Court involving the children or any of them? If so, please specify. (All relevant court orders relating to the children or any of them should be annexed hereto).

*Part IX*
*Declaration*

I,_____, Applicant/Respondent [delete as appropriate], declare that the information I have given herein is correct and complete to the best of my knowledge.


Signed: _____

Applicant/Respondent

Witnessed: _____

Date: _____

*Part X*
*Agreement of Respondent (where applicable)*

I, _____, Respondent, declare that the information given by the Applicant herein is correct and complete to the best of my knowledge and I agree with the arrangements and proposals contained herein.


Signed: _____

Respondent

Witnessed: _____

Date: _____

## Form No 7

### THE HIGH COURT

### FAMILY LAW

[INSERT AS APPROPRIATE]

### IN THE MATTER OF THE JUDICIAL SEPARATION AND FAMILY LAW REFORM ACT, 1989

### IN THE MATTER OF THE FAMILY LAW ACT, 1995

### IN THE MATTER OF THE FAMILY LAW (DIVORCE) ACT, 1996

BETWEEN ......................................................................................A.B. Applicant

and ...........................................................................................C.D. Respondent

#### NOTICE TO TRUSTEES

TAKE NOTICE that relief has been claimed by the Applicant/Respondent in the above entitled proceedings pursuant to section(s) 12 and/or 13 of the Family Law Act, 1995 or section 17 of the Family Law (Divorce) Act, 1996 or section 8B of the Family Law (Maintenance of Spouses) Act, 1976 and in particular in relation to _____ [here insert details of pension in respect of which relief is claimed].

AND FURTHER TAKE NOTICE that any representations to be made to the Court pursuant to section 12(18) or section 13(2) of the 1995 Act or section 17(18) of the 1996 Act may be made by way of Affidavit of Representation to be filed and served on all parties herein within 28 days of the date of service of this Notice upon you.

Dated the day of _____20 ___.

Signed: _____

Solicitors for the Applicant/Respondent


To: The County Registrar

and

To: The Trustees of the pension scheme concerned

and

To: Applicant/Respondent [or solicitors where appropriate]

_____

## [Form No 8

### THE HIGH COURT
### FAMILY LAW

IN THE MATTER OF THE _____ACT 19____ (AS THE CASE MAY BE)
AND IN THE MATTER OF SECTION 40(5), CIVIL LIABILITY AND COURTS
ACT 2004

BETWEEN.................................................................................... A.B. Applicant

and.............................................................................................. C.D. Respondent

Request for Court's permission to be accompanied by a person at the hearing of proceedings

1. Name of party applying to be accompanied at hearing _____
   *Applicant/Respondent

2. Name and address of person who it is proposed will accompany the *Applicant/Respondent _____

3. Relationship or connection of person referred to in paragraph 2 to *Applicant/ Respondent (*e.g. parent, brother/sister/ family friend etc*)_____

4. *have/*have not previously obtained the permission of the Court to be accompanied in these proceedings. (If permission has previously been granted, give details of the person who was permitted to accompany you)_____

Dated: _____ 20____

Signed:_____

Applicant/Respondent][1]

---

**Notes**

1   Form No 8 was inserted by SI 247/2005.

---

**[SCHEDULE 2
APPENDIX II**

**Form No 1**
THE HIGH COURT

O. 70B, rr, 5, 16(5)

CIVIL PARTNERSHIP

[OR, AS THE CASE MAY BE, COHABITATION]

IN THE MATTER OF SECTION OF THE CIVIL PARTNERSHIP AND CERTAIN RIGHTS AND OBLIGATIONS OF COHABITANTS ACT 2010

BETWEEN/..................................................................................A.B. Applicant

And ...................................................................................C.D. Respondent

AFFIDAVIT OF MEANS

I,...................., ............... [insert occupation], of.............., aged 18 years and upwards MAKE OATH and say as follows:—

1. I say that I am the applicant/respondent [delete as appropriate] in the above entitled proceedings and I make this affidavit from facts within my own knowledge save where otherwise appears and where so appearing I believe the same to be true.

2. I say that I have set out in the First Schedule all the assets, property and financial resources to which I am legally or beneficially entitled and the manner in which such assets, property and financial resources are held.

3. I say that I have set out in the Second Schedule all income which I receive, including any income or benefits to which I am entitled by or under statute, and the source(s) of such income, and details of my current employment and employment prospects.

4. I say that I have set out in the Third Schedule all my debts, liabilities, financial obligations and financial responsibilities and, where relevant, the persons to whom such debts and liabilities are due.

5. I say that details of my regular outgoings have been set out in the Fourth Schedule.

6. I say that to the best of my knowledge, information and belief, all pension information known to me relevant to the within proceedings is set out in the Fifth Schedule. [Where information has been obtained from the trustees of the pension scheme concerned under the Pensions Act 1990, such information should be exhibited and where such information has not been obtained, the Deponent should depose to the reason(s) why such information has not been obtained].

FIRST SCHEDULE

[Here set out in numbered paragraphs all assets, property and financial resources whether held in the applicant's/respondents sole name or jointly with another, whether held legally or beneficially, the manner in which the assets are held, whether they are

733

subject to a mortgage or other charge or lien and such further and other details as are appropriate].

## SECOND SCHEDULE

[Here set out in numbered paragraphs all the deponent's income including any income or benefits to which the deponent is entitled by or under statute, and the source(s) of all such income, and details of the deponent's current employment, if any, and future employment prospects].

## THIRD SCHEDULE

[Here set out in numbered paragraphs all debts, liabilities, obligations and responsibilities of the deponent and, where relevant, the person to whom each such debt, liability, financial obligation or financial responsibility is due].

## FOURTH SCHEDULE

[Here set out full details of regular personal outings].

## FIFTH SCHEDULE

[Here full details of nature of pension scheme, benefits payable thereunder, normal pensionable age and period of reckonable service should be listed to the best of the deponents knowledge, information and belief].

SWORN etc.

**Form No 2**
THE HIGH COURT

O. 70B, rr, 6(6), 16(5)

CIVIL PARTNERSHIP
[OR, AS THE CASE MAY BE, COHABITATION]
IN THE MATTER OF PARAGRAPH (A) OF SECTION *56(1) **179(1) OF THE
CIVIL PARTNERSHIP AND CERTAIN RIGHTS AND OBLIGATIONS OF
COHABITANTS ACT 2010

BETWEEN .......................................................A.B. Applicant /Maintenance Creditor

and ...................................................................C.D.Respondent /Maintenance Debtor

STATEMENT AS TO EARNINGS

I,...................., ............... [insert occupation], of.............., aged 18 years and upwards say
as follows:—

1. I am the respondent /maintenance debtor [delete as appropriate] in the above entitled
proceedings.

2. I have set out in the First Schedule the name and address of every employer by whom
I am employed, together with particulars enabling each such employer to identify me,
and particulars of my earnings and expected earnings from each such employment and
other sources, my resources and needs.

FIRST SCHEDULE

†Name and address of Employer(s) ..................................................................................

(or trustee of a pension scheme under .............................................................................

which the maintenance debtor is .......................................................................................

receiving periodical pension benefits).............................................................................

Commencement date. ........................................................................................................

Nature of work...................................................................................................................

Place of work.....................................................................................................................

Weekly earnings ................................................................................................................

Expected changes to weekly earnings ..............................................................................

Employee/contractor identification ..................................................................................

number/code (if any) .........................................................................................................

PPS number .......................................................................................................................

‡Income from any other sources.................................................................................

Nature of income...........................................................................................................

Source...........................................................................................................................

Identification/account number/code (if any)................................................................

Weekly income .............................................................................................................

‡Financial resources.....................................................................................................

Nature of resource........................................................................................................

Location (e.g. bank account) .......................................................................................

Gross value...................................................................................................................


Needs...........................................................................................................................

[Here set out full details of regular personal outings]................................................


Dated the_____ day of _____ 20____


Signed:_____


\*       For civil partnership law proceedings

\*\*      For cohabitation proceedings

†       Repeat for each separate employer, pension provider, or for income as self-employed

‡       Repeat for each separate income source or, as the case may be, resource

---

**Form No 3**

O. 70B, rr, 6(6), 16(5)

THE HIGH COURT

CIVIL PARTNERSHIP

[OR, AS THE CASE MAY BE, COHABITATION]

IN THE MATTER OF PARAGRAPH (A) OF SECTION *56(1) **179(1) OF THE CIVIL PARTNERSHIP AND CERTAIN RIGHTS AND OBLIGATIONS OF COHABITANTS ACT 2010

BETWEEN .....................................................A.B. Applicant /Maintenance Creditor

and ............................................................. C.D. Respondent /Maintenance Debtor

STATEMENT AS TO EARNINGS

I,...................., ............... [insert occupation], of.............., aged 18 years and upwards say as follows:—

1. I am the employer of the maintenance debtor in the above entitled proceedings (or a trustee of a pension scheme under which the maintenance debtor is receiving periodical pension benefits).

2. I certify the following particulars of the maintenance debtor:

FIRST SCHEDULE

Name and address of Employer(s) ..............................................................................

(or trustees)..............................................................................................................

Commencement date. ...............................................................................................

Nature of work..........................................................................................................

Place of work............................................................................................................

Weekly earnings .......................................................................................................

Expected changes to weekly earnings .......................................................................

Employee/contractor identification number/code (if any)
of the maintenance debtor ........................................................................................

P.P.S. number of the maintenance debtor................................................................ .

Dated: _____20_____

Signed _____

\*       For civil partnership law proceedings

\*\*      For cohabitation proceedings

737

**Form No 4**
## THE HIGH COURT

O. 70B, rr, 7(1), 8(3), 16(5)

### CIVIL PARTNERSHIP
[OR, AS THE CASE MAY BE, COHABITATION]
## IN THE MATTER OF SECTION OF THE CIVIL PARTNERSHIP AND CERTAIN RIGHTS AND OBLIGATIONS OF COHABITANTS ACT 2010

BETWEEN.................................................................................. A.B. Applicant

and.............................................................................................. C.D. Respondent

### NOTICE TO TRUSTEES

TAKE NOTICE that relief has been claimed by the applicant/respondent in the above entitled proceedings pursuant to the Civil Partnership and Certain Rights and Obligations of Cohabitants Act 2010 and in particular in relation to................. [here insert details of pension in respect of which relief is claimed].

AND FURTHER TAKE NOTICE that

†any representations to be made to the Court may be made by way of affidavit of representation to be filed and served on all parties herein within 28 days of the date of service of this notice upon you

†a request will be made to the court for you to provide the calculations referred to in section *126(2) **section 192 of the said Act.


Dated the_____ day of _____ 20____


Signed:_____

      Solicitors for the Applicant/Respondent

To: _____

      The Trustees of the pension scheme concerned

      and

      To: Applicant/Respondent [or solicitors where appropriate]

†    Delete where inapplicable

*    For civil partnership law proceedings

**   For cohabitation proceedings][1]


**NOTES**

1   Appendix II inserted by SI 348/2011.

# ORDER 133[1]

## CHILD ABDUCTION AND ENFORCEMENT OF CUSTODY ORDERS

Rule 1: For the purposes of this Order:

"the Act" means the Child Abduction and Enforcement of Custody Orders Act, 1991;

"the Hague Convention" means the Convention on the Civil Aspects of International Child Abduction, signed at the Hague on the 25th day of October, 1980 and set out in the First Schedule to the Act;

"The Luxembourg Convention" means the European Convention on Recognition and Enforcement of Decisions concerning Custody of Children and on Restoration of Custody of Children, signed at Luxembourg on the 20th day of May, 1980 and set out in the Second Schedule to the Act;

"Contracting State" means a State as defined by section 3 or section 17 of the Act, as the case may be;

"The Central Authority" means the Central Authority appointed by the Minister pursuant to section 8 or section 22 of the Act, as the case may be.

"Regulation No. 2201/2003" means Council Regulation (EC) No. 2201/2003 of 27 November 2003 (O.J. L. 338/1) concerning jurisdiction and the recognition and enforcement of judgments in matrimonial matters and the matters of parental responsibility.

References in this Order to the Hague Convention shall, where the context requires in relation to applications under the Hague Convention to which Regulation No. 2201/2003 relates, be deemed to include references to Regulation No. 2201/2003.

Rule 2:

(1) Any applications made pursuant to section 9(2), section 10(2), section 11, section 15, section 24 (2) or section 25 of the Act shall be brought by way of special summons which shall be a family law summons and shall be entitled:

" The High Court

Family Law,

In the Matter of the Child Abduction and Enforcement of Custody Orders Act, 1991 and In the Matter of the [X] Convention (as the case may be)

and In the Matter of [X], a minor,

Between

AB,

the applicant,

And

CD, the respondent".

Where an application under section 9(2) or section 10(2) of the Act is one to which Article 11 of Regulation No. 2201/2003 applies, the summons shall additionally be entitled "And in the matter of Council Regulation No. 2201/2003 (EC)."

(2) Where applications are brought by the Central Authority, the applicant shall be referred to as "the Minister for Justice, Equality and Law Reform, as the Central Authority for Ireland, ex parte (the applicant)".

(3) The indorsement of claim shall be entitled "Special Indorsement of Claim" and state, with all necessary particulars, the relief sought, each section of the Act under which the relief is sought and the grounds upon which the relief is sought. The indorsement shall, where possible, specify:

- (a) the name and (where available) the date of birth of the minor;

- (b) if known, the date on which the disputed removal or retention of the minor occurred;

- (c) the name of the minor's parents or guardians;

- (d) details of any decision relating to custody or access which is sought to be recognised or enforced;

- (e) the interest of the applicant in the matter;

- (f) the identity of the person alleged to have removed the minor and, if different, of the person with whom the minor is alleged to be;

- (g) the believed whereabouts of the minor.

Rule 3:

(1) In any proceeding pursuant to rule 2(1) above, an affidavit verifying such proceeding shall have regard to the matters specified in Article 8 of the Hague Convention and Article 13 of the Luxembourg Convention, as the case may be, and shall, where possible, be accompanied by all relevant documentation including that listed in Article 8 of the Hague Convention or Article 13 of the Luxembourg Convention, as the case may be.

(2) Notwithstanding the provisions of Order 38 rule 1, the special summons when issued shall be returnable before the Court. Proper proof of service shall be made available to the Court on the return date.

Rule 4:

(1) A respondent may deliver a replying affidavit and such replying affidavit shall be served on the applicant within seven days of the grounding affidavit having been served upon the respondent.

(2) The replying affidavit shall set out all grounds of defence being relied upon in opposition to the applicant's application.

(3) The applicant may file a further affidavit replying to any issue or matter raised by the respondent within seven days after the service upon the applicant of the respondent's affidavit.

Rule 5:

(1) The Court shall, at the earliest opportunity, give such directions as are necessary to provide for an expeditious hearing of the matter and all parties shall comply therewith.

(2) Applications shall be heard on the basis of affidavit evidence only. The Court, at its discretion, may, in exceptional circumstances, direct or permit oral evidence to be adduced.

Rule 6:

(1) Where an application is about to be made to the Court under Part II or Part III of the Act, the applicant may apply to the Court, pursuant to section 12(1), 12(2), 26(1) or 26(2) of the Act for interim directions.

(2) An application pursuant to section 12(2) or 26(2) may be made ex parte to the Court in any case where interim directions are required in a case of urgency. Such an application shall be heard on affidavit unless the Court otherwise directs. Where any oral evidence is heard by the Court in the course of any such application ex parte, a note of such evidence shall be prepared by the applicant or the applicant's solicitor and approved by the Court and shall be served upon the respondent forthwith together with a copy of the order made, if any, unless otherwise directed by the Court.

(3) Where a special summons has issued and been served, an application brought pursuant to section 12(1) or 26(1) of the Act shall be brought by notice of motion to the Court. Such notice shall be served upon the other party to the proceeding seven days before the return date and shall specify the directions or relief sought from the Court. The said notice shall be grounded upon the affidavit of the party concerned.

(4) Any application brought under the Act (not being an application mentioned in rule 2(1)) shall be brought by motion on notice in the proceedings.

Rule 7:

(1) An application made pursuant to section 31(1) of the Act shall be brought by way of notice of motion seeking the variation or revocation of the order of recognition or enforcement previously made by the Court. The said application shall be grounded upon affidavit served seven days before the return date. The said affidavit shall be accompanied by the documentation referred to at Article 13 of the Luxembourg Convention.

Rule 8:

(1) Where an application is made pursuant to section 36(3) of the Act, the said application shall be brought by way of an originating notice of motion. The said notice of motion shall be entitled:

"The High Court

Family Law,

In the Matter of Section 36(3) of the Child Abduction and Enforcement of Custody Orders Act, 1991

And in the matter of Foreign Proceedings entitled or to be entitled" "(as the case may be)."

(2) The said notice of motion shall be grounded on affidavit sworn by the applicant setting out:

    (a)  the applicant's interest in the matter;

(b)  the manner in which the minor has been taken from or sent or kept out of the State without the consent of any of the persons having the right to determine the child's place of residence under the law of that State;

(c)  the persons within the jurisdiction of the Court who may have relevant information;

(d)  the grounds for believing that the said persons may have relevant information;

(e)  the nature of the relevant information in respect of which an order for disclosure is sought.

Rule 9: The provisions of Order 119, rules 2 and 3 solely insofar as they relate to the wearing of a wig and gown shall not apply to any proceedings under this Order.

Rule 10: Where the Court makes an order of non-return pursuant to Article 13 of the Hague Convention in a case to which Article 11 of Regulation No. 2201/2003 applies, the Registrar shall cause the transmission, through the Central Authority, to the court with jurisdiction or central authority in the Member State of the European Union where the child was habitually resident before the wrongful removal or retention, of the documents specified in Article 11(6) of Regulation No. 2201/2003.

Rule 11:

(1) Where the Central Authority receives documents specified in Article 11(6) of Regulation No. 2201/2003 in respect of an order of non-return pursuant to Article 13 of the Hague Convention made concerning a child who was habitually resident in the State before his or her wrongful removal or retention, and no proceedings are in being before a Court in the State concerning the custody of or access to the child, the Central Authority shall issue an originating notice of motion entitled:

"The High Court

Family Law

In the Matter of Article 11(6) of Regulation No. 2201/2003

And In the Matter of the Foreign Proceedings entitled."

(2) The said originating notice of motion shall be grounded on an affidavit exhibiting the documents received pursuant to Article 11(6) of Regulation No. 2201/2003 and shall seek the directions of the Court for the purposes of Article 11(7) of Regulation No. 2201/2003. The originating notice of motion shall be served on the parties referred to in Article 11(7) of Regulation No. 2201/2003.

(3) Where the Central Authority receives documents specified in Article 11(6) of Regulation No. 2201/2003 in respect of an order of non-return pursuant to Article 13 of the Hague Convention made concerning a child who was habitually resident in the State before his or her wrongful removal or retention, and proceedings are in being before the Court concerning the custody of or access to the child, the Central Authority shall transmit the said documents to the appropriate office of the High Court or, as the case may be, to the Supreme Court Office.

(4) Where the Court receives documents specified in Article 11(6) of Regulation No. 2201/2003 in respect of an order of non-return pursuant to Article 13 of the Hague

Convention made concerning a child who was habitually resident in the State before his or her wrongful removal or retention (whether under sub-rule (3) of this rule or otherwise), and proceedings are in being before a Court in the State concerning the custody of or access to the child, the Court shall (i) if such proceedings are in being before the High Court or Supreme Court, cause the Registrar to transmit copies of such documents to the parties to those proceedings by registered post or in such other manner as the Court may direct or (ii) if such proceedings are in being before another court in the State, cause the Registrar to transmit such documents to the appropriate office of that court.

(5) Where the Court receives documents specified in Article 11(6) of Regulation No. 2201/2003 in respect of an order of non-return pursuant to Article 13 of the Hague Convention made concerning a child who was habitually resident in the State before his or her wrongful removal or retention, and no proceedings are in being before any Court in the State, concerning the custody of or access to the child, the Court shall cause the Registrar to transmit copies of such documents to the persons appearing to have an interest in such order by registered post or in such other manner as the Court may direct. Such persons shall also be notified of a date, within three months of the receipt of such documents, when the matter of the child shall be listed before the Court and any submissions by or on behalf of such persons heard. The title employed in proceedings in respect of the matter shall be the same title as in proceedings to which sub-rule (1) of this rule applies. Copies of the documents and notification referred to shall also be provided to the Central Authority, which shall be at liberty to appear and to apply to be heard on the date on which the matter of the child is listed before the Court. However, nothing in this rule shall be interpreted as requiring the Central Authority to appear or otherwise to participate in the matter or in any such proceedings.Rules of the Superior Courts (No 1) (Child Abduction and Enforcement of Custody Orders Act, 1991), 2001

**Notes**

1   Commencement: 13 July 2001.

# Part 4: European Union Legislation

# Council Regulation (EC) No 2201/2003

## of 27 November 2003 concerning jurisdiction and the recognition and enforcement of judgments in matrimonial matters and the matters of parental responsibility, repealing Regulation (EC) No 1347/2000

THE COUNCIL OF THE EUROPEAN UNION,

Having regard to the Treaty establishing the European Community, and in particular Article 61(c) and Article 67(1) thereof,

Having regard to the proposal from the Commission[1],

Having regard to the opinion of the European Parliament[2],

Having regard to the opinion of the European Economic and Social Committee[3],

Whereas:

(1) The European Community has set the objective creating an area of freedom, security and justice, in which the free movement of persons is ensured. To this end, the Community is to adopt, among others, measures in the field of judicial cooperation in civil matters that are necessary for the proper functioning the internal market.

(2) The Tampere European Council endorsed the principle of mutual recognition of judicial decisions as the cornerstone for the creation of a genuine judicial area, and identified visiting rights as a priority.

(3) Council Regulation (EC) No 1347/2000[4] sets out rules on jurisdiction, recognition and enforcement of judgments in matrimonial matters and matters of parental responsibility for the children of both spouses rendered on the occasion of the matrimonial proceedings. The content of this Regulation was substantially taken over from the Convention of 28 May 1998 on the same subject matter.[5]

(4) On 3 July 2000 France presented an initiative for a Council Regulation on the mutual enforcement of judgments on rights of access to children.[6]

(5) In order to ensure equality for all children, this Regulation covers all decisions on parental responsibility, including measures for the protection of the child, independently of any link with a matrimonial proceeding.

(6) Since the application of the rules on parental responsibility often arises in the context of matrimonial proceedings, it is more appropriate to have a single instrument for matters of divorce and parental responsibility.

(7) The scope of this Regulation covers civil matters, whatever the nature of the court or tribunal.

(8) As regards judgments on divorce, legal separation or marriage annulment, this Regulation should apply only to the dissolution of matrimonial ties and should not deal with issues such as the grounds for divorce, property consequences of the marriage or any other ancillary measures.

(9) As regards the property of the child, this Regulation should apply only to measures for the protection of the child, i.e. (i) the designation and functions of a person or body

having charge of the child's property, representing or assisting the child, and (ii) the administration, conservation or disposal of the child's property. In this context, this Regulation should, for instance, apply in cases where the parents are in dispute as regards the administration of the child's property. Measures relating to the child's property which do not concern the protection of the child should continue to be governed by Council Regulation (EC) No 44/2001 of 22 December 2000 on jurisdiction and the recognition and enforcement of judgments in civil and commercial matters.[7]

(10) This Regulation is not intended to apply to matters relating to social security, public measures of a general nature in matters of education or health or to decisions on the right of asylum and on immigration. In addition it does not apply to the establishment of parenthood, since this is a different matter from the attribution of parental responsibility, nor to other questions linked to the status of persons. Moreover, it does not apply to measures taken as a result of criminal offences committed by children.

(11) Maintenance obligations are excluded from the scope of this Regulation as these are already covered by Council Regulation No 44/2001. The courts having jurisdiction under this Regulation will generally have jurisdiction to rule on maintenance obligations by application of Article 5(2) of Council Regulation No 44/2001.

(12) The grounds of jurisdiction in matters of parental responsibility established in the present Regulation are shaped in the light of the best interests of the child, in particular on the criterion of proximity. This means that jurisdiction should lie in the first place with the Member State of the child's habitual residence, except for certain cases of a change in the child's residence or pursuant to an agreement between the holders of parental responsibility.

(13) In the interest of the child, this Regulation allows, by way of exception and under certain conditions, that the court having jurisdiction may transfer a case to a court of another Member State if this court is better placed to hear the case. However, in this case the second court should not be allowed to transfer the case to a third court.

(14) This Regulation should have effect without prejudice to the application of public international law concerning diplomatic immunities. Where jurisdiction under this Regulation cannot be exercised by reason of the existence of diplomatic immunity in accordance with international law, jurisdiction should be exercised in accordance with national law in a Member State in which the person concerned does not enjoy such immunity.

(15) Council Regulation (EC) No 1348/2000 of 29 May 2000 on the service in the Member States of judicial and extrajudicial documents in civil or commercial matters[8] should apply to the service of documents in proceedings instituted pursuant to this Regulation.

(16) This Regulation should not prevent the courts of a Member State from taking provisional, including protective measures, in urgent cases, with regard to persons or property situated in that State.

(17) In cases of wrongful removal or retention of a child, the return of the child should be obtained without delay, and to this end the Hague Convention of 25 October 1980 would continue to apply as complemented by the provisions of this Regulation, in particular

Article 11. The courts of the Member State to or in which the child has been wrongfully removed or retained should be able to oppose his or her return in specific, duly justified cases. However, such a decision could be replaced by a subsequent decision by the court of the Member State of habitual residence of the child prior to the wrongful removal or retention. Should that judgment entail the return of the child, the return should take place without any special procedure being required for recognition and enforcement of that judgment in the Member State to or in which the child has been removed or retained.

(18) Where a court has decided not to return a child on the basis of Article 13 of the 1980 Hague Convention, it should inform the court having jurisdiction or central authority in the Member State where the child was habitually resident prior to the wrongful removal or retention. Unless the court in the latter Member State has been seised, this court or the central authority should notify the parties. This obligation should not prevent the central authority from also notifying the relevant public authorities in accordance with national law.

(19) The hearing of the child plays an important role in the application of this Regulation, although this instrument is not intended to modify national procedures applicable.

(20) The hearing of a child in another Member State may take place under the arrangements laid down in Council Regulation (EC) No 1206/2001 of 28 May 2001 on cooperation between the courts of the Member States in the taking of evidence in civil or commercial matters.[9]

(21) The recognition and enforcement of judgments given in a Member State should be based on the principle of mutual trust and the grounds for non-recognition should be kept to the minimum required.

(22) Authentic instruments and agreements between parties that are enforceable in one Member State should be treated as equivalent to 'judgments' for the purpose of the application of the rules on recognition and enforcement.

(23) The Tampere European Council considered in its conclusions (point 34) that judgments in the field of family litigation should be 'automatically recognised throughout the Union without any intermediate proceedings or grounds for refusal of enforcement'. This is why judgments on rights of access and judgments on return that have been certified in the Member State of origin in accordance with the provisions of this Regulation should be recognised and enforceable in all other Member States without any further procedure being required. Arrangements for the enforcement of such judgments continue to be governed by national law.

(24) The certificate issued to facilitate enforcement of the judgment should not be subject to appeal. It should be rectified only where there is a material error, i.e. where it does not correctly reflect the judgment.

(25) Central authorities should cooperate both in general matter and in specific cases, including for purposes of promoting the amicable resolution of family disputes, in matters of parental responsibility. To this end central authorities shall participate in the European Judicial Network in civil and commercial matters created by Council Decision

2001/470/EC of 28 May 2001 establishing a European Judicial Network in civil and commercial matters.[10]

(26) The Commission should make publicly available and update the lists of courts and redress procedures communicated by the Member States.

(27) The measures necessary for the implementation of this Regulation should be adopted in accordance with Council Decision 1999/468/EC of 28 June 1999 laying down the procedures for the exercise of implementing powers conferred on the Commission.[11]

(28) This Regulation replaces Regulation (EC) No 1347/2000 which is consequently repealed.

(29) For the proper functioning of this Regulation, the Commission should review its application and propose such amendments as may appear necessary.

(30) The United Kingdom and Ireland, in accordance with Article 3 of the Protocol on the position of the United Kingdom and Ireland annexed to the Treaty on European Union and the Treaty establishing the European Community, have given notice of their wish to take part in the adoption and application of this Regulation.

(31) Denmark, in accordance with Articles 1 and 2 of the Protocol on the position of Denmark annexed to the Treaty on European Union and the Treaty establishing the European Community, is not participating in the adoption of this Regulation and is therefore not bound by it nor subject to its application.

(32) Since the objectives of this Regulation cannot be sufficiently achieved by the Member States and can therefore be better achieved at Community level, the Community may adopt measures, in accordance with the principle of subsidiarity as set out in Article 5 of the Treaty. In accordance with the principle of proportionality, as set out in that Article, this Regulation does not go beyond what is necessary in order to achieve those objectives.

(33) This Regulation recognises the fundamental rights and observes the principles of the Charter of Fundamental Rights of the European Union. In particular, it seeks to ensure respect for the fundamental rights of the child as set out in Article 24 of the Charter of Fundamental Rights of the European Union,

HAS ADOPTED THE PRESENT REGULATION:

---

**Notes**

1   OJ C 203 E, 27.8.2002, p. 155.

2   Opinion delivered on 20 September 2002 (not yet published in the Official Journal).

3   OJ C 61, 14.3.2003, p. 76.

4   OJ L 160, 30.6.2000, p. 19.

5   At the time of the adoption of Regulation (EC) No 1347/2000, the Council took note of the explanatory report concerning that Convention prepared by Professor Alegria Borras (OJ C 221, 16.7.1998, p. 27).

6   OJ C 234, 15.8.2000, p. 7.

7   OJ L 12, 16.1.2001, p. 1. Regulation as last amended by Commission Regulation (EC) No 1496/2002 (OJ L 225, 22.8.2002, p. 13).

8   OJ L 160, 30.6.2000, p. 37.

9   OJ L 174, 27.6.2001, p. 1.

10  OJ L 174, 27.6.2001, p. 25.

11  OJ L 184, 17.7.1999, p. 23.

# CHAPTER I

## SCOPE AND DEFINITIONS

*Article 1*

### Scope

1. This Regulation shall apply, whatever the nature of the court or tribunal, in civil matters relating to:

   (a)  divorce, legal separation or marriage annulment;

   (b)  the attribution, exercise, delegation, restriction or termination of parental responsibility.

2. The matters referred to in paragraph 1(b) may, in particular, deal with:

   (a)  rights of custody and rights of access;

   (b)  guardianship, curatorship and similar institutions;

   (c)  the designation and functions of any person or body having charge of the child's person or property, representing or assisting the child;

   (d)  the placement of the child in a foster family or in institutional care;

   (e)  measures for the protection of the child relating to the administration, conservation or disposal of the child's property.

3. This Regulation shall not apply to:

   (a)  the establishment or contesting of a parent-child relationship;

   (b)  decisions on adoption, measures preparatory to adoption, or the annulment or revocation of adoption;

   (c)  the name and forenames of the child;

   (d)  emancipation;

   (e)  maintenance obligations;

   (f)  trusts or succession;

   (g)  measures taken as a result of criminal offences committed by children.

*Article 2*

### Definitions

For the purposes of this Regulation:

1. the term '**court**' shall cover all the authorities in the Member States with jurisdiction in the matters falling within the scope of this Regulation pursuant to Article 1;

2. the term '**judge**' shall mean the judge or an official having powers equivalent to those of a judge in the matters falling within the scope of the Regulation;

3. the term '**Member State**' shall mean all Member States with the exception of Denmark;

4. the term '**judgment**' shall mean a divorce, legal separation or marriage annulment, as well as a judgment relating to parental responsibility, pronounced by a court of a Member State, whatever the judgment may be called, including a decree, order or decision;

5. the term '**Member State of origin**' shall mean the Member State where the judgment to be enforced was issued;

6. the term '**Member State of enforcement**' shall mean the Member State where enforcement of the judgment is sought;

7. the term '**parental responsibility**' shall mean all rights and duties relating to the person or the property of a child which are given to a natural or legal person by judgment, by operation of law or by an agreement having legal effect. The term shall include rights of custody and rights of access;

8. the term '**holder of parental responsibility**' shall mean any person having parental responsibility over a child;

9. the term '**rights of custody**' shall include rights and duties relating to the care of the person of a child, and in particular the right to determine the child's place of residence;

10. the term '**rights of access**' shall include in particular the right to take a child to a place other than his or her habitual residence for a limited period of time;

11. the term '**wrongful removal or retention**' shall mean a child's removal or retention where:

    (a) it is in breach of rights of custody acquired by judgment or by operation of law or by an agreement having legal effect under the law of the Member State where the child was habitually resident immediately before the removal or retention;

    and

    (b) provided that, at the time of removal or retention, the rights of custody were actually exercised, either jointly or alone, or would have been so exercised but for the removal or retention. Custody shall be considered to be exercised jointly when, pursuant to a judgment or by operation of law, one holder of parental responsibility cannot decide on the child's place of residence without the consent of another holder of parental responsibility.

# CHAPTER II

JURISDICTION

*Section 1*

**Divorce, legal separation and marriage annulment**

*Article 3*

**General jurisdiction**

1. In matters relating to divorce, legal separation or marriage annulment, jurisdiction shall lie with the courts of the Member State

    (a)  in whose territory:

       — the spouses are habitually resident, or

       — the spouses were last habitually resident, insofar as one of them still resides there, or

       — the respondent is habitually resident, or

       — in the event of a joint application, either of the spouses is habitually resident, or

       — the applicant is habitually resident if he or she resided there for at least a year immediately before the application was made, or

       — the applicant is habitually resident if he or she resided there for at least six months immediately before the application was made and is either a national of the Member State in question or, in the case of the United Kingdom and Ireland, has his or her 'domicile' there;

    (b)  of the nationality of both spouses or, in the case of the United Kingdom and Ireland, of the 'domicile' of both spouses.

2. For the purpose of this Regulation, '**domicile**' shall have the same meaning as it has under the legal systems of the United Kingdom and Ireland.

*Article 4*

**Counterclaim**

The court in which proceedings are pending on the basis of Article 3 shall also have jurisdiction to examine a counterclaim, insofar as the latter comes within the scope of this Regulation.

*Article 5*

**Conversion of legal separation into divorce**

Without prejudice to Article 3, a court of a Member State that has given a judgment on a legal separation shall also have jurisdiction for converting that judgment into a divorce, if the law of that Member State so provides.

*Article 6*

**Exclusive nature of jurisdiction under Articles 3, 4 and 5**

A spouse who:

    (a)  is habitually resident in the territory of a Member State; or

(b) is a national of a Member State, or, in the case of the United Kingdom and Ireland, has his or her 'domicile' in the territory of one of the latter Member States,

may be sued in another Member State only in accordance with Articles 3, 4 and 5.

## Article 7

### Residual jurisdiction

1. Where no court of a Member State has jurisdiction pursuant to Articles 3, 4 and 5, jurisdiction shall be determined, in each Member State, by the laws of that State.

2. As against a respondent who is not habitually resident and is not either a national of a Member State or, in the case of the United Kingdom and Ireland, does not have his 'domicile' within the territory of one of the latter Member States, any national of a Member State who is habitually resident within the territory of another Member State may, like the nationals of that State, avail himself of the rules of jurisdiction applicable in that State.

## Section 2

### Parental responsibility

## Article 8

### General jurisdiction

1. The courts of a Member State shall have jurisdiction in matters of parental responsibility over a child who is habitually resident in that Member State at the time the court is seised.

2. Paragraph 1 shall be subject to the provisions of Articles 9, 10 and 12.

## Article 9

### Continuing jurisdiction of the child's former habitual residence

1. Where a child moves lawfully from one Member State to another and acquires a new habitual residence there, the courts of the Member State of the child's former habitual residence shall, by way of exception to Article 8, retain jurisdiction during a three-month period following the move for the purpose of modifying a judgment on access rights issued in that Member State before the child moved, where the holder of access rights pursuant to the judgment on access rights continues to have his or her habitual residence in the Member State of the child's former habitual residence.

2. Paragraph 1 shall not apply if the holder of access rights referred to in paragraph 1 has accepted the jurisdiction of the courts of the Member State of the child's new habitual residence by participating in proceedings before those courts without contesting their jurisdiction.

## Article 10

### Jurisdiction in cases of child abduction

In case of wrongful removal or retention of the child, the courts of the Member State where the child was habitually resident immediately before the wrongful removal or retention shall retain their jurisdiction until the child has acquired a habitual residence in another Member State and:

(a) each person, institution or other body having rights of custody has acquiesced in the removal or retention;

or

(b) the child has resided in that other Member State for a period of at least one year after the person, institution or other body having rights of custody has had or should have had knowledge of the whereabouts of the child and the child is settled in his or her new environment and at least one of the following conditions is met:

  (i) within one year after the holder of rights of custody has had or should have had knowledge of the whereabouts of the child, no request for return has been lodged before the competent authorities of the Member State where the child has been removed or is being retained;

  (ii) a request for return lodged by the holder of rights of custody has been withdrawn and no new request has been lodged within the time limit set in paragraph (i);

  (iii) a case before the court in the Member State where the child was habitually resident immediately before the wrongful removal or retention has been closed pursuant to Article 11(7);

  (iv) a judgment on custody that does not entail the return of the child has been issued by the courts of the Member State where the child was habitually resident immediately before the wrongful removal or retention.

*Article 11*

**Return of the child**

1. Where a person, institution or other body having rights of custody applies to the competent authorities in a Member State to deliver a judgment on the basis of the Hague Convention of 25 October 1980 on the Civil Aspects of International Child Abduction (hereinafter 'the 1980 Hague Convention'), in order to obtain the return of a child that has been wrongfully removed or retained in a Member State other than the Member State where the child was habitually resident immediately before the wrongful removal or retention, paragraphs 2 to 8 shall apply.

2. When applying Articles 12 and 13 of the 1980 Hague Convention, it shall be ensured that the child is given the opportunity to be heard during the proceedings unless this appears inappropriate having regard to his or her age or degree of maturity.

3. A court to which an application for return of a child is made as mentioned in paragraph 1 shall act expeditiously in proceedings on the application, using the most expeditious procedures available in national law.

Without prejudice to the first subparagraph, the court shall, except where exceptional circumstances make this impossible, issue its judgment no later than six weeks after the application is lodged.

4. A court cannot refuse to return a child on the basis of Article 13b of the 1980 Hague Convention if it is established that adequate arrangements have been made to secure the protection of the child after his or her return.

5. A court cannot refuse to return a child unless the person who requested the return of the child has been given an opportunity to be heard.

6. If a court has issued an order on non-return pursuant to Article 13 of the 1980 Hague Convention, the court must immediately either directly or through its central authority, transmit a copy of the court order on non-return and of the relevant documents, in particular a transcript of the hearings before the court, to the court with jurisdiction or central authority in the Member State where the child was habitually resident immediately before the wrongful removal or retention, as determined by national law. The court shall receive all the mentioned documents within one month of the date of the non-return order.

7. Unless the courts in the Member State where the child was habitually resident immediately before the wrongful removal or retention have already been seised by one of the parties, the court or central authority that receives the information mentioned in paragraph 6 must notify it to the parties and invite them to make submissions to the court, in accordance with national law, within three months of the date of notification so that the court can examine the question of custody of the child.

Without prejudice to the rules on jurisdiction contained in this Regulation, the court shall close the case if no submissions have been received by the court within the time limit.

8. Notwithstanding a judgment of non-return pursuant to Article 13 of the 1980 Hague Convention, any subsequent judgment which requires the return of the child issued by a court having jurisdiction under this Regulation shall be enforceable in accordance with Section 4 of Chapter III below in order to secure the return of the child.

## *Article 12*

### Prorogation of jurisdiction

1. The courts of a Member State exercising jurisdiction by virtue of Article 3 on an application for divorce, legal separation or marriage annulment shall have jurisdiction in any matter relating to parental responsibility connected with that application where:

(a) at least one of the spouses has parental responsibility in relation to the child; and

(b) the jurisdiction of the courts has been accepted expressly or otherwise in an unequivocal manner by the spouses and by the holders of parental responsibility, at the time the court is seised, and is in the superior interests of the child.

2. The jurisdiction conferred in paragraph 1 shall cease as soon as:

(a) the judgment allowing or refusing the application for divorce, legal separation or marriage annulment has become final;

(b) in those cases where proceedings in relation to parental responsibility are still pending on the date referred to in (a), a judgment in these proceedings has become final;

(c)  the proceedings referred to in (a) and (b) have come to an end for another reason.

3. The courts of a Member State shall also have jurisdiction in relation to parental responsibility in proceedings other than those referred to in paragraph 1 where:

(a)  the child has a substantial connection with that Member State, in particular by virtue of the fact that one of the holders of parental responsibility is habitually resident in that Member State or that the child is a national of that Member State;

and

(b)  the jurisdiction of the courts has been accepted expressly or otherwise in an unequivocal manner by all the parties to the proceedings at the time the court is seised and is in the best interests of the child.

4. Where the child has his or her habitual residence in the territory of a third State which is not a contracting party to the Hague Convention of 19 October 1996 on jurisdiction, applicable law, recognition, enforcement and cooperation in respect of parental responsibility and measures for the protection of children, jurisdiction under this Article shall be deemed to be in the child's interest, in particular if it is found impossible to hold proceedings in the third State in question.

*Article 13*

**Jurisdiction based on the child's presence**

1. Where a child's habitual residence cannot be established and jurisdiction cannot be determined on the basis of Article 12, the courts of the Member State where the child is present shall have jurisdiction.

2. Paragraph 1 shall also apply to refugee children or children internationally displaced because of disturbances occurring in their country.

*Article 14*

**Residual jurisdiction**

Where no court of a Member State has jurisdiction pursuant to Articles 8 to 13, jurisdiction shall be determined, in each Member State, by the laws of that State.

*Article 15*

**Transfer to a court better placed to hear the case**

1. By way of exception, the courts of a Member State having jurisdiction as to the substance of the matter may, if they consider that a court of another Member State, with which the child has a particular connection, would be better placed to hear the case, or a specific part thereof, and where this is in the best interests of the child:

(a)  stay the case or the part thereof in question and invite the parties to introduce a request before the court of that other Member State in accordance with paragraph 4; or

(b)  request a court of another Member State to assume jurisdiction in accordance with paragraph 5.

2. Paragraph 1 shall apply:

   (a) upon application from a party; or

   (b) of the court's own motion; or

   (c) upon application from a court of another Member State with which the child has a particular connection, in accordance with paragraph 3.

A transfer made of the court's own motion or by application of a court of another Member State must be accepted by at least one of the parties.

3. The child shall be considered to have a particular connection to a Member State as mentioned in paragraph 1, if that Member State:

   (a) has become the habitual residence of the child after the court referred to in paragraph 1 was seised; or

   (b) is the former habitual residence of the child; or

   (c) is the place of the child's nationality; or

   (d) is the habitual residence of a holder of parental responsibility; or

   (e) is the place where property of the child is located and the case concerns measures for the protection of the child relating to the administration, conservation or disposal of this property.

4. The court of the Member State having jurisdiction as to the substance of the matter shall set a time limit by which the courts of that other Member State shall be seised in accordance with paragraph 1.

If the courts are not seised by that time, the court which has been seised shall continue to exercise jurisdiction in accordance with Articles 8 to 14.

5. The courts of that other Member State may, where due to the specific circumstances of the case, this is in the best interests of the child, accept jurisdiction within six weeks of their seisure in accordance with paragraph 1(a) or 1(b). In this case, the court first seised shall decline jurisdiction. Otherwise, the court first seised shall continue to exercise jurisdiction in accordance with Articles 8 to 14.

6. The courts shall cooperate for the purposes of this Article, either directly or through the central authorities designated pursuant to Article 53.

### Section 3

**Common provisions**

*Article 16*

**Seising of a Court**

1. A court shall be deemed to be seised:

   (a) at the time when the document instituting the proceedings or an equivalent document is lodged with the court, provided that the applicant has not subsequently failed to take the steps he was required to take to have service effected on the respondent;

   or

(b) if the document has to be served before being lodged with the court, at the time when it is received by the authority responsible for service, provided that the applicant has not subsequently failed to take the steps he was required to take to have the document lodged with the court.

*Article 17*

**Examination as to jurisdiction**

Where a court of a Member State is seised of a case over which it has no jurisdiction under this Regulation and over which a court of another Member State has jurisdiction by virtue of this Regulation, it shall declare of its own motion that it has no jurisdiction.

*Article 18*

**Examination as to admissibility**

1. Where a respondent habitually resident in a State other than the Member State where the action was brought does not enter an appearance, the court with jurisdiction shall stay the proceedings so long as it is not shown that the respondent has been able to receive the document instituting the proceedings or an equivalent document in sufficient time to enable him to arrange for his defence, or that all necessary steps have been taken to this end.

2. Article 19 of Regulation (EC) No 1348/2000 shall apply instead of the provisions of paragraph 1 of this Article if the document instituting the proceedings or an equivalent document had to be transmitted from one Member State to another pursuant to that Regulation.

3. Where the provisions of Regulation (EC) No 1348/2000 are not applicable, Article 15 of the Hague Convention of 15 November 1965 on the service abroad of judicial and extrajudicial documents in civil or commercial matters shall apply if the document instituting the proceedings or an equivalent document had to be transmitted abroad pursuant to that Convention.

*Article 19*

**Lis pendens and dependent actions**

1. Where proceedings relating to divorce, legal separation or marriage annulment between the same parties are brought before courts of different Member States, the court second seised shall of its own motion stay its proceedings until such time as the jurisdiction of the court first seised is established.

2. Where proceedings relating to parental responsibility relating to the same child and involving the same cause of action are brought before courts of different Member States, the court second seised shall of its own motion stay its proceedings until such time as the jurisdiction of the court first seised is established.

3. Where the jurisdiction of the court first seised is established, the court second seised shall decline jurisdiction in favour of that court.

In that case, the party who brought the relevant action before the court second seised may bring that action before the court first seised.

## *Article 20*

### Provisional, including protective, measures

1. In urgent cases, the provisions of this Regulation shall not prevent the courts of a Member State from taking such provisional, including protective, measures in respect of persons or assets in that State as may be available under the law of that Member State, even if, under this Regulation, the court of another Member State has jurisdiction as to the substance of the matter.

2. The measures referred to in paragraph 1 shall cease to apply when the court of the Member State having jurisdiction under this Regulation as to the substance of the matter has taken the measures it considers appropriate.

# CHAPTER III

## RECOGNITION AND ENFORCEMENT

### *Section 1*

### Recognition

### *Article 21*

### Recognition of a judgment

1. A judgment given in a Member State shall be recognised in the other Member States without any special procedure being required.

2. In particular, and without prejudice to paragraph 3, no special procedure shall be required for updating the civil-status records of a Member State on the basis of a judgment relating to divorce, legal separation or marriage annulment given in another Member State, and against which no further appeal lies under the law of that Member State.

3. Without prejudice to Section 4 of this Chapter, any interested party may, in accordance with the procedures provided for in Section 2 of this Chapter, apply for a decision that the judgment be or not be recognised.

The local jurisdiction of the court appearing in the list notified by each Member State to the Commission pursuant to Article 68 shall be determined by the internal law of the Member State in which proceedings for recognition or non-recognition are brought.

4. Where the recognition of a judgment is raised as an incidental question in a court of a Member State, that court may determine that issue.

### *Article 22*

### Grounds of non-recognition for judgments relating to divorce, legal separation or marriage annulment

A judgment relating to a divorce, legal separation or marriage annulment shall not be recognised:

(a) if such recognition is manifestly contrary to the public policy of the Member State in which recognition is sought;

(b) where it was given in default of appearance, if the respondent was not served with the document which instituted the proceedings or with an equivalent document in sufficient time and in such a way as to enable the respondent to arrange for his or her defence unless it is determined that the respondent has accepted the judgment unequivocally;

(c) if it is irreconcilable with a judgment given in proceedings between the same parties in the Member State in which recognition is sought; or

(d) if it is irreconcilable with an earlier judgment given in another Member State or in a non-Member State between the same parties, provided that the earlier judgment fulfils the conditions necessary for its recognition in the Member State in which recognition is sought.

*Article 23*

**Grounds of non-recognition for judgments relating to parental responsibility**

A judgment relating to parental responsibility shall not be recognised:

(a) if such recognition is manifestly contrary to the public policy of the Member State in which recognition is sought taking into account the best interests of the child;

(b) if it was given, except in case of urgency, without the child having been given an opportunity to be heard, in violation of fundamental principles of procedure of the Member State in which recognition is sought;

(c) where it was given in default of appearance if the person in default was not served with the document which instituted the proceedings or with an equivalent document in sufficient time and in such a way as to enable that person to arrange for his or her defence unless it is determined that such person has accepted the judgment unequivocally;

(d) on the request of any person claiming that the judgment infringes his or her parental responsibility, if it was given without such person having been given an opportunity to be heard;

(e) if it is irreconcilable with a later judgment relating to parental responsibility given in the Member State in which recognition is sought;

(f) if it is irreconcilable with a later judgment relating to parental responsibility given in another Member State or in the non-Member State of the habitual residence of the child provided that the later judgment fulfils the conditions necessary for its recognition in the Member State in which recognition is sought.

or

(g) if the procedure laid down in Article 56 has not been complied with.

## Article 24

### Prohibition of review of jurisdiction of the court of origin

The jurisdiction of the court of the Member State of origin may not be reviewed. The test of public policy referred to in Articles 22(a) and 23(a) may not be applied to the rules relating to jurisdiction set out in Articles 3 to 14.

## Article 25

### Differences in applicable law

The recognition of a judgment may not be refused because the law of the Member State in which such recognition is sought would not allow divorce, legal separation or marriage annulment on the same facts.

## Article 26

### Non-review as to substance

Under no circumstances may a judgment be reviewed as to its substance.

## Article 27

### Stay of proceedings

1. A court of a Member State in which recognition is sought of a judgment given in another Member State may stay the proceedings if an ordinary appeal against the judgment has been lodged.

2. A court of a Member State in which recognition is sought of a judgment given in Ireland or the United Kingdom may stay the proceedings if enforcement is suspended in the Member State of origin by reason of an appeal.

## Section 2

### Application for a declaration of enforceability

## Article 28

### Enforceable judgments

1. A judgment on the exercise of parental responsibility in respect of a child given in a Member State which is enforceable in that Member State and has been served shall be enforced in another Member State when, on the application of any interested party, it has been declared enforceable there.

2. However, in the United Kingdom, such a judgment shall be enforced in England and Wales, in Scotland or in Northern Ireland only when, on the application of any interested party, it has been registered for enforcement in that part of the United Kingdom.

## Article 29

### Jurisdiction of local courts

1. An application for a declaration of enforceability shall be submitted to the court appearing in the list notified by each Member State to the Commission pursuant to Article 68.

2. The local jurisdiction shall be determined by reference to the place of habitual residence of the person against whom enforcement is sought or by reference to the habitual residence of any child to whom the application relates.

Where neither of the places referred to in the first subparagraph can be found in the Member State of enforcement, the local jurisdiction shall be determined by reference to the place of enforcement.

*Article 30*

**Procedure**

1. The procedure for making the application shall be governed by the law of the Member State of enforcement.

2. The applicant must give an address for service within the area of jurisdiction of the court applied to. However, if the law of the Member State of enforcement does not provide for the furnishing of such an address, the applicant shall appoint a representative *ad litem*.

3. The documents referred to in Articles 37 and 39 shall be attached to the application.

*Article 31*

**Decision of the court**

1. The court applied to shall give its decision without delay.

Neither the person against whom enforcement is sought, nor the child shall, at this stage of the proceedings, be entitled to make any submissions on the application.

2. The application may be refused only for one of the reasons specified in Articles 22, 23 and 24.

3. Under no circumstances may a judgment be reviewed as to its substance.

*Article 32*

**Notice of the decision**

The appropriate officer of the court shall without delay bring to the notice of the applicant the decision given on the application in accordance with the procedure laid down by the law of the Member State of enforcement.

*Article 33*

**Appeal against the decision**

1. The decision on the application for a declaration of enforceability may be appealed against by either party.

2. The appeal shall be lodged with the court appearing in the list notified by each Member State to the Commission pursuant to Article 68.

3. The appeal shall be dealt with in accordance with the rules governing procedure in contradictory matters.

4. If the appeal is brought by the applicant for a declaration of enforceability, the party against whom enforcement is sought shall be summoned to appear before the appellate court. If such person fails to appear, the provisions of Article 18 shall apply.

5. An appeal against a declaration of enforceability must be lodged within one month of service thereof. If the party against whom enforcement is sought is habitually resident in a Member State other than that in which the declaration of enforceability was given, the

time for appealing shall be two months and shall run from the date of service, either on him or at his residence. No extension of time may be granted on account of distance.

*Article 34*

**Courts of appeal and means of contest**

The judgment given on appeal may be contested only by the proceedings referred to in the list notified by each Member State to the Commission pursuant to Article 68.

*Article 35*

**Stay of proceedings**

1. The court with which the appeal is lodged under Articles 33 or 34 may, on the application of the party against whom enforcement is sought, stay the proceedings if an ordinary appeal has been lodged in the Member State of origin, or if the time for such appeal has not yet expired. In the latter case, the court may specify the time within which an appeal is to be lodged.

2. Where the judgment was given in Ireland or the United Kingdom, any form of appeal available in the Member State of origin shall be treated as an ordinary appeal for the purposes of paragraph 1.

*Article 36*

**Partial enforcement**

1. Where a judgment has been given in respect of several matters and enforcement cannot be authorised for all of them, the court shall authorise enforcement for one or more of them.

2. An applicant may request partial enforcement of a judgment.

*Section 3*

**Provisions common to Sections 1 and 2**

*Article 37*

**Documents**

1. A party seeking or contesting recognition or applying for a declaration of enforceability shall produce:

    (a)  a copy of the judgment which satisfies the conditions necessary to establish its authenticity;

    and

    (b)  the certificate referred to in Article 39.

2. In addition, in the case of a judgment given in default, the party seeking recognition or applying for a declaration of enforceability shall produce:

    (a)  the original or certified true copy of the document which establishes that the defaulting party was served with the document instituting the proceedings or with an equivalent document;

    or

(b) any document indicating that the defendant has accepted the judgment unequivocally.

## Article 38

### Absence of documents

1. If the documents specified in Article 37(1)(b) or (2) are not produced, the court may specify a time for their production, accept equivalent documents or, if it considers that it has sufficient information before it, dispense with their production.

2. If the court so requires, a translation of such documents shall be furnished. The translation shall be certified by a person qualified to do so in one of the Member States.

## Article 39

### Certificate concerning judgments in matrimonial matters and certificate concerning judgments on parental responsibility

The competent court or authority of a Member State of origin shall, at the request of any interested party, issue a certificate using the standard form set out in Annex I (judgments in matrimonial matters) or in Annex II (judgments on parental responsibility).

## Section 4

### Enforceability of certain judgments concerning rights of access and of certain judgments which require the return of the child

## Article 40

### Scope

1. This Section shall apply to:

   (a) rights of access; and

   (b) the return of a child entailed by a judgment given pursuant to Article 11(8).

2. The provisions of this Section shall not prevent a holder of parental responsibility from seeking recognition and enforcement of a judgment in accordance with the provisions in Sections 1 and 2 of this Chapter.

## Article 41

### Rights of access

1. The rights of access referred to in Article 40(1)(a) granted in an enforceable judgment given in a Member State shall be recognised and enforceable in another Member State without the need for a declaration of enforceability and without any possibility of opposing its recognition if the judgment has been certified in the Member State of origin in accordance with paragraph 2.

Even if national law does not provide for enforceability by operation of law of a judgment granting access rights, the court of origin may declare that the judgment shall be enforceable, notwithstanding any appeal.

2. The judge of origin shall issue the certificate referred to in paragraph 1 using the standard form in Annex III (certificate concerning rights of access) only if:

(a) where the judgment was given in default, the person defaulting was served with the document which instituted the proceedings or with an equivalent document in sufficient time and in such a way as to enable that person to arrange for his or her defense, or, the person has been served with the document but not in compliance with these conditions, it is nevertheless established that he or she accepted the decision unequivocally;

(b) all parties concerned were given an opportunity to be heard; and

(c) the child was given an opportunity to be heard, unless a hearing was considered inappropriate having regard to his or her age or degree of maturity.

The certificate shall be completed in the language of the judgment.

3. Where the rights of access involve a cross-border situation at the time of the delivery of the judgment, the certificate shall be issued ex officio when the judgment becomes enforceable, even if only provisionally. If the situation subsequently acquires a cross-border character, the certificate shall be issued at the request of one of the parties.

*Article 42*

**Return of the child**

1. The return of a child referred to in Article 40(1)(b) entailed by an enforceable judgment given in a Member State shall be recognised and enforceable in another Member State without the need for a declaration of enforceability and without any possibility of opposing its recognition if the judgment has been certified in the Member State of origin in accordance with paragraph 2.

Even if national law does not provide for enforceability by operation of law, notwithstanding any appeal, of a judgment requiring the return of the child mentioned in Article 11(b)(8), the court of origin may declare the judgment enforceable.

2. The judge of origin who delivered the judgment referred to in Article 40(1)(b) shall issue the certificate referred to in paragraph 1 only if:

(a) the child was given an opportunity to be heard, unless a hearing was considered inappropriate having regard to his or her age or degree of maturity;

(b) the parties were given an opportunity to be heard; and

(c) the court has taken into account in issuing its judgment the reasons for and evidence underlying the order issued pursuant to Article 13 of the 1980 Hague Convention.

In the event that the court or any other authority takes measures to ensure the protection of the child after its return to the State of habitual residence, the certificate shall contain details of such measures.

The judge of origin shall of his or her own motion issue that certificate using the standard form in Annex IV (certificate concerning return of the child(ren)).

The certificate shall be completed in the language of the judgment.

*Article 43*

## Rectification of the certificate

1. The law of the Member State of origin shall be applicable to any rectification of the certificate.

2. No appeal shall lie against the issuing of a certificate pursuant to Articles 41(1) or 42(1).

*Article 44*

## Effects of the certificate

The certificate shall take effect only within the limits of the enforceability of the judgment.

*Article 45*

## Documents

1. A party seeking enforcement of a judgment shall produce:

    (a)  a copy of the judgment which satisfies the conditions necessary to establish its authenticity;

    and

    (b)  the certificate referred to in Article 41(1) or Article 42(1).

2. For the purposes of this Article,

    —  the certificate referred to in Article 41(1) shall be accompanied by a translation of point 12 relating to the arrangements for exercising right of access,

    —  the certificate referred to in Article 42(1) shall be accompanied by a translation of its point 14 relating to the arrangements for implementing the measures taken to ensure the child's return.

The translation shall be into the official language or one of the official languages of the Member State of enforcement or any other language that the Member State of enforcement expressly accepts. The translation shall be certified by a person qualified to do so in one of the Member States.

*Section 5*

## Authentic instruments and agreements

*Article 46*

Documents which have been formally drawn up or registered as authentic instruments and are enforceable in one Member State and also agreements between the parties that are enforceable in the Member State in which they were concluded shall be recognised and declared enforceable under the same conditions as judgments.

*Section 6*

## Other provisions

*Article 47*

## Enforcement procedure

1. The enforcement procedure is governed by the law of the Member State of enforcement.

2. Any judgment delivered by a court of another Member State and declared to be enforceable in accordance with Section 2 or certified in accordance with Article 41(1) or Article 42(1) shall be enforced in the Member State of enforcement in the same conditions as if it had been delivered in that Member State.

In particular, a judgment which has been certified according to Article 41(1) or Article 42(1) cannot be enforced if it is irreconcilable with a subsequent enforceable judgment.

*Article 48*

**Practical arrangements for the exercise of rights of access**

1. The courts of the Member State of enforcement may make practical arrangements for organising the exercise of rights of access, if the necessary arrangements have not or have not sufficiently been made in the judgment delivered by the courts of the Member State having jurisdiction as to the substance of the matter and provided the essential elements of this judgment are respected.

2. The practical arrangements made pursuant to paragraph 1 shall cease to apply pursuant to a later judgment by the courts of the Member State having jurisdiction as to the substance of the matter.

*Article 49*

**Costs**

The provisions of this Chapter, with the exception of Section 4, shall also apply to the determination of the amount of costs and expenses of proceedings under this Regulation and to the enforcement of any order concerning such costs and expenses.

*Article 50*

**Legal aid**

An applicant who, in the Member State of origin, has benefited from complete or partial legal aid or exemption from costs or expenses shall be entitled, in the procedures provided for in Articles 21, 28, 41, 42 and 48 to benefit from the most favourable legal aid or the most extensive exemption from costs and expenses provided for by the law of the Member State of enforcement.

*Article 51*

**Security, bond or deposit**

No security, bond or deposit, however described, shall be required of a party who in one Member State applies for enforcement of a judgment given in another Member State on the following grounds:

(a) that he or she is not habitually resident in the Member State in which enforcement is sought; or

(b) that he or she is either a foreign national or, where enforcement is sought in either the United Kingdom or Ireland, does not have his or her 'domicile' in either of those Member States.

*Article 52*

## Legalisation or other similar formality

No legalisation or other similar formality shall be required in respect of the documents referred to in Articles 37, 38 and 45 or in respect of a document appointing a representative ad litem.

## CHAPTER IV

### COOPERATION BETWEEN CENTRAL AUTHORITIES IN MATTERS OF PARENTAL RESPONSIBILITY

*Article 53*

## Designation

Each Member State shall designate one or more central authorities to assist with the application of this Regulation and shall specify the geographical or functional jurisdiction of each. Where a Member State has designated more than one central authority, communications shall normally be sent direct to the relevant central authority with jurisdiction. Where a communication is sent to a central authority without jurisdiction, the latter shall be responsible for forwarding it to the central authority with jurisdiction and informing the sender accordingly.

*Article 54*

## General functions

The central authorities shall communicate information on national laws and procedures and take measures to improve the application of this Regulation and strengthening their cooperation. For this purpose the European Judicial Network in civil and commercial matters created by Decision No 2001/470/EC shall be used.

*Article 55*

## Cooperation on cases specific to parental responsibility

The central authorities shall, upon request from a central authority of another Member State or from a holder of parental responsibility, cooperate on specific cases to achieve the purposes of this Regulation. To this end, they shall, acting directly or through public authorities or other bodies, take all appropriate steps in accordance with the law of that Member State in matters of personal data protection to:

(a) collect and exchange information:

    (i) on the situation of the child;

    (ii) on any procedures under way; or

    (iii) on decisions taken concerning the child;

(b) provide information and assistance to holders of parental responsibility seeking the recognition and enforcement of decisions on their territory, in particular concerning rights of access and the return of the child;

(c) facilitate communications between courts, in particular for the application of Article 11(6) and (7) and Article 15;

(d) provide such information and assistance as is needed by courts to apply Article 56; and

(e) facilitate agreement between holders of parental responsibility through mediation or other means, and facilitate cross-border cooperation to this end.

*Article 56*

**Placement of a child in another Member State**

1. Where a court having jurisdiction under Articles 8 to 15 contemplates the placement of a child in institutional care or with a foster family and where such placement is to take place in another Member State, it shall first consult the central authority or other authority having jurisdiction in the latter State where public authority intervention in that Member State is required for domestic cases of child placement.

2. The judgment on placement referred to in paragraph 1 may be made in the requesting State only if the competent authority of the requested State has consented to the placement.

3. The procedures for consultation or consent referred to in paragraphs 1 and 2 shall be governed by the national law of the requested State.

4. Where the authority having jurisdiction under Articles 8 to 15 decides to place the child in a foster family, and where such placement is to take place in another Member State and where no public authority intervention is required in the latter Member State for domestic cases of child placement, it shall so inform the central authority or other authority having jurisdiction in the latter State.

*Article 57*

**Working method**

1. Any holder of parental responsibility may submit, to the central authority of the Member State of his or her habitual residence or to the central authority of the Member State where the child is habitually resident or present, a request for assistance as mentioned in Article 55. In general, the request shall include all available information of relevance to its enforcement. Where the request for assistance concerns the recognition or enforcement of a judgment on parental responsibility that falls within the scope of this Regulation, the holder of parental responsibility shall attach the relevant certificates provided for in Articles 39, 41(1) or 42(1).

2. Member States shall communicate to the Commission the official language or languages of the Community institutions other than their own in which communications to the central authorities can be accepted.

3. The assistance provided by the central authorities pursuant to Article 55 shall be free of charge.

4. Each central authority shall bear its own costs.

*Article 58*

**Meetings**

1. In order to facilitate the application of this Regulation, central authorities shall meet regularly.

2. These meetings shall be convened in compliance with Decision No 2001/470/EC establishing a European Judicial Network in civil and commercial matters.

## CHAPTER V

### RELATIONS WITH OTHER INSTRUMENTS

*Article 59*

**Relation with other instruments**

1. Subject to the provisions of Articles 60, 63, 64 and paragraph 2 of this Article, this Regulation shall, for the Member States, supersede conventions existing at the time of entry into force of this Regulation which have been concluded between two or more Member States and relate to matters governed by this Regulation.

2.   (a)   Finland and Sweden shall have the option of declaring that the Convention of 6 February 1931 between Denmark, Finland, Iceland, Norway and Sweden comprising international private law provisions on marriage, adoption and guardianship, together with the Final Protocol thereto, will apply, in whole or in part, in their mutual relations, in place of the rules of this Regulation. Such declarations shall be annexed to this Regulation and published in the *Official Journal of the European Union*. They may be withdrawn, in whole or in part, at any moment by the said Member States.

  (b)   The principle of non-discrimination on the grounds of nationality between citizens of the Union shall be respected.

  (c)   The rules of jurisdiction in any future agreement to be concluded between the Member States referred to in subparagraph (a) which relate to matters governed by this Regulation shall be in line with those laid down in this Regulation.

  (d)   Judgments handed down in any of the Nordic States which have made the declaration provided for in subparagraph (a) under a forum of jurisdiction corresponding to one of those laid down in Chapter II of this Regulation, shall be recognised and enforced in the other Member States under the rules laid down in Chapter III of this Regulation.

3. Member States shall send to the Commission:

  (a)   a copy of the agreements and uniform laws implementing these agreements referred to in paragraph 2(a) and (c);

  (b)   any denunciations of, or amendments to, those agreements or uniform laws.

*Article 60*

**Relations with certain multilateral conventions**

In relations between Member States, this Regulation shall take precedence over the following Conventions in so far as they concern matters governed by this Regulation:

  (a)   the Hague Convention of 5 October 1961 concerning the Powers of Authorities and the Law Applicable in respect of the Protection of Minors;

(b) the Luxembourg Convention of 8 September 1967 on the Recognition of Decisions Relating to the Validity of Marriages;

(c) the Hague Convention of 1 June 1970 on the Recognition of Divorces and Legal Separations;

(d) the European Convention of 20 May 1980 on Recognition and Enforcement of Decisions concerning Custody of Children and on Restoration of Custody of Children; and

(e) the Hague Convention of 25 October 1980 on the Civil Aspects of International Child Abduction.

## *Article 61*

## Relation with the Hague Convention of 19 October 1996 on Jurisdiction, Applicable law, Recognition, Enforcement and Cooperation in Respect of Parental Responsibility and Measures for the Protection of Children

As concerns the relation with the Hague Convention of 19 October 1996 on Jurisdiction, Applicable law, Recognition, Enforcement and Cooperation in Respect of Parental Responsibility and Measures for the Protection of Children, this Regulation shall apply:

(a) where the child concerned has his or her habitual residence on the territory of a Member State;

(b) as concerns the recognition and enforcement of a judgment given in a court of a Member State on the territory of another Member State, even if the child concerned has his or her habitual residence on the territory of a third State which is a contracting Party to the said Convention.

## *Article 62*

## Scope of effects

1. The agreements and conventions referred to in Articles 59(1), 60 and 61 shall continue to have effect in relation to matters not governed by this Regulation.

2. The conventions mentioned in Article 60, in particular the 1980 Hague Convention, continue to produce effects between the Member States which are party thereto, in compliance with Article 60.

## *Article 63*

## Treaties with the Holy See

1. This Regulation shall apply without prejudice to the International Treaty (Concordat) between the Holy See and Portugal, signed at the Vatican City on 7 May 1940.

2. Any decision as to the invalidity of a marriage taken under the Treaty referred to in paragraph 1 shall be recognised in the Member States on the conditions laid down in Chapter III, Section 1.

3. The provisions laid down in paragraphs 1 and 2 shall also apply to the following international treaties (Concordats) with the Holy See:

(a) 'Concordato lateranense' of 11 February 1929 between Italy and the Holy See, modified by the agreement, with additional Protocol signed in Rome on 18 February 1984;

(b)   Agreement between the Holy See and Spain on legal affairs of 3 January 1979.

4. Recognition of the decisions provided for in paragraph 2 may, in Italy or in Spain, be subject to the same procedures and the same checks as are applicable to decisions of the ecclesiastical courts handed down in accordance with the international treaties concluded with the Holy See referred to in paragraph 3.

5. Member States shall send to the Commission:

(a)   a copy of the Treaties referred to in paragraphs 1 and 3;

(b)   any denunciations of or amendments to those Treaties.

# CHAPTER VI

## TRANSITIONAL PROVISIONS

### *Article 64*

1. The provisions of this Regulation shall apply only to legal proceedings instituted, to documents formally drawn up or registered as authentic instruments and to agreements concluded between the parties after its date of application in accordance with Article 72.

2. Judgments given after the date of application of this Regulation in proceedings instituted before that date but after the date of entry into force of Regulation (EC) No 1347/2000 shall be recognised and enforced in accordance with the provisions of Chapter III of this Regulation if jurisdiction was founded on rules which accorded with those provided for either in Chapter II or in Regulation (EC) No 1347/2000 or in a convention concluded between the Member State of origin and the Member State addressed which was in force when the proceedings were instituted.

3. Judgments given before the date of application of this Regulation in proceedings instituted after the entry into force of Regulation (EC) No 1347/2000 shall be recognised and enforced in accordance with the provisions of Chapter III of this Regulation provided they relate to divorce, legal separation or marriage annulment or parental responsibility for the children of both spouses on the occasion of these matrimonial proceedings.

4. Judgments given before the date of application of this Regulation but after the date of entry into force of Regulation (EC) No 1347/2000 in proceedings instituted before the date of entry into force of Regulation (EC) No 1347/2000 shall be recognised and enforced in accordance with the provisions of Chapter III of this Regulation provided they relate to divorce, legal separation or marriage annulment or parental responsibility for the children of both spouses on the occasion of these matrimonial proceedings and that jurisdiction was founded on rules which accorded with those provided for either in Chapter II of this Regulation or in Regulation (EC) No 1347/2000 or in a convention concluded between the Member State of origin and the Member State addressed which was in force when the proceedings were instituted.

# CHAPTER VII

## FINAL PROVISIONS

### *Article 65*

### Review

No later than 1 January 2012, and every five years thereafter, the Commission shall present to the European Parliament, to the Council and to the European Economic and Social Committee a report on the application of this Regulation on the basis of information supplied by the Member States. The report shall be accompanied if need be by proposals for adaptations.

### *Article 66*

### Member States with two or more legal systems

With regard to a Member State in which two or more systems of law or sets of rules concerning matters governed by this Regulation apply in different territorial units:

(a) any reference to habitual residence in that Member State shall refer to habitual residence in a territorial unit;

(b) any reference to nationality, or in the case of the United Kingdom 'domicile', shall refer to the territorial unit designated by the law of that State;

(c) any reference to the authority of a Member State shall refer to the authority of a territorial unit within that State which is concerned;

(d) any reference to the rules of the requested Member State shall refer to the rules of the territorial unit in which jurisdiction, recognition or enforcement is invoked.

### *Article 67*

### Information on central authorities and languages accepted

The Member States shall communicate to the Commission within three months following the entry into force of this Regulation:

(a) the names, addresses and means of communication for the central authorities designated pursuant to Article 53;

(b) the languages accepted for communications to central authorities pursuant to Article 57(2);

and

(c) the languages accepted for the certificate concerning rights of access pursuant to Article 45(2).

The Member States shall communicate to the Commission any changes to this information.

The Commission shall make this information publicly available.

*Article 68*

**Information relating to courts and redress procedures**

The Member States shall notify to the Commission the lists of courts and redress procedures referred to in Articles 21, 29, 33 and 34 and any amendments thereto.

The Commission shall update this information and make it publicly available through the publication in the *Official Journal of the European Union* and any other appropriate means.

*Article 69*

**Amendments to the Annexes**

Any amendments to the standard forms in Annexes I to IV shall be adopted in accordance with the consultative procedure set out in Article 70(2).

*Article 70*

**Committee**

1. The Commission shall be assisted by a committee (committee).

2. Where reference is made to this paragraph, Articles 3 and 7 of Decision 1999/468/EC shall apply.

3. The committee shall adopt its rules of procedure.

*Article 71*

**Repeal of Regulation (EC) No 1347/2000**

1. Regulation (EC) No 1347/2000 shall be repealed as from the date of application of this Regulation.

2. Any reference to Regulation (EC) No 1347/2000 shall be construed as a reference to this Regulation according to the comparative table in Annex V.

*Article 72*

**Entry into force**

This Regulation shall enter into force on 1 August 2004.

The Regulation shall apply from 1 March 2005, with the exception of Articles 67, 68, 69 and 70, which shall apply from 1 August 2004.

This Regulation shall be binding in its entirety and directly applicable in the Member States in accordance with the Treaty establishing the European Community.

Done at Brussels, 27 November 2003.

For the Council The President

R. CASTELLI

## ANNEX I

### CERTIFICATE REFERRED TO IN ARTICLE 39 CONCERNING JUDGMENTS IN MATRIMONIAL MATTERS1

1. Member State of origin
2. Court or authority issuing the certificate
    2.1. Name
    2.2. Address
    2.3. Tel/fax/e-mail
3. Marriage
    3.1. Wife
        3.1.1. Full name
        3.1.2. Address
        3.1.3. Country and place of birth
        3.1.4. Date of birth
    3.2. Husband
        3.2.1. Full name
        3.2.2. Address
        3.2.3. Country and place of birth
        3.2.4. Date of birth
    3.3. Country, place (where available) and date of marriage
        3.3.1. Country of marriage
        3.3.2. Place of marriage (where available)
        3.3.3. Date of marriage
4. Court which delivered the judgment
    4.1. Name of Court
    4.2. Place of Court
5. Judgment
    5.1. Date
    5.2. Reference number
    5.3. Type of judgment
        5.3.1. Divorce
        5.3.2. Marriage annulment
        5.3.3. Legal separation
    5.4. Was the judgment given in default of appearance?
        5.4.1. No
        5.4.2. Yes[2]
6. Names of parties to whom legal aid has been granted

7. Is the judgment subject to further appeal under the law of the Member State of origin?

    7.1.  No

    7.2.  Yes

8. Date of legal effect in the Member State where the judgment was given

    8.1.  Divorce

    8.2.  Legal separation

Done at.................................................................................................... , date

        Signature and/or stamp

---

**Notes**

1    Council Regulation (EC) No 2201/2003 of 27 November 2003 concerning jurisdiction and the recognition and enforcement of judgments in matrimonial matters and the matters of parental responsibility, repealing Regulation (EC) No 1347/2000.

2    Documents referred to in Article 37(2) must be attached.

---

## ANNEX II

### CERTIFICATE REFERRED TO IN ARTICLE 39 CONCERNING JUDGMENTS ON PARENTAL RESPONSIBILITY[1]

1. Member State of origin

2. Court or authority issuing the certificate

    2.1.  Name

    2.2.  Address

    2.3.  Tel/Fax/e-mail

3. Person(s) with rights of access

    3.1.  Full name

    3.2.  Address

3.3.Date and place of birth (where available)

4. Holders of parental responsibility other than those mentioned under 3[2]

    4.1.

        4.1.1.  Full name

        4.1.2.  Address

        4.1.3.  Date and place of birth (where available)

    4.2.

        4.2.1.  Full Name

        4.2.2.  Address

        4.2.3.  Date and place of birth (where available)

4.3.

    4.3.1. Full name

    4.3.2. Address

    4.3.3. Date and place of birth (where available)

5. Court which delivered the judgment

    5.1. Name of Court

    5.2. Place of Court

6. Judgment

    6.1. Date

    6.2. Reference number

    6.3. Was the judgment given in default of appearance?

        6.3.1. No

        6.3.2. Yes[3]

7. Children who are covered by the judgment[4]

    7.1. Full name and date of birth

    7.2. Full name and date of birth

    7.3. Full name and date of birth

    7.4. Full name and date of birth

8. Names of parties to whom legal aid has been granted

9. Attestation of enforceability and service

    9.1. Is the judgment enforceable according to the law of the Member State of origin?

        9.1.1. Yes

        9.1.2. No

    9.2. Has the judgment been served on the party against whom enforcement is sought?

        9.2.1. Yes

            9.2.1.1. Full name of the party

            9.2.1.2. Address

            9.2.1.3. Date of service

        9.2.2. No

10. Specific information on judgments on rights of access where 'exequatur' is requested under Article 28. This possibility is foreseen in Article 40[2].

    10.1. Practical arrangements for exercise of rights of access (to the extent stated in the judgment)

        10.1.1. Date and time

            10.1.1.1. Start

            10.1.1.2. End

10.1.2. Place

10.1.3. Specific obligations on holders of parental responsibility

10.1.4. Specific obligations on the person with right of access

10.1.5. Any restrictions attached to the exercise of rights of access

11. Specific information for judgments on the return of the child in cases where the 'exequatur' procedure is requested under Article 28. This possibility is foreseen under Article 40(2).

11.1. The judgment entails the return of the child

11.2. Person to whom the child is to be returned (to the extent stated in the judgment)

11.2.1. Full name

11.2.2 Address

Done at ................................................................................................................ , date

Signature and/or stamp

---

**Notes**

1  Council Regulation (EC) No 2201/2003 of 27 November 2003 concerning jurisdiction and the recognition and enforcement of judgments in matrimonial matters and the matters of parental responsibility, repealing Regulation (EC) No 1347/2000.

2  In cases of joint custody, a person already mentioned under item 3 may also be mentioned under item 4.

3  Documents referred to in Article 37(2) must be attached.

4  If more than four children are covered, use a second form.

---

## ANNEX III

### CERTIFICATE REFERRED TO IN ARTICLE 41(1) CONCERNING JUDGMENTS ON RIGHTS OF ACCESS[1]

1. Member State of origin

2. Court or authority issuing the certificate

2.1. Name

2.2. Address

2.3. Tel./fax/e-mail

3. Person(s) with rights of access

3.1. Full name

3.2. Address

3.3. Date and place of birth (where available)

4. Holders of parental responsibility other than those mentioned under 3[2,3]

  4.1.

    4.1.1.  Full name

    4.1.2.  Address

    4.1.3.  Date and place of birth (where available)

  4.2.

    4.2.1.  Full name

    4.2.2.  Address

    4.2.3.  Date and place of birth (where available)

  4.3.  Other

    4.3.1.  Full name

    4.3.2.  Address

    4.3.3.  Date and place of birth (where available)

5. Court which delivered the judgment

  5.1.  Name of Court

  5.2.  Place of Court

6. Judgment

  6.1.  Date

  6.2.  Reference number

7. Children who are covered by the judgment[4]

  7.1.  Full name and date of birth

  7.2.  Full name and date of birth

  7.3.  Full name and date of birth

  7.4.  Full name and date of birth

8. Is the judgment enforceable in the Member State of origin?

  8.1.  Yes

  8.2.  No

9. Where the judgment was given in default of appearance, the person defaulting was served with the document which instituted the proceedings or with an equivalent document in sufficient time and in such a way as to enable that person to arrange for his or her defence, or the person has been served with the document but not in compliance with these conditions, it is nevertheless established that he or she accepted the decision unequivocally

10. All parties concerned were given an opportunity to be heard

11. The children were given an opportunity to be heard, unless a hearing was considered inappropriate having regard to their age or degree of maturity

12. Practical arrangements for exercise of rights of access (to the extent stated in the judgment)

12.1.  Date and time

    12.1.1.  Start

    12.1.2.  End

12.2.  Place

12.3.  Specific obligations on holders of parental responsibility

12.4.  Specific obligations on the person with right of access

12.5.  Any restrictions attached to the exercise of rights of access

13. Names of parties to whom legal aid has been granted

Done at..................................................................................................... , date

        Signature and/or stamp

---

**Notes**

1   Council Regulation (EC) No 2201/2003 of 27 November 2003 concerning jurisdiction and the recognition and enforcement of judgments in matrimonial matters and the matters of parental responsibility, repealing Regulation (EC) No 1347/2000.

2   In cases of joint custody, a person already mentioned under item 3 may also be mentioned in item 4.

3   Please put a cross in the box corresponding to the person against whom the judgment should be enforced.

4   If more than four children are concerned, use a second form.

---

## ANNEX IV

### CERTIFICATE REFERRED TO IN ARTICLE 42(1) CONCERNING THE RETURN OF THE CHILD[1]

1. Member State of origin

2. Court or authority issuing the certificate

    2.1.  Name

    2.2.  Address

    2.3.  Tel./fax/e-mail

3. Person to whom the child has to be returned (to the extent stated in the judgment)

    3.1.  Full name

    3.2.  Address

    3.3.  Date and place of birth (where available)

4. Holders of parental responsibility[2]

    4.1.  Mother

        4.1.1.  Full name

        4.1.2.  Address (where available)

        4.1.3.  Date and place of birth (where available)

    4.2.  Father

        4.2.1.  Full name

        4.2.2.  Address (where available)

        4.2.3.  Date and place of birth (where available)

    4.3.  Other

        4.3.1.  Full name

        4.3.2.  Address (where available)

        4.3.3.  Date and place of birth (where available)

5. Respondent (where available)

    5.1.  Full name

    5.2.  Address (where available)

6. Court which delivered the judgment

    6.1.  Name of Court

    6.2.  Place of Court

7. Judgment

    7.1.  Date

    7.2.  Reference number

8. Children who are covered by the judgment[3]

    8.1.  Full name and date of birth

    8.2.  Full name and date of birth

    8.3.  Full name and date of birth

    8.4.  Full name and date of birth

9. The judgment entails the return of the child

10. Is the judgment enforceable in the Member State of origin?

    10.1.  Yes

    10.2.  No

11. The children were given an opportunity to be heard, unless a hearing was considered inappropriate having regard to their age or degree of maturity

12. The parties were given an opportunity to be heard

13. The judgment entails the return of the children and the court has taken into account in issuing its judgment the reasons for and evidence underlying the decision issued pursuant to Article 13 of the Hague Convention of 25 October 1980 on the Civil Aspects of International Child Abduction

14. Where applicable, details of measures taken by courts or authorities to ensure the protection of the child after its return to the Member State of habitual residence

15. Names of parties to whom legal aid has been granted

Done at ................................................................................................................ , date

       Signature and/or stamp

## Notes

1    Council Regulation (EC) No 2201 of 27 November 2003 concerning jurisdiction and the recognition and enforcement of judgments in matrimonial matters and the matters of parental responsibility, repealing Regulation (EC) No 1347/2000.

2    This item is optional.

3    If more than four children are covered, use a second form.

# ANNEX V

## COMPARATIVE TABLE WITH REGULATION (EC) NO 1347/2000

| Articles repealed | Corresponding Articles of new text | Articles repealed | Corresponding Articles of new text |
|---|---|---|---|
| 1 | 1, 2 | 27 | 34 |
| 2 | 3 | 28 | 35 |
| | 12 | 29 | 36 |
| 4 | | 30 | 50 |
| 5 | 4 | 31 | 51 |
| 6 | 5 | 32 | 37 |
| 7 | 6 | 33 | 39 |
| 8 | 7 | 34 | 38 |
| 9 | 17 | 35 | 52 |
| 10 | 18 | 36 | 59 |
| 11 | 16, 19 | 37 | 60, 61 |
| 12 | 20 | 38 | 62 |
| 13 | 2, 49, 46 | 39 | |
| 14 | 21 | 40 | 63 |
| 15 | 22, 23 | 41 | 66 |
| 16 | | 42 | 64 |
| 17 | 24 | 43 | 65 |
| 18 | 25 | 44 | 68, 69 |
| 19 | 26 | 45 | 70 |
| 20 | 27 | 46 | 72 |
| 21 | 28 | Annex I | 68 |
| 22 | 21, 29 | Annex II | 68 |
| 23 | 30 | Annex III | 68 |
| 24 | 31 | Annex IV | Annex I |
| 25 | 32 | Annex V | Annex II |
| 26 | 33 | | |

# ANNEX VI

Declarations by Sweden and Finland pursuant to Article 59(2)(a) of the Council Regulation concerning jurisdiction and the recognition and enforcement of judgments in matrimonial matters and matters of parental responsibility, repealing Regulation (EC) No 1347/2000.

Declaration by Sweden:

> Pursuant to Article 59(2)(a) of the Council Regulation concerning jurisdiction and the recognition and enforcement of judgments in matrimonial matters and matters of parental responsibility, repealing Regulation (EC) No 1347/2000, Sweden hereby declares that the Convention of 6 February 1931 between Denmark, Finland, Iceland, Norway and Sweden comprising international private law provisions on marriage, adoption and guardianship, together with the Final Protocol thereto, will apply in full in relations between Sweden and Finland, in place of the rules of the Regulation.

Declaration by Finland:

> Pursuant to Article 59(2)(a) of the Council Regulation concerning jurisdiction and the recognition and enforcement of judgments in matrimonial matters and matters of parental responsibility, repealing Regulation (EC) No 1347/2000, Finland hereby declares that the Convention of 6 February 1931 between Finland, Denmark, Iceland, Norway and Sweden comprising international private law provisions on marriage, adoption and guardianship, together with the Final Protocol thereto, will apply in full in relations between Finland and Sweden, in place of the rules of the Regulation.

# European Communities (Maintenance) Regulations 2011

*S.I. No. 274 of 2011*

*I, ALAN SHATTER, Minister for Justice and Equality, in exercise of the powers conferred on me by section 3 of the European Communities Act 1972 (No. 27 of 1972) and for the purpose of giving full effect to Council Regulation (EC) 4/2009 (OJ No. L7, 10.1.2009, p.1) of 18 December 2008 on jurisdiction, applicable law, recognition and enforcement of decisions and cooperation in matters relating to maintenance obligations make the following Regulations:*

## 1    Citation and commencement

(1) These Regulations may be cited as the European Communities (Maintenance) Regulations 2011.

(2) These Regulations come into operation on 18 June 2011.

## 2    Interpretation

(1) In these Regulations, except where the context otherwise requires—

"**Act of 1940**" means the Enforcement of Court Orders Act 1940 (No. 23 of 1940),

"**Act of 1976**" means the Family Law (Maintenance of Spouses and Children) Act 1976 (No. 11 of 1976),

"**Act of 1994**" means the Maintenance Act 1994 (No. 28 of 1994),

"**decision**" includes an authentic instrument and a court settlement,

"**enforcement order**" means an order for the recognition or enforcement of all or part of a decision where the order—

> (a)   is made by the Master of the High Court under Regulation 9, or
>
> (b)   is made or varied—
>
>> (i)   on appeal from a decision of the Master under that Regulation, or
>>
>> (ii)   on appeal from a decision of the High Court on such an appeal,

"**enforceable maintenance order**" means—

> (a)   a maintenance order respecting all of which an enforcement order has been made, or
>
> (b)   if an enforcement order has been made respecting only part of a maintenance order, the maintenance order to the extent to which it is so ordered to be enforced,

"**2007 Hague Protocol**" means the Hague Protocol of 23 November 2007 on the law applicable to maintenance applications,

"**maintenance**" means maintenance within the meaning of the Maintenance Regulation,

"**maintenance creditor**" means, in relation to a maintenance order, the person entitled to the payments for which the order provides, "**maintenance debtor**" means, in relation to a maintenance order, the person who is liable to make a payment under the order,

"**maintenance order**" means a decision relating to maintenance,

"**Maintenance Regulation**" means Council Regulation (EC) 4/2009¹ of 18 December 2008 on jurisdiction, applicable law, recognition and enforcement of decisions and cooperation in matters relating to maintenance obligations,

"**Member State**" means a Member State of the European Union other than the State or Denmark,

"**Member State not bound by the 2007 Hague Protocol**" means the United Kingdom or Denmark.

(2) References in these Regulations to numbered Chapters or Articles without qualification are references to the Chapters or Articles so numbered of the Maintenance Regulation.

(3) Unless provided otherwise, a word or expression used in these Regulations and in the Maintenance Regulation has the same meaning in these Regulations as it has in the Maintenance Regulation.

**3        Jurisdiction of Circuit and District Courts**

The Circuit Court or the District Court has jurisdiction for the purposes of Article 3(a) and (b) and the jurisdiction may be exercised by the judge for the time being assigned—

    (a)  in the case of the Circuit Court, to the circuit, and

    (b)  in the case of the District Court, to the district court district,

in which the creditor or debtor, as the case may be, is habitually resident.

**4        Choice of Court**

The Circuit Court or the District Court has jurisdiction for the purposes of Article 4.1. (a), 4.1. (b) and 4.1.(c)(ii) and the jurisdiction may be exercised by the judge for the time being assigned—

    (a)  in the case of the Circuit Court, to the circuit, and

    (b)  in the case of the District Court, to the district court district,

in which the creditor or debtor, as the case may be, habitually resides.

**5        Jurisdiction of High Court**

The High Court has jurisdiction for the purposes of Articles 7, 21 and 32.

**6        Jurisdiction of Dublin Circuit Court and Dublin Metropolitan District Court.**

Where the circumstances relating to the habitual residence of a creditor or debtor referred to in Regulations 3 and 4 do not apply, the creditor or debtor concerned shall be deemed to be habitually resident in the Dublin Circuit or the Dublin Metropolitan District, and a judge for the time being assigned to that Circuit or District shall have jurisdiction.

**7      Extract of decision**

Where a maintenance creditor is seeking to enforce a decision in a Member State, the court which made the decision concerned shall, on application to it by the maintenance creditor issue the extract from the decision in the form set out in Annex I to the Maintenance Regulation.

**8      Enforcement of decisions given in Member States bound by the 2007 Hague Protocol**

(1) A decision given in a Member State bound by the 2007 Hague Protocol shall be of the same force and effect as a judgment or decree of the District Court, and may be enforced, and proceedings taken on it, as if it were a judgment or decree of that Court.

(2) Section 8(7) of the Act of 1940 does not apply to proceedings for the enforcement of a decision referred to in paragraph (1).

(3) Paragraphs (1) and (2) apply even though an amount payable under the decision exceeds the maximum amount the District Court has jurisdiction to award under an enactment referred to in the Act of 1976.

(4) A decision to which paragraph (1) applies shall be deemed to be an antecedent order within the meaning of the Act of 1976.

**9      Applications for recognition or enforcement of decisions given in a Member State not bound by the 2007 Hague Protocol**

(1) An application under the Maintenance Regulation for the recognition and enforcement of a decision in a Member State not bound by the 2007 Hague Protocol shall be made to the Master of the High Court.

(2) The Master of the High Court shall determine an application referred to in paragraph (1) in accordance with the Maintenance Regulation.

(3) Where the application is for the enforcement of a decision, the Master of the High Court shall declare the decision enforceable immediately on completion of the formalities provided for in Article 28, without any review under Article 24 and shall make an enforcement order in relation to the decision.

(4) An order referred to in paragraph (3) may provide for the recognition or enforcement of all or part of the decision concerned.

(5) Where an application is made under paragraph (1), the Master of the High Court may by order declare the decision which is the subject of the enforcement order and which relates to—

(a)  a sum payable under the enforceable maintenance order as a periodic payment but not paid before the relevant enforcement order was made, or

(b)  a lump sum (not being a sum referred to in paragraph (a)) which is payable under the enforceable maintenance order,

to be of the same force and effect as a judgment of the High Court and such a decision may be enforced by the High Court and proceedings taken on it as if it were a judgment of that Court.

(6) No order shall be made under paragraph (5) unless the Master of the High Court considers it necessary for the effective enforcement of the enforceable maintenance order concerned.

(7) A maintenance order shall be regarded as a decision referred to in paragraph (1) if the District Court does not have jurisdiction to enforce it under Regulation 10.

(8) For the purposes of this Regulation references in Articles 31, 32, 34, 36, 37, 38, 39 and 48 to a declaration of enforceability are to be read as references to an enforcement order.

**10      Enforcement of enforceable maintenance orders given in a Member State not bound by the 2007 Hague Protocol**

(1) Subject to Regulation 14 and the restrictions on enforcement contained in Article 36(3), the District Court has jurisdiction to enforce an enforceable maintenance order.

(2) An enforceable maintenance order shall, from the date on which the maintenance order was made, be deemed for the purposes of—

    (a)    paragraph (1),

    (b)    section 98(1) (as amended by section 30(1) of the Act of 1976) of the Defence Act 1954 (No. 18 of 1954), and

    (c)    subject to the Maintenance Regulation, the variation or discharge of that order under section 6 (as amended by section 43(b) of the Act of 1995) of the Act of 1976,

to be an order made by the District Court under section 5, 5A (inserted by section 18 of the Act of 1987) or 21A (inserted by section 21 of the Act of 1987) of the Act of 1976, as may be appropriate.

(3) Paragraphs (1) and (2) apply even though an amount payable under the enforceable maintenance order exceeds the maximum amount the District Court has jurisdiction to award under an enactment referred to in pararaph (2).

(4) Where an enforceable maintenance order is varied by a court of a Member State not bound by the 2007 Hague Protocol, and an enforcement order has been made respecting all or part of the enforceable maintenance order as so varied, or respecting all or part of the order effecting the variation, the enforceable maintenance order shall, from the date on which the variation takes effect, be enforceable in the State only as so varied.

(5) Where an enforceable maintenance order is revoked by a court of a Member State not bound by the 2007 Hague Protocol, and an enforcement order has been made respecting the order effecting the revocation, the enforceable maintenance order shall, from the date on which the revocation takes effect, cease to be enforceable in the State except in relation to any sums under the order that were payable, but not paid, on or before that date.

(6) Subject to paragraphs (3) to (5) of Regulation 9, the following shall be regarded as being payable pursuant to an order made under section 5, 5A (inserted by section 18 of the Act of 1987), or 21A (inserted by section 21 of the Act of 1987) of the Act of 1976—

(a) any sum payable under an enforceable maintenance order but not paid before the relevant enforcement order was made;

(b) any costs of or incidental to the application for the enforcement order that are payable under Regulation 14(2).

(7) The jurisdiction vested in the District Court by this Regulation may be exercised by the judge of that Court for the time being assigned to—

(a) where the maintenance debtor under an enforceable maintenance order resides in the State, the district court district in which the debtor resides or carries on any profession, business or occupation, or

(b) where such a maintenance debtor does not so reside but is employed by a person residing or having a place of business in the State or by a body whose seat of management or control is in the State, the district court district in which the person resides or the body has its seat.

(8) Notwithstanding anything to the contrary in an enforceable maintenance order, the maintenance debtor shall pay any sum payable under that order to—

(a) in a case referred to in paragraph (7)(a), the district court clerk for the district court area in which the debtor for the time being resides, or

(b) in a case referred to in paragraph (7)(b), a district court clerk specified by the District Court, for transmission to the maintenance creditor or, if a public authority has been authorised by the creditor to receive the sum, to the public authority.

(9) Where a sum payable under an enforceable maintenance order is not duly paid and where the maintenance creditor so requests in writing, the district court clerk concerned shall make an application to the District Court respecting that sum under—

(a) section 8 (as amended by section 2(2) of the Enforcement of Court Orders (Amendment) Act 2009 (No. 21 of 2009) of the Act of 1940, or

(b) section 10 (as amended by section 43 of the Act of 1995) of the Act of 1976.

(10) For the purposes of paragraph (9)(a), a reference to an applicant in section 8 (other than subsections (4) and (5) of that section) of the Act of 1940 shall be construed as a reference to the district court clerk.

(11) Nothing in this Regulation shall affect the right of a maintenance creditor under an enforceable maintenance order to institute proceedings for the recovery of a sum payable to a district court clerk under paragraph (8).

(12) Section 8(7) of the Act of 1940 does not apply to proceedings for the enforcement of an enforceable maintenance order.

(13) The maintenance debtor concerned shall give notice of any change of address to the district court clerk for the district court area in which the debtor has been residing.

(14) A person who, without reasonable excuse, contravenes paragraph (13) is guilty of an offence and liable on summary conviction to a class C fine.

(15) Where there are two or more district court clerks for a district court area, a reference in this section to a district court clerk shall be construed as a reference to any of them.

(16) For the purposes of this Regulation the Dublin Metropolitan District is deemed to be a district court area.

(17) In this Regulation—

"Act of 1987" means the Status of Children Act 1987 (No. 26 of 1987),

"Act of 1995" means the Family Law Act 1995 (No. 26 of 1995).

**11      Proceedings to contest the decision given on appeal under Article 33**

A decision under Article 33 may be appealed on a point of law to the Supreme Court.

**12      Provisional, including protective, measures (Article 14)**

(1) The High Court may, on application to it pursuant to Article 14, grant any provisional measures, including protective measures, that the Court has power to grant in proceedings that, apart from this Regulation, are within its jurisdiction if—

    (a)  proceedings have been, or are to be, commenced in a Member State, and

    (b)  the subject matter of the proceedings is within the scope of the Maintenance Regulation (whether or not the Maintenance Regulation has effect in relation to the proceedings).

(2) On an application under paragraph (1) the High Court may refuse to grant the measures sought if, in the opinion of the Court, the fact that, apart from this Regulation, the Court does not have jurisdiction in relation to the subject matter of the proceedings makes it inexpedient for it to grant those measures.

(3) Subject to Article 36(3), an application to the Master of the High Court for an enforcement order respecting a judgment may include an application for any protective measures the High Court has power to grant in proceedings that, apart from these Regulations, are within its jurisdiction.

(4) Where an enforcement order is made, the Master of the High Court shall grant any protective measures referred to in paragraph (3) that are sought in the application for the enforcement order.

**13      Proof and admissibility of decisions and certain translations**

(1) For the purposes of Article 28 a document, duly authenticated, which purports to be a copy of a decision given in a Member State not bound by the 2007 Hague Protocol shall without further proof be deemed to be a true copy of the decision, unless the contrary is shown.

(2) A document purporting, under paragraph (1), to be a copy of a decision shall be regarded for those purposes as being duly authenticated if it—

    (a)  purports to bear the seal of the court or authority concerned, or

    (b)  purports to be certified by a judge or officer of the court or authority

to be a true copy of the decision.

(3) A document which—

   (a)  purports to be a transliteration or translation of—

      (i)  a decision given by a court of a Member State not bound by the 2007 Hague Protocol,

      (ii)  an authentic instrument or a court settlement within the meaning of Article 48(1), or

      (iii)  a form mentioned in Articles 40 and 48, and

   (b)  is certified as correct by a person competent to do so,

shall be admissible as evidence of the document of which it purports to be a translation.

## 14     Interest on decisions and payment of costs

(1) Where, on application for an enforcement order relating to—

   (a)  a decision for the payment of a sum of money, and

   (b)  in accordance with the law of the Member State in which the decision was given, interest on the sum is recoverable under the decision at a particular rate or rates and from a particular date or time,

the enforcement order concerned, where made, shall provide that the person liable to pay that sum shall also be liable to pay the interest, other than interest on costs recoverable under paragraph (2), in accordance with the particulars noted in the order, and the interest shall be recoverable by the applicant as though it were part of the sum.

(2) An enforcement order may provide for the payment to the applicant by the respondent of the reasonable costs of or incidental to the application for the enforcement order.

(3) A person required by an enforcement order to pay costs shall be liable to pay interest on the costs as if they were the subject of an order for the payment of costs made by the High Court on the date on which the enforcement order was made.

(4) Interest shall be payable on a sum referred to in subparagraph (1)(a) only as provided for in this Regulation.

## 15     Currency of payments under maintenance orders

(1) An amount payable in the State under a maintenance order shall be payable in the currency of the State.

(2) If the amount is stated in the maintenance order in any other currency, payment shall be made on the basis of the exchange rate prevailing on the date the enforcement order is made between the currency of the State and the other currency.

(3) For the purposes of this Regulation a certificate purporting to be signed by an officer of an authorised institution and to state the exchange rate prevailing on a specified date between a specified currency and the currency of the State shall be admissible as evidence of the facts stated in the certificate.

(4) In this Regulation, "authorised institution" means—

   (a)  a credit institution within the meaning of Directive 2006/48/EC of the European Parliament and of the Council of 14 June 2006 relating to the taking up and pursuit of the business of credit institutions (including a branch, within the meaning of Article 4(3) of that Directive, located in a Member State of a credit institution having its head office in or, in accordance with Article 38 of that Directive, elsewhere than in a Member State),

(b) a trustee savings bank within the meaning of the Trustee Savings Banks Acts 1989 and 2001, or

(c) An Post.

## 16 Designation of Central Authority

The Minister for Justice and Equality is designated as the Central Authority for the State for the purposes of the Maintenance Regulation.

## 17 Functions of Central Authority

(1) Where an application is made to the Central Authority pursuant to Article 56, the Central Authority shall, on behalf of the applicant, take any action which is required to be taken by it under the Maintenance Regulation and, in that context, references in the Maintenance Regulation to the applicant, to the party or to other analogous terms shall be construed, where appropriate, as references to the Central Authority.

(2) Without prejudice to the generality of paragraph (1), where the application is for recognition or for a declaration of enforceability of a decision, the Central Authority may, on receipt of that application, send it to the Master of the High Court for determination in accordance with Regulation 9.

(3) Where the Master of the High Court has determined an application in accordance with paragraph (2), the Master of the High Court shall cause the decision to be brought to the notice of the Central Authority and, if an enforcement order has been made, the Master shall cause notice thereof to be served on the maintenance debtor.

(4) (a) The notice to be served on a maintenance debtor under paragraph (3) shall include a statement of the provisions of Article 32 of the Maintenance Regulation.

(b) Service of the notice may be effected personally or in any manner in which service of a superior court document within the meaning of section 23 of the Courts Act, 1971 may be effected.

(5) Where no appeal has been made pursuant to Article 32, or the time allowed for an appeal has elapsed, the Central Authority shall, where appropriate, transmit a decision determined under paragraph (2) to the district court clerk for the district in which the debtor for the time being resides for the purposes of enforcement.

(6) The Central Authority may request that payments of maintenance be made directly to the maintenance creditor.

(7) Where the application is for the enforcement of a decision, paragraphs (4), (5) and (6) shall apply with any necessary modifications.

**18      Taking of evidence for proceedings in a Member State (Article 51(g))**

Where a request is made to the Central Authority by or on behalf of a court in a Member State to obtain the evidence of a person residing in the State for the purposes of any proceedings in that jurisdiction for the recovery of maintenance, the Central Authority shall forward the request to the District Court, which is competent to take evidence under the European Communities (Evidence in Civil or Commercial Matters) Regulations 2008 (S.I. No. 102 of 2008) pursuant to a request to which Article 1.1(a) of Council Regulation (EC) 1206/2001 (OJ No. L174, 27.6.2001, p.1) on co-operation between the courts of the Member States on the taking of evidence in civil or commercial matters applies.

**19      Obtaining, transmission and use of information**

(1) The Central Authority may, for the purposes of obtaining any information that is necessary or expedient for the performance of its functions, require any holder of a public office or body financed wholly or partly by means of moneys provided by the Oireachtas to provide it with any information in the possession or procurement of the holder or body as to the whereabouts, place of work, or location and extent of the assets, of a maintenance creditor or debtor and the holder or body shall, as soon as practicable, comply with the requirement.

(2) If the District Court, on application to it by the Central Authority, is of the opinion that any person or body (not being a person or body referred to in paragraph (1)) is likely to have information as to the matters referred to in that paragraph and that the Central Authority requires the information for the purposes so referred to, the Court may order that person or body to provide it to the Central Authority within such period as may be specified in the order.

(3) The jurisdiction conferred on the District Court by subsection (2) may be exercised by the judge of the District Court for the time being assigned to the district court district in which the person or body to whom the order sought is to be directed resides or carries on any profession, business or occupation.

(4) The Central Authority shall transmit the information referred to in Article 61(2) to the competent courts, the competent authorities responsible for service of documents and the competent authorities responsible for enforcement of a decision, as the case may be.

**20      Application of Article 68 (Relations with other Community Instruments)**

(1) The Maintenance Regulation, other than Chapters III and VII, applies to Denmark.

(2) Articles 2 and Chapter IX apply to Denmark to the extent that they relate to jurisdiction, recognition, enforceability and enforcement of judgments and the right to apply to the courts.

**21      Transitional Provision**

For the purposes of Article 75(2)(a) and (b), Regulations 5 (in so far as it relates to Article 32), and 9 to 15 apply.

**22    Application of Act of 1994 (Co-operation between Central Authorities)**

(1) The Maintenance Act 1994 shall cease to apply in relation to the State and Member States for the purposes of Chapter VII of the Maintenance Regulation with effect from 18 June 2011.

(2) The Act of 1994 applies to Denmark, except where a request for the recovery of maintenance is received under section 14 of that Act from the Central Authority of Denmark, the Central Authority shall transmit that request to the Master of the High Court for determination under Regulation 9.

**23    Amendment of European Communities (European Enforcement Order) Regulations 2005 (S.I. No. 648/2005)**

(1) Notwithstanding Regulation 7 of the European Communities (European Enforcement Order) Regulations 2005 (S.I. No. 648 of 2005), where a decision relates to a claim for periodical payments of maintenance, and has been certified as a European Enforcement Order in a Member State of origin, that decision shall be of the same force and effect as a judgment or decree of the District Court, and may be enforced, and proceedings taken on it, as if it were a judgment or decree of that Court.

(2) A decision to which paragraph (1) applies shall be deemed to be an antecedent order within the meaning of the Act of 1976.

**24    Restriction of European Communities (Civil and Commercial Judgments) Regulations 2002 (S.I. No. 52/2002)**

The European Communities (Civil and Commercial Judgments) Regulations 2002 (S.I. No. 52 of 2002) shall not apply to a maintenance order.

**25    Repeal of Maintenance Orders Act 1974**

The Maintenance Orders Act 1974 (No. 16 of 1974) is repealed.

# Part 5: Miscellaneous

# Child Abduction and Enforcement of Custody Orders Act 1991 (Section 4) (Hague Convention) Order 2008

*SI 220/2008*

[…]¹

---

**Notes**

1    SI 220/2008 repealed by SI 400/2011, Child Abduction and Enforcement of Custody Orders Act 1991 (Section 4) (Hague Convention) Order 2011.

---

# Child Abduction and Enforcement of Custody Orders Act 1991 (Section 4) (Hague Convention) Order 2011

*SI 400/2011*

I, *EAMON GILMORE, Minister for Foreign Affairs and Trade, in exercise of the powers conferred upon me by section 4 of the Child Abduction and Enforcement of Custody Orders Act 1991 (No. 6 of 1991), hereby order as follows:*

1. This Order may be cited as the Child Abduction and Enforcement of Custody Orders Act 1991 (Section 4) (Hague Convention) Order 2011.

2. It is declared—

   (a) that the states specified in Schedule 1 to this Order are Contracting States for the purposes of Part II of the Child Abduction and Enforcement of Custody Orders Act 1991;

   (b) that declarations (the texts of which in the English language are set out in Part 1 of Schedule 2 hereto) have been made to the Ministry of Foreign Affairs of the Kingdom of the Netherlands pursuant to Articles 39 and 40 of the Convention; and

   (c) that reservations (the texts of which in the English language are set out in Part 2 of Schedule 2 hereto) have been made to the Ministry of Foreign Affairs of the Kingdom of the Netherlands pursuant to Articles 24 and 26 of the Convention.

3. The Child Abduction and Enforcement of Custody Orders Act 1991 (Section 4) (Hague Convention) Order 2008 (S.I. No. 220 of 2008) is revoked.

4. This Order shall come into operation on 20 July 2011.

## SCHEDULE 1

| | | |
|---|---|---|
| Albania | Finland | Paraguay |
| Argentina | France | Peru |
| Armenia | Former Yugoslav Republic of Macedonia | Poland |
| Australia | Georgia | Portugal |
| Austria | Germany | Romania |
| Bahamas | Greece | Saint Kitts & Nevis |
| Belarus | Guatemala | San Marino |
| Belgium | Honduras | Serbia |
| Belize | Hungary | Seychelles |
| Bosnia & Herzegovina | Iceland | Slovakia |

| | | |
|---|---|---|
| Brazil | Israel | Slovenia |
| Bulgaria | Italy | South Africa |
| Burkina-Faso | Latvia | Spain |
| Canada | Lithuania | Sri Lanka |
| Chile | Luxembourg | Sweden |
| China (Convention applicable to Hong Kong and Macao Special Administrative Regions only) | Malta | Switzerland |
| Colombia | Mauritius | Thailand |
| Costa Rica | Mexico | Trinidad and Tobago |
| Croatia | Moldova | Turkey |
| Cyprus | Monaco | Turkmenistan |
| Czech Republic | Montenegro | Ukraine |
| Denmark | Morocco | United Kingdom of Great Britain and Northern Ireland |
| Dominican Republic | Netherlands | United States of America |
| Ecuador | New Zealand | Uruguay |
| El Salvador | Nicaragua | Uzbekistan |
| Estonia | Norway | Venezuela |
| Fiji | Panama | Zimbabwe |

## SCHEDULE 2

### PART 1

#### Australia

"The Convention extends to the legal system applicable only in the Australian States and mainland Territories." — 29 October 1986

#### Canada

"... in accordance with the provisions of Article 40, the Government of Canada declares that the Convention shall extend to the Provinces of Ontario, New Brunswick, British Columbia and Manitoba." — 2 June 1983

"... in accordance with the provisions of Article 40, the Government of Canada declares that the Convention shall extend to the Province of Nova Scotia." — 24 February 1984

"... in accordance with the provisions of Article 40, the Government of Canada declares that the Convention shall extend to the Province of Newfoundland." — 5 July 1984

"... in accordance with the provisions of Article 40, the Government of Canada declares that the Convention shall extend to the Province of Quebec." — 9 October 1984

"... in accordance with the provisions of Article 40, the Government of Canada declares that the Convention shall extend to the Yukon Territory." — 15 November 1984

"... in accordance with the provisions of Article 40, the Government of Canada declares that the Convention shall extend to the Province of Prince Edward Island." — 11 February 1986

"... in accordance with the provisions of Article 40, the Government of Canada declares that the Convention shall extend to the Province of Saskatchewan." — 7 August 1986

"... in accordance with the provisions of Article 40, the Government of Canada declares that the Convention shall extend to the Province of Alberta." — 4 November 1986

"... in accordance with the provisions of Article 40, the Government of Canada declares that the Convention shall extend to the Northwest Territories." — 25 January 1988

"In accordance with the provisions of Article 40 of the Convention, the Government of Canada declares that, in addition to the provinces of Ontario, New Brunswick, British Columbia, Manitoba, Nova Scotia, Newfoundland, Quebec, Prince Edward Island, Saskatchewan, Alberta, the Yukon Territory and the Northwest Territories, the Convention shall extend to Nunavut. The Government of Canada further declares that the Convention now extends to all the territorial units of Canada." — 26 October 2000

## Denmark

"... pursuant to the provisions of Article 39, paragraph 1, the Convention shall not be applicable to the territories of the Faroe Islands and Greenland..." — 17 April 1991

## France

"... 4) In accordance with the provisions of Article 39, the Government declares that the Convention shall extend to the whole of the territory of the French Republic." — 16 September 1982

## United Kingdom of Great Britain and Northern Ireland

"In accordance with Article 39 of the Convention, the United Kingdom will notify the depositary in due course of the territories for the international relations of which it is responsible, to which the Convention is to be extended." — 20 May 1986

"The Isle of Man" — 28 June 1991

"Falkland Islands" — 26 March 1998

"Cayman Islands" — 8 May 1998

"Montserrat" — 8 December 1998

"Bermuda" — 21 December 1998

"Jersey" — 19 December 2005

"Anguilla" — 13 June 2007

## PART 2

### Albania

"In accordance with Article 42 of the Convention, the Republic of Albania reserves the right that it shall not be bound to assume any costs referred to in the second paragraph of Article 26 of the Convention resulting from the participation of legal counsel or advisers or from court proceedings, except insofar as those costs may be covered by its system of legal aid and advice." — 4 May 2007

### Armenia

"1. With regard to Article 24, applications, communications or other documents sent to the Central Authority of the Republic of Armenia shall be in original languages and shall be accompanied by a translation into Armenian or, where that is not feasible, a translation into English.

2. With regard to Article 26, the Republic of Armenia shall not be bound to assume any costs referred to in Article 26, second paragraph, resulting from the participation of legal counsel or advisers or from court proceedings, except insofar as those costs may be covered by its system of legal aid and advice." — 1 March 2007

### Belarus

"The Republic of Belarus declares that it shall not be bound to assume any costs referred to in paragraph 2 of Article 26 of this Convention resulting from the participation of legal counsel or advisers or from our court proceedings, except insofar as those costs may be covered by its system of legal aid and advice." — 12 January 1998

### Belize

"1. Any application or other documents transmitted to the Central Authority under the Convention must be accompanied by a translation in English and not in French and

2. Belize will not be bound to assume any costs relating to applications under the Convention resulting from the participation of legal counsel or advisers, or from court proceedings, except insofar as these costs may be covered by its system of legal aid and advice." — 22 June 1989

### Brazil

"... with a reservation as provided for in Article 24 of the said Convention (permitted under Article 42), to the effect that foreign documents appended to legal instruments must be accompanied by a translation into Portuguese done by a sworn translator." — 19 October 1999

### Bulgaria

"In accordance with Article 42, paragraph 1, of the Convention, the Republic of Bulgaria declares it shall not be bound to assume any costs and expenses resulting from proceedings or, where applicable, those arising from the participation of legal counsel and those of returning the child." — 20 May 2003

## Canada

"In accordance with the provisions of Article 42 and pursuant to Article 26, paragraph 3, the Government of Canada declares that, with respect to applications submitted under the Convention concerning the Provinces of Ontario, New Brunswick and British Columbia, Canada will assume the costs referred to in paragraph 2 of Article 26 only insofar as these costs are covered by the system of legal aid of the Province concerned." — 2 June 1983

"In accordance with the provisions of Article 42 and pursuant to Article 26, paragraph 3, the Government of Canada declares that, with respect to applications submitted under the Convention concerning the Province of Nova Scotia, Canada will assume the costs referred to in paragraph 2 of Article 26 only insofar as these costs are covered by the system of legal aid of the Province of Nova Scotia." — 24 February 1984

"In accordance with the provisions of Article 42 and pursuant to Article 26, paragraph 3, the Government of Canada declares that, with respect to applications submitted under the Convention concerning the Province of Newfoundland, Canada will assume the costs referred to in paragraph 2 of Article 26 only insofar as these costs are covered by the system of legal aid of the Province of Newfoundland." — 5 July 1984

"In accordance with the provisions of Article 42 and pursuant to Article 24, paragraph 2, translation in the French language will be required for any application, communication or other document concerning the Province of Quebec when the original language is neither French nor English. In accordance with the provisions of Article 42 and pursuant to Article 26, paragraph 3, the Government of Canada declares that, with respect to applications submitted under the Convention concerning the Province of Quebec, Canada will assume the costs referred to in paragraph 2 of Article 26 only insofar as these costs are covered by the system of legal aid of the Province of Quebec." — 9 October 1984

"In accordance with the provisions of Article 42, and pursuant to Article 26, paragraph 3, the Government of Canada declares that, with respect to applications submitted under the Convention concerning the Yukon Territory, Canada will assume the costs referred to in paragraph 2 of Article 26 only insofar as these costs are covered by the system of legal aid of the Yukon Territory." — 15 November 1984

"In accordance with the provisions of Article 42, and pursuant to Article 26, paragraph 3, the Government of Canada declares that, with respect to applications submitted under the Convention concerning the Province of Prince Edward Island, Canada will assume the costs referred to in paragraph 2 of Article 26 only insofar as these costs are covered by the system of legal aid of the Province of Prince Edward Island." — 11 February 1986

"In accordance with the provisions of Article 42, and pursuant to Article 26, paragraph 3, the Government of Canada declares that, with respect to applications submitted under the Convention concerning the Province of Saskatchewan, Canada will assume the costs referred to in paragraph 2 of Article 26 only insofar as these costs are covered by the system of legal aid of the Province of Saskatchewan." — 7 August 1986

"In accordance with the provisions of Article 42, and pursuant to Article 26, paragraph 3, the Government of Canada declares that, with respect to applications submitted under the Convention concerning the Province of Alberta, Canada will assume the costs referred to in paragraph 2 of Article 26 only insofar as these costs are covered by the system of legal aid of the Province of Alberta." — 4 November 1986

"In accordance with the provisions of Article 42, and pursuant to Article 26, paragraph 3, the Government of Canada declares that, with respect to applications submitted under the Convention concerning the Northwest Territories, Canada will assume the costs referred to in paragraph 2 of Article 26 only insofar as these costs are covered by the system of legal aid of the Northwest Territories." — 25 January 1988

"In accordance with the provisions of Article 42, and pursuant to Article 26, paragraph 3, the Government of Canada declares that, with respect to applications submitted under the Convention concerning Nunavut, Canada will assume the costs referred to in paragraph 2 of Article 26 only insofar as these costs are covered by the system of legal aid of Nunavut." — 26 October 2000

### China, Hong Kong Special Administrative Region only

"The Government of the Peoples Republic of China also makes the following declaration...In accordance with the provisions of Article 42 of the Convention, the Hong Kong Special Administrative Region will not be bound to bear any costs referred to in paragraph 2 of Article 26 of the Convention resulting from the participation of legal counsel or advisers or from court proceedings, except insofar as those costs may be covered by its system of legal aid and advice." — 13 June 1997

### Czech Republic

"Having examined this Convention and knowing that the Parliament of the Czech Republic has given its consent thereto, we hereby ratify and confirm it with the reservation according to Article 42 of the Convention, that the Czech Republic shall not be bound to assume any costs referred to in Article 26, paragraph 2, of the Convention, resulting from the participation of legal counsel or advisers or from our court proceedings, except insofar as those costs may be covered by its legal system of legal aid and advice." — 15 December 1997

### Denmark

"... pursuant to the provisions of Article 42, paragraph 1,

a the Kingdom of Denmark objects to the use of French in any application, communication or other document sent to its Central Authority (cf. Article 24, paragraph 2); and

b it shall not be bound to assume any costs resulting from the participation of legal counsel or advisers or from court proceedings, except insofar as those costs may be covered by its system of legal aid and advice (cf. Article 26, paragraph 3)..." — 17 April 1991

## El Salvador

"1. The Government of the Republic of El Salvador shall not be bound to assume the costs referred to in Article 26, paragraph 3, except insofar as those costs may be covered by its system of legal aid and advice;

2. (...)

3. (...)

4. The Government of the Republic of El Salvador declares that all documentation sent to El Salvador in application of the said Convention must be accompanied by an official translation into Spanish." — 5 February 2001

## Estonia

(...)

2. pursuant to Article 42 and Article 24, paragraph 2, of the Convention the Republic of Estonia only accepts English language with regard to applications, communications or other documents;

3. pursuant to Article 42 and Article 26, paragraph 3, of the Convention the Republic of Estonia will not accept obligations with regard to expenses referred to in Article 26, paragraph 2, which result from the participation of a legal counsel or advisers or from court proceedings, except insofar as those costs may be covered by its system of legal aid and advice." — 18 April 2001

## Finland

"1. Finland declares, according to Article 42 and Article 24, paragraph 2, of the Convention, that it accepts only the use of English in applications, communications and other documents sent to its Central Authority.

2. Finland declares, according to Article 42 and Article 26, paragraph 3, of the Convention, that it shall not be bound to assume any costs referred to in Article 26, paragraph 2, resulting from the participation of legal counsel or advisers or from court proceedings, except insofar as those costs may be covered by its system of legal aid and advice." — 25 May 1994

## France

"2. In accordance with the provisions of Article 42 and pursuant to Article 24, paragraph 2, the Government will consider only those applications which are drawn up in French, or are accompanied by a translation into French, and will require a translation into French of any communication or document sent to its Central Authority.

3. In accordance with the provisions of Article 42 and pursuant to Article 26, paragraph 3, the Government declares that it will assume the costs referred to in paragraph 2 of Article 26 only insofar as those costs are covered by the French system of legal aid..." — 16 September 1982

### Germany

"The Federal Republic of Germany declares in accordance with the third paragraph of Article 26 that it is not bound to assume any costs referred to in the second paragraph of Article 26 resulting from the participation of legal counsel or advisers or from court proceedings, except insofar as those costs may be covered by its regulations concerning legal aid and advice.

The Federal Republic of Germany assumes that, in accordance with the first paragraph of Article 24, applications from other Contracting States shall regularly be accompanied by a translation into German." — 27 September 1990

### Greece

"1. In accordance with Article 42 of the Convention on the Civil Aspects of International Child Abduction, Greece declares that it shall not be bound to assume any costs referred to in the second paragraph of Article 26 resulting from the participation of legal counsel or advisers or from court proceedings, except insofar as those costs concern cases of free legal aid.

2. In accordance with Article 42 of the above-mentioned Convention Greece declares that it objects to the use of the French language in any application, communication or other document sent to its Central Authority." — 19 March 1993

### Guatemala

"1. The Republic of Guatemala oppose itself to the use of French in all the requests, communication and other documents to be sent to the Central Authority, based in the second paragraph of Article 24 of the Convention (if applicable).

2. The Republic of Guatemala is not obligated to assume any kind of expenses mentioned in the second paragraph of Article 26 of the Convention, derived from the participation of a lawyer, legal advisors or the judiciary procedure, except insofar as those costs may be covered by its system of legal aid and advice." — 6 February 2002

### Honduras

"Under the reservation of Article 26, paragraph 3." — 20 December 1993

### Iceland

"1. In accordance with Article 42, paragraph 1, and Article 24, paragraph 2, of the Convention, Iceland makes a reservation with regard to Article 24, paragraph 1, and objects to the use of French in any application, communication or other document sent to its Central Authority.

2. In accordance with Article 42, paragraph 1, and Article 26, paragraph 3, of the Convention, Iceland makes a reservation that it shall not be bound to assume any costs referred to in Article 26, paragraph 2, resulting from the participation of legal counsel or advisers or from court proceedings, except insofar as those costs may be covered by its system of legal aid and advice.

The other provisions of the Convention shall be inviolably observed." — 14 August 1996

## Israel

"In accordance with Articles 26 and 42 of the Convention, the State of Israel hereby declares that, in proceedings under the Convention, it shall not be bound to assume any costs resulting from the participation of legal counsel or advisers or from court proceedings, except insofar as those costs may be covered by its system of legal aid and advice." — 4 September 1991

## Latvia

"In accordance with Article 42 and Article 24, paragraph 2, of the Convention on the Civil Aspects of International Child Abduction the Republic of Latvia declares that it accepts only the use of English in any application, communication or other document sent to its Central Authority." — 15 November 2001

## Lithuania

"1. Pursuant to Article 42 and paragraph 2 of Article 24 of the Convention, the Republic of Lithuania consents to using only the English language for any application, communication or other document sent to its Central Authority;

2. Pursuant to Article 42 and paragraph 3 of Article 26 of the Convention, the Republic of Lithuania shall not be bound to assume any costs referred to in paragraph 2 of Article 26 of the Convention resulting from court proceedings or from the participation of legal counsel or advisers, except insofar as those costs may be covered by the system of legal aid and advice of the Republic of Lithuania." — 5 June 2002

## Luxembourg

"The Grand-Duchy of Luxembourg declares that it shall not be bound to assume any costs referred to in Article 26, paragraph 2, of the Convention, namely the costs resulting from the participation of legal counsel or advisers or from court proceedings, except insofar as those costs are covered by the Luxembourg system of legal aid and advice." — 8 October 1986

## Mauritius

"The Republic of Mauritius declares that it shall not be bound to assume any costs referred to in paragraph 2 of Article 26 resulting from the participation of legal counsel or advisers or from court proceedings, except insofar as those costs may be covered by its system of legal aid and advice." — 23 March 1993

## Moldova

"In accordance with the provisions of Article 42 of the Convention, pursuant to Article 26, paragraph 3, the Republic of Moldova declares that the Republic of Moldova will assume the costs referred to in paragraph 2 of Article 26 only insofar as these costs are covered by the national system of legal and judicial aid." — 10 April 1998

## Monaco

"In conformity with Article 26, paragraph 3, of the Convention, the Principality of Monaco declares that it shall not be bound to assume any costs referred to in Article 26, paragraph 2, resulting from the participation of legal counsel or advisers or from court proceedings, except insofar as those costs may be covered by its system of legal aid and advice." — 12 November 1992

## Netherlands

"The Kingdom of the Netherlands shall not be bound to assume any costs referred to in the second paragraph of Article 26 of the Convention on the Civil Aspects of International Child Abduction, done at The Hague on 25 October 1980, resulting from the participation of legal counsel or advisers or from court proceedings, except insofar as those costs may be covered by its system of legal aid and advice." — 12 June 1990

## New Zealand

"The Government of New Zealand hereby declares in accordance with Article 24 and Article 42 of the Convention that any application, communication or other document sent to its Central Authority should either be in the English language or accompanied by a translation thereof in the English language; and the Government of New Zealand hereby further declares in accordance with Article 26 and Article 42 of the Convention that it reserves the right not to be bound to assume the costs referred to in Article 26 resulting from the participation of legal counsel or advisers or from court proceedings, except insofar as those costs may be covered by its system of legal aid and advice." — 31 May 1991

## Norway

"1. In accordance with Articles 24 and 42, the Norwegian Government reserves the right not to accept applications, communications or other documents sent to the General Authority in French.

2. In accordance with Articles 26 and 42, Norway makes the reservation that it shall not be bound to assume any costs resulting from the participation of legal counsel or advisers or from court proceedings, except insofar as those costs may be covered by Act of 13 June 1980 relating to free legal aid." — 9 January 1989

## Panama

"... the Republic of Panama declares that it shall not be bound to assume any costs referred to in the first paragraph of Article 26 of the Convention resulting from the participation of legal counsel or advisers or from court proceedings, except insofar as those costs may be covered by its system of legal aid and advice." — 2 February 1994

## Poland

"In accordance with Article 42, the Republic of Poland makes the reservation pursuant to Article 26, paragraph 3, of the Convention and declares that it shall not be bound to assume any costs referred to in the preceding paragraph, resulting from court proceedings, except insofar as those costs may be covered by its system of legal aid and advice." — 10 August 1992

### Saint Kitts and Nevis

"Saint Kitts and Nevis is not bound to assume any costs resulting under the Convention from the participation of legal counsel or advisers or from court proceedings in terms of paragraph 3 of Article 26 of the Convention." — 31 May 1994

### San Marino

"In conformity with Article 26, paragraph 3, of the Convention, the Republic of San Marino declares that it shall not be bound to assume any costs referred to in Article 26, paragraph 2, resulting from the participation of legal counsel or advisers or from court proceedings, except insofar as those costs may be covered by its system of legal aid and advice." — 14 December 2006

### Slovakia

"The Slovak Republic avails itself of the possibility to make a reservation under Article 42 of the Convention of 25 October 1980 on Civil Aspects of International Child Abduction and, in accordance with its Article 26, paragraph 3, declares that is shall not be bound to assume any costs referred to in Article 26, paragraph 2, resulting from the participation of legal counsel or advisers or from court proceedings, except insofar as those costs may be covered by its system of legal aid and advice." — 7 November 2000

### South Africa

"(a) That the use of French in any application, communication or other document sent to the Central Authority of the Republic of South Africa, as provided for in Article 24 of the Convention, is objected to, and that such documents shall not be accepted in French.

(b) That the Republic of South Africa shall not be bound to assume any costs referred to in paragraph 2 of Article 26 of the Convention resulting from the participation of legal counsel or advisers or from court proceedings, except those costs which may be covered by the system of legal aid in terms of the Legal Aid Act, 1969 (Act No. 22 of 1969)." — 8 July 1997

### Sri Lanka

"For purposes of Article 24, the documents should be in the English language.

For purposes of Article 26(3) Sri Lanka should not be bound to assume any costs referred to in the preceding paragraph resulting from the participation of Legal Counsel or advisers or from Court proceedings except in so far as those costs may be covered by the legal aid and advice system of Sri Lanka." — 28 September 2001

### Sweden

"In accordance with the provisions of Article 42 and pursuant to Article 42 and pursuant to Article 26, Sweden declares that it shall not be bound to assume any costs referred to in Article 26, paragraph 2, resulting from the participation of legal counsel or advisers or from court proceedings, except insofar as those costs may be covered by the Swedish system of legal aid." — 22 March 1989

**Thailand**

"(...) subject to the reservation, made pursuant to Articles 24 and 42 thereof, that it accepts only the use of the English language in any application, communication or other document sent to its Central Authority, (...) — 14 August 2002

**Turkey**

"... that in accordance with paragraph 3 of Article 26, the Republic of Turkey shall not be bound to assume any costs and expenses of the proceedings or, where applicable, those arising from the participation of legal counsel or advisers and those of returning the child." — 31 May 2000

**United Kingdom of Great Britain and Northern Ireland**

"... in accordance with the provisions of Article 42 of the Convention, the United Kingdom declares that it shall not be bound to assume any costs referred to in the second paragraph of Article 26 of the Convention resulting from the participation of legal counsel or advisers or from court proceedings, except insofar as those costs may be covered by its system of legal aid and advice." — 20 May 1986

**United States of America**

"1. Pursuant to the second paragraph of Article 24, and Article 42, the United States makes the following reservation: All applications, communications and other documents sent to the U.S. Central Authority should be accompanied by their translation into English.

2. Pursuant to the third paragraph of Article 26, the United States declares that it will not be bound to assume any costs or expenses resulting from the participation of legal counsel or advisers or from court and legal proceedings in connection with efforts to return children from the United States pursuant to the Convention except insofar as those costs or expenses are covered by a legal aid program." — 29 April 1988

**Uzbekistan**

"The Republic of Uzbekistan shall not be bound to assume any costs referred to in paragraph 2 of Article 26 and resulting from the participation of legal counsel or from court proceedings." — 31 May 1999

**Venezuela**

"All communications to the Central Authority should be drawn up in the Spanish language. The Republic of Venezuela is not bound to assume any costs referred to in Article 26, paragraph 3." — 16 October 1996

**Zimbabwe**

"... subject to the reservation that the costs mentioned in the second paragraph of Article 26 of the aforesaid Convention shall not be borne by the State." — 4 April 1995

GIVEN under my official seal at Dublin,
20 July 2011.
EAMON GILMORE,
Tánaiste and Minister for Foreign Affairs and Trade.

## Explanatory Note

(This note is not part of the Instrument and does not purport to be a legal interpretation.) Section 4 of the Child Abduction and Enforcement of Custody Orders Act 1991 enables the Minister for Foreign Affairs to declare which states are Contracting States to the Convention on the Civil Aspects of International Child Abduction, done at The Hague on the 25th day of October 1980 and that a declaration or reservation has been made to the Ministry of Foreign Affairs of the Kingdom of the Netherlands. This Order specifies which States are Contracting States and sets out the texts of the declarations and reservations which have been received by the Ministry of Foreign Affairs of the Kingdom of the Netherlands.

# Index

All references are to the provisions of the relevant legislation

*Garda Síochána (contd)*
power to detain child at risk of
abduction, CAECOA 1991, s 37
receipt of domestic violence orders,
DVA 1996, s 11
***Guardian ad litem*, appointment of,**
GIA 1964, s 28
**Guardians and guardianship**
agreement on, adjournment to assist,
GIA 1964, s 22
alternatives to, GIA 1964, ss 20, 21
appointment of father, GIA 1964,
s 6A
appointment and removal by court,
GIA 1964, s 8
child, paramount welfare of, GIA
1964, ss 3,11, 25
court applications by, GIA 1964, s 11
parents, rights of, GIA 1964, s 6
powers and duties, GIA 1964, s 10
registered father, appointment as,
CCR 2001, Ord 59, r 4 (13)
testamentary guardians, parents, GIA
1964, s 7
two or more appointed, GIA 1964, s 9
**Hague Convention**
Central Authority
appointment, CAECOA 1991, s 8;
CAECOA 1991, Sch 1, Ch II,
co-operation, CAECOA 1991, Sch
1, Ch II,
provision of information, CAECOA
1991, s 14
court jurisdiction for purposes of,
CAECOA 1991, s 7
interim powers of court under,
CAECOA 1991, s 12
legal effect of, CAECOA 1991, s 6
notice and stay of proceedings,
CAECOA 1991, s 13
precedence of Council Regulation
2201/2003, CR(EC) 2201/2003,
Arts 60–62

provision of documents by court,
CAECOA 1991, s 16
return of child under, CAECOA 1991,
Sch 1, Ch III
right of access, CAECOA 1991, Sch
1, Ch IV
scope of, CAECOA 1991, Sch 1, Ch I
wrongful removal declaration,
CAECOA 1991, ss 15, 16
**Health Service Executive**
domestic violence, power to apply for
orders, DVA 1996, ss 6–7
private foster care
notification, GIA 1964, s 22
supervision orders
**High Court**
Community judgments, enforcement
by, JCEJA 1998, ss 8, 13
jurisdiction of, FLA 1995, s 38;
CPCROCA 2010, ss 139,196
**Holy See, Treaties with, Council
Regulation 2201/2003 and,** CR(EC)
No 2201/2003, Art 63
**Household allowance, property in,**
FL(MSC)A 1976, s 21; CPCROCA
2010, s 66
**Income tax, maintenance orders and,**
FL(MSC)A 1976, s 24; CPCROCA
2010, s 64
**Interim maintenance,** FL(MSC)A
1976, s 7
**Joint custody,** GIA 1964, s 11A
**Judicial separation**
adultery and unreasonable behaviour,
proof of, JSFLRA 1989, s 4
alternatives to, awareness of, JSFLRA
1989, s 5
collusion, condonation, recrimination,
connivance, JSFLRA 1989, s 44
decree
application for, JSFLRA 1989, s 2
grant of, JSFLRA 1989, s 2